RAVE REVIEWS

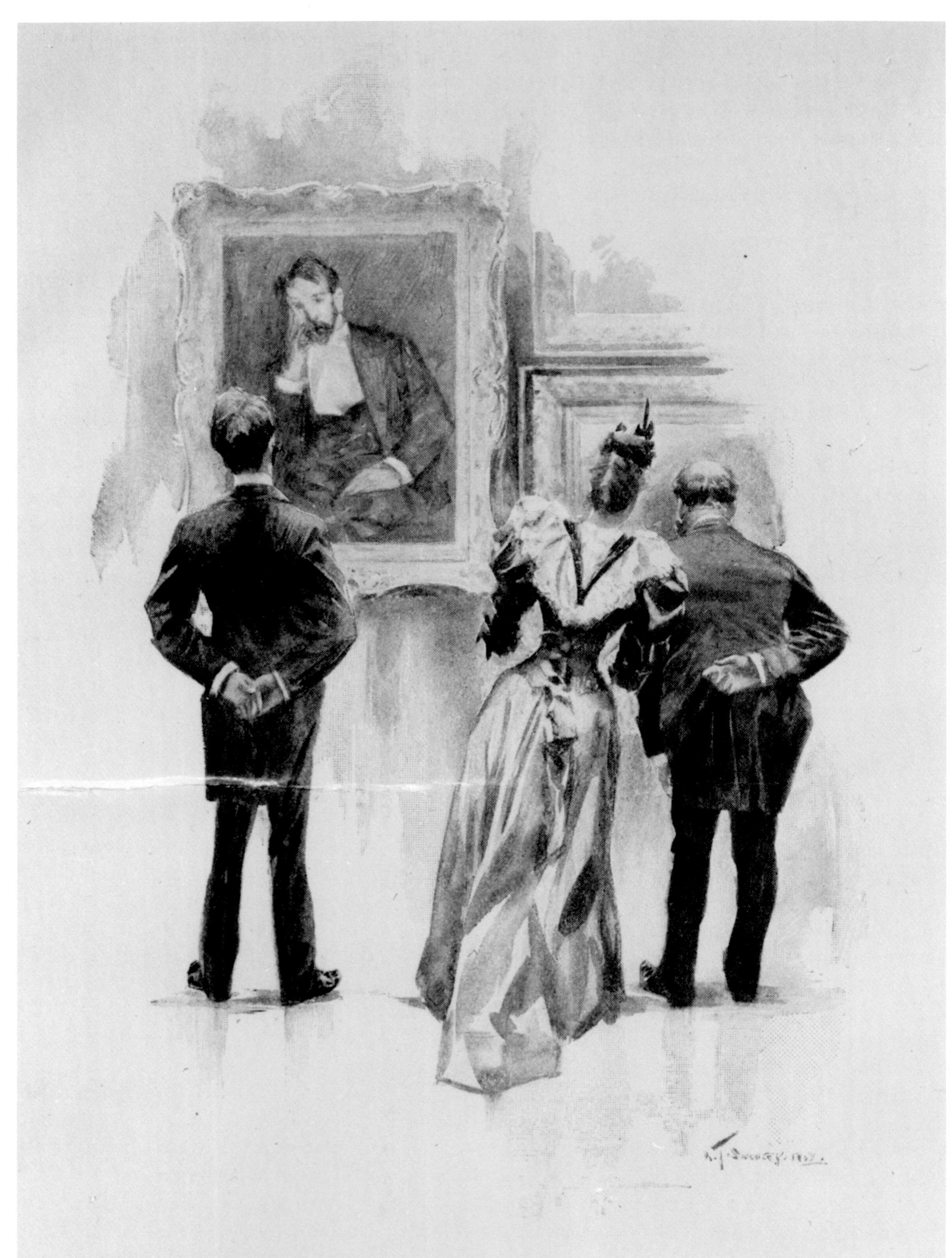

"MR. RUPERT DE RUYTER COULD NOT BE KEPT AWAY FROM HIS OWN PORTRAIT."

RAVE REVIEWS

American Art and Its Critics, 1826–1925

DAVID B. DEARINGER, *Editor*

With essays by
Avis Berman
Margaret C. Conrads
David B. Dearinger
William H. Gerdts
Trudie A. Grace
Sarah J. Moore
Kenneth John Myers

NATIONAL ACADEMY OF DESIGN · NEW YORK · 2000

Distributed by University Press of New England · Hanover and London

The National Academy of Design
1083 Fifth Avenue
New York, New York, 10128

EXHIBITION ITINERARY

National Academy of Design, New York
September 20–December 31, 2000

Gilcrease Museum, Tulsa, Oklahoma
January 31–April 1, 2001

Indianapolis Museum of Art
April 29–July 1, 2001

Funding for the catalogue was provided by The Lucelia Foundation.

Rave Reviews: American Art and Its Critics, 1826–1925 was made possible by a generous grant from The Henry Luce Foundation.

Additional support has been provided by New York State Office of Parks, Recreation and Historic Preservation and the office of Senator Roy M. Goodman.

Distributed by the University Press of New England, Hanover, New Hampshire, and London, England.

Printed in the United States of America by Penmor Lithographers, Lewiston, Maine.

Binding by Acme Book Bindery, Charlestown, Massachusetts.

Book design by Christopher Kuntze.
Composed in Minion and Golden Cockerel types.
Edited by Nancy Preu.

FRONT COVER: William St. John Harper, "In the National Academy of Design," *Harper's Weekly,* April 29, 1882, Archives, National Academy of Design

BACK COVER: Charles Kurtz, *National Academy Notes and Complete Illustrated Catalogue,* detail of title page (New York, 1889), Archives, National Academy of Design

FRONTISPIECE: "Mr. Rupert De Ruyter Could Not Be Kept Away From His Own Portrait," *Harper's New Monthly Magazine,* March 1894, Archives, National Academy of Design

LIBRARY OF CONGRESS CATALOGING-IN-PUBLICATION DATA

Rave Reviews : American art and its critics, 1826–1925 / David B. Dearinger, editor ; with essays by Avis Berman . . . [et al.].
    p. cm.
   Catalog published in conjunction with an exhibition held at the National Academy of Design, New York, Sept. 20, 2000–Dec. 31, 2000.
   Includes bibliographical references.
   ISBN 1-887149-04-x (cloth : alk. paper) — ISBN 1-887149-05-8 (pbk. : alk. paper)
   1. Art, American—Exhibitions. 2. Art, Modern—19th century—United States—Exhibitions. 3. Art, Modern—20th century—United States—Exhibitions. 4. Art criticism—United States—History—19th century. 5. Art criticism—United States—History—20th century.
I. Dearinger, David B. (David Bernard), 1950– II. Berman, Avis.
III. National Academy of Design (U.S.)
N6510.R38 2000
701'.18'097309034—dc21   00-064311

It would be a happy thing for the world if *Artists* were to be made the sole judges of the *Arts*—
but we are favoured with canonists and nobility as arbitrators who are quite unacquainted with
our concerns, and these again have certain *managers,* as they are termed on the stage, or,
as Æschines calls them, *pettifoggers of the forum,* who cajole the public.

—ARISTOTLE, as quoted on the cover of the National Academy of Design's
Catalogue of the Seventeenth Annual Exhibition, 1842

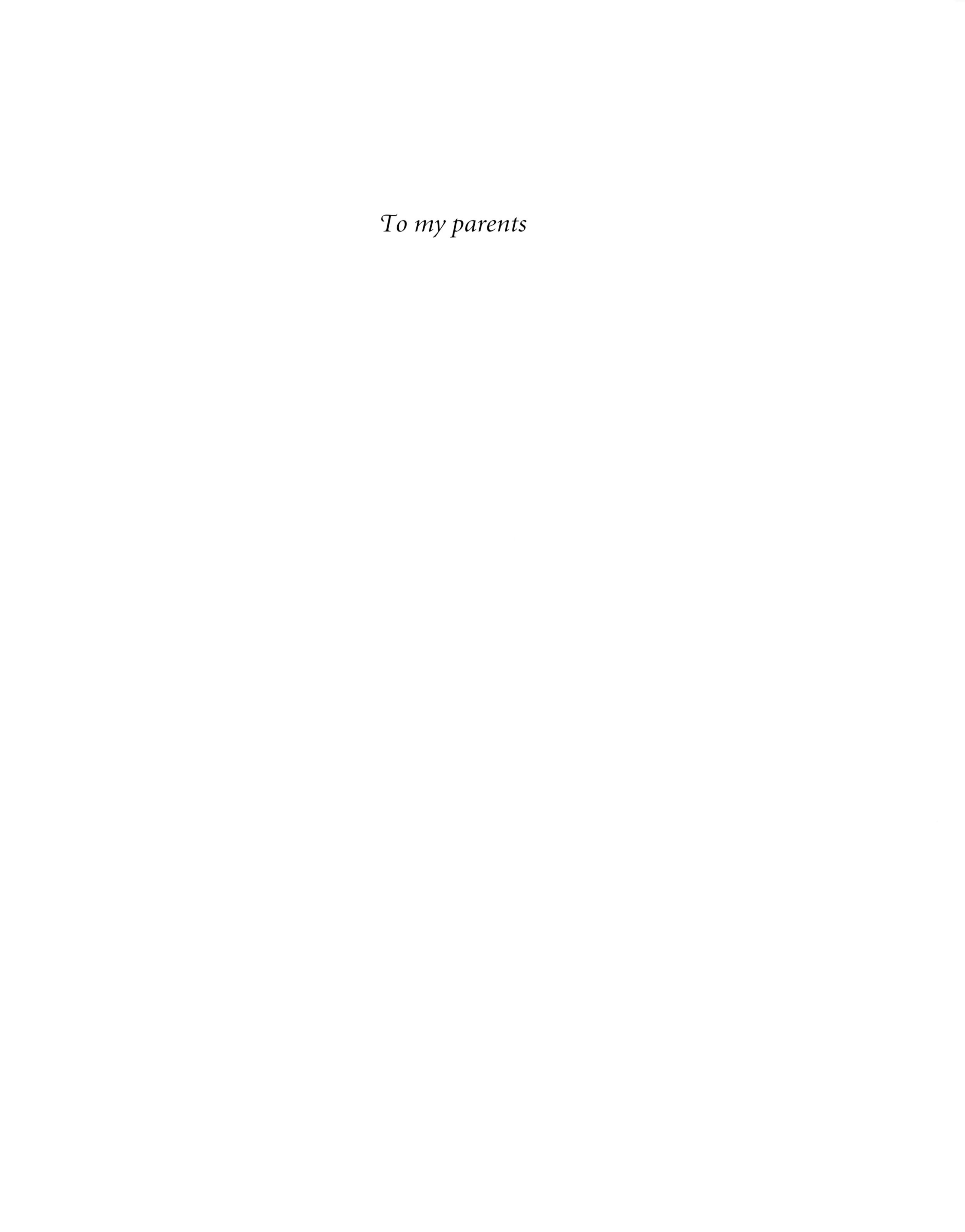

To my parents

Contents

Foreword | 11

Acknowledgments | 13

Lenders to the Exhibition | 15

An Introduction to the History of American Art Criticism to 1925 | 17
David B. Dearinger

The Public Display of Art in New York City, 1664–1914 | 31
Kenneth John Myers

Annual Exhibitions and the Birth of American Art Criticism to 1865 | 53
David B. Dearinger

"In the Midst of an Era of Revolution": The New York Art Press and the
Annual Exhibitions of the National Academy of Design in the 1870s | 93
Margaret C. Conrads

The National Academy of Design and the Society of American Artists:
Rivals Viewed by Critics, 1878–1906 | 107
Trudie A. Grace

A "Salon of America"? Defining Nationalism at the
National Academy of Design, 1909–1915 | 123
Sarah J. Moore

"As National as the National Biscuit Company":
The Academy, the Critics, and the Armory Show | 131
Avis Berman

Ekphrasis: A Non-critical Look at Early Nineteenth-century
Portraiture through Poetry | 145
William H. Gerdts

Catalogue of the Exhibition | 159

Notes to the Reader | 160

Appendix A: The Critics | 273

Appendix B: National Academy of Design Annual Exhibitions, 1826–1925 | 276

Reviews of the Annual Exhibitions of the National Academy of Design, 1826–1925 | 277

Index to Artists and Works in the Exhibition | 301

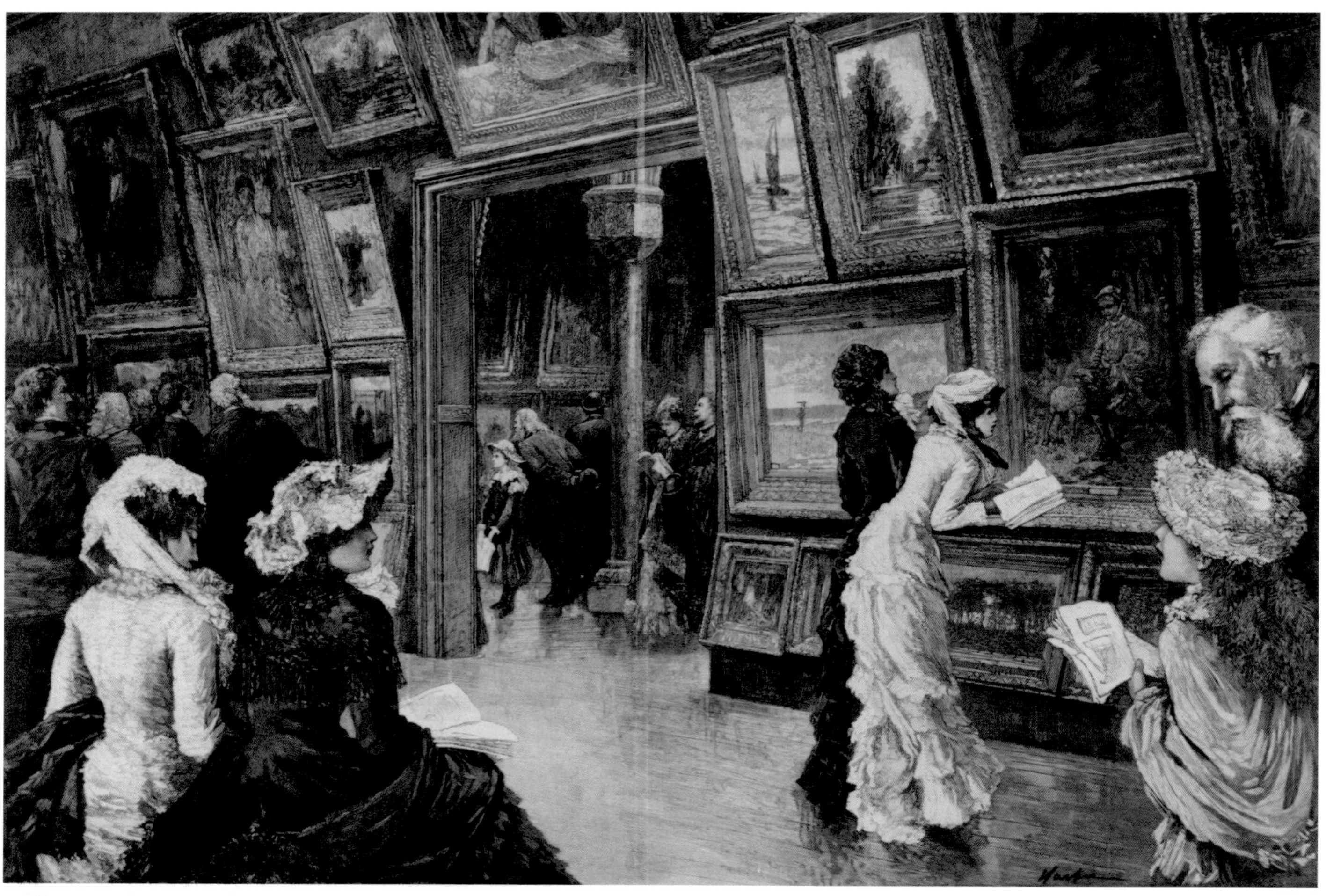

William St. John Harper, "In the National Academy of Design," *Harper's Weekly*, April 29, 1882, Archives, National Academy of Design

Foreword

"I love criticism just so long as it is unqualified praise," the witty actor, writer, and composer Noel Coward commented after rave reviews of his 1929 operetta, *Bitter Sweet,* appeared. Most artists would agree.

Beginning in 1826, American artists were afforded the opportunity to exhibit their work regularly at the annual exhibitions of the newly founded National Academy of Design. Critical reviews of these annuals began immediately and with that, the field of American art criticism was born. The Academy's founding fathers rented space to hold their exhibitions of contemporary art, which were open to any American artist whose work was accepted by the jury of selection. Because of their seriality, the National Academy of Design annual exhibitions provide an armature for examining not only the evolution of American art but also the development of art criticism in the United States, the primary focus of this volume.

Using the annuals, the largest and most important continuing contemporary art exhibitions in this country, Dr. David Dearinger, principal author and editor of this volume and Chief Curator at the National Academy of Design, in his two essays, traces the history of early periodicals that featured reviews. He discusses some of the important critics and comments on changes in art criticism from its bland descriptive beginnings to more critical analysis. Dr. Kenneth Myers, Assistant Curator of American Art at the Freer Gallery of Art in Washington, D.C., reveals the wider context in which the annuals took place, writing about other public venues, cultural attitudes, and taste. Dr. Margaret Conrads, Samuel Sosland Curator of American Art at the Nelson-Atkins Museum in Kansas City, Missouri, focuses on the years following the Civil War, the important transitional period of the 1870s. She discusses the emergence of the critic as an identifiable personality and the rise of several major artists such as Winslow Homer and George Inness. The establishment of newer, less traditional art organizations such as the Society of American Artists in 1877, is the subject of the essay by Dr. Trudie Grace, Adjunct Assistant Professor, Department of Art History, Fashion Institute of Technology, State University of New York. She contrasts the ideas of younger, European-trained artists with those of more conventional National Academicians. Dr. Sarah Moore, Associate Professor of Art at the University of Arizona in Tucson, tracks the development of American art during the first decades of the twentieth century, centering on the Academy presidency of John White Alexander. Avis Berman, an independent art historian and author, sums up the negative attitudes of critics toward the academy during the first quarter of the twentieth century. These later reviewers promote more progressive elements in the art world and oppose the conservatism in evidence at Academy annuals. And finally, a bonus from Dr. William H. Gerdts, Professor Emeritus, Ph.D. Program in Art History, City University of New York, who writes insightfully on another manner of art criticism: ekphrastic poetry, that is poems written expressly about paintings, in particular some examples accompanying paintings exhibited at the Academy.

The art included in the exhibition that this book accompanies is illustrated herein, appearing with entries that specify and quote from period criticism. These entries are expertly written and researched by David Dearinger, Trudie Grace, Andrea Husby, Sarah Kelly, Mark Mitchell, and Zachary Ross.

While this exhibition tells some of the Academy's long history and includes the work of many of its members, it is, in fact, about art criticism as it occurred between 1826 and 1925. In this year 2000, the Academy can boast 175 years of uninterrupted annual exhibitions and concomitant criticism. Artists from across the country still participate, hoping to be accepted by the juries of Academicians, professional artists who have been elected to membership by their peers. At this time the Academy rules have evolved to exhibiting the work of Academicians exclusively one year and opening the galleries to all qualified artists on alternate years. That this annual tradition endures, and approximately two thousand artists vie for admission and prizes, bears witness to its vitality and significance. Today's Academicians are working to modernize this 175-year-old tradition so that critics can continue to hone their specialty.

The Academy is pleased to share this exhibition with the Gilcrease Museum in Tulsa, Oklahoma, and the Indianapolis Museum in Indiana and thanks their directors Brooks Joyner and Bret Waller and their staff for their commitment to the project. The exhibition was conceived by David Dearinger, who has spent three years working diligently on it; we applaud his effort and congratulate him on the result. Others on the staff who have been intimately involved and to whom David and I are indebted for their many hours of work are: Anne Rehkopf Townsend, Director of Development, whose persistence in writing grant proposals to fund the exhibition and catalogue was exemplary; Simone Manwaring, former Registrar, and Wendy Rogers, current Registrar, who organized the shipping, insurance, and loans; Lucie Kinsolving, Chief Conservator, and Nadia Ghannam, Associate Conservator, who restored paintings and supervised the condition reports;

Barbara Suhr, the exhibition designer, who made the exhibition come alive; Nancy Preu, tireless editor of the accompanying book; and Christopher Kuntze for his remarkable book design. Furthermore, all of the essayists and entry writers mentioned above are acknowledged for their insightful and timely contributions to this catalogue. As is well known, there are many museum staff members who work behind the scenes and I want to acknowledge and thank all of them: Deena Abu-Lugod, Charles Biada, Cecilia Bonn, Nancy Cafferty, Jonah Ellis, Monique Leblanc, Joanna Sternberg, and Thomas Sembros.

We are grateful, too, to the many museums, galleries, and private collections that have been so cooperative in agreeing to lend major works from their holdings for this exhibition. The names of these lenders appear on a separate page in this book, but I would like to express my gratitude to all of them here.

Without the sponsorship and financial aid of The Henry Luce Foundation and The Lucelia Foundation this book and the exhibition it complements could not have occurred. We are indebted in particular to Henry Luce III and Elizabeth Gosnell for their support, confidence, and encouragement. We are especially gratified that, as a result of its generous participation in *Rave Reviews,* The Lucelia Foundation has established The Lucelia Foundation Fund for Publication at the National Academy of Design, which will provide the Academy with long-term support for future publications.

Annette Blaugrund, Ph.D.
Director

Curator's Acknowledgments

This book and the exhibition for which it was produced would never have happened without the generous support and assistance of many people. The staff of the National Academy of Design has been a consistent and reliable support team for this project, and I would like to add my thanks to all of the individuals cited in the Director's Foreword. In addition, I would like to thank Annette Blaugrund, Director of the Academy, who has given generously of her time, energy, and advice.

The amount of research that was necessary for this project could not have been contemplated without the assistance of William H. Gerdts and Abigail Booth Gerdts. They generously opened their amazing library, which includes copies of hundreds of reviews of nineteenth-century exhibitions, to me. Without access to the Gerdts American Art Research Library, neither the exhibition nor this book could have been realized.

I would also like to thank the members of the National Academy of Design, especially those who have served on the Council and the Exhibition Committee during the period in which this project was being planned. I am especially grateful for the support of Raoul Middleman, current president of the Academy and former chairman of the Exhibition Committee; and Paul Resika, current chairman of the Exhibition Committee. In addition, I wish to acknowledge Edward Gallagher, former director of the Academy, who gave *Rave Reviews* his enthusiastic support at its inception.

Several scholars willingly agreed to join an advisory panel for the exhibition, and I am grateful to them for their support. They are Dr. Carrie Rebora Barratt, Associate Curator, American Paintings and Sculpture, Metropolitan Museum of Art; Avis Berman, independent art historian; Dr. Margaret Conrads, Samuel Sosland Curator of American Art, Nelson-Atkins Museum of Art, Kansas City; Dr. William H. Gerdts, Professor Emeritus, Ph.D. Program in Art History, City University of New York; and Dr. Kenneth Myers, Assistant Curator, Freer Gallery of Art, Washington, D.C. Drs. Conrads, Gerdts, and Myers, and Ms. Berman, along with Dr. Sarah Moore, Professor of Art History at the University of Arizona, Tucson, and Dr. Trudie Grace, Adjunct Assistant Professor, Fashion Institute of Technology, New York, also contributed essays to this book. I thank all of them for their hard work and unflagging enthusiasm. Likewise, I thank the authors who produced the short essays that make up the catalogue section of this book: Trudie Grace, Andrea Husby, Sarah Kelly, Mark Mitchell, and Zachary Ross. I would also like to thank Margo Hensler, Curatorial Assistant at the Academy, who helped to compile label text for the exhibition; and the three research

assistants who have contributed to various aspects of the project: Kathy Fieramosca, Jennifer Wagelie, and especially Elizabeth Barry. I am deeply grateful for the patience and wisdom of Nancy Preu, who edited this book; the good taste of Christopher Kuntze who designed it; and the talent of Barbara Suhr who designed the exhibition.

From the beginning of this project three years ago, I have had the gratifying cooperation of many colleagues in institutions around the country, and I wish to thank them all for their assistance:

Linda Merrill, and Jody Cohen, High Museum of Art, Atlanta; Jackie Day and Tracy N. Meehan, Adirondack Museum, Blue Mountain Lake, New York; Theodore E. Stebbins and Erica E. Hirshler, Museum of Fine Arts, Boston; Linda Ferber, Barbara Gallati, and Ken Moser, Brooklyn Museum of Art, New York; James M. Wood, Daniel Schulman, and Carrie Ann Schweiger, Art Institute of Chicago; Barbara K. Gibbs, Anita Ellis, John Wilson, Julie Aronson, and Gretchen Shie, Cincinnati Art Museum; Kathleen D. Stocking, New York State Historical Association, Cooperstown, New York; Graham W. J. Beal, James Tottis, Sylvia Inwood, and Michelle Peplin, The Detroit Institute of Arts; Judith O'Toole and Barbara L. Jones, Westmoreland Museum of American Art, Greensburg, Pennsylvania; Bret Waller and Harriet Warkel, Indianapolis Museum of Art; Jean Stern, The Irvine Museum, Irvine, California; Russell Bowman and Leigh Albritton, Milwaukee Art Museum; Mary Sue Sweeney Price and Amber Woods Germano, The Newark Museum, Newark, New Jersey; Warren Adelson, Adelson Galleries, Inc., New York; Frederick Hill and Bruce Weber, Berry-Hill Gallery, New York; John Howat, H. Barbara Weinberg, William S. Lieberman, Peter M. Kenny, Anna Seroff, Suzanne L. Shenton, and Ida Balboul, The Metropolitan Museum of Art, New York; Carol Lowry and the members of the National Arts Club, New York; Kimberly M. Terbush, and Laird Ogden, New-York Historical Society, New York City; Robert Rainwater, Eileen Coffey, and Russell Drisch, The New York Public Library; Alex Boyle and the members of the Art Committee, Union League Club, New York; William J. Hennessey, The Chrysler Museum, Norfolk, Virginia; Jeffrey Cooley, The Cooley Gallery, Old Lyme, Connecticut; Pierre Théberge and Carole Lapointe, National Gallery of Canada, Ottawa; Daniel Rosenfield and Lorena K. Sehgal, Pennsylvania Academy of the Fine Arts, Philadelphia; Anne d'Harnoncourt, Darrel Sewell, and Nancy Wulbrecht, Philadelphia Museum of Art; Michael W. Schantz and Mildred O. Staib, Woodmere Art Museum, Philadelphia; Michael Ryan, University of Pennsylvania, Philadelphia;

Richard Armstrong, Carnegie Museum of Art, Pittsburgh; Carmen T. Ruiz-Fischler, Museo de Arte de Ponce, Puerto Rico; John R. Porter and Mireille Arsenault, Musée du Québec, Canada; Grant Holcomb III, Marjorie Searl, Monica Simpson, and Kathy Ertsgaard, Memorial Art Gallery of the University of Rochester, Rochester, New York; Mark S. Weil and Jane E. Neidhardt, Washington University Gallery of Art, St. Louis, Missouri; Harry S. Parker III, Steven A. Nash, and Timothy A. Burgard, The Fine Arts Museums of San Francisco; Paul Ivory and Linda Wesselman Jackson, Chesterwood, Stockbridge, Massachusetts; Deborah Johnson and Joshua Ruff, The Museums at Stony Brook, Stony Brook, New York; Richard Manoogian and Joan Barnes, Masco Corporation, Taylor, Michigan; Lawrence W. Nichols, Patricia J. Whitesides, and Roger Berkowitz, The Toledo Museum of Art, Toledo, Ohio; Ellwood C. Parry III, University of Arizona, Tucson; Deborah Burke and Michael Sudbury, Gilcrease Museum, Tulsa, Oklahoma; Paul Schweizer and Debora Ryan, Munson-Williams-Proctor Institute, Utica, New York; David C. Levy, Jacquelyn Serwer, Sarah Cash, and Kimberly S. Liddle, Corcoran Gallery of Art, Washington, D.C.; Rachel Doggett and Lori Johnson, Folger Shakespeare Library, Washington, D.C.; Earl A. Powell III, National Gallery of Art, Washington, D.C.; Margaret Grandine, National Museum of American History, Smithsonian Institution, Washington, D.C.; Beverly Cox, The National Portrait Gallery, Smithsonian Institution, Washington, D.C.; Melissa M. Heaver, National Trust for Historic Preservation, Washington, D.C.; Michael Moss, David M. Reel, and Pat Dursi, West Point Museum, United State Military Academy, West Point, New York; Michael Conforti, Richard Rand, and Martha Asher, Sterling and Francine Clark Art Institute, Williamstown, Massachusetts; and David Brigham and Laura Mills, Worcester Art Museum, Worcester, Massachusetts.

Finally, I wish to thank my friends Darrell Ung, Greg Christiansen, and Timothy Gura; my siblings Kevin Lane Dearinger and Pam Hutton; and, especially, my parents, John A. and Anna Lane Dearinger, for their love and support.

David B. Dearinger
Chief Curator
National Academy of Design

Lenders to the Exhibition

Adirondack Museum, Blue Mountain Lake, New York

Annenberg Rare Book & Manuscript Library, University of Pennsylvania, Philadelphia

Art Institute of Chicago

Boston Public Library

Brooklyn Museum of Art

The Carnegie Museum of Art, Pittsburgh, Pennsylvania

Chesterwood National Historic Site, National Trust for Historic Preservation, Stockbridge, Massachusetts

The Chrysler Museum of Art, Norfolk, Virginia

Cincinnati Art Museum

The Cooley Gallery, Old Lyme, Connecticut

Corcoran Gallery of Art, Washington D.C.

Detroit Institute of Arts

The Fine Arts Museums of San Francisco

Folger Shakespeare Library, Washington, D.C.

High Museum, Atlanta, Georgia

Joan Irvine Smith Fine Arts, Inc., Irvine, California

Manoogian Collection, Taylor, Michigan

Memorial Art Gallery, University of Rochester, Rochester, New York

Metropolitan Museum of Art, New York City

Milwaukee Art Museum

Munson-Williams-Proctor Institute, Utica, New York

Musée du Québec, Canada

Museo de Arte de Ponce, Ponce, Puerto Rico

Museum of Fine Arts, Boston

National Arts Club, New York City

National Gallery of Art, Washington, D.C.

National Gallery of Canada, Ottawa

National Museum of American History, Smithsonian Institution, Washington, D.C.

Newark Museum, Newark, New Jersey

The New-York Historical Society

The New York Public Library, Astor, Lenox, and Tilden Foundations

New York State Historical Association, Cooperstown, New York

Pennsylvania Academy of the Fine Arts, Philadelphia

Philadelphia Museum of Art

Private Collection, New York City

Sterling and Francine Clark Art Institute, Williamstown, Massachusetts

The Museums at Stony Brook, Stony Brook, New York

The Toledo Museum of Art, Toledo, Ohio

Union League Club, New York City

Washington University Gallery of Art, St. Louis, Missouri

West Point Museum, United States Military Academy, West Point, New York

Westmoreland Museum of American Art, Greensburg, Pennsylvania

Whitney Museum of American Art, New York City

Woodmere Art Museum, Philadelphia

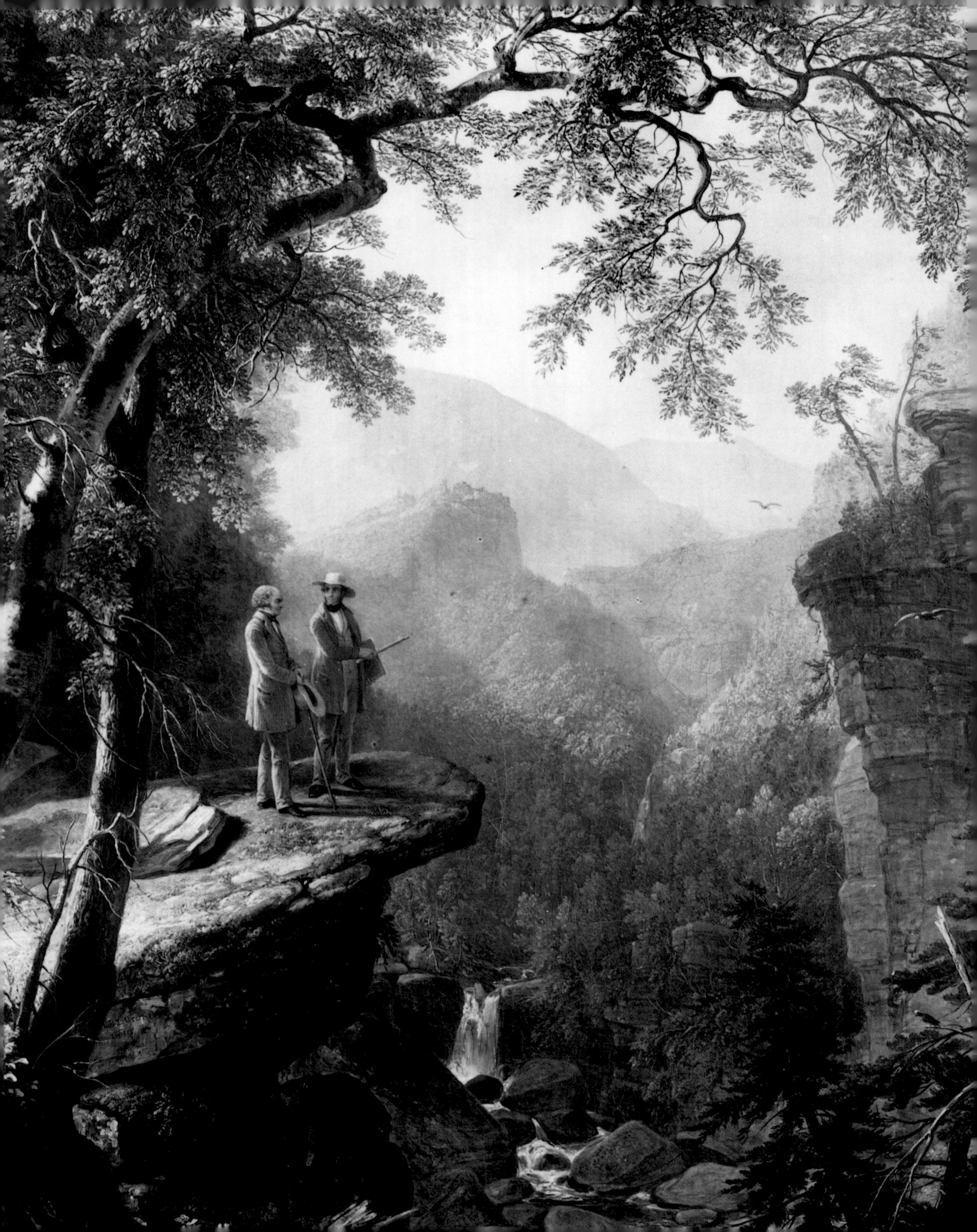

An Introduction to the History of American Art Criticism to 1925

DAVID B. DEARINGER

"A wise skepticism is the first attribute of a good critic."
JAMES RUSSELL LOWELL, *Shakespeare Once More*

Criticism has been defined as "the art of evaluating or analyzing with knowledge and propriety works of art or literature."[1] Since relatively little art was produced in America during the Colonial and early Federal periods—and far less was publicly displayed—the erudition and refinement required for such evaluation and analysis was slow to develop here. Before 1800, almost no criticism of the aesthetics or stylistic development of American artists or analyses of their works was published, nor were there many reliable venues for the printing of such critical expression even if it had been formulated. Most scholars have agreed that this situation began to change with the coming of the nineteenth century. Nevertheless, they have considered most art criticism published in this country during the first half of the nineteenth century to be cursory and superficial. Prevailing opinion has been that these early critics relied mostly on simple description and emphasized subject matter over almost everything else. They have been accused of having had no strong opinions, no sense of humor, and only a modicum of literary style. In fact, it has been written, these critics were seldom analytical or concerned with the formal or aesthetic qualities of a work of art and, therefore, did not deserve to be called critics at all.[2] Their writings have been dismissed as "either indiscriminate praise or ignorant ridicule."[3]

This may have been true during the first few decades of the nineteenth century; but a closer examination of art reviews published in this country during the second quarter of the century reveals that such assumptions have been too hastily made. These assessments overlook or ignore the abilities of certain writers of the period who were dedicated and highly capable professionals and whose writings make it clear that they understood that it was their duty as writers to show an interest in and knowledge of contemporary American art. In other words, while they may not have considered themselves to be professional art critics, most of them took their jobs seriously, educated themselves about art, and did their best to formulate logical and elucidating theories about it.[4]

Published articles on art in general greatly increased in this country between 1800 and 1850. In part, this was a direct result of the establishment of annual exhibitions of art at various venues in Philadelphia, New York, and Boston during the 1810s and 1820s (see the essay "Annual Exhibitions and the Birth of American Art Criticism to 1865" in this book). Once these more-or-less reliable venues were established, the professional critic began to find a place in the cultural life of the nation. Newspapers and periodicals, most of which were primarily political or literary, began to print articles on art more consistently. Admittedly, most of these "reviews" of art exhibitions were simply lists of objects with brief descriptions or comments attached. Easily understood representational symbolism, pride in American-born artists, and biographical anecdotes characterized many of these early articles. Subject matter often attracted more critical attention than style. Distinctive personalities or philosophies of individual art critics were rarely perceptible.

While some of these qualities remained characteristic at least until the Civil War, noticeable improvements in American art criticism began to appear during the 1830s and 1840s. Partially due to the increasing popularity of paintings of the Hudson River School—a distinctively *American* movement established under the leadership of Thomas Cole (see fig. 1)—writers for newspapers and periodicals became more experienced in viewing art. Consequently, their tastes became more sophisticated. As American art increased in quantity and in quality, and as its very existence seemed less tenuous, critics were more willing and better able to make astute and precise observations and to move beyond puffery and hyperbole. Consequently, the critic's power and stature in the world of journalism—and in the cultural world at large—increased. New periodicals, several of which were dedicated to art, began to appear. Likewise, reviews in newspapers, especially in New York, increased in length and became more detailed in content. By 1850, it was not uncommon for an exhibition review to be published serially, continued from one issue of a newspaper to another, sometimes stretching over as many as eight issues. Several paragraphs or even a whole article might be devoted to a single work of art or to one artist. While by-lines for the authors of these reviews remained rare, individual personalities and writing styles became more apparent. In some cases, it is possible to make an educated guess, based on style or external evidence, as to the identity of a specific author.

The trend toward professionalism continued after the Civil War when the art critic—widely recognized by name and

OPPOSITE: Detail of *Kindred Spirits* (fig. 6).

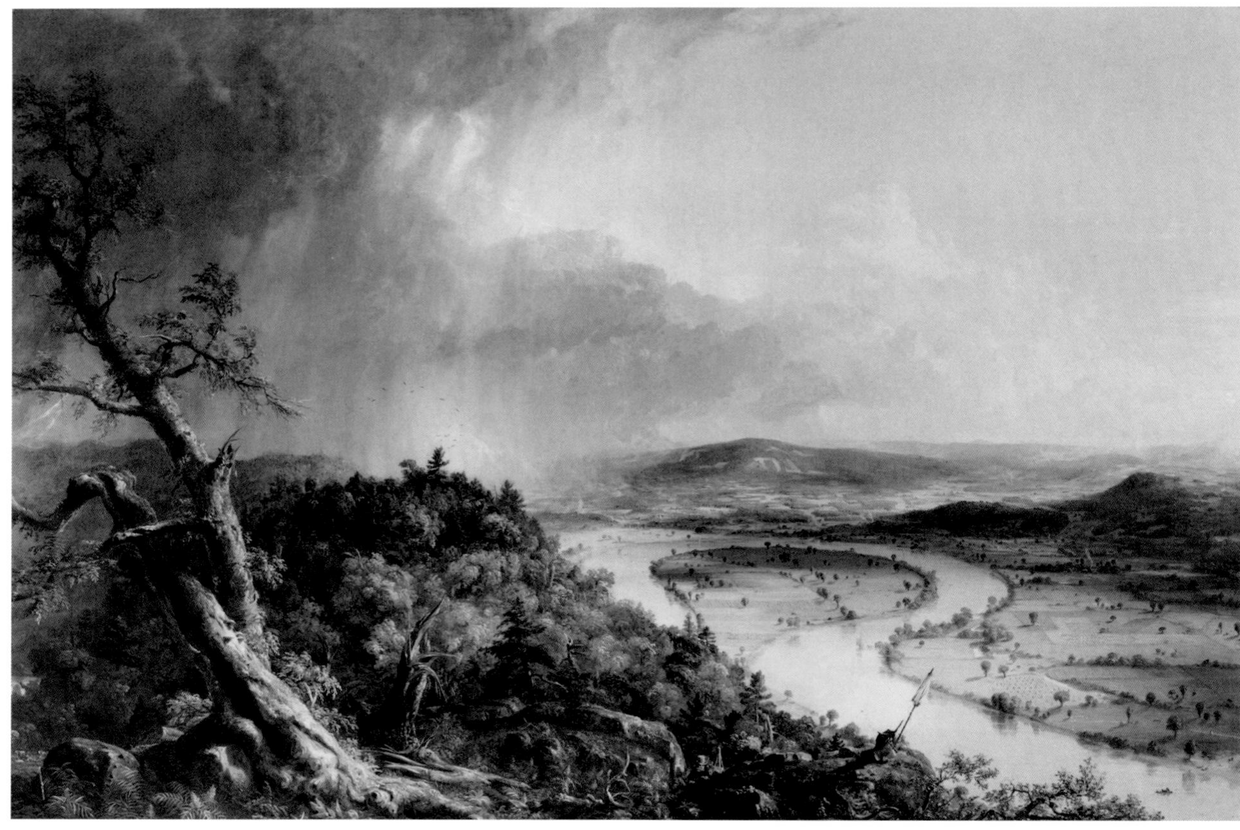

Fig. 1 Thomas Cole, *View from Mount Holyoke, Northampton Massachusetts, after a Thunder Storm (The Oxbow),* 1836, oil on canvas, 51½ x 76, The Metropolitan Museum of Art, Gift of Mrs. Russell Sage, 1908 (National Academy of Design, 11th Annual Exhibition, 1836, no. 149)

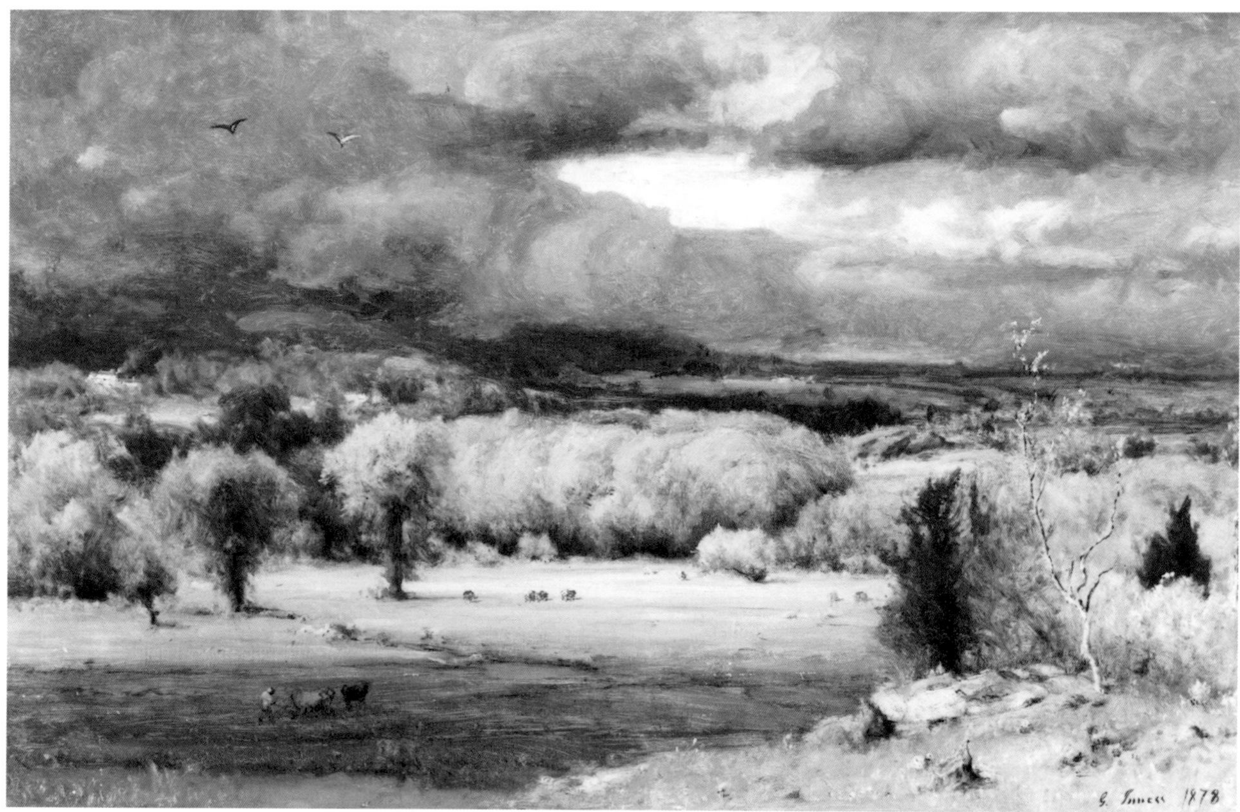

Fig. 2 George Inness, *The Coming Storm,* 1878, oil on canvas, 26 x 39, Albright-Knox Art Gallery, Buffalo, New York, Albert H. Tracy Fund, 1900 (National Academy of Design, 55th Annual Exhibition, 1880, no. 351)

attitude—finally emerged. Men—and eventually women—began to find long-term employment as "the" art critic or art editor for a particular journal or newspaper. The reasons for this change are many. Certainly, it was related to the postwar departure of many younger American artists for Europe, where they often studied, worked, and traveled for several years. Energized by their cosmopolitan experience, they returned to this country beginning in the 1870s, ready to expound a new aesthetic that emphasized formal and expressive qualities over subject matter (see fig. 2). New ways of creating and looking at art demanded new forms of art criticism. Art reviews became more impersonal and began to focus on the object and its style rather than on the personality of the artist.

The last three decades of the nineteenth century were also the time of the birth of the modern American art museum and the growth of commercial art galleries. As economics began to play a greater role in art, participants in the art world in general became smarter and more professional. Encouraged by their European experiences, American artists were more self-consciously aware of themselves as professionals living in a highly competitive world, while their patrons became more knowledgeable about artistic trends on both sides of the Atlantic. Not surprisingly, those writing about art—the art critics—followed suit.

No comprehensive study of the history of American art criticism has been published, although a number of important works that cover parts of the story exist. By way of introduction to the topic, the remainder of this essay will identify the several kinds of sources in which American art criticism appeared from its beginnings to the early twentieth century.

TREATISES AND DISCOURSES

The birth of art criticism in this country can be traced to a group of treatises, published in the eighteenth and early nineteenth centuries, that were meant to raise the cultural acumen of Americans in general. Some of these were designed to function as teaching aids to art students by providing art historical background and theoretical advice. The earliest were imported from Europe and included William Hogarth's *The Analysis of Beauty* (1753), Edmund Burke's *An Inquiry into the Origin of Our Ideas of the Sublime and Beautiful* (1757), and Archibald Alison's *Essays on the Nature and Principles of Taste* (1790).[5] Among the pedagogical discourses were those delivered by Sir Joshua Reynolds and Benjamin West to the students and members of the Royal Academy in London. These, too, were published and available on both sides of the Atlantic and, like the others named here, remained influential well into the nineteenth century.[6]

These British authors were followed and, to some degree, emulated by a small group of Americans who wrote, delivered, and often published their own treatises or "discourses" on art, usually focusing on the art of their own country.[7]

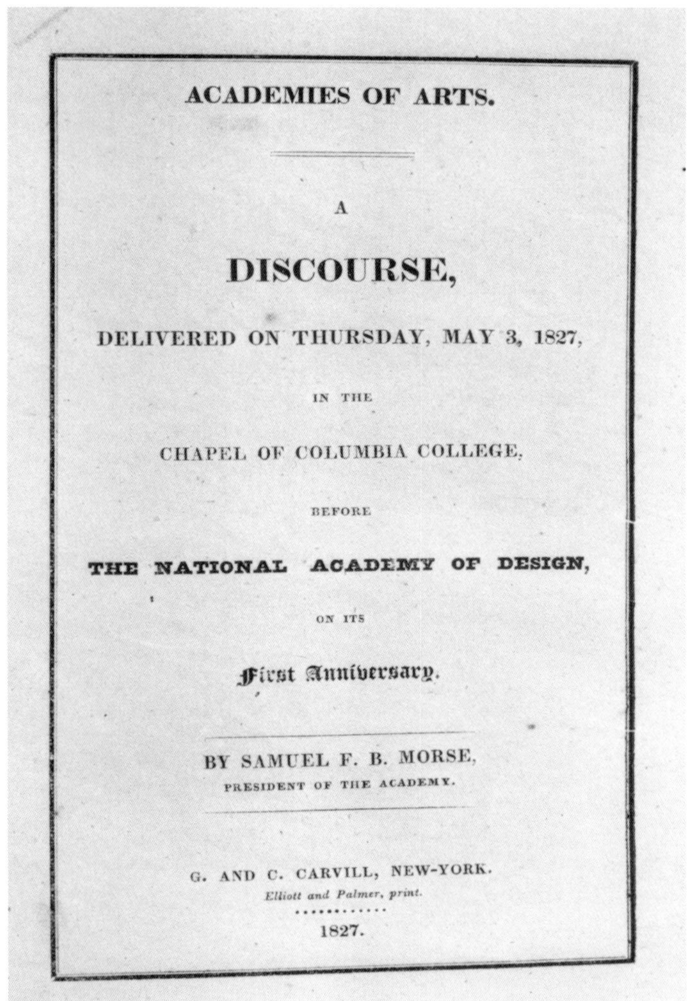

Fig. 3 Samuel F. B. Morse, *Academies of Arts. A Discourse, Delivered on Thursday, May 3, 1827, in the Chapel of Columbia College, Before The National Academy of Design on Its First Anniversary* (New York, 1827), Archives, National Academy of Design

These were often published in pamphlet form, although some were reprinted in periodicals such as Philadelphia's *Port Folio*, which published several during the early 1800s. Connoisseurs, collectors, and poets often wrote these discourses, among them being Joseph Hopkinson (whose discourse on art was published in 1810), De Witt Clinton (1816), and William Cullen Bryant (1865). Artists were just as likely to do so, however: architect Benjamin Henry Latrobe (1811); painters Samuel F. B. Morse (1827; fig. 3) and Thomas Cole (1836); and sculptor Horatio Stone (1858) all delivered and published discourses prior to the Civil War.[8]

The typical discourse began with a rather lengthy history of Western art, sometimes tracing back to the Greeks and Romans and then forward again to the art of the New World. If the discourse originated as a lecture or address, the importance of the organization before which it was initially delivered—the Pennsylvania Academy of the Fine Arts or the National Academy of Design, for example—was touted.

When artists were mentioned by name, the great American success stories received their due. Depending on the date of the lecture, the most popular of these were Benjamin West, John Singleton Copley, John Trumbull, Gilbert Stuart, John Vanderlyn, Washington Allston, and Thomas Cole.[9]

PERIODICALS[10]

For the earliest published art criticism in this country, one might point to Mather Byles's poem written as a tribute to John Smibert, a portrait painter who had immigrated to America from Scotland in 1728. The poem was published in Philadelphia in the *American Weekly Mercury* two years after Smibert's arrival.[11] The first essay on art printed in this country was "Of the knowledge of Painting," which appeared in 1745 in the *American Magazine and Historical Chronicle*, which had begun publication in Boston two years earlier.[12] Benjamin West (fig. 4) was the first American-born artist to be mentioned by name in the American press.[13] Again, this attention came in the form of poetry and appeared in the *American Magazine and Monthly Chronicle for the British Colonies*, a short-lived journal published by the College of Philadelphia from 1757 to 1758.[14] All three of these magazines were general in nature, with articles on science, literature, music, and politics. None specialized in articles on the fine arts, and the poems about Smibert and West were adulatory to the extreme, "mawkish doggerel," as one modern historian has called it.[15]

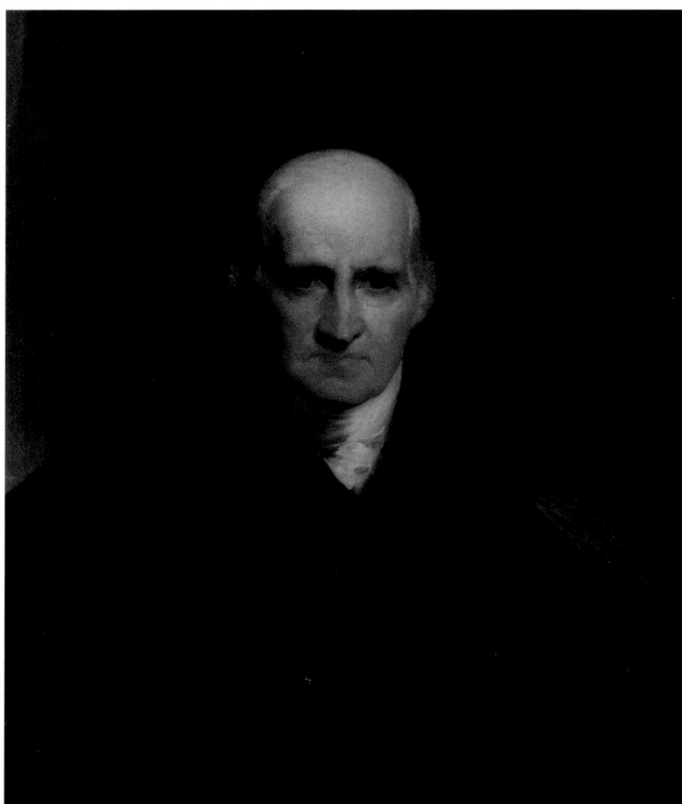

Fig. 4 Samuel F. B. Morse, after Sir Thomas Lawrence, *Benjamin West*, n.d., oil on canvas, 30 x 25, National Academy of Design

The art magazine and formal art criticism would not appear in America for a number of decades.

Nevertheless, as more periodicals of a general nature began to be produced in the new United States in the 1780s and 1790s, more articles on art appeared.[16] *The Boston Magazine* included essays on taste and beauty and, in the mid 1780s, reprinted sections of Sir Joshua Reynolds's famous *Discourses*.[17] In Philadelphia, the *American Museum* printed similar articles on taste, including a long essay by Rev. Timothy Dwight, and art-related poems similar to those mentioned above.[18] In fact, most articles published from 1780 to 1810 either addressed very general topics—such as "beauty" or "taste"—or suggested reasons for the slow growth of art in America and offered plans for its "improvement."[19] Something slightly different, however, appeared in 1809 when the *Port Folio* published a brief item that gave the whereabouts and activities of several American artists, including Benjamin West and John Vanderlyn.[20] This type of informative notice would eventually become a staple of American art periodicals.

The earliest articles to discuss American landscape painting date from this period, too; they appeared in the *New Haven Gazette* and *Connecticut Magazine* in 1787 and the *New-York Weekly Magazine* in 1796.[21] A landscape painter was also a protagonist in the first documented art dispute in this country. It occurred in Baltimore in 1807 between the artist Francis Guy and the editor of the *Observer,* Eliza Godefroy, who wrote under the name of Beatrice Ironsides. Godefroy called Baltimore "the Siberia of the arts" and Guy "an Amateur." As might be expected, a vicious battle, chronicled elsewhere, ensued.[22]

It has been estimated that only about fifty periodicals were published in America before 1800; most of these were short-lived and had a small circulation. Between 1800 and 1825, however, that number almost doubled, and by 1850 approximately six hundred periodicals were being produced here. While the vast majority of these included articles on a variety of topics, they published increasing numbers of articles on art.[23] Among the more significant of those dating from the first half of the nineteenth century were two New York publications: the *New-York Mirror* (1823–1847), founded by George Pope Morris and eventually illustrated with engravings, many of which were based on paintings by American artists, and the *Knickerbocker* (1833–1865), which reached prominence under the editorship of Lewis Gaylord Clark, a friend of artists and writers.[24] In Boston, the *North American Review* (1815–1940) had articles on art and taste in its earliest issues;[25] and in Philadelphia, *Sartain's Union Magazine* (1847–1852) featured a series of "Art Notices" written by the artist and editor John Sartain. Also of note was *Graham's Magazine* (1841–1858), named for its founder George Rex Graham, who had abandoned a law career in favor of publishing. Not only did Graham hire many of this country's most important writers as contributors to his magazine—Edgar Alan Poe, James Greenleaf Whittier, Seba Smith, and James Russell Lowell, for example—he also commissioned original woodcuts, engravings, and mezzotints for the magazine. Articles about art often supplemented these illustrations. Notable here are eleven pieces written by Estelle Anna Lewis and published in *Graham's* from 1854 to 1856 under the general title "Art and Artists of America."[26] Other magazines from the antebellum period that carried articles about art were *Gentleman's Magazine* (1837–1840); the *United States Magazine and Democratic Review* (1837–1859); *Littell's Living Age* (1844– 1896); the *American Whig Review* (1845–1852); and the *Literary World* (1847–1853).[27]

All of these were published in the larger cities on the East Coast, but the provinces were not bereft of similar journals. In the antebellum period, Cincinnati was the publishing center of the west and produced a surprising number of literary journals, many of which published articles on art. Among these were the *Western Monthly Review* (1827–1830), the *Cincinnati Mirror* (1831–1836), the *Hesperian* (1838–1839), and the *Ladies' Repository* (1841–1876).[28] Another important regional journal was Richmond, Virginia's, *Southern Literary Messenger* (1834–1864), which published over fifty articles on art during its thirty-year run. Sculptors Hiram Powers, William Barbee, and, especially, Thomas Crawford were the subject of articles in the magazine, as were painters Thomas Cole and Frederic E. Church. Reviews of books by Washington Allston and Christopher Pearse Cranch and serial essays by George Cooke and Charles Lanman appeared there. Although occasional references were made to local events, the magazine always maintained a national scope in its coverage.[29]

It was not until 1839 that the first publication devoted to art appeared in this country. This was the *Transactions* of the Apollo Association, which, in 1844 became the American Art-Union. In 1848, the organization also began publishing its *Bulletin*, edited by the engraver William J. Hoppin. Both publications continued until the Art-Union folded in 1852.[30] Similar ones were produced for brief periods in the late 1840s and early 1850s by art unions in Cincinnati, Philadelphia, and Boston. All of these organizations sought to promote and distribute American art through a lottery system that was eventually judged illegal. With circulation limited to members or "subscribers," the art union publications favored news items over true criticism. When criticism did appear, it was decidedly nationalistic and optimistic in tone.[31]

Similar to these serials in basic content and purpose, the *Cosmopolitan Art Journal* was larger in format and broader in scope. It was published as the organ for another art union, the Cosmopolitan Art Association, from 1856 to 1861. Its mission was to bring art "to the people," and it favored articles of an art historical nature, including summaries of "schools" of art and brief biographies of American artists written in an informal, sometimes gossipy language.

The *Cosmopolitan Art Journal* was one of about nine new journals devoted to art that appeared in this country during the 1850s. The most important of these was the *Crayon*, which began publication in New York in 1855. Edited by William James Stillman and John Durand, both of whom were artists as well as writers, it had a respectable circulation and lasted until 1861.[32] The *Crayon* was the first art magazine in America to align itself with a particular aesthetic, one that had been formulated and promoted in the writings of the great British artist and art theorist John Ruskin.[33] The magazine included essays, exhibition reviews, travel notes, poems, book reviews, fiction, and scripts for plays, most of which were directly or indirectly related to art. Several sections were devoted to brief news items, tracking the movements and progress of American artists around the world. Contributors included William Cullen Bryant, Lydia Sigourney, Rembrandt Peale, Asher Brown Durand, William Page, and Horatio Greenough. The *Crayon* was one of the first American art journals to publish articles about the art of criticism itself.[34] These articles attempted to define the role of the art critic, amateur or professional, and the effect criticism had on individual artists. As might be expected, this elicited response, some quite caustic, from writers for other journals. Although no issues were resolved in the debate, the fact that the *Crayon* bothered to publish on the subject at all suggests that the role of the art critic was at least beginning to be acknowledged and even beginning to be taken seriously.[35]

With the demise of both the *Cosmopolitan Art Journal* and the *Crayon* in 1861, a new periodical stepped into the breach. Initiated that same year, the *New Path* was, like the *Crayon*, decidedly Ruskinian in its outlook. In fact, during the two and a half years of its existence, it functioned as the mouthpiece for the Society for the Advancement of Truth in Art, an American version of England's Pre-Raphaelite Brotherhood.[36] The periodical eschewed news items for criticism and, in fact, picked up where the *Crayon* left off by actually writing about the art critic as a professional. An important article on the subject by Russell Sturgis appeared in the journal in 1864. The successful critic, Sturgis lectured, has "a familiar and intimate knowledge of nature, and not only a practical knowledge to be gained by observation and experience, but also a scientific knowledge." While the artist can afford to be emotional, the critic must be "cool, considered, moderate" and yet show "independence and boldness."[37]

Following the Civil War, American art periodicals grew in number and size—many were published in a larger format. As competition increased, wood engravings and even fine prints and chromolithographs became a staple in many of them. This was a characteristic of the *Aldine*, published in New York between 1868 and 1879. It started life with a literary focus but in 1876, under the editorship of James Sutton, Jr., shifted its emphasis to the fine arts.[38]

Another important periodical of the period was the *Art Journal*, which ran for thirteen volumes between 1875 and 1887. While it included a number of articles on contemporary art, it published many that were more art historical. Also dating from the 1870s were the *Magazine of Art* (1878–1904), a

British publication with an American supplement; *Art Interchange* (1878–1904), which dealt with both the decorative and the fine arts; the *American Art Review* (1879–1881), which was more scholarly than the others (an aspect that may have contributed to its relatively quick demise); and the *Art Amateur* (1879–1903), which, with an eventual circulation of over ten thousand, was one of the most popular art periodicals of the time.[39]

The proliferation of improved art journals continued into the 1880s. Dating from those decades were the *Studio* (1881–1894), which, thanks to the leadership of the art critic Clarence Cook, changed from a musical review to an art journal in 1884; and the *Art Age* (1883–1889), which featured more articles on architecture than did most art journals at the time. Also of note was the *Collector* (1889–1897), which was dominated by its editor and publisher Alfred Trumble. The *Collector* lived up to its name by providing information particularly useful to buyers, sellers, or collectors of art; typical topics were the art market, private collections, exhibitions, and book reviews.[40]

The final decade of the century saw the introduction of such influential journals as the *Art Student* (1892–1907) and the *Monthly Illustrator* (1893–1897). A number of regional art journals, some with a nation-wide circulation, were also being produced, notably in the Midwest. Among the most significant of these was Chicago's *Brush and Pencil* (1897–1907), which was well illustrated with drawings and reproductions of modern and old master paintings and featured learned editorials by Charles Francis Browne and William F. Morton.[41] Browne was a landscape painter as well as a journalist, as was James William Pattison, who edited another Chicago art periodical, the *Fine Arts Journal* (1899–1919). Another interesting though short-lived Chicago serial was called simply *Arts* and was edited by Mrs. T. Vernette Morse in 1893–94. It featured many articles and illustrations by women critics and artists. In 1894, it became the official organ of the Central Art Association, which eventually renamed the publication *Arts for America*. Its articles were historical and educational, and it even supplied its readers with bibliographic information. Among its contributors were sculptor Lorado Taft and painter Alexander Van Laer. Although *Arts for America* ceased publication in 1900, it has recently been cited as having been "one of the finest art periodicals in the country."[42]

In addition to these art periodicals, of course, the nineteenth century continued to see the rise and fall of a number of extremely popular journals of a general nature that printed articles on art and artists in many issues. The second half of the century gave birth to four of the most popular magazines this country has ever seen: *Harper's New Monthly Magazine* (1850–1900); *Scribner's Monthly* (1870–1881), which continued as the *Century* (1881–1929); and *Scribner's Magazine* (1887–1939).[43] Like the earlier journals named above, these periodicals were aimed at an audience of diverse interests and varying levels of education and are notable for their fine journalism and longevity. However, even these giants of publishing history had plenty of competition in the form of *Putnam's Magazine* (1853–1870); the *Nation* (1865–present); the *Galaxy* (1866–1878); *Lippincott's Magazine* (1868–1916); and *Appleton's Journal* (1869–1881).

N E W S P A P E R S

Eighteenth-century newspapers in America were even less likely to contain articles on art than were periodicals of the day.[44] Most were aligned with a particular political faction, and politics was their main topic. During the 1790s, this political emphasis was expanded to include items of mercantile and economic interest. It has been pointed out, for example, that all eleven weekly newspapers being published in New York in 1800 were dependent on commercial interests for their existence, a fact reflected in the types of articles they carried.[45] Lists of ship arrivals and departures, stock and bond quotations, and real estate transactions, all printed in small type densely arranged in long columns, were typical. Topics that were not directly related to business or politics, such as the arts, rarely received coverage. This limited range of subject matter undoubtedly contributed to the low circulation of most newspapers. In 1820, for example, neither of the two largest papers in New York, the *Commercial Advertiser* and the *Evening Post*, had a daily circulation of more than two thousand copies.[46]

In the 1820s, American newspapers underwent a dramatic change, signaling the beginning of what has come to be known as the Golden Age of American journalism. Like periodicals, newspapers greatly increased in number: in 1800, there were about two hundred newspapers in the United States; by 1830 there were over twelve hundred.[47] At the same time, under the leadership of a new breed of visionary editors and publishers, newspapers greatly expanded their missions by covering all types of contemporary events and interests. A sign of this change was the appointment in 1826 of William Cullen Bryant as editor of New York's *Evening Post*, which had been founded in 1801 by Alexander Hamilton.[48] Bryant, who would hold his position at the *Post* until 1870, was this country's leading poet, not a journalist. He was an intimate friend of artists such as Samuel Morse, Asher Brown Durand, and Thomas Cole, and his presence at the *Post* had an immediate and palpable impact on the paper, giving it a cultural slant that it had not had.[49]

Another sign of change—one that signaled the arrival of newspapers with much larger circulation—was the merger in 1829 of two New York papers to form the *Courier and Enquirer*, published under the leadership of James Watson Webb (1802–1884). Until it was consolidated with the *New York World* in 1861, it was one of the largest and most powerful papers in the country, with a circulation that far exceeded the paltry numbers of earlier newspapers. This was true, too, of the *Courier*'s first major competitor, the *New York Sun*, founded in 1833. Printed in a smaller format and costing only a penny a copy, the *Sun* soon had a circulation that equaled that of the powerful *Courier*. Although its popularity waned during the Civil War, it experienced a major revival when it was purchased in 1868 by Charles A. Dana.[50] The success of these papers only sparked more competition in the form of the *New York Herald*, founded by James Gordon Bennett in 1835; and the *New York Tribune*, begun by Horace Greeley in 1841 and edited by him for over thirty years.[51] These two papers dominated American journalism for decades. By 1853, the *Herald*'s circulation was over fifty-two thousand, making it the most widely read daily newspaper in the country, and the *Tribune* was close behind.[52] By that time, though, they had a new rival in the form of the *New-York Times*, which began publication in 1851. As we shall see in the essay "Annual Exhibitions and the Birth of American Art Criticism to 1865" in this book, these newspapers gave unprecedented coverage to the fine arts.

Meanwhile, other major American cities were seeing similar activity. During the 1820s and 1830s in Boston, for example, "the air seemed to quiver with new dailies," as one historian has put it.[53] The most enduring of these were the *Transcript*, the *Post*, the *Traveller*, and the *Daily Advertiser*. The last, founded in 1813, was edited by Nathan Hale, nephew and namesake of the patriot, and was the first successful daily paper in New England. Among its contributors were Edward Everett, Jared Sparks, and William Ellery Channing.[54] Probably the most successful of these Boston papers, at least in terms of circulation, was the *Transcript*. It was founded in 1830 and by the time of the Civil War, it was Boston's leading paper. Although it was better known for criticism of literature and drama, it did publish reviews of exhibitions, notably those at the Boston Athenaeum. Later in the century, it employed professional writers such as Ralph Adams Cram and William Howe Downes to write about the fine arts.[55] Also important in Boston was the *Courier* (1824–1864), founded by the printer and author Joseph T. Buckingham. Buckingham's deep interest in literature and the theater earned the *Courier* distinction as "the most lively and literary of the city's dailies."[56]

By the 1830s, Philadelphia had more than a dozen daily newspapers, the most enduring of which proved to be the *Inquirer*, founded in 1829. One of its chief rivals was the *Public Ledger*. Founded in 1836, the *Ledger* achieved its greatest circulation after it was purchased in 1864 by George W. Childs, one of this country's best-known publishers and philanthropists.[57] Meanwhile, Baltimore, which by 1830 was the second largest city in the nation, had two daily newspapers with wide circulations—the *American*, which ran for 129 years beginning in 1799, and the *Sun*, founded in 1837—and a weekly, *Niles' Weekly Register* (1811–1849), which had a national circulation.[58] The first was more likely to run articles on art, but the other two had occasional notices on the subject.

During the antebellum period, Washington, D.C., was dominated by the *Daily National Intelligencer*. It was the capital's leading daily from 1813 through the Civil War and, at the time, was nationally recognized as one of the country's best newspapers. As of 1830, its major rival was the *Globe*, founded

that year as a radical counter to the *Intelligencer*'s basically moderate tone. As such, the *Globe* was more blatantly political, leaving the *Intelligencer* as the city's more likely publisher of articles on the arts.[59] Notable here is the paper's fairly detailed coverage of the U.S. government's attempts to commission works of art for the Capitol.[60]

For the most part, the attention newspapers began to give to American artists during the 1820s and 1830s came in one of two forms. The first was the exhibition review, a type of article made more or less mandatory by the instigation of the various annual exhibitions. These regular, dependable, and predictable events provided newspapers with the opportunity to publish lively and timely commentary that would be of immediate interest to readers. As will be seen in the essays that follow, it also allowed writers to compare one year's exhibition to those of the past and thereby to track the "progress" of American art.

The second type of article common in nineteenth-century American newspapers took the form of a column that typically appeared under titles such as "Sketchings," "Art Matters," or simply "Fine Arts." More often than not, these were anthologies of brief, informative items—often ten or more—that told readers of the travels of artists and the identity of specific paintings or sculptures on which they were working. While similar articles appeared in many art periodicals, they were more common to newspapers. They were rare in journals of a general nature.

Some of America's early important writers on art are more accurately called historians than critics.[61] The best known of these was the painter William Dunlap (fig. 5), who wrote the first history of American art, *History of the Rise and Progress of the Arts of Design in the United States*, published in two volumes in 1834. For the most part, it consists of a series of biographies, many of which were based on facts Dunlap gleaned directly from his subjects; its overall tone is very positive.[62] It was followed in 1846 by Charles Edwards Lester's *The Artists of America*. Lester borrowed freely from Dunlap, but with only seven chapters, each devoted to a single artist, his book was not nearly so comprehensive as his predecessor's.[63]

The following year, 1847, Henry T. Tuckerman published *Artist Life, or Sketches of American Painters*, which he expanded into *Book of the Artists* in 1867.[64] Like Lester, Tuckerman followed Dunlap's basic biographical approach,[65] but he was more willing to draw some theoretical conclusions about his topic. These were affected by his belief that an American artistic style, based on close observation and adherence to the rules of nature, actually does exist.[66] In fact, of these authors, Tuckerman was probably the closest to being a true critic. He had begun his writing career as an author of European travel books, and, in 1843, was editor for the short-lived *Boston Miscellany of Literature and Fashion*. He has been credited with writing some of the best articles for the *North American*

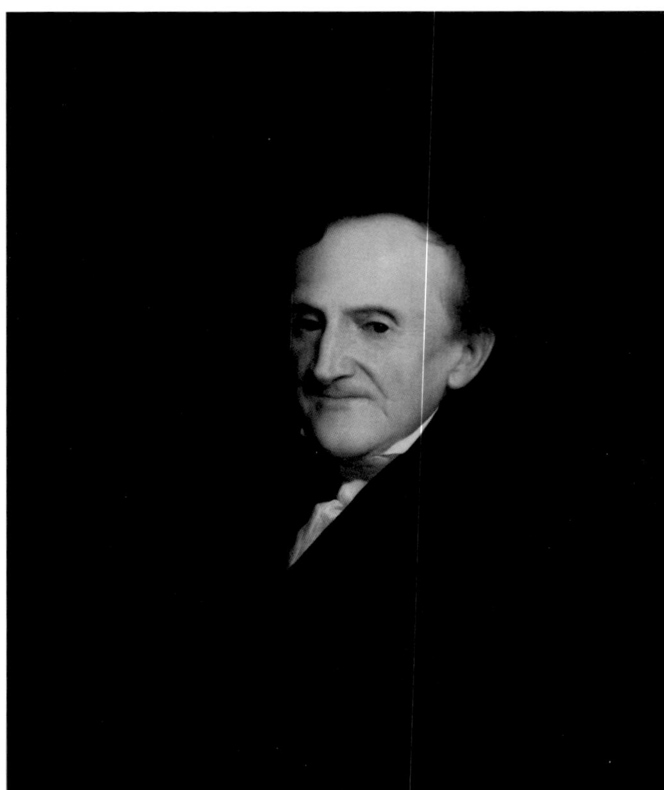

Fig. 5 Charles Cromwell Ingham, *William Dunlap*, 1838–39, oil on canvas, 30 x 25, National Academy of Design (National Academy of Design, 15th Annual Exhibition, 1840, no. 195)

Review from the 1840s to the 1860s.[67] He was personally acquainted with many American artists, and this was certainly part of his reason for eventually turning his attention to them. *Book of the Artists* is said to be one of the first art historical works to have sold well in this country.[68]

The earliest books that surveyed the history of American sculpture appeared at mid-century as well, both published in Boston in the 1850s. The first was Pickering Dodge's *Sculpture and the Plastic Arts*, which summarized the history of sculpture from the ancient world to modern times. While the contents were decidedly Eurocentric, Dodge devoted his final chapter to sculpture in the United States. He briefly mentioned Horatio Greenough, Robert Ball Hughes, Thomas Crawford, and Hiram Powers; but his favorite American sculptor, Shobal Clevenger, earned a more lengthy account, probably because that sculptor's early death had touched Pickering deeply.[69]

Similar to and contemporary with Dodge's book was Hannah F. Lee's *Familiar Sketches of Sculpture and Sculptors*, published in 1854. Like Dodge, Lee surveyed the entire history of sculpture, which included, in a final chapter, American sculptors. After writing about some of her more recent European favorites—Antonio Canova, Bertel Thorwaldsen, Anne Seymour Damer, and John Flaxman—she turned to the Americans. Among these she preferred Horatio Greenough, Henry Dexter, and John C. King, and, in a final chapter devoted to them, the women sculptors Caroline Wilson, Mary Anne Dubois, and Harriet Hosmer.[70]

The early American art histories by Dunlap, Lester, and Tuckerman included substantial information on American artists, both living and dead. Later surveys tended to ignore or gloss over the earlier years. They might have begun by making some brief statements about West, Allston, Stuart, or Cole, but then they quickly leapt forward to the art of more recent times. Notable here is Samuel W. G. Benjamin's *Art In America*, published in 1880; Sadakichi Hartmann's *History of American Art* (1901); Lorado Taft's *History of American Sculpture* (1903); Samuel Isham's *History of American Painting* (1905); and Charles Caffin's *American Masters of Painting* (1907). Of these, Taft's and Isham's are the most comprehensive. Both authors were artists, and they reviewed the history of American sculpture and painting, respectively, in terms of artistic education, influences, patronage, and stylistic development. Their books had a wide enough following that both were revised and reissued. A revised edition of Taft's book was published in 1924, followed by a new edition with an additional chapter by Adeline Adams in 1930. A new edition of Isham's book appeared in 1927, with five additional chapters written by the critic Royal Cortissoz.

OTHER SOURCES OF
AMERICAN ART CRITICISM

If we return to the definition of criticism given at the start of this essay, we find that it does not restrict the type of vehicle by which an evaluation or analysis of a work of art may be given. Admittedly, criticism most often comes in the form of a review published in a magazine or newspaper; but there are other, less expected methods of critical expression.

One of these is poetry, which was mentioned briefly above and which is the topic of William H. Gerdts's essay elsewhere in this book. Among other things, poetry is an expression of opinion, and as such can be taken as a form of criticism. Admittedly, since poetry written about paintings or sculptures usually grows out of admiration or even awe for the works of art, the opinion expressed or implied is almost always positive; but that does not prevent poetry from being an interesting, if eccentric, form of criticism. The associations between art and poetry in America have often been strong, and they were especially so during the first half of the nineteenth century. In fact, a number of American artists were also published poets—the painters Washington Allston, Christopher Pearse Cranch, and Thomas Buchanan Read, and the sculptors Joel Tanner Hart and Alexander Galt published poems in major periodicals and anthologies.[71] Friendships existed between artists and poets—that of Thomas Cole and William Cullen Bryant, memorialized in Asher Brown Durand's painting *Kindred Spirits* (fig. 6), immediately comes to mind. Their relationship, in fact, is a good example of how inspiration can work in both directions. Bryant wrote a poem

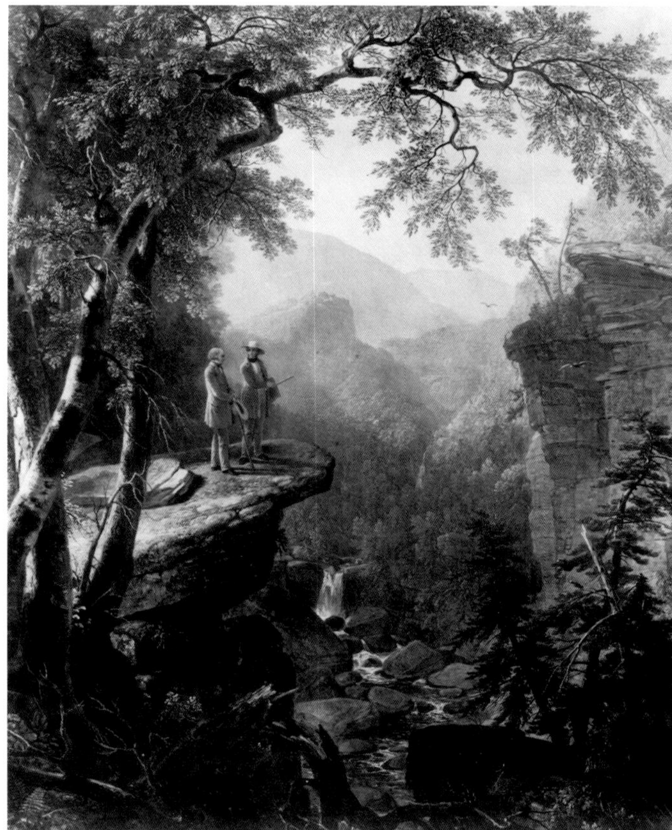

Fig. 6 Asher Brown Durand, *Kindred Spirits,* 1848, oil on canvas, 46 x 36, New York Public Library Collection of The New York Public Library, Astor, Lenox and Tilden Foundations (National Academy of Design, 24th Annual Exhibition, 1849, no. 180)

about Cole's departure for Europe, and Cole found inspiration for his paintings in Bryant's poetic concepts of nature. Durand, too, was inspired by Bryant both in general and in particular: Bryant's poem, "Thanatopsis," inspired a painting by Durand (see no. 17).[72] Finally, some writers who were better known as art historians or critics were also admired for their poetry—critic John Neal's poems, for example, were credited with having "the unquestionable stamp of genius," while those of historian and critic Henry T. Tuckerman were called "expressions of graceful and romantic sentiment."[73]

Another type of art criticism can be found in many of the hundreds of travel books that were published in this country in the nineteenth century, especially from the 1820s through the 1860s. American artists and their works were the subject of sections of many of these books, which were written by participants in the Grand Tour of Europe. Among the authors of travel books with significant commentary on American art were Rembrandt Peale (whose travel book was published in 1831), Henry T. Tuckerman (1837), Catherine Sedgwick (1841), Horace Greeley (1851), William Cullen Bryant (1851), Harriet Beecher Stowe (1854), and Nathaniel Hawthorne (1871). All of these travelers visited the studios of American artists living in Europe, notably in Florence or Rome, and wrote about what they saw there.[74] Europeans, especially the British, who visited America also wrote about American art in their travel books. The most famous of these were Frances Trollope and Charles Dickens, but there were many others besides these two.[75]

Although it was short-lived, one other published source for a type of art criticism in America should be mentioned. The idea for these publications originated with the British journalist and art historian Henry Blackburn, who, beginning in 1875, published a series of small volumes under the general title *Academy Notes.* Following the basic format of an exhibition catalogue, these volumes included listings for and engraved illustrations of many of the works in the then-current annual exhibition of the Royal Academy. Small maps of the Academy's galleries, marked with the location of works of art in the exhibition, were also included. The purpose of the *Notes* was to edify those who could not attend the exhibitions and to provide a memento for those who did. According to Blackburn, his *Notes* were meant to be descriptive rather than critical; but he often expressed an opinion anyway, albeit briefly. For example, in the first entry in the first edition of the *Notes,* Blackburn wrote that a painting was "pleasant, carefully painted . . . without pathos." Another had a "graceful composition" and included "noble, and lovely" figures painted with a "dexterous use of low tones."[76] Some of the illustrations in the *Notes* were taken from photographs or drawings provided by the artists, but most were engraved from sketches made by Blackburn himself, based on his own "memory notes" since sketching was not permitted in the Royal Academy's galleries.[77]

The American version of these volumes was published in New York from 1881 through 1889 by author and journalist Charles M. Kurtz, first under the title *American Academy Notes,* then as *Illustrated Art Notes,* and finally as *National Academy Notes* (fig. 7).[78] All nine volumes were published in New York in conjunction with the annual exhibitions of the National Academy of Design, and each was intended to be "an independent supplement to the official catalogue" of the exhibition. In the first volume, Kurtz acknowledged his indebtedness to Blackburn's *Notes,* which, he reported, "have been received with such great favor on both sides of the Atlantic, as to encourage the belief that 'Notes' somewhat similar in character, devoted to the annual exhibitions of the American National Academy, would meet with like approval."[79]

"Similar" is exactly what Kurtz's *Notes* are. By including illustrations of and commentary on many of the works in the National Academy's exhibitions, as well as detailed maps of its galleries, Kurtz followed Blackburn's format almost exactly (fig. 8). When his editions proved popular, Kurtz expanded them. In 1882, he began to include brief biographies of artists and, two years later, he provided a history of the National Academy. In 1885 he incorporated an appendix that listed museums, galleries, private collections, and the dates and locations of other exhibitions in New York.

Like Blackburn's volumes, Kurtz's were successful with the public. Several issues appeared in more than one edition, and some were available with an attractive hardcover binding.

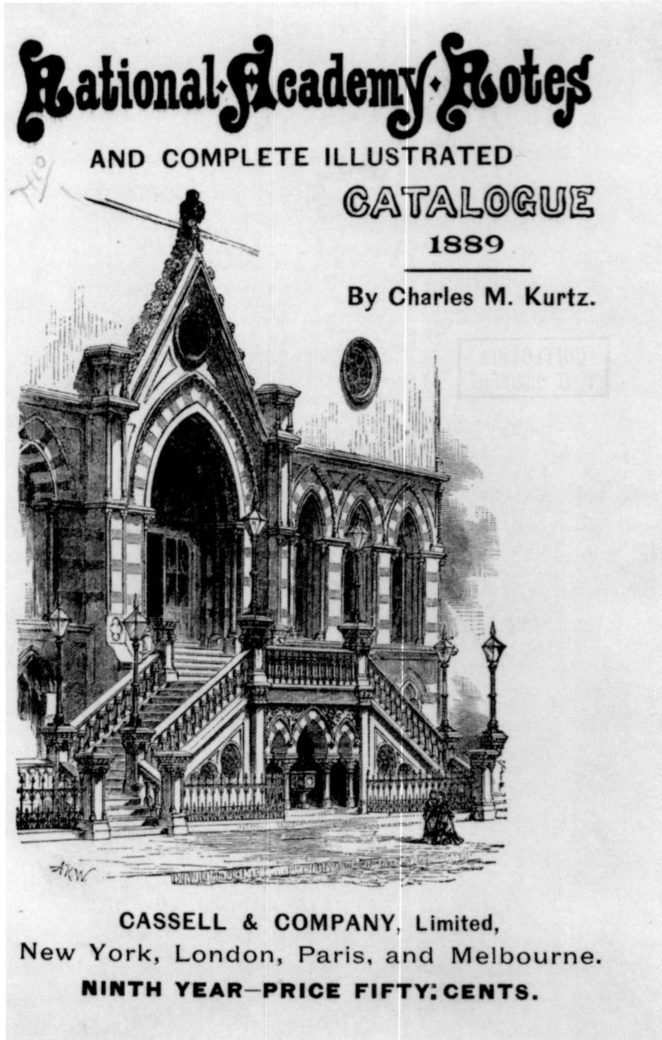

Fig. 7 Charles Kurtz, *National Academy Notes and Complete Illustrated Catalogue*, title page (New York, 1889), Archives, National Academy of Design

Kurtz improved upon Blackburn's publications, however, when he convinced a majority of artists to contribute original sketches of their paintings for publication in his *Notes*. Of the 122 illustrations in the issue of 1881, for example, only 25 were not provided by the artists who created the paintings that they illustrated.[80] At least in the early years, the commentary Kurtz provided was similar to Blackburn's, too, in that it was part description and part opinion. For example, in 1883, Kurtz devoted a comparatively lengthy paragraph to Gilbert Gaul's *Silenced* (location unknown), which he called "one of the most striking pictures in the exhibition." Gaul, he reported, "has succeeded in painting the effect of violent death with startling and horrible realism." That same year, Kurtz called Charles Ulrich's *The Glassblowers* (see no. 48) "an exceptionally excellent picture" executed with "surpassingly fine technique."[81] In later volumes, Kurtz reduced such commentary to simple descriptions of only one or two sentences. The reasons for this noticeable change are unknown. Perhaps it was simply a matter of space, or maybe Kurtz found himself being criticized for his comments, as so often happens to art critics.

NOTES

1. *Webster's Third New International Dictionary of the English Language* (Springfield, Massachusetts, 1981), 538.

2. The best history of early art criticism in this country is still John Peter Simoni, "Art Critics and Criticism in Nineteenth Century America" (Ph.D. diss., Ohio State University, 1952). Also see Janice Reed Hellman's excellent "American Art Criticism in the Mid-Nineteenth Century: 1840–1860" (M.A. thesis, George Washington University, 1972); and, for the antebellum period, Anne Farmer Meservey, "The Role of Art in American Life: Critics' Views on Native Art and Literature, 1830–1865," *American Art Journal* 10 (May 1978): 73–89. For later periods see Arlene R. Olson, *Art Critics and the Avant-Garde, New York 1900–1913* (Ann Arbor, Michigan, 1975); Peninah R. Y. Petruck, "American Art Criticism: 1910–1939" (Ph.D. diss., New York University, 1979); Linda Docherty, "A Search for Identity: American Art Criticism and the Concept of the 'Native School,' 1876–1893" (Ph.D. diss., University of North Carolina at Chapel Hill, 1985); Cynthia H. Prebus, "Transitions in American Art and Criticism: The Formative Years of Early American Modernism, 1895–1905" (Ph.D. diss., Rutgers, The State University of New Jersey, New Brunswick, 1994); and JoAnne Marie Mancini, "Enabling Modernism: American Art Criticism, 1865–1913" (Ph.D. diss., The Johns Hopkins University, Baltimore, 1996).

3. Simoni, 2. Simoni was not the first to summarize early American art criticism in this way. Henry T. Tuckerman, writing in the 1860s, referred to contemporary criticism as consisting of "exaggerated praise and newspaper puffs" (Henry T. Tuckerman, *Book of the Artists* [New York: Charles Scribner, 1864], 38).

4. There seems to have been a feeling in the United States, particularly during the antebellum years, that styling oneself a critic was a pretentious thing to do. Not surprisingly then, those who took on the role of critic were often criticized themselves. In 1841, for example, a writer for the *New World* expressed frustration and exhaustion at the words being repeatedly used by the press to describe works of art. The examples he gave—"hard," "stiff," "cold," "rigid," and others—were, he thought, evidence of a woefully small vocabulary ("World of Art. National Academy of Design," *New World* 2 [May 22, 1841]: 365). In 1853, the *Knickerbocker* denounced most of the art criticism that was appearing in the American press as "twaddle." The writer complained that the typical "critic" in this country had made one visit to Paris, Florence, or Rome and consequently presumed "a 'knowledge of art' which, being conceded, enables him to sit in judgment upon the works of artists who could tell him more of the true spirit and aim of art than he could acquire in five years" ("Exhibition of the National Academy of Design," *Knickerbocker* 42 [July 1853]: 93–96).

5. See Janice G. Schimmelman, "A Checklist of European Treatises on Art and Essays on Aesthetics Available in America through 1815," *Proceedings of the American Antiquarian Society* 93 (1983): 95–195.

6. The impact of Reynolds's and West's discourses on similar lectures sponsored by the American Academy of the Fine Arts in New York is discussed in Carrie Rebora, "The American Academy of the Fine Arts, New York 1802–1842" (Ph.D. diss., City University of New York, 1990), 217–34.

7. The term *discourse* was first applied to these writings by William H. Gerdts. See his "The American 'Discourses': A Survey of Lectures and Writings on American Art, 1770–1858," *American Art Journal* 15 (Summer 1983): 61–79, which provides an introduction to the subject and a useful bibliography.

8. Gerdts, "The American 'Discourses'," 79.

9. For references to specific artists, Henry Gilpin's *An Annual Discourse before the Pennsylvania Academy of the Fine Arts, Delivered . . . on the 29th of November, 1826* (Philadelphia: H. C. Carey and I. Lea, 1827) is especially rich.

10. The best history of American periodicals remains Frank Luther Mott's *A History of American Magazines*, 4 vols. (Cambridge, Mass.: Belknap Press of Harvard University, 1957). Another very useful reference work is Edward E. Chielens, ed., *American Literary Magazines: The Eighteenth and Nineteenth Centuries* (New York: Greenwood Press, 1986). For the more general reader, there is John Tebbel, *The American Magazine: A Compact History* (New York: Hawthorn Books, 1969), and John Tebbel and Mary Ellen Zuckerman, *The Magazine in America 1741–1990* (New York and Oxford: Oxford University Press, 1991).

11. Richard Saunders, *John Smibert: Colonial America's First Portrait Painter* (New Haven and London: Yale University Press, 1995): 68. The entire poem is reprinted in John W. McCoubrey, *American Art 1700–1960, Sources and Documents* (Englewood Cliffs, New Jersey: Prentice-Hall, Inc., 1965), 6–8.

12. "Of the Knowledge of Painting," *American Magazine and Historical Chronicle* 2 (March 1745): 114–17. This article is the focus of Albert Ten Eyck Gardner, "A Majestik Shape—1745," *Metropolitan Museum of Art Bulletin* 8 (1949): 74–80. The *American Magazine and Historical Chronicle* was the first magazine in

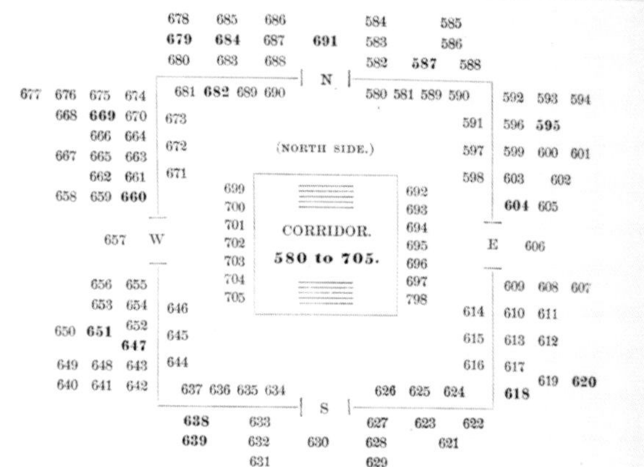

The Corridor, as well as the North-west Gallery, contains a better class of paintings than usual. Among the exhibits here will be noticed pictures by Messrs. Wyant, Perry, Ward, Beckwith, Healey, Millet, Thomas Moran, Eakins, Alden Weir, Crane, and many others whose works have become familiar to visitors to the exhibitions.

The numbering of the pictures in the Corridor begins at the right-hand side of the doorway leading into the North Gallery.

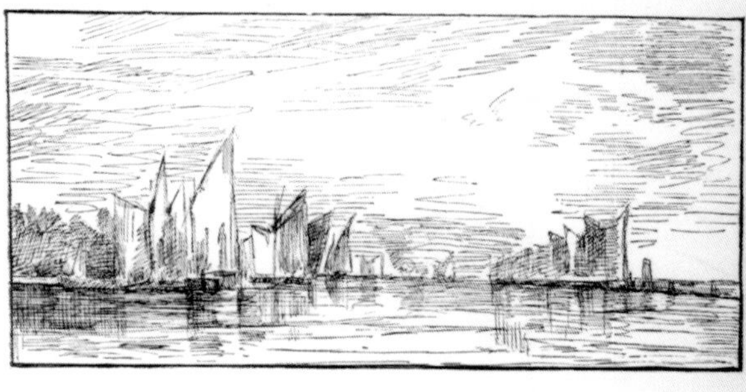

No. 587.   16 x 25.

No. 587.   *Giardini Pubblici, Venezia.*—WILLIAM GEDNEY BUNCE.

View near the public gardens of Venice (green in extreme left of picture), in the morning. Boats with bright-colored sails, glowing sky, smooth water.

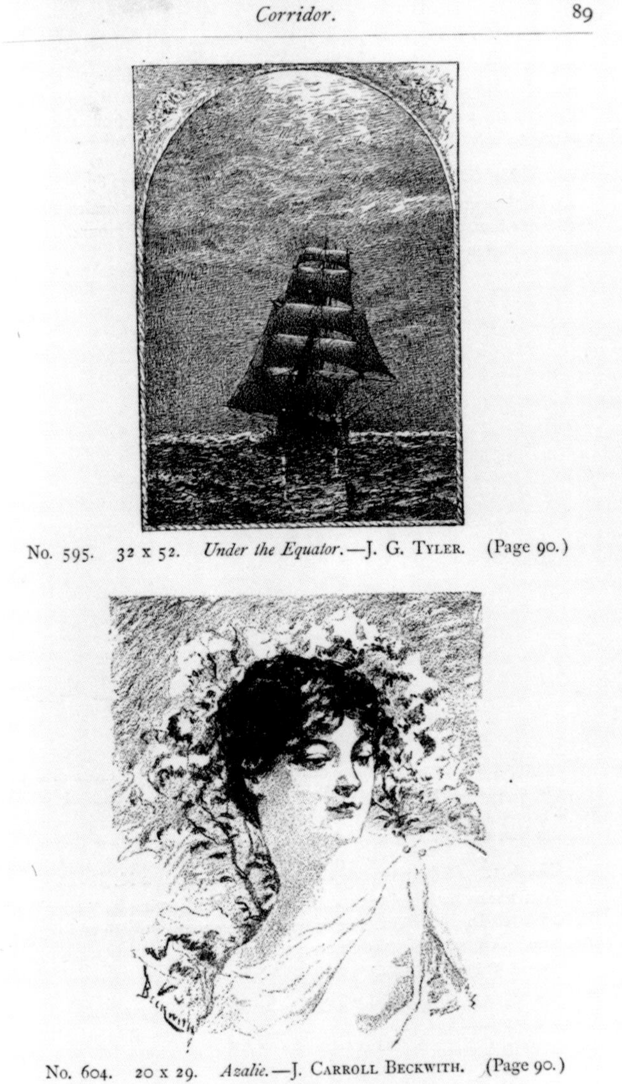

Corridor.   89

No. 595.   32 x 52.   *Under the Equator.*—J. G. TYLER.   (Page 90.)

No. 604.   20 x 29.   *Azalie.*—J. CARROLL BECKWITH.   (Page 90.)

Fig. 8 Page from Charles Kurtz, *Illustrated Art Notes upon the Fifty-Seventh Annual Exhibition of the National Academy of Design, New York* (New York, 1882), Archives, National Academy of Design

this country to last longer than six months (Mott, *History of American Magazines*, 1: 78–79).

13. West continued to be the most often mentioned American artist in the American press for many decades, and the facts of his career were given numerous times, sometimes in detail. See, for example, the extensive account, "Biographical Notice of Benjamin West, Esq. President of the Royal Academy of London," *Analectic Magazine* 8 (July 1816): 36–60.

14. "Upon seeing the Portrait of Miss **—** by Mr. West," *American Magazine and Monthly Chronicle for the British Colonies* 1 (February 1758): 258. The poem and the periodical in which it appeared are discussed briefly in Ann Uhry Abrams, *The Valiant Hero: Benjamin West and Grand-Style History Painting* (Washington, D.C.: Smithsonian Institution Press, 1985), 61–65. Abrams points out that the *American Magazine* contained articles on topics ranging from earthquakes and sea creatures to love and politics.

15. Saunders, *Smibert*, 68.

16. No comprehensive compilation of such articles has been made; but some idea of the numbers and kinds of articles published during the period can be gleaned from the bibliographies and endnotes in J. Meredith Neil, *Toward a National Taste: America's Quest for Aesthetic Independence* (Honolulu: The University Press of Hawaii, 1975) and Lillian B. Miller, *Patrons and Patriotism: The Encouragement of the Fine Arts in the United States, 1790–1860* (Chicago: The

University of Chicago Press, 1966). Neil's bibliography includes a useful list of periodicals published in America during the Colonial and Federal periods (Neil, 359–68).

17. "An Essay on Taste. From a New Work," *Boston Magazine* 1 (October 1783): 27–29; Dr. Blair, "On Criticism and Genius," *Boston Magazine* 1 (December 1783): 56–59; "An Essay on Beauty," *Boston Magazine* 2 (July 1784): 362–66 (continued in subsequent issues); and "On Genius and Taste. From Reynold's Academical Discourses," *Boston Magazine* 2 (March 1784): 169–71.

18. Timothy Dwight, "Essay on Taste," *American Museum or Universal Magazine* 10 (July 1791): 51–53; William Smith, "On Art and Nature," *American Museum or Repository* 1 (February 1787): 165–66. See Helene Emylou Roberts, "American Art Periodicals of the Nineteenth Century" (M.A. thesis, University of Washington, Seattle, 1961), 7–8. Roberts's thesis remains an indispensable source for the study of art periodicals of the period.

19. For example, "On the Causes that have promoted or retarded the Growth of the Fine Arts," *Massachusetts Magazine* 7 (April 1795): 43–45; and "Plan for the Improvement and Diffusion of the Arts, Adapted to The United States," *Literary Magazine* 3 (March 1805): 181–83.

20. "Anecdotes of American Painters," *Port Folio* 1 (1809): 274–75. The *Port Folio* was published in Philadelphia from 1801–25. Its founder, James Dennie, who edited it until 1809, defined it as "not quite a Gazette, nor wholly a Magazine, with

something of politics to interest Quidnuncs, and something of literature to engage Students" (quoted in Tebbel and Zuckerman, 8). Among its contributors were Joseph Hopkinson, John Quincy Adams, and Charles Brockden Brown.

21. William H. Gerdts, "American Landscape Painting: Crucial Judgments, 1730–1845," *American Art Journal* 17 (Winter 1985): 29–30.

22. The story is told in Stiles Tuttle Colwill, *Francis Guy, 1760–1820* (Baltimore, 1981), and in Gerdts, "American Landscape Painting." As the latter points out, the *Observer* printed other articles on art during the first decade of the 1800s.

23. Roberts, 14–15.

24. For these two magazines, see Mott, *History of American Magazines,* 1: 320–30, 606–14; and Chielens, ed., 189–94, 272–79. The *Knickerbocker* published an early article on art criticism, "A Letter. To Critics on the Art of Painting," *Knickerbocker* 16 (September 1840): 230–33, which was signed by "Pictor."

25. See for example "Miscellaneous and Literary Intelligence," *North American Review* 2 (March 1816): 434; and Walter Channing, "On the Fine Arts," *North American Review* 3 (July 1816): 194–201.

26. For *Graham's Magazine,* see Chielens, ed., 156–61.

27. All of these magazines are discussed in the first volume of Mott's *History of American Magazines.*

28. Mott, *History of American Magazines,* 1: 386–89.

29. For the *Southern Literary Messenger,* see Benjamin Blake Minor, *The Southern Literary Messenger, 1834–1864* (New York and Washington: Neale Publishing Company, 1905); and David K. Jackson, *The Contributors and Contributions to the Southern Literary Messenger (1834–1864)* (Charlottesville: Historical Publishing Co., 1960).

30. See Charles E. Baker, "The American Art-Union," and Mary Bartlett Cowdrey, "Publications of the American Art-Union," in Cowdrey, *American Academy of Fine Arts and American Art Union* (New York: New-York Historical Society, 1953), 95–240 and 241–293 respectively; and Maybelle Mann, *The American Art-Union* (Jupiter, Fla.: ALM Associates, 1977).

31. Roberts, 54–59.

32. An analysis of the types of criticism found in the *Crayon* and especially Stillman's role in its formulation is in Simoni, 60–119. Also see Janice Simon, "*The Crayon* 1855–1861: The Voice of Nature in Criticism, Poetry, and the Fine Arts" (Ph.D. diss., University of Michigan, 1990); and the exhibition catalogue by Marion Grzesiak, *The Crayon and the American Landscape* (Montclair, N. J.: The Montclair Museum, 1993).

33. The influence of John Ruskin—British writer, critic, artist, and art historian—on American art is the focus of Roger B. Stein, *John Ruskin and Aesthetic Thought in America 1840–1900* (Cambridge, Mass.: Harvard University Press, 1967).

34. For other early articles on criticism in America in general, see Simoni, 25-56, 539-44.

35. Among the articles are "The Basis of Criticism," *Crayon* 1 (March 21, 1855): 177; "Nothing if Not Critical," *Crayon* 1 (April 25, 1855): 266–67; "Sketchings," *Crayon* 1 (May 30, 1855): 348; "Newspaper Criticism of the Fine Arts," *Crayon* 1 (June 27, 1855): 410–11; and "The Critical Standard," *Crayon* 2 (December 12, 1855): 367–68. Stillman was probably the author of most of these articles.

36. See Linda S. Ferber and William H. Gerdts, *The New Path: Ruskin and the American Pre-Raphaelites* (New York: The Brooklyn Museum, 1985).

37. Russell Sturgis, "Art Criticism," *The New Path* 1 (April 1864): 153–57.

38. Roberts, 75.

39. Roberts, 100.

40. Roberts, 127–30.

41. Roberts, 161–62.

42. William H. Gerdts, *Art Across America: Two Centuries of Regional Painting 1710–1920* (New York: Abbeville Press, 1990), 2: 302–3.

43. *Scribner's* provides a typical example of the range of art topics covered in these general serials. Approximately ninety articles on the fine arts were published in *Scribner's* alone between 1887 and 1900. These were on topics such as Barbizon art, the art of Japan, American illustration, Greek vase painting, portraits of Napoleon, the decoration of the new Boston Public Library, the writings of John Ruskin, art of the World's Columbian Exposition, and modern Scandinavian painters. Monographic articles included pieces on Elihu Vedder, Albert Moore, Claude Monet, Theodore Robinson, Washington Allston, Sir Joshua Reynolds, Kenyon Cox, Giuseppe Segantini, Edwin A. Abbey, John La Farge, and Mary Cassatt.

44. For the history of newspapers in the United States, see Frank Luther Mott, *American Journalism: A History of Newspapers in the United States Through 250 Years 1690 to 1940* (New York: Macmillan Company, 1941), and John Tebbel, *The Compact History of the American Newspaper* (revised; New York: Hawthorn Books, Inc., 1969).

45. Richard Kluger, *The Paper: The Life and Death of the New York Herald Tribune* (New York: Alfred A. Knopf, 1986), 23.

46. Edwin G. Burrows and Mike Wallace, *Gotham: A History of New York City to 1898* (New York: Oxford University Press, 1999), 439.

47. Mott, *American Journalism,* 167.

48. Actually, Bryant was made acting editor of the *Post* in 1826; officially, he assumed the role of editor-in-chief in 1829. See Allan Nevins, *The Evening Post: A Century of Journalism* (New York: Russell & Russell, 1922): 121–38. When he retired in 1870, he was succeeded by his son-in-law and associate editor Parke Godwin.

49. The idea of a poet running a newspaper struck some journalists as odd and led one rival to refer to Bryant and William Leggett, Bryant's colleague at the *Post,* as "the chanting cherubs" of American journalism. (Quoted in Nevins, 139). The reference is to Horatio Greenough's marble group *Chanting Cherubs* (location unknown), which received much attention in the press when it was exhibited in the United States in the 1830s.

50. Mott, *American Journalism,* 374–78, 421–22.

51. Mott, *American Journalism,* 229–35; Burrows and Wallace, 523–25; and Tebbel, *Compact History of the American Newspaper,* 93–124. Greeley was succeeded as editor of the *Tribune* by Whitelaw Reid in 1873.

52. Burrows and Wallace, 677.

53. Joseph E. Chamberlin, *The Boston Transcript: A History of its First Hundred Years* (Boston: The Boston Transcript, 1930), 7.

54. Mott, *American Journalism,* 187.

55. Chamberlin, 212.

56. Mott, *American Journalism,* 187.

57. Ibid., 450.

58. Ibid., 188.

59. Tebbel, *Compact History of the American Newspaper,* 71–72, 88–89.

60. For example, the events surrounding the commission for Horatio Greenough's colossal statue of George Washington for the Rotunda of the Capitol were reported in the *Intelligencer.* See Nathalia Wright, *Horatio Greenough: The First American Sculptor* (Philadelphia: University of Pennsylvania Press, 1963), 329–41. Another example of the type of art article that appeared in the *Intelligencer* is "The Art and Artists of Italy," which appeared in the paper on April 26, 1836.

61. For early American art histories, see Elizabeth Johns, "Scholarship in American Art: Its History and Recent Developments," *American Studies International* 22 (October 1984): 3–40; and, by the same author, "Histories of American Art: The Changing Quest" *Art Journal* 44 (Winter 1984): 338–44.

62. For an analysis of Dunlap's history, see Maura Lyons, "William Dunlap's History of the Rise and Progress of the Arts of Design in the United States" (Ph.D. diss., Boston University, 1998).

63. C. Edwards Lester, *The Artists of America* (New York: Baker and Scribner, 1846).

64. Tuckerman is discussed in more depth in the esaay "Annual Exhibitions and the Birth of Art Criticism to 1865" in this book.

65. At least one book review from the period compared Dunlap's and Tuckerman's histories. See "Art. III.—The Fine Arts in America," *Southern Quarterly Review* 15 (July 1849): 333–55.

66. Johns, "Scholarship in American Art," 5–6.

67. Chielens, ed., 71.

68. Hellman, "American Art Criticism in the Mid-Nineteenth Century: 1840–1860."

69. Dodge had already written *Painting, Its Rise and Progress from the Earliest Ages to the Present Time,* published in 1846. It was meant to be used as a compendium of art history by Americans traveling abroad. Its chapter on American art was basically a summary of Dunlap's history.

70. Lee was a nationally known author, although her fame was as a novelist, not as an art historian. In 1837, her *Three Experiments in Living* rivaled Dickens's *Pickwick Papers* and Hawthorne's *Twice-Told Tales* as that year's best-selling book in the United States. See Frank Luther Mott, *Golden Multitudes: The Story of Best Sellers in the United States* (New York: The Macmillan Company, 1947), 103. Lee's experience of American sculpture was first-hand and, presumably personal: she actually owned several works by American neoclassic sculptors. For that aspect of Lee's life, see my own "American Neoclassic Sculptors and Their Private Patrons in Boston (Ph.D. diss., City University of New York, 1993).

71. One of the most important anthologies of the antebellum period is Rufus Wilmot Griswold, *The Poets and Poetry of America* (Philadelphia: Parry and

McMillan, 1854). It includes poems by all three of the painters named here. In fact, the entire volume is dedicated to Washington Allston.

72. Bryant's "To Cole, the Painter, Departing for Europe" was written in 1829 and is reprinted in McCoubrey, 96. His "Thanatopsis" is in Griswold, 160.

73. Griswold, 152, 433. In his book *The Artists of America,* cited above, C. Edwards Lester reprinted poems dedicated to Washington Allston (1), Henry Inman (33), Benjamin West (65), and Gilbert Stuart (115).

74. For these and other travel books written following the Grand Tour, see William H. Gerdts, "Celebrities of the Grand Tour: The American Sculptors in Florence and Rome," in Theodore E. Stebbins, Jr., *The Lure of Italy: American Artists and the Italian Experience 1760–1914* (Boston: Museum of Fine Arts, New York, 1992), 66–93. For a particularly amusing critique of travel books, written when they were at their peak of popularity, see Henry T. Tuckerman, *America and Her Commentators* (New York: Charles Scribner, 1864). Tuckerman expressed his frustration with the seemingly incessant publication of travel books about the United States, especially those that take a negative or sarcastic view of the country.

75. See my own "British Travelers' Views of American Art Before the Civil War," *American Art Journal* 23 (1991): 39–69.

76. Henry Blackburn, *Academy Notes 1875. With Illustrations of Some of the Principal pictures at Burlington House* (London: Chatto and Windus, 1875), 5–7.

77. Blackburn, 54. Blackburn also published *Academy Sketches* beginning in 1883 (Sidney C. Hutchison, *The History of the Royal Academy 1768–1968* [New York: Taplinger Publishing Company, 1968], 140–41).

78. Arlene Panza-Graham is writing a dissertation on Charles M. Kurtz for the Graduate School of the City University of New York.

79. Charles M. Kurtz, ed., *American Academy Notes* 1 (New York: Cassell, Petter, Galpin & Co., 1881): 3.

80. Kurtz retained possession of many of the sketches he acquired for his *Notes,* and some of these are now in the collection of the National Academy of Design. For some years, a selection of the engravings was used by *Harper's Weekly* to illustrate articles on the Academy's exhibitions. For example, see *Harper's Weekly* 32 (April 7, 1888): 259.

81. Charles M. Kurtz, ed., *Illustrated Art Notes Upon the Fifty-Eighth Annual Exhibition of the National Academy of Design, New York* (New York: Cassell, Petter, Galpin & Co., 1883), 19, 23

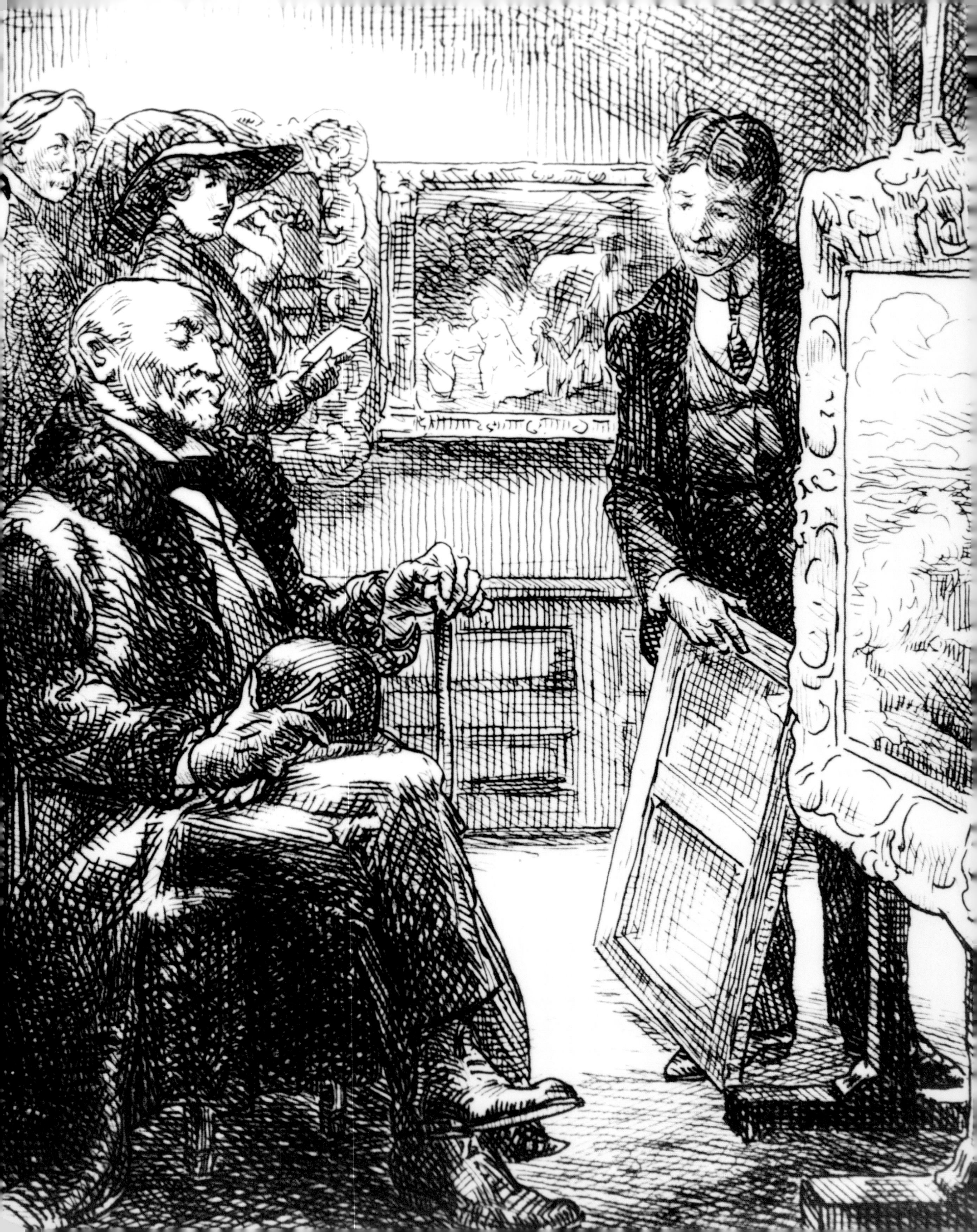

The Public Display of Art in New York City, 1664–1914

KENNETH JOHN MYERS

Founded by Dutch traders in 1626, New York City was already two hundred years old when the National Academy of Design opened its first annual exhibition in 1826. The establishment of the Academy, the success of its annual exhibitions, indeed its trumpeting of the accomplishments of American artists are commonly credited with creating a discerning audience for American art. In fact, the process by which New York City was transformed from a provincial outpost with a tiny market for art imported from Europe into a national center for the production, display, sale, and interpretation of art was lengthier, more diffuse, and more complex. A confluence of factors—geographic, social, political, economic, and historical—brought together the many artists, dealers, buyers, critics, museums, commercial galleries, private clubs, schools, and arts organizations that by the close of the nineteenth century made art in New York City something to rave about.

ART IN EARLY NEW YORK: 1664–1815

The Dutch founders of New Amsterdam carried a rich pictorial tradition with them. Estate records and surviving paintings suggest that prosperous Dutch settlers and their descendents decorated their homes and public buildings with painted and engraved still-lifes, landscapes, religious scenes, and portraits. The 1685 inventory of the estate of a New York barber and surgeon named Jacob DeLange, for example, lists a dozen prints and fifteen or so paintings, including still-lifes, landscapes, banquet scenes, a portrait, and a biblical scene of Abraham and Hagar. Since engravings were not produced in North America until the eighteenth century, DeLange's prints, as well as many of his paintings, must have been brought from Europe. But some art was locally produced by resident artisans such as Gerrit Duyckinck, who painted occasional portraits and religious scenes in oil while making his living as a glazier and enameler.[1]

England conquered the Dutch colony of the New Netherlands in 1664, renaming both the colony and its leading city New York. English rule was confirmed at the end of the third Anglo-Dutch War in 1674. But despite the exceptional quality of its harbor, New York grew slowly. In 1730, it was still a small provincial port with a population of about nine thousand.

Unlike the Dutch, the English had little interest in the visual arts except for portraiture. They had turned away from religious subjects after the break with the Church of Rome in 1535 and did not develop significant traditions of still-life, genre, or history painting until the eighteenth century. Most English immigrants to New York settled in Manhattan and other southern parts of the colony, where they often intermarried with the Dutch. Netherlandish pictorial traditions decayed in these areas of the colony, although they remained stronger in the central and upper Hudson Valley, where English immigration had less impact.[2]

The nascent market for art in New York did not begin to recover from the effects of the English conquest until the 1740s, when the development of large-scale industrial manufacturing in England and prolonged war with Spain and France created profitable new opportunities for New York merchants, ship captains, and privateers. By the end of the French and Indian Wars in 1763, New York had passed Boston to become the second largest city in the colonies with a population of over eighteen thousand—Philadelphia was substantially larger with a population of almost twenty-four thousand. As trade increased and travel across the Atlantic became more common, many New Yorkers developed both the financial means and the desire to look and act genteel. By 1750, wealthy New Yorkers were making their refinement visible by wearing fashionable clothes, purchasing private coaches, and building stylish homes filled with costly furnishings.

The spread of refined standards of sociability transformed the organization and furnishing of upper-class homes. In these new "Spacious Genteel Houses," each room served a specialized private or public function. Dining rooms were outfitted with large sideboards loaded with English china, crystal glassware, and as much silver as the owner could afford. Private chambers displayed canopied beds hung with expensive fabrics. No drawing room was complete without a finely carved game table and a painted family portrait.[3] Some of these family portraits were painted in Europe, but most were locally produced by itinerant portrait painters who settled in New York for a few weeks or years until they exhausted the market and moved on to fresher climes in search of unpainted faces. In the 1740s, paint supply shops and bookstores began to advertise copperplate engravings for sale, suggesting that local gentry had already started to use them to decorate walls.[4]

The growth of polite society also affected the organization and appearance of public spaces. The beautification of the city began in 1732, when three prominent citizens leased a small plot of publicly owned land at the south end of Broadway and developed it as a public park with walks and a bowling green. By 1760, the blocks facing the park had become one of the most fashionable residential neighborhoods in the city. Other beautification projects soon followed. Beginning in the late 1740s, leading New Yorkers funded construction of several large neoclassical churches, including St. George's Chapel (1752), St. Paul's (1766), and the North Dutch Church (1769). In the 1750s, the Common Council of New York and several wealthy citizens funded construction of a new civic building known as the Royal Exchange. The open ground floor of the Exchange was used as a covered market. The second story was divided into several chambers, including a large ornate hall with a twenty-foot ceiling that was used for government meetings, dinners, concerts, and balls. Like the main halls of English country houses after which it was modeled, the main chamber of the Royal Exchange was hung with appropriate portraits, including a painting of William Pitt donated in 1766. Social gatherings were also held in taverns. Until the 1740s, most taverns were small and utilitarian, associated with drinking, cursing, and other plebeian vices. In the 1750s, local entrepreneurs such as Samuel Fraunces recognized the growing demand for more refined establishments and began to establish elegant taverns with large well-appointed "long rooms." Like the main room in the Royal Exchange, many of these rooms were decorated with fine furnishings, including painted wallpapers imported from Europe and framed art. The public display of art in colonial New York reached a climax of sorts on April 26, 1770, when Lieutenant Governor Cadwallader Colden dedicated an equestrian statue of King George III. Commissioned by the General Assembly of the colony of New York and cast from a design by the English sculptor Joseph Wilton, the statue was prominently displayed on a pedestal in the Bowling Green until July 6, 1776, when it was toppled by a throng of patriotic soldiers and civilians.[5]

The American Revolution had a devastating effect on New York, which was occupied by British forces from September 1776 until 1783. Before the war began, the city's population had reached twenty-five thousand. In 1783 it had fallen to twelve thousand. A contemporary observer described the remaining inhabitants as a "heterogeneous set, composed of almost ruined exiles, disbanded soldiery, mixed foreigners, disaffected Tories, and the refuse of the British army." Thousands of people poured into the city in the years following the final British evacuation on November 25, 1783. The city grew even faster in the 1790s, when war between England and France disrupted European agricultural production, creating new markets for American farm products and spurring settlement of previously thinly populated sections of upstate New York. Increased trade in agricultural products attracted tens of thousands of new residents to the city. Most came from other parts of the northeastern United States, but many were immigrants from the British Isles and Europe. By 1800, returning residents and newcomers had revitalized the local economy, and New York had become a bustling city of sixty thousand. By 1810, it had passed Philadelphia to become the largest city in the country, with a population of almost one hundred thousand.[6]

Newspaper advertisements evidence a steady increase in activities related to the arts during this period, as economic growth and the increasing refinement of middling and wealthy New Yorkers created new opportunities for artists and dealers. The greatest demand was for portraits. Buyers could choose among a wide variety of sizes, mediums, and prices, including silhouettes, pastel miniatures on paper, watercolor miniatures on ivory, cabinet portraits in crayon, half-length oils, and full-length oils painted by famous visitors such as Ralph Earl or John Trumbull.[7] As before the Revolution, most artists were itinerants who moved on after exhausting the local market. The first professional artists to become permanent residents of the city appear to have been the brothers Archibald and Alexander Robertson. The Robertsons immigrated to New York from Scotland in 1791 and soon founded a drawing school that they named the Columbian Academy of Painting, which they ran for at least twenty years. Several of their students became famous, including the writer Washington Irving and the painter John Vanderlyn.[8]

Except for portraits, most of the art sold in New York was produced elsewhere and brought to the city by dealers. Many of the first dealers were itinerants who would arrive in the city with an assortment of paintings and prints that they would sell through a local shop or at auction. The intended market for these works is clearly named by an advertisement placed during the Revolution, which announced the sale of "SIX ELEGANT PICTURES of the following Dock-Yards for his Majesty's Navy, viz. Portsmouth, Plymouth, Chatham, Woolwich, Sheerness, Deptford. Illuminated with very elegant frames, they are very large, and may be thought proper furniture for the Halls of the first Personages of this city."[9] The first local shopkeepers to carry a significant amount of art in inventory were the booksellers Henry Caritat and David Longworth, each of whom was advertising the availability of substantial collections of engravings by 1800.[10] Another important source was an Italian gilder and looking-glass manufacturer named Corti. Corti arrived from London in 1797 and was soon advertising the availability of "a very large assortment of Italian Paintings and Drawings, superior in point of elegance to anything of the kind ever imported, also, a Large and Elegant Collection of London Prints with and without Gilt Frames."[11] The most successful, or at least the longest lasting, of these early dealers was Michael Paff, who began selling engravings by 1801 and opened his first art gallery in 1811. Paff continued to sell what he claimed were old master paintings until his death in 1838. The second-floor shop sign for his gallery at 221 Broadway is visible in Hugh Reinagle's 1832 lithograph *The Old Broadway Stages, New York* (fig. 9).[12]

From 1783 until after the turn of the century, City Hall was one of the most important public venues for the display of art

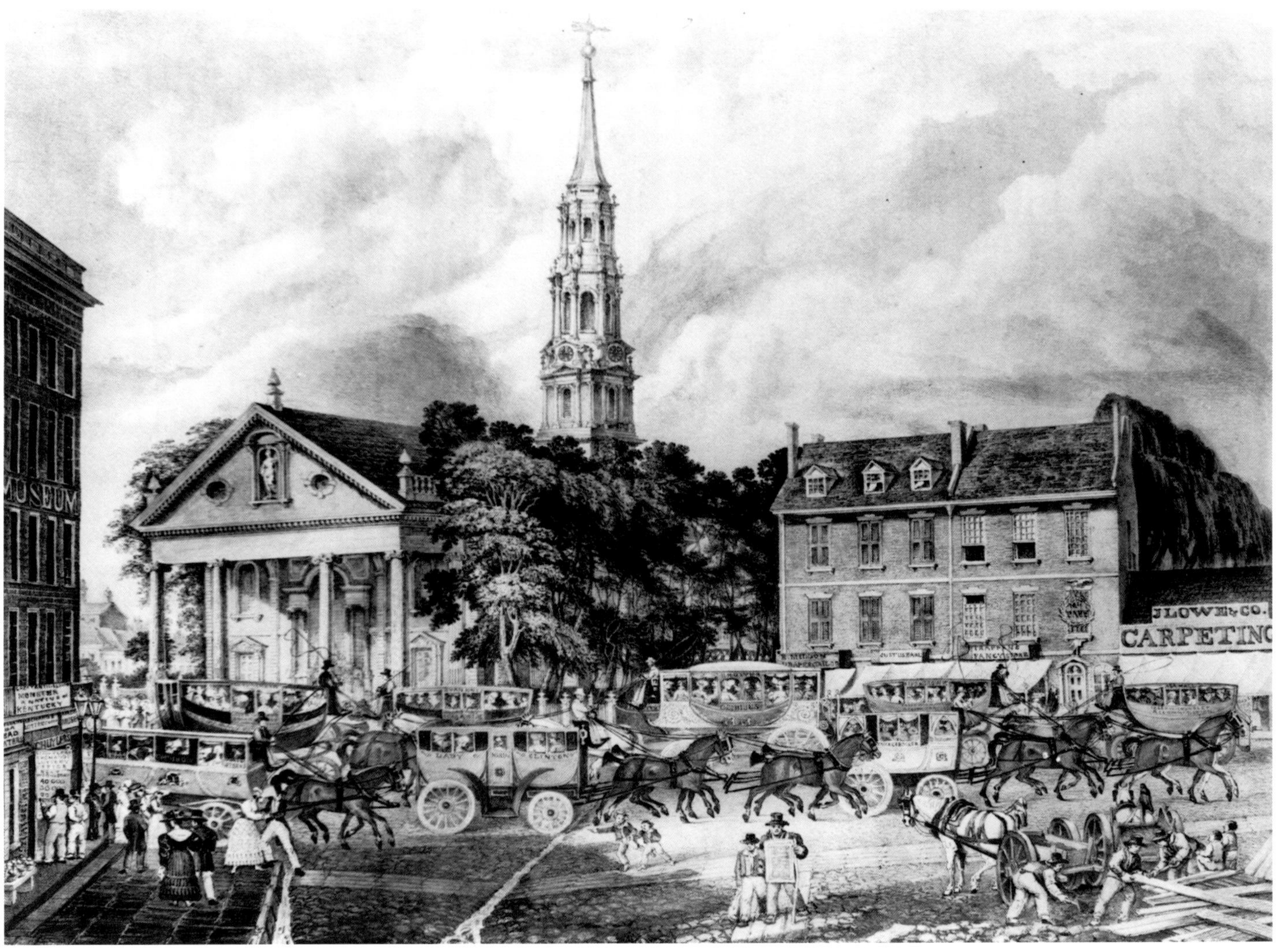

Fig. 9 Hugh Reinagle, *The Old Broadway Stages, New York,* 1831, engraved by John Pendleton, The Museum of the City of New York

in the city. The Common Council of New York began commissioning portraits of political and military leaders soon
after the end of the Revolution. The portraits were originally
displayed in the main chamber of Federal Hall. One of the
first paintings commissioned for the collection was John
Trumbull's 1790 portrait of George Washington, which shows
the general on November 25, 1783, as the last British forces in
the United States completed their evacuation from New York.
In 1812, the collection was moved to the Governor's Room of
the new (and current) City Hall in City Hall Park (fig. 10). The
collection grew rapidly during the 1810s and 1820s. Important
additions included six large portraits of American military
heroes from the War of 1812 by John Wesley Jarvis and Samuel
F. B. Morse's influential portrait of the *Marquis de Lafayette*
(see no. 3).[13]

Another important early venue for the public display of art
was the museum organized by the Tammany Society in 1791.
The first museum in the city, it was originally located in
Federal Hall but was soon moved to a larger space on Broad
Street. The Tammany Society relinquished control of the

Museum in 1795, when it was taken over by the Keeper of
Collections, Gardiner Baker. Like other contemporary museums, it was designed both to enlighten and to entertain.
Collections were mixed and included everything from geological specimens and stuffed animals to Indian artifacts,
wax-work statues of historical figures, engravings, and paintings. Baker expanded operations in 1797, when he opened a
second building, the New Panorama, at 222 Greenwich Street.
In that facility, he offered changing exhibitions of large
painted panoramas and established a small commercial art
gallery. According to one of Baker's newspaper advertisements, his "Print Shop" was "well furnished with 200 different
engravings, a number of fine Paintings, and a large collection
of American Butterflies and other insects in frames." After
Baker's death in 1798, William Waldron operated both the
museum and the panorama. The Massachusetts engraver and
portrait painter Edward Savage purchased the museum collections in 1802 and installed them in his new Columbian
Gallery of Paintings and City Museum in a building known as
the Pantheon at 80 Greenwich Street.[14]

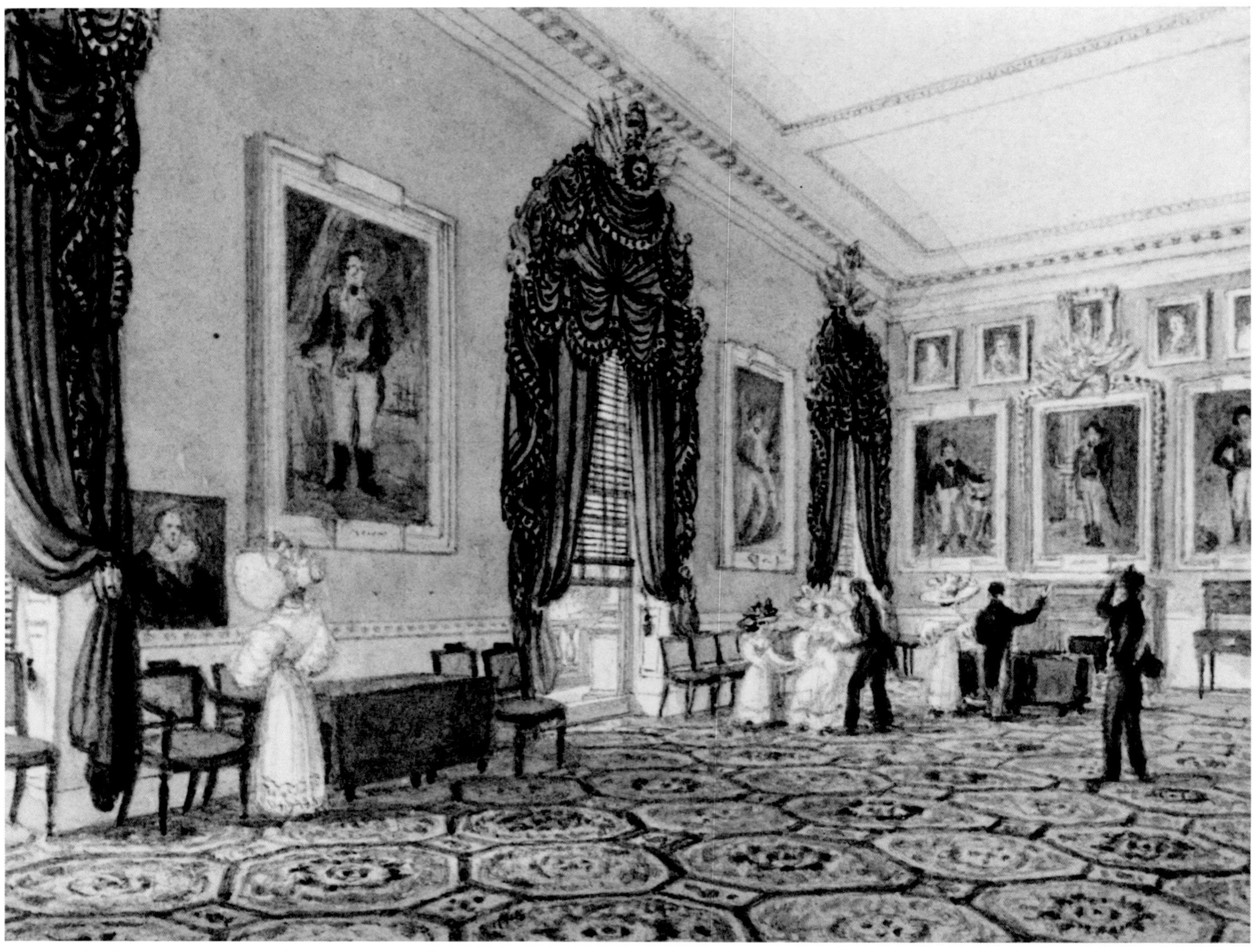

Fig. 10 Charles Burton, *Governor's Room, City Hall, New York*, 1831, sepia watercolor on paper, The New-York Historical Society, Gift of Mrs. Ralph Smillie, 1968

From autumn 1802 until its demolition in the spring of 1805, the Pantheon was at the center of the city's art life. Originally built as Rickett's Amphitheatre in 1797, the Pantheon contained a riding stable, theater, and several residential apartments. Savage remodeled the building, transforming the theater into an exhibition space. In November 1802, he opened a large temporary exhibition of over two hundred "Italian, Flemish, French, English, and American" works. The exhibition mixed "ancient and modern Paintings, Prints, and Sculpture," including his own group portrait of *The Washington Family* (1796; National Gallery of Art, Washington, D.C.). Although some of the works were borrowed from private collections, advertisements explained that the "price of each of those pieces marked for sale in the Gallery, may be known at the door." Savage's show seems to have been the first major exhibition of ancient and contemporary paintings in New York, and it was also the first to be extensively reviewed in the daily press.[15]

Savage continued to exhibit paintings and prints in the old theater until the summer of 1803, when he rented the space to the American Academy of the Fine Arts. The first non-profit arts organization in the city, the American Academy had been founded in the spring of 1802 by a small group of wealthy men led by Robert R. Livingston (United States minister to France) and his brother Edward (mayor of New York). Created and managed by genteel art patrons, the Academy sought to inspire local artists and uplift the general public by displaying art that would promote civic virtue. The Academy's first major acquisition was a collection of twenty plaster casts of antique sculpture that arrived in New York in the spring of 1803. The collection included casts of the Borghese Gladiator, the Laocoön, the Capitoline Venus, and the Apollo Belvedere. Unfortunately, the first exhibition of the casts coincided with a yellow fever epidemic, and they failed to attract many paying visitors. In March of 1805, Savage moved his museum to 166 Greenwich Street, and the Academy's casts were put into storage until 1810, when they were installed in the Academy's new rooms at the Government House on lower Broadway, facing Bowling Green.[16]

THE GRAND COMMERCIAL EMPORIUM: 1815–1840

Economic and aesthetic activities in New York slowed drastically in December 1807, when congressional efforts to keep the United States out of the war between Britain and France led to passage of the Embargo Acts, closing down foreign trade. Economic conditions remained difficult until 1815, when the end of the war with Britain set the stage for the renewal of rapid growth and the reinvigoration of local arts activities. Even before the War of 1812, New York craftsmen had begun to cut costs and increase production by dividing the manufacture of goods into simple tasks that could be performed by teams of less skilled workers. By the end of the 1820s, the introduction of these industrial techniques and the consequent shift from artisanal to wage labor had made the city into an international center for the production of inexpensive clothes, moderately priced furniture, and leather. Geographical location enabled New York merchants and wholesalers to seize initial control over much of the national market for imported British manufactured goods, but they consolidated their position by convincing the state legislature to slash import fees and to adopt new laws guaranteeing merchants from rural areas the lowest possible wholesale prices. Bankers and stockbrokers were equally innovative, developing new systems for marshalling investment capital that enabled local businesses to dominate the trade in cotton and other basic agricultural commodities produced in southern states. By the early 1820s, the unprecedented growth of financial services made it possible for New Yorkers to fund construction of a canal linking the Hudson River with Lake Erie and the booming grain producing regions of the Midwest. Completed in 1825, the Erie Canal gave New Yorkers control over the movement of most goods to and from the Midwest, assuring the city's position as the commercial and financial capital of the new nation. Increased commercial activity created thousands of new jobs, leading to further population growth. By 1830, New York's population had doubled to more than 200,000, making it one of the largest cities in the world. By 1840, it had reached 313,000.[17]

Economic growth quickly attracted many new portrait painters to the city. John Wesley Jarvis and Samuel Waldo had remained in New York during the war. John Trumbull returned from England in 1815, and John Vanderlyn arrived from France in the same year. Charles Cromwell Ingham emigrated from Dublin with his family in 1816. After serving in the militia during the war, William Dunlap returned to the city in 1817. Samuel F. B. Morse arrived in 1823.[18] The New York art market was now large enough and sophisticated enough to attract artists other than portraitists. The English engraver

and art teacher John Rubens Smith moved to the city in 1816 and immediately opened an influential drawing school. The landscape painter, picture restorer, and engraver Gherlandio Marsiglia emigrated from Italy in 1817, and the landscape painter William Guy Wall arrived from Dublin in 1818. Asher Brown Durand opened his own engraving shop in 1820. The French lithographer Anthony Imbert emigrated in 1824 or 1825. The English landscape painter Thomas Cole arrived by way of Ohio and Philadelphia in 1825.[19]

The influx of painters soon led to the establishment of several new art galleries. William A. Colman opened a two-story bookstore and art gallery at the corner of Broadway and Wall Street in the spring of 1824. The store was on the first floor; on the second was a "Gallery of Fine Arts," selling paintings "of the ancient and modern schools." Colman's greatest contribution to the history of American art occurred in October 1825, when he placed several new landscape paintings by Thomas Cole in his shop window, where they were "discovered" by William Dunlap, John Trumbull, and Asher Brown Durand. By 1828, Colman had relocated to a larger and more elegant space on the second floor of the Park Place House.[20] Perhaps even more important to the growth of American art in New York was the three-story looking-glass and picture-frame manufactory established by Lewis P. Clover and his partner John Parker at 180 Fulton Street around 1820. In 1872, an elderly New York writer recalled that because of the shop's convenient location and Clover's "naturally refined mind, pleasant manners, and strict integrity," it had soon become an important meeting place for local artists and patrons. Professionals and social celebrities such as Dr. David Hosack, who lived in Vesey Street, and diarist Philip Hone, whose residence was opposite City Hall Park, on Broadway, found it convenient in their "evening walks" to drop in at 180 Fulton Street. There "they met each other and the artists, and indulged in animated discussions and told pleasant reminiscences."[21] By 1830, Parker and Clover had become small-scale art dealers and were publishing copperplate engravings of good quality.

The city's rapid growth also attracted the attention of museum operators from other cities. In 1825, Charles Willson Peale's son Rubens Peale moved to New York and opened a branch of the family's Philadelphia museum. Located across from City Hall Park, at 252 Broadway, Peale's Museum offered a wide variety of entertainments, ranging from glass-blowing demonstrations and Egyptian mummies to an art gallery containing portraits of eminent men.[22]

After the War of 1812, a group of leading citizens concerned that the city was not doing enough to promote republican virtue among the people of the city convinced the Common Council to convert the old municipal almshouse into New York's first non-profit cultural center. Located on Chambers Street behind City Hall, the new facility was formally known as the New York Institution for the Promotion of the Arts and Sciences (fig. 11). The original tenants were the American

Academy of the Fine Arts, the Literary and Philosophical Society, the New-York Historical Society, and John Scudder's American Museum. Each of these organizations paid an annual rent of "one Pepper Corn if lawfully demanded." The American Academy occupied six rooms on the two upper stories. The American Museum had the west wing. Scudder's establishment was mainly devoted to the natural sciences, although he also showed wax figures, mechanical curiosities, painted panoramas, and some paintings and engravings.[23]

The galleries occupied by the American Academy immediately became the most important venue for the public display of art in the city. The leaders of the Academy organized their first annual exhibition in October 1816 (see the essay "Annual Exhibitions and the Birth of American Art Criticism to 1865" in this book). Jonathan Trumbull became president of the Academy in late 1816 or early 1817 and immediately assumed responsibility for organizing the exhibitions, which included ancient as well as modern works by European and American artists. The annual exhibitions originally stayed up for a year, but Trumbull quickly realized that attendance dropped off after the first few months. In order to maintain attendance and generate income, he began to rent the galleries to artists and dealers to use for special exhibitions. Following a practice begun in Paris and London, many of the special exhibitions consisted of a single important painting. The first of these opened in October 1818 and featured Trumbull's *Declaration of Independence* (1817), which had been commissioned by the United States Congress for installation in the Capitol. Subsequent single-painting exhibitions were devoted to Samuel F. B. Morse's full-length portrait of President Monroe (November 1820) (1820; Collection of City Hall, Charleston, South Carolina), Rembrandt Peale's *Court of Death* (December 1820–February 1821) (1819–20; Detroit Institute of Arts), Trumbull's *Surrender of General Burgoyne at Saratoga* (January 1822) (1816; Yale University Art Gallery), William Dunlap's *Death on a Pale Horse* (November 1825) (1825; presumed destroyed), and the first American showing of Jacques-Louis David's 1822 replica of his 1805–07 *Coronation of Napoleon* (February 1826) (Versailles; Musée National du Château). The first dealer to lease the space was an itinerant Florentine named Antonio Sarti. In 1829, Sarti leased the three main exhibition rooms to show his collection of over two hundred Italian paintings. The Sarti exhibition was well reviewed and attracted substantial crowds. It was on display

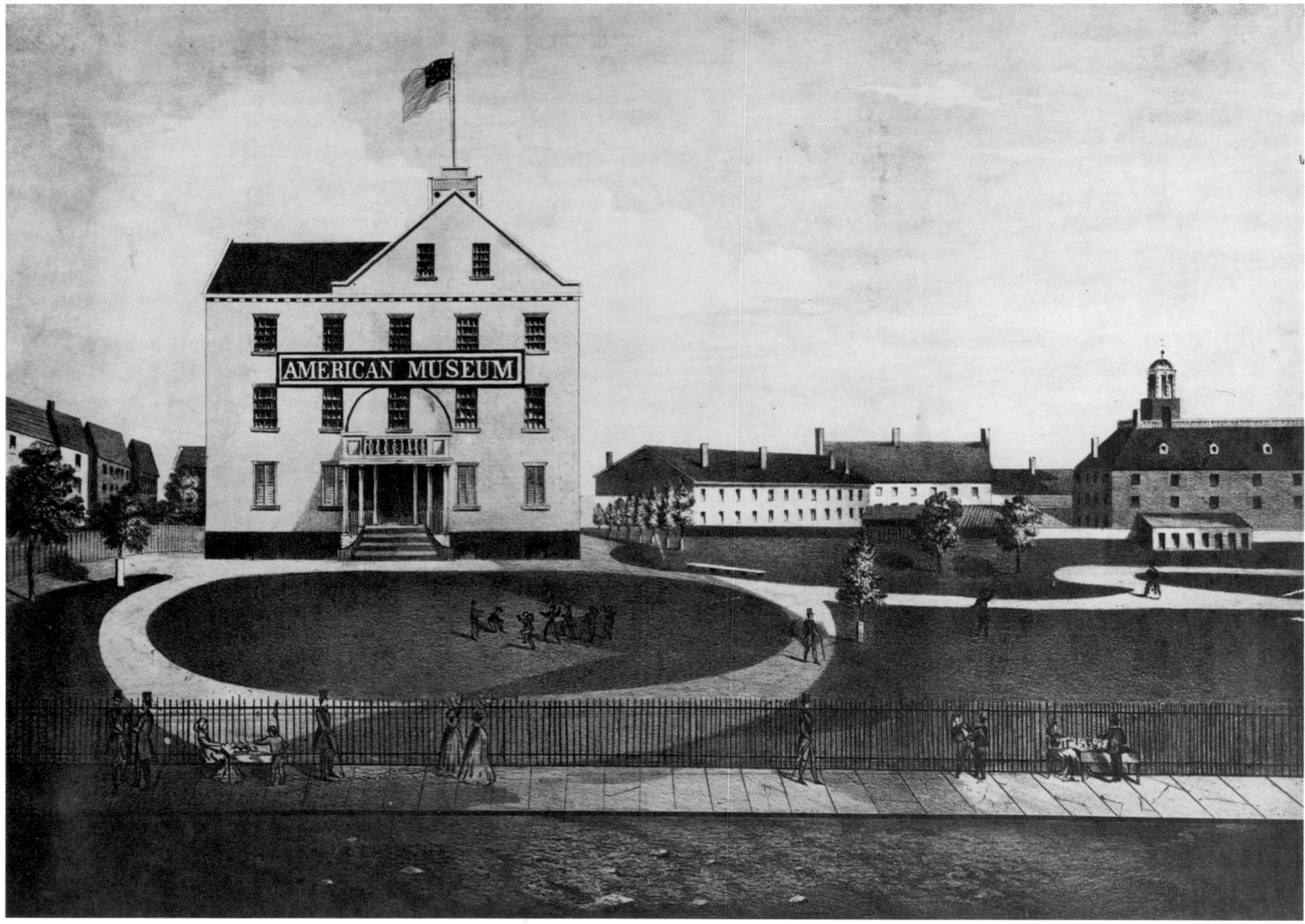

Fig. 11 Alexander Jackson Davis, *New York City Hall Park, North End*, 1825, lithograph, National Academy of Design

from December 1828 until April 1829, when the entire collection was sold at auction. In 1830, an English firm impressed by Sarti's success leased all the main galleries to show a collection of old master paintings put together by a London dealer named Richard Abraham.[24]

The Governor's Room in City Hall and the New York Institution were not the only cultural facilities in City Hall Park. In 1817, the Common Council granted John Vanderlyn a nine-year lease on a site next to the New York Institution to erect a building for the display of panoramas and other works of art. Although Vanderlyn was responsible for all construction costs, the city subsidized his operations by charging him the token rent of one peppercorn per year. While in Europe, Vanderlyn had been impressed by the popularity of panoramas. He hoped that income from a panorama would enable him to develop the building into a national gallery of fine art. Vanderlyn named his building the Rotunda. Based on the design of the Pantheon, it was fifty-six feet in diameter and forty-five feet in height. Entrance was through a Doric portico with a triangular pediment (fig. 12). The Rotunda opened to the public in October 1818 with a showing of Thomas Barker's *View of the Interior of the City of Paris*. Exhibits changed regularly. In January 1819, he was showing Henry Barker's *Attack of the Allied Force on Paris March 30, 1814*, which was replaced in April by Robert Ker Porter's *Battle of Lodi*. In June, he installed his own *Panoramic View of the Palace and Gardens of Versailles*

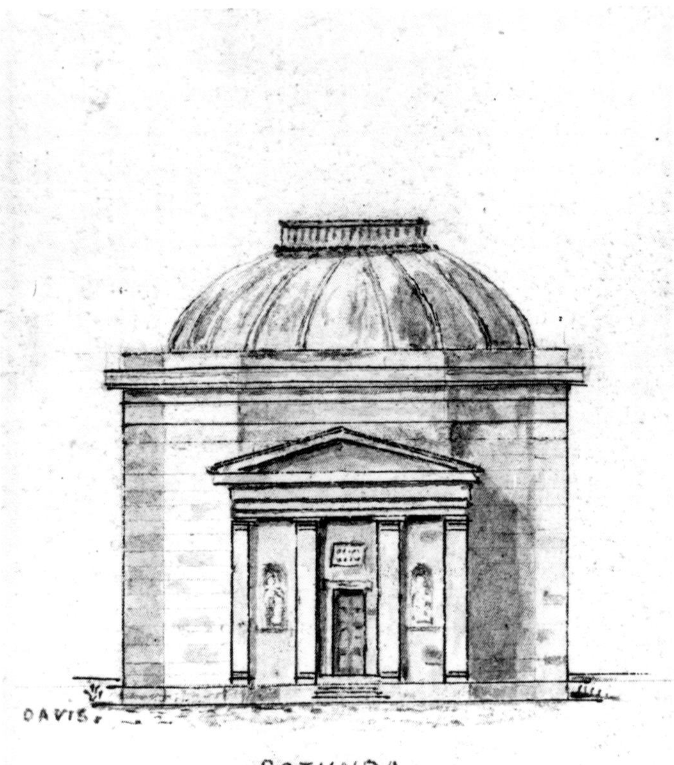

Fig. 12 Alexander Jackson Davis, *The Vanderlyn Rotunda, Chambers Street*, 1828, wash drawing, Collection of the New-York Historical Society

(1818; Metropolitan Museum of Art). Vanderlyn continued to exhibit panoramas in the Rotunda until October 1829.[25]

Establishment of the National Academy of Design in 1825 was made possible by and contributed to the growth of the New York art market. Unlike the older American Academy, which was run by patrons primarily concerned with the promotion of civic virtue, the new National Academy was organized and directed by artists who were mainly interested in the training of young artists and the promotion of contemporary American art. The artists running the new Academy organized their first annual exhibition in May 1826. Unlike the annual exhibitions at the American Academy, the National Academy exhibitions were limited to new works not previously shown in public. The number of New Yorkers with the means and desire to purchase art was still small in comparison even to the art market of the 1850s, but the young American painters associated with the National Academy benefited from widespread concerns about the authenticity of many of the purported old masters for sale in the city and from a pervasive cultural nationalism that encouraged potential buyers to support the work of native artists.[26]

The Academy's first annual exhibition was held in a twenty-five by fifty-foot room on the second floor of a private residence located at the corner of Broadway and Reade Street. A more suitable location was found the following year, when the exhibition was held in a similarly sized room on the top floor of the Arcade Baths on Chambers Street (fig. 13). In the spring of 1831, the exhibition was moved to the second floor of a new building known as Clinton Hall (fig. 14), located at the corner of Beekman and Nassau streets. That structure was built to house the New York Mercantile Library, which operated one of the largest circulating libraries in the city. By 1838, with attendance at the exhibitions rising, the leadership of the Academy began to look for a larger and more elegant space. In 1840, the Academy joined forces with the New York Society Library, which was completing a new building at the corner of Broadway and Leonard Street, five blocks north of City Hall Park. Academy members designed and decorated their new gallery, which offered four hundred running feet of wall space lit by a skylight, with gaslights for night viewing. The Academy stayed at the Society Library for nine years, until it purchased a building of its own in 1850.[27]

During the summer of 1829, the Common Council decided not to renew the leases held by any of the cultural organizations in City Hall Park. This decision marked a major turning point in the history of the arts and sciences in the city. Until the War of 1812, cultural activities in the city were dominated by a small group of wealthy men who valued them as a source of spiritual fulfillment but also understood them as important means of controlling the potentially dangerous passions of poor and middling citizens. By the end of the 1820s, rapid economic growth and the democratization of gentility were producing a more entrepreneurial and egalitarian society in which cultural activities were impossible to direct in this way.

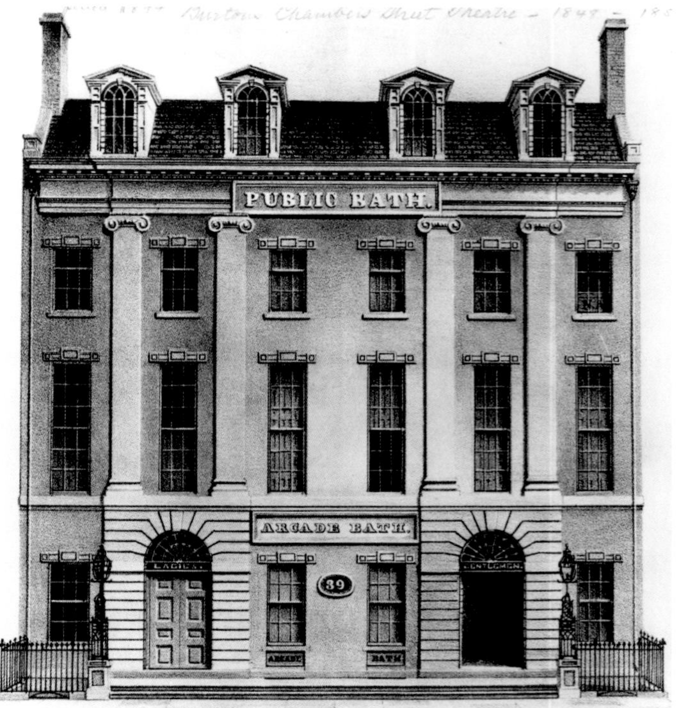

Fig. 13 Alexander J. Davis, *The Baths, 39 Chambers Street, New York,* n.d., lithograph, The Museum of the City of New York

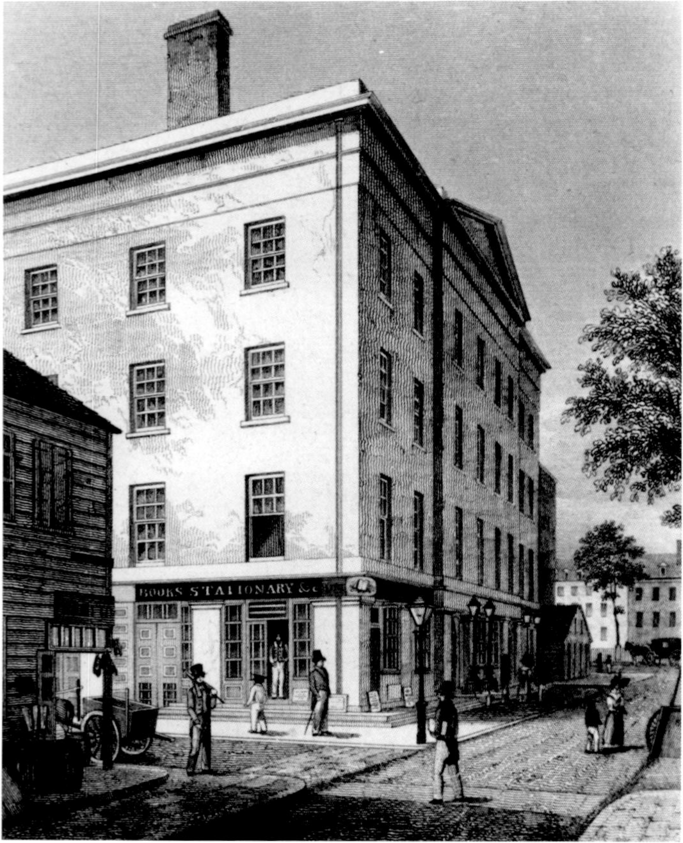

Fig. 14 Charles Burton, *Clinton Hall, Beekman Street, Corner of Nassau Street,* 1831, engraving, published by Charles Burton, Collection of The New-York Historical Society. The National Academy of Design's annual exhibitions were held in rented rooms here from 1831 through 1840. From 1832 to 1835, Clinton Hall also served as the first home of the University of New York (now New York University).

Well-to-do New Yorkers continued to use cultural activities as a means of influencing the actions of poorer and middling citizens, but the Common Council's decision not to renew the leases marked the moment when the patrician model of culture ceased to be dominant.[28]

In July 1830, Scudder's American Museum moved from the New York Institution to a new five-story building located just south of City Hall Park, at the corner of Broadway and Ann Street. The new building can be seen at the extreme left of Hugh Reinagle's *The Old Broadway Stages, New York* (see fig. 9). The American Academy of the Fine Arts stayed in the New York Institution until November 1831, when they completed construction of a new gallery at 8½ Barclay Street. Built on land leased from Dr. David Hosack, the three-story brick building contained three exhibition rooms and a studio for John Trumbull. The new galleries were well reviewed, but the public was already growing tired of annual exhibitions that featured familiar selections of portraits, history paintings, and European old masters leavened by a few new works by local artists. Needing to keep up with their rent and facing increased competition from the National Academy of Design and other local venues, the American Academy became increasingly dependent on rental income. For much of the time from 1832 to 1837, the galleries were leased to a British art dealer named John Watkins Brett. In 1832–33, 1834, and 1837, Brett leased the three exhibition rooms to display his large collection of "old master" paintings. In 1833 and 1836, he rented one of the galleries to exhibit two large religious paintings by Claude-Marie Dubufe.[29] Despite the success of some of Brett's exhibitions, the American Academy was on its last legs. Trumbull resigned as president in January 1836. No one stepped forward to organize the next annual exhibition, so it was cancelled. In March 1837, the building was badly damaged in a fire. A small group of local artists and architects tried to reinvigorate the institution, and the galleries were rented for occasional exhibitions until the spring of 1840. These efforts failed, however, and by January 1842, the lease had been cancelled and all the collections sold.[30]

EMPIRE CITY: 1840–1865

The American Academy died because most local artists would not support an organization reflecting the hierarchical values of an older patrician elite, but its death was hastened by economic hard times that undermined the vitality of the entire art world in the late 1830s and early 1840s. By the mid-1830s, American production of cotton was far outstripping British demand. In the summer of 1836, cotton prices dropped sharply, and the Bank of London cut off the easy credit that had fueled the rapid growth of the American economy. The crisis came to a head in the spring of 1837. Cotton producers could not pay their debts, merchants holding uncollectible cotton debts failed, American banks restricted credit to protect hard currency reserves, imports slowed dramatically, ships were idled, factories closed, commodity prices fell, and workers swelled the ranks of the unemployed as the nation slid into an unusually severe depression. The effects of the crash were especially harsh in New York, where mass bankruptcies led to mass unemployment. In April 1837, one survey reported that half the population of the city was not making enough to live on and that one-third had no work at all.[31]

The New York economy began to revive in the mid-1840s. Cotton prices recovered, creating new opportunities for New York bankers, insurers, shippers, and merchants. Crop failures in Ireland and England brought renewed demand for midwestern corn and wheat. The rate of growth accelerated after 1848, when gold from California helped finance the importation of European consumer and capital goods, including railroad iron. In 1851, New York's control over trade with western parts of the country was confirmed by completion of the Hudson River Railroad, connecting Manhattan with Albany, and the New York & Erie Railroad, joining the Great Lakes with the Hudson River just north of Albany. Local production boomed, speculative construction within the city revived, and the value of land shot back up. The city once again became a magnet for immigrants. In 1850, the population of Manhattan was about half a million. By 1860, it had surged to more than eight hundred thousand.[32]

The number of professional artists living in New York remained small throughout the 1830s. For example, as late as 1840, Thomas Cole was the only full-time professional landscape painter based in the city. The ranks of local artists grew in the mid-1840s, however, as improved economic conditions convinced aspiring young men (almost all were men) that they could make a living as professional painters. Although a few members of this generation became sculptors or history painters, most specialized in portraiture, landscape, or genre. Some, including Asher Brown Durand and John Casilear, were experienced engravers or portrait painters in their thirties or forties, eager to make the leap into landscape or genre painting. Others, such as the genre painter Francis Edmonds, were businessmen who began to paint as an avocation. But most were younger men from rural parts of the Northeast and Midwest, born after the War of 1812, who did not decide to become artists until the economic recovery had already begun. It was members of this generation who dominated the New York art scene from the late 1840s until the end of the Civil War. Leading figures included Daniel Huntington, John Frederick Kensett, Worthington Whittredge, Thomas Hicks, Sanford Gifford, Jasper Cropsey, Eastman Johnson, and Frederic Edwin Church.

The success of these artists was made possible by and contributed to the growth of a new generation of local collectors. Unlike the rich men who had backed the American Academy, the most active collectors in this period tended to be entre-preneurs who had prospered in trade, manufacturing, real estate, finance, or transportation. Charles Leupp made his fortune manufacturing leather. Jonathan Sturges made his in dry goods and then became a major investor in railroads. Marshall O. Roberts began as a grocery clerk but ended up owning transatlantic steamboats and telegraph cables. William T. Blodgett manufactured varnish and made a killing in Manhattan real estate. Alexander T. Stewart transformed shopping into a pleasurable leisure activity and built a small retail shop into one of the world's first great department stores.[33] Much wealthier than earlier generations of New York collectors, these men had access to more art, lived in bigger homes, and had both the means and the desire to put together significantly larger collections. Eastman Johnson's understated group portrait of William T. Blodgett's family in a corner of their home at 27 West Twenty-fifth Street shows only four paintings but implies the presence of the much larger collection filling the house (fig. 15). Indeed, when the painting was exhibited at the National Academy of Design in 1865, many viewers would have known that Blodgett owned several major American paintings, including Frederic Edwin Church's mammoth *The Heart of the Andes* (1859; Metropolitan Museum of Art), which he had purchased in 1859 for ten thousand dollars, at that time the highest sum ever paid for an American landscape painting.[34]

Economic growth and increased arts activity led to expansion of existing arts institutions and the establishment of new

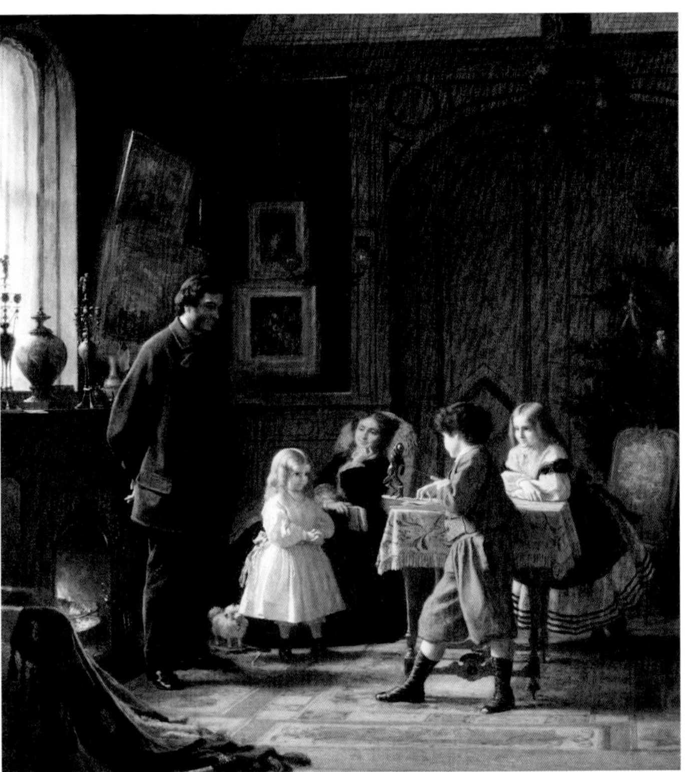

Fig. 15 Eastman Johnson, *Christmas Time (The Blodgett Family)*, 1864, oil on canvas, 30 x 25, The Metropolitan Museum of Art, Gift of Mr. and Mrs. Stephen Whitney Blodgett, 1983 (National Academy of Design, 40th Annual Exhibition, 1865, no. 376)

ones. In the 1840s, most of this activity continued to focus on Broadway near City Hall Park. In December 1841, a Yankee showman with a genius for promotion, Phineas Taylor Barnum, purchased Scudder's Museum. P. T. Barnum also purchased Peale's Museum, moving Peale's collection to Scudder's Broadway building, which he enlarged in 1843 and again in 1850. Like the earlier museum operators, Barnum offered an eclectic array of attractions that emphasized curiosities but always incorporated some more serious exhibits, including a "picture gallery contain[ing] several hundred portraits of the great men of America." Barnum quickly made his museum into the most famous and popular attraction in the city. Barnum's success and the proximity of the elegant Astor House hotel attracted other purveyors of leisure activities, including most of the city's first photographers. Matthew Brady's Daguerrean Miniature Gallery was located in a building at the corner of Broadway and Fulton Street. Eager to establish the gentility and desirability of "instantaneous" photographic portraiture, Brady and other daguerreotypists went to great expense to create elegant reception rooms decorated with paintings and prints—and samples of the photographers' best work.[35]

By the mid-1840s, the focus of art collecting in New York had shifted from old masters to contemporary European and American art. Contemporary European art was generally sold through commercial art galleries, the most important of which were located along Broadway, a few blocks north of City Hall Park. The first major New York gallery to specialize in contemporary European art was a branch of the French firm Goupil, Vibert and Co., which opened at 289 Broadway, on the corner of Duane Street, in 1846. The company specialized in the manufacture and sale of European prints, although it also sold paintings by contemporary French artists. In the 1840s and early 1850s, Goupil's specialized in sentimental works by older painters such as Horace Vernet and Ary Scheffer, but by the end of the 1850s they were selling works by Ernest Meissonier, Edouard Frère, and Rosa Bonheur. Two of Goupil's earliest New York agents were a young Frenchman named Michel Knoedler and a young German named William Schaus, each of whom went on to become influential New York dealers in European art. Knoedler left Goupil's by 1859, when he opened M. Knoedler and Co. in the old A. T. Stewart mansion at 772 Broadway.[36] Contemporary French art was also shown at temporary exhibitions organized by the London dealer Ernest Gambart in the late 1850s and early 1860s, and by several local auctioneers and dealers including Henry H. Leeds and the firm of Williams, Stevens, and Williams. One of the most important of these exhibitions occurred in October 1857, when the latter showed Bonheur's widely discussed painting *The Horse Fair* (1853; Metropolitan Museum of Art). A local collector and entrepreneur had purchased the painting from Gambart the previous winter and immediately set about recouping his investment by sending the painting on an extended American tour.[37]

The most influential foreign school of art in the city during the 1850s was German. American artists began to study in the German city of Düsseldorf in the early 1840s. By the end of the decade, Düsseldorf had become a magnet for younger American painters, many of whom eventually settled in New York. Artists who later had major New York careers who studied at Düsseldorf included Emanuel Leutze, Albert Bierstadt, Eastman Johnson, and Worthington Whittredge. In 1849, a successful German-American wine merchant named John Godfrey Boker opened a large gallery of Düsseldorf art in New York. Located on the second floor of the Church of the Divine Unity at 548 Broadway, between Spring and Prince Streets, Boker's "Düsseldorf Gallery" was, for the next decade, the city's most important venue for the display of contemporary European art. In 1853, Carroll and Hutchinson opened a gallery across the street, at 547 Broadway, dedicated to Belgian art, but this venture was less successful and soon closed. Boker operated the Düsseldorf Gallery until 1857, when he sold it to an American dealer named Henry W. Derby, who in 1860 moved it to a larger space in the Institute of Fine Arts, at 625 Broadway. Derby soon discovered that both artists and collectors were losing interest in the hard finish and sentimental genre subjects characteristic of the Düsseldorf school. He sold the remaining Düsseldorf collections at auction in 1862 and renamed his gallery the Derby Atheneum.[38]

From the mid-1840s until the Civil War, many of the most active New York collectors were primarily interested in contemporary American art. Several of the galleries specializing in European art, including Knoedler and Williams, Stevens, and Williams, recognized the trend and began to offer some American art. As in the 1810s and 1820s, contemporary American art was also available from local art supply stores and frame shops. One of the most important of these sources was the framer John Snedecor, who was selling a substantial amount of new American art by the late 1850s. Older American works were occasionally offered at local estate auctions. What seems to have been the first art gallery dedicated to the sale of American art was started by the portrait painter and print-seller James Herring in 1838. Herring's Apollo Gallery was located above his lending library, at 410 Broadway. But commercial sources for American art remained limited because collectors preferred to buy American works directly from the artist. Herring's experience was typical—his Apollo Gallery lasted less than a year. With collectors and buyers living near each other in the same city, the market for American art remained small and highly personalized, with artists bearing the primary responsibility for the sale of their work.[39]

The most important new arts organization formed during the 1830s and 1840s was the American Art-Union. The Art-Union grew out of the ashes of James Herring's Apollo Gallery. In 1839, Herring reorganized his gallery as a noncommercial joint stock company. Except for Herring, who eventually gave up his position in the Art-Union, the managers were merchants and professional men committed to patrician ideas of stewardship and moral uplift. Herring and the other managers raised capital by selling annual subscriptions that cost five dollars. With these funds, they published a magazine, commissioned engravings, and purchased recent American paintings and sculptures that were put on display in the organization's exhibition room. Artists were not allowed to serve as managers because the organizers believed they would politicize the purchase of art. Members received free admission to the exhibition, a subscription to the magazine, a copy of the year's engraving, and a chance to receive one of the art works, which were distributed by lottery at the end of each year. Non-members paid for admission to the exhibition—a one-time ticket cost twenty-five cents.[40]

The American Art-Union struggled during the lean years of the late 1830s and early 1840s, but boomed along with the economy in the late 1840s. During the early years the exhibitions were held in a variety of spaces, including Herring's gallery at 410 Broadway and the National Academy of Design rooms in Clinton Hall. By 1847, increased sales of subscriptions enabled the managers to build a new facility with a large exhibition room at 497 Broadway (fig. 16). Perhaps even more importantly, increased sales enabled them to eliminate all fees for admission to the exhibition. At the end of 1848, the managers reported that they had sold almost seventeen thousand subscriptions, that they had spent over forty thousand dollars on the purchase of 454 works of art, and that the new "free" gallery had attracted more than half a million visitors. The following year, they leased the adjoining lot and built a second large exhibition room. At the end of 1849, the managers reported that they had spent forty-five thousand dollars on the purchase of 460 works of art and that the exhibition had attracted approximately three-quarters of a million visitors. [41]

Attendance figures and press reports suggest that the free exhibitions at the American Art-Union attracted the patronage of an unusually broad spectrum of the local population and played an important role in the popularization of American art in the nation as a whole and especially in New York. But the success of the Art-Union was short-lived. In 1852, anti-gambling organizers convinced the New York State Court of Appeals that the annual distributions violated state laws prohibiting lotteries. In 1856, Henry Derby tried to circumvent this ruling by organizing the Cosmopolitan Art-Union, which held its exhibitions at the Institute of Fine Arts but was legally based in Ohio, where lotteries were not prohibited. Derby's Cosmopolitan Art-Union survived until 1861 but never achieved the popularity or influence of the American Art-Union.[42]

Although New York was rapidly becoming the nation's arts center, it still did not have a permanent non-commercial art gallery or museum. In 1844, a group of wealthy businessmen led by Jonathan Sturges purchased a large collection of

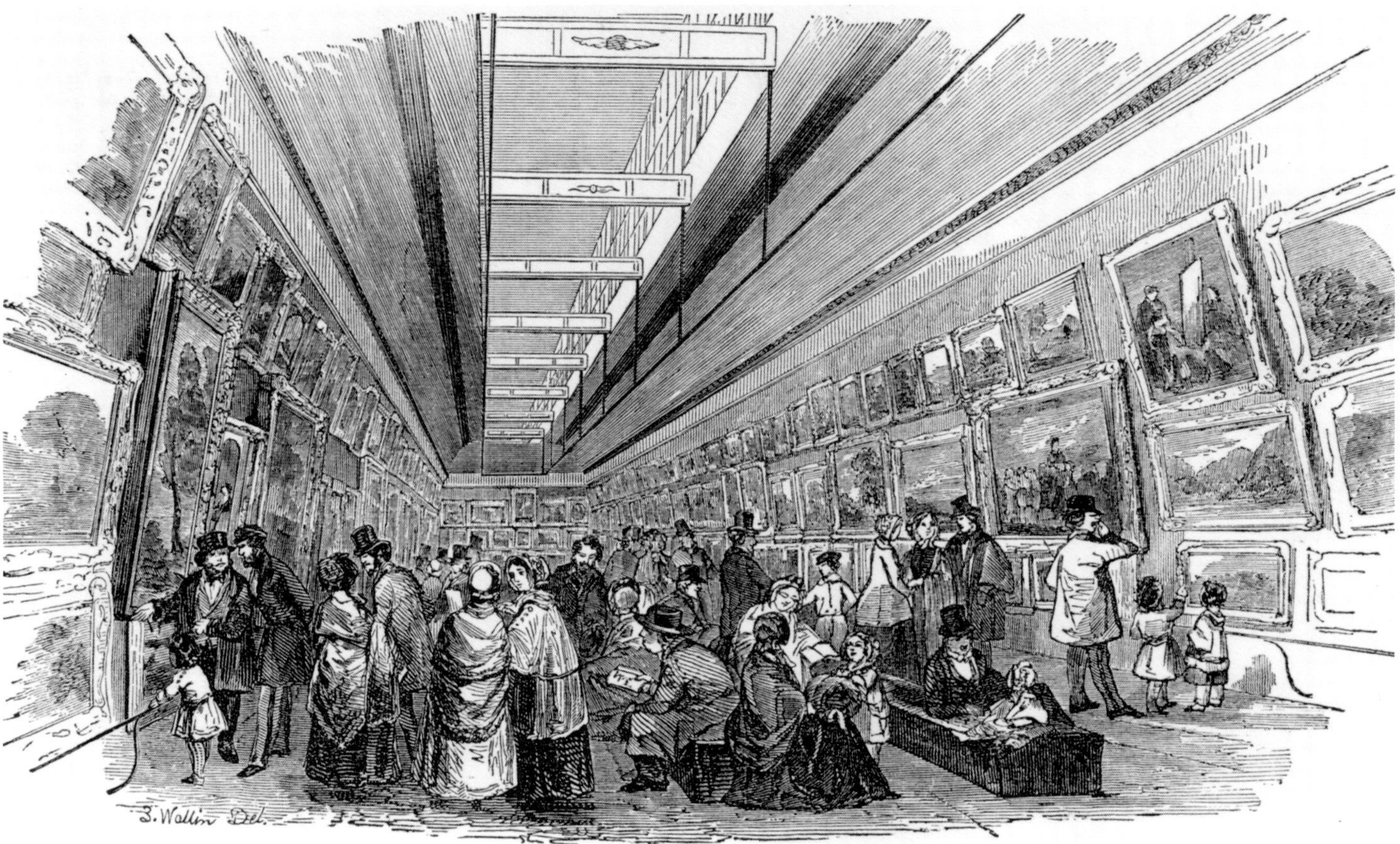

Fig. 16 Samuel Wallin, *Gallery of the Art-Union,* from *Bulletin of the American Art-Union* 2 (May 1849), frontispiece, Archives, National Academy of Design

European and American art assembled by Sturges's former partner Luman Reed and opened a non-profit museum they called the New-York Gallery of the Fine Arts. Reed was born in rural New York in 1785. By the mid-1820s, he had become one of the most successful wholesale dry goods merchants in New York. He probably began to collect art in the late 1820s. By the early 1830s, he had begun to focus on contemporary American art and especially on works by the New York painters George Whiting Flagg, Thomas Cole, and William Sidney Mount. Reed died in 1836, at the age of forty-one. His family maintained the collection for eight years, until they sold it to the group led by Sturges. The first exhibition of the New-York Gallery of the Fine Arts was held in rooms leased from the National Academy of Design during the winter of 1844–1845. After extensive lobbying, the leaders of the new organization secured a lease on Vanderlyn's Rotunda for the token fee of one dollar per year. The collection was on continuous display at the Rotunda from July 1845 until June 1848, when the City Council reclaimed the Rotunda for use as offices. Reed's paintings were subsequently displayed at the National Academy of Design, but Sturges and his colleagues were unwilling to subsidize the acquisition and operation of a permanent facility, and in 1852 they placed the collection in storage.[43]

The demise of the New-York Gallery of the Fine Arts coincided with the reinvigoration of the New-York Historical Society, which soon became one of the most important venues for the display of art in the city. In the mid-1850s, the leaders of the Historical Society decided "to enlarge and extend their Art Collections with a view of providing a public gallery of art in this city."[44] In 1858, the leaders of the moribund Gallery of the Fine Arts donated their entire collection to the Historical Society so that it could be exhibited in the Society's new building at the corner of Second Avenue and Eleventh Street. The Society's collection grew again in 1867, when Thomas Bryan donated almost four hundred "old master" paintings dealing with religious themes. The Bryan paintings were already familiar to many New Yorkers, who could have seen them in the "Gallery of Christian Art" that Bryan had operated out of his home at Broadway and Thirteenth Street since 1853. By 1868, the Historical Society had outgrown its Second Avenue building and received permission from the New York state legislature to build on a large site on the eastern edge of Central Park, between Eighty-first and Eight-fourth streets. But the leaders of the Historical Society failed to raise the necessary funds. Construction had still not begun in 1872, when the state legislature changed its mind and gave the Historical Society rights to its current site on Central Park West.[45]

The rapid growth of the city created a new physical geography of art production. In the nineteenth century, as today, artists tended to live in or near their studios. Up to the mid-1840s, artists' studios, art supply stores, frame shops, the most important art institutions—including the National Academy of Design—and the major galleries and auction houses were all clustered within a few blocks of City Hall Park. The small size of the neighborhood encouraged a sense of community among the artists and facilitated sales by enabling potential buyers to move easily between exhibitions, galleries, and studios. This community began to fragment in the late 1830s, when several leading artists found studios in the recently completed New York University Building at the northeast corner of Washington Square Park in Greenwich Village. The breakup of the old arts neighborhood accelerated during the boom years of the late 1840s and early 1850s, when artists followed the northward movement of their patrons and arts-related businesses and institutions. By the end of the Civil War, Union Square had replaced City Hall Park as the center of civic life. The timing of this shift is clearly suggested by the history of the National Academy of Design, which stayed in the Society Library building on Broadway at Leonard Street until 1850. In 1851, the Academy moved to Greenwich Village, where the Academicians purchased a building at 663 Broadway, between Bleecker and Amity streets. Within a few years, the Academy sold this building at a substantial profit and moved even further north, renting space on the corner of Fourth Avenue and Tenth Street. But the Academy did not stay on Tenth Street long. By 1865, the Academicians had used the profits from the sale of 663 Broadway to construct a large building at Fourth Avenue and Twenty-third Street (fig. 17; see the essay "Annual Exhibitions and the Birth of American Art Criticism to 1865" in this book).[46]

By the end of the 1850s, the focus of artistic life had shifted north to Greenwich Village, with many of the leading artists congregating in a handful of older buildings in which developers had created studio spaces. In 1859, eleven artists had studios in the Society Library, which had been purchased by the publishing firm of D. Appleton and Co. and was known as the Appleton Building. John Kensett and several of his close friends worked out of the Waverly, at 697 Broadway, on the corner of Fourth Street. Others rented space in the Dodsworth Building, at 806 Broadway between Eleventh and Twelfth streets. [47] The most influential of these enclaves, however, was the Studio Building, on Tenth Street between Fifth and Sixth avenues, the first building anywhere in the world specifically designed for the use of artists (fig. 18). The brainchild of James Boorman Johnston, a prominent real estate developer with close ties to many leading artists and collectors, the Studio Building opened in January 1858. It contained about twenty studios on three floors surrounding a central gallery. The gallery was thirty by forty feet, covered by a large glass ceiling. In 1858, the *Crayon* reported that "gas-burners, of a fan-pattern flame, and projecting horizontally, are arranged within the lower edge of the skylight-well; and being very numerous, and the light, in a measure, concentrated, there is an ample supply of it. We have never seen a better night-light for pictures, nor a better constructed exhibition room." The Civil War slowed the development of studio buildings, but immediately after the war, the YMCA completed a large building that included twenty studios and an exhibition

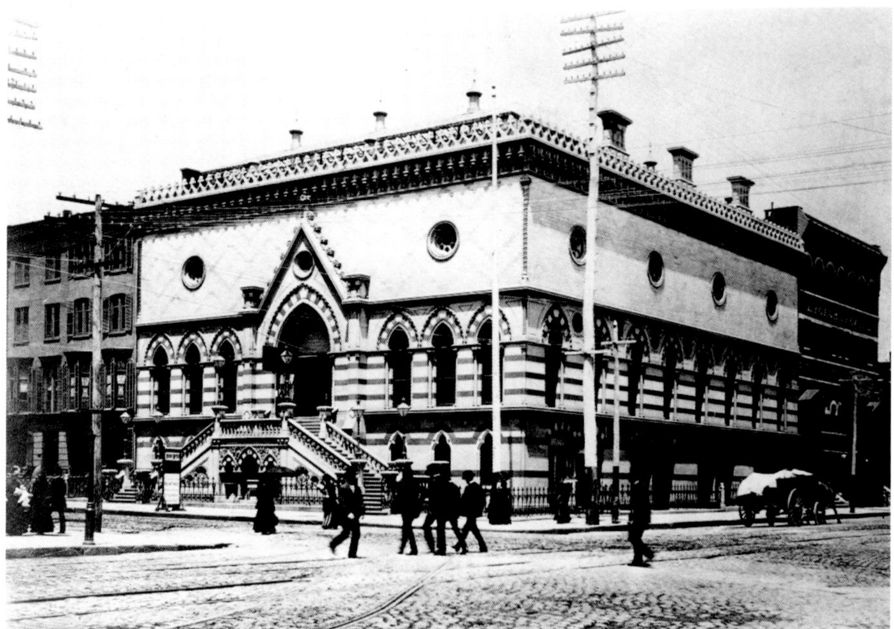

Fig. 17 Peter B. Wight, *National Academy of Design, Twenty-third Street and Fourth Avenue,* 1863–65, Archives, National Academy of Design.

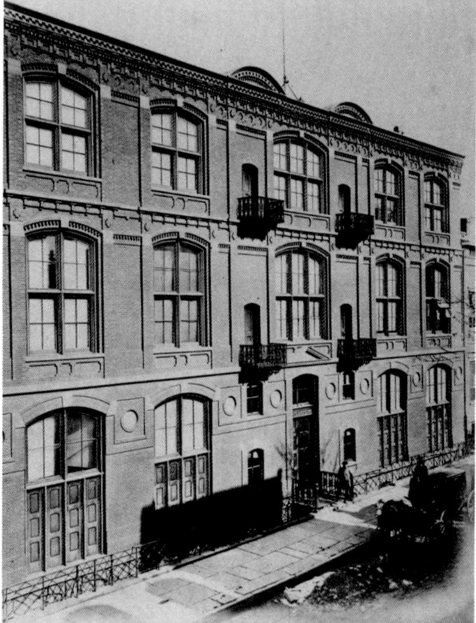

Fig. 18 *Tenth Street Studio Building,* about 1858, The Octagon, The Museum of the American Architectural Foundation, Washington, D.C.

gallery modeled on the one in the Tenth Street Studio. Often referred to as the Association Building, it was located across Twenty-third Street from the National Academy of Design (fig. 19).[48]

Development of the studio buildings transformed the marketing of contemporary American art in the city as artists joined together to host evening receptions in which all the artists in a building would invite friends, clients, and potential clients to see their recent work. Receptions were held in all the studio buildings, but they were most closely identified with the Tenth Street Studio Building, in which the gallery served as a central space for the display of art. Artists' receptions were generally held shortly before the spring exhibitions at the National Academy, allowing potential buyers to see new works and works-in-progress before they were shown to the general public (fig. 20). The gallery was also used for special exhibitions. Frederic Church rented it to display *The Heart of the Andes* in the spring and fall of 1859. In 1863, Albert Bierstadt used the space to exhibit his similarly large canvas, *The Rocky Mountains, Lander's Peak* (1863; Metropolitan Museum of Art). Sometimes it was used for group shows, such as the exhibition of English art organized by Ernest Gambart in 1867.[49]

NEW YORK INCORPORATED: 1865–1914

From the 1820s until the Civil War, New York thrived by placing itself at the center of the nation's trade, dominating the marketing of manufactured goods imported from Europe and the export of agricultural products from both the Midwest and the South. The southern trade was especially profitable, with New York banks, insurance companies, com-

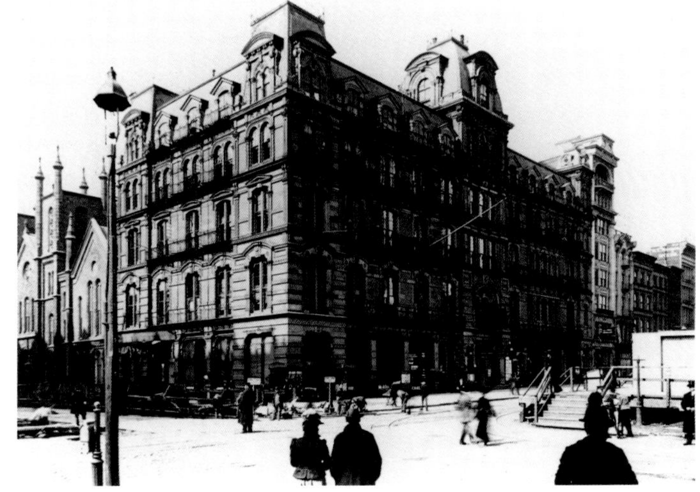

Fig. 19 Robert Louis Bracklau, photographer, *Young Men's Christian Association Building, Fourth Avenue and Twenty-third Street, New York,* Archives, National Academy of Design

modities brokers, warehouse operators, and shippers earning about forty cents on every dollar Europeans spent on American cotton. By early 1861, however, many New Yorkers were worrying that the political crisis over slavery threatened local dominance of the cotton trade and the economic health of the city. As a writer for the *New-York Times* put it, losing the southern trade would mean that "we shall not only cease to see marble palaces rising along Broadway, but [we shall be] reduced from a national to a merely financial metropolis, our shipping will rot at the wharves, and grass will grow in the streets."[50] The beginning of the Civil War, in April 1861, initially fulfilled the worst of these fears, leading to a severe panic

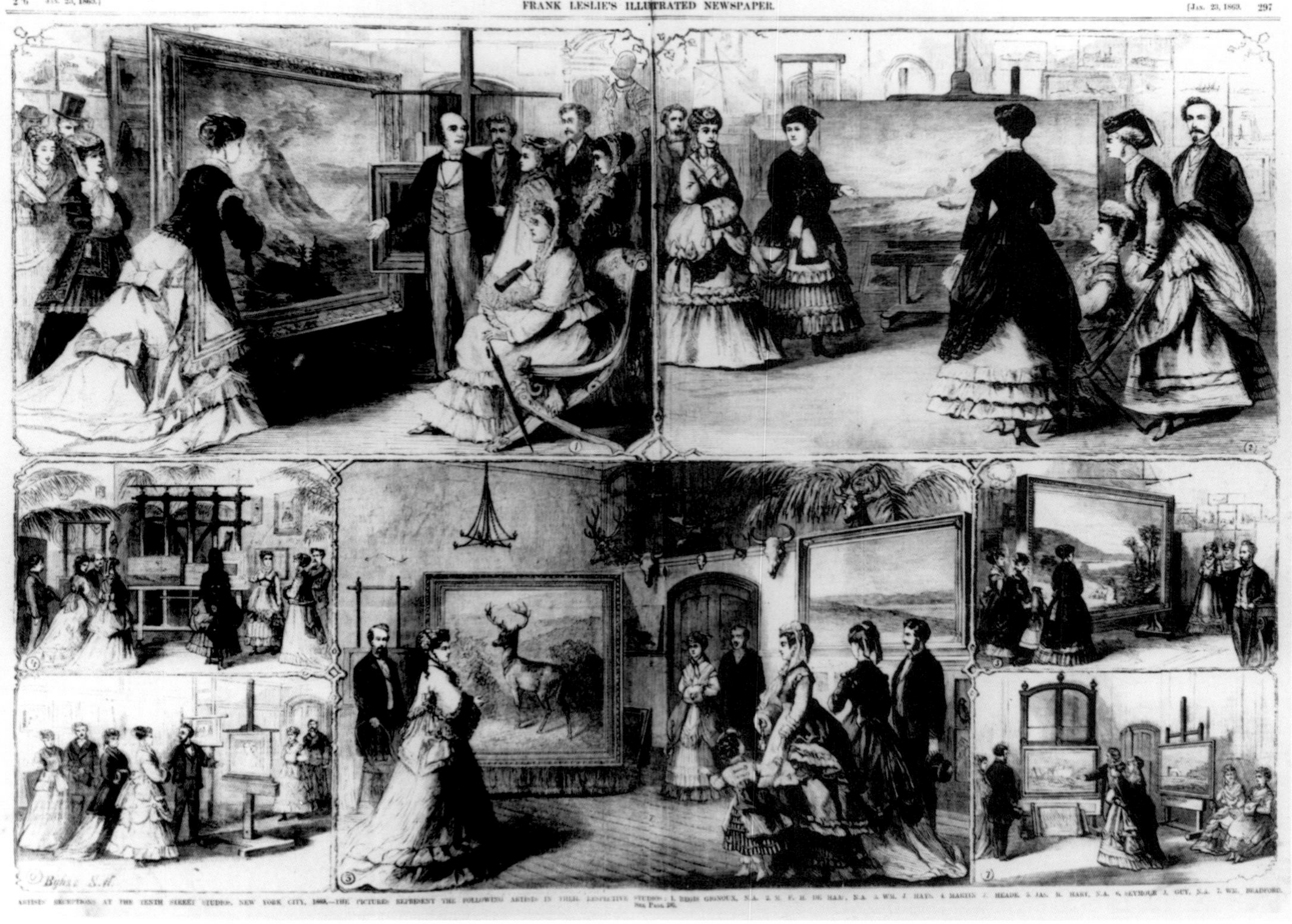

Fig. 20 "Artists' Receptions at the Tenth Street Studio, New York City, 1869," *Frank Leslie's Illustrated Newspaper*, January 3, 1869, The New York Public Library, Astor, Lenox and Tilden Foundations

as southern debts went unpaid and local importers and manufacturers were stuck with inventories they could not sell. Trade with the south did not return to pre-war levels until after the end of Reconstruction in 1879. But by then, the cotton trade represented a much smaller portion of a much larger economic pie.

Turning adversity to opportunity, New York's leading businessmen refocused the local economy by expanding trade with the western parts of the nation. Before the Civil War, much western grain, cattle, and hogs had been shipped to market by way of New Orleans. When the war closed the Mississippi River, New Yorkers, eager to gain control over this trade, modernized the Erie Canal, improved the Hudson River Railroad, and extended the Erie Railroad through to Cincinnati. The effect of these improvements was dramatic. At the beginning of the Civil War, annual exports of wheat, wheat flour, and corn from New York totaled nine million bushels. By 1865, they had surged to fifty-seven million bushels. New York's leading competitor was Philadelphia, which shipped only five million bushels. The War was also good for local manufacturing, spurring production of a wide range of goods necessary to the war effort, including ships, engines, boilers, munitions, wagons, uniforms, boots, and pharmaceuticals. Leading manufacturers and financiers became millionaires seemingly overnight. At the beginning of the war, the city had only a few dozen millionaires. By the end of the war, there were hundreds.[51]

Changes in the local economy that began during the Civil War accelerated in the years after it. The lead industry was railroads. The first transcontinental railroad was completed in 1869. By 1873, twenty-four thousand miles of track crossed the nation. In the next four years, another fifty-five thousand miles of track were added. The explosive growth of the rail system required massive new investments in mining, iron production, and manufacturing. Unprecedented expansion of extractive industries and manufacturing drew vast numbers of foreign immigrants, fueling urban growth and the further extension of commercial agriculture. By the end of the 1870s, railroad construction had knit the nation together into a continental marketplace. New York banks, insurance companies, merchants, and manufacturers were at the center of these interrelated developments, funding industrial growth, directing the flow of western commodities to European and East Coast consumers, and sending locally manufactured and imported goods west. But unplanned development also led to construction of unnecessary railroads and manufacturing plants, resulting in cutthroat competition and financial instability. In the 1880s, industrialists, bankers, and lawyers invented the corporate holding company, which enabled competing businesses to combine, resulting in previously unimaginable concentrations of economic and social power in the hands of business tycoons and financiers. Many of the new corporations grew out of older New York businesses. Others began elsewhere but relocated to New York in order to secure direct access to the nation's most important investment banks and legal talent. By 1900, Manhattan's population had grown to almost 1.9 million, and New York was poised to overtake London as the hub of the global economy.[52]

Most of the best-known American painters thrived during the boom years of the Civil War, but even before the fighting ended the winds of aesthetic change were blowing. In 1863, a group of mostly young New York artists formed a new arts organization that they grandly named the Association for the Advancement of Truth in Art. The first self-conscious "school" of artists to form in the United States, these self-described American Ruskinians immediately established a monthly art journal in which they attacked the leading American painters as formalists who thought they were painting nature but were only marshalling a set of outmoded pictorial conventions. The editor of the group's journal was a Harvard-educated architect named Clarence Cook. Cook gained a more prominent pulpit in 1864, when he became art critic for the *New York Tribune* and quickly established himself as the most influential commentator of his generation. Except for a year in the early 1870s, Cook stayed at the *Tribune* until 1883, when he took over an arts magazine called the *Studio*. Although Cook abandoned his Ruskinian insistence on minute fidelity to observed nature by the end of the 1860s, he continued to criticize many of the better-known American painters as provincial artists whose work lacked the creative power of the best contemporary European art.[53]

Cook's criticism expressed a new cosmopolitanism that transformed the New York art world in the decades following the Civil War. The transatlantic cable, faster steamships, and the great wealth amassed by New York's industrial and financial tycoons shrank the Atlantic Ocean. In 1867, many of the most important New York collectors of American art lent paintings to the American art section of the Universal Exposition in Paris. They followed their paintings to Paris, met leading European artists, and returned home eager to acquire more European art. Sales of European art boomed. Threatened by the growing demand for foreign art, American artists sought government protection by lobbying Congress for increased tariffs. Cook and other leading art journalists derided these efforts, insisting that American artists had lived too long in a protected provincial market and were "in serious

need of competition and rivalry." Cook even claimed to believe that the best American artists welcomed the challenge:

> *. . . the successive importation of foreign pictures during the last ten years, especially those made by the house of Goupil, have been a great advantage to the whole body of artists, and have greatly advanced the public taste, while even the second and third rate productions have been far superior in some technical qualities to the best of the pictures painted here. Indeed, if we may speak frankly, we believe it is just here, in the improvement of public taste, that the difficulty lies. The majority of our artists have been left behind by it, and are indisposed or unable to make the necessary exertions to catch up with it, and regain the public favor.*

Not surprisingly, by the early 1870s, both wealthy collectors and ambitious young artists were flocking to Europe, usually making a beeline for Munich and Paris.[54]

From the mid-1860s until World War I, most of the major New York collectors focused their buying on European art that they displayed in large private galleries in their palatial homes. One of the earliest of these large-scale collectors was A. T. Stewart. Wealthy before the Civil War, Stewart became much wealthier supplying uniforms to the army and navy. In the late 1860s, he built a grand mansion at the corner of Fifth Avenue and Thirty-fourth Street. Stewart's collection included some major mid-century American works such as Hiram Powers's *Greek Slave* (1847; Newark Museum, Newark, New Jersey) and Frederic Church's *Niagara from the American Side* (1867; National Gallery of Scotland). Stewart continued to purchase American works in the late 1860s, but after the war he began to focus on contemporary French art, acquiring numerous important works, including Roas Bonheur's *Horse Fair* (1853; Metropolitan Museum of Art) and Meissonier's *Friedland 1807* (1875; Metropolitan Museum of Art). When Stewart died in 1876, his collection included over two hundred and fifty major paintings and sculptures, of which only twenty-one were by Americans. William H. Vanderbilt's collecting followed the same trajectory. As the dealer Samuel P. Avery later explained, Vanderbilt patronized local artists when he was young, but by the end of the Civil War, "he was able to buy the best and most costly in the world. He decided . . . to buy nothing that was not important." For Vanderbilt and for many other post–Civil War collectors, if not for Avery himself, no American work of art was truly "important." Major collectors like J. P. Morgan and the Havemeyers, who did not enter the art market until the 1880s and 1890s, often skipped this American "phase" almost entirely.[55]

Increased demand for European art spurred expansion of the commercial art market. Several of the new dealers announced that they were going to specialize in American art, but until the 1890s everyone who tried to do so discovered that the market was too weak to be relied on. The career of Samuel P. Avery is representative. Born in New York in 1822,

Avery worked as an engraver until the late 1850s, when he began to buy paintings for several private collectors. Avery opened a Broadway gallery specializing in American art in 1864 but soon recognized the drift of the market. After organizing the American art section at the 1867 Universal Exposition in Paris, he spent six months meeting European artists and buying art before returning home to open a new gallery at 88 Fifth Avenue, on the corner of Fourteenth Street. Although Avery continued to handle some American art, he specialized in contemporary European figure paintings and French Barbizon landscapes. Like the other major dealers in contemporary European art, he also sold "old masters" when he could get them. By the end of the 1860s, Avery was firmly established as an influential arbiter of taste, organizing exhibitions, and advising major collectors including August Belmont, John Taylor Johnston, and William H. Vanderbilt.[56]

The American Art Gallery on Madison Square went through a similar evolution. Founded in 1879 by James Sutton and Rufus Moore, the gallery was originally dedicated to the exhibition of contemporary American art. Moore quit the partnership in 1882, when Sutton and Thomas Kirby reorganized it as the American Art Association. Kirby was an auctioneer, and by 1885, the American Art Association had joined Leavitt's, Ortgies & Co., and Robert Somerville as one of the leading art auction firms in the city. In the spring of 1885, Sutton went to Europe in search of fresh merchandise and convinced the Parisian dealer Paul Durand-Ruel to help the American Art Association mount the first major American exhibition devoted to the Impressionists. Durand-Ruel sent three hundred paintings. As a bow to established New York taste, he included a group of Barbizon landscapes for which he had first become known. But the bulk of the exhibition consisted of Impressionist paintings—three by Seurat, fifteen by Sisley, seventeen by Manet, twenty-three by Degas, forty-two by Pissarro, and forty-eight by Monet. *Works in Oil and Pastel by the Impressionists of Paris* stayed at the American Art Association for a month, when it was moved to the National Academy of Design. Durand-Ruel sold $18,000 worth of paintings, including half of the Monets, and quickly agreed with Sutton to mount another New York exhibition. The second Durand-Ruel exhibition opened at the National Academy of Design in May 1887. A few years later, Sutton resigned from active management of the American Art Association in order to become a full-time dealer in contemporary French art. Under Kirby's management, the American Art Association functioned solely as an auction house.[57]

One year after his second Impressionist exhibition with Sutton, Durand-Ruel opened his own New York gallery. Managed by Durand-Ruel's sons, the gallery was located north of the old arts district, at 297 Fifth Avenue. Durand-Ruel moved to a larger space at 315 Fifth Avenue, on the corner of Thirty-second Street, by 1892, before moving into an extensively renovated pre–Civil War mansion at 389 Fifth Avenue, on the corner of Thirty-sixth Street, in November 1894. Durand-Ruel's landlord, and one of his most important clients, was the sugar magnate H. O. Havemeyer. Other dealers jumped into the market Durand-Ruel had pioneered, opening fancy galleries on Fifth Avenue between Thirtieth and Thirty-ninth streets, which had become the most fashionable retail neighborhood in the city. Boussod, Valadon, and Co. (successor to Goupil, Vibert, and Co.) opened a gallery specializing in contemporary French art on Fifth Avenue near Thirty-first Street in 1888. M. Knoedler and Co. moved to Fifth Avenue at the corner of Thirty-fourth Street by the mid-1890s.[58]

The most important new arts institution created in the post–Civil War period was the Metropolitan Museum of Art. From the end of the eighteenth century, New York collectors and artists had repeatedly tried to establish a permanent art gallery or museum. In the spring of 1864, a group of prominent New York artists and their patrons, including Henry Blodgett, John Taylor Johnston, Samuel P. Avery, John Frederick Kensett, and Frederic Church, had organized a large temporary exhibition of European and American art to raise funds for the care of wounded and sick Union soldiers. The exhibition was held in the Fourteenth Street Armory and was known as the Metropolitan Fair. Five years later, many of the same artists and collectors joined to form the Metropolitan Museum of Art. Incorporated by act of the state legislature in April 1870, the new museum opened in a gallery on the top floor of a converted row house at 681 Fifth Avenue in February 1872. The following year, the Central Park Commissioners offered the new museum the large site on the east side of Central Park between Seventy-ninth and Eighty-fourth streets that had previously been promised to the New-York Historical Society. In October 1873, the museum moved from Fifth Avenue to a substantially larger space in a converted mansion at 128 West Fourteenth Street. The museum stayed on Fourteenth Street until March 1880, when it inaugurated its new building in Central Park. The board of the new museum was dominated by men who had begun to collect before the Civil War, were interested in American as well as European art, respected the leading New York artists, and conceived of the museum as an educational institution. As Rufus C. Choate put it in his speech marking the opening of the 1880 building, the Metropolitan Museum of Art would "gather together a more or less complete collection of objects illustrative of the history of art in all its branches . . . which should serve not only for the instruction and entertainment of the people, but should also show to the students and artisans of every branch of industry, in the high and acknowledged standards of form and color, what the past has accomplished for them to imitate and excel." But the museum's board was soon influenced by changes sweeping the local art market. By the end of the 1880s, local artists had been dropped from the board, which was rapidly losing interest in the education of artists and artisans as it focused on the collection and display of great and original masterpieces of European art.[59]

The last quarter of the nineteenth century was a difficult time for most American artists. The old art market founded on the personal encounter of the individual artist with a buyer was passing away. A more highly structured and depersonalized art market focusing on the dealer as mediating expert was being born. James McNeill Whistler, William Merritt Chase, and a few other leading artists were able to take advantage of the new mass media to turn themselves into well-known celebrities. But even artists who attained celebrity could not command the high prices paid for important old master and contemporary French art. This gap bred dissatisfaction, as American artists remembered the heady days of the 1850s and early 1860s when leading native artists had been able to command top dollar.[60]

For many American artists, one of the first clear signs that the art market was changing was the unexpected decline of the studio receptions. The receptions thrived through the Civil War, but potential buyers began to loss interest in them in the late 1860s. The loss of public interest surprised the artists. Thomas Seir Cummings, long-time treasurer of the National Academy of Design, suggested that the public grew tired of the receptions because artists had hosted too many of them. But the decline of the reception was probably due to more fundamental cultural factors. By the end of the 1860s, the members of the art-buying public had become used to shopping in luxury department stores like A. T. Stewart's, in which buyers were free to browse without the supervision of hovering salespeople and prices were set so that haggling was unnecessary. This more impersonal shopping environment appealed to potential buyers of art who lacked confidence in their aesthetic taste or bargaining skills and felt threatened by the intimacy of the evening receptions, which did little to conceal the economic reality that the artists were hawking their own wares. This would have been especially true of women buyers, who were assuming increasing responsibility for home decoration.[61]

Artists sought to reinforce the fraying bonds linking them with their patrons by inventing new social occasions in which they could display their work to potential buyers. Beginning in 1858, the artists of the National Academy of Design held gala receptions to celebrate the opening of the annual exhibition. The galas had been abandoned during the Civil War but were renewed soon after it and quickly became important social events.[62] The most important institutional innovation of the post–Civil War period, however, was the development of temporary exhibitions sponsored by several of the city's leading men's clubs. The Union League Club organized the first of these in February 1867. By the late 1870s, it was mounting exhibitions every month from October until May in a large gallery in its clubhouse on Madison Square. Another influential club, the Century, began organizing monthly exhibitions in 1870, after adding an art gallery to its clubhouse at 109 East Fifteenth Street. The Salmagundi Club began monthly exhibitions in 1887. The Lotos Club, the National Arts Club, and several artists' clubs also hosted exhibitions. Although all the clubs that mounted regular exhibitions showed some European art, as a group they remained strikingly loyal to the work of native artists.[63]

The club exhibitions were a peculiar hybrid, less intimate than the studio receptions, but more private than exhibitions at the National Academy of Design or the commercial galleries. Exhibitions were generally organized by a committee, which often included artists or art dealers. Except for special loan exhibitions borrowed from members or other collectors, exhibited works were generally for sale. Because the exhibitions were private events, the clubs did not let the critics review them. Nevertheless, they received publicity. Because the clubs played such an important role in the social life of the wealthiest New Yorkers, the exhibitions were widely noticed on the society and arts pages of local newspapers and magazines. At a time when many leading newspaper and magazine reviewers frequently were dismissive of the work of well-known local artists, the club exhibitions were a safe haven in which artists could show their work and garner favorable publicity free from the poisoned pens of carping critics. The exhibitions also served the needs of aesthetically insecure buyers, reassuring them that exhibited works met the high standards of the most aesthetically knowledgeable members of the club. The organizing committee mediated the artist's relationship with potential buyers, playing the role that a dealer might have played in a more fully commercialized art market.

Even the best-connected New York artists realized that the private club exhibitions did not offer a long-term solution to their difficulties. During this period, numerous artists tried to take the marketing of their work into their own hands by forming new artist-run organizations, the main purpose of which was to mount annual exhibitions. The first of these new organizations was the Artists' Fund Society. Founded in 1860, it held exhibitions and auctions in order to raise funds for the support of indigent artists and their families. It was followed by the Brooklyn Art Association in 1861, the American Watercolor Society in 1866, and the Society of American Artists in 1877. Recognizing the need for more venues, the National Academy of Design experimented with summer exhibitions in 1870 and 1871, organized annual autumn exhibitions from 1882 until 1898, and began a series of winter exhibitions in 1906.[64]

The establishment of more annual exhibitions enabled New York artists to reach larger numbers of potential buyers, but by the end of the 1870s even the most stalwart local artists realized that they needed professional help with the marketing of their work. As a frustrated Jervis McEntee confided to his diary in 1878, "the more I think of it, the more I am convinced of the necessity of business management of the sale of our pictures."[65] The market for American art bottomed out in the mid-1880s. In the late 1880s, a new generation of collectors, led by Thomas B. Clarke, William T. Evans, George A.

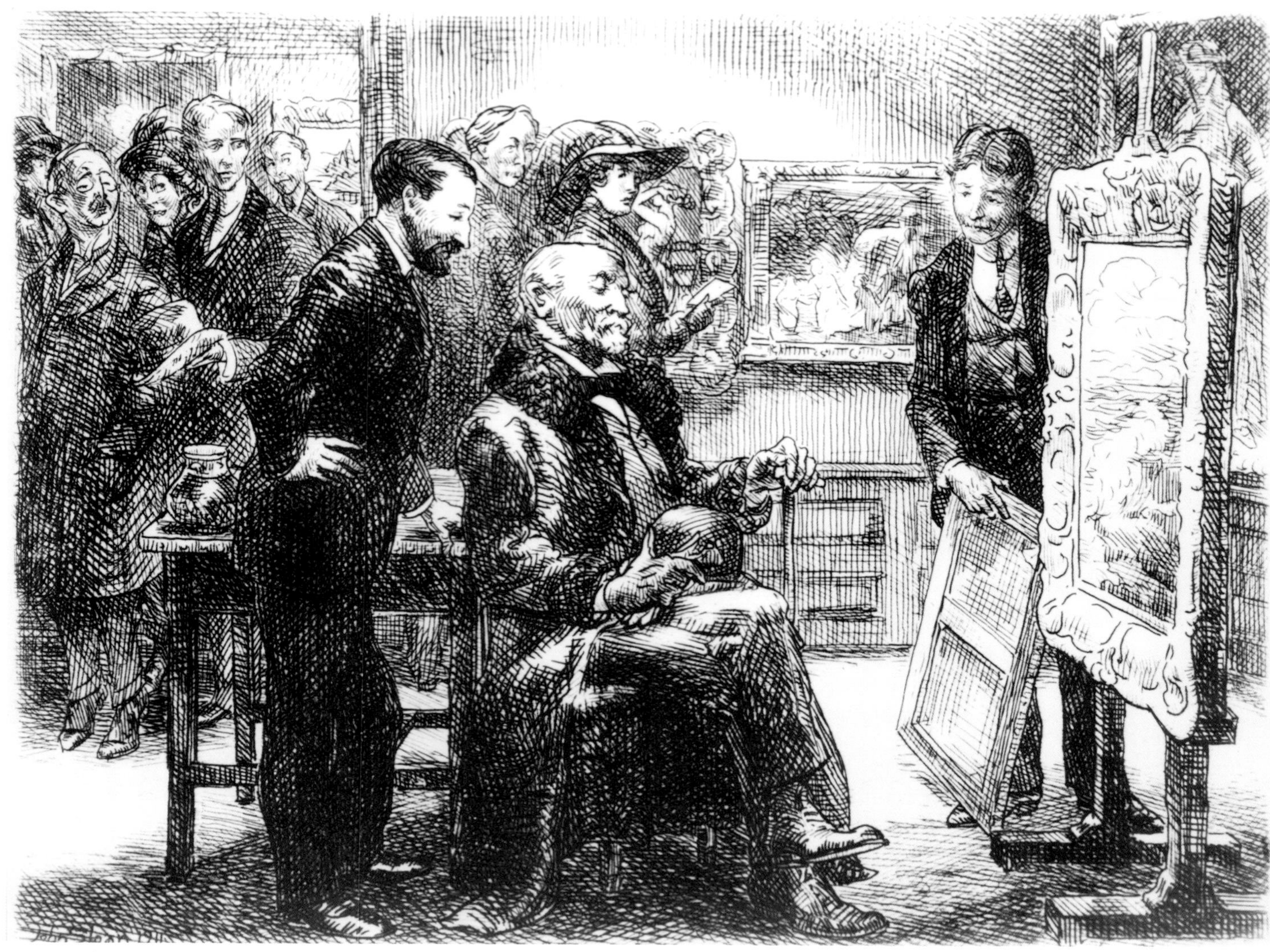

Fig. 21   John Sloan, *The Picture Buyer*, 1911, etching, 5 5/16 x 7 1/6, Bowdoin College Museum of Art, Brunswick, Maine, Bequest of George Otis Hamlin

Hearne, and John Gellatly, began to focus on contemporary American art.[66] By then, the New York art scene was dominated by a new generation of more cosmopolitan artists who accepted the fact that they would never tower over the local market the way Cropsey, Church, and Bierstadt had. In 1892, William Macbeth founded the first successful commercial gallery for American art. Macbeth survived where Avery and Sutton had failed by seeking out more nationalistic collectors outside of New York who could be convinced to buy American. Macbeth struggled for a decade, but by 1906 he was able to move out of his modest storefront at 237 Fifth Avenue and into a much more substantial space at 450 Fifth Avenue, near Fortieth Street. A famous etching by John Sloan shows Macbeth "purring" into the ear of a client (fig. 21).[67] The tide had turned by the end of the 1890s, and even the most important European galleries began to handle some American art. In 1897, M. Knoedler and Co. started showing the paintings of Winslow Homer. The following year, Durand-Ruel hosted the first exhibition of the upstart group of American Impressionists known as The Ten.[68]

NOTES

1. On the early history of New York, see, Edwin G. Burrows and Mike Wallace, *Gotham: A History of New York City to 1898* (New York: Oxford University Press, 1999), 141–49. For the DeLange inventory, see Kenneth Scott and James A. Owre, *Genealogical Data From Inventories of New York Estates, 1666–1825* (New York: New York Genealogical and Biographical Society, 1970), 39. On the visual arts in Dutch New York, see Roderic H. Blackburn and Ruth Piwonka, *Remembrance of Patria: Dutch Arts and Culture in Colonial America, 1609–1776* (Albany: Albany Institute of History and Art, 1988), 209–55. Gerrit Duyckinck's father and son also painted. On the Duyckinck family, see especially Waldron P. Belknap, Jr., *American Colonial Painting: Materials for a History* (Cambridge: Harvard University Press, 1959), 63–128. On printmaking in the colonies, see Lawrence C. Wroth, *The Colonial Printer* (1931; reprint, Charlottesville: University Press of Virginia, 1964), 283–95; and Wendy Shadwell, *American Printmaking: The First 150 Years* (New York: Museum of Graphic Art, 1969).

2. On the impact of the English conquest on the visual culture of New York, see Wayne Craven, "Painting in New York City, 1750–1775," in *American Painting to 1776: A Reappraisal*, Ian M. G. Quimby ed. (Charlottesville: University Press of Virginia, 1971), 251–53; and Richard H. Saunders "The Portrait in America, 1700–1750," in Richard H. Saunders and Ellen G. Miles, *American Colonial Portraits: 1700–1776* (Washington, D.C.: Smithsonian Institution Press, 1987), 1–8.

3. Burrows and Wallace, *Gotham*, 177. Also see Richard Bushman, *The Refinement of America: Persons, Houses, Cities* (New York: Vintage, 1993), 139–80; T. H. Breen, "An Empire of Goods: The Anglicization of Colonial America, 1690–1776," *Journal of British Studies* 25 (1986): 467–99; and *Of Consuming*

Interests: The Style of Life in the Eighteenth Century, Cary Carson, Ronald Hoffman, and Peter Albert eds. (Charlottesville: University Press of Virginia, 1994).

4. Portrait painters active in New York between 1740 and 1770 include John Singleton Copley, John Durand, Lawrence Kilburn, Thomas McIlworth, John Mare, and John Wollaston. In addition to Belknap, *American Colonial Painting,* and Saunders and Miles, *American Colonial Portraits,* see Frank Kelly, "The Portraits of John Durand," *The Magazine Antiques* 122 (November 1982): 1080-87; Wayne Craven, "John Wollaston: His Career in England and New York City," *American Art Quarterly* 7 (1975): 19–31; Helen Burr Smith, "John Mare (1739–c. 1795), New York Portrait Painter," *New-York Historical Society Quarterly* 35 (October 1951): 355–99; and William Sawitzky and Susan Sawitsky, "Thomas McIlworth," *New-York Historical Society Quarterly* 35 (April 1951): 117–39. The earliest advertisement I know of announcing numerous single sheet engravings available for purchase was published in the *New-York Gazette,* April 24, 1749, and is reproduced in Rita Gottesman, *The Arts and Crafts in New York: 1726–1776* (New York: New-York Historical Society, 1938), 14. For later announcements offering numerous engravings for sale, see idem, 15.

5. Burrows and Wallace, *Gotham,* 175–77. For the portrait of Pitt in the Royal Exchange, see Saunders and Miles, *Colonial American Portraits,* 55–56. For the equestrian statue, see Arthur S. Marks, "The Statue of King George III in New York and the Iconology of Regicide," *American Art Journal* 13 (Summer 1981): 61–82.

6. Burrows and Wallace, *Gotham,* 333–52; Robert Albion, *The Rise of New York Port: 1815–1860* (1939; reprint, Boston: Northeastern University Press, 1984); and Sean Wilentz, *Chants Democratic: New York City and the Rise of the American Working Class, 1788–1850* (Oxford: Oxford University Press, 1984).

7. Rita Gottesman, *The Arts and Crafts in New York: 1777-1799* (New York: New-York Historical Society, 1954), 3-11, 15-19; Rita Gottesman, *The Arts and Crafts in New York: 1800–1804* (New York: New-York Historical Society, 1965), 3–16.

8. Kenneth Myers, "Alexander Robertson," in *The Catskills: Painters, Writers, and Tourists in the Mountains, 1820-1895* (Yonkers, New York: Hudson River Museum of Westchester, 1987), 178-80; John Stillwell, "Archibald Robertson, Miniaturist," *New-York Historical Society Quarterly Bulletin* 13 (1929), 1–33; and Mrs. Warren Goddard, "Archibald Robertson, Founder of the First Art School in America," *New York Genealogical and Biographical Record* 51, no. 2 (1920), 130–37.

9. Gottesman, *Arts and Crafts in New York: 1777–1799,* 25.

10. Gottesman, *Arts and Crafts in New York: 1800–1804,* 13, 19, 20, 52, 62, 73.

11. Gottesman, *Arts and Crafts in New York: 1777–1799,* 32–33. Corti seems to have continued selling prints and paintings for at least five years. See, Gottesman, *Arts and Crafts in New York: 1800–1804,* 37–39, 56. On 56, "Porri" seems to be a printers mistake for the Italian "Corti."

12. J. & M. Paff were showing wax portraits by John Rauschner at their shop at 112 Broadway in December 1798. Michael Paff opened a gallery of paintings at 208 Broadway in 1811. In an 1812 prospectus, he claimed that he had been collecting his paintings for "more than twelve years." Paff relocated to 221 Broadway in 1812, but only stayed two years before moving on to 124 Cedar Street. He returned to 112 Broadway in 1820, where he stayed until the building was demolished in 1834. The Astor House was built on the site. The main sources of information are I.N.P. Stokes, *Iconology of Manhattan Island,* 1498–1909, 6 vols. (New York: R. H. Dodd, 1915–28), 3: 610–11; Gottesman, *Arts and Crafts in New York: 1777–1799,* 36; and Gottesman, *Arts and Crafts in New York: 1800–1804,* 59.

13. Peter Kenny, *Honoré Lannuier: Cabinetmaker from Paris* (New York: Metropolitan Museum of Art, 1998), 139–42; William H. Gerdts, "Natural Aristocrats in a Democracy: 1810–1870," in Michael Quick, *American Portraiture in the Grand Manner: 1720–1920* (Los Angeles: Los Angeles County Museum of Art, 1982), 38–44; Edith Gaines, "Portraits in New York's City Hall," *The Magazine Antiques* 80 (October 1961), 346–49; Edith Holzer and Harold Holzer, "Portraits in City Hall, New York," *The Magazine Antiques* 110 (November 1976), 1030–39; and Harold E. Dickson, *John Wesley Jarvis: American Painter 1780–1840* (New York: New-York Historical Society, 1949).

14. [New York] *Weekly Museum,* February 4, 1797, in Rita Gottesman, *The Arts and Crafts in New York: 1777–1799* (New York: New-York Historical Society, 1954), 23. The best history of Baker's museum is Robert M. McClung and Gale S. McClung, "Tammany's Remarkable Gardiner Baker," *New-York Historical Society Quarterly* 42 (1958): 142–169.

15. Quotations are from the *New York Commercial Advertiser,* November 18, 1802; and the [New York] *Chronicle Express,* November 25, 1802; both reproduced in Rita Gottesman, *The Arts and Crafts in New York: 1800–1804* (New York: New-York Historical Society, 1965), 25, 27. The most useful secondary sources of infor-

mation are Loyd Haberly, "The American Museum from Baker to Barnham," *New-York Historical Society Quarterly* 43 (1959): 272–87; and Rita Gottesman, "New York's First Major Art Show as Reviewed by its First Newspaper Critic in 1802 and 1803," *New-York Historical Society Quarterly* 43 (1959): 288–305. Information concerning Rickett's Amphitheatre is from Carrie Rebora, "The American Academy of the Fine Arts, New York, 1802-1842" (Ph.D. diss., City University of New York, 1990), 1: 10.

16. New York Academy of Arts, "Account of Statues, Busts, &c in the Collection of the Academy of Arts," (New York: Morning Chronicle, 1803); Rebora, "American Academy of the Fine Arts," 11–14; and Theodore Sizer, "The American Academy of the Fine Arts," in Mary B. Cowdrey, *American Academy of the Fine Arts and American Art-Union* (New York: New-York Historical Society, 1953), 1: 13.

17. Burrows and Wallace, *Gotham,* 409–28, 736; Douglass C. North, *The Economic Growth of the United States: 1790–1860* (New York: Norton, 1966), 46–60, 177–88.

18. William Dunlap, *History of the Rise and Progress of the Arts of Design in the United States* (1834; reprint, New York: Dover, 1969), 2: 207, 216, 273, 315, 321; Rebora, "American Academy of the Fine Arts," 61, 261.

19. Myers, *The Catskills,* 117, 127–28, 162, 183–84, 188.

20. "A Card," [Philadelphia] *United States Gazette,* June 7, 1824, 3:2; photocopy supplied by Merle M. Moore, Jr. For Coleman's second establishment, see Ellwood C. Parry III, *The Art of Thomas Cole: Ambition and Imagination* (Newark: University of Delaware Press, 1988), 87–88. The best treatment of Cole's "discovery" is Ellwood C. Parry III, "Thomas Cole's Early Career: 1818–1829," in Edward Nygren, *Views and Visions: American Landscape Before 1830* (Washington, D.C.: Corcoran Gallery of Art, 1986), 167–72.

21. Thomas Bangs Thorpe, "New-York Artists Fifty Years Ago," *Appleton's Journal* 7 (May 25, 1872): 572–575; Alexander W. Katlan, *American Artists' Materials. Vol. II. A Guide to Stretchers, Panels, Millboards, and Stencil Marks* (Madison, Conn: Sound View Press, 1992), 493–501; and Richard Koke, *American Landscape and Genre Paintings in the New-York Historical Society* (New York: New-York Historical Society, 1982), 182.

22. Haberly, "American Museum," 276–83. Also see Charles C. Sellers, *Mr. Peale's Museum: Charles Willson Peale and the First Popular Museum of Natural Science and Art* (New York: Norton, 1980).

23. Rebora, "American Academy of the Fine Arts," 1:34–36; and Sizer, "American Academy," 26. Before it moved to City Hall Park, Scudder's American Museum had been located at 21 Chatham Street. Within a few years, the original tenants had been joined by John Griscom's chemistry laboratory, the Lyceum of Natural History, the Deaf and Dumb Institution, and the New York Bank for Savings. Fitz-Green Halleck commented on this situation in his poem "Fanny," quoted in Winifred Howe, *History of the Metropolitan Museum of Art* (New York: Metropolitan Museum of Art, 1913), 20:

> *. . . It remains*
> *To bless the hour the Corporation took it*
> *Into their heads to give the rich in brains*
> *The worn-out mansion of the poor in pocket,*
> *Once the old almshouse, now a school of wisdom,*
> *Sacred to Scudder's shells and Dr. Griscom.*

24. Sizer, "American Academy," 20–52; Rebora, "American Academy of the Fine Arts," 346–98.

25. Kevin Avery and Peter Fodera, *John Vanderlyn's Panoramic View of the Palace and Gardens of Versailles* (New York: Metropolitan Museum of Art, 1988), 19–29.

26. See, for example, Neil Harris, *The Artist in American Society: The Formative Years, 1790–1860* (New York: Braziller, 1966), 102–105.

27. Eliot Clark, *History of the National Academy of Design: 1825–1953* (New York: Columbia University Press, 1954), 20–21, 29, 64, and 68; and Benson J. Lossing, *History of New York City* (New York: Perine Engraving, 1884), 1: 152–53, 167–68, 180–82. For the Mercantile Library, see John Hassard, "The New York Mercantile Library," *Scribner's Monthly* 1 (February 1871): 353–67; and *Fiftieth Anniversary of the Mercantile Library* (New York: Nesbitt, 1871). For the Society Library, see Austin Keep, *History of the New York Society Library* (New York: De Vinne, 1908); and Marion King, *Books and People: Five Decades of New York's Oldest Library* (New York: Macmillan, 1954).

28. See Thomas Bender, *New York Intellect: A History of Intellectual Life in New York From 1750 to the Beginning of our Own Time* (Baltimore: Johns Hopkins University Press, 1987), 62–95.

29. Rebora, "American Academy of the Fine Arts," 388, 396–414, 468. For the Dubufe exhibition, see Kendall Taft, "Adam and Eve in America," *Art Quarterly* 23

(Summer 1960): 171–79. For Brett's collection of "old masters," see *Descriptive Catalogue of the Paintings, by the Ancient Masters, Including Specimens of the First Class, by the Italian, Venetian, Spanish, Flemish, Dutch, French, and English Schools* (New York: Mitchell, 1832); and *Descriptive Catalogue of the Collection of Celebrated Paintings, Including Works of the First Class by the Old Masters* (New York: Van Norden, 1835).

30. Rebora, "American Academy of the Fine Arts," 468–93. For one of the last large exhibitions held at the Barclay Street space, see *Synopsis of Mr. Sanguinetti's Collection of Ancient Italian Paintings, Engravings, and other Valuable Articles of the Fine Arts* (New York: Clayton, 1838).

31. North, *Economic Growth of the United States,* 189–204; Burrows and Wallace, *Gotham,* 611–17.

32. North, *Economic Growth of the United States,* 208–12; Burrows and Wallace, *Gotham,* 649–66.

33. Harris, *Artist in American Life,* 279–81, 402; Alan Wallach, "Thomas Cole: Landscape and the Course of American Empire," in *Thomas Cole: Landscape Into History,* William Truettner and Alan Wallach, eds. (New Haven: Yale University Press, 1994), 38–42; and Calvin Tomkins, *Merchants and Masterpieces: The Story of the Metropolitan Museum of Art* (New York: Dutton, 1970), 33–36. For A. T. Stewart, see Burrows and Wallace, *Gotham,* 666–68.

34. Suzaan Boettger, "Eastman Johnson's *Blodgett Family* and Domestic Values During the Civil War Era," *American Art* 6 (Fall, 1992), 50–67; and Kevin Avery, *Church's Great Picture: The Heart of the Andes* (New York: Metropolitan Museum of Art, 1993), 34.

35. J. C. Myers, *Sketches on A Tour Through the Northern and Eastern States* (Harrisonburg, Virginia: Wartmann, 1849), 59. For Barnum, see Neil Harris, *Humbug: The Art of P. T. Barnum* (Chicago: University of Chicago Press, 1973), 31–90; and A. H. Saxon, *P. T. Barnum: The Legend and the Man* (New York: Columbia University Press, 1989). For the decoration of photographic studios, see Katherine C. Grier, *Culture & Comfort: Parlor Making and Middle-Class Identity, 1850–1930* (Washington, D.C.: Smithsonian Institution Press, 1988), 50–53.

36. For Goupil, Vibert, and Co., see Hélène Lafont-Couturier, "The Dissemination of Rosa Bonheur's Works by the House of Goupil," in Dahesh Museum, *Rosa Bonheur: All Nature's Children* (New York: Dahesh Musuem, 1998), 52–53. For Schaus, see Harris, *Artist in American Society,* 262; and Frances Weitzenhoffer, *The Havemeyers: Impressionism Comes to America* (New York: Abrams, 1986), 53. For Michel Knoedler, see Lois Marie Fink, "French Art in the United States, 1850–1870: Three Dealers and Collectors," *Gazette des Beaux-Arts* 92 (September 1978): 87–88; and Charles R. Henschel, "A Catalogue of an Exhibition of Paintings and Prints of Every Description on the Occasion of Knoedler One Hundred Years 1846–1946" (New York: Knoedler, 1946). For Leeds, see Thomas Cummings, *Historic Annals of the National Academy of Design* (Philadelphia: George W. Childs, 1865), 292. For overviews of the reception of nineteenth-century French art in the United States, see Laura Meixner, *French Realist Painting and the Critique of American Society* (Cambridge; Cambridge University Press, 1995); and Alexandra Murphy, "French Paintings in Boston: 1800–1900," in Museum of Fine Arts, *Corot to Braque: French Paintings from the Museum of Fine Arts, Boston* (Boston: Museum of Fine Arts. 1979), xvii–xlvi.

37. For Gambart, see Jeremy Maas, *Gambart, Prince of the Victorian Art World* (London: Barrie & Jenkins, 1975); and Susan Casteras, "The 1857–58 Exhibition of English Art in America: Critical Responses to Pre-Raphaelitism," in *The New Path: Ruskin and the American Pre-Raphaelites,* Linda S. Ferber and William H. Gerdts, eds. (New York: Shocken Books, 1985), 109–33.

38. Raymond L. Stehle, "The Düsseldorf Gallery of New York," *New-York Historical Society Quarterly* 58 (1974), 304–17; High Museum of Art, *The Düsseldorf Academy and the Americans* (Atlanta: High Museum of Art: 1972); and Kunstmuseum Düsseldorf: *The Hudson and the Rhine* (Düsseldorf Kunstmuseum Düsseldorf, 1976). On Derby, see William H. Gerdts, "The Düsseldorf Connection," in *Grand Illusions: History Painting in America,* William H. Gerdts and Mark Thistlewaite, eds. (Fort Worth, Texas: Amon Carter Museum, 1988), 163–64. For the Belgian Gallery, see Gerdts, "American Art Exhibitions and Their Catalogues," xxx.

39. For Herring, see Charles Baker, "The American Art-Union," in Cowdrey, *American Academy of Fine Arts and American Art-Union,* 98–100. For Williams, Stevens, and Williams, see Gerdts, "American Art Exhibitions," xxix.

40. Rachel N. Klein, "Art and Authority in Antebellum New York City: The Rise and Fall of the American Art-Union," *Journal of American History* 81 (March 1995): 1537–42; and Baker, "American Art-Union," 203. See also, Patricia Hills, "The American Art-Union as Patron for Expansionist Ideology in the 1840s," 314–39, in *Art in Bourgeois Society, 1790–1850,* Andrew Hemingway and William Vaughan, eds. (Cambridge: Cambridge University Press, 1998).

41. Baker, "American Art-Union," 137, 161, 208–17, 227.

42. Baker, "American Art-Union," 219–40; Gerdts, "American Art Exhibitions," xxx.

43. Ella M. Foshay, *Mr. Luman Reed's Picture Gallery: A Pioneer Collection of American Art* (New York: Abrams, 1990); Abigail Booth Gerdts, "Newly Discovered Records of the New-York Gallery of the Fine Arts," *Archives of American Art Journal* 26 (1981): 2-9; and Maybelle Mann, "The New-York Gallery of the Fine Arts: 'A Source of Refinement,'" *American Art Journal* 11 (1979), 76–86.

44. Robert Hendre Kelby, *The New-York Historical Society, 1804–1904* (New York: New-York Historical Society, 1893), 52.

45. Howe, *Metropolitan Museum of Art,* 35–45; Kevin Guthrie, *The New-York Historical Society: Lessons from One Nonprofit's Long Struggle for Survival* (San Francisco: Jossey-Bass, 1996), 9–19; and Robert W. G. Vail, *Knickerbocker Birthday: A Sesqui-Centennial History of the New-York Historical Society* (New York: New-York Historical Society, 1954). For the Bryan collection, see Sotheby's, *Important Old Master Paintings: The Property of the New-York Historical Society. Sale 6653* (New York: Sotheby's, January 12, 1995); and Thomas Jefferson Bryan, "Companion to the Bryan Gallery of Christian Art," (New York: Baker, Godwin, 1853).

46. Clark, *National Academy of Design,* 68-83, 142–47.

47. Harris, *Artist in American Life,* 267-69; and Annette Blaugrund, *The Tenth Street Studio Building: Artist-Entrepreneurs from the Hudson River School to the American Impressionists* (Southampton, New York: The Parrish Art Museum, 1997), 14–15.

48. Quoted in, Blaugrund, *Tenth Street Studio,* 22. See also, Christine Oaklander, "Studios at the YMCA, 1869–1903," *Archives of American Art Journal* 32 (1992): 14–22.

49. Blaugrund, *Tenth Street Studio,* 60–71, 101 (fn 19).

50. Quoted in Burrows and Wallace, *Gotham,* 868.

51. Burrows and Wallace, *Gotham,* 872–78; and Russell Bourne, *Floating West: The Erie and Other American Canals* (New York: Norton , 1992), 188–90.

52. Burrows and Wallace, *Gotham,* 908–11, 1044–46.

53. Linda Ferber, "'Determined Realists': The American Pre-Raphaelites and the Association for the Advancement of Truth in Art," in Linda S. Ferber and William H. Gerdts, eds., *The New Path: Ruskin and the American Pre-Raphaelites* (New York: Shocken 1985) 11–38; Jo Ann W. Weiss, "Clarence Cook: His Critical Writings" (Ph.D. diss., Johns Hopkins University, 1976); and Roger B. Stein, *John Ruskin and Aesthetic Thought in America, 1840–1900* (Cambridge: Harvard University Press, 1967).

54. Clarence Cook, "The Cry From the Studios," *Galaxy* 3 (February 15, 1867): 439–40.

55. Samuel P. Avery, quoted in Linda H. Skalet, "The Market for American Painting in New York: 1870–1915" (Ph.D. diss., Johns Hopkins University, 1980), 2. For the Stewart and Vanderbilt collections, see Earl Shinn, *The Art Treasures of America* (1879–1882; reprint, New York: Garland, 1977); *Artistic Houses: Being a Series of Interior Views of a Number of the most Beautiful and Celebrated Homes in the United States* (New York: D. Appleton, 1883–1884); and *Catalogue of the A. T. Stewart Collection of Paintings, Sculptures, and Other Objects of Art* (New York: American Art Association, 1887).

56. *The Diaries 1871–1882 of Samuel P. Avery, Art Dealer,* Madeleine F. Beaufort, Herbert L. Kleinfield, and Jeanne K. Welcher , eds. (New York: Arno, 1979); and Madeleine F. Beaufort and Jeanne K. Welcher, "Some Views of Art Buying in New York in the 1870s and 1880s," *Oxford Art Journal* 5 (1982): 48–55. John Snedecor and Gustav Reichard both advertised some American art during the 1870s, but like Avery, they survived by showing European art, which made up the bulk of their sales. For Snedecor and Reichard, see Skalet, *Market For American Painting,* 188–89.

57. Weitzenhoffer, *The Havemeyers,* 38–46, Skalet, "Market for American Painting," 191–200; and Hans Huth, "Impressionism Comes to America," *Gazette des Beaux-Arts* 29 (March 1946): 225–52.

58. Weitzenhoffer, *The Havemeyers,* 57–58, 60–61, 84, 94–95; and idem., "The Earliest American Collectors of Monet," in *Aspects of Monet: A Symposium on the Artist's Life and Times,* John Rewald and Frances Weitzenhoffer , eds. (New York: Abrams, 1984), 74–91; Henschel, "Knoedler One Hundred Years," [2].

59. Choate is quoted in Tomkins, *Merchants and Masterpieces,* 21. See also, Morrison H. Heckscher, *The Metropolitan Museum of Art: An Architectural History* (New York: Metropolitan Museum of Art, 1995), 5–20.

60. On the transformation of the art market, see Skalet, "Market for American Painting;" Saul Zalesch, "Competition and Conflict in the New York Art World, 1874–1879," *Winterthur Portfolio* 29 (1994): 103–120; and Sarah Burns, *Inventing the Modern Artist: Art and Culture in Gilded Age America* (New Haven: Yale University Press, 1996).

61. Cummings is quoted in Skalet, "Market for American Painting," 18. On the decline of the receptions, see also Blaugrund, *Tenth Street Studio,* 78–80.

62. Lois Marie Fink and Joshua C. Taylor, *Academy: The Academic Tradition in American Art* (Washington, D.C.: Smithsonian Institution Press, 1975), 46; and Skalet, "Market for American Painting," 24.

63. For the private club exhibitions, see Skalet, "Market for American Painting," 73–121.

64. On the growth of new arts organizations, see Skalet, "Market for American Painting," 9–66; and Blaugrund, *Tenth Street Studio*, 80–82.

65. Jervis McEntee, Diary, February 13, 1878, Archives of America Art.

66. See especially, William Truettner, "William T. Evans, Collector of American Paintings," *American Art Journal* 3 (Fall 1971): 50–79; and H. Barbara Weinberg, "Thomas B. Clarke: Foremost Patron of American Art from 1872 to 1899," *American Art Journal* 8 (May 1976): 52–83.

67. Skalet, "Market for American Painting," 201–11; and especially, Gwendolyn Owens, "Art and Commerce: William Macbeth, The Eight and the Popularization of American Art," in Elizabeth Milroy, *Painters of a New Century: The Eight and American Art* (Milwaukee: Milwaukee Art Museum, 1991), 61–84. In a letter, Macbeth identified the seated buyer as H. H. Benedict, the president of Remington Typewriter. The figure next to the easel is Macbeth's nephew, and the gallery's third director, Robert McIntyre. For the identification of these figures, see Owens, "Art and Commerce," 72–73.

68. Weinberg, "Thomas B. Clarke," 70. For "The Ten," see H. Barbara Weinberg, Doreen Bolger, and David Park Curry, *American Impressionism and Realism: The Painting of Modern Life: 1885–1915* (New York: Metropolitan Museum of Art, 1994), 22–24.

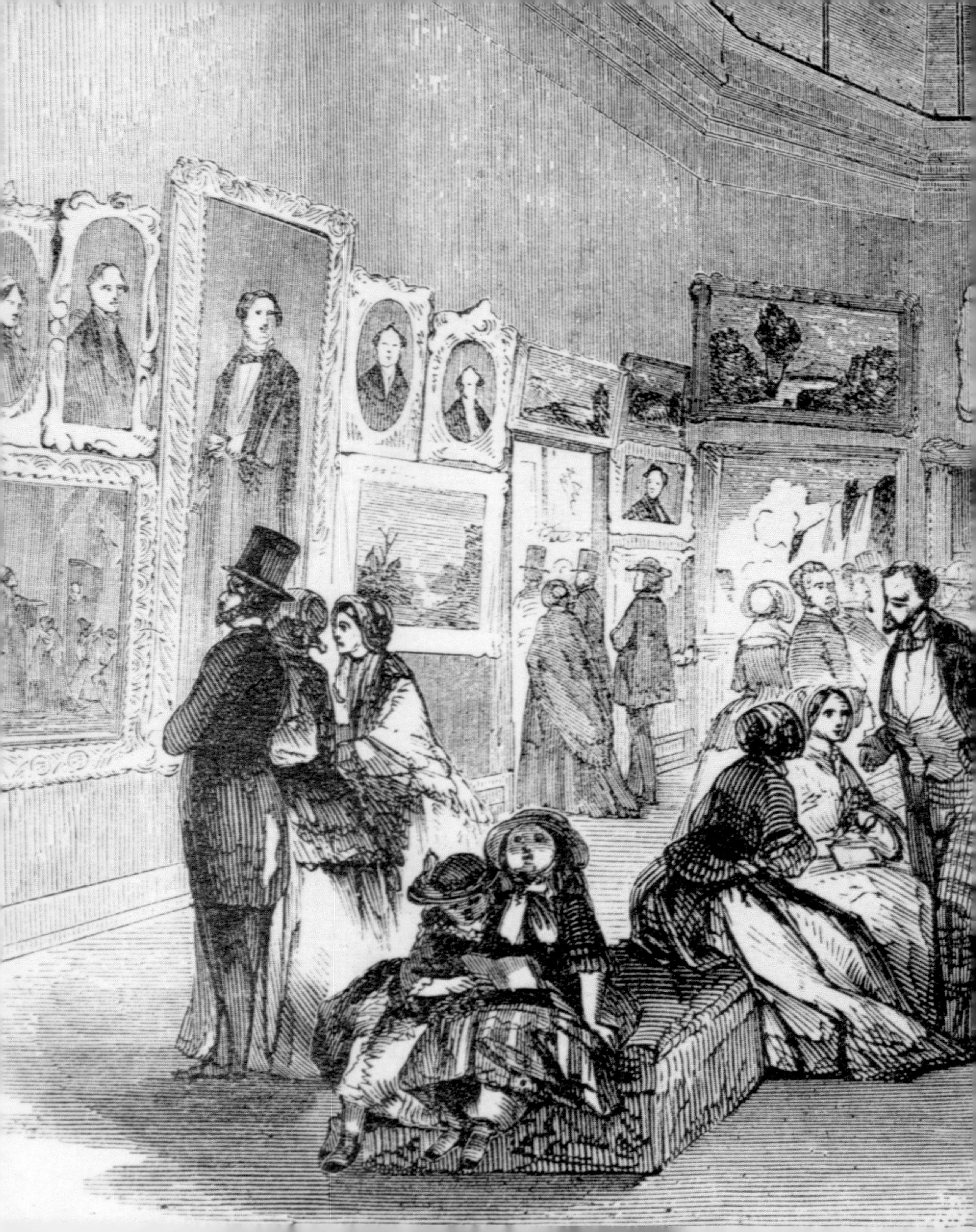

Annual Exhibitions and the Birth of American Art Criticism to 1865

DAVID B. DEARINGER

The history of American art criticism is directly linked to the history of annual art exhibitions in this country. It is, of course, also linked to the rise in importance of journalism and the press in this country. Annual exhibitions date back to those held in France and England in the eighteenth century and to those introduced in several major cities in the United States, specifically Philadelphia, New York, and Boston, in the first third of the nineteenth century. Of these, the annual exhibitions of the National Academy of Design were the longest lived, starting in 1826 and continuing to the present, and the most significant (fig. 22). By the time of the Civil War, the Academy's annuals had become an established part of the American art world. This period, from the 1820s through the 1860s, coincided with journalism's Golden Age. These were the years when newspapers and magazines began to stake out their subject matter and to increase their circulation to a truly national level. The developing relationship between art and the press—and between annual exhibitions and art criticism—can be seen in a survey of the individual journals and newspapers that began to publish significant numbers of art reviews during this period.

SERIAL EXHIBITIONS

The concept of serial art exhibitions was initially a French one. Its earliest manifestation was an exhibition of works by

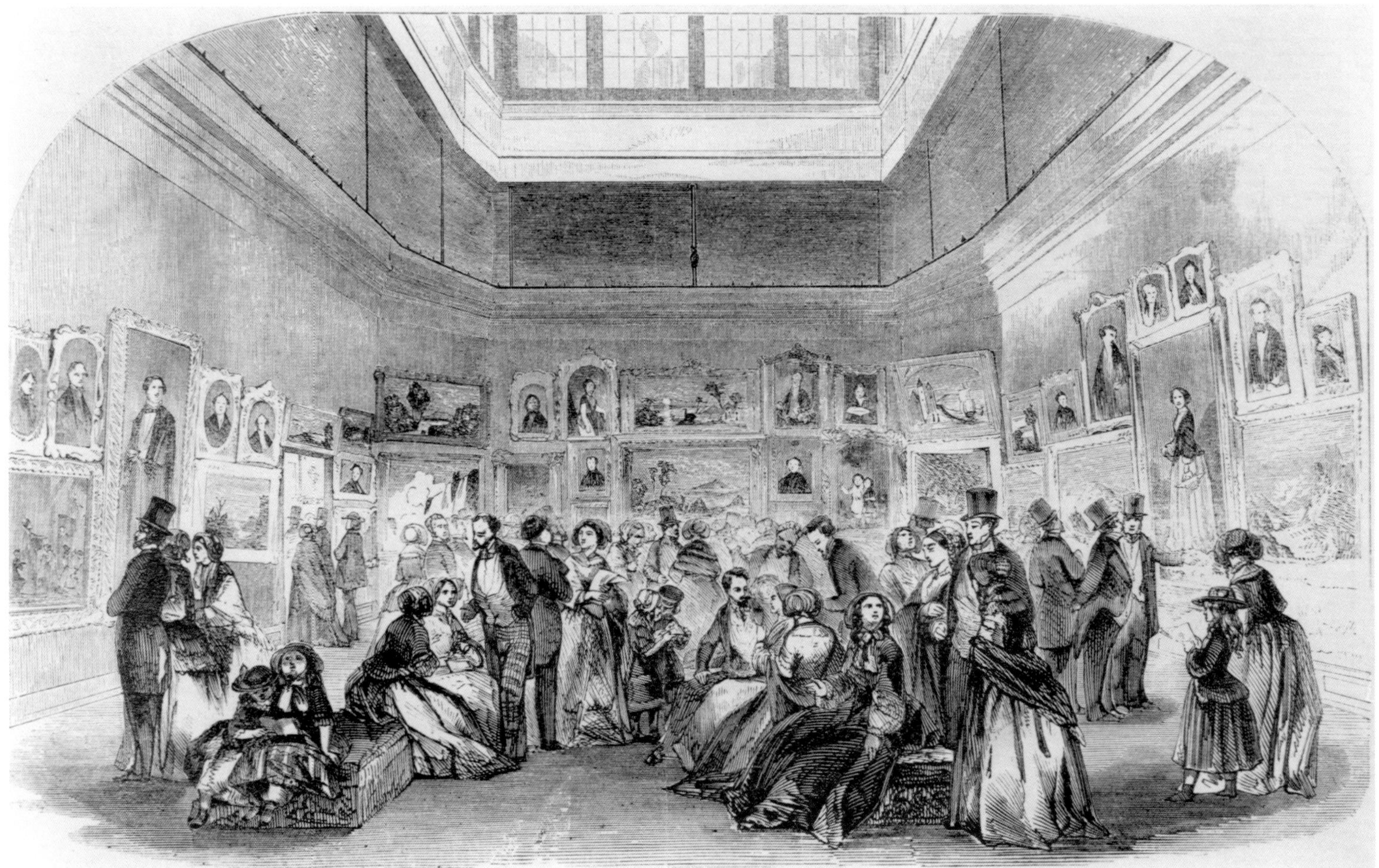

Fig. 22 "National Academy of Design—The Principal Room," *Illustrated News* (May 7, 1853): 296, Archives, National Academy of Design (detail opposite). In 1853, the Academy's annual exhibition was held in rented rooms at 663 Broadway in New York.

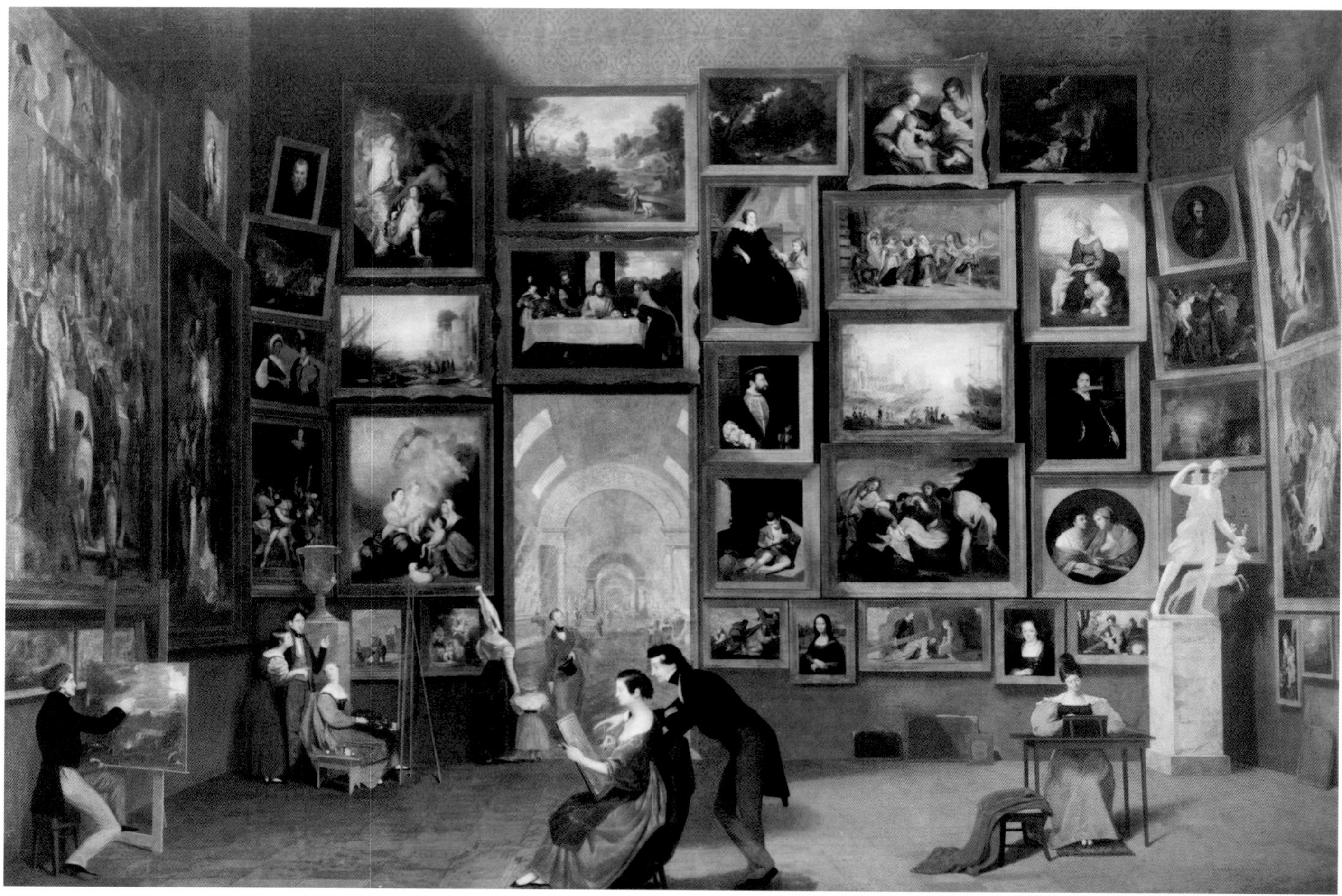

Fig. 23 Samuel F. B. Morse, *The Gallery of the Louvre*, 1831–33, oil on canvas, 73¾ x 108, Terra Foundation for the Arts, Daniel J. Terra Collection, Terra Museum of American Art, Chicago. The setting is the Louvre's Salon Carré.

members of the French Royal Academy of Painting and Sculpture held at the Hôtel Richelieu (now the Palais-Royal) in Paris in 1667. This and the exhibitions that followed over the next three decades were relatively simple affairs; but in 1699, a much larger, more inclusive, and more impressively arranged display was held in the Louvre under the patronage of Louis XIV. The location, size, and sponsorship of the event verified its official status, and subsequent exhibitions were planned on the same grand scale. Beginning in 1737, the exhibitions became annual events, and in 1755 they moved into the Louvre's Grand Salon—the famous Salon Carré (fig. 23)— prompting the historical appellation now applied to all exhibitions in the series, "Salons." With the abolition of the French Academy in 1795, the Salons were held under the aegis of the newly formed National Institute of France, but their grandiose scale and established format remained unchanged. By then, they had become part of academic tradition.[1]

It is clear then, that in France, the Royal Academy gave birth to the annual exhibitions. In England, it was, in a sense, the reverse. The saga began in about 1746 when British artists such as William Hogarth and Thomas Gainsborough donated paintings to decorate London's new Foundling Hospital. The hospital generously opened this fortuitously acquired art col-lection to the public and it soon became one of the attractions of London. Its success inspired the painter Robert Edge Pine—who later worked in America—to propose in 1759 that Britain's Society of Artists hire a room for regular exhibitions of works by contemporary artists. While no immediate action was taken on the suggestion, it resurfaced later that year at a meeting of the artists who had contributed to the Foundling Hospital. Such an exhibition, it was decided, would "raise to distinction [artists] who otherwise might languish in obscu-rity" and establish "a provident fund for the support of infirm and aged artists."[2]

A committee was formed to carry out the plan; the Society of Artists agreed to host the event; and the exhibition opened in the spring of 1760. It was the first organized public exhibi-tion ever held in England and was a popular and financial suc-cess. It inspired the establishment of a more permanent and formal body that would, among other things, sponsor similar exhibitions on an annual basis. This was the formation of the Royal Academy of Arts, which was given official status and royal sanction when George III signed an Instrument of Foundation in 1768.[3] The Academy's dual purpose, as stated therein, was to establish "a well-regulated School or Academy of Design, for the use of students in the Arts, and an Annual

Exhibition, open to all artists of distinguished merit."[4] Its first annual exhibition opened in the spring of 1769. The series has continued ever since.

Philadelphia

The earliest attempt at annual art exhibitions in the United States was made in Philadelphia in 1794 by the Columbianum, an organization founded that year under the leadership of artist and entrepreneur Charles Willson Peale (fig. 24). Article IX of the Columbianum's constitution mandated that "an exhibition of Paintings, Sculptures, Models and Drawings of every kind, &c., shall be opened on the first day of May, every year" and run for six weeks. The exhibitions were to be limited to works by "modern Artists" that had not been previously exhibited in this country.[5] The Columbianum's first exhibition opened in the spring of 1795, but the demise of the society later that year ended all hopes of establishing a series, as planned. Although a catalogue was printed, no published critical response to the exhibition is known.[6]

The Columbianum was a failure, but Philadelphia got a second chance to be the birthplace of annual exhibitions in this country with the founding in 1810 of the Society of Artists of the United States. The Society's constitution clearly stated that it was "to establish an annual Exhibition of . . . works of art." Amateurs as well as professionals could participate in these exhibitions, the contents of which were not restricted to American art. Even good copies and drawings were welcome.[7]

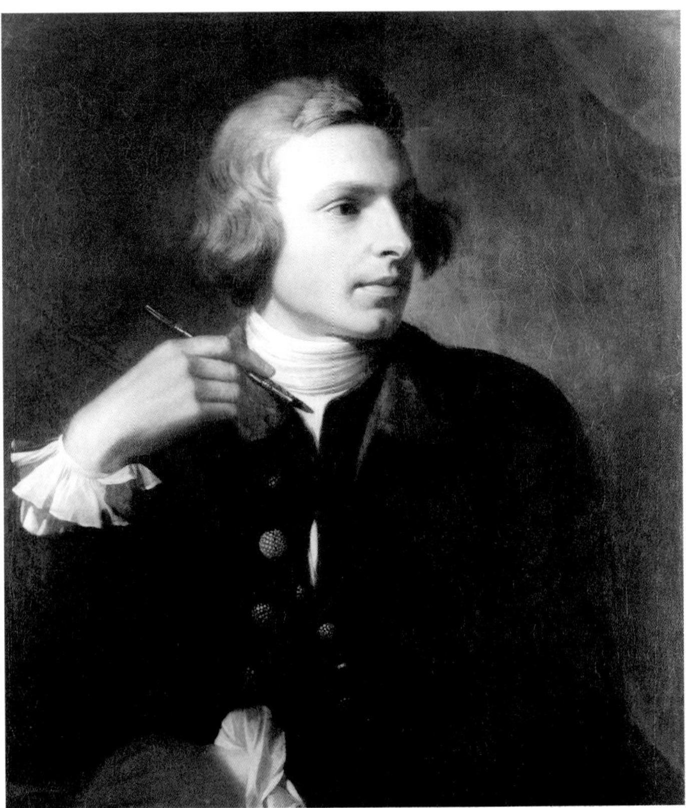

Fig. 24 Benjamin West, *Charles Willson Peale*, c. 1767–69, oil on canvas, 28¼ x 23, Collection of The New-York Historical Society, Gift of Thomas J. Bryan, 1867

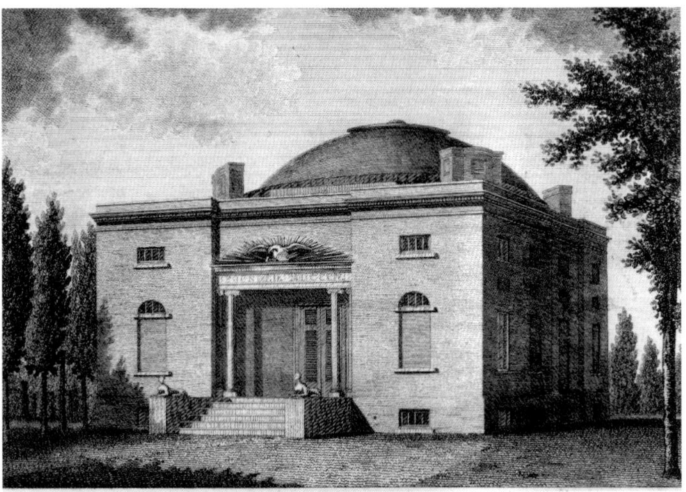

Fig. 25 Benjamin Tanner, *The Pennsylvania Academy of the Fine Arts [First Building]*, 1809, engraving and etching on ivory paper, 4¹¹⁄₁₆ x 6½, Pennsylvania Academy of the Fine Arts, The John S. Phillips Collection

Meanwhile, another art organization had already been established in Philadelphia. This was the Pennsylvania Academy of the Fine Arts, founded in 1805 (fig. 25). The Academy's goals were clearly defined in its Articles of Agreement, written the following year. Among these was the promotion and

> *cultivation of the Fine Arts, in the United States of America, by introducing correct and elegant copies from works of the first masters in sculpture and painting . . . and also by occasionally conferring moderate but honourable premiums, and otherwise assisting the studies and exciting the efforts of the artists gradually to unfold, enlighten and invigorate the talents of our countrymen.*[8]

The mission of the Pennsylvania Academy, then, was to create a study collection and to establish monetary prizes to help young artists get a start in the professional world. The sponsorship of annual exhibitions was not initially mandated. Reminiscent of the manner in which exhibitions hosted by London's Society of Artists evolved into the annual exhibitions of the Royal Academy, however, those of the Philadelphia's Society of Artists quickly became joint efforts with the Pennsylvania Academy. The first of these exhibitions opened in 1811, and by the following year it was obvious that they were collaborative efforts. By 1815, the two organizations had merged.[9]

The exhibitions at the Pennsylvania Academy were not limited to American artists, especially in the early years. Visitors were as likely to see works by the old masters—or copies after them—as they were paintings by contemporary American artists. This began to change in favor of the latter during the late 1830s, and by 1855 approximately half of the works in the annuals were by Americans.[10] Except for the years from 1870 through 1875, when the Academy was constructing its present building, it sponsored annual exhibitions until 1969.

Chronologically, the next organization to establish annual exhibitions in the United States was the American Academy of Fine Arts, founded in New York in 1802 by Robert R. Livingston, the United States minister to France, and others.[11] Livingston believed that it was the duty of civic leaders to promote aesthetics among artists and the general public. To that end, he purchased a group of plaster casts of antique sculptures in Europe and shipped them back to America. The American painter John Vanderlyn added more casts and copies of paintings by old masters to Livingston's purchases to form a public gallery of art. The gallery opened to the public in August 1803, but it was not a success. During the following years, financial problems made it necessary to move the collection from site to site and, since its contents did not change, the public soon became bored with it.

The American Academy did not really begin to function on a meaningful level until 1813, when De Witt Clinton, the inimitable mayor of New York City, became its president.[12] Like Livingston, Clinton felt that the best way to enlighten the public about art and to improve the cultural life of the city was to mount exhibitions; but he understood the desirability of having changing displays rather than the static installations that the Academy had been hosting thus far. With the assistance and financial support of philanthropist John Pintard and other of Clinton's friends and political cronies, new quarters for the American Academy were established at New York's almshouse (see fig. 11), which was centrally located near City Hall. There, in 1816, the Academy opened its first annual exhibition. Unlike the displays of casts and copies for which the organization had been previously known, this exhibition consisted of loans from the city's most prominent collectors—Mrs. Robert Fulton, David Hosack, and John Jacob Astor were among the lenders. In addition, the painter and future president of the organization, John Trumbull, sent a group of his own paintings. Generally speaking, however, the works of contemporary artists were in the minority, and those who were well represented—William Dunlap, John Wesley Jarvis, and John Rubens Smith, for example—were closely affiliated with the management of the organization.[13] The American Academy's exhibitions continued, fundamentally unchanged in either their purpose or the kinds of works included, well into the 1830s.[14]

Boston

In Boston, the first organization to plan and execute annual art exhibitions was the Boston Athenaeum. It was founded in 1807 as a literary society with the primary purpose of providing members with a library for the study of literature and science. It had an educational mandate, as well, and although the initial focus of its members was scientific, by the 1820s they were calling for facilities for the study and enjoyment of the fine arts. A turning point came in 1821 when new quarters were purchased on Pearl Street in Boston (fig. 26).

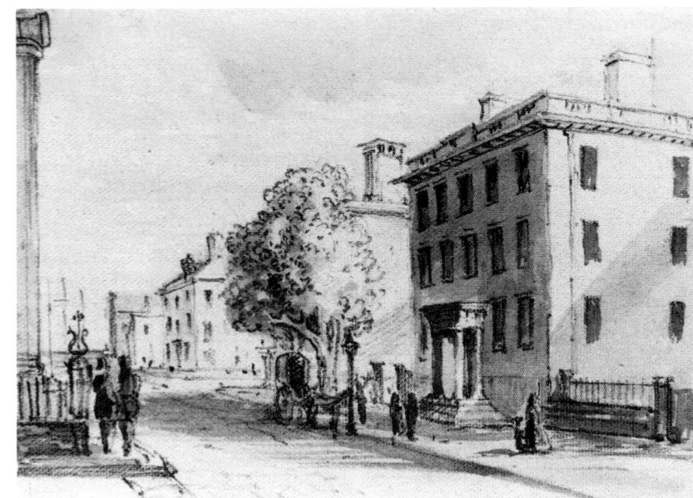

Fig. 26 *The Boston Athenaeum in Pearl Street,* 1830, pencil and wash drawing, 3 x 4, Collection of the Boston Athenaeum

Less than two years later, construction began on an auxiliary building that featured laboratories and a lecture hall that could double as an art gallery. With the completion of these facilities, the leaders of the Athenaeum decided to initiate a series of loan exhibitions. In 1826, a committee chaired by Boston's most important art patron, Thomas H. Perkins, was formed for that purpose. The local press kept the public abreast of the situation so that by the time the exhibition opened in May 1827, all of Boston was eager to see it. The result was that over two thousand season tickets, as well as a large number of single admission tickets, were sold during the first eight days of the exhibition.[15]

The Athenaeum's annuals followed the system established at the Pennsylvania Academy in that they were not limited to contemporary American art. In fact, among the 165 works in the first Athenaeum exhibition, many were said to be by old masters such as Canaletto, Teniers, Ruysdael, Poussin, or Murillo. These were touted by the press as genuine, although at least some of them were undoubtedly copies.[16] Despite the presence of Europeans here, American artists dominated the first exhibition. For example, Gilbert Stuart was represented by eighteen paintings, Washington Allston by twelve, Rembrandt Peale by three, and Thomas Doughty by five.[17] A large group of portraits by the long expatriated and by then deceased John Singleton Copley was even included. Many of the works in the first exhibition—especially those that were owned by the Athenaeum itself—were shown in subsequent annuals, some ten or more times.[18] This was one of several features that made the Athenaeum's exhibitions different from those held elsewhere in this country.

When the Athenaeum's first exhibition closed in July 1827, it was declared a success; it made money and, it was said, had roused conservative Bostonians to take a keener interest in art.[19] The press had given it much favorable coverage. *The North American Review,* for example, thought it was "a fine collection" and only regretted that this type of public display had not been introduced in Boston earlier. It had proved, the journal concluded, that annual exhibitions are "obviously the best mode of encouraging the arts."[20] The exhibition's success assured the perpetuation of the series, which continued through 1874. Reviews of the Athenaeum's exhibitions became regular features in the *North American Review* and, beginning in the 1850s, in periodicals such as *Dwight's Journal of Music* and the *Boston Literary Magazine*.

The National Academy of Design

As reported by its first historian and one of its founding members, Thomas Seir Cummings (1804–1894), the National Academy of Design was

the first institution in this city, and indeed in the country, established by, and under the exclusive control and management of the professional Artists, in whom alone it was contended could Art, and its general dissemination be properly placed.[21]

The National Academy grew out of the New York Association of Artists (also called the New-York Drawing Association), an informal body of artists that first met in November 1825.[22] In January of the following year, the leader of that group, Samuel F. B. Morse (fig. 27), had convinced his colleagues to upgrade the organization into a bona fide academy of art. Using the Royal Academy of Arts in London as a model, the founders of the National Academy, who included Morse himself, the painters Asher Brown Durand, William Dunlap, and Henry Inman, architect Ithiel Town, and sculptor John Frazee, defined the organization's purpose as "the general promotion of knowledge in the arts of Design." (Since "design" meant drawing, the founders of the National Academy were expressing their desire that the organization would concentrate on the traditional fine arts for which drawing is fundamental: painting, sculpture, engraving, and architecture). The methods by which the Academy would achieve its goals were set forth in its first constitution, adopted and published in December 1826. Article VII of that document states simply, "There shall be an annual exhibition of the works of living artists." The by-laws clarified the time of year in which the exhibitions were to be held—the spring—and assured that each exhibition would be different from its predecessors—works of art "that have been once in the Exhibition, can never be exhibited again at the Annual Exhibition."

From the start, then, the National Academy's annuals were limited to *contemporary* American art. While the shows were open to all artists, the National Academicians themselves formed the hanging committees and, when necessary, the juries that selected the works. This meant that, since membership in the Academy was limited to professional artists, its exhibitions were planned and executed *by* contemporary artists *for* contemporary artists.[23] Partly due to these regulations, which made the exhibitions somewhat exclusive, they quickly became the most desirable exhibitions for artists and,

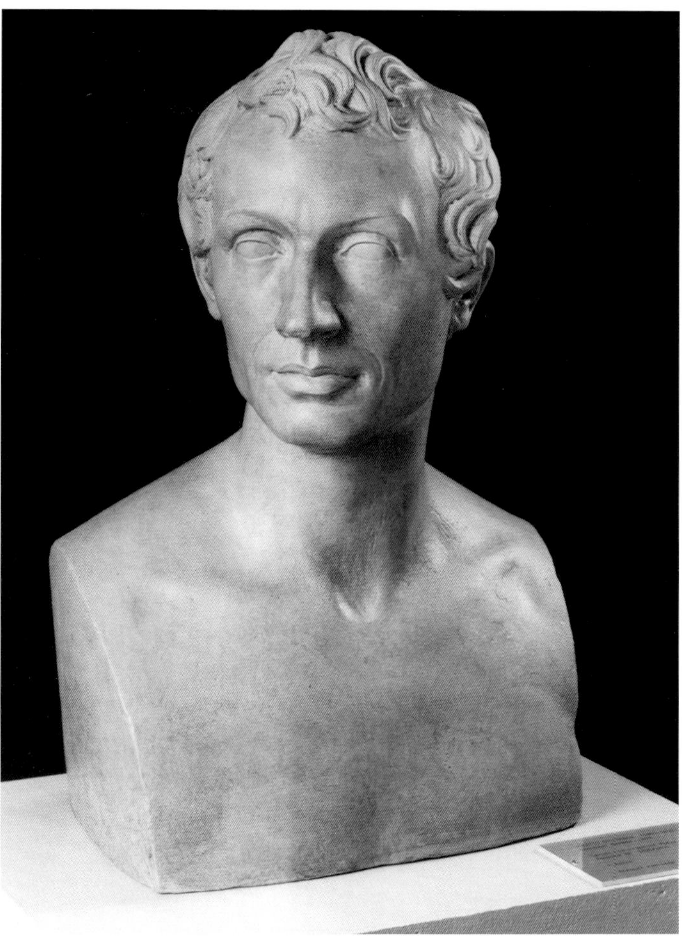

Fig. 27 Horatio Greenough, *Samuel F. B. Morse*, 1831, plaster, 21⅛ x 13⅛ x 9½, National Academy of Design (A version of this sculpture was included in the National Academy of Design, 8th Annual Exhibition, 1833, no. 205.)

in terms of the history of American art, the most influential of all serial exhibitions in this country, at least during much of the nineteenth century. Because works of art could not be shown in more than one of the Academy's annuals, each exhibition was guaranteed to consist of new works by a wide range of contributors. This, in turn, assured a lively attendance by an audience eager to see what the exhibition would bring in each succeeding year.[24]

The unique qualities of the National Academy's annuals and their importance to the cultural development of the nation were recognized almost as soon as the exhibitions began. In 1829, three years after their establishment, several New York publications lauded their structure. A writer for the *Critic* congratulated the Academy on its decision to concentrate on contemporary American art and to ban "the trash, under the name of old pictures, which was imported . . . into the city from the garrets and lumber-rooms of Europe."[25] In the same vein, the *New-York Mirror* reported that the Academy's rule that no work could be shown twice in its galleries had had desirable effects. The *Evening Post* noted that the Academy's exhibitions had the advantage over those of other organizations in that they "formulate a kind of annual record of the progress of the fine arts among us."[26] This was reiterated the following year by the *Morning Courier*, which proclaimed the association to be "a real academy" since it had both students and exhibitions. Because of this, the writer concluded, the Academy's exhibitions were fair representations of the state of art in the United States.[27]

Such proclamations continued through the 1830s and 1840s. In 1831, when the Academy held a retrospective exhibition of selected works from its five previous annuals, the *Evening Post* reported that the result "surpasses in merit any collection of merely modern pictures that has ever been seen in this country."[28] By the time of the tenth exhibition in 1835, the *American Monthly Magazine* could declare that it was time for "exultation" because the Academy's exhibitions had settled the question of whether American art was capable of rising to a high level.[29] Several years later, the *Knickerbocker* decreed that the Academy's success was due to the exertions of its members and to the funds they had raised through their exhibitions. "This speaks well for the artists," the author concluded, "and as well for the public."[30] In 1849, the *Home Journal* called the exhibitions the "favorite annual display of the struggles and trophies of our artists."[31]

The Academy's established importance in American culture at mid-century was even touted internationally. In a review originally published in the *London Art Union,* the American correspondent for that periodical reported that he had attended the Academy's 1847 exhibition. Impressed with what he saw there, he assured his British readers of the Academy's significance. "There are annual exhibitions of original paintings in Philadelphia and in Boston," he reported, "but the great exhibition of the country, in which its best productions may be found, is that of the National Academy of New York."[32]

By the 1840s, almost every periodical and newspaper in New York, as well as many from other cities that professed to have a literary bent, reviewed the exhibitions. As seen in the above citations, many journalists of the day used the Academy's annuals as a barometer to measure the success or failure of American art. In turn, the regular and reliable coverage that these journalists gave the exhibitions provides us with a rational means to chart the advent and development of the professional writers who covered the exhibitions—that is, the earliest art critics in America. For the remainder of this essay, several key newspapers and journals will be discussed individually in order to suggest how and when the art critic emerged in American journalism. From the many periodicals published at the time, those that lasted for at least a few years and that gave fairly consistent coverage to the Academy's exhibitions have been singled out for this investigation.

Before beginning this analysis, however, it might be useful to remind ourselves that the journalists who wrote about these exhibitions rarely arrived at a consensus about them. For every opinion expressed in the contemporary press, it is easy to find an opposing view. An endless point of discussion was the worth of the exhibitions individually and as a group. In almost any given year, they were proof of the improvement of American art for one writer, and evidence of its deterioration to another. Proclamations that an exhibition was better than that of the year before—or that it was the worst one yet—were constantly being made. The presence of so many portraits was either a bore or was happy proof of American patronage of the arts. The lack of good historical works in the exhibitions was bemoaned, or the dominance of landscape, which should naturally supersede history painting in America, was declared a matter of national pride. Some critics found it unfortunate that a number of our best artists were not represented in this or that year, while others found it refreshing to see works by so many young artists. The exhibitions were amazingly well attended, or the crowds consisted of nothing but simpering girls, preening women, and old men. The galleries were badly lit, or they were beautifully carpeted and filled with natural light. The works were apparently hung based on their size and the shape of their frames, or the hanging committee had taken extra care that adjacent works complimented each other.

THE NATIONAL ACADEMY OF DESIGN: CRITICAL REACTIONS

The first annual exhibition of the National Academy of Design opened on the evening of May 13, 1826, in a rented room on the second floor of 287 Broadway in New York. It consisted of 181 paintings, sculptures, watercolors, and drawings by thirty-two artists. The largest number of works—approximately 88—were portraits; landscapes ran a distant second, numbering around 36. When the exhibition closed on July 16, it was immediately clear that it was not a financial success. A deficit of $163 announced to the Academy's governing council by its president, Samuel Morse, had to be covered by an assessment of seven dollars from each Academy member.[33] None of this seems to have discouraged the Academicians, for early in 1827, they began planning their second annual exhibition. Their optimism was rewarded: the Academy managed to cover the expenses of its annual exhibition for most of the rest of the century.

Whatever the financial or popular success of that first exhibition, it is difficult to say whether it was a critical success, since only a few publications responded to it. The *New York Post* thought it should make New Yorkers proud because it was evidence that it was "an auspicious time for art" in the city. "Nothing will tend more to make artists put forth their strength," the newspaper predicted, " . . . than that union, blended with liberal competition, which has taken place in the formation of the National Academy of Design."[34]

The only publication to give the first exhibition coverage of any depth was the *New-York Mirror*, which, like the *Post,* lauded the birth of the Academy and its plan to make these

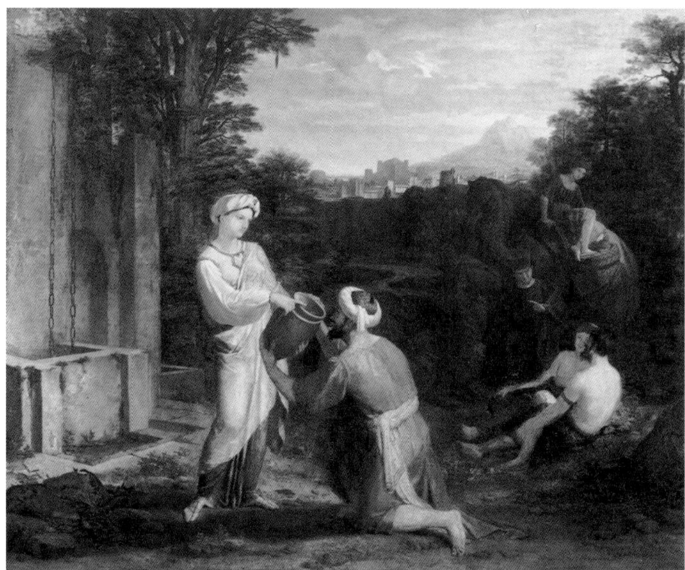

Fig. 28 Washington Allston, *Rebecca at the Well*, 1816, oil on canvas, 29¾ x 35½, Fogg Art Museum, Harvard University, The Washington Allston Trust (National Academy of Design, 1st Annual Exhibition, 1826, no. 14)

exhibitions annual events. The writer—who probably was George Pope Morris, the *Mirror's* founder and editor—noted the success of such ventures in England and, going the *Post* one better, he linked the exhibition to civic *and* national pride. In fact, Morris wrote, it would be a matter of "national disgrace and loss" if the genius of American artists was allowed "to fade and pass away." Although he failed to identify many of the artists in the Academy's exhibition by name—a frustrating lacunae that was corrected in future issues—he wrote at some length about selected works. It is clear that he preferred historical paintings, such as Washington Allston's *Rebecca at the Well* (fig. 28), which he called "rich and gorgeous";[35] but his favorite was a group of studies done for a large painting of the Crucifixion by William Dunlap. He admired the "sublime simplicity" of the composition of one of the studies and praised the manner in which Dunlap captured the emotions of the figures of St. John, Mary, and Mary Magdalene. In another work, the "head, attitude, and expression of the Savior are in the best style."[36] Morris complained about the sparse attendance at the exhibition—which would explain why it lost money—and encouraged his fellow New Yorkers to give their full support to the new institution.[37]

The United States Review and Literary Gazette (1826–1827)

The first review of an Academy exhibition of substantial length and erudition appeared in the *United States Review and Literary Gazette*[38] in July 1827 in response to the Academy's second annual, held on an upper floor of the Arcade Baths on Chambers Street in New York (see fig. 13).[39] The title of the article reads liked a bibliographic citation for the exhibition's catalogue— "Review. *The Exhibition of the National Academy of Design*, 1827. *The Second.* New York. D. Fanshaw. 1827."[40]

The "D. Fanshaw" of the title is Daniel Fanshaw, publisher of the catalogue. The inclusion of his name in the title of the article has caused several modern historians to identify him as its author, but this is incorrect.[41] In fact, the author was Samuel F. B. Morse, founding member and president of the Academy. Morse sent the review to his friend William Cullen Bryant (fig. 29) who, as of October 1826, was the New York editor of the *United States Review*. For obvious reasons, Bryant was concerned that it be published anonymously, which it was.[42] Despite the blatant conflict of professional interest that Morse's authorship of the article implies, it has been identified as this country's "earliest concrete statement on the scope of art criticism, together with an outline of criteria to be used in the evaluation of art."[43]

Morse began the article with a lengthy quotation from the Academy's exhibition catalogue that explained the purposes of the annual exhibitions. These were three: to show the state of modern art in America; to give young artists a chance to exhibit their work with that of mature artists; and to energize the art market. He then outlined the criteria of art, which, in brief, reflect the traditional and accepted hierarchy of artistic subject matter established in the Renaissance and codified, first in the seventeenth century by André Félibien in France, and then, in the late eighteenth century by Sir Joshua Reynolds in England.[44] As far as is known, Morse's article was the first explanation of the hierarchy to be published in this country, and therein lies its significance. In the hierarchy, the most

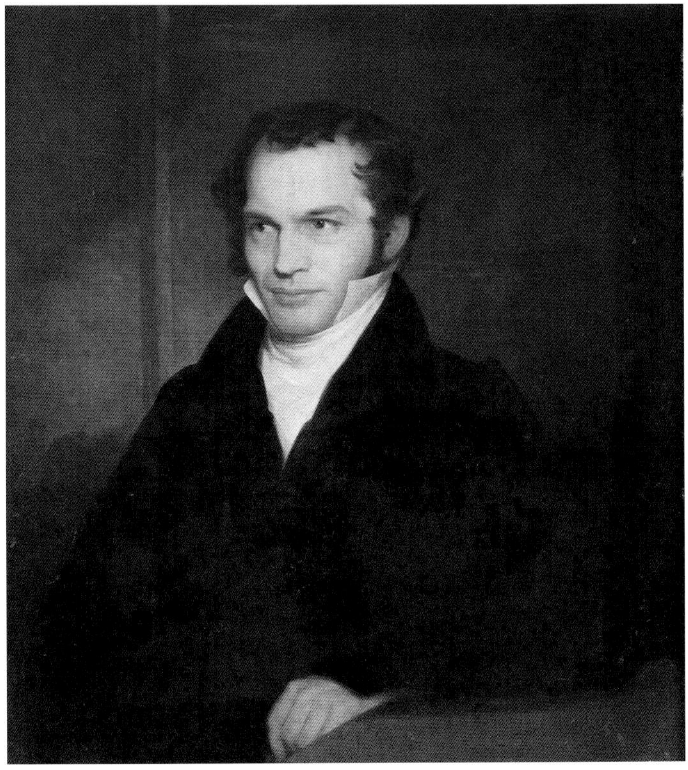

Fig. 29 Samuel F. B. Morse, *William Cullen Bryant,* [1828–29], oil on canvas, 30 x 25, National Academy of Design (National Academy of Design, 4th Annual Exhibition, 1829, no. 56)

elevating, inspirational, and pedagogically successful subjects—the historical and the religious—were at the top. These were followed, in descending order of importance, by historical portraits, historical landscapes, common portraits, common landscapes, genre images, and still-lifes. Having thus set the stage, Morse stated that criticism had "two duties to perform, to *censure* and to *praise*," and he then proceeded to do just that, using the criteria that he had just clarified. Unfortunately, the few historical works in the exhibition—a sketch for a religious painting by Dunlap, Gerlando Marsiglia's *Telemaque and Calipso* (location unknown), and a painting of *Sampson Shorn of His Locks* by Durand (location unknown), for example—did not live up to Morse's standards. But in an amazing piece of self-promotion, Morse praised his own *House of Representatives* (fig. 30)—a history painting with a contemporary, distinctly American theme. The painting, he declared, was without error, but he recognized that the American public was not ready for it. Appreciation of a grand manner painting such as *House of Representatives* required "a more highly cultivated taste in painting than is common in this country." He concluded that the painting would have a better chance of success if it were sent to England.[45]

If Morse was disappointed by the few historical works in the exhibition—and by the public's lack of understanding of them—he was impressed with the two major entries in the next category on the hierarchical scale, historical portraiture. These were (again) his own *Marquis de Lafayette* (1826; City Hall, New York City; see no. 3) and Henry Inman's *William Charles Macready as William Tell* (1827; location unknown, see no. 2). Both portraits, Morse thought, had fine compositions and incorporated symbolism of admirable simplicity. In addition, he declared Inman's portrait to be so well executed that it could easily pass as the work of a more mature artist.[46] Further down the hierarchical scale, the writer praised landscapes by Thomas Cole and William Guy Wall, but he especially liked the paintings of Thomas Doughty for their purity of color, careful finish, and freshness of atmosphere (see fig. 32).[47] With Bryant as its editor and contributions being made by writers such as Morse, the *United States Review and Literary Gazette* promised to be a publication in which art criticism would be nurtured and allowed to mature. That makes it especially unfortunate that it ceased to exist within months of publishing Morse's article. Fortunately, another journal with equal promise—the *New-York Mirror, and Ladies' Literary Gazette*—lived on.

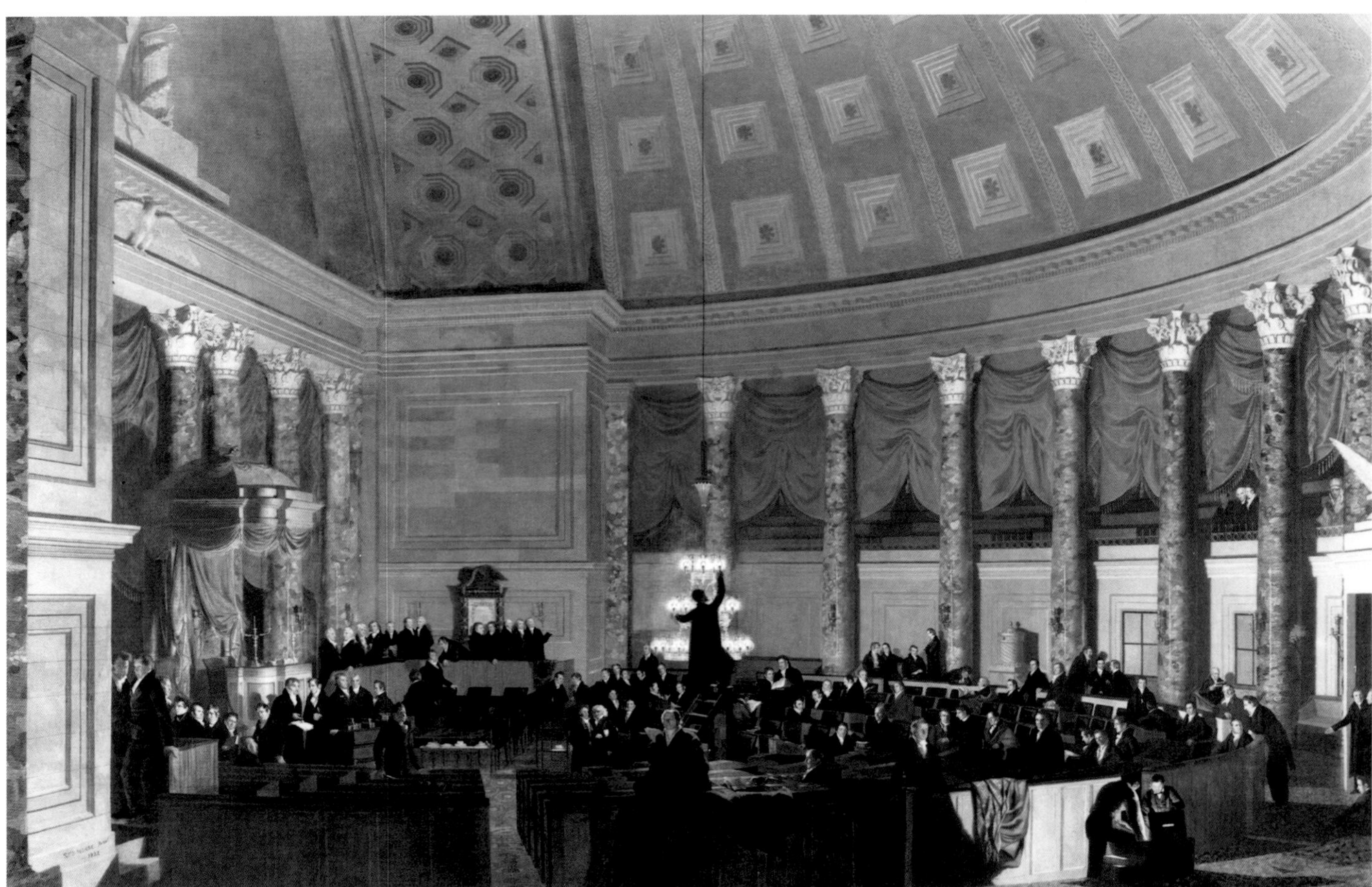

Fig. 30 Samuel F. B. Morse, *The House of Representatives,* 1822, oil on canvas, 86½ x 130¾ , Collection of the Corcoran Gallery of Art, Washington, D.C., Museum Purchase, Gallery Fund (National Academy of Design, 2nd Annual Exhibition, 1827, no. 51)

The New-York Mirror was a weekly literary magazine founded in 1823 by George Pope Morris (1802–1864) (fig. 31). As the new journal's publisher, Morris immediately hired Samuel Woodworth (1785–1842) as its editor.[48] Both men were writers and poets as well as journalists, and Morris even had some renown as a novelist and songwriter. In the first issue of the *Mirror*, the men stated their intention to make it "literally and emphatically, *American*."[49] Woodworth's affiliation lasted only a year, after which Morris took complete control, acting as editor and publisher until his retirement in 1846. It was probably Morris, too, who wrote many of the critical articles that appeared in the *Mirror*.[50] Evidently, he was equipped to do so. Artist and historian William Dunlap recognized Morris as a supporter of the arts and in his 1834 history of American art, wrote that Morris was deserving of "our notice and thanks as a friend of artists, and the arts of design."[51] The catalogues of the annual exhibitions of the National Academy indicate that Morris lent several works from his collection to the exhibitions. These were Robert Weir's *Hoboken Walk* (location unknown), which was in the exhibition of 1832; Horatio Greenough's bust of Nathaniel P. Willis (1832; private collection), which was in the exhibition of 1835; John Gadsby Chapman's *Scene from Knickerbocker* (location unknown), which was in the 1836 exhibition; and portraits of Morris by William Dunlap (location unknown), in the 1835 exhibition,

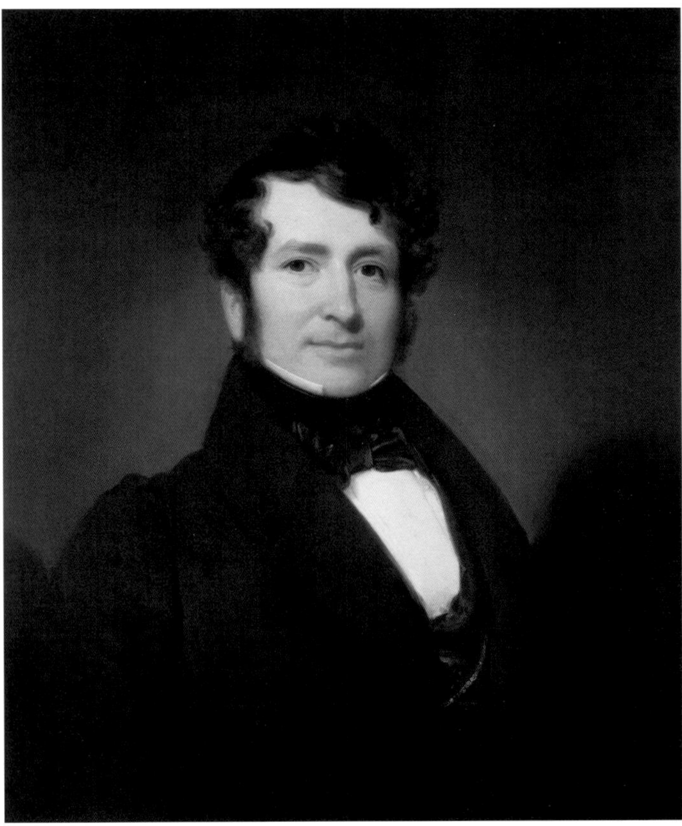

Fig. 31 Henry Inman, *George Pope Morris*, 1836, oil on canvas, 30 x 25, National Gallery of Art, Washington, D.C., Andrew W. Mellon Collection (National Academy of Design, 11th Annual Exhibition, 1836, no. 146)

and by Henry Inman (fig. 31) in the 1836 exhibition.[52] He also owned George Flagg's *Scene from N. P. Willis' Play of "Fortesa the Usurer"* (location unknown), a portrait of President James Madison by Asher Durand (location unknown), and William Dunlap's *The Historic Muse* (location unknown).[53] William Sidney Mount was evidently one of Morris's favorite artists: he owned Mount's *Studious Boy* (1834; location unknown) and *The Sportsman's Last Visit* (1835; The Museums at Stonybrook, Stonybrook, New York). Mount painted a view of Morris's home on the Hudson[54] and, although it was never fulfilled, Morris commissioned the artist to paint an image based on his famous poem "Woodman Spare That Tree."[55] Other American artists produced illustrations for some of Morris's books. David Claypoole Johnston, for example, illustrated Morris's *Little Frenchman and His Water Lots,* a collection of humorous sketches published in Phildelphia in 1839; and Robert W. Weir and John Gadsby Chapman did the same for a collection of Morris's poems, *The Deserted Bride,* which was published in New York by Adlard and Saunders in 1838.

Having been one of only a few journals and newspapers to notice the Academy's first exhibition, the *Mirror's* coverage of subsequent ones became longer and more detailed. By the 1830s the journal was publishing Academy reviews serially in as many as eight issues a year.[56] Although the commentary was sometimes brief, the writer—presumably Morris—considered the exhibitions "with care," as Frank Luther Mott has observed.[57] Morris's articles were thoughtful, logical, articulate, and fair—meaning they were not always positive. Already in 1827, for the second annual exhibition, Morris expressed disappointment and, "with some unwillingness," confessed that "the present collection, both in point of beauty and interest, falls far short of its predecessor—not so much, perhaps, in the dearth of talent as in the misapplication of it." He limited his attention to seven paintings that he felt were the best or at least the most interesting. Like Samuel Morse, George Pope Morris clearly preferred historical works and called attention to many of the same ones that the other periodical noticed—Morse's *House of Representatives,* Marsiglia's *Telemaque and Calipso,* and Durand's *Samson Shorn of His Locks.* Morris described these in clear, often rather lyrical language. Landscape painting also got his attention. Of those in the 1827 exhibition, he preferred Doughty's *Landscape: Delaware Water Gap* (fig. 32) to Cole's landscape, *Last of the Mohicans,* which was popular with other writers (see no. 4). Doughty's painting was "the sweetest picture in the room," Morris thought, and promised great things for landscape painting in America. Like Morse in the *United States Review,* Morris understood the hierarchy of artistic subject matter, predicting that "if landscape painting be not one of the highest branches of the art, such works as [Doughty's] will go far to convince that it is at least one of the most delightful."[58]

Despite this early preference for Doughty, Cole soon became one of Morris's favorite artists. Cole's *Subsiding of the Waters from the Deluge* (fig. 33) was singled out by Morris for

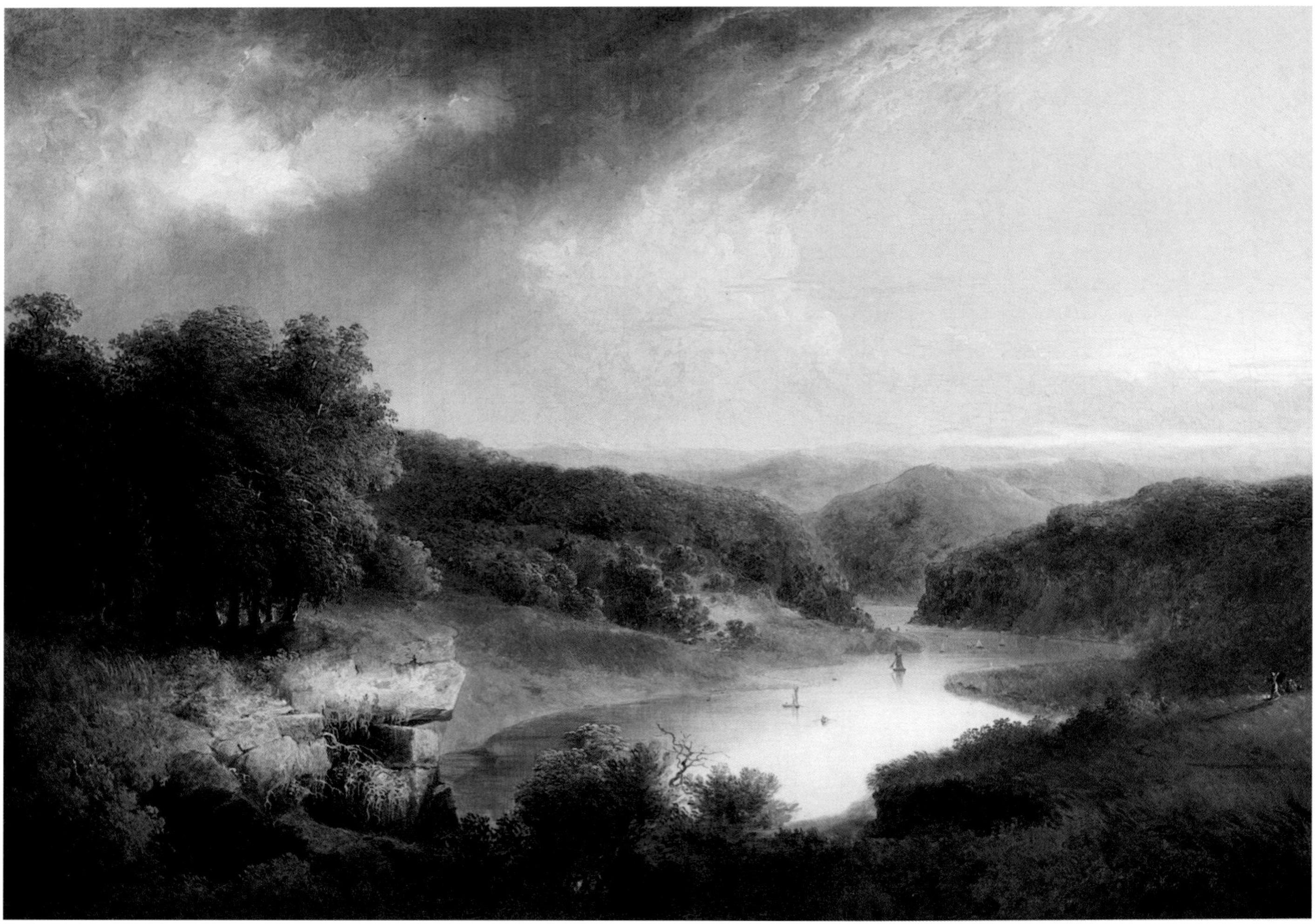

Fig. 32 Thomas Doughty, *Landscape: Delaware Water Gap*, 1826, oil on canvas, 20¹/₁₀ x 28, Collection of the Boston Athenaeum, Bequest of Martha G. Watriss (National Academy of Design, 2nd Annual Exhibition, 1827, no. 21)

praise when it appeared in the Academy's exhibition of 1829,[59] and he continued to applaud Cole's work in subsequent years. In 1830, he thought the artist's *A View of Lake Windermere, England* (location unknown) was one of the most attractive works in the exhibition; and in 1837, Cole's *View of Florence* (1837; Cleveland Museum of Art) received a long paragraph in which Morris praised the artist for painting "with a truth, with reality and history."[60]

In a number of his reviews in the *Mirror*, Morris claimed to have little knowledge of art and no talent at art criticism. This, he said, was the reason that he often made only brief comments about works in the exhibitions; but in fact, he often gave comparatively lengthy commentary on selected works. For the Academy's retrospective exhibition of 1831, for example, he devoted a whole paragraph to Robert Weir's *The Vintage* (location unknown). In this and other passages, Morris often made it clear that he had seen—and remembered—a number of paintings by the artist being discussed. This allowed him to write insightfully, to put the works under discussion into the context of the artist's development, and to compare it to other works. He did all of this in his analysis of Weir's painting.[61]

Other examples of this occurred in 1833 when Morris wrote specifically about Samuel Morse's *Amalfi from the Grotto of the Capuchin Convent* (location unknown), which was in the exhibition that year. By way of comparison, Morris recalled the artist's portrait of Thorwaldsen (1830–31; His Majesty the King of Denmark) which was then in the collection of Philip Hone. Likewise, when he wrote about Thomas Cole's *View of Tivoli* (private collection) that same year, he discussed the artist's earliest productions and his development during and after his trip to Italy.[62] It is probably safe to say that, at least in part, Morris gained this broader knowledge, and a more complete art-historical education, from visiting the Academy's annuals.

In fact, Morris, who was a true professional, often prepared himself in advance for writing about the Academy's exhibitions. In 1835, he anticipated the coming show by visiting a number of studios in order to get a preview of the works the artists intended to send to the Academy. This allowed him to get a jump on the competition and to be able to announce, in advance, that major new works by Ingham, Morse, Page, and others would be in the exhibition that year. He also took the opportunity to review the status of American art *vis-à-vis* the Academy:

> *To the "National Academy of Design" our country is indebted for painters and engravers that rival any in the world; to that institution they are indebted for the opportunities of study which have raised them to this proud eminence; they are now repaying the debt, by enhancing the reputation of the institution, and by the attractions of their works at the annual exhibitions; thus increasing, yearly, the only source of that fund which supports the schools of art, and then generous emulation of our artists. . . . We announce the annual exhibition of the "National Academy," for 1835, as one that will call for the strongest testimonies of publick [sic] approbation, and for a generous support to an institution that does honour to our country, and has forwarded, incalculably, the progress of those arts which distinguish the civilized man from the savage or barbarian.[63]*

Despite these encomiums, it must not be thought that Morris was blinded by his desire to see improvements in the cultural life of the nation or by his friendship with the Academicians. When an exhibition did not live up to his standards, he said so. In 1830, for example, he complained about the "great number of portraits" in the exhibition, although he quickly stated that this was not the fault of the artists but of "the egotistical particles which make up the public."[64] The exhibition of 1838, Morris pointed out, was void of works by established artists such as Allston, Morse, Weir, and Sully, and he found this disturbing. He worried that if this became a trend, "serious injury will result both to the arts and the artists." The works of "older and abler heads" were necessary for the proper education of young artists and for the edification of the public. The press had a role here, too, Morris believed, but it could not do the job alone: "Honest and impartial criticism may do much toward correcting this evil, but one good picture, by the hand of a first-rate artist, is worth more than all the remarks we can publish in a month."[65]

Morris's review of the 1835 annual was distinctive: it was one of the first to give notable attention to sculpture. The impetus for this was the display that year of two busts by Horatio Greenough, of Lord Byron and Nathaniel Parker

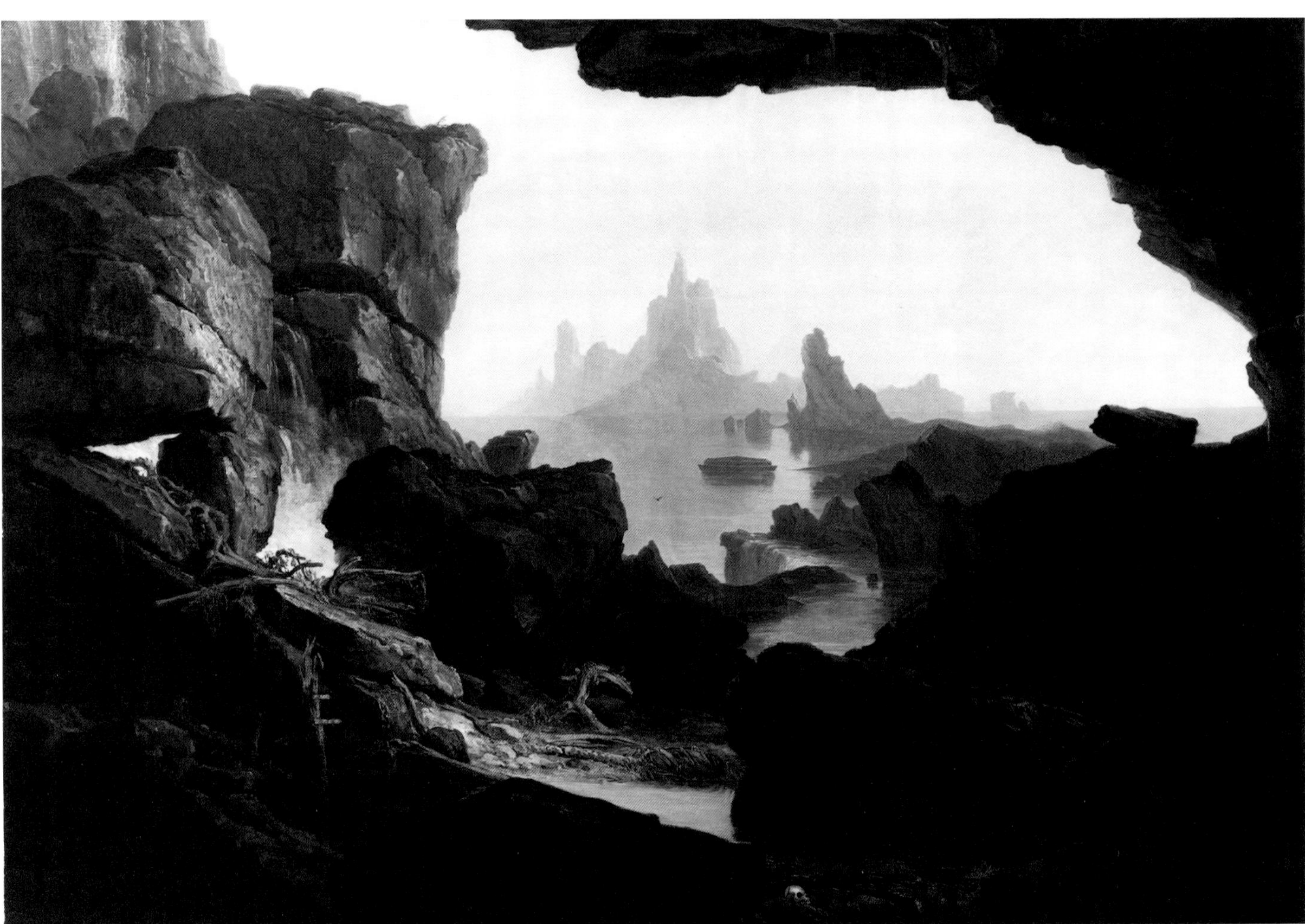

Fig. 33 Thomas Cole, *Subsiding of the Waters from the Deluge*, 1829, oil on canvas, 36 x 48, National Museum of American Art, Smithsonian Institution, Gift of Mrs. Katie Dean in memory of Minnebel S. and James Wallace Dean and museum purchase through the Smithsonian Institution Collections Acquisition Program (National Academy of Design, 4th Annual Exhibition, 1829, no. 60; and 6th Annual Exhibition, 1831, no. 7)

Willis, respectively. These, Morris wrote, were "interesting, and both beautifully executed." Morris then took the opportunity to write a brief history of public sculpture in this country, starting with the sculptures of George III and the Earl of Chatham in New York.[66]

The following year, Morris called attention to miniature painting. While such images had been a part of the Academy's annual exhibitions from the beginning (see the essay "Ekphrasis: A Non-Critical Look at Early Nineteenth-century Portraiture through Poetry" herein), they had received little notice. After admiring one by Thomas S. Cummings, Morris, in his review of the 1836 exhibition, went on to praise the genre in general. He believed that the "delicacy, high finish and force, which may be given to painting on ivory, make good miniature-portraits peculiarly attractive; and we know nothing in art more captivating than the image of beauty so delineated."[67] The attention Morris gave to these two neglected categories of art—sculpture and miniature painting—suggests that he was more astute and had a deeper knowledge of American art than some of his journalistic colleagues.[68]

Despite a healthy circulation, the *Mirror's* financial status was shaken by the economic panic of 1837, and the magazine never fully recovered. By 1843, Morris was forced to reorganize. He began publishing the journal in a smaller format, reduced its price, and changed its title, first to the *New Mirror*, and then, in 1844, to the *Evening Mirror*. As others—notably Nathaniel P. Willis and Hiram Fuller—began to take more editorial control, the journal's focus shifted to articles that would have a greater appeal for New York's social elite.[69] Until that happened, however, the long and thoughtful reviews of the Academy's exhibitions that were a hallmark of Morris's editorship continued, at least sporadically. One of these was published in four issues of the *New Mirror* in 1843. It begins by recounting the history of the Academy and ends with a long quotation taken from an address by Samuel Morse, the institution's president, to the Academy membership. Obviously the author of the *Mirror* article—again, probably Morris—was either on intimate terms with the leaders of the Academy or had done some in-depth research.[70]

Morris left the *Mirror* in January 1846, but the journal continued for another nineteen months.[71] The reviews that it published during 1846 and 1847 were as selective and detailed as any of the time. Hiram Fuller (c. 1815–1880) was sole editor by then, but whether he was the author of these final reviews or not, is not known.[72] Whoever did write them gave an extraordinary amount of space to a few works in the exhibition that year. For example, William Page's *The Mother and Child* (c. 1834; Pennsylvania Academy of the Fine Arts) was the subject of almost two whole columns in the *Mirror's* review of 1847.[73]

After leaving the *Mirror*, Morris, with his friend Nathaniel Parker Willis, founded the *Home Journal* and served as its editor until his death in 1864. While space does not permit a thorough analysis of that periodical, it should be noted that it did publish reviews of the Academy's exhibitions. These were written in the same supportive, optimistic spirit as had been those in the *Mirror* and it might safely be assumed that Morris was again the author.[74]

The Evening Post (1801–present)

If the *Mirror* was the most reliable weekly magazine to cover the Academy's early exhibitions, New York's *Evening Post* was the most reliable newspaper to do so. In fact, throughout the nineteenth century, the *Post* rarely failed to cover the exhibitions and often printed its reviews of them on its front page. Like the *Mirror*, the *Post* sometimes ran the reviews serially in five or more issues. This level of attention was assured almost from the newspaper's inception, for in the summer of 1826—the year of the Academy's first annual exhibition—William Cullen Bryant, poet and friend of artists, joined the staff of the *Post*. Three years later, he became the paper's editor-in-chief. As his son-in-law Parke Godwin later noted, Bryant's presence at the newspaper immediately resulted in an increase in the number of book and art reviews and articles on individual artists and their works.[75]

It is impossible to know how many of the *Post's* reviews of the Academy's exhibitions were written by Bryant, but it seems likely that many were, especially in the early years of his employment there. Being a close friend of several of the founders of the National Academy, including Samuel Morse and Asher Brown Durand, Bryant was predictably supportive of the young organization and even somewhat protective of it. When he was in London in 1845, he visited the annual exhibition of the Royal Academy, and in a letter home, wrote that he saw "nothing in it to astonish one who has visited the exhibitions of our Academy of the Arts of Design in New York …."[76] This attitude is reflected in the *Post's* coverage of the National Academy's exhibitions, whether Bryant was the actual author of the reviews or not. In a brief notice of the Academy's first annual, for example, the *Post* admitted reluctance to name specific artists, stating that it would be "invidious" to do so "where so many are deserving."[77] In 1828, it was impressed with the large proportion of landscapes and historical works in the exhibition, stating that it was even greater than at the Royal Academy's annual that year.[78] In 1829, the paper announced that the Academy's exhibitions were definitely superior to others in the United States in that they formulate an "annual record of the progress of the fine arts among us." In addition, the newspaper believed, the exhibitions proved that New York City was the center of the nation's artistic talent and congratulated the Academy on giving young artists, such as William Sidney Mount, a chance to exhibit their works.[79]

In 1831, the Academy deviated from its usual policy of showing only works of art that had not been previously exhibited in New York. Instead, that year's exhibition was a retrospective display of the best works from the previous five annuals.[80] The decision to do this was favorably received by the press in general but especially by the *Post*, which published no less than four articles on the event. It also happened to be the first exhibition held in the Academy's new headquarters in Clinton Hall (see fig. 14).[81] Obviously charmed by this new venue, the *Post* writer—probably Bryant—praised everything he saw there. The main gallery, he reported, "is so well lighted from above, that not a single picture is left in the shade; and so spacious as to admit of all being placed low enough to be seen to advantage." He even flattered the other visitors to the exhibition who, he said, were "of the first respectability and fashion."[82] The soft lighting of the rooms not only complimented the pictures, but "had the same effect . . . on the complexions and costumes of the ladies who were present to view them."[83]

Whenever the situation required it, the *Post* went even further and cast itself in the role of defender of the Academy against what it termed "falsehood and malignant enmity."[84] Its defense against such slander was often vigorous. For example, in 1836, when the short-lived *Evening Star* gave the Academy's exhibition a bad review, the *Post* responded by calling the offending article "a display of consummate ignorance." On the contrary, the *Post* declared, the exhibition was one of the largest and most beautiful the city had ever seen.[85]

Evidently, the *Post's* protective attitude toward the Academy was widely recognized. In 1835, a writer for the *American Monthly Magazine,* possibly its founder and editor Henry William Herbert (1807–1858),[86] generally praised the Academy's exhibition, but he was unhappy with the manner in which it had been arranged. Artists should not be involved in the hanging of the exhibitions, he wrote, because doing so puts them in the role of critics, a role they are not qualified to assume. He was also displeased with the apparent preference given to well-known artists over younger ones who deserved a chance. His case in point was John Gadsby Chapman, many of whose twelve contributions to the exhibition that year— mostly views of the exterior and interior of Mount Vernon— had been placed high or in dark corners.[87]

A member of the Academy's hanging committee responded to this article, but interestingly, that response was published in the *Post*, not in the *American Monthly Magazine*. Possibly, the writer felt that the *American Monthly* would not print his letter, and since he called the magazine's comments "*unjust and uncharitable,*" he was probably right. In his response, he explained the method used in arranging the Academy's galleries, pointing out that, since there was not much space, every inch of the walls, from floor to ceiling, had to be used. The first step in arranging the pictures, he wrote, was to put one work by each artist "on the line"—a double row of paintings hung at eye level. The rest were then arranged in the remaining space. He pointed out that four of the twelve paintings Chapman sent to the exhibition that year were hung on the line. Furthermore, works by better-known artists such as Henry Inman, William Dunlap, Asher Brown Durand, and Samuel Morse, were hung in corners. The writer concluded by responding to the statement that artists should have nothing to do with the hanging. When it is proven that others can do it better, he declared, the artists will relinquish the duty.[88]

The *Post* supported the Academy again in the 1840s when it seemingly was threatened by the establishment of the American Art-Union, an organization that bought paintings, held exhibitions, and then distributed the works by lottery to its members. The Art-Union's popular appeal made it the Academy's first major competitor but, according to the *Post*, the threat was a weak one at best. This was proven by the Academy's exhibition of 1848, which, the *Post* claimed, was a gratifying display of true American talent. The history of the Academy had been one of "uninterrupted progress and success," and the organization had created an *esprit de corps* among artists. The Art-Union may have existed to *create* taste, but the Academy's *raison d'etre* was to *preserve* it. "The influence of the Academy has been to check charlatanism," the *Post's* critic wrote, "improve the taste and increase the cause of the artist, in offering him the prospect of fame, in the chance of rivalry it has afforded him with all his competitors."[89]

For the most part, the *Post* continued to lavish this kind of high praise on the Academy and its various functions through the 1850s. Only occasionally did it publish a discouraging word. One of these came in reference to the annual of 1839, which the *Post* thought included too many portraits and was arranged so that "gaudy subjects destitute of all taste or merit [are] side by side with more modest superior works of true genius." Having said this, though, the review ended with the kind of positive statement that had become standard for the *Post*:

> *Before we conclude we must pay a just tribute to this highly useful and creditable institution, which, in spite of all other arguments, has a much deeper and influential effect upon the spirit of the age—upon the morals and taste of the people, than a cursory observer would at first imagine.*[90]

The *Post's* concern about the number of portraits in the exhibitions was a common one, expressed by almost every periodical and newspaper at one time or another during the antebellum years. In 1845, a writer for the *Post* prefaced such a complaint by stating that he did not want to wound "the sensibilities of a class of men proverbially sensitive," but that the "habit of indiscriminate praise . . . will not help the advance of the arts." Although he eventually found some "jewels among the rubbish" in the Academy's exhibition that year, he had to admit that, on entering its galleries, he had been struck with the "undue proportion of portraits."[91] A few years later, in 1851, the *Post* made a related complaint about the lack of sculpture in the exhibitions, noting that only one, a bust of a child by Erastus Dow Palmer, was included in that year's annual.[92]

Individual works could also come under fire, although the *Post's* remarks were seldom cutting to the extreme. A rare exception came in 1856 when the critic, who had a discernible preference for landscape painting, singled out several figural

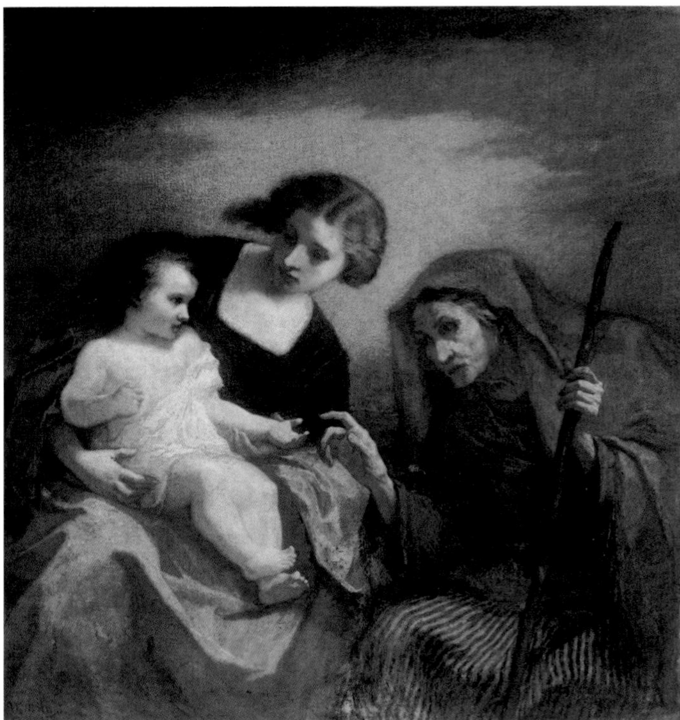

Fig. 34 William Morris Hunt, *The Fortune Teller,* 1852, oil on canvas, 55 x 51, Museum of Fine Arts, Boston, Bequest of Miss Elizabeth Howes (National Academy of Design, 31st Annual Exhibition, 1856, no. 30)

works for unusual ridicule. He quipped that a painting called *Hal* by Henry Peters Gray (location unknown) depicted "a boy in whose veins, apparently, water, not blood, is supposed to flow," and he called William Morris Hunt's *The Fortune Teller* (fig. 34) "repulsive and false." To him, it resembled "some aboriginal illumination of a rhinoceros hide."[93]

Prior to 1860, these were rare complaints for the *Post*. The paper was always ready to reiterate its belief that the activities of the Academy, and even the fact of its continued existence, were a strong indication of the increase of taste for art in the United States.[94]

Unqualified praise of the Academy began to slip at the *Post* during the late 1850s. While the editorial staff may have retained positive feelings toward the institution, they seem to have been more willing to publish letters and articles by correspondents that reflected a less charitable attitude. Some of this criticism resulted from the Academy's move in 1858 to new quarters at the corner of Tenth Street and Fourth Avenue in New York.[95] The *Post's* opinion of the rooms there was very different from that expressed in 1831 when the organization moved into Clinton Hall. According to the *Post,* the new Tenth Street galleries were too small. They did not provide "the opportunity for a grand *coup d'oeil*" or permit the visitor to stand an appropriate distance from the larger pictures.[96] More negative commentary came the following year when the newspaper printed a two-part review of the Academy's exhibition written by an unidentified correspondent. The writer declared that only two artists whose works were in the exhibi-

tion—Eastman Johnson and William Oliver Stone—showed any improvement in style or technique. This writer was also one of only a handful of critics to comment on the presence—or absence—of women artists in any exhibition of this period. The quantity of women artists represented in the exhibition, he or she said, was one of its "noticeable peculiarities." Unfortunately, the writer was not impressed with the quality of their work and decided that it would be necessary to wait for "more striking proof than we have yet witnessed that, in the distribution of her gifts, the Genius of Art establishes no disabilities of sex."[97]

During the 1860s, the style of the *Post's* reviews of the Academy's exhibitions changed. Overall, they reflected more balanced opinions, more articulately expressed. The writers were less likely to gush or to use hyperbole. Instead of trying to mention every work in an exhibition, they focused on the works that they found most significant or interesting. With fewer than ten works discussed per article, each could be analyzed more thoroughly than in previous years. Compare, for example, the following two passages. The first, part of a discussion of Thomas Cole's *Protestant Burying Ground* (fig. 35), is from a review of 1834:

> *If ever Mr. Cole's pictures deserve praise, it is now they should have it. With his strong natural talent, he has combined study from nature of the most arduous description; he has journeyed across the Atlantic to the land of ART, and culled the merits from her standard works. He has returned to us a more finished painter and decidedly more attached to America than before he departed, and he has since his return painted such landscapes as have not before appeared in this country, either from native or foreign pencils.*[98]

The second was written thirty years later, in 1864; after discussing *Twilight in the Adirondacks* (fig. 36), a painting by one of Cole's aesthetic descendants, Sanford Gifford, the reviewer turns to William H. Beard, whose *The Argument* (location unknown) was in the Academy's exhibition that year. The tone of his remarks is far more negative and even eccentric than that used in the *Post's* earlier art reviews:

> *We sometimes despair of ever seeing this gentleman elevate himself to saints on their toe-nails, decomposing stone-breakers, marine orphans with mildewed pantaloons, seamstresses with lamp-black shadows, or flat perspective martyrs. Perhaps the artist who once gets into a feeling for obscene goats, bestial bears, reckless rabbits, trivial terrapins and demoralizing donkeys, never more has mercy extended to him and must keep on painting atmosphere and perspective and distance, with the kindred falsehoods, until he awakes in a world of verity veritas where the firmament has been put under an air pump, and the only difference between an eagle in the sky and a fly on one's nose is the tickling.*[99]

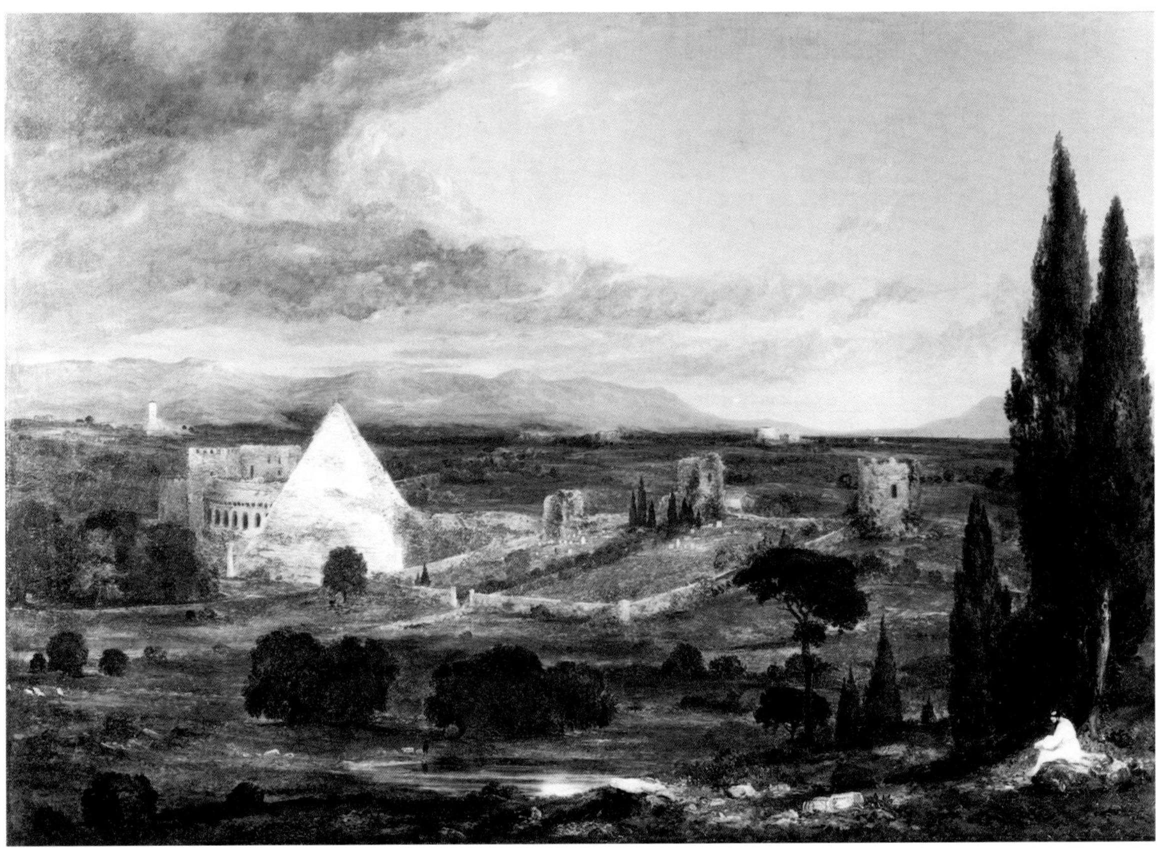

Fig. 35 Thomas Cole, *View of the Protestant Burying Ground, Rome,* n.d., oil on canvas, New York State, Office of Parks, Recreation and Historic Preservation, Olana State Historic Site (National Academy of Design, 9th Annual Exhibition, 1834, no. 27)

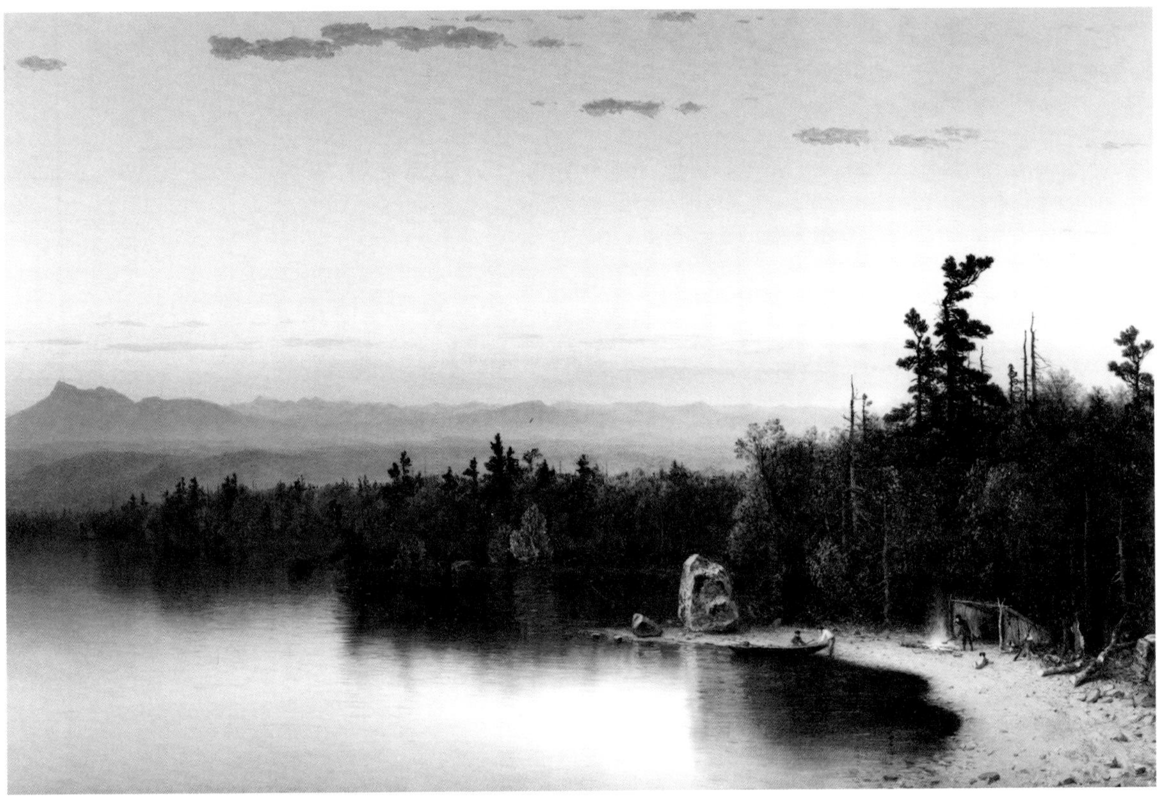

Fig. 36 Sanford Robinson Gifford, *Twilight in the Adirondacks,* 1864, oil on canvas, 24 x 26, Adirondack Museum, Blue Mountain Lake, New York (National Academy of Design, 39th Annual Exhibition, 1864, no. 250)

The reason for this change at the *Post* in the 1860s is difficult to determine. It seems likely that it was at least partly due to a change in staff or contributors; but perhaps it is also linked to the great national conflict that was then in process, an event of such national consequence that it certainly affected every mode of contemporary life and attitude, including the mood of art critics.

The Knickerbocker Magazine (1833–1865)

For most of its life, the *Knickerbocker* was dominated by Lewis Gaylord Clark (1810–1873), who was editor and publisher of the magazine from 1834, when he bought the journal from its founder, Charles Fenno Hoffman, until 1860 when he retired.[100] Clark was outgoing and congenial and had all the necessary literary connections to make the venture a success. He quickly developed an impressive list of distinguished contributors that included Washington Irving, from whose writings the title of the magazine was taken, James Fenimore Cooper, William Cullen Bryant, William Dunlap, Bayard Taylor, Henry Wadsworth Longfellow, and Nathaniel Hawthorne. Clark preferred articles of a humorous nature, even blatant sarcasm and parody; but he also published poetry, literary criticism, and excerpts from other books and magazines.[101]

Clark himself was responsible for much, although not all, of the literary and art criticism published in the *Knickerbocker*, especially that found in "The Editor's Table," a mostly humorous column that eventually dominated the publication.[102] Although it never gave the Academy the kind of undying support that Bryant's *Post* did, Clark's *Knickerbocker,* which had a close association with the entire set of Knickerbocker writers, was predisposed to see the Academy as an integral part of the cultural life of the city. This opinion was expressed in the *Knickerbocker's* reviews and articles about the Academy, most of which were probably written by Clark. In 1842, for example, Clark suggested that his readers might not be aware of all the functions of the Academy, pointing to the organization's valuable collection of casts of antique sculptures and its library "containing some of the most rare and costly works on the arts." He went further by giving credit to the Academy's exhibitions for "the growth of taste and the establishment of correct feeling among us for the arts."[103] In a review of the Academy's 1837 exhibition, the *Knickerbocker* reminded readers that, although the founding of the Academy may have been a hazardous venture, the organization had overcome all dangers. Its exhibitions were "highly creditable to the city and the country" and its influence could be measured in the increasing numbers of exhibitors. In fact, the *Knickerbocker* declared, the exhibitions had grown so large and so important that they presented a considerable challenge to critics, who were finding it increasingly difficult to select and give attention to those works that deserved it.[104]

Thematically, Clark preferred landscape painting over other subject categories. Certainly his magazine's close affil-iation with Romantic poets and writers such as Bryant and Cooper, who glorified Nature in their writings, coupled with the fact that the magazine was born just as American landscape painting was coming into its own, makes this predictable. For example, the magazine's review of the Academy's 1834 exhibition implied that the landscape paintings there saved the exhibition from mediocrity. Going further, the *Knickerbocker* observed that when Thomas Cole or others of his stature failed to participate, the exhibitions suffered.[105] Nor would the magazine accept second-rate substitutes. In a *Knickerbocker* review of the Academy's 1839 exhibition, artist and journalist John Kenrick Fisher (1807–1874) wrote of his disappointment at the lack of paintings by Cole there. Unmollified by landscapes by other artists, Fisher called Charles Cromwell Ingham's *The Great Adirondack Pass* (see no. 12), a "daub" and monotonous; he found it to be void of "all true substance."[106] Once Cole returned to the exhibitions, the *Knickerbocker* noted, matters improved. Although the journal thought that, on the whole, the Academy's exhibition of 1840 was "mediocre," it gave high praise to Thomas Cole's *A View of the Mountain Pass Called the Notch of the White Mountains* (fig. 37). The author, again almost certainly Clark, wrote that it was "truly an American picture." He went on to admire the "boldness of the scenery itself, the autumnal tints which are spread over the forest, and the wild appearance of the heavens" and called Cole "a master, without rival among his own countrymen."[107]

Despite this, Clark's support for the Academy had its limits. In fact, he never really gave much priority to the critical articles that reported on its exhibitions. These reviews appeared only sporadically and, when they were published, their length varied widely from one issue to another. It is often obvious—and Clark rather guiltily admitted this—that longer submissions in this category had been heavily edited and sometimes omitted altogether due to lack of space. It seems that the *Knickerbocker's* concerns that the exhibitions were often more than a critic could handle were well founded and that, indeed, the magazine itself was not always able to rise to the challenge. With Clark's retirement in 1860 and the advent of the Civil War the following year, the *Knickerbocker's* coverage of art exhibitions waned. One of its last reviews of an Academy exhibition of any length appeared in 1858, but most of it was in the form of a letter to the editor.[108]

The New York Herald (1835–1924)

The *Herald* was founded in 1835[109] by James Gordon Bennett (1795–1872), who emigrated from Scotland, worked for a number of newspapers in Charleston and Washington, and finally settled in New York. His earlier experiences, including a stint on the staff of New York's *Courier and Enquirer,* had left him discouraged with politics. When he founded the *Herald,* he decided to eschew politics altogether in favor of economics. In fact, his new newspaper's initial success was due to its "money column," a daily financial report

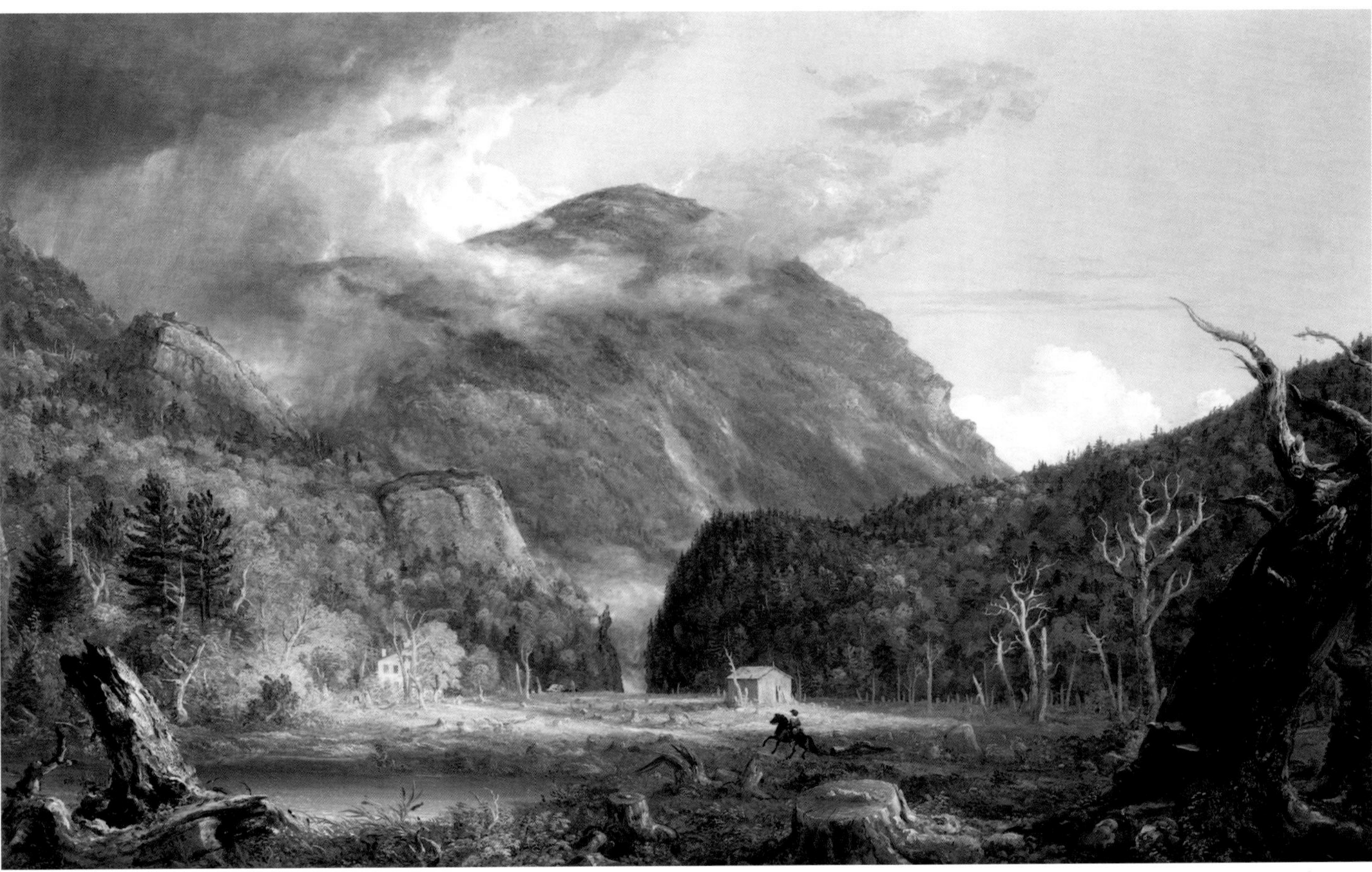

Fig. 37 Thomas Cole, *A View of the Mountain Pass Called the Notch of the White Mountains*, 1839, oil on canvas, 40 x 60½, National Gallery of Art, Washington, D.C., Andrew W. Mellon Fund, 1967 (National Academy of Design, 15th Annual Exhibition, 1840, no. 49)

written by Bennett himself. After only six months in operation, the presses of the printing company that produced the *Herald* were destroyed by fire, but Bennett was not discouraged. He resurrected the *Herald* as a more independent and exuberant journal. "More exuberant, indeed," writes historian Frank Luther Mott. "Its columns sparkled. Everything was personalized. Wit supplanted dignity; recklessness took the place of conservatism. Objective reporting suffered and news reports were editorialized. . . . the *Herald* came to be thought of as 'spicy' and 'saucy'—adjectives it liked to apply to itself."[110]

In its new, expanded form, the *Herald* immediately showed an interest in art by reviewing the National Academy's 1836 annual exhibition. The review appeared serially in five issues and was written by a correspondent who identified himself as John More Anon. The *Herald* called More Anon "piquant and racy." Whether he was actually those things or not, his writing does have a generally sarcastic tone. He wrote and submitted his review to the *Herald,* he said, because he presumed that the paper wished "to be known as having due regard for the arts." In form and content, the review was fairly typical for the time. More Anon mentioned almost every work in the exhibition, adding a few lines of commentary for each. Adjectives such as "rich," "bold," "soft," "harmonious," "easy," and "natural" abound in his writing; and phrases like "full of humor and

excellence," "a little gem," "lack of atmosphere," and "happy management of chiaroscuro" are coined and then repeated.[111]

As far as is known, this was John More Anon's one and only article for the *Herald;* but its irreverent tone was characteristic of the *Herald* in general and continued to be used in the paper's art reviews for some time. In 1837, for example, a report on the opening reception of the Academy's exhibition was more about the guests than about the art. "There was not an ugly woman in the room," the writer stated,

nay, more, there was not one that would not be considered beautiful. What can be the reason? Is it that those who are not so pretty dislike to put themselves in comparison with the beautiful portraits on the walls? Pshaw! They need not fear that, for where there is one handsomer, we will be sworn there are six not half so good looking.[112]

Once he got around to discussing the works of art, the critic was unapologetic. "When we proposed to notice the pictures in this exhibition," he wrote, "we promised to give our own unprejudiced opinions. . . . Let our opinions go for what they are worth—go and see if you can find fault with them."[113]

Occasionally, the *Herald's* reviews took unusual formats. For example, in 1838, the writer pretended to have overheard a conversation between an elderly gentleman and his beautiful young daughter as they viewed the Academy's exhibition. Their discussion functions as a review of the exhibition, but it is peppered with the same kind of sarcastic and even caustic remarks mentioned above.[114] In fact, the *Herald* was far more likely to criticize the Academy's exhibitions than was the *Post*. It even subtitled one review "Cutting Criticism."[115] In 1839, the paper declared that the Academy's exhibition "contains more trash than ever seen in the same space before." Of the 296 works in the show, 13 were "excellent," 20 "good," 75 "passable," 84 "indifferent," and 91 "potboilers."[116] (Presumably, the rest were not even worth inspecting.) The following year, the paper serialized its review in six issues; but almost all of its comments were negative, and for the most part, the writer did not even bother to identify the artists by name. Remarks such as "a ridiculous affair," "too high up to see," "too dark," and "an unfortunate subject," were commonplace. One of the few paintings to receive any praise was Francis W. Edmonds's *City and Country Beaux* (see no. 13), which was admired for its humor.[117]

The sarcasm of these early years was toned down to some degree by the mid-1840s, and some of the paper's commentary became more thoughtful and detailed. A hint of a new seriousness—and the term is relative—is seen in a review of the 1845 exhibition. In direct contrast to remarks made about Edmonds in 1840, those in the 1845 review had "little feeling" for that artist's *Facing the Enemy* (1845; location unknown). "The fine arts," the critic wrote, "should have a higher aim than producing laughter."[118] The 1848 exhibition was criticized by the *Herald* for containing too many portraits— "commonplace faces painted in a commonplace manner," as the writer put it. But instead of simply making a brief comment about the situation, as it might have done in earlier years, the *Herald* gave reasons for its displeasure. "What on earth can be the motive of people," it stated,

> *who are themselves of no consequence to the public, to put their resemblances out for the public gaze, we never could imagine. Portraits of noted warriors, statesmen, literary men, etc., are interesting to the public, and there is a propriety in placing them in a public hall for exhibition, but in the other case it must arise from a miserable vanity on the part of the originals of the pictures, and of the artists who produce them.*[119]

A similar complaint was made again in 1856 when the paper bemoaned the lack of good historical paintings and landscapes, a more-or-less chronic lament at the time. Patrons and the art market—not the artists—were blamed, "for there is talent enough amongst our painters to produce good compositions if they could obtain fair prices for them."[120]

In some of its reviews of the exhibitions during the 1850s, the *Herald* did what the *Post* was doing at the same time: it focused on fewer works and gave these a more detailed analysis. In 1850, the review singled out fewer than ten paintings for discussion; and in 1852, it discussed only eight works.[121] This

did not mean that the *Herald* had lost its old audacity. In 1858, its critic complimented the Academy on its new rooms at Tenth Street and Fourth Avenue, but he reported that most works in the exhibition were "crude," "common," or "rubbish." He later admitted, however, that the exhibition was not a total disaster and exempted Durand, Edmonds, Coleman, Elliott, Huntington, Gifford, and a few others from his vitriol. In fact, when he got around to discussing specific works, he was less caustic.[122] This became something of a standard for the *Herald* during the 1860s: several opening paragraphs expressed an almost unequivocal negativity toward the exhibitions, a ploy, perhaps, to get the reader's attention. These remarks were followed by discussions of individual works that were usually quite brief, more passive, more charitable and, at times, quite positive.

Beginning in the late 1850s, expressions of disappointment in the paucity of historical paintings became a particular characteristic of the *Herald's* reviews. Once war was declared in 1861, this only increased. "The interest of the events daily transpiring throughout the country," the paper wrote in 1863, "and the multiplicity of subjects which they suggest, would, it was supposed, have stimulated somewhat the ambitions of our historical painters." As the paper pointed out, only a handful of paintings in the exhibition dealt with the great contemporary event. Judging by the titles listed in the exhibition catalogue that year, of the 471 paintings and sculptures, only 9 had titles that clearly indicate that their themes were related to the War.[123] Whether this was the fault of the artists or of the Academy's hanging committee is difficult to say.[124]

The New York Tribune (1841–1924)

Horace Greeley (1811–1872) (fig. 38) founded the *New York Tribune* in 1841 and subsequently became one of the most famous journalists in American history. He had entered the field of journalism as a printer, but in 1834, he founded a weekly paper of his own called the *New-Yorker*. It was a journal of "Literature, Politics, Statistics and General Intelligence" that sought "to blend the lessons of Science, History, Morality and sound Criticism."[125] It was known for its attractive format, eclectic range of subjects, editorial brashness, and high quality of writing, most of which was by Greeley himself.[126]

Among the topics covered by the *New-Yorker* were the arts. During its seven-year life span, the journal consistently reported on the National Academy's annual exhibitions and usually looked upon them with favor. In 1836, for example, the *New-Yorker* announced that it was the duty of every New Yorker to visit the Academy's exhibition, where they would be rewarded with "a refined and refining pleasure." That year at least, the journal declined to "inflict the ordinary ten columns of criticism upon the collection, item by item—particularly as we are not sufficiently conversant with the art to pretend to criticize its productions."[127]

This reluctance had evaporated by the following year when the *New-Yorker* not only reviewed the Academy's exhibition,

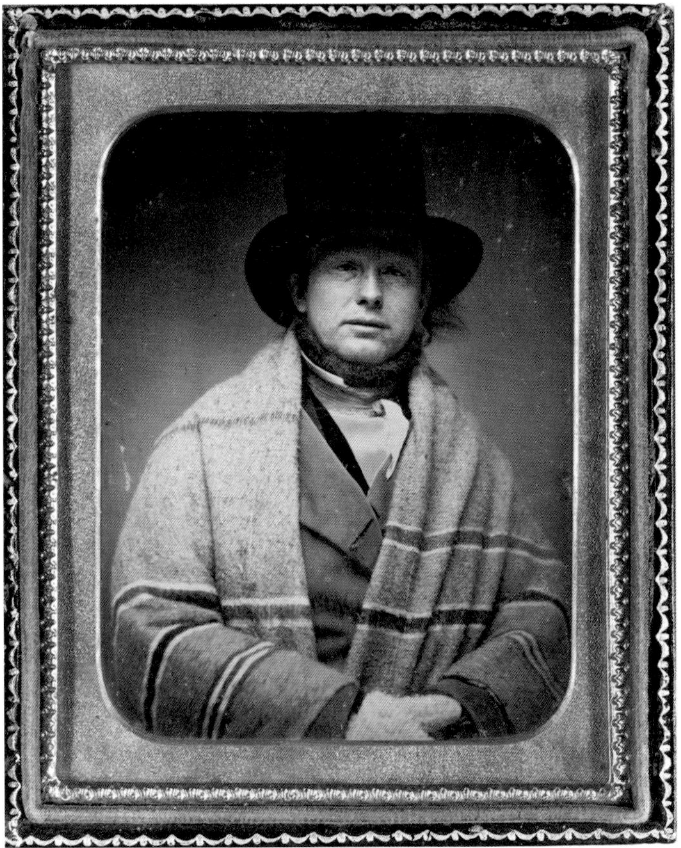

Fig. 38 Unidentified artist, *Horace Greeley*, c. 1850, daguerreotype, 4³/₁₆ x 3¼, National Portrait Gallery, Smithsonian Institution

but did so serially in five issues. While the author is unidentified, it was almost certainly Greeley. He showed a preference for landscape painting and praised Asher Durand, Thomas Cole, Joshua Shaw, and Daniel Huntington.[128] In subsequent years, he lauded the effects that art criticism itself was having on American art. "Since the criticisms of connoisseurs have been brought to bear upon the productions of the American pencil," he editorialized in 1838, "a lively competition has been excited amongst our distinguished artists, and the strife for superiority during the past year has enabled the Academy to present a number of pictures, which, for real merit, surpasses any they have heretofore exhibited."[129]

Not all was rosy, though. The next year the *New-Yorker* turned vicious when reviewing the Academy's annual. The dramatically different tone and attitude suggest that the author was not the same as that of the previous year's review—perhaps Greeley had turned the task over to one of his associate editors, Park Benjamin or Henry J. Raymond being the most likely candidates. Whoever the author was, he felt that the Academy's exhibition of 1839 indicated that the progress of art in America had been slow; that the Academy had done little to help the situation; and that the initials "N. A." actually meant "No Artist" instead of "National Academician." While he thought the exhibition as a whole was "miserably meagre of merit," he was particularly vicious about the "ragged regi-

ment" of portraits and the landscapes by Durand and Ingham. He suggested the former return to engraving and called the latter's *Great Adirondack Pass* (see no. 12) the *Great Abominable Pass*.[130] This brand of alliterative sarcasm was not really characteristic of the *New-Yorker* and was not in keeping with Greeley's own writing style. The next year the journal returned to its more positive attitude toward the Academy and its contributions to the cultural life of New York City.[131]

As he was writing and editing these reviews, Greeley obviously was gaining experience in thinking about art. In fact, it is likely that the National Academy's annual exhibitions served as an educational tool for him, as it probably did for others. Visiting the exhibitions regularly in order to write about them, or editing reviews written by others, would surely have heightened Greeley's awareness of art and helped to form his tastes.[132] By the time he founded the *New York Tribune* in 1841, he probably took the inclusion of articles on art as a matter of course.

Like its predecessor, the *New-Yorker,* and its rival, the *Herald,* the *Tribune* was a consistent reviewer of Academy exhibitions, eventually publishing some of its criticism serially over as many as seven issues. On occasion, these reviews began with an acknowledgment of the Academy's importance, if not culturally, then socially.[133] Generally, the *Tribune's* reviews were similar to those in the *Herald.* During the 1840s, they tended to do little more than list works in the exhibitions with brief comments for each. Nevertheless, the paper often tried to give attention to those categories of art that were usually neglected by its competition. One of these was miniature painting, which was the subject of several paragraphs in the *Tribune's* review of 1843. Similarly, sculpture at the Academy was the subject of an entire article in 1850.[134] In fact, the paper's 1850 review of the annual exhibition at the Academy was far more introspective than what had come before. The writer began with a discussion of the significance of criticism in the development of the arts. "Art cannot thrive under the dispensation of indiscriminate praise," he wrote, "whether dictated by ignorance, bad taste or personal partiality. Artists are not benefited nor the public instructed by criticism, unless it breathe a manly sincerity." He then took up a number of issues, including the Academy's new building, which he said looked more like an oyster shop than the headquarters of a major art organization. Its brick facade, he believed, should have been covered with granite and decorated with allegorical sculptures in order to suggest more accurately the purpose of the interior. While he approved of the distribution of the galleries and the inclusion of several artists studios on the top floor, he regretted the many steps one had to climb to reach the galleries and the inadequate lighting and blood red carpet and walls he found there.[135]

This writer also had definite opinions about the manner in which art should be displayed and viewed. As part of his 1850 review, he advised the Academy to plan its installations more carefully so that adjacent works would compliment each

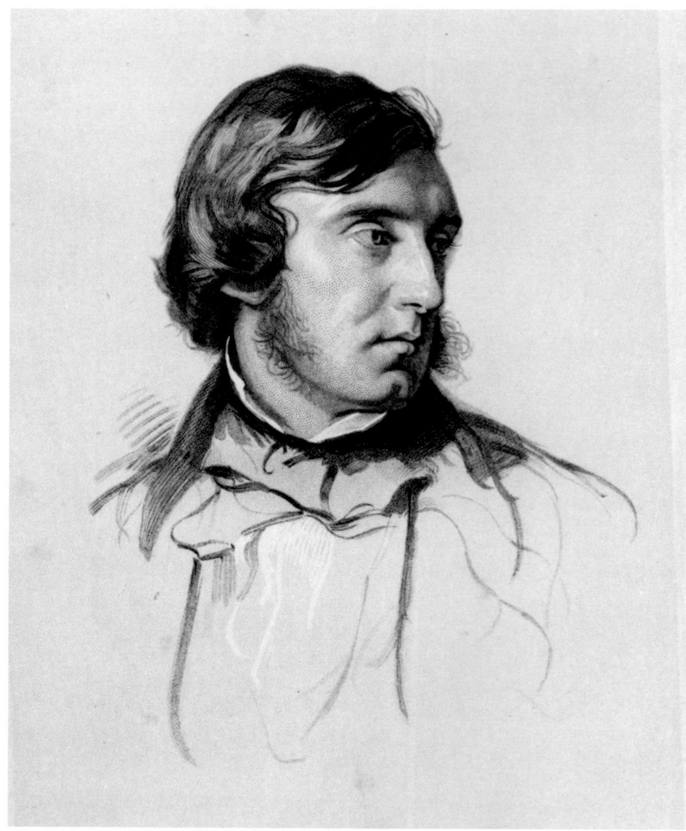

Fig. 39 H. B. Hall, after Samuel Lawrence, *George William Curtis*, frontispiece from George William Curtis, *The Potiphar Papers* (New York: G. P. Putnam and Company, 1856), Private collection, New York

other. He lectured that the shape and size of frames should be considered.[136] In a discussion of landscape painting, he professed that the first requirements of painting are beauty, appropriateness of form, and a picturesque treatment. Paintings should have a close resemblance to nature; but, he observed, no American artist had been able to live up to these requirements since the death of Cole. Nevertheless, some of his followers, such as Asher Brown Durand, came close in paintings such as *Thanatopsis* (see no. 17), to which the critic devoted a long paragraph of mostly positive remarks.[137]

Another issue that disturbed the *Tribune's* critic—he discussed it twice in the course of reviewing the 1850 exhibition—was the threat of the American Art-Union to the Academy. The latter has been in "rapid decline" in recent years, he claimed, due to the former's free exhibitions of and "liberal dissemination of pictures." This rivalry was regrettable and would not exist, he thought, if the Academy were not controlled by a "close group of individuals." Since the Academy was forced to charge admission to its exhibitions in order to survive, the critic suggested that the Art-Union agree not to open its shows while the Academy's were in progress. This would prevent friction between the two organizations.[138]

Thoughtful reviews such as the one just discussed became the norm at the *Tribune* in 1851 when the young George William Curtis (1824–1892) (fig. 39) joined the staff. With his arrival, the *Tribune* began publishing much longer and more interesting reviews. These ran serially in as many as seven issues and covered more topics, both general and specific, than did most other such articles of the period.[139] Curtis, who was at the beginning of a brilliant career in 1851, was "one of the most graceful and eloquent writers of the times." He provided "reliable guidance to . . . middle-class audiences on art, manners, and especially, politics."[140]

Curtis was a native of Rhode Island and began his literary career as a writer of romantic novels. With his brother Burrill, he spent the early 1840s at the transcendentalist community of Brook Farm and in Concord, Massachusetts. In 1846, he went to Europe, where he and his brother spent most of their time in Italy, Germany, France, and the Near East. He reported on his travels in a series of letters to the *Courier and Enquirer* back in New York. Meanwhile, he was also contributing articles to other magazines, including the *Knickerbocker*. When he returned to the United States in 1850, he spent a year writing an account of his travels and then, in 1851, joined the editorial staff of the *Tribune*.[141] By that time, he was personally acquainted with many of this country's leading political, business, and literary figures. He was also a friend of many artists, some of whom he had met in Europe.[142] Among them was John F. Kensett who, in 1852, provided illustrations for Curtis's *Lotus-Eating: A Summer Book* (fig. 40), an anthology of essays

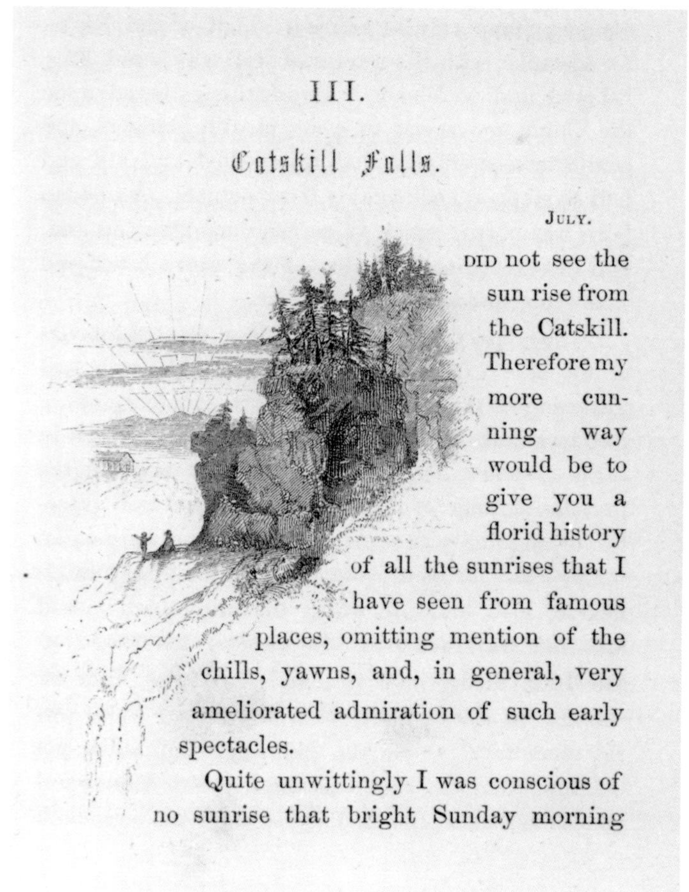

Fig. 40 John Frederick Kensett, illustration for George William Curtis, *Lotus-Eating: A Summer Book* (New York: Harper & Brothers, 1852), Collection of Kevin Lane Dearinger, New York

on the scenic beauties of the northeastern United States.[143] Curtis was amazingly prolific and served as correspondent for several periodicals simultaneously. In 1853, he began writing the column known as "The Editor's Easy Chair" for *Harper's Monthly* and continued to do so for forty years. It made him famous. He also founded *Harper's* column known as "The Lounger," in which he often reviewed art exhibitions during the late 1850s and early 1860s.[144] Meanwhile, from 1853 to 1857, he was an associate editor and writer for *Putnam's Monthly Magazine*, and, in 1857, he became an editor of *Harper's Weekly*.[145] Besides being a journalist, his interests and connections led him to politics. His power and influence in that field were assured in 1856 when he delivered an oration at Wesleyan University in Middletown, Connecticut, in reaction to the caning of Charles Sumner on the floor of the United States Senate. The text of Curtis's speech was published in its entirety by Horace Greeley in the *Tribune*.[146]

Curtis wrote his first review of a National Academy exhibition shortly after joining the editorial staff of the *Tribune* in 1851. In April of that year, he recorded in his diary that he was "already in labor with the critiques upon the Academy Exhibition." This, and the reviews to follow, were characterized by one of his contemporaries as "clever, agreeable, bright, never violent or ugly." [147] This opinion is certainly supported by Curtis's seven-part review of the 1851 Academy exhibition. He declared the show to be the finest that he could remember. He was "charmed with the freshness and promise of the pictures," pleased that far fewer portraits of unidentified subjects were present, and satisfied with the quality of the landscapes, which, he wrote, had also never been seen in such quantity.[148] In fact, the first four installments of the review were devoted to landscape paintings, specifically those of Durand (fig. 41), Cropsey, Kensett, Church, and the Düsseldorf artist B. L. Koek Koek. While Curtis acknowledged that he was personally acquainted with many of the artists whose works were at the Academy, he made it clear that his review was "aimed at the service of Art and not at the satisfaction of friendship."[149]

Curtis's review of the Academy's exhibition of 1852 was again serialized, this time in seven issues, with each installment of considerable length and erudition. Generally, he was pleased with the exhibition and thought that the best artists of the previous year—Henry Peters Gray, Thomas Hicks, Daniel Huntington, John F. Kensett, and Thomas P. Rossiter—had only improved. In order to suggest the difficulties art critics have in being taken seriously, Curtis began by recounting a two-hour conversation about painting that he had had with an artist at the church of San Miniato in Florence. Evidently, the conversation was interesting and edifying for both parties

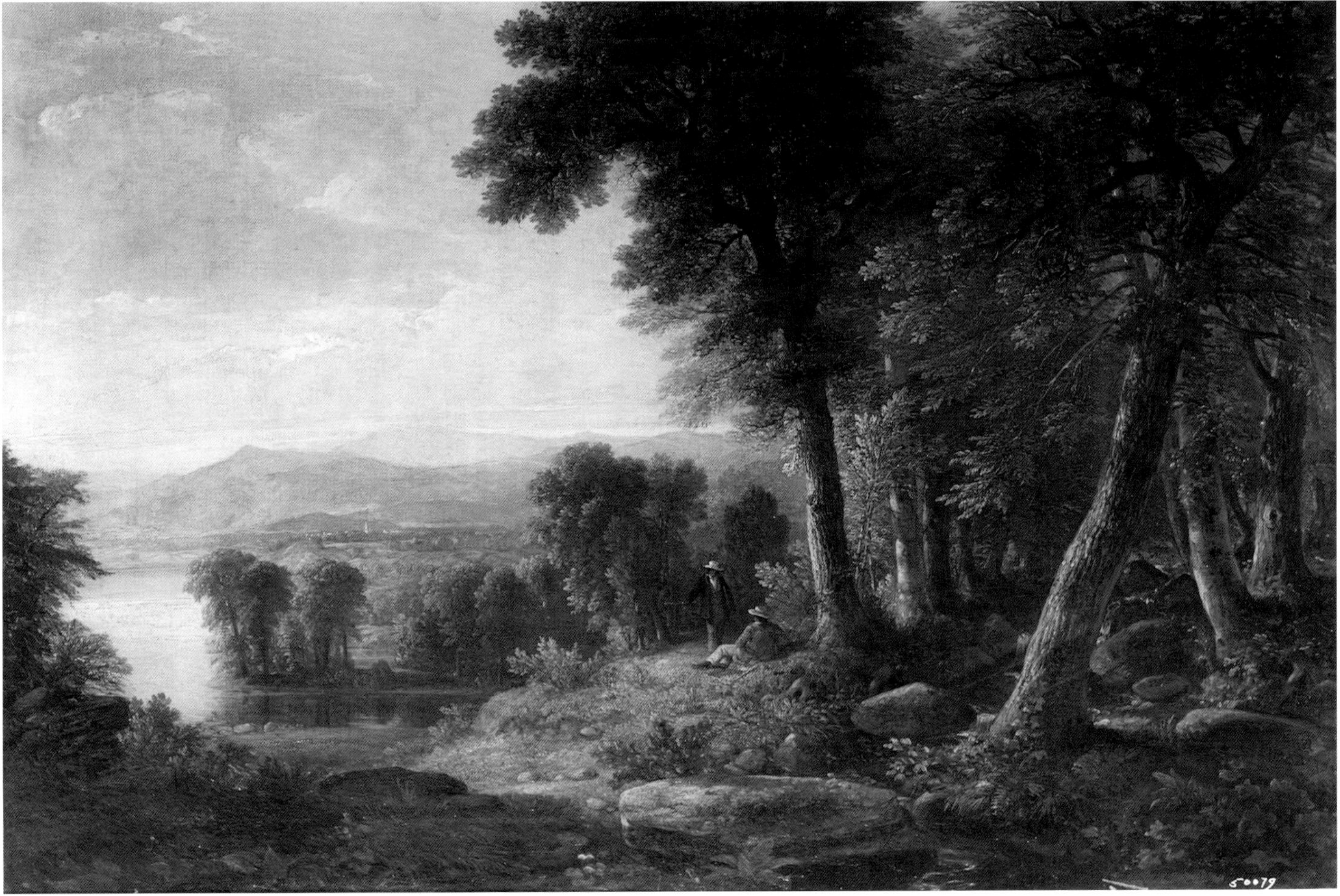

Fig. 41 Asher Brown Durand, *Landscape,* 1850, 27¼ x 38½, National Academy of Design, Bequest of James A. Suydam, 1865 (National Academy of Design, 26th Annual Exhibition, 1851, no. 343)

until the artist realized that Curtis was not himself a painter, at which time the artist declared that he had wasted two hours of his time and stalked away. In response to this memory, Curtis assured his readers, in his usual graceful and poetic way, that art was not as elitist as the actions of the artist at San Miniato might suggest. "Art is essentially democratic," he wrote.

> *Like flowers, and the forms of clouds, and the beauty of the landscape, it addresses the humblest sense and out-reaches the most aspiring imagination. A picture, like a person, is what the observer sees in it.*[150]

Curtis's art reviews were the finest published by the *Tribune* in the years before the Civil War, but by 1855, he was no longer writing them.[151] Instead, an author identified only by the initials "R. T." wrote the review for that year and, judging by the writing style, was almost certainly the author of the review of the following year. Whoever R. T. was, he was much less thoughtful and far more caustic—one might even say less fair—than Curtis. While he praised the landscapes in the 1855 exhibition, he was not particularly receptive to the Academy in general or positive about its role in American culture. He called it a "poor excuse for an Institution which ought to answer to its title of National" and declared that its failure was proof that the United States had made progress in every branch except art.[152] He was clearly prejudiced against the Academy as seen in his review of the following year. To support his dislike of the institution, he dredged up the rivalry between it and the older American Academy that had led—sadly, he believed—to the demise of the latter. He totally disapproved of an art organization being managed by artists. Art "is not for the benefit of artists, but for the world; and an institution designed to foster it and promote its growth, could best be managed by men who have a knowledge of affairs, and who would be wholly free from preference, jealousies, and fantastic theories and rivalries."[153] He went so far as to suggest that the National Academy "disband, shut up, and give the artists an opportunity to form a new institution, or to get along as well as they can without any aid."[154]

A more balanced view of the exhibitions was taken by the anonymous writer or writers for the *Tribune* in the early years of the war. In 1862, for example, the paper optimistically announced that, despite the war, more works had been submitted to the Academy's annual than ever before. As a whole, the exhibition was "fully equal to any preceding one" and "the well-lighted, spacious, and elegant gallery produces a very cheerful feeling." The writer marveled at the longevity of some of the founders of the Academy, such as Charles Cromwell Ingham, who were represented in the exhibition, and reported that the improvement evident in works by some of the younger artists was "in the highest degree gratifying."[155] Similar observations were expressed the following year when the paper declared that the exhibition was the best yet. In fact, the *Tribune* believed that the Academy's 1863 exhibition was proof that the war "has been anything but damaging to the interests of Art." Instead, "the spirit of the times has imparted boldness and vigor" to artists, both young and old. The paper noted that the war had furnished artists with fresh subjects and, unlike the *Herald,* the *Tribune* believed that paintings dealing with the war were well represented in the 1863 exhibition. The writer particularly praised Jervis McEntee's *Virginia* and Louis Lang's *The Soldier's Widow.*[156]

After George Curtis's departure from the *Tribune,* no critic with his articulate and poetic style wrote art reviews for the paper until Clarence Cook joined the staff in 1864. Cook had a temperament that was very different from Curtis's. From 1854 to 1856, he had been the regular art critic for the New York-based *Independent.* His articles and reviews for that weekly newspaper show that he already had an unfavorable opinion of the Academy. The institution did not serve the public as well as it could, he felt, and its exhibitions were selected according to the reputations of the artists rather than the quality of the work. The shows were poorly hung, were not open long enough, and had an admission price that was too high.[157] Cook's review of the 1855 exhibition is typical. There, he made it clear that he would not waste his time "on pictures of which nothing good can be said by artists of whom nothing good will come." Cook preferred paintings that resulted from a close examination of nature. A case in point was Samuel Colman, Jr. (1832–1920) who, according to Cook, showed great promise. If Colman continued "the most careful, minute, and conscientious study of a particular scene in nature . . . with the most laborious exactness, the most literal truth," the critic predicted, that promise would be fulfilled.[158]

In other words, Cook was already showing his preference to the aesthetics of Pre-Raphaelitism,[159] a British art movement founded by John Ruskin that espoused an almost microscopic examination of nature. American artists who were acolytes of the Pre-Raphaelites formed the Society of the Advancement of Truth in Art, which published its own periodical, *The New Path.* Cook was editor of that journal from 1863 to 1864, when he left to become the art critic for the *Tribune,* a position he held for twenty years.[160]

After joining the *Tribune,* Cook maintained his Pre-Raphaelite views, a fact made clear in the first review of a National Academy exhibition that he wrote for the paper; it appeared serially in seven issues of the *Tribune* in 1864. The "only test of Art," Cook stated simply, "is its Truth to nature." Art must be "a presentation of Beauty—not the so-called 'Beauty' of the schools, which is, for the most part mere prettiness or gracefulness—but the supreme Beauty of Nature, whether expressed in landscape, or in human character." Rather than improving upon nature, the idealization of it—and this, Cook reiterated, includes the idealization of the human figure—actually leeches all beauty from it. Ultimately, Cook declared, Beauty cannot be separated from Truth.[161]

Besides maintaining his Pre-Raphaelite pose, Cook also brought his rather precise tastes and sharp tongue to the

Tribune. In this same 1864 review of the Academy's exhibition, he immediately began his attack—John La Farge happened to be his first target. In a long diatribe, Cook called La Farge's *Brenton's Cove, Newport; Fog Blowing In* (location unknown) an almost incomprehensible "muddle" of color that could just as easily have been hung upside down for all the sense it made. For Cook, what it lacked, of course, was Truth—to him, its "color" looked like nothing in nature. This, according to Cook, was the same problem with the work of Jasper Cropsey, whose *Greenwood Lake* (1862; Newington-Cropsey Foundation, Hastings-on-Hudson, New York) was in the exhibition. Cropsey, Cook wrote, "cannot do anything with [color] that is not painful . . . aggressively bad, harsh, raw and discordant," and he wished that the artist could find a way to express himself with something that did not involve the use of color at all.[162]

Cook was not totally negative about the exhibition, however. He managed to find a few artists who lived up to his standards, or at least appeared to be trying to do so. For example, having been encouraged by a friend to examine Worthington Whittredge's *The Old Hunting Ground* (Reynolda House Collection, Winston-Salem, North Carolina), Cook found himself pleasantly surprised. Whittredge, Cook admitted, was an artist whose work he normally ignored, but *The Old Hunting Ground* suggested that Whittredge had changed his ways. The artist, it seemed, was actually turning to Nature to seek "her Truth and Beauty" as he strove "with all his might to interpret her aright to men."[163] Likewise, two paintings by Thomas Farrar in the exhibition—*A Buckwheat Field on Thomas Cole's Farm* (fig. 42) and *The Catskills from the Village* (location unknown)—greatly pleased Cook, and for the same reasons. "These two pictures," he wrote of Farrar's landscapes,

"are made forever precious and valuable by the faithful record of the truth of Nature that is in every square inch of them." Cook went further: he declared that, because of their fidelity to nature, "the exhibition of these two pictures marks an era in the history of American Art. . . . "[164]

Cook began his serialized review of the Academy's 1865 exhibition by focusing on portraiture which, he said, is usually "so little cared for by the general public." Nevertheless, he especially liked Thomas Hicks's portrait of the New York businessman Pelatiah Perit, done for the Seaman's Savings Bank, as a good example of Hicks's talents as a draftsman and of his good sense when choosing accessories. On the other hand, he derided Daniel Huntington's portraits, which, he thought, given Huntington's long years of experience, should display a greater variety of technique. After admitting that he was "sometimes accused of an unnecessary hostility to the Academy," Cook blamed this on the Academy itself, which, he felt, encouraged sameness and mediocrity.[165] His favorite painting in the exhibition, however, was a group portrait, Eastman Johnson's *Christmas Time (The Blodgett Family)* (see fig. 15). In fact, Cook wrote that if the Academy's building was burning, this was the painting he would save, and he gushed over it as he seldom did over any work of art:

> *We have long held this name in great respect, as our readers ought to know, but we did not know, till now, how much we have in him to be proud of. This beautiful picture will, we are sure, win so many hearts, that the place of first painter of children in the country, will be his, before the exhibition closes, by acclamation.[166]*

Cook devoted the second installment of his 1865 review to a long discussion of the work of women artists, a rarity in the

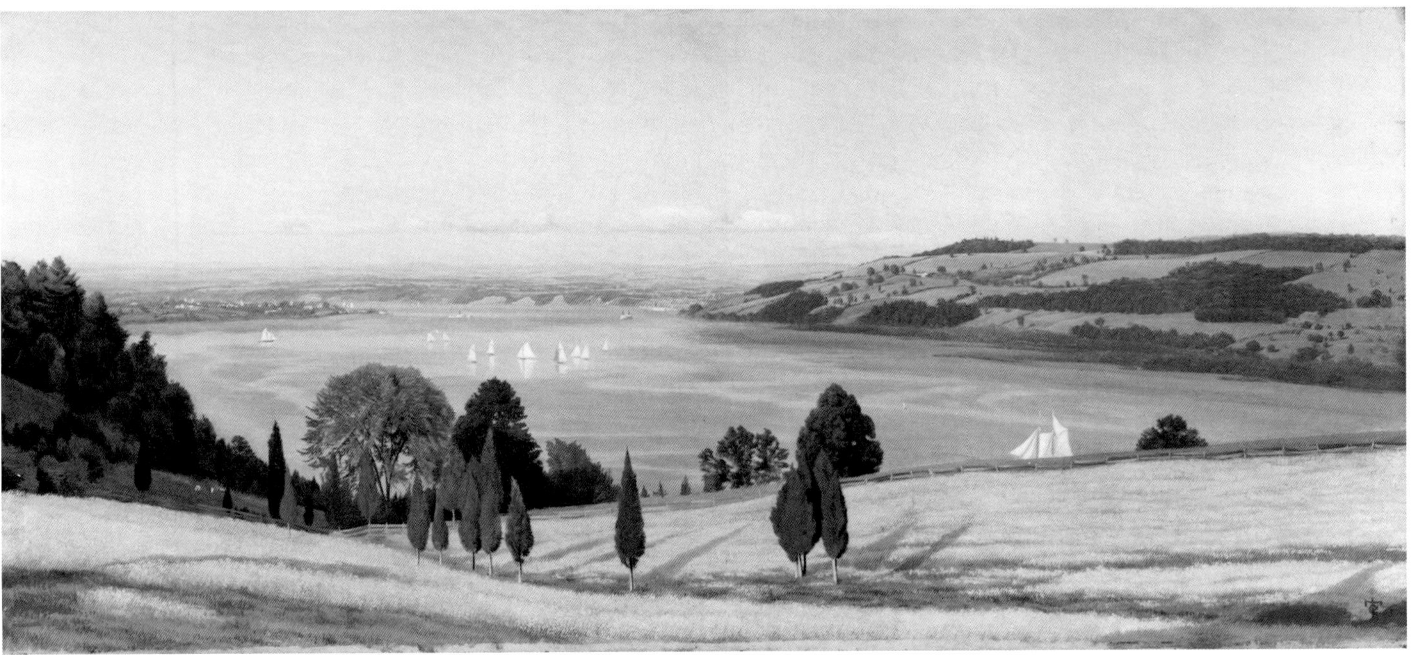

Fig. 42 Thomas Farrar, *A Buckwheat Field on Thomas Cole's Farm*, 1863, oil on canvas, 11¾ x 25¼, Museum of Fine Arts, Boston, Gift of Maxim Karolik for the M. and M. Karolik Collection of American Paintings, 1815–1865 (National Academy of Design, 39th Annual Exhibition, 1864, no. 114)

art criticism of the time. He applauded the progress women had made in the field during the previous ten years and predicted that their improvement would continue. The Academy's 1865 annual exhibition was the perfect time to discuss women artists, he wrote, because their representation that year was exceptional in both quantity and quality. While he gave none of the women unqualified praise—that would have been rare for Cook in any case—he focused his analysis on five artists, three painters and two sculptors: Juliana Oakley, Adelaide E. Rose, Sarah W. Wenzler, Harriet Hosmer, and Anne Whitney. Oakley, he believed, showed more improvement than did any other artist in the show, and he praised the simplicity and honesty of her still-lifes and studies of nature. He favorably compared Rose's flower paintings with those of John La Farge; and he admired the meticulousness that made Wenzler's grapes look "painfully good." While he thought that Hosmer's *Puck* (see no. 34) was not much more than a "pretty toy" and had little to do with Shakespeare, he felt that it could stand its own against any other sculpture in the room. On the other hand, Whitney's *Africa*, which she later destroyed, rose above the confectionery quality of much contemporary sculpture, including Hosmer's, and Cook admired the "vastness of the theme" and the "imaginative treatment" of the allegorical figure.[167]

Since the terminus date of this essay is 1865, we must leave Cook here, at the beginning of his affiliation with the *New York Tribune*. It should be noted, however, that he would serve as the *Tribune's* art critic until 1883, producing hundreds of articles on American and European art, including many more reviews of the National Academy's exhibitions.

The Literary World (1847–1853)

Except for a brief period in 1847–48 when Charles Fenno Hoffman was its editor, the weekly *Literary World* was edited and published by Evert A. Duyckinck (1816–1878) with the assistance, until 1857, of his brother George (1823–1863).[168] The primary function of the magazine was the publication of book reviews, but it also featured departments on the fine arts, drama, and music. Although many of its contributors are unknown, the journalist and historian Henry T. Tuckerman (1813–1871) wrote at least some of its art criticism.[169] Evidently, the Duyckincks were great admirers of Tuckerman—they called him one of the few "thoroughbred men" in the literary world of the 1840s.[170] Not surprisingly, they entrusted him with writing the art reviews for their journal.

Tuckerman was born in Boston and educated at Harvard. He made a number of trips to Europe, notably to Italy. The first of these was in 1833–34 and was the inspiration for his *Italian Sketchbook*, published in 1835.[171] In 1843, he served briefly as editor of the *Boston Miscellany of Literature and Fashion* while simultaneously contributing articles to many of the major periodicals of the day. These included the *New-England Magazine, The North American Review, Graham's Magazine, Godey's Lady's Book, The Southern Literary Mes-senger, The Democratic Review, The Southern Quarterly Review, Columbian's Lady's and Gentleman's Magazine, The American Whig Review,* and *The Union Magazine.*[172] By the time Tuckerman moved from Boston to New York in 1845, he was acquainted with most of the major American journalists of the day. He also had met many American artists, both here and abroad, and in 1847, his *Artist Life or Sketches of American Painters* was published. (He expanded it into *Book of the Artists* in 1867, and that is the work for which he is best remembered today).[173] By the late 1840s, he was well equipped to write art reviews for the Duyckincks—or for anyone else.

In the *Literary World's* first year—1847—it published a detailed, serial review of the Academy's exhibition that ran for nine issues.[174] It seems likely that it was written by Tuckerman. Early in the article, the author stated his philosophy about criticism and its effect on artists:

> *We disclaim all intention to wrong any man who figures in the catalogue. From judicious observation, when called for, an artist has to fear nothing, and may profit much; but it should ever be remembered that the professional merit must be humble indeed which does not render the possessor superior to his self-constituted judge, who is himself not an artist.*[175]

Tuckerman was particularly impressed with the portraits of Charles Loring Elliott and Charles Cromwell Ingham, the genre paintings of William Sidney Mount, and the landscapes of Asher Brown Durand and Thomas Cole. Evidently, he was no slave to the traditional hierarchy of artistic subject matter for he believed superior paintings to be those "that are low in tone, pure and simple in composition, and elevated in sentiment." His example of what painting should *not* be was Peter F. Rothermel's *Cortés Burning His Ships before Marching on Mexico* (1846; destroyed), which he vilified in two separate articles. This is "the very worst school of art," he said, "and is hardly equal to the signs and banners that are every day hung out to dry." He then launched into a long discussion of artists who produce flashy works just to get attention in exhibitions. He used Rothermel's painting to introduce a discussion of the components of a successful history painting, which, he stated, depends upon the careful selection of a story worth telling and the telling of it worthily.[176]

This same review featured an unusually lengthy discussion of sculpture. In fact, one entire article in the series was devoted to the topic, which, the author acknowledged, rarely received equal attention with painting in the exhibitions. He granted that this was partially due to the fact that, so far, the progress of sculpture in the United States had rested in the hands of only a few competent artists. He heralded the emergence of Hiram Powers and the return of Henry Kirke Brown from Europe as signs that sculpture was beginning to come into its own and that it had great promise.[177]

This long series of long articles ended gracefully with the following comment:

The following year, 1848, Tuckerman reiterated some of the same points made in the 1847 review. Genre and landscapes were generally praised, history painting was not. Singled out for particular abuse that year was William Powell's *Columbus Before the Council of Salamanca* (location unknown), which "possesses few of the requisites of a first class work of Art."[179] Again, Tuckerman gave what attention he could to the sculpture in the exhibition, although, as he pointed out, the show was "lamentably deficient" in it.

Some rather sophisticated theories about art begin the *Literary World's* review of the 1850 Academy, suggesting again that Tuckerman may have been the author.[180] That year, two whole articles were devoted to the landscape paintings at the Academy, and it was these that received most of what praise was given. The writer began his lengthy review with a summary of his own theories on the special powers of landscape paintings that can give the viewer a different—and often more satisfying—experience from looking at the actual landscape. Such paintings, the critic wrote, must have more to them than the simple transcription of nature; they must reflect the "creative energy" of the artist. If it does possess these qualities, the painting will have a visual power that "goes beyond the text which nature lends it in its subject." Thus the viewer will find "his highest satisfaction in the recognition, not of the life-like features and startling imitation of nature, but of the embodied thoughts and feelings of which they are only the vehicles and accessories."[181]

Like so many nineteenth-century literary journals, the *Literary World* had a devoted following, but a circulation too low to make it profitable. While periodicals such as *Harper's New Monthly Magazine* and *Putnam's* were growing more popular, the *Literary World* succumbed to financial trouble in 1853.

The Albion (1822–1875)

The *Albion* was founded in New York in 1822 by John Sherren Bartlett (1790–1863), a native of England who had previously practiced journalism in Boston before moving to New York. His weekly journal was one of a group of eclectic periodicals dating from the first half of the nineteenth century that specialized in digesting articles from British journals; it was noted for its conservatism.[182] Bartlett's main interest appears to have been politics, and the magazine did not really cover art in any depth until he relinquished the editorship in 1848. Major evidence of this was the impressive amount of attention the magazine was giving to the annual exhibitions of the National Academy of Design within a year

of Bartlett's departure. The Academy's annual, the *Albion* declared, was "*the* annual exhibition in the city."[183]

The magazine's British roots undoubtedly affected its view of the Academy's exhibitions, and its writers often attempted to place the shows into an international context. Reporting on the Academy's annual of 1849, for example, the *Albion* stated:

In the 1849 Academy show, the writer found the number of portraits wearisome. Having made that statement, however, he, like many of his contemporaries, went on to praise individual works in the field. He particularly liked Henry Peters Gray's *Portrait of a Lady in Italian Costume* (location unknown), and he identified the best painting in the entire exhibition as being Charles Loring Elliott's *Portrait of an Artist* (1849; National Gallery of Art, Washington, D.C.).[185] Durand's *Kindred Spirits*—which combines portraiture with landscape, genre, and history painting—was a "graceful and appropriate compliment to the poet and the painter, and a happy testimony to the kindly feeling subsisting between them." In the area of pure landscape, he declared Frederic Church's *West Rock, New Haven* (1849; New Britain Museum of American Art, New Britain, Connecticut) "a masterpiece."[186]

While the *Albion's* writer or writers were just as likely to admire portraits or genre images as they were landscapes, the magazine's overall conservatism is reflected in its preference for historical works. In 1851, for example, the *Albion* found "great merit" in Peter Rothermel's *Murray's Defence of Toleration* (location unknown). The following year it praised Edwin White's *The Requiem of De Soto* (location unknown) for its "marked ability" and gave noteworthy attention to Jasper Cropsey's *The Spirit of War* and *The Spirit of Peace* (see nos. 19 and 20). While decrying the "decided lack of pictures of this class in the collection," the journal called its readers' attention to Asher Brown Durand's *God's Judgment Upon Gog* (fig. 43). This painting, the critic said, deserves "earnest study" because of its place in the "higher order" of art.[187] Given this preference, it follows that the *Albion* would not appreciate the efforts of artists such as the Pre-Raphaelites, who, the journal complained, were so literal in their interpretations of nature that their work was vulgar.[188]

Ultimately, the *Albion* despaired of the Academy's ability to improve American art and reiterated its earlier summation that, so far, the only area in which the Americans excelled was sculpture. In 1855, the *Albion* summarized the Academy's annual thus:

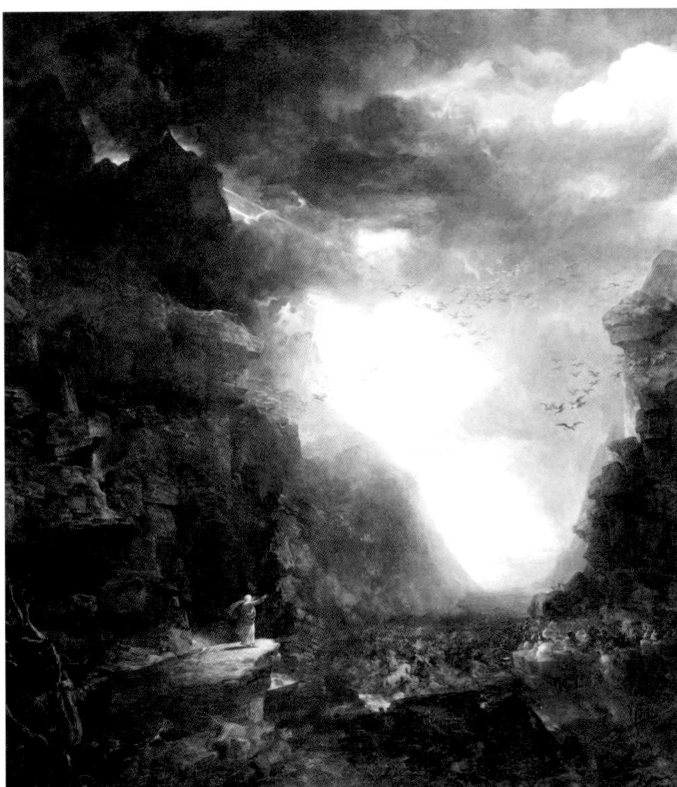

Fig. 43 Asher Brown Durand, *God's Judgment upon Gog*, c. 1851–52, oil on canvas, 60¾ x 50½, The Chrysler Museum, Norfolk, Virginia, gift of Walter P. Chrysler, Jr. (National Academy of Design, 27th Annual Exhibition, 1852, no. 139)

him; we shall all of us talk connoisseurship, during a few weeks, very knowingly; and in the end the season will pass away, leaving the American School of Painting just where it was—that is to say, much below its School of Sculpture, and greatly below the place that we should wish to see it occupy.[189]

The New-York Times (1851–present)

The *New-York Times* was founded in 1851 with Henry J. Raymond as editor and George Jones as business manager.[190] The two men had met a decade earlier when they worked for the *Tribune,* and they now wanted to establish a paper that was more conservative, less eccentric, and more devoted to pure news than was their former employer. The idea paid off. The *Times* was an immediate success and by the time of the Civil War, its circulation equaled that of Greeley's powerful paper.[191]

One of the first notable reviews of the National Academy's annual exhibitions to be published by the *Times* appeared in 1854. That year, the paper reported, the National Academy had decided to open its exhibition earlier than usual because of the chance that the building at 633 Broadway in which it was being held would be razed to make way for a new music hall.[192] A number of the city's leading artists were caught off guard and, having not yet finished works that they had hoped to send to the exhibition, were not represented in it.[193] Despite

this, the *Times* critic found pleasure in Asher Brown's Durand's *Strawberrying* (1854; location unknown), which he called a "gem—a tranquil, beautiful gem—on which we may gaze for an hour without winking." This, and William Sidney Mount's *Coming to the Point* (see no. 22), were the writer's obvious favorites, undoubtedly due to their nationalistic appeal. In fact, the latter was described by the *Times* as "peculiarly National and characteristic. The incident is American, the scene American, and the faces American—American of the most obvious type."[194]

The following year, the exhibition did not fare as well in the eyes of the *Times.* Plans for the new building were still unrealized, and the show was being staged in the former quarters of the Düsseldorf Gallery, "the crowded garret of Dr. Chapin's Church," at 548 Broadway. The *Times* bemoaned the fact that so few works were in the exhibition (278) and that the Academy's school had been forced to close due to lack of space and had not yet reopened. Frustrated, the newspaper simply reported that the exhibition, crammed into one large room and one small one, showed a "depressing sameness," and left it at that.[195]

The *Times* review of the 1856 exhibition is different in style and tone from those of previous years. It is signed "C. C.," and given the thoughtfulness—and extremely caustic nature—of the writing, it seems very likely that the author was Clarence Cook, who, as we have seen, wrote his last article as critic for the *Independent* that same year.[196] The following passage from the *Times* review is typical of Cook's attitude toward the Academy, already expressed at the *Independent* and soon to be repeated at the *Tribune:*

Let us take this "National Academy of Design"—so called, every constituent word of whose title is a misnomer—let us look at its insufficiency, its weakness, its want of breadth, its want of national, of American feeling—then let us look at its languishing state internally, look at the slack support by the people; at the indifference of the press, of society to it, and see if these facts have not a correlation, if they do not mean something very clear and pertinent.[197]

According to Cook, the Academy blamed public apathy for these problems, but he felt that the American people were perfectly capable of appreciating "free, noble, and individual" works by artists such as Washington Allston, Thomas Cole, Thomas Crawford, and Henry Kirke Brown. Instead, it is the fault of those artists who, with the encouragement of the Academy, "give us Shakespeare, and Byron, and Europe and the Sandwich Islands, till we are sick and sick—men whom America does not touch nor move." Artists must put something of "America, and the thought of America" into their paintings and sculptures, Cook preached, if they expect the public to respond.[198] As a case in point, he devoted almost one entire article in his serialized review to Asher Brown Durand, who, he says, failed to capture the essence and the "soul" of nature, despite his attention to detail. Hope for an honest and an "American" art, Cook believed, was in the hands of younger artists such as Samuel Colman, Aaron Draper Shattuck, James Suydam, and Jasper Cropsey.[199]

The following year, Cook confirmed that these and other younger artists had survived their "candidacy" and ascended "to a stable rank." The first artist to get the critic's attention in 1857 was Frederic Church. Cook compared Church's South American landscapes, three of which where at the Academy that year, to the works of J. M. W. Turner, noting that Church was in no way inferior to Turner. According to Cook, Church "handles the grandest effects of nature as lightly as the least" and paints "what he sees, and not what he thinks he ought to see, or imagines that he has seen, or fancies that somebody else will expect to see . . . ." Cook especially admired Church's "point of view," recalling the success of the artist's *Niagara*. For that painting, Church carefully selected his point of view, which, as in the work of the Pre-Raphaelites, gives a truthful view of the scene, "not the truth of a photograph, but pure, pictorial truth—truth, that is, to the *perceptions of a human being*." Church used this device to good effect again, Cook notes, in his *Andes of Equador* (1855; Reynolda House, Museum of American Art, Winston-Salem, North Carolina) and *View on the Magdalena River* (fig. 44), both in the 1857 exhibition. Cook found the latter to be "exquisite" and "one of

the freshest, and sweetest, and most seducing pictures of the exhibition."[200]

The truthfulness of Church's work was contrasted by Cook to the paintings of Thomas Rossiter, which, to Cook, were melodramatic, unimaginative, and dishonest. Nine of these were in the 1857 exhibition, and Cook was especially critical of *Primitive Life* (location unknown) for its falseness ("[W]here did he ever see such a moon in such a sky?") and *The Wise and Foolish Virgins* (location unknown), which seemed to have nothing to do with the parable that it is supposed to illustrate. Rossiter came under fire again later in the same review, as did Emanuel Leutze. Both artists, as far as Cook was concerned, gave inappropriate or inaccurate interpretations to historical and literary subjects. For example, the accessories in Leutze's *Rose of Alhambra* (location unknown) made no sense to Cook, and Rossiter's *Giorgione and His Friends Going to the Lido* (location unknown) was hardly suggestive of Giorgione's actual life or character. Both paintings fell short of the standard set, again, by J. M. W. Turner in such paintings as his *Temeraire*. (1838; National Gallery, London).[201]

Of the figural works in the exhibition, Cook preferred the paintings of William Morris Hunt, especially that artist's *La Bouquetière* (*The Violet Girl*) (fig. 45) and of John J. Ehninger, notably his *The Foray* (location unknown). Neither painting,

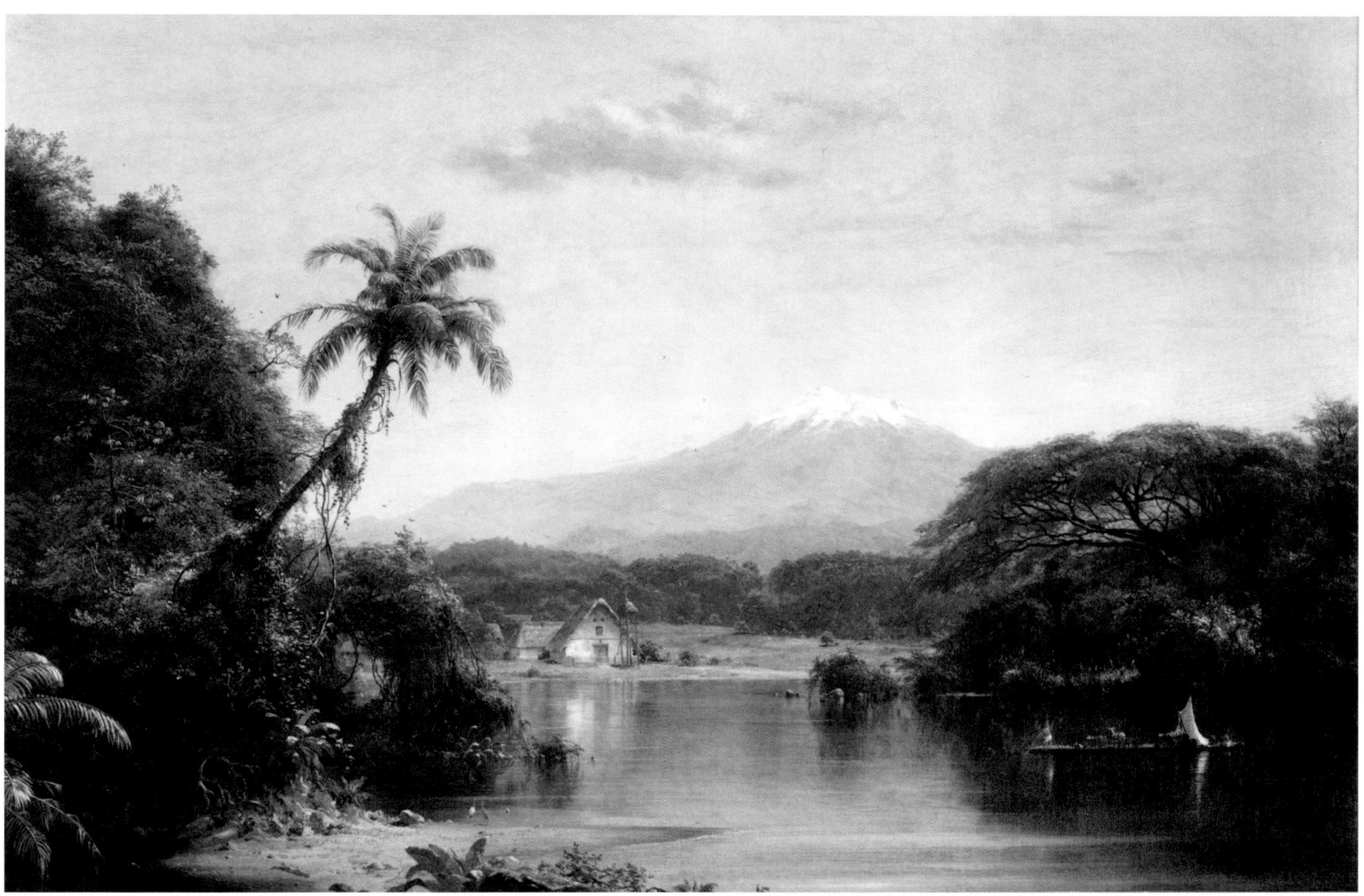

Fig. 44 Frederic Edwin Church, *View on the Magdalena River,* 1857, oil on canvas, 24 x 36, The Manoogian Collection (National Academy of Design, 32nd Annual Exhibition, 1857, no. 522)

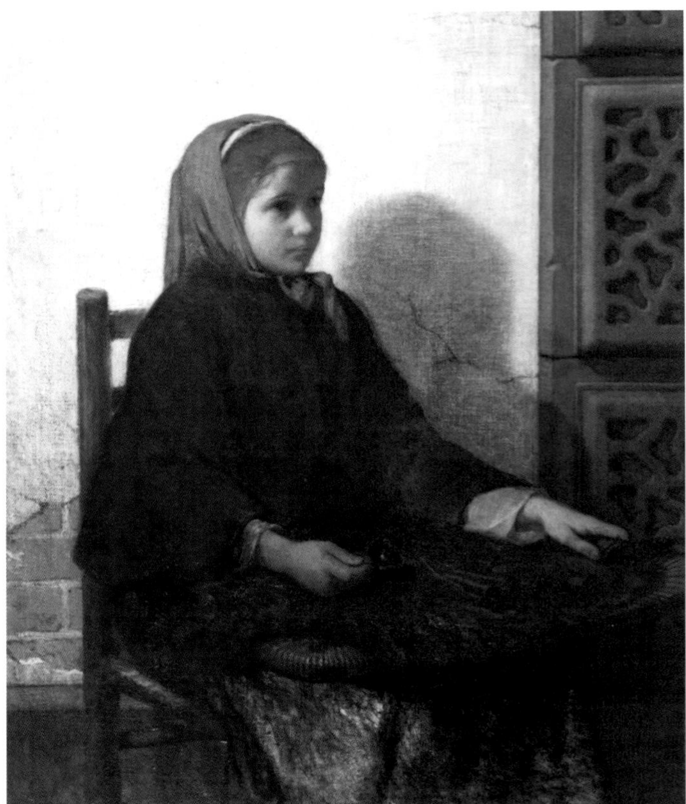

Fig. 45 William Morris Hunt, *La Bouquetière (The Violet Girl)*, 1856, oil on canvas, 32¼ x 39⅝, Museum of Art, Rhode Island School of Design, Gift of Mrs. S. Foster Damon (National Academy of Design, 32nd Annual Exhibition, 1857, no. 88)

Cook wrote, pretends to be more than it is. He found the emotion and attitude of the figures to be honest and true to reality. This, Cook believed, came from the artists' understanding of their subject, "clearness of conception," and simplicity of treatment.[202] He praised the same characteristics when they appeared in the landscapes of John F. Kensett, his *Coast Scene* (location unknown), for example; William Hart, especially his *October Afternoon on the Esopus* (location unknown); and William J. Stillman, notably his *Nightfall in the Wilderness* (location unknown).[203]

The attack on the Academy continued in the *Times* in 1858, when the paper's critic—probably still Cook—dismissed the entire collection of 636 works in the Academy's exhibition as unworthy, called the galleries shabby, and mocked the exhibition's opening reception. This so-called "private viewing," he wrote, was anything but that; instead, it was a "rout" and a "jam."[204] Likewise, the following year, the Academy's decision to hold the exhibition in rooms on Tenth Street was compared with putting "the Goddess of Beauty in a stye." The artists' "fecundity," which, according to Cook, was "rather out of proportion to their intellectual development," came under fire: the exhibition contained a record 815 works, most of which were not worth mentioning. One of the few exceptions was Church's *Twilight—A Sketch* (1858; Olana State Historic Site, Hudson, New York), which was praised for its "rare and beautiful atmosphere" and "truths of color."[205] Landscapes continued to be about the only kind of art that the *Times* praised. In

1861, for example, it was Sanford Gifford's *A Twilight in the Catskills* (location unknown) that received most attention, praised for the truthfulness of its "Golden haze, aerial sheen, rich mists and dreams of 'cloud-land, gorgeous-land.'"[206]

In 1862 and 1863, the format of the *Times*'s reviews of the Academy's annuals returned to the older method of listing many works in the exhibition with a sentence or two of commentary attached. The resulting reviews were less cogent—and less caustic—than those in the *Times* in the preceding years. This is almost certainly an indication that Cook was no longer writing art reviews for the paper.

The Crayon (1855–1861)

As noted elsewhere in this catalogue, the *Crayon* (fig. 46) was founded in 1855 by John Durand, son of painter Asher Brown Durand, and William J. Stillman, an artist and writer, and these men were responsible for most if not all of its articles on art.[207] In one of the magazine's early reviews of the National Academy's annual exhibitions, its criteria for criticism were clarified. "The only standard we are conscious of having raised, by which to measure the works in the exhibition," it was noted, "is that of *purpose*. We have demanded only, that the work should have some final object beyond picture making."[208] In other words, landscape painting was expected to fulfill the same traditional purpose of art—to

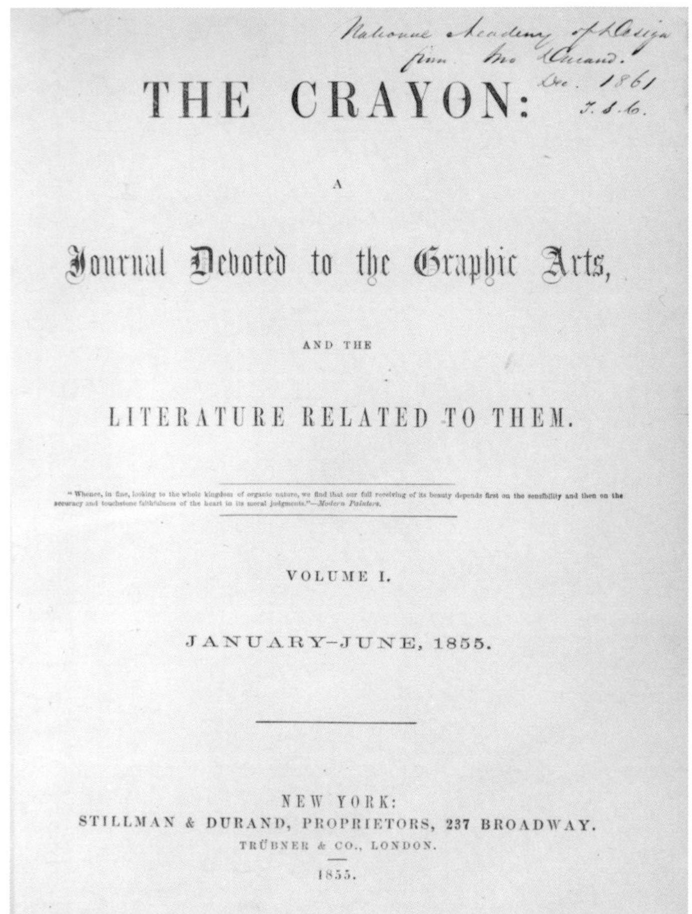

Fig. 46 Title page, *The Crayon*, vol. 1, January–June, 1855, Archives, National Academy of Design, New York

teach and inspire—as the greatest historical and religious works. Thus would landscape be raised to the same lofty levels as those branches of artistic subject matter.

John Durand's and Stillman's affiliations, professional and otherwise, predicted a special sensibility to landscape painting and related issues. One of their first reviews of an Academy exhibition takes up the discussion of landscape vs. historical paintings.[209] Both men admired the detailed style of the Pre-Raphaelites, whose cause was supported by the great British critic and artist John Ruskin. This preference is readily apparent in the *Crayon's* reviews of the National Academy's annual exhibitions. The first of these was serialized in the magazine's first volume, and it set the tone for the reviews that followed. It becomes immediately apparent that landscape will be the star in the journal's reviews. In 1855, for example, after registering the usual complaint about the number of portraits in that year's exhibition, the *Crayon* went on to praise the landscapes there. Asher Brown Durand's *In the Woods* (fig. 47) was one of the most popular attractions of the exhibition, and the painting was discussed in several issues that year. In fact, one article was devoted almost exclusively to it. In its depiction of pure wilderness, the *Crayon* noted, *In the Woods* was "something new in Landscape art," prompting the writer to declare that it "satisfies us more entirely than any landscape he has ever painted."[210] Whether the author of these words was Stillman or John Durand, this opinion is in keeping with their admiration of the Pre-Raphaelites, a fact made clear by a direct reference to the similarity of *In the Woods* to the work of the Pre-Raphaelites.[211] This led the writer to credit American landscape painters with "an honesty of purpose and, generally, a straight-forwardness which is an excellent feeling to found study on."[212]

These interests and concerns were stated even more explicitly in the *Crayon's* Academy reviews in the following year, 1856. Landscape "is the only genuine Art we possess as yet," the magazine stated. But then the writer complained that, with a few minor exceptions, "there is no evidence of a determined effort to realize a perfect truth of Nature," such as can be found in the work of John Ruskin, an example of which was actually—and somewhat unusually—included in the Academy's exhibition that year.[213] Using Ruskin's work—evidently, it was a drawing—as a case in point, the journal clarified its position: the drawing was not "high Art" and there was nothing in it "that is more profound than simple truth"; furthermore, it was no more detailed than a photograph, perhaps even less so. But a photographer would only know the *location* of the rock; the artist "understands the nature of the stone, the laws of its formation, the characteristics of the plants which hold their existence in its crevices. . . ." This, the writer concluded, is "the secret of the value of that refinement of study which is with us known as pre-Raphaelitism. . . ."[214]

When the *Crayon* turned its attention to portraiture, as it did in its review of the Academy's 1857 exhibition, it looked for the same level of detail and truth to nature that it did in landscape. Interestingly, among its favorite portraits that year were

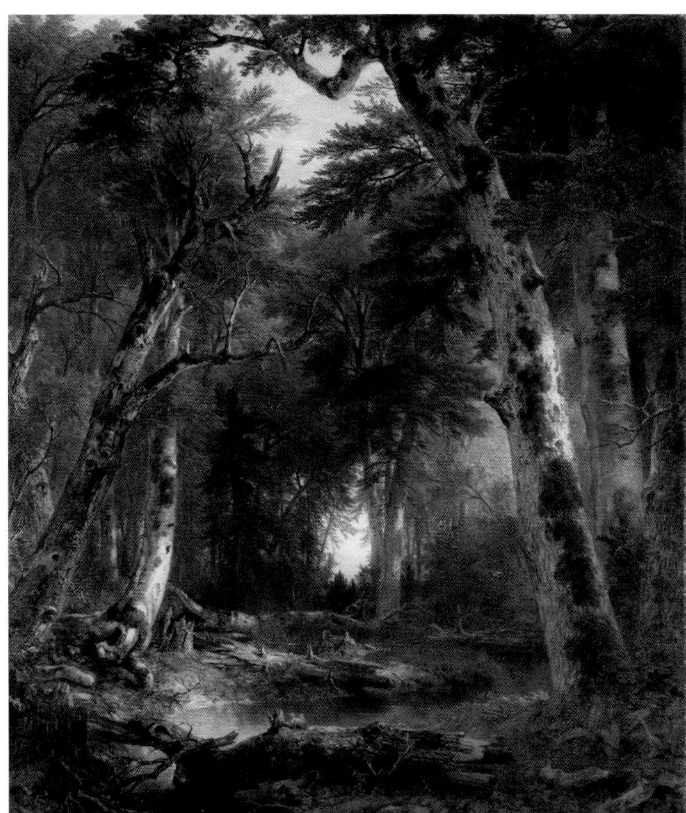

Fig. 47 Asher Brown Durand, *In the Woods,* 1855, oil on canvas, 60½ x 49, The Metropolitan Museum of Art, Gift in memory of Jonathan Sturges by his children, 1895 (National Academy of Design, 30th Annual Exhibition, 1855, no. 113)

six by Samuel W. Rowse, all of which were typical of him in that they were drawings. Their style was forceful but delicate, the *Crayon* noted, so that "we do not *see* a single feature defined, yet we *feel* that forms are adequately expressed." Works such as these, the writer concluded, "teach us what Art is."[215]

In 1858, the *Crayon* devoted the first of its two articles on the Academy's exhibition to landscape painting, pointing out that the largest number of works in the show were in this category. Judiciously passing over the paintings of Asher Brown Durand, the writer—probably Durand's son—gave his first attention to the paintings of John Kensett, whose appeal to the public, he said, was growing. Kensett's paintings, eight of which were in the exhibition, were thought admirable "for refinement of taste, treatment of distances, rendering of atmospheric effect, and a happy expression of the broad light of day and of a specific time of day." He then praised James and William Hart, Sanford Gifford, and Richard W. Hubbard, and called George Boughton's *Winter Twilight* (see no. 25), which was a general favorite that year, one of the best works in the show.[216] Before turning to a summary discussion of portraiture and figure painting, the writer concluded his discussion of landscape by stating that it was the only category of artistic subject matter that was "actively encouraged by the community." This, he explained, was a natural outgrowth of "the peculiar aspects of American scenery" and the general appreciation that Americans had for it.[217]

During the *Crayon's* last several years, the Academy's exhibitions became so large, with close to six hundred works in each exhibition, that the magazine was somewhat overwhelmed. For the thirty-fourth annual exhibition in 1859, the *Crayon* simply listed artists and titles in its first review, with brief commentary for each.[218] In a second article that year, however, the writer waxed more philosophical, beginning his discussion of specific works with some thoughts on art and art exhibitions. The latter, he said, were less a display of the merits of particular works and more about "the nature of public taste, or rather the character of artistic thought which the public chooses to manifest through its encouragement of Art."[219] By way of explanation, he stated that artists "must live like other people" and could not always paint what they wanted to paint. They had constantly to consider what would sell. Similarly, the writer felt that art criticism was useless unless it contextualized art by considering the tastes and concerns of the community in which it was produced. This discussion continued through several long paragraphs in which the author outlined the criteria of art criticism. "Criticism took its rise in admiration," he declared, "it originated with *lovers* of Art, not *judges;* it aimed to quicken the perceptions of beauty, not to set forth defects." It is a work of art's success or failure at depicting *beauty*—"the true end of Art"—that finally must be judged to determine its value. He felt that landscape painting revealed beauty in a more subtle way, one that is hard to avoid or criticize because it is such a part of man's spirit. Figure painting he found useful, too, and pointed out that it could afford "an opportunity to illustrate principles of Art with more precision." The writer's case in point was Eastman Johnson's *Negro Life at the South* (see no. 26), on which he lavished high praise. His admiration stemmed from the painting's ability to convey beauty, which, in this case, was not found in the "forms and objects" but in the painting's "sentiment . . . for imitation and expression are vitalized by conveying to our mind the enjoyment of human beings in new and vivid aspects."[220]

In 1860, the *Crayon* was again impressed with the number of works in the Academy's exhibition—668 works by 265 artists—and resorted to mentioning most of them only briefly. Its favorite landscape that year was Albert Bierstadt's *Base of the Rocky Mountains, Laramie Peak* (location unknown), which it described as "a faithful artistic transcript of a beautiful and peculiar aspect of natural scenery." Its preferred figure paintings were Emanuel Leutze's *Princess Elizabeth in the Tower* (1860; New York Public Library) and Eastman Johnson's *Marguerite* (location unknown).[221] The following year, just months before its demise, the *Crayon* published its last Academy review. Again, the writer preferred landscapes, such as Sanford Gifford's *Twilight in the Catskills* and William Trost Richards's *In the Valley of the Wyoming* (location unknown), and figural works, such as three by Eastman Johnson and Frank Howland's *Gems for the Market* (location unknown). But he was confounded by the color and composition of the work of William Page. Page's paintings

were "based upon views of art so entirely different from our own" that he admitted that he could not comprehend the artist's style. The review ended on an optimistic note, however, with urgings that the reader visit the exhibition often and "congratulate himself that Art remains to place before the eye symbols of time, place and circumstance more consoling and more harmonious with true progress than the abortive tests of politics and commerce."[222]

The *Crayon*, this country's first true art magazine, ceased publication in July, 1861, a victim of the Civil War.

THE FORTIETH ANNUAL EXHIBITION: 1865

In 1860, following a decade of peregrination and debate, the National Academy took positive steps toward erecting a permanent headquarters for itself. In that year, it purchased land at the corner of Twenty-third Street and Fourth Avenue in New York from William Niblo and, three years later, broke ground for its new building. The structure (fig. 48), designed in a Venetian Gothic Revival style by Peter Bonnat Wight

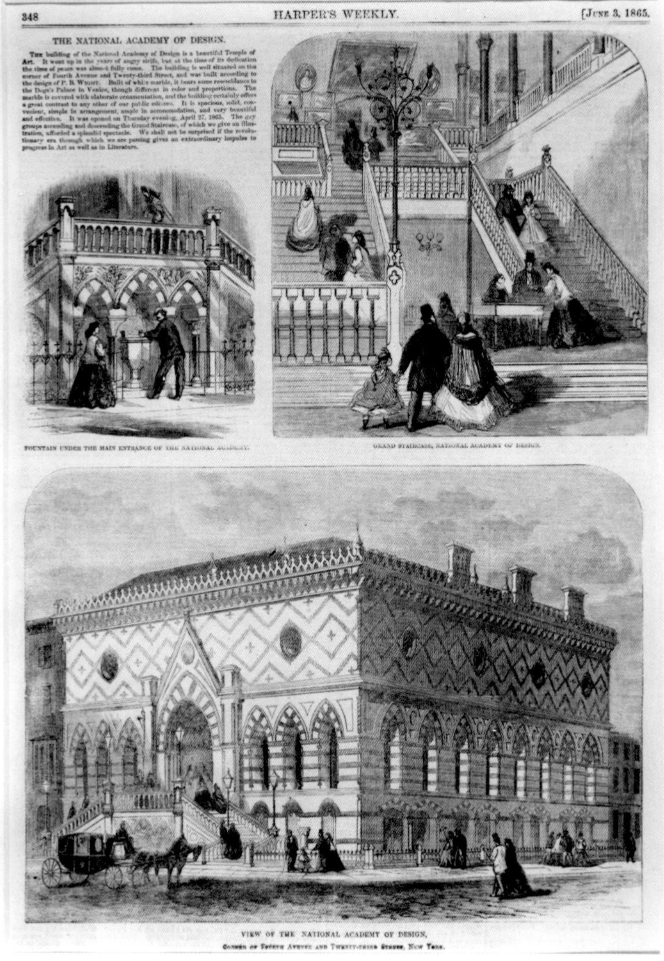

Fig. 48 "View of the National Academy of Design," *Harper's Weekly* (June 3, 1865), Archives, National Academy of Design. Designed by Peter B. Wight, the Academy's building was begun in 1863 and opened to the public in 1865. It stood at the corner of Twenty-third Street and Fourth Avenue in New York City until it was razed in 1900. The site is now occupied by the Metropolitan Life Insurance Building.

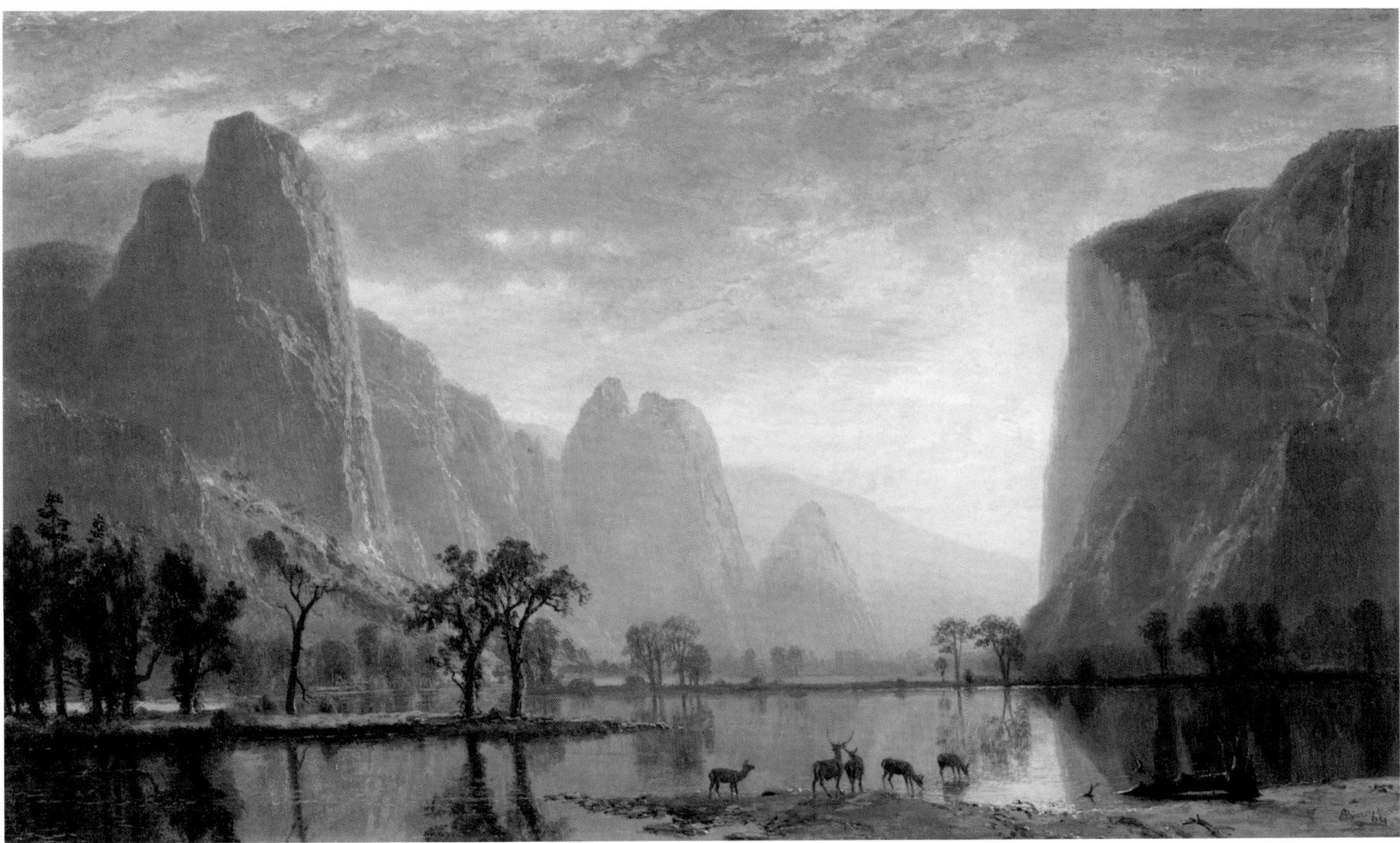

Fig. 49 Albert Bierstadt, *Valley of the Yosemite,* oil on paperboard, Museum of Fine Arts, Boston, Gift of Martha C. Karolik for the M. M. Karolik Collection of American Paintings, 1815–1865 (Replica of a painting shown at the National Academy of Design, 40th Annual Exhibition, 1865, no. 436.)

(1838–1925), was opened to the public for the Academy's fortieth annual exhibition on April 27, 1865.[223] The event, which was covered in detail by the press, came just days after the end of the Civil War and the assassination of President Lincoln, a fact not lost on most journalists. A writer for *Harper's,* for example, saw the opening of the Academy's new building as indication of "the soft dawn of returning peace."[224] Whatever its perceived symbolic links to the political situation in this country, the event certainly marked a turning point in the Academy's history—and, in a sense, in the history of American art in general.

Because the 1865 exhibition had a new and exciting location, some critics gave it special attention. The *New York Leader,* for example, had at least three different authors write about the exhibition. The first of these was George Arnold (1834–1865). Arnold was a native New Yorker and had studied there in his youth to be a portrait painter. He abandoned that career in favor of a literary one, however, and his short stories, poems, biographical sketches, and art criticisms appeared in *Vanity Fair* and the *Leader,* among other publications.[225] Arnold wrote two articles in which he discussed the Academy's exhibition of 1864.[226] These articles, and those he wrote in 1865, were rather typical of the time.[227]

Articles on art written before the 1870s that can definitely be attributed to women writers are very rare. This makes several other reviews that appeared in the *New York Leader* in 1865 of particular interest. One of these, published in two parts, was identified in its title as being by a woman, and was written under the pseudonym "Esperance." Evidently in response to her, a Cara Montane—and this name is probably a pseudonym—submitted "Another Woman's View of the New Academy of Design" to the *Leader.* While neither woman strictly limited her discussion to a single artist or subject, both showed a propensity for works by or about women. Esperance, for example, joined Clarence Cook, cited above, in praising Anne Whitney's sculpture *Africa,* an allegorical representation of that continent in female form. The sculpture "not only attracts attention," she wrote, "it rivets the astonished gaze." For her, the other most admirable sculpture in the show was also by a woman, Harriet Hosmer's *Puck* (see no. 34). That sculpture, the critic stated, was "delightful" and Hosmer "a faithful, a conscientious, and a brilliant and successful artist. . . ."[228]

In actuality, this brand of praise was unusual for Esperance. The other article she wrote for the *Leader* that year—in which she discussed the Academy's building and the paintings on view—was almost completely negative. "The inauguration of a new building devoted to their interests," she wrote, "has not stimulated the artists of New York to a transcendant effort." She acknowledged that Bierstadt's *Looking Down Yosemite Valley* (see fig. 49) was receiving more attention than any other work in the exhibition, but she did not

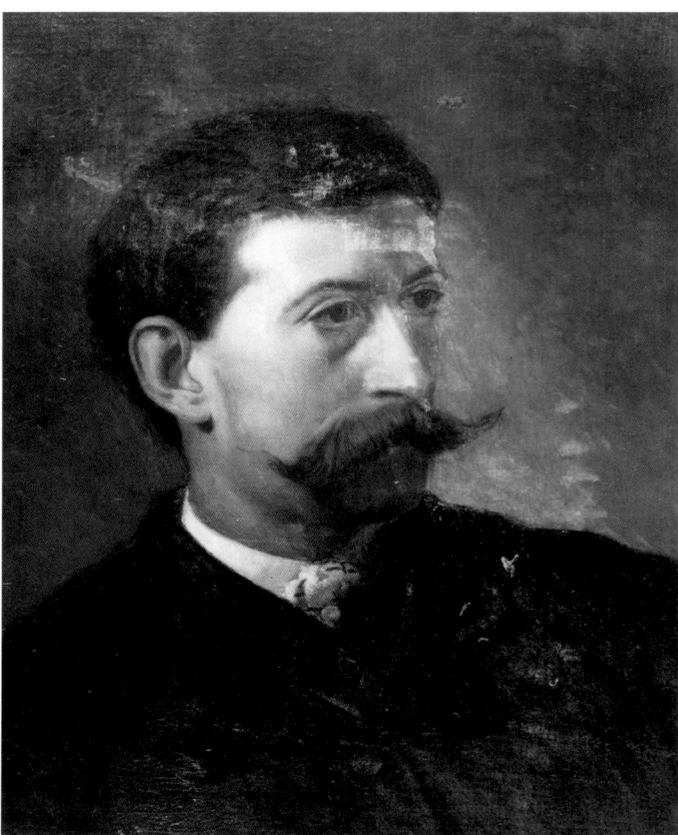

Fig. 50 Oliver Lay, *Winslow Homer*, 1865, oil on canvas, 20⅛ x 16⅛, National Academy of Design (National Academy of Design, 40th Annual Exhibition, 1865, no. 439)

think the painting deserved it. She much preferred the understated simplicity of the landscapes of artists such as Casimir Griswold. Likewise, in portraiture, she was unimpressed with George P. A. Healy's flashy image of the Archbishop of New York, preferring the simpler, bust portrait of Winslow Homer by Oliver Lay (fig. 50).[229]

Like Esperance, Cara Montane—the other woman writer for the *Leader*—remains unidentified. Her favorite portrait in the exhibition was one of a child, *Eddie,* by William Oliver Stone (location unknown), which she called "a perfect jewel." In figural works, she praised two images, both of which depicted distressed women: Alfred Fredericks's *The Sear and Yellow Leaf* (location unknown), a painting of an old woman walking in the woods with the aid of a cane; and Elihu Vedder's *A Lost Mind* (fig. 51), which shows an obviously disturbed young woman in a wild landscape. Montane found the latter image painful in its truthfulness. She noted that the subject's eyes "have a strange, fascinating glitter, withal, inexpressibly pathetic, that draws you to them, and follows you, hauntingly, through the gallery." Likewise, in Mrs. A. T. Oakes's miniature interpretation of Ophelia from Shakespeare's *Hamlet,* the "melting sadness of the hapless maid is most exquisitely rendered, being conceived in the spirit of poetry and strewn all over with the melancholy richness of a grieving fancy." On a happier note, in Edward D. E. Greene's *Dreams,* the visage of another young woman is a "sweet, pure

countenance . . . a vision of grace, that being once seen haunts the imagination ever."[230]

While images of women caught much of Montane's attention, she also discussed several war-related paintings in her 1865 review. Constance Mayer's *North and South—an Episode of the War* was "worthy of careful examination," she thought; and James Beard's *The Night Before the Battle* (see no. 30) was "startlingly wild" and "original." Thomas Nast's *General Sherman's March through Georgia—His Advance Arriving at a Plantation,* a "rough and homely" subject, was "treated in a most subtle and delicate manner" with "a touch of pathos and humor."[231]

Of the three critics writing for the *Leader* in 1865, only one—Esperance—gave much attention to the organization's new venue. Other writers for other journals, however, gave the building its due, although not always favorably. For example, a writer for the *Albion* did not balk at listing the new structure's defects, including the entrance staircase, the stunted

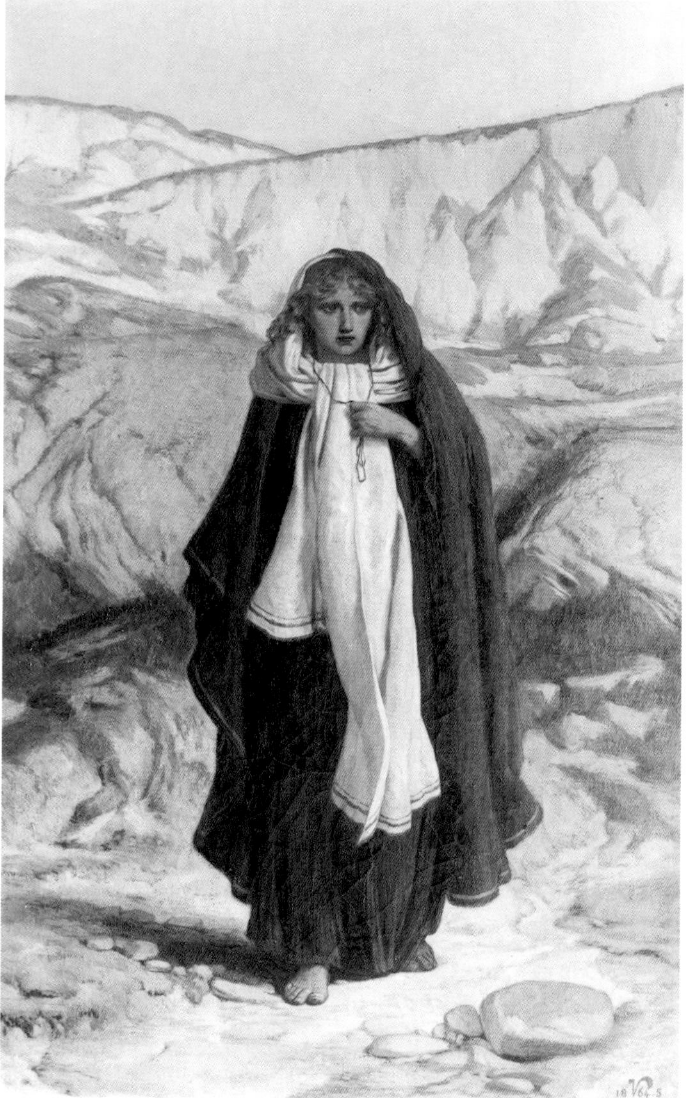

Fig. 51 Elihu Vedder, *A Lost Mind,* 1864–65, oil on canvas, 39⅛ x 23¼, The Metropolitan Museum of Art, Bequest of Helen L. Bullard in memory of Laura C. Bullard, 1921 (National Academy of Design, 40th Annual Exhibition, 1865, no. 601)

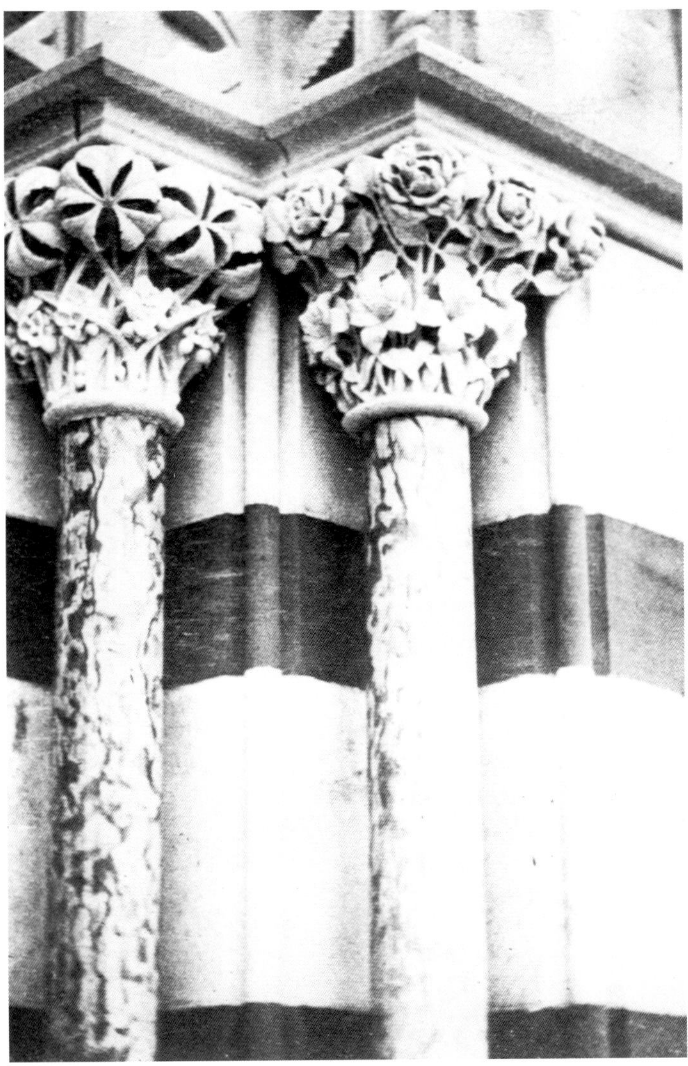

Fig. 52 Photographer unknown, *Capitals on Jamb Columns, Portal of the National Academy of Design by Peter B. Wight*, Archives, National Academy of Design

columns, and the building's proximity to those around it. Despite these and other problems, though, the writer praised the interior, especially the galleries, declaring them "all that is desirable," with "moderate dimensions" and perfect lighting. "May their walls be garnished hereafter," he hoped, "with many a master-piece!"[232]

The writer for the *Albion* also perceived the influence of John Ruskin in the faux-Gothic decorative detailing of the structure, especially in the plant forms on which many of them were based (fig. 52).[233] Not surprisingly, another journal that commented on this aspect of Wight's building was the Ruskinian *The New Path*. Its unidentified critic wrote at length about the building, mostly in positive tones. The writer praised the structure's "unity and grace"; the carvings of plants that adorned the exterior, quite profusely in some places; the wrought iron railings; and even the drinking fountain that was built into the area under the main exterior staircase. "This solidly and admirably built, richly decorated building," the critic concluded, "a noble design well carried out, will remain

for ages, unless fire destroy it; its lesson ought not to be lost upon this generation. It will not be lost upon the next."[234]

While these hopes were eventually dashed—the building was razed in 1900—the critic's sentiments were shared by many. As it had been since 1826, the *New York Evening Post* was supportive of the Academy and announced the opening of its new building with excitement and approval. Like other writers, the *Post's* compared the happy occasion to recent historic events. "During all the tumults of a dark and fluctuating national life," he reported,

> in the midst of fears and ecstasies that have alternately dominated the heart of a people battling for existence, the building of the National Academy of Design has grown under the hands of skilled workmen, and its interests have been lovingly cared for by our intelligent and liberal citizens, and our untiring artists. All honor to each. . . .[235]

Likewise, *Harper's* was impressed by the "gay and flashing groups" of fashionable New Yorkers who turned out for the opening of the exhibition and building, which it called "spacious, solid, convenient, simple in arrangement, ample in accommodation, and very beautiful and effective."[236]

With its new building complete, open, and immediately famous, the Academy was riding high. Even its financial problems were solved, at least temporarily, when its beloved member, James Augustus Suydam (fig. 53), died, bequeathing the

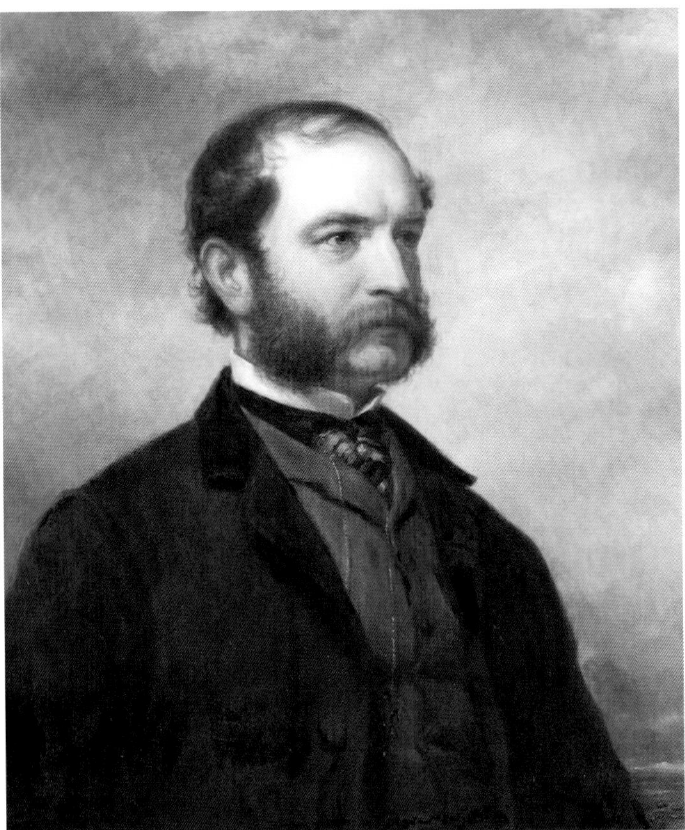

Fig. 53 Daniel Huntington, *James Augustus Suydam*, c. 1862, oil on canvas, 30 x 25¼, National Academy of Design, Bequest of James A. Suydam (National Academy of Design, 38th Annual Exhibition, 1863, no. 221)

institution a substantial collection of American and European paintings—and the useful sum of fifty thousand dollars. The latter allowed the Academy to pay off the mortgage on its new home almost overnight, thereby relieving it of what would have been a worrisome, and possibly even fatal, burden.[237]

But the state of art in America and the nature of the New York art world was on the brink of changing dramatically and forever. Within the coming decade, more American artists would seek training in Europe and, on their return to this country in the late 1870s and 1880s, would bring new styles and fresh subject matter that would have an immediate impact on American art. Ultimately, this would fuel the first serious challenge to the Academy's authority, as will be discussed in the following chapters.

NOTES

1. A concise history of the French Salons can be found in Lois Marie Fink, *American Art at the Nineteenth-Century Paris Salons* (Washington, D.C.: National Museum of American Art, 1990), 1–6. From 1751 to 1791, the Salons were biennial rather than annual.

2. Derek Hudson and Kenneth W. Luckhurst, *The Royal Society of Arts 1754–1954* (London: John Murray, 1954), 3–35.

3. Hudson and Luckhurst, 40. One source has stated that the exhibition of works at the Foundling Hospital, "was the germ of the Royal Academy. . . and the first experiment, the exhibition held in 1760 . . . revealed a new source of wealth, a money-making power hitherto unknown. Annual exhibitions of pictures under such promising circumstances were continued, and have gone on until they have attained the present portentous results" (J. E. Hodgson and Frederick A. Eaton, *The Royal Academy and Its Members 1768–1830* [London: John Murray, 1905], 9).

4. Quoted in Sidney C. Hutchison, *The History of the Royal Academy 1768–1968* (New York: Taplinger Publishing Company, 1968), 43.

5. *The Constitution of the Columbianum, or American Academy of the Fine Arts* (Philadelphia: Francis & Robert Bailey, 1795), 7.

6. Edgar P. Richardson, Brooke Hindle, and Lillian B. Miller, *Charles Willson Peale and His World* (New York: Harry N. Abrams, Inc., 1983), 87–88, 262.

7. Quoted in Anna Wells Rutledge, *Cumulative Record of Exhibition Catalogues The Pennsylvania Academy of the Fine Arts 1807–1870* (Philadelphia: American Philosophical Society, 1955): 2. This indispensable source was reprinted, with revisions and additions, in 1988 under the editorship of Peter Falk as *The Annual Exhibition Record of the Pennsylvania Academy of the Fine Arts 1807–1870* (Madison, Conn.: Sound View Press, 1988).

8. Quoted in Rutledge, 1.

9. For the history of the Pennsylvania Academy, see Helen W. Henderson, *The Pennsylvania Academy of the Fine Arts* (Boston: L. C. Page & Company, 1911); and *In This Academy* (Philadelphia: Pennsylvania Academy of the Fine Arts, 1976).

10. See "Introduction to the Revised Edition" in Peter Falk's revision of Rutledge, viii.

11. The most recent history and analysis of the American Academy of the Fine Arts is Carrie Rebora's superb "The American Academy of the Fine Arts, New York 1802–1842" (Ph.D. diss., City University of New York, 1990), and it is upon that source that I have relied for most of the information given here.

12. Rebora, 9–13.

13. Carrie Rebora has pointed out, that the "exclusivity of the American exhibitors strongly suggests that the committee on arrangements juried in work by themselves and their closest colleagues" (Rebora, 343).

14. Rebora, 14–15. Rebora argues that the success of the American Academy and its exhibitions depended on the continuity of its leadership. From the time Clinton became president until the Academy closed, it remained "a silk-stocking, generational project, a rather insular fraternity of wealthy professionals—merchants, physicians, landowners, and politicians . . . (Rebora, 15)." For an analysis of the contents of the American Academy's exhibitions and a discussion of the critical reaction to them, see Chapter 7 in Dr. Rebora's dissertation, "The Academy's Exhibitions Under Trumbull" (337–421).

15. Mabel Munson Swan, *The Athenaeum Gallery 1827–1873: The Boston Athenaeum as an Early Patron of Art* (Boston: Boston Athenaeum, 1940), 19–20. Other sources on the history of the Boston Athenaeum are Josiah Quincy, *The History of the Boston Athenaeum, with Biographical Notices of its Deceased Founders* (Cambridge: Metcalf and Company, 1851); *The Athenaeum Centenary: The Influence and History of the Boston Athenaeum from 1807–1907* (Boston: Boston Athenaeum, 1907); and *A Climate for Art: The History of the Boston Athenaeum Gallery, 1827–1873* (Boston: The Boston Athenaeum, 1980).

16. Swan, 21.

17. *A Catalogue of the First Exhibition of Paintings, in the Athenaeum Gallery: Consisting of Specimens by American Artists, and a Selection of the Works of the Old Masters* (Boston, 1827), passim.

18. See Robert F. Perkins, Jr., and William J. Gavin III, *The Boston Athenaeum Art Exhibition Index 1827–1874* (Boston: The Library of the Boston Athenaeum, 1980).

19. Swan, 33.

20. "Exhibition of Pictures at the Boston Athenaeum," *North American Review* 25 (July 1827): 227–30.

21. Thomas S. Cummings *Historic Annals of the National Academy of Design* (Philadelphia: George W. Childs, 1865), 5. Cummings's book is the earliest published history of the Academy; the only other one is Eliot Clark, *History of the National Academy of Design 1825–1953* (New York: Columbia University Press, 1954).

22. No thorough study of the Academy's annual exhibitions has been made. The basic sources of information for them are the original exhibition catalogues, a complete set of which is in the Archives of the National Academy. (These catalogues are the only documentation of the exhibitions that the Academy collected). The exhibitions are discussed to some degree in Cummings, and in Clark, cited above, and in Lois Marie Fink and Joshua Taylor, *Academy: The Academic Tradition in American Art* (Washington, D.C.: Smithsonian Institution Press, 1975). Also see Paul Douglas Schweizer, "The Genteel Manner: A Study of the Major Styles and Classes of American Painting Exhibited at the National Academy of Design's Annual Exhibitions, Between 1891 and 1910" (Master's thesis, University of Delaware, 1974).

23. This was one of a number of organizational ideas that the National Academy borrowed directly from the Royal Academy in London. For a discussion of the regulations governing the annual exhibitions of the latter and a description of the way in which its exhibitions were hung, see Allen Staley, "The Victorian Royal Academy," in Christopher Forbes, *The Royal Academy (1837–1901) Revisited* (New York: Forbes Magazine, 1975), 7–8.

24. Another similarity between the Royal Academy's and the National Academy's annuals is their longevity. With only one exception, the Academy has held an annual exhibition in every year since the first in 1826. In 1939, the Academy's Council decided to forego the annual and, in its place, to organize a large, historic exhibition. The impetus for this was the upcoming New York World's Fair. After reviewing the plans for the display of art at that event, the Academicians became concerned that they would be poorly represented in the galleries there. (As it turned out, no works by living artists, American or otherwise, were included in the exhibition at the fair. See Walter Pach, *Catalogue of European & American Paintings 1500–1900* [New York: New York World's Fair, 1940].) Under the leadership of their president, Jonas Lie, they formulated their own historic exhibition at a series of meetings in 1938, the minutes of which are in the Academy's archives. (See especially the meetings of May 6, December 6, and December 21, 1938). With the title *Special Exhibition of the National Academy,* the exhibition opened in the Academy's galleries on West Fifty-seventh Street in New York on May 8, 1939. It consisted of hundreds of paintings and sculptures by National Academicians, living and dead, borrowed from public and private collections, and a large group of artifacts and archival material that helped celebrate the historical significance of the Academy.

25. "Fine Arts. National Academy of Design. Fourth Annual Exhibition," *Critic* 2 (May 23, 1829): 46.

26. "Fine Arts. Fourth Annual Exhibition of the National Academy of Design," *New-York Mirror* 6 (May 16, 1829): 354; "Exhibition of the National Academy of Design," *New York Evening Post*, May 9, 1929.

27. "Living Artists. National Academy of Design," *New York Morning Courier*, May 28, 1830.

28. "Exhibition of the National Academy of Design," *New York Evening Post*, April 27, 1831.

29. "Fine Arts in America. National Academy of Design," *American Monthly Magazine* 5 (June 1835): 312–18.

30. "Editor's Table. National Academy of Design," *Knickerbocker* 19 (June 1842): 588. The author of this article was presumably Lewis Gaylord Clark, editor of the magazine from 1834 to 1860 (Mott, *History of American Magazines*, 1: 606–8).

31. "The National Academy of Design," *Home Journal*, April 18, 1849.

32. Reprinted in "The Fine Arts," *Literary World* 1 (July 3, 1847): 517–18.

33. NAD Minutes.

34. "Fine Arts," *New York Post*, May 6, 1826.

35. "The National Academy of the Arts of Design," *New-York Mirror* 3 (June 10, 1826): 366.

36. "Fine Arts," *New-York Mirror* 3 (June 17, 1826): 375, and (July 1, 1826): 391.

37. "The National Academy of the Arts of Design," *New-York Mirror* 3 (June 10, 1826): 366.

38. In October 1826, the Boston-based *United States Literary Gazette* merged with the *New-York Review and Atheneum Magazine.* The new serial was published simultaneously in Boston and New York with Charles Folsom as its Boston editor and William Cullen Bryant as its New York editor. Bryant had been among the major poets whose works appeared in the *U.S. Literary Gazette;* thus his appointment to the staff of the *U.S. Review* (Mott, *History of American Magazines,* 1: 331–33). As a recent historian has noted, Bryant, who had many responsibilities at the magazine, found time "to write many of the reviews, two short narratives, five original poems, and three Spanish translations for the *Review and Literary Gazette.* He also secured original poetry from, among others, Fitz-Greene Halleck" (see Timothy J. Conley's entry on the *United State Literary Gazette* in Edward E. Chielens, ed., *American Literary Magazines: The Eighteenth and Nineteenth Centuries* [New York, Westport, Conn., and London: Greenwood Press, 1986], 419).

39. The Arcade Baths building was across Chambers Street from what is now City Hall Park in New York. The Academy's annual exhibitions were held there from 1827 to 1830, inclusive.

40. [Samuel F. B. Morse], "Review. *The Exhibition of the National Academy of Design, 1827. The Second.* New York. D. Fanshaw. 1827," *United States Review and Literary Gazette* 2 (July 1827): 241–63. Fanshaw also published the catalogue for the Academy's first exhibition. Later, in 1840–42, he was publisher of the *New-York Mirror* (Mott, *History of American Magazines,* 1:320).

41. To my knowledge, the first to give Fanshaw credit for having written the article was John Peter Simoni in "Art Critics and Criticism in Nineteenth Century America" (Ph.D. diss., Ohio State University, 1952), 29–34.

42. Morse is identified as the author by Bryant in a letter to his coeditor at the *United States Review,* Charles Folsom, c. June 5, 1827, in William Cullen Bryant II and Thomas G. Voss, *The Letters of William Cullen Bryant* (New York: Fordham University Press, 1975), 1: 243.

43. Simoni, 29.

44. André Félibien, *Conférences de l'Académie royale de peinture et de sculture* (Portland, Oregon, 1972), x–xxi; Joshua Reynolds, *Discourses on Art* (repr., New York, 1961), 55–56.

45. [Morse], "Review," *United States Review* 2 (July 1827): 251–52. The appearance of the painting at the National Academy inspired the *Evening Post* (June 7, 1827) to reprint an article about it from the *Boston Daily Advertiser.*

46. [Morse], "Review," *United States Review* 2 (July 1827): 247–48.

47. [Morse], "Review," *United States Review* 2 (July 1827): 256.

48. Mott, *History of American Magazines,* 1: 320–21. As poets, Morris is remembered for his "Woodman, Spare that Tree" (1830) and Woodworth for "The Bucket" ("The Old Oaken Bucket"); Morris's most successful novel was *Brier Cliff* (1826). After leaving the *Mirror,* Woodworth edited the short-lived magazine *Parthenon* and wrote poetry and librettos for operettas, but with little success (*Appleton's Cyclopedia of American Biography,* 6: 608).

49. Quoted in Mott, *History of American Magazines,* 1:322.

50. At one time or another, the editorial staff of the *Mirror* included John Inman, brother of the painter; Nathaniel Parker Willis, whose 139 letters from Europe were published in the *Mirror* in 1833–35 as "Pencilings by the Way"; and Charles Fenno Hoffman, whose stories were often illustrated with fine engravings. The magazine was published under the title *New Mirror* in 1843–44 and as the *Weekly Mirror* from 1844 until 1847 when it ceased publication.

51. William Dunlap, *A History of the Rise and Progress of the Arts of Design in the United States* 2:465.

52. In addition, a portrait of Morris by Julius Gollman (location unknown) was lent to the Academy's 1856 annual by Gen. Elijah Ward. A *Portrait of a Lady* by Gollman, owned by Morris (location unknown) and possibly a portrait of his wife, was in that same exhibition.

53. James L. Yarnall and William H. Gerdts, *Index to American Art Exhibition Catalogues from the Beginning through the 1876 Centennial Year* (Boston: G. K. Hall & Company, 1986), 1107, 1122, 1267.

54. The painting was lent by John A. Brownlee to the St. Louis Agricultural & Mechanical Association exhibition in 1859 (Yarnall and Gerdts, 2501).

55. Albert Frankenstein, *William Sidney Mount* (New York: Harry N. Abrams, Inc., 1975), 26, 27, 232, 234; Deborah J. Johnson, *William Sidney Mount: Painter of American Life* (New York: The American Federation of Arts, 1999), 130. Mount did make an oil study for *Woodman Spare that Tree,* a photograph of which is reproduced in Frankenstein, 241.

56. In 1833, for example, the *Mirror's* review of the Academy's exhibition extended over eight issues and in each of the years 1836, 1837, and 1838, it ran in seven installments. One of the few years in which the magazine did not report on the Academy's annual was 1840.

57. Mott, *History of American Magazines,* 1: 324.

58. "The Fine Arts. National Academy of Design," *New-York Mirror* 4 (June 2, 1827): 351. Morris proved his understanding of the hierarchy of art again, ten years later, when he recognized what Samuel Morse was attempting to do in his portrait of his daughter (*The Muse: Susan Walker Morse,* 1836–37, Metropolitan Museum of Art), which was shown at the Academy in 1837. In the painting, the young woman, who has a large pad in her lap and a pencil in her hand, pauses to seek inspiration. Morris astutely praised Morse "for combining with portraiture those qualities which belong to historical composition ("National Academy of Design," *New York Mirror* 14 [May 27, 1837]: 383).

59. "Fine Arts. The Fourth Annual Exhibition of the National Academy," *New-York Mirror* 6 (May 16, 1829): 354–55.

60. "The Fine Arts. National Academy of Design," *New-York Mirror* 7 (May 15, 1830): 359; "Fine Arts. National Academy of Design. Third Notice," *New-York Mirror* 14 (May 13, 1837): 365.

61. "The Fine Arts. National Academy of Design," *New York Mirror* 8 (May 7, 1831): 350. Weir was one of Morris's favorite artists. See, for example, "A Glance at the Exhibition of the Academy of Design," *New-York Mirror* 16 (May 11, 1839): 367, in which Morris gives particular attention to Weir's *Indian Captives.* In addition, Morris owned at least one painting by Weir.

62. "National Academy of Design. First Notice," *New-York Mirror* 10 (May 18, 1833): 366.

63. "Exhibition of the National Academy," *New-York Mirror* 12 (May 2, 1835): 351.

64. "The Fine Arts. National Academy of Design," *New-York Mirror* 7 (May 15, 1830): 359.

65. "The Fine Arts. National Academy of Design," *New-York Mirror* 15 (May 26, 1838): 382.

66. "The Fine Arts. Exhibition of the National Academy of Design. Fourth Notice," *New-York Mirror* 12 (June 6, 1835): 390. Today's sensitivity to conflict of interest evidently did not apply in 1835: Morris was the owner of the very bust of Willis that he praised in this review, and Willis himself was the foreign correspondent and one of the editors of the *Mirror* at various times from 1831 to 1847.

67. "The Fine Arts. National Academy of Design. Third Notice," *New-York Mirror* 13 (May 21, 1836): 375.

68. "The Fine Arts. Exhibition of the National Academy of Design. Fourth Notice," *New-York Mirror* 12 (June 6, 1835): 390. Morris's admiration for Greenough is suggested by the fact that he published several articles about the sculptor and his work. See, for example, "Greenough the Sculptor," *New-York Mirror* 14 (August 27, 1836):70; and "Greenough's Chanting Cherubs," *New-York Mirror* 9 (November 19, 1831): 155.

69. Bruce I. Weiner, "The New-York Mirror," in Chielens, ed., 277.

70. "Arts and Artists. History of the National Academy of Design," *New Mirror* 1 (May 6 1843): 76–78.

71. Weiner, "The New-York Mirror," in Chielens, ed., 277–79. After leaving the *Mirror,* Morris evidently had a brief stint as editor of the *Home Journal.* Perhaps he was the impetus behind or even the author of a review of the National Academy's exhibition that appeared there in 1849 ("National Academy of Design," *Home Journal* 18 [April 18, 1849]: 2).

72. Before moving to New York in 1843, Fuller was a bookseller in Providence, Rhode Island. He was best known in his own time as author of a series of humorous letters said to be written by a fictional society matron, "Belle Brittan" from Newport. In his later years, he lived in London and Paris (*Appleton's Cyclopedia of American Biography,* 2: 560). His travel book, *Sparks from a Locomotive,* in which he recounts his visits in 1859 to the studios of American artists in Florence and Rome, among other things, was published in New York later that same year.

73. "Exhibition at the National Academy," *New-York Mirror* 5 (May 15, 1847): 90.

74. For example, see "National Academy of Design," *Home Journal* 18 (April 18, 1849): 2.

75. Nevins, 125. William James Stillman wrote on art for the *Post* beginning in 1854; but, since no articles published there bear his byline, the extent of his contributions to the paper is difficult to determine. Since he was involved in preparing the first issue of the *Crayon* in 1854-55, it seems unlikely that he contributed much to the *Post.*

76. William Cullen Bryant, *Letters of a Traveller, or, Notes of Things Seen in Europe and America* (New York: G. P. Putnam, 1851), 165. In this travel book, Bryant makes it clear that he had an abiding interest in American art and cared a great deal about American artists. Among those he took the time to visit while in Europe in 1845 were Hiram Powers, Horatio Greenough, Henry Peters Gray, George L. Brown, Thomas Rossiter, and Henry Kirke Brown.

77. "National Academy," *New York Evening Post*, May 15, 1826.

78. "National Academy of Design," *New York Evening Post*, May 6, 1828. Bryant was not in London in 1828, so if he was the author of this review, he probably made his deductions about the Royal Academy's 1828 show by examining a copy of the exhibition catalogue.

79. "Exhibition of the National Academy of Design," *New York Evening Post*, May 9, 1829; "Fine Arts," *New York Evening Post*, June 6, 1829; "Exhibition of the National Academy of the Arts of Design," *New York Evening Post*, May 1, 1830. It appears that the *Post* went out of its way, at least sometimes, to notice the works of younger artists. For example, it began a review of the Academy's 1838 exhibition by stating that most of the article would focus on "younger aspirants for graphic honors" ("National Academy," *New York Evening Post*, May 26, 1838).

80. One might presume that the Academy decided to have such a retrospective out of pride in its achievements. However, Thomas Cummings, the Academy's first historian, recalled that it grew out of an anxiety that few first-rate works would be submitted to the 1831 exhibition. The organization's president, Samuel Morse, was in Europe; one of its more influential and admired officers, Henry Inman, had left town; and, according to Cummings, a "general luke-warmness" pervaded "the art body." Enemies of the Academy were predicting the organization's imminent demise. In order to forego a possible debacle, Cummings suggested that the Academicians organize a "review exhibition," with works submitted by invitation. All reports indicate that the resulting exhibition was a popular success; Cummings reported that it was a financial one (Cummings, 120–21; NAD Council Minutes, December 13, 1830).

81. The Academy took possession of four rooms at Clinton Hall in October, 1830, and occupied them until August, 1840. The dimensions of these spaces were as follows: exhibition room—50 square feet; school room—50 x 38 feet; library—36 x 20 feet; Keeper's room—36 x 20 feet (Cummings, 119; NAD Council Minutes, May 5, 1830, August 10, 1840). By 1836, the Academy's annual exhibitions were requiring more space, and it was decided to expand the show into the school room when necessary (NAD Council Minutes, July 26, 1836). When the Academy was not using the exhibition room, it sublet the space for fifty dollars per month (NAD Council Minutes, December 2, 1833).

82. The Academy's galleries became a fashionable place to meet during the 1830s. Clinton Hall was only a block from City Hall Park, and the major thoroughfare of Broadway and the fashionable Broadway Hotel were nearby. In 1831, the *New York Morning Courier* reported on the popularity of the new gallery of art and advised visitors from out of town that there was no better place to spend a pleasant morning ("National Academy of Design," *New York Morning Courier*, May 6, 1831).

83. "Exhibition of the National Academy of Design," *New York Evening Post*, April 27 and April 28, 1831.

84. Apollo, "The National Academy of Design," *New York Evening Post*, May 7, 1831; T, "The Progress of the Arts in Our Country," *New York Evening Post*, May 9, 1831.

85. "National Academy of Design," *New York Evening Post*, May 25, 1836. Several papers called the *Star*, or some variation on that name, have been published in New York. This one was founded by writer Mordecai M. Noah in 1833 and ran until 1840 (Mott, *American Journalism*, 229n).

86. Herbert was born in England and, after graduating from Oxford, came to the United States in 1830. When the *Knickerbocker* rejected an article he had written, he established the *American Monthly Magazine*. He wrote novels, historical works, and, under the name of Frank Forester, articles on sports for *Graham's Magazine*, among others. Herbert left the *American Monthly* in 1835; Charles Fenno Hoffman and Park Benjamin served as its editors until the magazine's demise in 1838. See Mott, *History of American Magazines*, 1: 618–21, who says that Herbert was the author of the *American Monthly's* theater and art reviews; and John Grant Wilson and John Fiske, eds., *Appleton's Cyclopedia of American Biography* (New York: D. Appleton and Company, 1888), 3: 179–80.

87. "Fine Arts in America. National Academy of Design," *American Monthly Magazine* 5 (June 1835): 312–18. Chapman painted nine pictures of Virginia sites associated with George Washington from which engravings were made to illustrate poet James Kirke Paulding's *Life of Washington* (New York: Harper & Brothers, 1835). The original paintings are in a private collection. See Ben L. Bassham, *Conrad Wise Chapman: Artist & Soldier of the Confederacy* (Kent, Ohio: The Kent State University Press, 1998), 12–13.

88. *New York Evening Post*, June 24, 1835.

89. "The Twenty-Third Exhibition of the National Academy," *New York Evening Post*, May 13, 1848; "National Academy of Design. Twenty-Third Annual Exhibition," *New York Evening Post*, May 25 and 30, 1848. Since it often bought paintings from the Academy's annual exhibitions, the Apollo Association/ American Art-Union certainly benefited many of the artists who participated in those shows. In 1842, for example, the *Post* reported that the Art-Union had purchased at least eight paintings from the Academy's exhibition that year ("The Fine Arts," *New York Evening Post*, July 9, 1842).

90. "National Academy of Design," *New York Evening Post*, May 14, 1839.

91. "The Fine Arts," *New York Evening Post*, May 10, 1845.

92. "City Intelligence. Exhibition of the Academy of Design," *New York Evening Post*, April 21, 1851. The bust was almost certainly Palmer's *Infant Ceres* (1849–50; private collection, Santa Barbara, California).

93. "National Academy of Design. No. 2," *New York Evening Post*, April 7, 1856.

94. "The Annual Exhibition of the National Academy of Design," *New York Evening Post*, April 2, 1847; "The Exhibition of the Academy of Design," *New York Evening Post*, March 16, 1855.

95. From 1841 through 1849, the Academy rented rooms in a building at Broadway and Leonard Street; from 1850 through 1854, and again in 1857, they did the same at 663 Broadway; in 1855 and 1856 they were at 548 Broadway. Its earlier homes and these addresses were not far from City Hall Park, making the move to Tenth Street something of a geographic leap.

96. "The National Academy of Design," *New York Evening Post*, April 22, 1858.

97. "The Thirty-Fourth Exhibition of the Academy of Design," *New York Evening Post*, April 25, 1859; "National Academy of Design. Thirty-Fourth Exhibition," *New York Evening Post*, May 14, 1859. This exhibition included Eastman Johnson's *Negro Life at the South* (New-York Historical Society).

98. "National Academy of Design," *New York Evening Post*, June 5, 1834.

99. "The National Academy of Design. Thirty-Ninth Annual Exhibition," *New York Evening Post*, May 21, 1864.

100. *Appleton's Cyclopedia of American Biography*, 1:629–30. Clark was a friend of American artists and had at least a small collection of paintings, including a portrait of a child by Edward Ludlow Mooney; a portrait of a lady, "à la Madonna," by Cephas G. Thompson; another portrait of a lady by Charles Loring Elliott; and, appropriately, a painting, also by Elliott, called *"Old Knick,"* which was a common nickname for the *Knickerbocker Magazine*. Clark lent each of these to annual exhibitions at the National Academy (see New-York Historical Society, *National Academy of Design Exhibition Record, 1826–1860* [1943], passim).

101. Mott, *History of American Magazines*, 1: 606-14. Mott points out that the heyday of the *Knickerbocker* was the first ten years of his editorship (1834–44) and that the magazine had clearly deteriorated by 1850. For a useful bibliography on the *Knickerbocker*, see Benjamin Franklin Fisher IV, "The Knickerbocker," in Chielens, ed., 189–94.

102. Mott, *History of American Magazines*, 1: 611.

103. [Lewis Gaylord Clark?], "Editor's Table. National Academy of Design," *Knickerbocker* 19 (June 1842): 588.

104. [Lewis Gaylord Clark?], "Editor's Table. Exhibition of the National Academy," *Knickerbocker* 9 (June, 1837): 617.

105. [Lewis Gaylord Clark?], "National Academy of Design," *Knickerbocker* 3 (May 1834): 399.

106. J[ohn] K[enrick] F[isher], "Editor's Table. The Fine Arts. National Academy of Design," *Knickerbocker* 13 (June 1839): 545–49. Fisher was a portraitist and historical painter. He studied in England, exhibited at the Royal Academy in London, the Boston Athenaeum, and the American Art-Union in New York. He was best known for a large collection of copies of old master paintings that he brought back from Europe in 1848 and exhibited to the public in his studio ("Art Items," *Literary World* [November 4, 1848]: 792, [March 17, 1849]: 254). He sent three portraits to the National Academy's annual exhibition in 1834 and one, of C. Van Doren, to the exhibition of 1853. Besides being an artist, he was something of an art critic as well. For example, he wrote a series of articles for the *Literary World* promoting the dissolution of the American Art-Union and the establishment of a public art gallery ("Fine Arts, Galleries, Exhibitions, Etc.," *Literary World* [February 9, 1850] 132–33, [February 23, 1850]: 182, [March 2, 1850]: 206–7), and another on the state of the arts in this country for the *Southern Literary Messenger* ("Culture of the Fine Arts, *Southern Literary Messenger* 6 [December, 1840]: 842–46). During the early 1850s, he was a regular contributor to the *Photographic and Fine Arts Journal*. I wish to thank Dr. William H. Gerdts for calling my attention to Fisher and identifying him as "J. K. F," the author of the *Knickerbocker's* review of the Academy's 1839 exhibition.

107. [Lewis Gaylord Clark?], "National Academy of Design," *Knickerbocker* 16 (July 1840): 81–83.

108. "Editor's Table," *Knickerbocker* 52 (July 1858): 81–84.

109. Literally speaking, both the *New York Herald* and the *New York Tribune* ceased to exist in 1924; in actuality, they lived on until 1966 as the product of their merger, the *New York Herald Tribune.* For the history of both the *Herald* and the *Tribune,* see Richard Kluger, *The Paper: The Life and Death of the New York Herald Tribune* (New York: Alfred A. Knopf, 1986).

110. Mott, *American Journalism,* 232.

111. More Anon, "National Academy," *New York Herald,* May 9, 12, 14, 17, and 19, 1836.

112. "National Academy of Design," *New York Herald,* May 8, 1837.

113. "National Academy—Second Notice," *New York Herald,* May 25, 1837.

114. "National Academy of Design," *New York Herald,* May 5, 10, 16, 1838; June 1, 14, 1838.

115. "National Academy of Design—Cutting Criticisms," *New York Herald,* June 13 and 16, 1842.

116. "The National Academy," *New York Herald,* May 4, 1839. Like the writer for the *Knickerbocker,* cited above, the *Tribune* critic especially disliked Charles Cromwell Ingham's *Great Adirondack Pass*, which he classified as a potboiler. The only works he praised were landscapes by Andrew Richardson and H. C. Selous.

117. "National Academy," *New York Herald,* June 4, 19, 25, and 27, July 2 and 4, 1840.

118. "National Academy of Design," *New York Herald,* April 29, 1845. The painting depicted an old man staring at a bottle of liquor, "the enemy." See H. Nicholas B. Clark, *Francis W. Edmonds: American Master in the Dutch Tradition* (Washington, D.C.: Smithsonian Institution Press for the Amon Carter Museum, 1988), 80–81.

119. "The Fine Arts. Exhibition at the National Academy of Design," *New York Herald,* April 19, 1848.

120. "The Fine Arts. The Academy of Design," *New York Herald,* March 18, 1856.

121. "The Fine Arts. National Academy of Design," *New York Herald,* May 12, 1850; "Academy of Design. Twenty-Eighth Annual Exhibition," *New York Herald,* May 8, 1853.

122. "The National Academy of Design—Annual Exhibition," *New York Herald,* April 13, 1858; and "National Academy of Design," *New York Herald,* April 23, 1858.

123. These are Victor Nehlig's *An Episode of the War: The Cavalry Charge of Lt. Harry B. Hidden;* Charles Elliott and J. B. Stearns's *Lieut. Harry Hidden at Sangster's Station, Va., March 9, 1862;* Constant Mayer's *Sisters of Charity Removing a Wounded Soldier from the Battle Field;* Granville Perkins *Escape of Contrabands to the U.S. Bark Kingfisher, off the Coast of Florida;* Edwin White's *Major Anderson Raising the Flag on the Morning of his Taking Possession of Fort Sumter, Dec. 27, 1860;* Jervis McEntee's *Virginia;* Louis Lang's *The Soldier's Widow;* John Rogers's *The Union Refugees;* and John Q. A. Ward's *The Freedman.* There were others in the exhibition, such as Henry P. Gray's *America in 1862* and Thomas Le Clear's *Young America,* that had patriotic themes.

124. It has been estimated that, from 1861 to 1865 inclusive, the works of art with war-related subjects in the Academy's exhibitions never exceeded 4.5 percent of the total number of works on display. See Lucretia Giese, "Harvesting the Civil War: Art in Wartime New York," in Patricia M. Burnham and Lucretia Hoover Giese, eds, *Redefining American History Painting* (New York: Cambridge University Press, 1995), 64–81.

125. Quoted in Mott, *American Journalism,* 358–59.

126. Kluger, 26.

127. "National Academy of Design," *New-Yorker* 1 (June 18, 1836): 205.

128. "Exhibition. National Academy of Design," *New-Yorker* 3 (May 6, 1837): 109; (May 13, 1837): 127; (May 20, 1837): 143; (June 3, 1837): 175; (June 17, 1837): 205. For Greeley and the *New-Yorker,* see William Harlan Hale, *Horace Greeley, Voice of the People* (New York: Harper & Brothers, 1950), 25–30.

129. "National Academy of Design," *New-Yorker* 5 (May 26, 1838): 157–58.

130. "Exhibition of the National Academy of Design," *New-Yorker* 7 (May 4, 1839): 109; (May 11, 1839): 125.

131. "The National Academy," *New-Yorker* 9 (June 20, 1840): 221–22.

132. Greeley's attitudes toward art had been defined by the time he made his first trip to Europe in 1851. During that Grand Tour, he acted as a foreign correspondent for the *Tribune,* regularly writing letters to his editors that were then published in the paper. Later that same year, his letters were reprinted in the form of a travel book entitled *Glances At Europe* (New York: Dewitt and Davenport, 1851). While abroad, Greeley visited a number of major art collections, notably those in Italy, where he preferred what he saw in Rome to what he saw in Venice. Also in that country, he took time to visit the studios of a number of American artists, including painter William Page and sculptors Joel Tanner Hart, Alexander Galt, Randolph Rogers, and Hiram Powers, whose work Greeley particularly admired (Greeley, *Glances At Europe,* 216–18). In London, he visited the Great Exhibition at the Crystal Palace and, in one of his letters home, reacted to negative criticism that American art had received on the occasion of the exhibition from the London press. In that letter, Greeley wondered if the "self-constituted arbiters who thus tell the American people that Art is not their province" were really impartial judges. "Are they not palpably speaking in the interest of the rival product of Europe, alarmed by the rapid growth and extension of American Art?," he asked. "Would they have taken so much trouble with us if American taste and skill were really the miserable abortions they represent them?" (Greeley, *Glances At Europe,* 147).

133. In 1843, for example, the Academy's annuals were called "a central point of attraction for the fair and fashionable of the City" ("The Exhibition of the National Academy of Design," *New York Daily Tribune,* May 19, 1843).

134. "The Exhibition of the National Academy of Design," *New York Daily Tribune,* May 19, 1843; "National Academy of Design. Twenty-Fifth Annual Exhibition," *New York Daily Tribune,* July 7, 1850.

135. "National Academy of Design. Twenty-Fifth Annual Exhibition," *New York Daily Tribune,* May 1, 1850.

136. "National Academy of Design. Twenty-Fifth Annual Exhibition," *New York Daily Tribune,* May 1, 1850.

137. "National Academy of Design. Twenty-Fifth Annual Exhibition," *New York Daily Tribune,* June 20, 1850.

138. "National Academy of Design. Twenty-Fifth Annual Exhibition," *New York Daily Tribune,* July 7, 1850.

139. The *Tribune's* serial review of the Academy's annual exhibition of 1851 was signed with the initials "G. W. C." But the tone and language of the reviews of several subsequent years, suggest that Curtis was the author of them as well.

140. Mott, *American Journalism,* 379; Thomas Bender, *New York Intellect* (New York: Alfred A. Knopf, 1987), 177. Like so many art writers of his day, Curtis has been dismissed, quite unfairly, in recent times as a bland writer who had no "substantial knowledge of art, design, technique or style" (Barbara Jean Stephanic, "Clarence Cook's Role as Art Critic, Advocate for Professionalism, Educator, and Arbiter of Taste in America" [Ph.D. diss, University of Maryland, 1997], 58). Considering Curtis's substantial contribution to American letters and his influence on American journalism, such a cursory analysis of him is, I believe, irresponsible.

141. See Edward Cary, *George William Curtis* (Boston: Houghton, Mifflin, and Company, 1894). Curtis was also a contributing writer to the *Harbinger,* a transcendentalist journal published by George Ripley at Brook Farm from 1845 to 1849. With the demise of that periodical, Ripley joined the staff of the *Tribune,* as did another former Brook-Farmer, Charles A. Dana (Henry Golemba, "The Harbinger," in Chielens, ed., 164; Hale, 84).

142. His friend and biographer, Edward Cary, stated that, while in Europe, Curtis "saw many pictures, knew many artists of various races, and had obviously a keen enjoyment of their works" (Cary, 49).

143. George William Curtis, *Lotus-Eating: A Summer Book* (New York: Harper and Brothers, 1852). *Lotus-Eating,* a compilation of reportorial letters by Curtis published in the *New York Tribune,* is a veritable travel guide to locations dear to the painters of the Hudson River School. It includes essays on places such as the Hudson River, Niagara Falls, Catskill Falls, Nahant, Massachusetts, and Newport, Rhode Island. Cary identified Kensett, the book's illustrator, as Curtis's "warm friend," and Curtis himself called the artist "the genial Kensett" (Cary, 76, 89).

144. Curtis's writings were anthologized a number of times during the nineteenth century. In addition to *Lotus-Eating,* for example, see his *Literary and Social Essays* (1894; reprinted Kennikat Press, Port Washington, N. Y., 1968) and *From the Easy Chair* (New York: Harper and Brothers, 1893).

145. *Appleton's Cyclopedia of American Biography,* 2: 35–36.Chielens, ed., 168, 333. Curtis was also something of a collector of art. He owned some watercolor sketches by James B. Wandersford and two paintings, *Autumn* and *The Harem,* by Hamilton Gibbs Wilde, all of which he lent to the National Academy's annual exhibition of 1854. He also owned several marble sculptures: Harriet Hosmer's bust of *Medusa* and Martin Milmore's of Charles Sumner (1864). The latter was given to Curtis by the State of Massachusetts in appreciation of his having delivered the eulogy at Sumner's funeral in 1874. Curtis's widow, Anna Shaw Curtis, gave it to the U.S. government, and it is now the Senate wing of the U.S. Capitol. See George William Curtis, "Charles Sumner: A Eulogy," *Harper's Weekly* 18 (June 20, 1874): 525–31; and David B. Dearinger, "American Neoclassic Sculptors and Their Private Patrons in Boston" (Ph.D. diss., City University of New York, 1993), 461–63, 682.

146. Bender, 178. Curtis's eventual stature in American journalism and politics is indicated by the fact that, after his death, a committee was formed to com-

mission a bust of him from John Quincy Adams Ward, one of this country's leading sculptors of the day, for presentation to the New York Public Library, in which collection it remains (Lewis I. Sharp, *John Quincy Adams Ward: Dean of American Sculpture* [Newark, Delaware: University of Delaware Press, 1985], 254–55).

147. Quoted in Cary, 75.

148. G. W. C., "The Private View of the Academy Exhibition," *New York Daily Tribune,* April 10, 1851.

149. G. W. C., "The Fine Arts. The National Academy of Design. VI," *New York Daily Tribune,* June 21, 1851. Curtis had done the Grand Tour in 1847, had met many American artists in Florence and Rome, and often returned to Italy in the summers.

150. "The Fine Arts. National Academy of Design. I," *New York Tribune,* April 17, 1852.

151. Evidently, Curtis's attitude toward the Academy became more negative as time went on. In 1855, in an early edition of his soon-to-be famous column for *Harper's,* he derided the Academy's attempt, in that year's annual exhibition catalogue, to defend its school. Curtis sarcastically called it "a hilarious account of the condition and prospects of the Academy" and demanded a more serious appraisal of the Academy's condition (George W. Curtis, "Editor's Easy Chair," *Harper's New Monthly Magazine* 10 [May 1855]: 840). Curtis's writings on art after he left the *Tribune* deserve further study.

152. R. T., "Exhibition of the National Academy of Design," *New York Tribune,* April 18 and 27, May 7, 1855. The author was not the only one to carp about the inclusion of the word *national* in the Academy's title. Similar complaints began as early as 1827 when the *North American Review* chided the Academy for failing to live up to its name, one that implied "a public institution, founded and supported by the nation." Instead, the Boston periodical claimed, the Academy was "simply a society of artists in the City of New-York, organized for the purposes of exhibition and instruction" (quoted in Cummings, 45).

153. "The National Academy of Design. [First Article]," *New York Tribune,* April 9, 1856

154. "National Academy of Design. [Fifth and Last Notice]," *New York Tribune,* May 10, 1856.

155. "The National Academy of Design. Thirty Seventh Annual Exhibition," *New York Tribune,* April 14, 1862.

156. "Annual Exhibition of the National Academy of Design," *New York Tribune,* April 17, 1863.

157. Jo Ann W. Weiss, "Clarence Cook: His Critical Writings" (Ph.D. diss., The Johns Hopkins University, 1977), 31–32.

158. Clarence Cook, "The Fine Arts. The National Academy of Design," *Independent,* April 5 and 19, May 10, 1855. Coleman showed two works at the Academy that year, *Study from Nature* and *The Evening Walk.*

159. The American Pre-Raphaelite movement, its journal, and Cook's role in it have been thoroughly examined in Linda S. Ferber and William H. Gerdts, *The New Path: Ruskin and the American Pre-Raphaelites* (New York: The Brooklyn Museum, 1985).

160. Weiss, 37. Weiss suggests that Cook's employment by the *Tribune* may have been influenced by his friendship with George Ripley, who was its long-time literary editor.

161. [Clarence Cook], "National Academy of Design. The Thirty-Ninth Exhibition. [Second Article]," *New York Daily Tribune,* April 30, 1864.

162. [Clarence Cook], "National Academy of Design. The Thirty-Ninth Exhibition," *New York Daily Tribune,* April 23, 1864.

163. [Clarence Cook], "National Academy of Design—The Thirty-Ninth Exhibition. [Third Article]," *New-York Daily Tribune,* May 7, 1864.

164. [Clarence Cook], "National Academy of Design—The Thirty-Ninth Exhibition. [Fifth Article]," *New-York Daily Tribune,* May 21, 1864.

165. [Clarence Cook], "National Academy of Design. Fortieth Annual Exhibition," *New York Daily Tribune,* May 13, 1865.

166. [Clarence Cook], "National Academy of Design—Fortieth Annual Exhibition. [First Article]," *New York Daily Tribune,* May 13, 1865.

167. [Clarence Cook], "National Academy of Design. Fortieth Annual Exhibition. [Second Article]," *New York Daily Tribune,* May 20, 1865.

168. Sons of a publisher, the Duyckincks both trained for careers in the law but soon gave that up for careers in literature. Evert was a contributor to the *New York Review* before taking over the *Literary World.* During the mid 1830s, New York's most gifted writers often gathered at his house, thus leading to the formation of the Knickerbocker literary circle. He was known for his love of New York and especially its cultural features such as public libraries and art exhibitions. He was the author of many books and, at his death, was working with William Cullen Bryant on the manuscript for an edition of the works of William Shakespeare (*Appleton's Cyclopedia of American Biography,* 2:278; Bender, 141).

169. Mott, *History of American Magazines,* 1: 766–68; Donald Yannella, "The Literary World," in Chielens, ed., 224–30. Of the two brothers, Evert was the more literary- minded; George was business manager of the periodical.

170. Quoted in Debra Brown, "The Boston Miscellany of Literature and Fashion," Chielens, ed., 71.

171. Tuckerman's book was published in Philadelphia by Key and Biddle.

172. Mott, *History of American Magazines,* 1: passim. In an essay on the *North American Review,* John B. Mason writes that Tuckerman's "judicious and balanced" contributions to the *Review* were among "its best writing in the three decades before the Civil War" (Chielens, ed., 293).

173. James Thomas Flexner, "Tuckerman's *Book of the Artists,*" *American Art Journal* 1 (Fall 1969): 53–57. Also see Wilson, *Bryant and His Friends,* 416–17.

174. In addition, it reprinted a review of the exhibition from the *London Art Union* ("The Fine Arts," *Literary World* 1 [July 3, 1847]: 517–18).

175. "The Fine Arts: Exhibition at the National Academy," *Literary World* 1 (May 8, 1847): 322–23.

176. "The Exhibition of the National Academy," *New York Evening Mirror,* April 13, 1847; "The Fine Arts. Exhibition at the National Academy," *Literary World* 1 (April 27, 1847): 279–80. The negative view of Rothermel expressed here is similar to that given by Tuckerman in his *Book of the Artists,* supporting the assumption that these reviews in the *Literary World* were by Tuckerman. In his book, Tuckerman says that Rothermel's "facility of composition and his aptitude for grouping, costume, and scenic effects, have led him to produce a large number of works with a rapidity incompatible with grand permanent results, however indicative of talent and knowledge" (Tuckerman, *Book of the Artists* [1867], 437).

177. "The Fine Arts," *Literary World* 1 (June 19, 1847): 467.

178. "The Fine Arts," *Literary World* 1 (June 19, 1847): 468. The article purports to be a critique of the *catalogue,* not of the exhibition, so that it could qualify for publication in a periodical devoted to book reviews.

179. "The Fine Arts. National Academy Exhibition. (Concluded)," *Literary World* 3 (June 3, 1848): 350–51.

180. The theories proposed in these articles are not unlike some expressed in Tuckerman's history of American art, published in 1867, 27–28. This further supports the assignment of the 1850 *Literary World* articles to him.

181. "The Fine Arts. The National Academy. A First View. Durand and the Landscapes," *Literary World* 7 (April 27, 1850): 424. The author deplored the quantity of portraits in the exhibition—"Who cares how Timothy Hodgson or Paul Jenkins, Esq., look . . . ?"—but he was pleased with the thirteen sculptures by Henry Kirke Brown on display. The exception in that category was Brown's bust of William Cullen Bryant which, the critic thought, had "more of the Evening Post than of Thanatopsis in the face" ("The Fine Arts. The National Academy. Third View—The Portraits—The Sculpture," *Literary World* 7 [May 18, 1850]: 497–98).

182. Mott, *History of American Magazines,* 1: 131. The *Albion's* conservatism was evidently widely recognized at the time; the *Knickerbocker,* for one, referred to it in 1854 ("The National Academy of Design," *Knickerbocker* 43 (May, 1854): 539–40). After Bartlett left the *Albion,* he established a similar publication, *The Anglo-American,* in Boston in 1855. He later served as British consul at Baltimore (*Appleton's Cyclopedia of American Biography,* 2:184).

183. "Fine Arts. National Academy of Design," *Albion* 14 (March 24, 1855): 141.

184. "National Academy of Design," *Albion* 8 (April 14, 1849): 177.

185. According to the *Bulletin of the American Art Union* (2 [May 1849]: 13–15), this was a portrait of William Sidney Mount.

186. "National Academy of Design," *Albion* 8 (April 14, 1849): 177.

187. "Fine Arts. The National Academy of Design," *Albion* 10 (April 19, 1851): 189; "Fine Arts. National Academy of Design," *Albion* 11 (April 24, 1852): 201-202; "Fine Arts. The National Academy of Design—No. III," *Albion* 11 (May 8, 1852): 225–26.

188. "Fine Arts. The National Academy of Design," *Albion* 13 (April 8, 1854): 165.

189. "Fine Arts. The National Academy of Design," *Albion* 14 (March 24, 1855): 141.

190. Raymond began his writing career with contributions to Greeley's *New Yorker.* When Greeley founded the *Tribune* in 1841, he made Raymond his assistant editor, a post he held until 1843, when he began working for the *Courier and Enquirer.* After a trip to Europe in 1851, he founded the *Times.* He was active in the Republican party and held a number of public offices (*Appleton's Cyclopedia of American Biography,* 5:192–93).

191. Mott, *American Journalism,* 278–81. The paper was called the *Daily Times* until 1857. Mott deemed it "the culmination and highest achievement of the cheap-for-cash newspaper movement" (280).

192. According to *Putnam's*, the Academy, which had built the building, had sold it for a fifty thousand dollar profit, raising hopes that the inadequate galleries there would be replaced by better ones in a new building ("The Fine Arts. The National Academy," *Putnam's Monthly Magazine* 3 [May 1854]: 566–68). The structure at 633 Broadway was not demolished—at least not right away—and, in 1857, the Academy, having temporarily rented it back from its owner, held its annual exhibition there.

193. In fact, the exhibition of 1854 contained almost four hundred works, which was not substantially less than the number of works shown in previous years. Actually, it was the following year—1855—that saw a dramatic decrease in the number of works in the shows. The catalogue for that year's exhibition apologized for the situation and explained that it was due to the "limited capacity of the rooms" and should not be interpreted as an "intimation that the Institution is losing strength" ("The Academy: A Glance at Its Career and Character," in *Catalogue of the Thirtieth Annual Exhibition of the National Academy of Design* [New York, 1855], iii).

194. "The National Academy of Design. Number One," *New-York Times*, March 31, 1854; "The National Academy of Design. Second Notice," *New-York Times*, April 4, 1854.

195. "National Academy of Design," *New-York Daily Times*, April 12, 1855.

196. Neither Simoni nor Weiss include the *New-York Times* article in their bibliographies of Cook's writings, but both state that Cook often signed himself with his initials (Simoni , 434 and 441; Weiss, 316–21).

197. C[larence] C[ook], "National Academy of Design. Thirty-first Yearly Exhibition. First Article," *New-York Times*, March 24, 1856.

198. C[larence] C[ook], "National Academy of Design. Thirty-first Yearly Exhibition. First Article," *New York-Times*, March 24, 1856.

199. [Clarence Cook], "National Academy of Design. Thirty-First Annual Exhibition. Second Article," *New- York Times*, April 4, 1856.

200. [Clarence Cook], "The National Academy Exhibition," *New-York Times*, May 27, 1857.

201. [Clarence Cook], "Academy Exhibition. Second Notice," *New-York Times*, June 16, 1857.

202. [Clarence Cook], "Academy Exhibition. Second Notice," *New-York Times*, June 16, 1857. Cook's praise of Hunt in this review was rare. He often singled Hunt out as a target for his special brand of nastiness. See Martha J. Hoppin, "William Morris Hunt and His Critics," *American Art Review* 2 (September–October 1975): 79–91.

203. [Clarence Cook], "Exhibition of the National Academy. Third Notice," *New-York Times*, June 20, 1857.

204. [Clarence Cook?], "The Opening of the Academy of Design. The Fine Arts in the City," *New-York Times*, April 13, 1858.

205. [Clarence Cook?], "The Academy of Design. The Thirty-fourth Exhibition of the Academy of Design," *New-York Times*, April 20, 1859.

206. [Clarence Cook?], "National Academy Exhibition. The Landscapes of the Present Year," *New-York Times*, April 21, 1861.

207. The most thorough study of the *Crayon* is Janice Simon, "*The Crayon* 1855–1861: The Voice of Nature in Criticism, Poetry, and the Fine Arts" (Ph.D. diss., The University of Michigan, 1990). Simon states that Durand became sole editor of the magazine after 1856 and was responsible for the column called "Sketchings," in which many of the reveiws of the National Academy's exhibitions appeared. He was probably also the author of the column called "Domestic Art Gossip" (Simon, 6).

208. "Exhibition of the National Academy. Second Article," *Crayon* 3 (May 1856): 145–50.

209. "Sketchings. Exhibition of the Academy of Design. No. II," *Crayon* 1 (April 4, 1855): 218–19.

210. "Sketchings. The National Academy of Design," *Crayon* 1 (March 21, 1855): 186.

211. Ibid., 186. For an analysis of the painting, see John Caldwell's catalogue entry in *American Paintings in the Metropolitan Museum of Art* (New York: Metropolitan Museum of Art, 1994) 1: 424–28.

212. "Sketchings. Exhibition of the Academy of Design. No. III," *Crayon* 1 (April 11, 1855): 234–35.

213. The work by Ruskin in the Academy's 1856 exhibition was titled *Water, Rock & Foliage* and was number 246 in the exhibition catalogue. (It was probably similar to Ruskin's watercolor, *Fragment of the Alps* [c. 1854–56, Fogg Art Museum, Harvard University, Cambridge, Massachusetts]). Although in principal the Academy's exhibitions were limited to the work of American artists, works by European artists were occasionally included. Another work by Ruskin, *View Near Naples,* was lent to the exhibition of 1855 by E. L. Magoon.

214. "Exhibition of the National Academy. Second Article," *Crayon* 3 (May 1856): 145–50.

215. "Sketchings. National Academy of Design," *Crayon* 4 (July 1857): 220–24.

216. "Sketchings. Exhibition of the National Academy of Design," *Crayon* 5 (May 1858): 147.

217. "Sketchings. Exhibition of the National Academy of Design. (Concluded)," *Crayon* 5 (June 1858): 175–76.

218. "Sketchings. National Academy of Design," *Crayon* 6 (May 1859): 152–53.

219. "National Academy of Design. Second Notice," *Crayon* 6 (June 1859): 189.

220. Ibid., 191.

221. "Sketchings. National Academy of Design. First Notice," *Crayon* 7 (May 1860): 140; "Sketchings. National Academy of Design. Second Notice," *Crayon* 7 (June 1860): 171.

222. "Sketchings. National Academy of Design," *Crayon* 8 (April 1861): 94–95.

223. For the history of the Academy's Twenty-third Street building, see Cummings, 332–53; Clark, 79–86; and Sarah Bradford Landau, *P. B. Wight: Architect, Contractor, and Critic, 1838–1925* (Chicago: The Art Institute of Chicago, 1981), 16–21.

224. "The Exhibition of the National Academy," *Harper's Weekly* 9 (May 13, 1865): 291. In memory of the slain president, the tympanum over the entrance to the building, designed to hold sculpture, was temporarily filled with the seal of the United States draped in black ("National Academy of Design—Fortieth Annual Exhibition," *New Path* 2 [June 1865]: 81).

225. *Appleton's Cyclopedia of American Biography*, 1: 96.

226. George Arnold, "The Academy Exhibition," *New York Leader*, April 23, April 30, 1864.

227. George Arnold, "Art Matters," *New York Leader*, June 3, June 10, June 24, 1865.

228. Esperance, "Academy of Design," *New York Leader*, June 17, 1865; Cara Montane, "Another Woman's View of the New Academy of Design," *New York Leader*, June 3, 1865.

229. Esperance, "A Woman's View of the New Academy of Design," *New York Leader*, May 27, 1865.

230. Cara Montane, "Another Woman's View of the New Academy of Design," *New York Leader*, June 3, 1865.

231. Cara Montane, "Another Woman's View of the New Academy of Design," *New York Leader*, June 3, 1865.

232. "Fine Arts. The New National Academy of Design," *Albion* 43 (May 6, 1865): 213. For the critic, the new Academy building was not alone in its faults. He was also critical of the public art buildings in London, Paris, and Munich.

233. For a discussion of the Academy's building and its relation to Ruskin, see Landau, 16–21.

234. "National Academy of Design—Fortieth Annual Exhibition," *New Path* 2 (June, 1865): 81–85.

235. "Forthcoming Exhibition of the National Academy of Design," *New York Evening Post*, April 13, 1865.

236. "The Exhibition of the National Academy," *Harper's Weekly* 9 (May 13, 1865): 291.

237. See Eliot Clark, *A History of the National Academy of Design 1825–1953* (New York: Columbia University Press, 1954), 84–104.

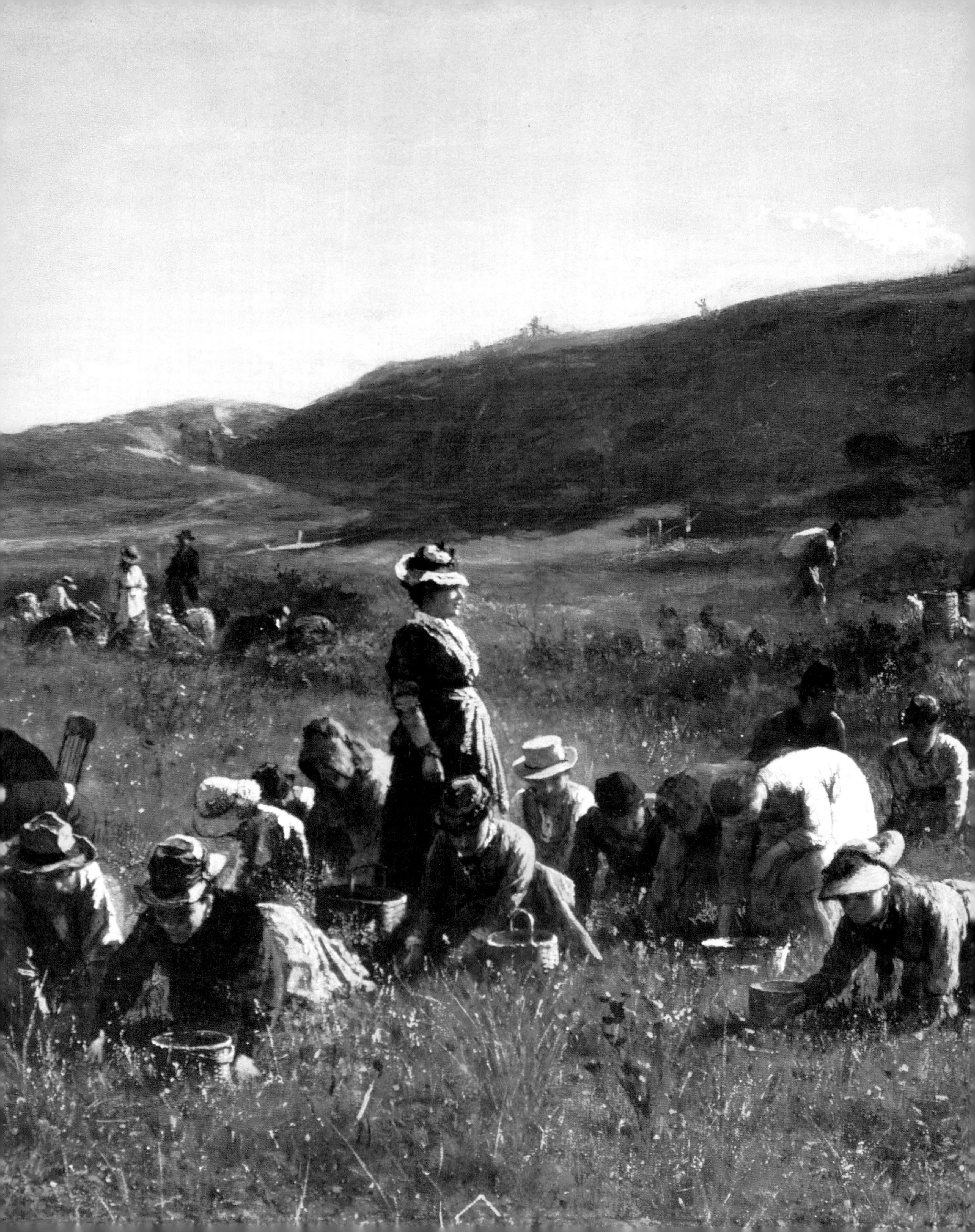

"In the Midst of an Era of Revolution": The New York Art Press and the Annual Exhibitions of the National Academy of Design in the 1870s

MARGARET C. CONRADS

On the occasion of the National Academy of Design's fiftieth annual exhibition in 1875, Clarence Cook exclaimed: "[W]e are in the midst of an era of revolution."[1] While his comments stemmed from his reaction to specific works of art, Cook's proclamation recognized that the upheaval that was strikingly apparent at the Academy exhibition was part of larger fundamental changes that had been taking place in American art for some time. The course of this revolution was at its peak between 1867 and 1880 and was manifested on the walls of the Academy. It was charted and debated in the pages of the many New York newspapers and magazines that reported on art in the 1870s.

Writers on art assumed new prominence and power during the 1870s and were instrumental in constructing and articulating American attitudes toward art. As newspapers dropped their tight political allegiances, the positions of art editor and art writer/critic became more important and formalized.[2] The result was that art writing in daily papers swiftly moved beyond straightforward reporting to a greater degree of criticism and commentary on issues. Magazines, already established as the critical forum for the visual arts, experienced a similar expansion.[3] With regard to art criticism, the most important development in periodicals was the blossoming in the 1870s of art magazines as a new genre. The *Aldine*, *American Art Review*, *Art Amateur*, *Art Interchange*, and the New York edition of the *Art Journal* were all newcomers during this period. With the exception of the *Aldine*, they all began publication between 1875 and 1878.[4] These changes heralded a new era for art criticism, one that coincided with the rapid growth of public interest in art. By the end of the 1870s the amount of attention that the press gave to art had skyrocketed.

The event that commanded the greatest percentage of critical attention during this period was the exhibition held each spring at the National Academy of Design. Despite the significance of this intersection of the press and the Academy through the reviews of these yearly exhibitions, the topic has received only cursory attention. This essay thus presents an overview of the critical response to the spring annuals of the 1870s. It examines the seminal issues of the era from the vantage point of the critics and journalists who, along with artists

and patrons, formed a dynamic trio in the New York art world. While such an approach runs the risk of extracting elements of the debates from the larger context, it offers a window onto how the majority of the art-interested public was engaged in the complex artistic issues of the day.

That significant transformations in American art began in the 1860s is well known. By the close of the Civil War, the Hudson River School of landscape painting, which had held supremacy for three decades, began to wane. No single aesthetic replaced it.[5] Rather, a variety of principles arose, chiefly due to an expanded awareness of European art. John Ruskin and the Pre-Raphaelitism of England, as well as British academic painting; the Barbizon and academic schools of France; the academy at Munich and the more radical strains produced in that city in the studios of artists such as Wilhelm Leibl; the art of Mariano Fortuny and his followers; and the aesthetic and decorative movements, all had a noteworthy impact on the development of American art. Thus, the expansion of acceptable artistic modes was a primary characteristic of American art of the 1870s.

Similarly, there was no tight, linear progression in the critical thinking of the period. However, a survey of the criticism written between 1868 and 1880 reveals a number of persistent themes that pervaded the multiple threads of thought.[6] Chief among them was the definition and concept of a national art. The question of what did or should constitute American art formed an umbrella over the debate about the purpose of art; what comprised "progress"; what benchmarks indicated its presence; and what were appropriate subjects, media, and methods of treatment for its expression. Tightly tied to all these debates was the discussion of what was American art's appropriate relationship to that of Europe. The primary forum for these discussions was the reviews of the yearly exhibitions at the National Academy of Design.

Writers who reviewed the Academy's annuals in the 1870s had the same concerns that American critics of these events had had for decades. Evaluating the present state of American art; assessing the position of the National Academy as the body in charge of mediating that state; and debating what elements contributed to a national art were the larger issues that formed the armature for the discussions of nearly every

Academy annual exhibition. Closely linked to these issues were comparisons of younger artists to older ones and examinations of the relationship of American to European art—both qualitatively and with regard to influence. Debates surrounding the definition of truth, finish, and completeness also repeatedly occurred during the period. With these issues setting the parameters of the reviews, writers critiqued individual works and artists.

As the first annual exhibition after the Paris Exposition of 1867, the Academy's 1868 show serves as a useful starting point for this essay. Carol Troyen has suggested that the response to the Exposition widened the already existing gap between artistic generations. The perceived inferiority of the American section at Paris may have encouraged younger artists to pursue alternate types of training and artistic influences, particularly French.[7] In 1868, at the Academy, the strong appearance by younger artists was of greatest interest to the critics because it created a more visible division between the older and younger artistic generations.[8] Clarence Cook noted that the split actually had been recognizable for some time. "The Exhibitions of the last five years," he wrote, "have given evidence that the Fine Arts in this country are in a state of revolution." Cook's evidence for this conclusion was that the preeminent artists of the previous decade—Thomas Rossiter, Thomas Hicks, Asher Brown Durand, David Huntington, and John Kensett, for example—were no longer at the center of discussions on art. Cook reasoned that this shift was connected to the greater presence of European art in this country.[9] On a separate occasion, the *World* noticed differences between the rising generation of figure painters and their older peers and suggested that the divide, which was noticeably along generational lines, had to do with the younger artists' maturation during the Civil War.[10]

Whatever the reasons, by 1868, hope for American art was seen to be in the "younger men." This new generation was a loosely defined group. It was clearer who they were not than who they were. As the writer for the *Mail* pointed out,

Church and Bierstadt and their fellow artists have done all for American art that they will do. Their genius has been felt, and its influence, good or bad, is at work. . . . As to whether they die to-day or to-morrow, American art, as a profession has little interest. . . . It is to younger men, younger in artistic reputation, we mean, to whom we must look for future development and progress. . . .[11]

At the Academy's 1870 annual exhibition, evidence of progress was the issue around which many reviewers framed their reactions.[12] Most effusive in its praise was the *Evening Mail*, which stated that the Academy exhibition was "the best, to our mind, where the evidences of progress are most numerous. . . . At this one . . . we pronounce not a step forward merely but a stride."[13] The opposing opinion was voiced by the *Telegram*, which simply saw no improvement, in any

capacity, from the previous year.[14] Tied to these assessments of progress was the consideration of truth in art. A lack of truthfulness throughout the show bothered a number of critics. Although it was agreed that greater study was the remedy for this problem, both the problem itself and the proper solution were articulated in multiple ways.[15] On a philosophical level, the discussion was based on the role of truth in art; its practical correlative was concerned with how it could best be achieved in visual presentations.[16] Some writers continued to cling to Ruskinian-inspired thinking, which Clarence Cook had aptly delineated in 1864 with his pronouncement, "[T]he only test of Art is its truth to Nature." Consequently, they fretted over the lack of thorough study of the material object being pictured.[17] The *Telegram* expressed such an attitude in its criticism of technique: "The greatest evident fault seems to lie in a proneness to overpaint. . . . Another fault seems to be . . . a sharpness of outline. . . . For instance, three daubs of a brush . . . will not make a figure."[18]

The opposing point of view had its roots in the writings of James Jackson Jarves, who, in *Art Hints* (1855), asserted that art should be based in universal truths through which nature is interpreted.[19] *The New York Post* echoed Jarves in 1870 when it stated that the job of an artist is to define "the true relationship between matter and spirit." Thus, the paper suggested that something other than a rendering of detail was needed: "[T]here is too little study of the picturesque and too much indifference in the matter of ideas."[20] These discussions continued the decades-long debate over a material or spiritual basis for truth in art. Increasingly, however, they came to be framed around stylistic issues rather than those of subject matter.

In 1870, such debate was particularly focused on landscape painting, which still dominated the walls of the Academy's exhibitions and the reviews that covered them. Landscape was considered the genre in which the best work was being accomplished.[21] As it had throughout the 1860s, the discussion revolved around the rivalry between Albert Bierstadt and Frederic Church; but the landscape that commanded the greatest praise from the widest range of critics in 1870 was Sanford Gifford's *San Giorgio*.[22] Bierstadt's *Sierra Nevada Mountains* (1870; Gilcrease Museum, Tulsa, Oklahoma), a panoramic, transcriptive painting in the style of the Hudson River School similar to *Among the Sierra Nevada, California* (fig. 54), received mainly negative criticism for its artificiality.[23] Church's *The After Glow* (1867; Olana State Historical Site), a more modest canvas that combined a detailed foreground with an intensely colored atmospheric effect, garnered mixed reactions. Some critics found the work a truthful attempt to suggest the phenomenon of sunset; others thought it false.[24] Gifford's *San Giorgio*, however, came closest to interweaving the variety of acceptable artistic means and philosophical viewpoints and also suggested to the critics how fact and poetry might coexist in a single canvas.[25] The *World* summed it up this way:

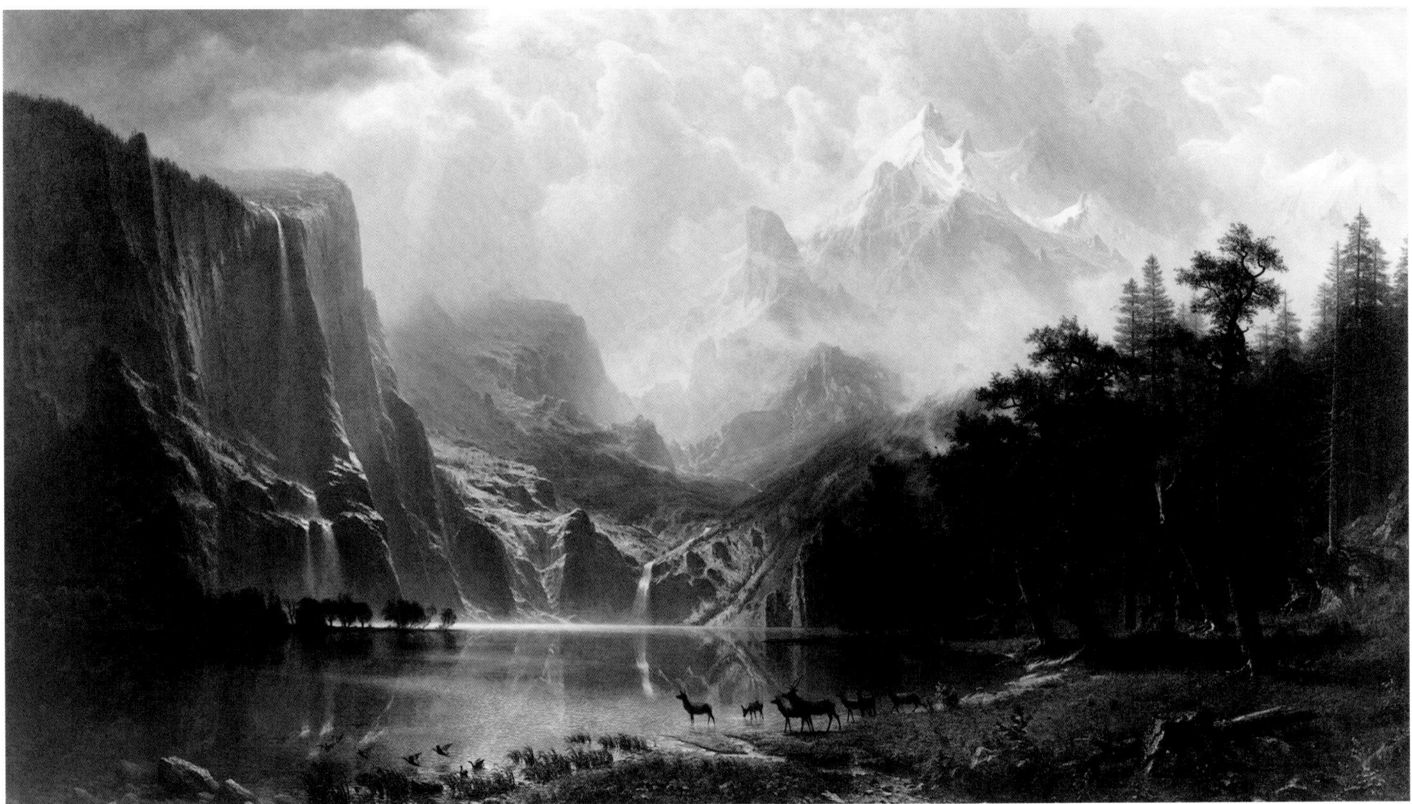

Fig. 54 Albert Bierstadt, *Among the Sierra Nevada, California,* 1868, oil on canvas, 72 x 120, National Museum of American Art, Smithsonian Institution, Bequest of Helen Huntington Hull, granddaughter of William Brown Dinsmore, who acquired the painting in 1873 for "The Locusts," the family estate in Dutchess County, New York

Perhaps no other picture in the exhibition conveys so fully an idea of completeness; that charm of totality perfected and intelligible by reason of its unity. The subject involves no technical difficulties; placid water and clear reflections of masonry are not in themselves to be reckoned among the few things in nature which forever elude the painter; but these materials have been transfused by the artist with a life of color, and he has shown rare sagacity in the use of his limited details. The consequence is that the "San Giorgio" burns like a shaft of southern sunshine in this cold marble hall.[26]

Gifford had blended careful drawing, based on particular knowledge, with an evocation of emotion through color, light, and design. For nearly every critic—no matter where his opinion lay on the spectrum of defining truth in art—such artistic strategies satisfied the notion of completion.

By 1872, the Academy's annual exhibition lost its distinction as the only art event of the spring season, and the volume of reviews covering the show, while substantial, was not as extensive as in the recent past.[27] While news of the party conventions for the 1872 presidential campaign may have curtailed the number of art reports, the expansion of art-world activities was more likely the cause of the drop in attention. As the *Mail* remarked, "The season, already so prolific of really fine exhibitions of works of Art, promises to sustain its good character to the end."[28] On view at the same time as the Academy exhibition were a show of European pictures that had been contributed to support the victims of the Great Chicago Fire; the sale of LeGrand Lockwood's collection; the Vanderlip Collection sale; and important dealers' sales by Avery, Snedecor, and Leavitt.[29] From this point in the decade, the Academy increasingly jockeyed for preeminence among art venues. By 1880, its status had considerably altered.

The reviews of 1872 also made it apparent that conflicts were brewing within the Academy. The absence of entries by important artists, or their appearance with only minor work, was seen as an indication of the organization's unsettled state.[30] Most of those repeatedly cited in this list of absentees were landscapists and included Church, Bierstadt, William and James Hart, Samuel Colman, and George Inness.[31] Whatever their reasons for staying away, their absence caused the proportion of landscapes in the annual exhibition to be smaller than usual. The ratio of landscape to genre paintings in 1872 reflected a shift in subject matter that had been growing in the Academy's shows. The number of landscape subjects decreased and figure subjects increased, each by ten percent, between 1867 and 1874.[32] Not surprisingly, this shift in the make-up of the exhibitions caused figure painters, including specialists in genre, to be noticed more. This is seen in the

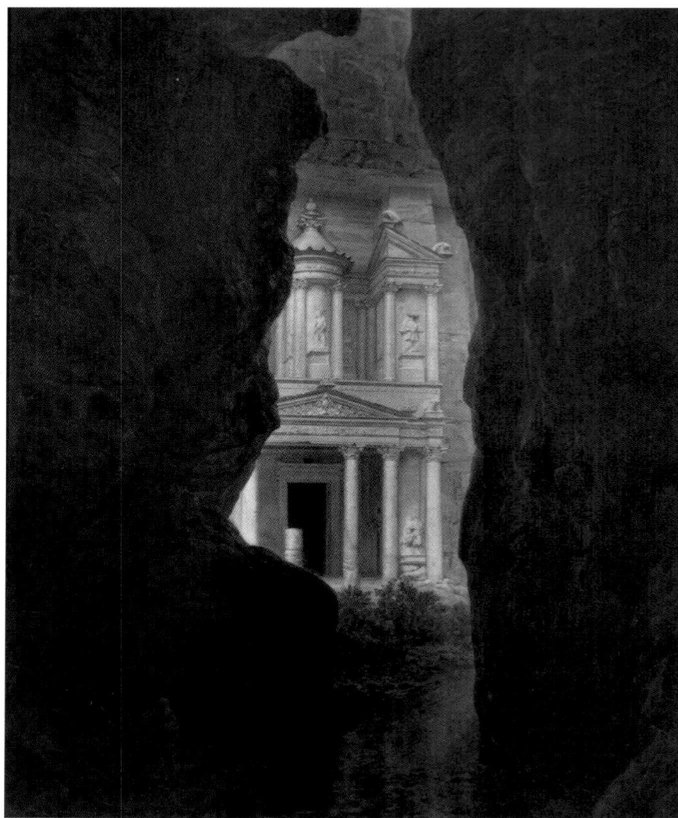

Fig. 55 Frederic Edwin Church, *El Khasne, Petra*, 1874, oil on canvas, 60½ x 5½, New York State, Office of Parks, Recreation and Historic Preservation, Olana State Historic Site (National Academy of Design, 49th Annual Exhibition, 1874, no. 320)

increase of column inches devoted to subject pictures in periodicals and newspapers, and the level of seriousness with which they were treated. Thus at the 1872 annual, Winslow Homer, Eastman Johnson, Seymour Guy, John Beaufain Irving, and Enoch Wood Perry were repeatedly discussed—not just mentioned in passing—as individuals and as a cohesive group of genre artists.

In contrast to the Academy's exhibition of 1872, that of 1874 received considerable attention, including praise for the Academy's efforts to convince the public that it was a vital organization.[33] The *Herald* understood that this effort was not intended simply to redeem the Academy as an institution, but also was related to the position of American art.[34] Thus, despite the praise given to the exhibition that year, the concern for the state of American art was raised by individual writers. In this context, some debated whether the most admired artists, such as Frederic Church, William Page, and George Inness, were sending their best work.[35] Even so, it was the dramatic canvases, including Church's *Petra* (fig. 55), Page's *Shakespeare Reading* (see no. 38 herein), and George Boughton's *The March of Miles Standish* (c. 1874; location unknown) that received most of the attention.

Looming above the selection of American paintings, however, was the placement of a foreign canvas in the exhibition's place of honor. The reactions to August Schenck's *Lost—Souvenir of Auvergne* (c. 1874; location unknown) were various in terms both of its quality and its being hung in the central spot in the most prominent gallery.[36] The *Mail* simply considered Schenck's subject hackneyed and could not agree with its prominent placement.[37] Clarence Cook questioned the canvas's placement, not because he disliked the painting but because he preferred some of the American pictures.[38] For the *Herald*, the central installation of *Lost* was praised because it was the best picture, regardless of its origin, and its prominent placement indicated the Academy had not pandered to its own or the public's sentiments.[39]

Amid the turmoil caused by Schenck's canvas and the lack of consensus about the American pictures, some writers noted that they sensed something else stirring, both within the Academy and among the artists. The *Tribune* called the show a "new departure."[40] *Scribner's* suggested that "something has waked up the artists."[41] Contributing to this notion of change was the shared belief that the younger artists continued to progress and, therefore, were responsible for the better quality of the show.[42]

The National Academy of Design's 1875 annual exhibition celebrated the institution's fiftieth anniversary. The import of this milestone was reflected in the voluminous assessments of the show.[43] In the main, writers noted progress, but fewer than one-third of the publications reviewing the show were forthrightly positive in their assessments. A reiteration and expansion of the old rule that forbade the inclusion of any previously shown work was the focus of much of the commentary, and it was generally agreed that the restriction severely compromised the selection of canvases. It was complained that the rule was not evenly applied and that it caused some of the best-known artists to boycott the exhibition.[44] Clarence Cook found that the rule further deepened the rut into which the Academy was sinking.[45] Only the *Sun* saw a positive effect from the requirement, crediting it with creating a "freshness" in the exhibition.[46]

While the Academy's anniversary and the implementation of the "no previous show" rule were topics written about repeatedly, the appearance of a large number of paintings by young Americans studying abroad, especially in Munich, created a visible change in the character of the exhibition. With the 1875 annual, a greater variety of styles and interests in American art were fully apparent, and the critics took special note. So marked was the effect of these works that Clarence Cook made the statement quoted at the beginning of this essay, "[W]e are in the midst of an era of revolution."[47] The 1875 annual presented, for the first time, the younger generation of European-trained artists—William Merritt Chase, David Neal, Toby Rosenthal, Frederick Bridgman, Wyatt Eaton, Edgar Ward, and others—as a new coalition. Their strength, in numbers and images, forced them into the forefront of most critics' articles. Thus, the revolution was waged not only on canvas but in words. A multiplicity of aesthetic preferences grew among the critics, and the viewpoints reflected in their reviews illuminated the issues that would receive increasing attention to the end of the decade. The paintings and sculptures in the 1875 exhibition and the reaction to them marked a watershed in American art history. The questions fostered by the visibility of so much foreign training became paramount and included: its general value; the relative virtues and vices of German and French art and the implications of their influence; and the desirability of home or foreign subjects. In this context, discussions of the merits of differing technical applications arose, as did discussions concerning subject matter and its relationship to style. Heated debates quickly ensued with increased frequency and fervor.

The critics generally approved of foreign study. In an atmosphere of frequent complaints that the technical flaws of American painting were caused by lack of training and the absence of full-service art schools, foreign influence provided the much sought after "look of training," as Earl Shinn called it.[48] However, Susan Nichols Carter, writing for the *Post*, noted that Munich-influenced paintings by Munich-trained American artists could be unsettling because she was not used to seeing the results of the influence of the Dutch or Flemish masters on American art.[49] Henry James liked the directness and reality of the Munich-trained artists, but he found their subjects ugly.[50] Clarence Cook had mixed reactions to the broad brushwork, earthy palette, and inelegant subjects of the style. Like Shinn and James, he acknowledged the earnestness and evidence of careful training in the foreign-schooled artists' pictures, and he admitted that the best work came from foreign-trained hands. On the other hand, he was "not much pleased" with most American members of this group because, to his eye, they imitated the German style to the point of being copyists.[51] Believing that American art should represent national cultural accomplishment, the *Tribune* critic complained that artists who had trained abroad were noticed to the exclusion of those who had stayed at home.[52] How American art could absorb the best of European aesthetics and technique while retaining its originality and independence was the crux of the matter for both critics and artists. Ultimately related to freedom, democracy, and a national identity different from that of the Old World, originality became an increasingly sought after quality in art. [53]

Due to the opening of the International Centennial Exhibition in Philadelphia in early May 1876, that year's National Academy of Design annual exhibition suffered a noticeable lack of attention. The reactions that did appear were varied. The *Times*, for example, being especially bothered by the absence of Frederic Church and Albert Bierstadt, as well as by the generally lackluster contributions of the older generation, decried the Academy's show as inferior.[54] In contrast, for a number of other critics, the absence of these artists struck a positive note.[55] Clarence Cook, in his review for the *Tribune*, was the most excited by what he saw. "The present exhibition of the Academy," he wrote,

. . . is not only much above the exhibitions of late years in general excellence, but it will make itself remembered, we are inclined to think, as one in which for the first time the influence of the new generation of painters had made itself distinctly felt. . . . [Despite reflecting much foreign influence,] there is so much independence and feeling shown as to justify the hope that the tide has turned and that we shall soon be no more bound in the flats and shallows of the last ten years.[56]

In 1875, the younger men had provided "the shock of the new"; a year later, they were embraced as the saviors of American art. Commentary often focused on the parity American artists were achieving with their European counterparts, rather than on what they were actually painting.[57] The political situation at the Academy was also part of this discussion. Both Clarence Cook and an unidentified writer for the *Atlantic* noted the improved treatment of younger artists by the Academy.[58] On the other hand, the *Express* saw evidence of jealousies in the arrangement of the exhibition. Although it considered the show an improvement overall, it felt the exhibition did not represent American or metropolitan art and called for the Academy to "wake up."[59]

In 1875, the sobriquet of "new men" was virtually synonymous with those studying in Munich; in 1876 its definition was broadened to include American artists studying in Paris, as well as some of those working at home. The names repeatedly mentioned in this context included Edward Moran, Charles H. Miller, Daniel Ridgway Knight, Thomas Hovenden, Enoch Wood Perry, Maria Oakey, A. T. Bricher, William Magrath, and Winslow Homer.[60] Although this diverse group of painters was praised *en masse*, there was great variety of opinion as to which were the best pictures, subjects, and styles. Eastman Johnson's *Husking Bee* (fig. 56; also see no. 40) received the greatest and most positive attention. Earl Shinn explained:

[An] artist who has dared to put his completeness in to his plan and not into his penciling is Mr. Eastman Johnson, whose 'Husking Bee' (285) is more vital than anything he has given us since 'Stage Coach,' and perhaps a little in advance of that … the sentiment of the scenery is what is paramount. The figures, very properly, are viewed as we view figures in a landscape, as parts of the general effect. [61]

Shinn found Johnson's design to be successfully integrated in idea, proper relation of figures, compositional design, and light, in a way increasingly sought after by the critics.

The uproar caused by the National Academy's exhibition of 1877 is well known and has been studied elsewhere.[62] Among the works that created the stir were the Turkish page subjects by William Merritt Chase and Frank Duveneck (fig. 57) as well as Walter Shirlaw's *Sheep Shearing in the*

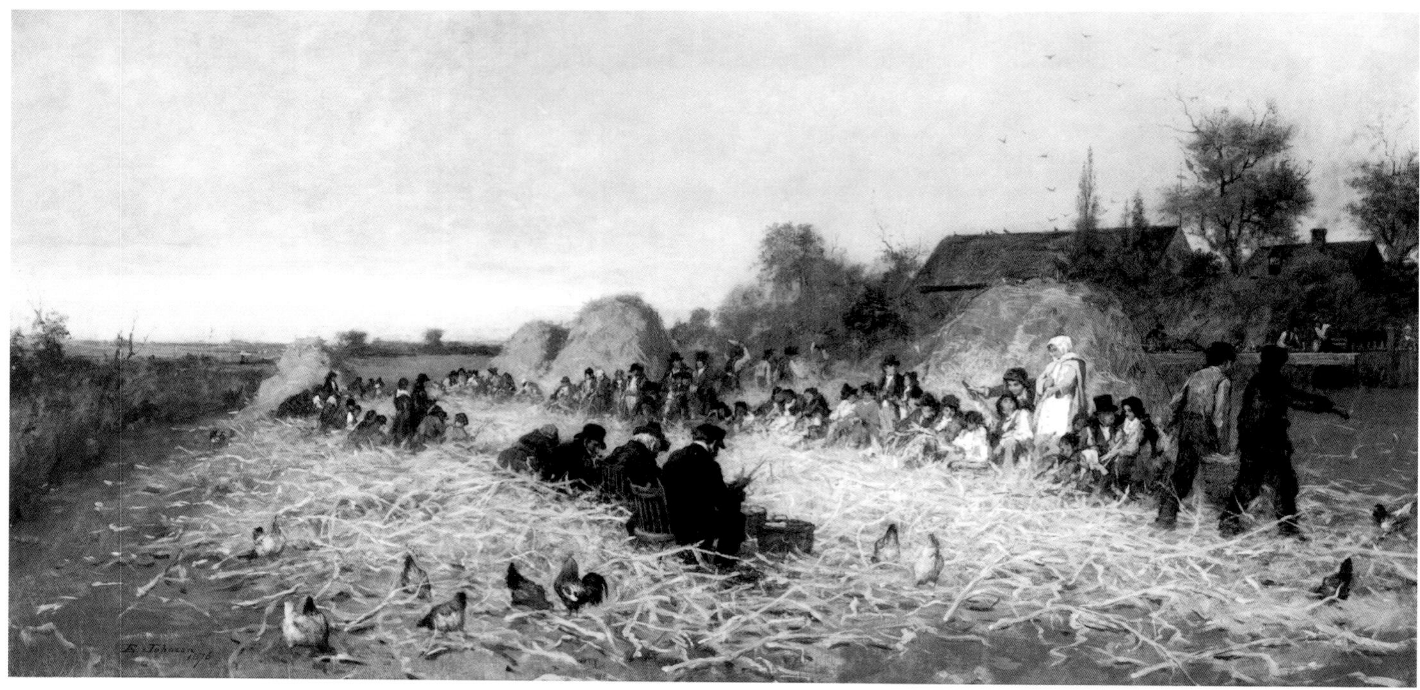

Fig. 56 Eastman Johnson, *Husking Bee, Island of Nantucket*, 1876, oil on canvas, 27¼ x 54³/₁₆, Art Institute of Chicago, Potter Palmer Collection, 1922 (National Academy of Design, 51st Annual Exhibition, 1876, no. 285)

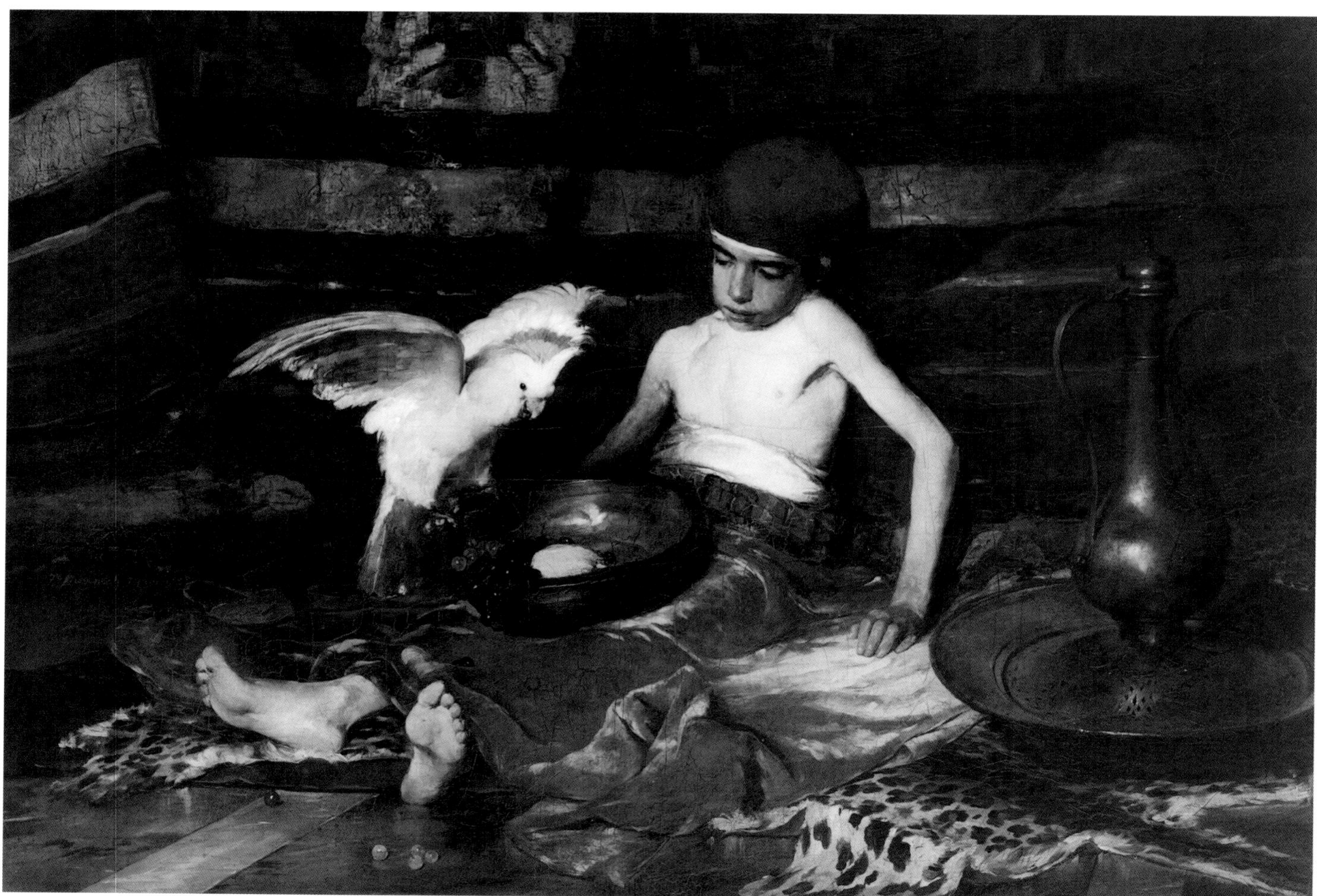

Fig. 57 Frank Duveneck, *Turkish Page*, 1876, oil on canvas, 45 x 59¾, Pennsylvania Academy of the Fine Arts (National Academy of Design, 52nd Annual Exhibition, 1877, no. 431)

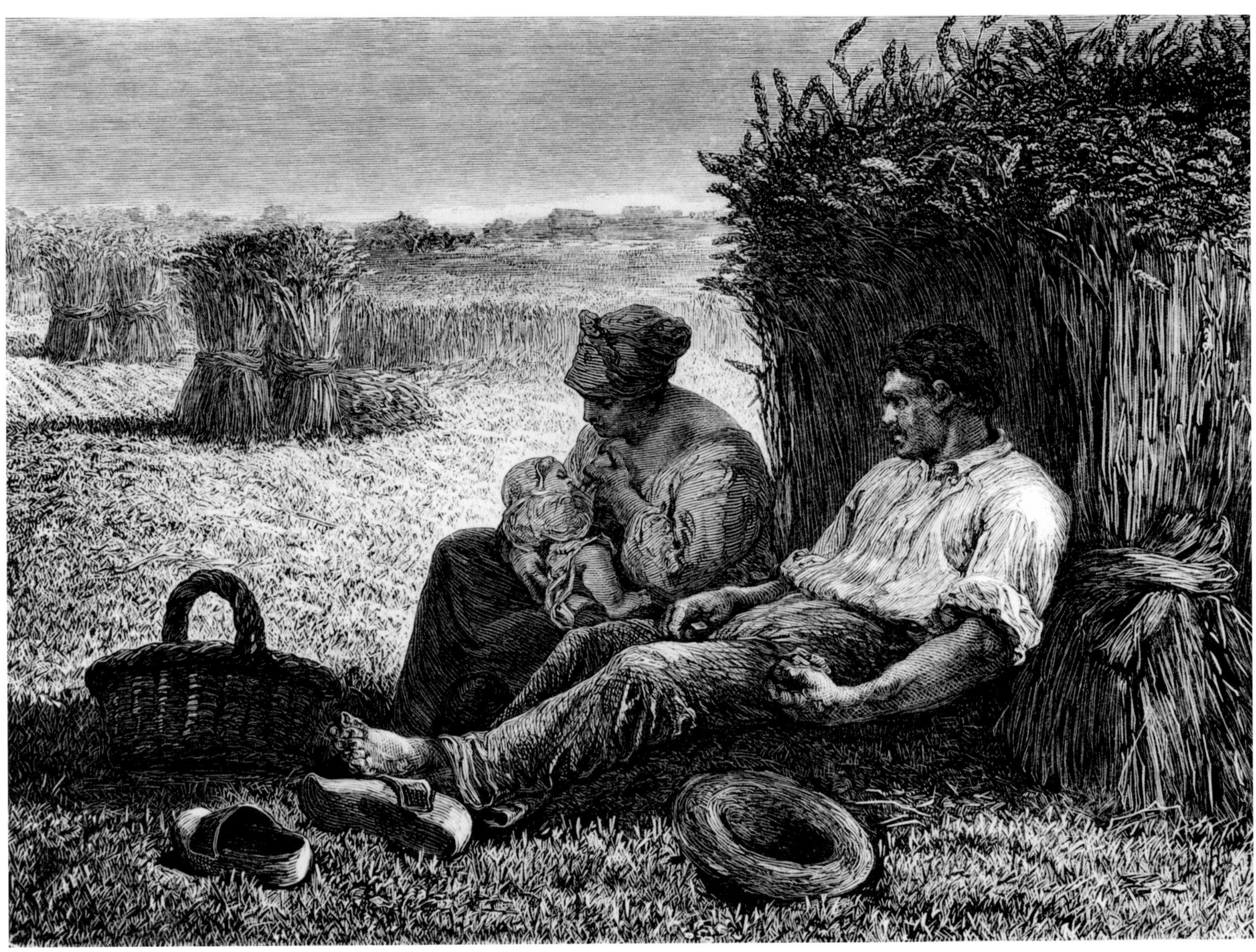

Fig. 58 Charles Wyatt Eaton, *Harvesters at Rest*, c. 1877, oil on canvas, location unknown; illustrated in G. W. Sheldon, *American Painters* (New York: D. Appleton and Co., 1879), Archives, National Academy of Design (The original painting was shown in the National Academy of Design, 52nd Annual Exhibition as no. 215.)

Bavarian Highlands (c. 1877; private collection), all of which represented the Munich-trained faction. The compositions by French-trained artists, which added to the discussion, included Wyatt Eaton's *Harvesters at Rest* (fig. 58); Daniel Ridgway Knight's *Harvest Scene* (c. 1877; location unknown); Edgar Ward's *Sabot Maker* (c. 1877; location unknown); and Will Low's *Reverie* (c. 1877; location unknown). Amid all this talk about Europe, however, home artists made their own impact on the show. Winslow Homer's *Answering the Horn* (1876; Muskegon Museum of Art, Michigan) and George Inness's *Autumn* (c. 1877; location unknown) also received repeated high praise for their American qualities.[63]

The inclusion of a large number of European-trained younger artists and the hanging of many of their works "on the line" and in other coveted spots were the most noted features of the exhibition.[64] The selection and installation together heightened the perception of a "new departure" in American art.[65] Variety of theme and treatment were its

defining features. The division between generations also appeared more distinctly. Whether an artist was considered old or young no longer depended simply on such factors as birth date, place of training, current address, choice of subjects, or methods used, but on an individual's whole approach to art. This split was defined by the *World*:

> *All men who care for art at all, and who think about it at all divide roughly into two classes. Consciously or unconsciously they care for what we call imitation (in its narrower and conventional sense) or for what we call ideality, for logic or for feeling, for truth (also in its narrower sense) or for beauty, for reason or for poetry, for exactness or for freedom, for reproduction or for production, for the tangible thing or for the suggestive thing, for representation or for illusion.*[66]

The *World* continued to assert that the old school was to be understood as grounded in imitation, factual truth, reason, exactness, and the correct reproduction of tangible things, while the new departure was based on capturing the suggestion of things in order to express feeling, beauty, and poetry.[67]

Most critics embraced this new departure as a positive stimulus despite the notably varied responses to individual artists and particular works. Many reviewers gave their recipe for what would make an American school to be proud of, and reiterated frequently that the ingredient of European training was essential. While there was nearly unanimous agreement on the importance of European training, there were disagreements as to which of the European schools provided the best models. The *World* was among the most enthusiastic voices for the Munich-trained artists.[68] The *Tribune* continued to prefer the more carefully drawn efforts of French-trained painters and rejected those of the Munich men, especially Duveneck's, as ugly and imitative.[69]

In the spring of 1878, the National Academy found itself in a new position: for the first time, its annual exhibition had a direct and serious competitor—the first annual exhibition of the Society of American Artists.[70] Another concern was the Paris Exposition of 1878, which would open in early summer. Due to these events, the Academy's 1878 exhibition had a somewhat different cast than it had had in the previous two years. Munich-trained artists were less visible than in 1877, while Paris-trained artists, including Wyatt Eaton, Abbott Thayer, Julian Alden Weir, Thomas Eakins, and Mary Cassatt, were in greater evidence. Paintings concerned with the poetic and the imagination, such as canvases by John La Farge, George Inness, Homer Martin, and George Fuller, captured a greater share of the attention. Well-known academicians, including Winslow Homer, Seymour Guy, Eastman Johnson, John George Brown, Robert Swain Gifford, and Thomas Waterman Wood, also appeared in the exhibition.

Having just completed critiquing the Society of American Artists' exhibition, the press found the 1878 Academy exhibition to be simply less exciting than in the past.[71] There were no heated discussions of either its excellence or its inferiority. Writers who had less than positive reactions to the exhibition noted that it would have been difficult to live up to the previous year's showing. The *World* pointed out the conservatism of the hanging committee, which consisted of Aaron Draper Shattuck, John Casilear, and Henry Augustus Loop. It also discussed the "8-foot rule," a short-lived resolution that guaranteed a certain amount of desirable space for the works of the Academicians. It had been adopted in reaction to the inclusion of so many younger artists in the 1877 exhibition. This rule, the *World* felt, signaled a "return of the natives" and resulted in a much less interesting exhibition. Clarence Cook, too, found the show tame compared with that of the previous year, although he gave the members of the Academy credit for trying hard. He confessed, however, that he preferred the Society of American Artists' exhibition.[72] The lack of any truly notable works—such as Duveneck's *Turkish Page* (fig. 57), which was on view at the Society—was also cited as a decided weakness of the Academy's show. In fact, Cook criticized the figural paintings in general and the seemingly less ambitious efforts of older and younger artists alike.[73]

If the Academy's 1879 exhibition did not generate the excitement of 1877, it overcame the malaise of that of 1878. Even though the Society's exhibition diluted the power of the Academy show, the latter was thoroughly reviewed.[74] In the main, the exhibition was considered to be a success. However, some critics felt the younger artists were not following up on the promise they had shown two years earlier. The *Independent* remarked that the "impulse of fresh blood, which promised so much two years ago . . . has not quickened its pulse one jot."[75] The *Post* agreed and pointed out that there were "no new bravura passages in the new schools' display like those . . . two years ago."[76] Whatever the critics felt about the younger artists—which now included more women—on the whole, it was clear that the younger generation's contributions created a contest between those trained in Munich and those trained in Paris. Shirlaw, Chase, and Duveneck were frequently compared with James Carroll Beckwith, J. Alden Weir, Wyatt Eaton, Edgar Ward, and the newcomer, John Singer Sargent, who exhibited *Neapolitan Boys Bathing* (see no. 43).[77]

The topic most prominently discussed in 1879 was the need for more thought and completeness in American painting. *Appleton's*, the *Tribune*, the *Times*, and *American Architect and Building News* all asserted that substantial meaning was lacking in the canvases on display and that meaning was one of the most critical elements in art—if not *the* most. Although *Appleton's* found a fairly high proportion of noteworthy pictures in the show, it commented that "none are absolutely great; a few have national character, but none of them exert absolute power over the sympathies of the people . . . . very little if anything . . . 'stirs the heart,' takes possession of the imagination or . . . affections."[78] For most critics of the day, technique needed to play a subordinate but supportive role to subject matter that elicited an emotional response.

An overemphasis on technical excellence, especially since the return of American students from Munich, drove a number of art writers to plead for deeper thought in art. No one questioned the importance of good methods, or even that, perhaps, they were best learned in a European setting. Some worried, however, that their usefulness as the means to an end—that is, to enable the presentation of a completed thought—had been forgotten. This concern was at the heart of Susan Nichols Carter's comments on the Academy's exhibition. She found that the "difficulty with many of the new men, as they are called, is not that they do not know how to use color, that they are deficient, in the technical requirements of Art, but they rest their efforts there . . . [We] see no character, no force, beyond the cleverness of the *technique*." She found a similar lack of deep conception among the home and older artists. She felt that "simple subjects . . . simply treated" had been the ambition of home artists for some time, and that this focus had suppressed imagination "and the mere subject stated all there was to tell."[79] Mariana Griswold van Rensselaer felt similarly and tied her remarks directly to the sketch-versus-finish debate, writing,

> *[It] is not the sketchiness I blame. . . . A dozen outline strokes may be sufficient unto themselves. . . . But a picture which starts to be a definite rendering and stops half-way cannot be more satisfactory than a half-written book, no matter how clever or a block-out statue, though genius held the mallet. . . . Finish for the sake of finish is not desirable, but neither is incompleteness for the sake of supposed vigor.*[80]

The question was not which methods were best but to what purpose they were put.

From these general platforms, the critics still reacted variously to Munich-trained artists. Noticeable, however, is their consistent praise for French-trained artists, especially James Carroll Beckwith, John Singer Sargent, and Wyatt Eaton. Earl Shinn (writing as Edward Strahan) concisely outlined the reasons. He explained that Munich students were more showy and popular as a result of their technical flair. He also admitted that Munich-inspired canvases were clever and that those on the Academy walls were attractive. Yet, to his mind and eye, they gave attention to the wrong qualities and ultimately were superficial. In contrast, he said, the French system was "austere, thorough, and honorable . . . [an] ideal is to be planted on anatomical accuracy."[81] For Shinn, as well as for a number of his peers, the influence of Munich created an art of the surface—both of paint and thought—while the French methods produced an art of more depth, both in construction and ideas.

In this atmosphere, the artist who received the broadest praise was George Fuller, for his two entries in the Academy's exhibition, *The Romany Girl* (c. 1879; location unknown) and especially *And She Was a Witch* (fig. 59). A number of critics praised Fuller for the Americanness of his subjects, as well as

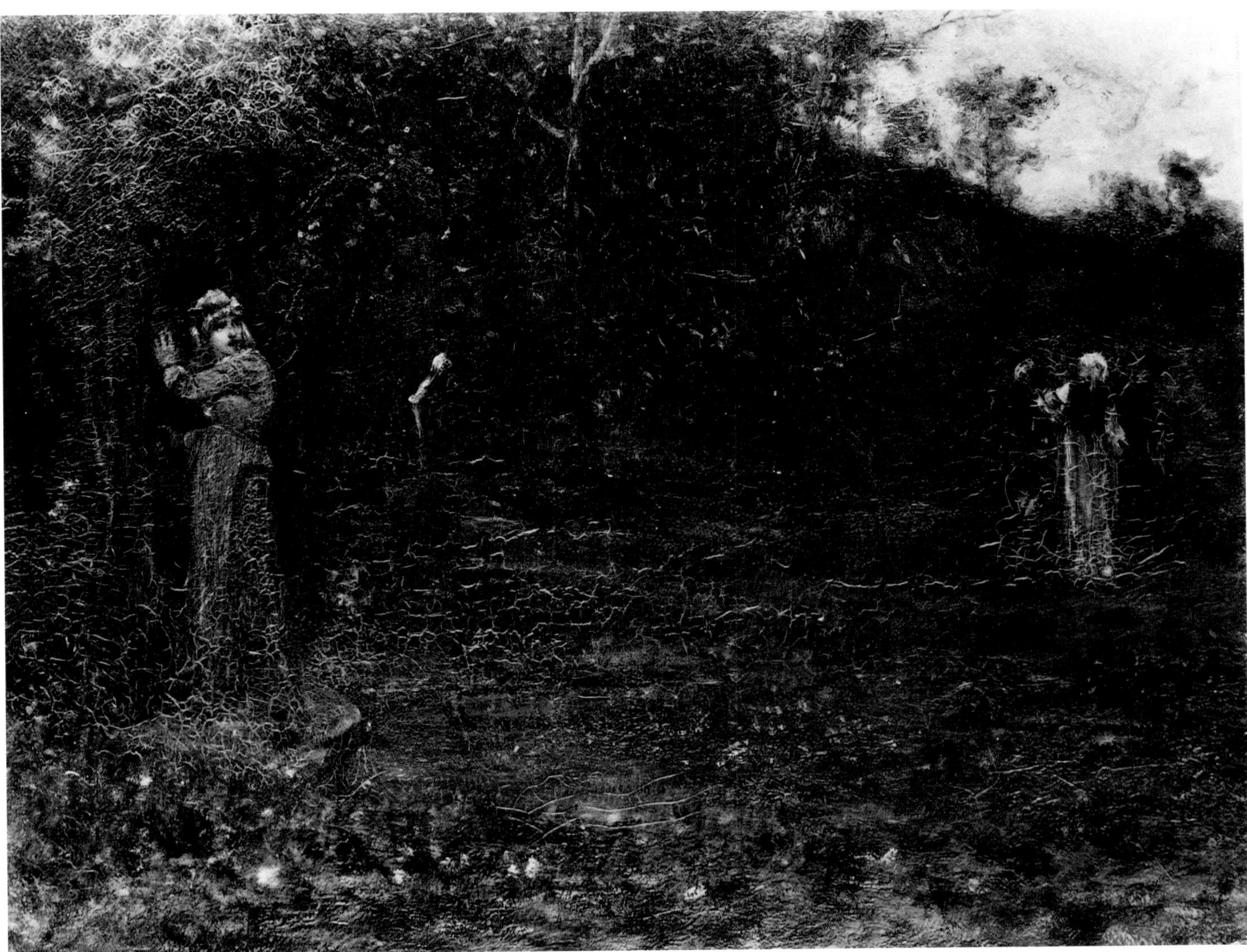

Fig. 59 George Fuller, *And She Was a Witch*, 1877/83, oil on canvas, 30 x 40, The Metropolitan Museum of Art, Gift of George I. Seney, 1887 (National Academy of Design, 54th Annual Exhibition, 1879, no. 421)

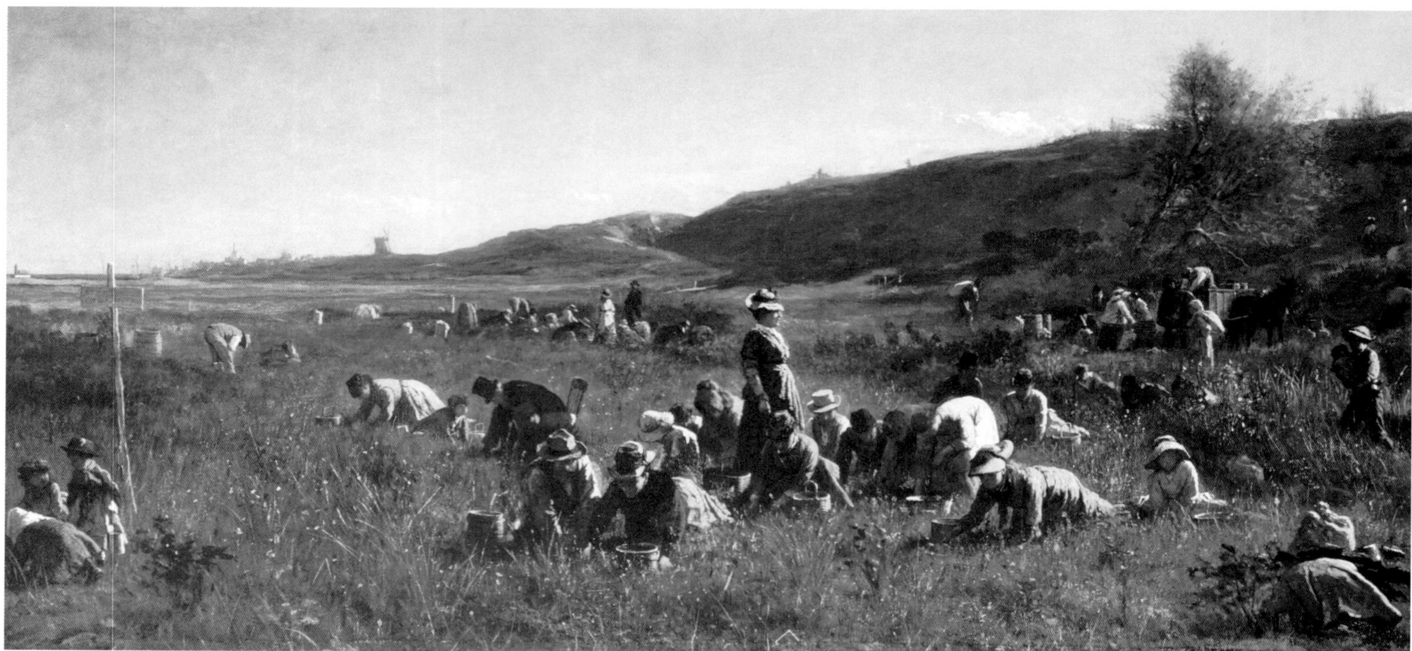

Fig. 60 Eastman Johnson, *Cranberry Harvest, Nantucket*, 1880, oil on canvas, 27 x 55, The Putnam Foundation, Timken Museum of Art, San Diego (National Academy of Design, 55th Annual Exhibition, no. 382)

his ability to render them with sympathy, drama, imagination, subjectivity, and a literary quality.[82] He satisfied the requirements of both the most cosmopolitan and the nationalistic critics. As art historian Sarah Burns has suggested, Fuller's success came from his combining the local character so admired in the work of an artist like Winslow Homer with the poetry found in the canvases of the French-trained William Morris Hunt. It was a combination that pleased almost everyone.[83]

By 1880, it was clear that the National Academy of Design's annual exhibitions no longer held the prominence they had in the past.[84] A number of critics noted that the 1880 exhibition was neither the only important exhibition nor the most interesting that year. Comparisons of the Academy with the Society of American Artists, both as organizations and as representatives of opposing artistic camps, became more frequent (see the essay "The National Academy of Design and the Society of American Artists: Rivals Viewed by Critics, 1878–1906" in this book). The *Independent* noted specifically that the Academy had been harmed by the success of other venues.[85] The Academy was seen as an institution unable to generate excitement, display the vitality of art, or suggest a sense of progress.[86]

The 1880 annual show was deemed mediocre at best by most critics. For many, it was compromised by the absence of a number of key younger artists—especially the Munich-trained trio of William Merritt Chase, Walter Shirlaw, and J. Frank Currier—and important older contributors, such as George Inness and Frederic Church. Fewer artists who were members of the Society showed at the Academy that year, and with no works by either Inness or Church to laud or con-

demn, the overall exhibition had fewer extremes than in the recent past. Most noticeable was that visual investigations of outdoor light and color hung next to tonal images replete with poetry and sentiment. Among them, Eastman Johnson's *Cranberry Harvest, Nantucket* (fig. 60) and George Fuller's *Quadroon Girl* (1880; The Metropolitan Museum of Art, New York) appeared at the top of nearly every critic's list.

Johnson's painting was nearly unanimously considered the best of the older artists' work. The canvas pictured, in glittering light and with vivid color, a sunny moment of everyday life on Nantucket. At the same time, the machine-less harvesting image resonated with the memories of a simpler past.[87] It had elements that satisfied both those who needed the comfort of the older genre tradition and those who preferred accomplished technique reflective of European-inspired methods. While the expression of external nature through dazzling light and color elicited rave reviews for Johnson's canvas, poetic sentiment and tonal palettes continued their rise in acceptance and praise. For these qualities, Fuller's *Quadroon Girl* received high marks for its combination of beauty and artistic harmony.[88]

While no particular issues generated debate in the 1880 Academy exhibition, one thing was clear: no matter how one felt about artists, old or young, the art world had changed. Most noticeable, perhaps, was that by 1880 the younger artists were no longer a sensation, an observation made by William Cary Brownell, among others, in his seminal article "The Younger Painters of America." They were a generally accepted part of the fabric of American art.[89] As the state of American art became increasingly framed in a cosmopolitan context, the definition of progress shifted from one based on technical proficiency to one grounded in content, especially emotional. The art press, which had undergone its own expansion and change of generations in the 1870s, had closely followed this remarkable revolution. It was a revolution most visible at the annual exhibitions of the National Academy of Design.

NOTES

1. "Fine Arts. The National Academy of Design. Fiftieth Annual Exhibition. Third Notice," *New York Tribune*, April 29, 1875.

2. Frederic Hudson, *Journalism in the United States from 1690–1872* (New York: Harper Brothers, 1873), 778. In 1870, ten daily New York newspapers included art writing in their pages. These were the *Commercial Advertiser, Evening Express, Evening Mail, Evening Post, Evening Telegram, New York Daily Tribune, New York Herald, New York Times, New York World*, and *Sun*. Three of these papers had only begun publication after 1860. The *World* was established in 1861, and the *Mail* and *Telegram* in 1867. The *Independent* was a weekly and, although it was published in 1868–69, art articles only appeared from 1870. The *Daily Graphic*, founded in 1873, printed writings on art from that date.

3. Through the 1870s, eight general magazines had ongoing commitments to art, and five of them only began publication after 1865. The general magazines included *Appleton's Journal, Atlantic Monthly, Galaxy, Harper's New Monthly Magazine, Harper's Weekly, Nation, Putnam's Monthly*, and *Scribner's Monthly*.

4. Although not exclusively devoted to the fine arts, *American Architect and Building News* contributed important art writing from the end of the decade.

5. On the rise and fall of the Hudson River School, see John K. Howat et al., *American Paradise: The World of the Hudson River School* (New York: Metropolitan Museum of Art, 1987).

6. For a more lengthy investigation of the aesthetic identities of the critics and the serials they worked for, see Margaret C. Conrads, "Winslow Homer and His Critics in the 1870s" (Ph.D. diss., City University of New York, 1999).

7. Carol Troyen, "Innocents Abroad: American Painters at the 1867 Exposition Universelle, Paris," *American Art Journal* 16 (Autumn 1984): 13–22.

8. See, for example, "Notes on Art," *New York Herald*, April 20, 1868, and "The National Academy. The Reception," *New York Mail*, April 15, 1868.

9. "The National Academy of Design. Forty-Third Annual Exhibition, " *New York Tribune*, May 4, 1868.

10. "Art in New York. Past and Present," *New York World*, January 2, 1868.

11. "The National Academy. The Reception," *New York Mail*, April 15, 1868.

12. Those that focused on progress included "National Academy of Design. Reception and Private View—The Forty-Fifth Annual Exhibition," *World*, April 15, 1870; "The Spring Exhibition. Forty-Fifth Annual Exhibition of the N.A.D.," *Mail*, April 18, 1870; and "The Exhibition At The Academy Of Design," *Albion*, 48 (May 21, 1870).

13. *Mail*, April 18, 1870.

14. "Fine Arts. National Academy of Design—Critical Review of a Portion of the Pictures on Exhibition," *Telegram*, April 23, 1870.

15. Only the *World* felt otherwise, suggesting more than usual care and thought could be seen in the show, especially in the landscapes (*World*, April 15, 1870).

16. In a similar manner, Laura Meixner has outlined the different camps of critics writing around 1865–70, but her focus was their response to French art. See Meixner, *French Realist Painting and the Critique of American Society, 1865–1900* (New York: Cambridge University Press, 1995), 142.

17. "National Academy of Design," *Tribune*, April 30, 1864.

18. *Telegram*, April 23, 1870.

19. Jarves wrote that the "failures . . .of Art generally arise chiefly from commencing at the wrong end. Instead of first studying the great principles of Nature, upon which all Art is founded, and working from them *outwardly*, artists too commonly are led by their blind impulses; and looking first to external expression, begin on the *outside* of Art, applying to it primarily the technical rules of material excellence; as it were, building their house before they knew what kind of spirit is to occupy it. This is working in the dark. The meaning of the work must first be considered" (James Jackson Jarves, *Art Hints* [New York: Harper and Brothers, 1855], 310).

20. "Art Notes," *Evening Post*, October 13, 1870; "National Academy of Design. Third Notice," *Evening Post*, June 10, 1870.

21. On the high esteem in which landscape was held, see, for example, *World*, April 15, 1870; "Art Notes. National Academy of Design," *Herald*, April 24, 1870; and "Art Notes. The Academy of Design," *Albion* 48 (April 23, 1870), 267.

22. Ila Weiss, *Poetic Landscape: The Art and Experience of Sanford R. Gifford* (Newark: University of Delaware Press, 1987), 328, lists *San Giorgio* (1869–70) as formerly in the collection of Richard Butler, but now unlocated.

23. Such complaints about Bierstadt were aired in "Art Gossip," *Mail*, April 20, 1870; "Art Notes. National Academy of Design," *New York Herald*, May 8, 1870; and *Albion* 48 (April 23, 1870): 267.

24. See, for example, "Fine Arts. The Exhibition of Paintings at the National Academy of Design," *Telegram*, April 28, 1870; "Fine Arts," *New York Times*, April 17, 1870; "Fine Arts," *Times*, April 24, 1870; *Mail*, April 18, 1870; and *Albion* 48 (April 23, 1870): 267.

25. Just a few critics found aspects to condemn in Gifford's work. The *Mail* complained the painting was too showy, while the *Nation* confessed it liked the picture very much, but found the atmosphere too artificial. "Art Gossip," *Mail*, April 20, 1870, and "Forty-Fifth Exhibition of the National Academy of Design. Second Notice," *Nation* 10 (2 June 1870): 357.

26. "Academy of Design. Second Article," *World*, May 8, 1870.

27. For example, while the *World, Tribune,* and *Mail* printed a minimum of three reviews each, two or more of them were only short references rather than the extensive multiple reviews that had appeared in 1870.

28. "Art Gossip," *Mail*, March 23, 1872.

29. Mentions of these events were made in, among others, *Mail*, March 23, 1872; "Fine Arts," *Times*, April 14, 1872; and "Art Matters. LeGrand Lockwood Collection," *Express*, April 13, 1872. How the commerce of art was conducted was rapidly changing in this era. This is a topic needing further, in-depth study. It has been covered generally in Linda Skalet, "The Market for American Painting in New York, 1870–1915" (Ph.D. diss., Johns Hopkins University, 1980). A more recent overview of it can be found in Gerald D. Bolas, "The Early Years of the American Art Association" (Ph.D. diss., City University of New York, 1998), 12–98.

30. Those reviews that made reference to the Academy conflicts in this regard included "Fine Arts," *Tribune*, April 12, 1872; "The Spring Exhibition of the Academy of Design," *Herald*, April 14, 1872; and "Gallery Gossip. The Academy of Design," *World*, April 28, 1872.

31. See, for example, *Herald*, April 14, 1872; "The Academy Exhibition," *World*, April 12, 1872; *Times*, April 14, 1872; "The Spring Exhibition of the National Academy," *Appleton's Journal* 7 (May 25, 1872): 578–80; and "Art Reception," *Mail*, April 12, 1872. Church, in particular, was criticized for what appeared as snubbing the exhibition, since he chose to show his new magnum opus, *The Parthenon* (1871; The Metropolitan Museum of Art), in a solo exhibition. Clarence Cook severely criticized Church in the *Tribune*, April 12, 1872. Eleanor Harvey has noted that Church never exhibited his "Great Pictures" at the Academy (Eleanor Jones Harvey, *The Painted Sketch: American Impressions from Nature 1830–1880* [Dallas: Dallas Museum of Art, 1998], 67).

32. Theodore E. Stebbins, Jr., "Luminism in Context: A New View," in *American Light: The Luminist Movement, 1850–75* (Washington, D.C.: National Gallery of Art, 1980), 215. Stebbins's estimate was based on titles and thus not authoritatively accurate, but the numbers give a reasonable idea of the change. Why it occurred is a subject for its own study, yet scholars have touched on the significant reasons. Nicolai Cikovsky has suggested that the destruction of so much land during the Civil War damaged the concept of the landscape as the location for national beliefs (Nicolai Cikovsky, "School of War," in *Winslow Homer* [Washington, D.C.: National Gallery of Art, 1995], 72). At the same time, as Sarah Burns has noted, genre became an increasingly appropriate vehicle for exploring the issues of the day. The increased interaction of populations fostered human interaction as a worthy subject (Sarah Burns, *Pastoral Inventions: Rural Life in Nineteenth Century American Art and Culture* [Philadelphia: Temple University Press, 1989], 6).

33. The exhibition was covered by at least ten newspapers and six magazines. For reviews of a positive nature, see, for example, "Art at the Academy," *Telegram*, April 11, 1874; "The Academy Exhibition," *World*, April 9, 1874; and "Fine Arts. The Academy Exhibition," *Times*, April 6, 1874. In no review was there a truly dissenting voice.

34. "The Spring Exhibition of the Academy of Design," *Herald*, April 7, 1874.

35. In the case of Church's *Petra*, the *Post* praised it for its "rare force and beauty," while the *World* criticized it as unworthy of the artist's brush because it was neither pictorial nor interesting ("National Academy of Design," *Post*, April 8, 1874, and "National Academy of Design. First Article," *World*, April 19, 1874). "The New Departure at the National Academy," *Mail*, April 9, 1874, and "Art at the

Academy," *Telegram*, April 11, 1874, agreed with the *Post*, while "Fine Arts. The Exhibition at the Academy of Design," *Sun*, April 15, 1874, and [Earl Shinn], "Fine Arts. The National Academy Exhibition. II," *Nation* 18 (May 14, 1874): 320–21, concurred with the *World*.

36. The painting was described as "a woman—presumably a shepherd girl—clinging to a wayside cross in the midst of a terrible snow storm. In the foreground are crowded together a flock of sheep wild with terror. On the left, two dogs crouch together, blinded and frightened by the violence of the tempest" (*Sun*, April 15, 1874).

37. "Fine Arts. The Exhibition at the Academy of Design," *Mail*, April 25, 1874. The *Mail* was the only paper that truly disliked the painting, though others were critical of particular aspects.

38. "Fine Arts. National Academy of Design. Forty-Ninth Annual Exhibition. Second Article," *Tribune*, April 11, 1874.

39. "The Academy of Design. Some Gems of the Present Exhibition," *Herald*, April 20, 1874.

40. "Fine Arts," *Tribune*, April 9, 1874.

41. "Culture and Progress. The Academy Exhibition," *Scribner's* 8 (June 1874): 245.

42. "Fine Arts. Annual Exhibition of the National Academy of Design," *Daily Graphic*, April 9, 1874; "The Academy of Design. The Private View—List of Pictures Sold," *Times*, April 9, 1874; and *Mail*, April 9, 1874.

43. Eleven newspapers and six magazines covered the exhibition in depth.

44. See, for example, "Art Matters. Academy of Design—The Fiftieth Annual Exhibition," *Express*, April 8, 1875; "Academy of Design. Opening of the Fiftieth Annual Exhibition," *Herald*, April 8, 1875; and "The Fine Arts. The Exhibition at the Academy of Design," *Times*, April 17, 1875. A listing of some of the works already shown appeared in "The Academy and the Clubs," *Tribune*, April 10, 1875.

45. "Fine Arts. The National Academy of Design–Fiftieth Annual Exhibition–Private View," *Tribune*, April 9, 1875. Cook was clear that it was the Academy that was in the rut and not the whole of American art, which he felt was not adequately represented, due, in part, to the rule.

46. "The National Academy of Design. A Half Century of American Painting," *Sun*, April 21, 1875.

47. "Fine Arts. The National Academy of Design. Fiftieth Annual Exhibition. Third Notice," *Tribune*, April 29, 1875.

48. [Shinn], *Nation* 20 (April 22, 1875): 281–82. Among those concurring were *Herald*, April 8, 1875, and "Fine Arts," *Independent*, April 29, 1875.

49. S. N. C. [Susan Nichols Carter], "The Academy Exhibition. I. The Portraits and Fancy Heads," *Post*, April 17, 1875.

50. Henry James, "On Some Pictures Lately Exhibited," *Galaxy* 20 (July 1875): 94–95.

51. *Tribune*, April 29, 1875. It was the fine draftsmanship of the French-trained Frederick Bridgman and Wyatt Eaton that inspired Cook's praise for foreign-trained artists, although he admired Munich-trained David Neal.

52. *Tribune*, April 9, 1874.

53. Originality was a complex notion that occupied the center of much thinking in American arts and letters during the nineteenth century. It was seen, especially in literature, as a crucial component in the creation of a distinct American idiom. On American literature's relationship with nationalism, see Benjamin T. Spencer, *The Quest for Nationality* (Syracuse, New York: Syracuse University Press, 1957).

54. "Academy of Design. The Fifty-First Annual Exhibition—Private View and Reception," *Times*, March 28, 1876.

55. See, for example, "The National Academy of Design. First Notice," *Art Journal* 2 (May 1876): 157; "Fine Arts. The Fifty-First Academy Exhibition," *Mail*, March 30, 1876; and "The Art Exhibition. The Annual Display of the National Academy," *Daily Graphic*, March 29, 1876.

56. "Fine Arts-Music-The Drama. Fine Arts. Fifty-First Annual Exhibition of the National Academy of Design," *Tribune*, March 28, 1876.

57. Linda Jones Docherty, "A Search for Identity: American Art Criticism and the Concept of the 'Native School,' 1876–1893" (Ph.D. diss., University of North Carolina, Chapel Hill, 1985), 67.

58. "Fine Arts. National Academy of Design. Fifty-First Annual Exhibition," *Tribune*, April 1, 1876, and "Art," *Atlantic* 37 (June 1876): 758.

59. "Art Matters. A Hasty Glance at the Academy Exhibition," *Express*, May 6, 1876.

60. See, for example, "Academy of Design. The Fifty-First Annual Exhibition—Private View and Reception," *Times*, March 28, 1876; "The Arts. Representative Pictures at the Academy," *Appleton's* 15 (April 15, 1876): 508–10; and "Fifty-First

Exhibition of the National Academy," *Sun*, March 28, 1876. Munich-trained artists were, in fact, somewhat in the background as their numbers were fewer this year.

61. [Earl Shinn], "Fine Arts. Exhibition of the National Academy of Design," *Nation* 22 (April 6, 1876): 234. Among those who also praised Johnson's canvas in this way were *Art Journal* 2 (May 1876): 159; *Daily Graphic*, March 29, 1876; and *Appleton's* 15 (April 15, 1876): 508–9.

62. For a description of the events surrounding this show, see Jennifer A. Bienenstock, "The Formation and Early Years of the Society of American Artists, 1877-1884" (Ph.D. diss., City University of New York, 1983), 1–57.

63. See, for example, "Fine Arts. The Academy Exhibition. II," *Mail*, April 23, 1877, and "The Academy of Design. Some Landscapes in the Fifty-Second Annual Exhibition," *Post*, April 21, 1877. While Homer and Inness were praised for their American qualities, it cannot be ignored that they achieved such notice with paintings reverberating with French influence.

64. Critics considered the contents of the exhibition to be among the finest or even *the* finest ever, but they considered the installation by hanging committeemen Charles H. Miller, Thomas LeClear, and Wordsworth Thompson to be controversial and the worst ever. That was the feeling, for example, in "The Academy Exhibition. I," *World*, April 10, 1877; "The Academy of Design. The Pictures and Sculpture in the Fifty-Second Annual Exhibition. First Paper," *Post*, April 10, 1877; and "Pictures in the Spring Exhibition. The Present Attractions of the Academy of Design—Works by Representative Artists," *Daily Graphic*, April 6, 1877.

65. The phrase "new departure" was specifically used by *World*, April 10, 1877, and "American Art. The Academy of Design. A Second View of the Exhibition—Landscapes by the Younger Artists," *New-York Times*, April 8, 1877, and articulated by description or suggestion in "At the Academy. II. Figure Pictures and Portraits," *Tribune*, April 7, 1877; "Fine Arts. The Academy Exhibition. I," *Mail*, 16 April 16, 1877; "The Academy Exhibition," *Art Journal* 3 (May 1877): 157; and "Culture and Progress. The National Academy Exhibition," *Scribner's* 14 (June 1877): 263. The *Art Journal* noticed that what some saw as a suddenness of change was just a reaction to surface differences, but, in fact, had been in progress for some time (*Art Journal* 3 [May 1877]: 157).

66. *World*, April 10, 1877.

67. Ibid.

68. "The Academy Exhibition. II," *World*, April 14, 1877.

69. *Tribune*, April 7, 1877.

70. As Jennifer Bienenstock has pointed out, the Society of American Artists played a pivotal role in shifting American artistic identity away from one defined by subject matter, especially landscape and inventive individualism, to a more universal concept of art that shared the history of Western civilization (Bienenstock, "Society of American Artists," 1–8).

71. Some periodicals completely lost interest in the Academy. *Atlantic* and *Scribner's* did not report on it at all, choosing instead to focus on the Paris Exposition.

72. Considering Cook's pivotal role in the formation and support of the Society, it would have been strange for him not to have such a response. "Art at the Academy. The Fifty-Third Annual Exhibition," *Tribune*, April 2, 1878.

73. See, for example, "Fine Arts. The Fifty-Third Exhibition of the Academy of Design," *Nation* 26 (April 18, 1878): 265–66; "The Academy of Design. Opening of the Fifty-Third Annual Exhibition," *Post*, March 30, 1878; "The Academy Exhibition. Portraits," *Times*, April 7, 1878; and "The National Academy of Design. I," *Sun*, April 7, 1878.

74. Twenty-one magazines and newspapers covered the show. Of them, the *Times* and the *Herald* devoted the greatest number of articles to it—eight each, although not all were long. In addition to these two papers, the *Tribune*, *World*, *Telegram*, and *Sun*, as well as the *Art Journal*, *Appleton's*, *Art Amateur* (new on the scene), and the *Nation* gave it especially full attention.

75. "Fine Arts. National Academy," *Independent*, April 10, 1879.

76. "The Academy Exhibition. First Impression and a Hasty Tour of the Galleries," *Post*, March 30, 1879.

77. An especially cogent discussion outlining the differences can be found in Edward Strahan [Earl Shinn], "The Art Gallery. The National Academy of Design. First Notice," *Art Amateur* 1 (June 1879): 4–5.

78. "Editor's Table. The Academy Exhibition," *Appleton's* 6 (May 1879): 471. Charles De Kay and Clarence Cook offered similar reactions in "America in Pictures," *Times*, April 16 1879, and "Academy of Design. Fifty-Fourth Annual Exhibition. Fourth Article," *Tribune*, April 26, 1879.

79. Susan Nichols Carter, "The Academy Exhibition," *Art Journal* 5 (May 1879): 158.

80. M. G. van Rensselaer, "The Spring Exhibition in New York. The National Academy of Design—The Society of American Artists, Etc.," *American Architect and Building News* 5 (May 10, 1879): 148.

81. Strahan, *Art Amateur* 1 (June 1879): 26–29.

82. Praise for Fuller appeared in "Preparing the Pictures. The Artist's Varnishing Day," *Times*, March 30, 1879; *Tribune*, April 26, 1879; "The Academy Exhibition. III," *World*, April 27, 1879; *Post*, March 30, 1879; "Fine Arts. Exhibition of the Academy of Design. II," *Nation* 28 (May 22, 1879): 359; *Scribner's* 18 (June 1879): 313; "The National Academy," *Sun*, April 20, 1879; Carter, *Art Journal* 5 (May 1879): 158; and "The Studio. The Spring Exhibition—National Academy of Design. Second Notice," *Art Interchange* 3 (April 16, 1879): 58.

83. Burns, *Pastoral Inventions*, 222.

84. In the newspapers, especially, there were fewer extended series of reviews. Most papers had one or two reviews of the show.

85. "Fine Arts. National Academy of Design. Fifty-Fifth Annual Exhibition," *Independent*, April 8, 1880.

86. Such beliefs were expressed in [William Crary Brownell], "Fine Arts. National Academy of Design—Fifty-Fifth Annual Exhibition—I," *Nation* 30 (April 15, 1880): 295; "National Academy of Design. Fifty-Fifth Annual Exhibition," *Tribune*, March 27, 1880; M. G. van Rensselaer, "Spring Exhibition and Picture Sales In New York. I," *American Architect and Building News* 7 (May 1, 1880): 190; and "Exhibition of the Academy of Design," *Art Amateur* 2 (May 1880): 112.

87. Sarah Burns has made this point with other harvesting images. Burns, *Pastoral Inventions*, 36–38.

88. S. G. W. Benjamin, "The Exhibitions. V—National Academy of Design. Fifty-Fifth Exhibition. First Notice," *American Art Review* 1 (May 1880): 308; S. G. W. Benjamin, "The Exhibitions. V—National Academy of Design. Fifty-Fifth Exhibition. Second Notice," *American Art Review* 1 (June 1880): 348; "The New York Spring Exhibitions. The National Academy Exhibition," *Art Journal* 6 (May 1880): 153; Strix [George Hows], "Our Feuilleton. The Academy Exhibition. Concluding Article," *Express*, May 15, 1880; and William Crary Brownell, "The Younger Painters of America. First Paper," *Scribner's* 20 (May 1880): 15.

89. Brownell, *Scribner's* 20 (May 1880): 3.

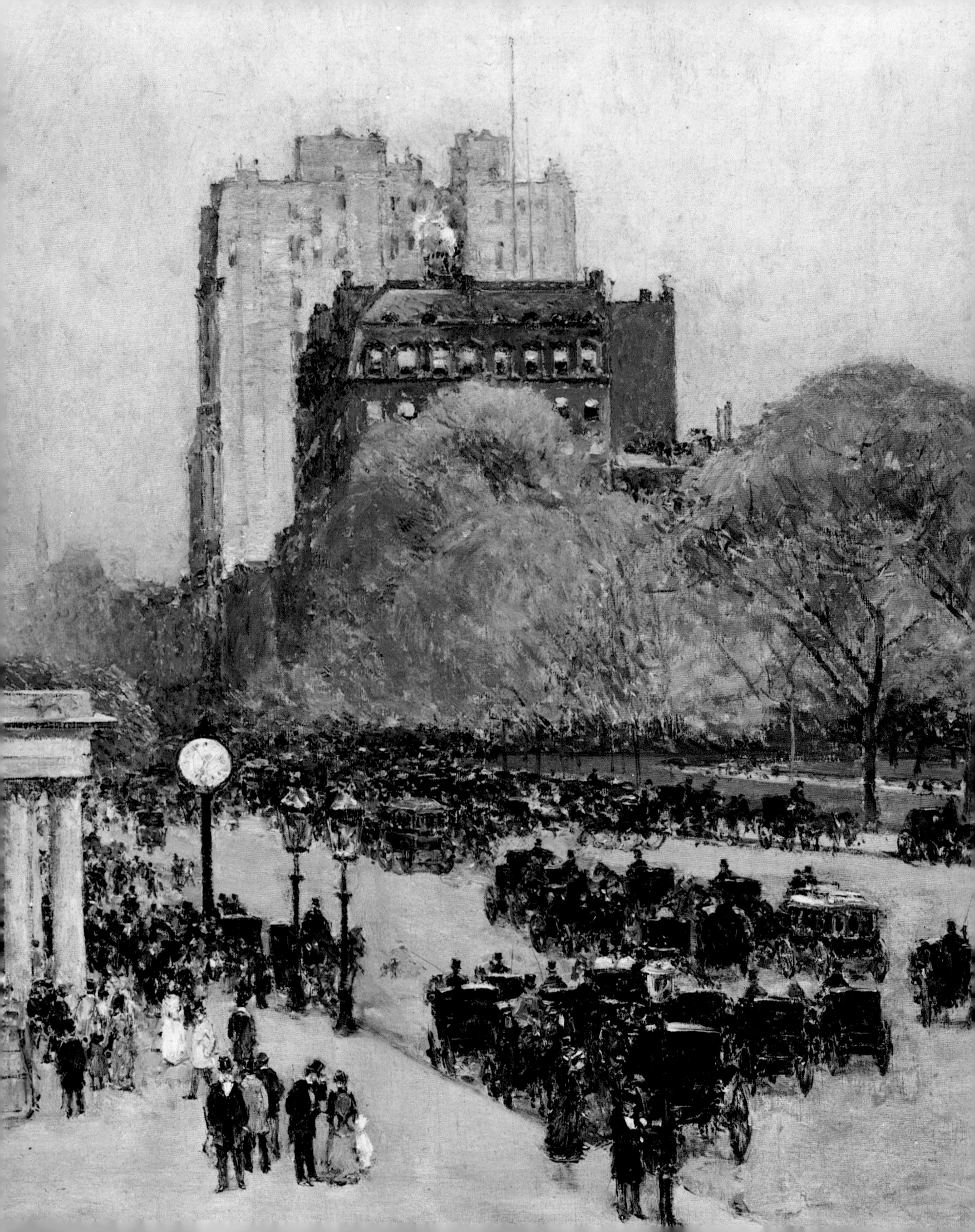

The National Academy of Design and the Society of American Artists: Rivals Viewed by Critics, 1878–1906

TRUDIE A. GRACE

The twenty-nine year rivalry between the National Academy of Design and the Society of American Artists, as evidenced by their annual exhibitions, provided art critics with abundant material for commentary about the state of American art. The period was one of significant stylistic changes, due primarily to European influence, and hence offered reviewers challenging and rich possibilities for analysis. Changes in methods of selecting and exhibiting works were also occurring and drew the attention of the press. The reviews were often enhanced by the use of each organization as a foil for the other. Considerable praise was forthcoming for both; however, criticism was frequently harsh and expressed at times long-term frustration over one issue or another. There never seemed to be a consensus on any point. The story began with the 1877 founding of the Society by a group of artists. Of the first twenty-two members (half of whom were thirty-six or younger in 1878), all but one had shown previously with the Academy and nine were members. They reacted to what they perceived to be unfair practices in the selection and hanging of works at the Academy annuals and hoped to present exhibitions of higher general quality and smaller scale.[1]

In the reviews of the annuals of the Academy and the Society, an abiding concern was the overall level of quality, which the critics typically linked to the standards employed in the selection processes and the sizes of the exhibitions. Because the Academy was committed to hosting as large a show as its space would allow and had adopted multi-level arrangements of works (the Salon style), it was vulnerable on the issues of quality and standards and was often roundly criticized for both. (It showed as many as 843 works, in 1886, and as few as 314, in 1900, and averaged 692 through 1889, and 413 after that.)[2] Although reviewers always found works that pleased them, their remarks frequently indicated that persistence was required. In 1878, the *New York Mail* reported that the Academy's display revealed "many hidden beauties not discovered on first view."[3] The same year, Susan Nichols Carter at the *Art Journal* conceded that, after overcoming confusion generated by the heterogeneous mass of pictures, one realized moment by moment that there was "a great deal of good work in the exhibition."[4] In the 1890s, the story was basically the same. *Harper's* reported in 1891 that much was

"worth looking at twice," that is, after one "recovered from the shock" produced by "the incongruous mixing up of good and bad" and examined each picture.[5]

Occasionally critics defended the Academy for holding large exhibitions by explaining the aims of the organization. A writer for the *Boston Daily Evening Transcript*, who noted in 1878 that all styles were represented among the seven hundred works on view, addressed his comments to "the people who object to having anything on the walls that does not please them." He recommended that they "remember that the Academy aims to reflect the present condition of American art, and not merely to gather a collection of attractive pictures." It was his opinion that, "Where a young artist of fair ability shows progress from year to year, he should be accorded the privilege of submitting his work to the judgment of the public and the tender mercies of the critics of the daily papers."[6] Also in 1878, for the *American Architect and Building News*, Mariana Griswold Van Rensselear wrote that, "more than ever before," the Academy merited "the epithet 'national' because its list of names embraces many states."[7]

The Society was often applauded for significantly restricting the number of works in its annuals, particularly in its earlier years, and for its high standards. (It showed as many as 479 works, in 1905, and as few as 88 in 1884, and averaged 143 through 1889, and 331 after that.)[8] Space restrictions at a variety of locations did influence the total count, far more so than in the case of the Academy; yet, when the Society's exhibitions became larger at the time of its move into more spacious facilities in 1892, many critics still felt that the standards remained high.[9]

When addressing the issue of standards at both the Academy and the Society exhibitions, the press frequently quoted the number of submitted versus selected works. Figures for the former suggest an admission rate of over sixty-percent during many years, although about twenty-five percent seems to have been the case with the smaller, later exhibitions. The rate of acceptance at the Society was often close to twenty-five percent and sometimes was considerably lower. On what would appear to be the majority of occasions, both organizations dealt with over twelve hundred submissions. Although the Academy never openly publicized the number

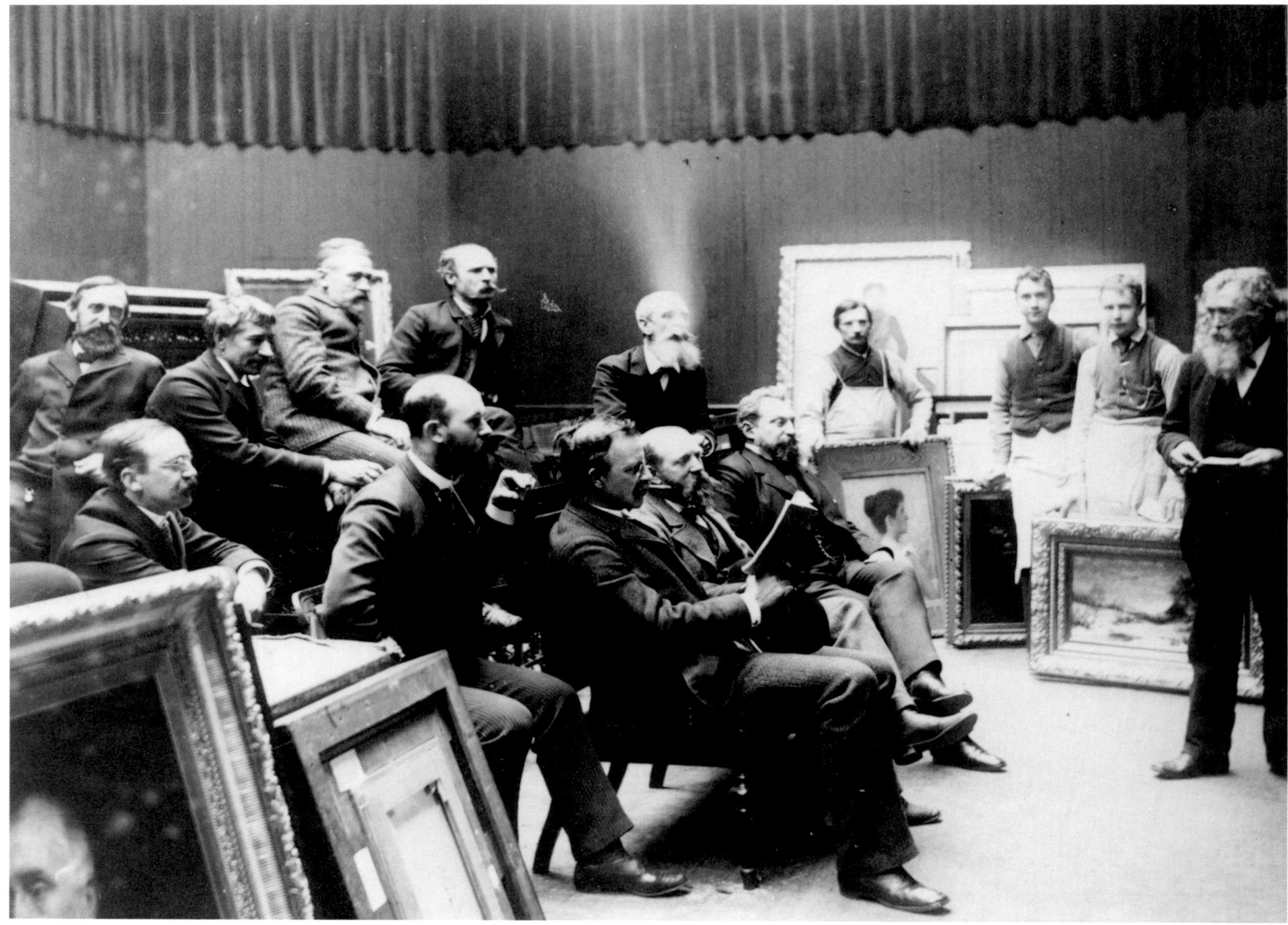

Fig. 61 *Jury of Selection, 64th Annual Exhibition, 1889, National Academy of Design,* Archives, National Academy of Design, Gift of J. C. Nicoll

Back row, left to right: J. C. Nicoll, Hamilton Hamilton, John Q. A. Ward, and Frederick Dielman *Front row, left to right:* Louis Moeller (behind portrait), J. Francis Murphy, Frederick Stuart Church, Robert Swain Gifford, and Charles H. Miller *Standing at rear:* Thomas Moran (with beard) and three unidentified art handlers. *At far right:* James M. Hart

of submissions, the figures were likely to turn up in the press when the ratio suggested a more rigorous selection process. The figures for the Society appeared more commonly, probably because the organization had good reason to make them known. The high number of artists on the Society's selection committees (twenty-seven from 1887 on according to the names listed in its catalogues) also frequently attracted the attention of critics, who saw the figure, as the Society expected them to, as a means of insuring fairness in the selection process.[10] With fewer members as jurors, usually from five to nine, the Academy generally did not receive attention in this area.[11] A photograph taken during the selection of its 1889 annual (fig. 61) pictures eleven of the twelve members listed in the Academy's catalogue.

If the Society deviated from its goal of high standards and fairness in the selection process, critics pounced. The best example of this occurred in 1884. The Society's exhibition included six works by William Merritt Chase, among them, *Courtyard of a Dutch Orphan Asylum* (fig. 62), as well as many

works by students of his.[12] An incensed critic for the *Art Interchange* reminded his readers that the Society had "received hearty approval from all quarters in its opposition to the unfairness of the National Academy" and then shouted: "That unfairness however has never equaled the evident partiality of the Society. . . ." He pressed on with complaints that Chase's work was for the most part "bizarre, theatric, and coarse," that his students felt his influence, and that, as a consequence, "the moral effect on the exhibition" was "disastrous."[13] The *Art Amateur* regarded the episode as "the greatest exhibition of charlatanry that the public of New York has ever been amused with."[14] The *New York Sun* reacted strongly as well: "The Academy never was so arrogant in its pretensions, or so selfish in its exclusiveness as the younger body. . . ."[15] The uproar most likely contributed to the cancellation of the Society's next show as its members rethought policy.

The press was alert to other anomalies within the Society's selection process, as well, and works borrowed to improve shows and attract audiences produced especially strong feel-

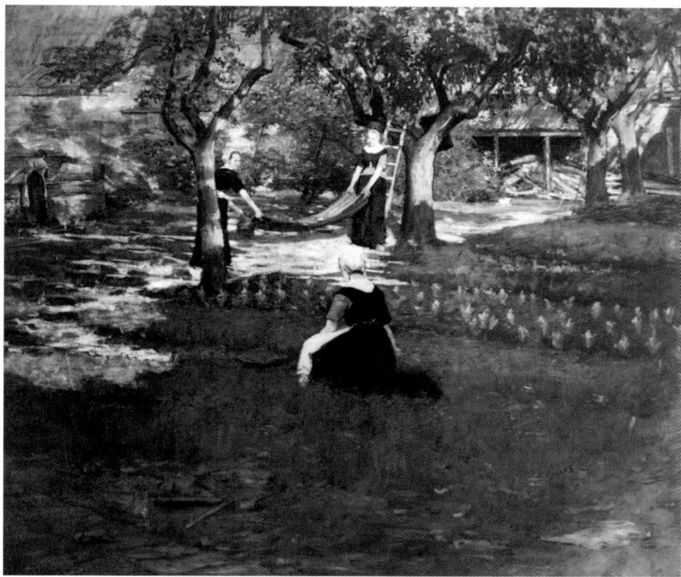

Fig. 62 William Merritt Chase, *Courtyard of a Dutch Orphan Asylum,* c. 1884, oil on canvas on board, 66⅞ x 78⅛, Washington University Gallery of Art, St. Louis, University purchase, Subscription Fund, 1885

ings, both positive and negative. In 1899, Charles Caffin at *Harper's* was among many critics who praised *Christ and the Disciples at Emmaus* (fig. 63) by the prominent French painter P. A. J. Dagnan-Bouveret.[16] The *Art Collector* declared, though, that the work was created "to make a sensation" and was loaned to the Society for the same purpose.[17] The *Commercial Advertiser* complained that it overshadowed all other works in the exhibition.[18] A reviewer for *Town Topics* lambasted all aspects of the work, including the artist's depiction of himself, his wife, and son in modern dress along the right side. He seemed offended by the work's position in the place of honor occupied the year before by John Singer Sargent's *Portrait of Mr. and Mrs. I. N. Phelps Stokes* (1897; The Metropolitan Museum of Art). In summarizing, he must have generated either chuckles or horrified gasps by writing that there was "certainly a loose screw" in the work and that it was "one of the worst pictures of the century." He even criticized Henry Clay Frick for purchasing the painting for one hundred thousand dollars and for giving it "for the purpose of advertising" to the Pittsburg [*sic,* Carnegie] Art Galleries in Pittsburgh, from which it was borrowed for the exhibition.[19]

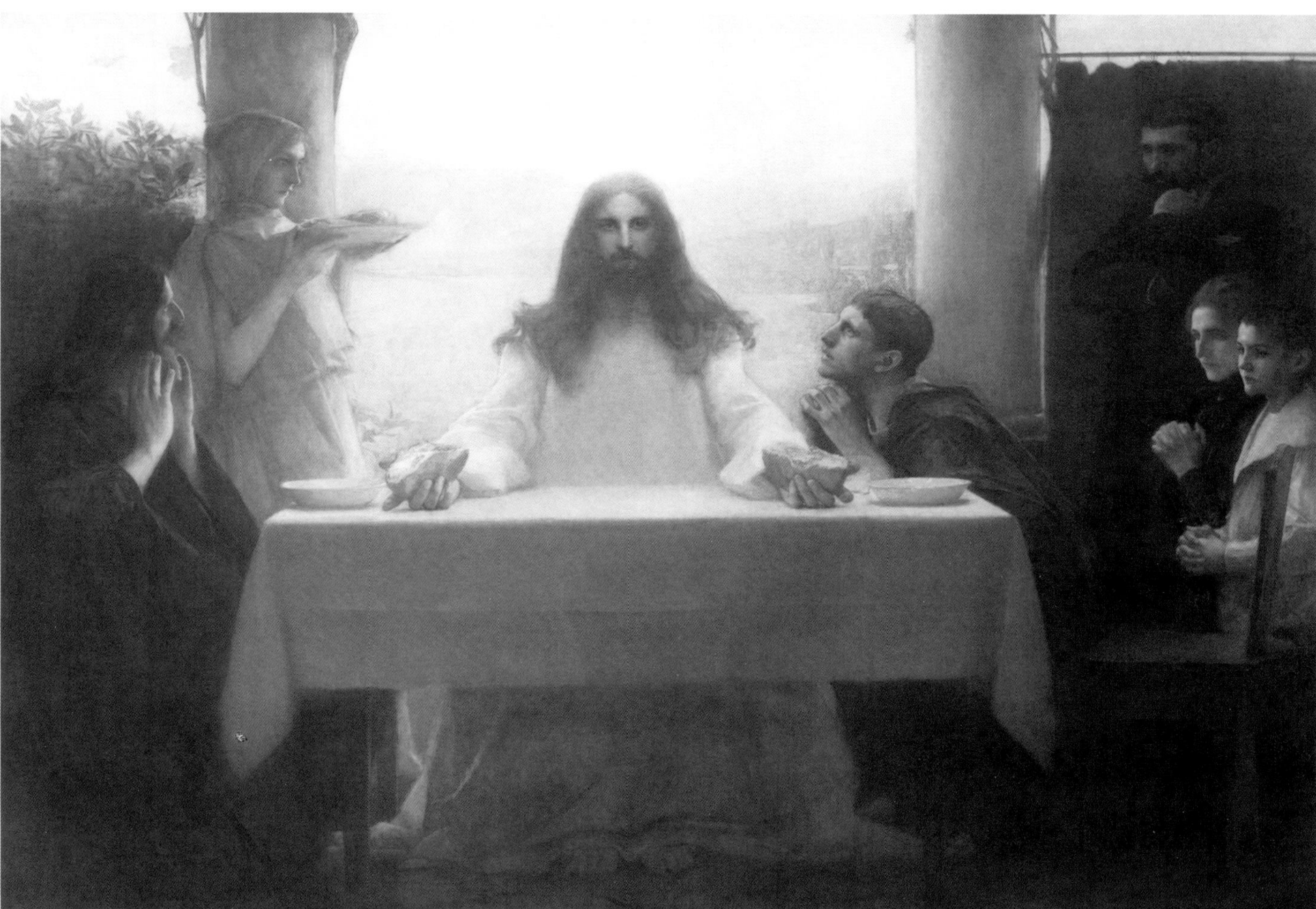

Fig. 63 Pascal-Adolphe-Jean Dagnan-Bouveret, *Christ and the Disciples at Emmaus,* 1896–97, oil on canvas, 78 x 110½, Carnegie Museum of Art, Pittsburgh, Gift of Henry Clay Frick

Writers were also sensitive to how the Academy and the Society annuals were hung and frequently strongly condemned the Academy's general policy of giving privileged places to its members. A critic for the *Nation* wrote in 1878 of the "forcing of tedious Academicians on the eye, according to the rights guaranteed them by an unfortunate caste-system." Then he described a method used to subvert the Academy's hanging policy: "The wary look no longer . . . at the picture hung upon the eye-line, but confine their attention to works which the hanging committee endeavor to conceal; so that by attending strictly to exhibits placed in the second and third rows they can partly defeat the efforts of the tyrant."[20] Repeated visits to the Academy's 1880 exhibition by a *New York Herald* critic confirmed in him "the belief that a broad statement" could "be made that the pictures are hung in an inverse ratio to their merit. . . ."[21] In 1896, the same complaint was still being made in a *Times* article reporting that "as usual . . . many wretchedly incompetent things" were evident "in prominent places."[22] Some writers detected prejudice in the hanging of works by non–New Yorkers. In 1891, the *Art Interchange* thought that paintings by Frederick Porter Vinton of Boston and Thomas Eakins of Philadelphia were "hung in the corridor with the Academy's usual hospitality to strangers."[23]

Scattered voices did acknowledge the difficulties faced by the Academy's hanging committee. In 1878, with 747 works on view, the *New York Mail* believed that the committee "fulfilled its difficult and thankless task with excellent judgment."[24] When the Academy was more selective than usual in 1893, having taken 450 out of 1200 works, the *Sun* sympathized with the hanging committee: " . . . fancy the embarrassment of these well-meaning and conscientious gentlemen when confronted by the awful 'N.A.'"[25] Various critics referred to the traditional nature of the Academy's hanging policies, as did a writer for the *Art Interchange* who noted in 1881 that the "well-worn, respected names" were placed "where visitors' eyes may find them with least effort" and that the hanging committee was loyal "as might be expected, to their fraternity, the academicians. . . ." Because this was "patent to everyone," no harm would result. The procedure merely illustrated "in a pleasant way, the harmonious state of the happy family of academicians."[26] The press continued to explain the procedures, in the 1890s, with William A. Coffin indicating in *Harper's,* albeit with regret, that there were "traditions and rights to be respected" in the placement of works."[27]

In contrast, reviewers often raved about the presentation of the Society's annuals, including its use of fewer levels of paintings than were found at the Academy and even of single-row hanging. Typical was the report of the *Tribune* in 1880 that the Society's committee had tried to place each picture where it would "look best and be best seen" and that there had been "no attempt to make 'places of honor,'" a policy which most readers knew contrasted with the Academy's.[28] Three years later, the *Tribune* again issued praise, saying that, as expected, the 142 paintings were hung with "care and excellent judgment." It also provided a musical analogy: "The collection imparts an impression which a musician might liken to that produced by a nocturne of Chopin's or perhaps a symphony by Mozart, without rising to the grandeur of Beethoven or the dramatic force of Wagner."[29] When the Society's annual of 1886, with 120 works by 83 artists, had an unusually long run on a one-time basis at the Metropolitan Museum of Art in New York, the *Critic* maintained that "never was an exhibition of American paintings more interesting in itself or more satisfactorily placed before the public than this."[30]

Although compared to the European avant-garde, the Society showed many works of a conservative nature, the press frequently touted it as a "progressive organization."[31] The use of painterly effects and lighter tonalities in a far greater percentage of works distinguished its annuals from those of the Academy. In 1887, the *New York World* ran the title "By the Younger Artists" for a Society review and called the group "the band of young irrepressibles who, fresh from the foreign studios, were the first to stir, ten years ago, the stagnant pool of American art."[32] The Society's periodic inclusion of one or more works by the expatriate James McNeill Whistler supported the idea of progressiveness and helped to bring attention to its exhibitions. *Symphony in Violet and Blue* (n.d.; Harvard University Art Museums) in 1898 and *Nocturne in Black and Gold* in 1902 (fig. 64) were among those on view.[33]

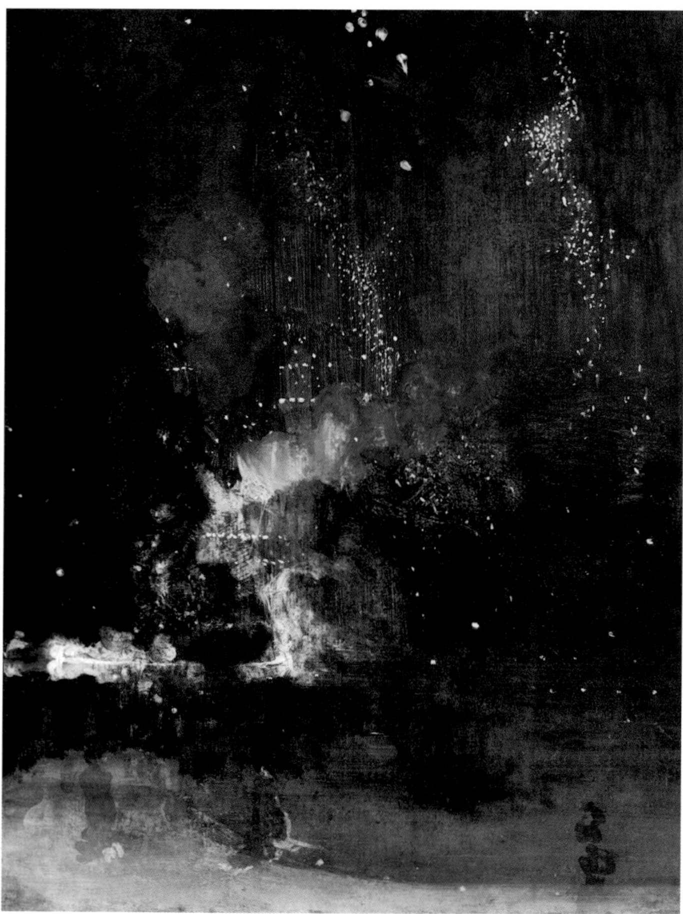

Fig. 64 James McNeill Whistler, *Nocturne in Black and Gold (The Falling Rocket),* c. 1875, oil on canvas, The Detroit Institute of Arts, Gift of Dexter M. Ferry, Jr.

The *Tribune* called the latter a "beautiful little pyrotechnical study."[34] (The Academy showed works by Whistler only twice over the course of the artist's career, in 1868 and 1874, before the establishment of the Society.) Paintings by John Singer Sargent that demonstrated his typical painterly bravura also strongly reinforced the Society's status as a progressive venue. His now famous *Oyster Gatherers of Cancale* (1878; Museum of Fine Arts, Boston) was in the Society's first annual, and some of his most noteworthy portraits were exhibited during his eighteen years of showing with the organization. (Although he was made an Academician in 1897, his work appeared at the Academy only five times during the Society's existence.)

Most critics responded positively to the policies and spirit of the Society, but many did not like what they saw at its exhibitions. There was, for example, a significant negative reaction in 1880 to the unfinished look, or unfinished state, of many of the works on view. The *Times* wrote that "plenty" of works were "bad," "inefficient," "sloppy," "immature," "ill-considered," and "at times slightly impertinent." However, the Society's exhibition was free of "the desolation of sterility" that "unfortunately reigned on most of the Academy walls."[35] In the same year, at the *Art Journal*, Susan Nichols Carter felt that J. Alden Weir had tackled "one of the most ambitious of subjects" in his painting *The Good Samaritan* (fig. 65)—a subject "of the class to which the great masters brought all their skill in drawing, composition, and colour"—but had "not attempted anything more than the most simple treatment of his subject, apart from a very difficult foreshortening of the figure."[36] In 1883, G. W. Sheldon from *Harper's* observed that there had been an advance in quality "made in the teeth of several obstacles." "Most of the exhibitors are young," he wrote, "and there are certain indispensable matters of technique and sentiment in which the young do not, because they can not, excel. . . ."[37] At the same time, a *New York Sun* critic found that older artists like Alexander Wyant and George H. Smillie had begun to do work "full of vitality and force," in part because of the examples set by younger men like Chase and Weir, but that no picture in the exhibition would have been awarded a first-class place in the Paris Salon.[38]

When stylistic changes began to occur at the Academy soon after the Society was founded, the press responded. The *New York Evening Express* thought in 1880 that it was "particularly pleasing . . . to see how the older men [had] bestirred themselves" and explained that they were painting "with more expression" because they were painting "with more liberal ideas." Their work combined "native enthusiasm with foreign technique."[39] The following year, a critic for the same paper, claiming to have attended Academy exhibitions for fifteen or twenty years, was amazed by the change he saw: " . . . the advance made within the last year is more than noteworthy—it is remarkable." Not only had "the spirit of progress" developed in the "new men," the "elder men" seemed also "to have become imbued with it." The latter had contributed work that

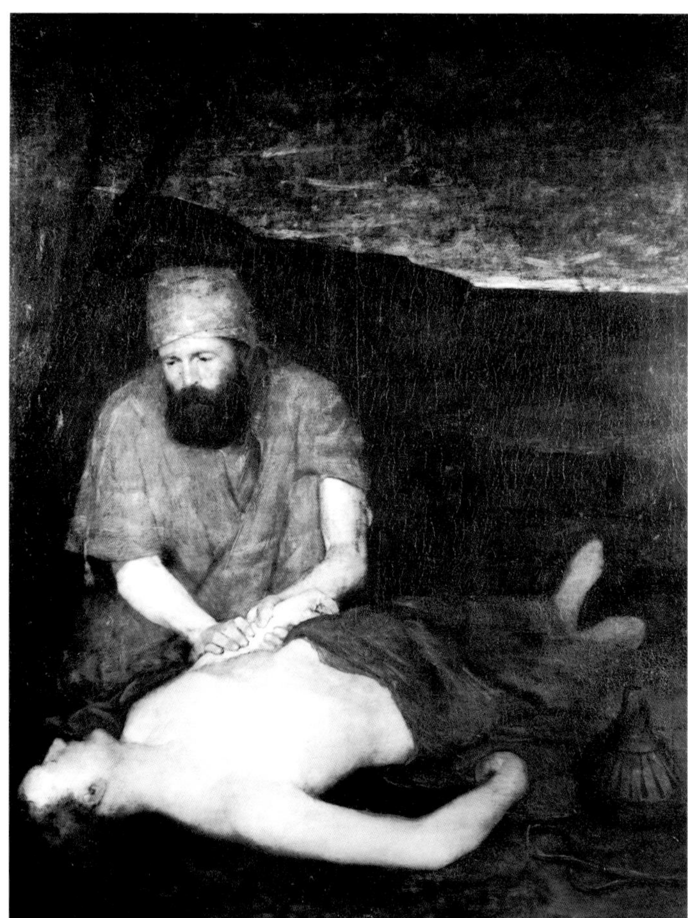

Fig. 65 Julian Alden Weir, *The Good Samaritan*, 1880, oil on canvas, 72 x 53, St. Paul's Episcopal Church, Windham, Connecticut

showed "how much the infusion of a new element [had] quickened their energies and brightened their perceptions."[40] *Harper's* indicated that a distinguishing feature of the exhibition was "the unmistakable tendency of many of the contributors to paint more broadly than heretofore, to consult the movement and proportion of masses rather than the trivial carefulness of details." The writer summed up with a catchy phrase: "Nature, in a word, is not so prigged up as she used to be, say two or even five years ago, on similar occasions. . . ." He ascribed the change to the influence of American artists who had lately studied or were then studying in Europe.[41] After four hours of viewing the show, a critic for the *Herald* proclaimed that it bore "strong evidence of an encouraging advance in American art."[42] The *Commercial Advertiser* reported that the Academy's exhibition was "drawing crowds" of the "best" citizens every day and comprised "the best collection of paintings ever produced by American artists." This contrasted strikingly with the paper's negative exclamation about the Society's annual, matched by others that year: "Some of the worst trash ever offered to purchasers of pictures may be found in the majority of works at the exhibition. . . ."[43]

Eastman Johnson's genre picture/double portrait *The Funding Bill* (fig. 66) elicited praise from several sources at the

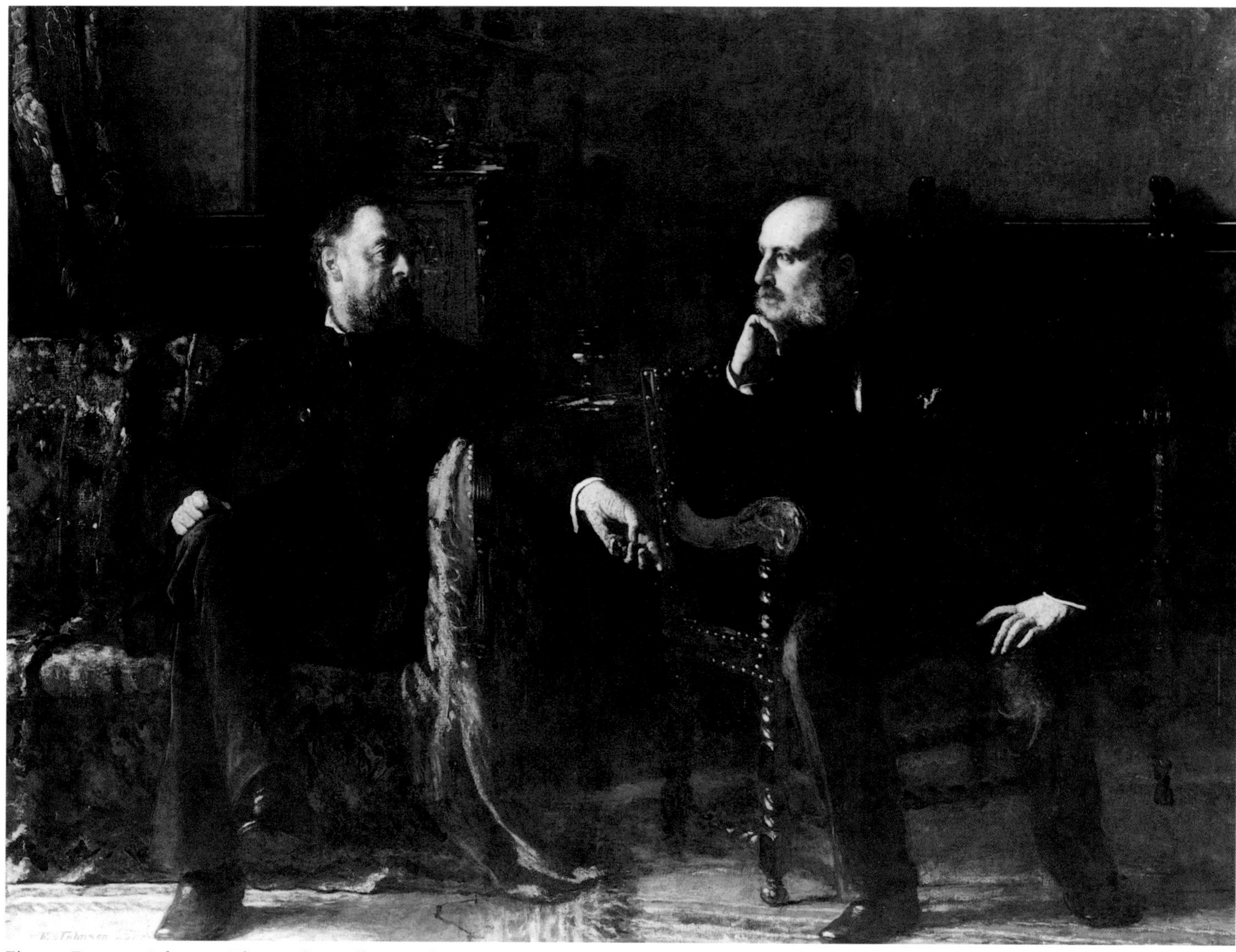

Fig. 66 Eastman Johnson, *The Funding Bill*, 1881, oil on canvas, 60½ x 78¼, The Metropolitan Museum of Art, Purchase, Robert Gordon Gift, 1898 (National Academy of Design, 56th Annual Exhibition, 1881, no. 216)

time. *Harper's* said that Johnson, who was fifty-six, was notable among some of the older Academicians who had "never painted so admirably."[44] The *Art Amateur* was of the opinion that Johnson had "produced one of the best pictures in his life, filled with swift energy and decision in the painting, and treated with altogether masterly brio in a scale unusual for him."[45] The *Nation* responded to the theme when calling the work "perfection" in the type of painting "so often urged upon unpatriotic American artists who repair to Venice and Brittany for inspiration, and neglect the possibilities with which our own life and land teem. . . ."[46] In 1882, the *Magazine of Art* revealed that both the Academy and the Society were claiming Johnson as their own.[47] He had shown at the Academy seventeen times since 1861 and been a full member since 1860; he had not exhibited with the Society before 1881, the year he became one of its members.

The Academy and the Society both held their exhibitions in the spring, and on sixteen occasions their shows overlapped to some extent. Occasionally critics informed their readers that some artists were members of, and showed with, both organizations. In 1879, Thomas Eakins's large, somewhat loosely painted, ambitiously complex *Portrait of Dr. Gross (The Gross Clinic)* (1875; Medical College of Thomas Jefferson University, Philadelphia) was presented at the Society's exhibition and was mentioned in a review of the Academy's show, which opened three days after the other closed and included the artist's *The Pair-Oared Shell* (1872) (see no. 44), a smaller work, painted with more precision and considerable emphasis on the natural setting. In 1887, when forty-one of eighty-five members of the Society exhibited at the Academy, Charles De Kay at the *Art Review* noted that most of the "Society men" were represented at the Academy's exhibition, that the Society did not constitute "a camp apart," and that the only difference between the two annuals that year was the "absence of a mass of really poor paintings" at the Society's exhibition.[48] When the exhibitions overlapped in 1888, the *Times* was moved to declare "an epoch of conciliation," explaining that "the olive branch has been waved in the orthodox camp to such effect that the younger men line the galleries of the old institution with their canvases."[49] That year, the Academy elected eight members of the Society to its associate level.

Although critics noted the presence of Impressionism in some works shown by the Society in the 1880s, they had many opportunities to respond to modern characteristics or tendencies in the late 1880s and into the 1890s. The Society, being more influenced by French Impressionism and in general by the loose brushwork favored by many European painters, continued to be more advanced artistically than the Academy. Numerous paintings in the Impressionist vein were shown by the Society in the 1890s, including examples by William Merritt Chase, Theodore Robinson, John Twachtman, J. Alden Weir, and Childe Hassam. In 1891, the latter's *Spring Morning in the Heart of the City* (fig. 67) not only emphasized light and movement but also utilized the elevated view for cityscapes favored by the French Impressionists. In 1892, a writer for the *Critic* noted that it was "to be expected that many should answer the Impressionist summons who were not called," but added, "how little evil, how much good has come of it!" He went on to praise paintings by John Twachtman and Edmund Tarbell, who along with six other artists in the exhibition would be among those to form the American Impressionist group, The Ten, and to show independently for the first time in 1898.[50]

Many critics truly disliked Impressionism. In 1894, a writer for *Town Topics* claimed that a person had to "wear his smoked glasses" whichever way he turned in the Society's

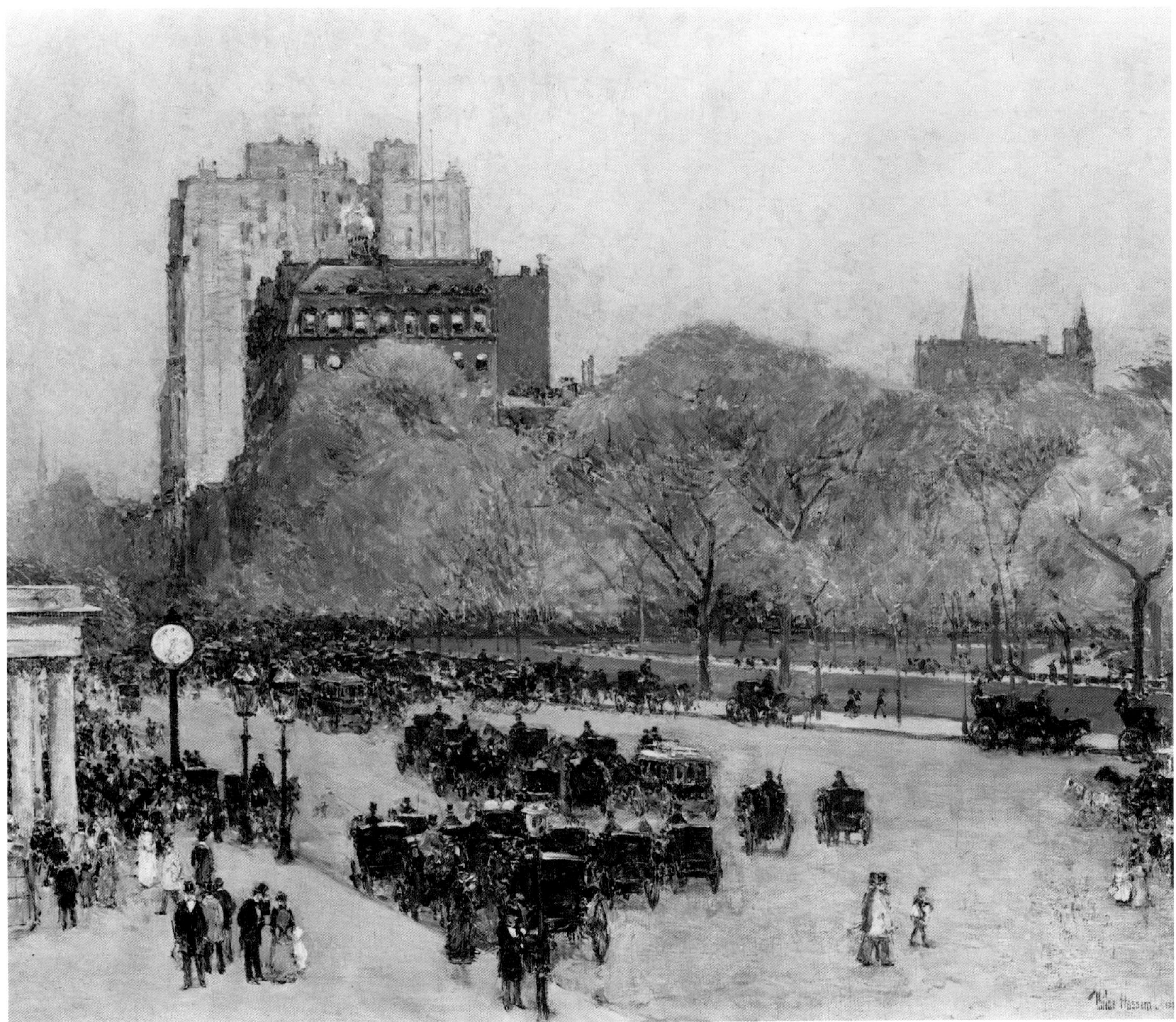

Fig. 67 Frederick Childe Hassam, *Spring Morning in the Heart of the City,* oil on canvas, 18⅛ x 20¾, The Metropolitan Museum of Art, Gift of Miss Ethelyn McKinney, 1943, in memory of her brother Glenn Ford McKinney

"garish galleries, lest he stumble over purple boulders or blunder up against blue trees, over which green skies shed their yellow effulgence." He felt that the Society painters had "always presented the results of the latest experiment or fad" and thusly had left the "calm looker-on [to] put up with their painterliness and garish affectation." However, some good had come from the showing of "brainless pictures"—"the staid old Academy" might "get some cheer out of the comparative failure of the society to show any serious advance." Implying change at the Academy, he bluntly stated: "Technical jugglery without ideas may be as bad in its way as the dry rot that had threatened the older institution."[51] In 1895, the *Times* reported that the Society "had been struck by a great wave of impressionism," but close inspection revealed "lack of purpose in much of the work."[52] In agreement, the *Sun* saw a "frivolous gayety—the bizarre achievements of the half-baked impressionists." Like other members of the press, the reviewer also chafed at the lack of originality in American art and expressed frustration over artists working under the influence of a European movement. For him, the show was "full of extravagances, misdirected imitations of Monet, etc."[53]

Writers responded to the stylistic changes that occurred at the Academy in the late 1880s and 1890s, too. An 1889 review in the *New York Herald* was even entitled "All for Arts Sake," a variation of Whistler's "Art for Art's Sake."[54] Many writers pointed out an influx of Impressionist works in the early 1890s; paintings by eight of the future members of The Ten were shown during at least one year from 1890 through 1892, for example.[55] In 1892, a critic for the *Evening Post* described

the jostling of the old and new styles: "Here are plein air pictures of the most pronounced tendencies elbowing those of the 'Hudson River School,' which insist upon their right to be seen...." He deemed this combination "the oft-tried process of mixing oil and water."[56] For examples, he might have used Jasper F. Cropsey's *The Gates of the Hudson* (fig. 68) and Twachtman's *Brook in Winter* (fig. 69), quite possibly the work listed in the Society's catalogue and mentioned by critics.[57]

From the mid-1890s on, the press reported the narrowing of differences between the Society and Academy annuals. When the two organizations had exhibitions on view simultaneously for about five weeks in 1896, Augustus van Cleef of the *Illustrated American* offered this summation: "... the Academy has become more and more liberal, and the Society somewhat more conservative," an observation often repeated in the press thereafter.[58] In 1897, Royal Cortissoz, for the *Tribune*, pointed out that, although the Impressionists were "still considerably in evidence" at the Society, the exhibition was "formed with more catholicity than usual." There was a "refreshing absence of the youthful crudity" that had "so often disfigured the walls."[59] A *Herald* reviewer noticed that the 1897 Society exhibition was larger than those before, with 374 works, and also remarked that it had "fewer 'freak' pictures than usual."[60] In 1899, the *Times* seemed pleased with developments at the Society's annuals, saying that it had "taken many of ... twenty-one years for the society to strike what may be called a decorous gait—to outlive fads and fancies and to become a dignified institution."[61] At the time of the Society's 1899 annual, the *Times* observed that the organization had "grown

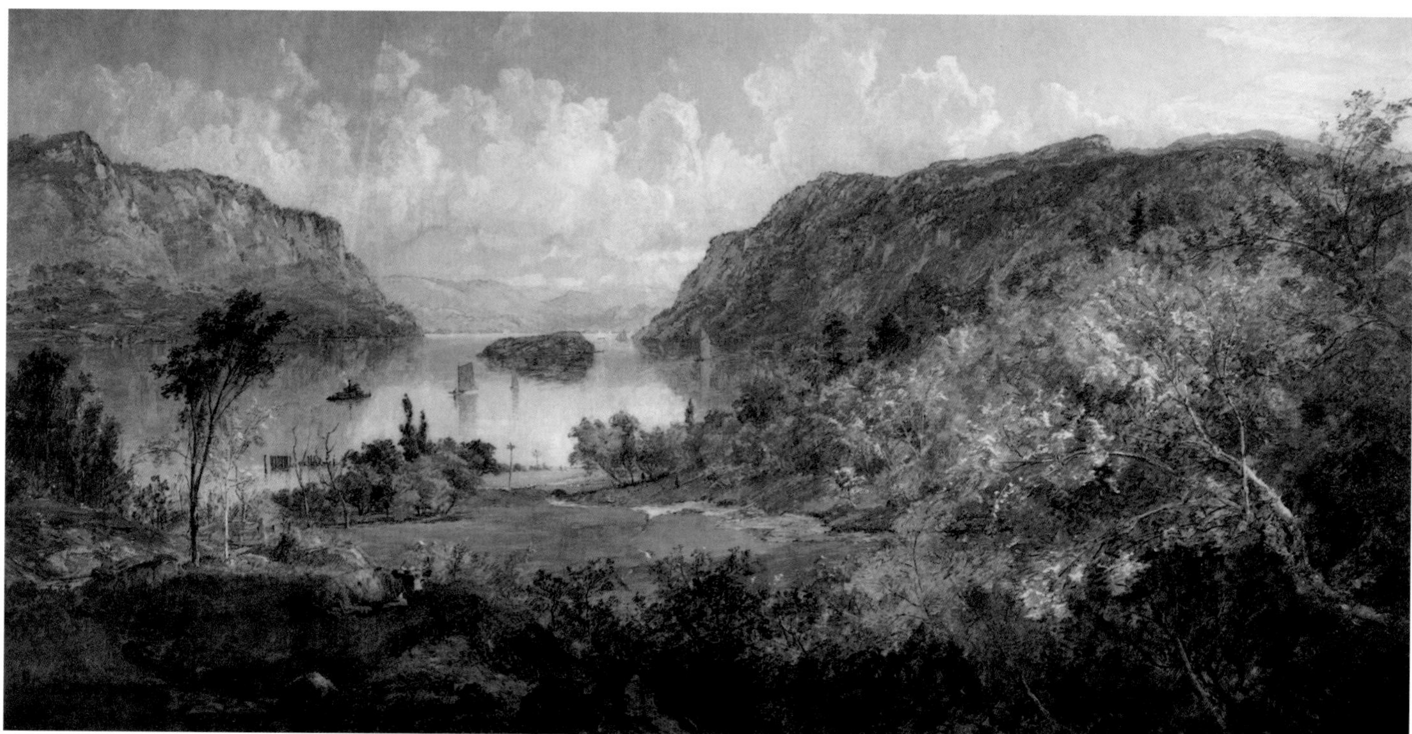

Fig. 68 Jasper F. Cropsey, *The Gates of the Hudson,* oil on canvas, 23½ x 43½, Newington-Cropsey Foundation, Hastings-on-Hudson, New York (National Academy of Design, 67th Annual Exhibition, 1892, no. 76)

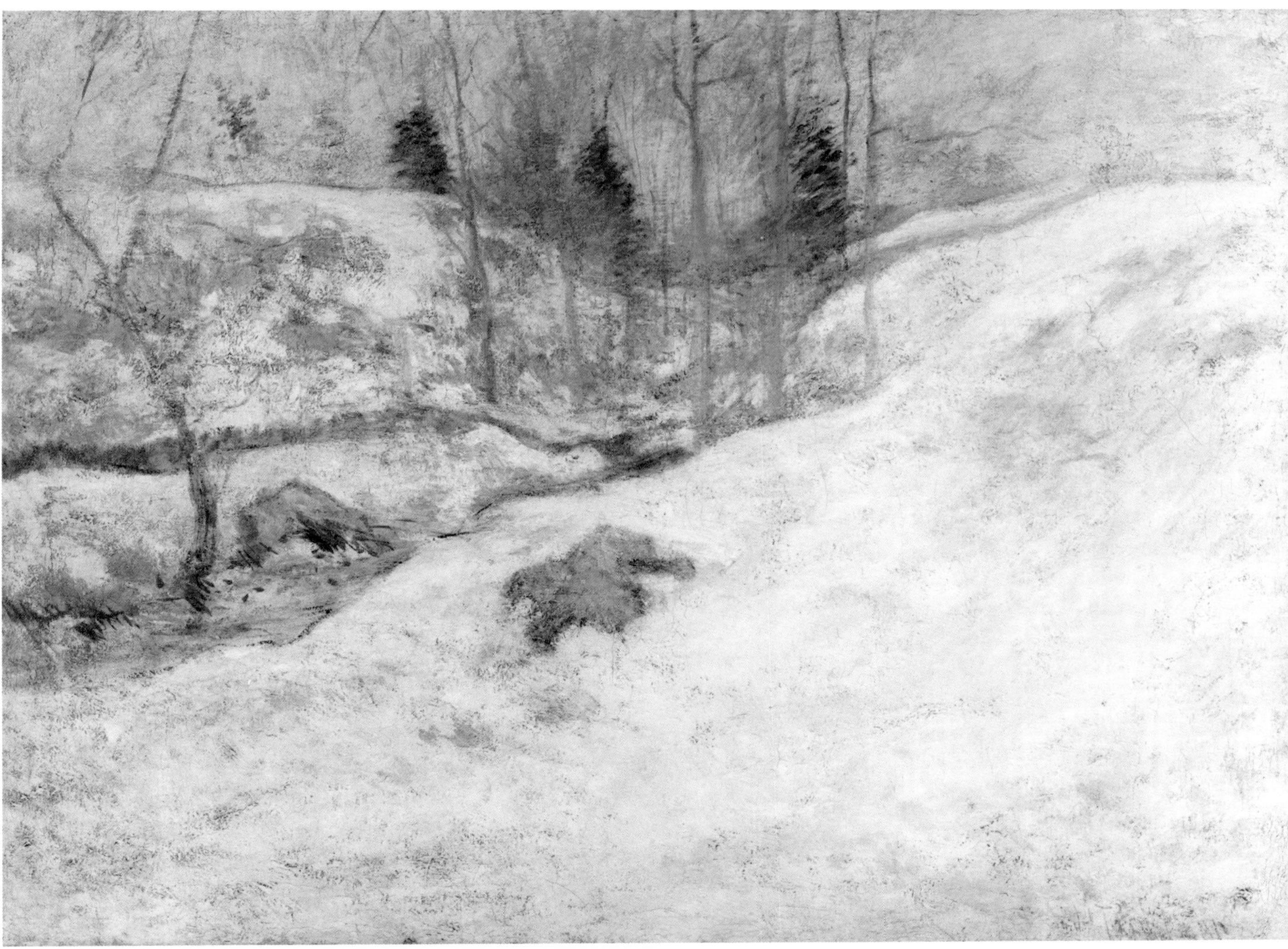

Fig. 69 John Henry Twachtman, *Brook in Winter*, c. 1892, oil on canvas, 36⅛ x 48⅛, Museum of Fine Arts, Boston, The Hayden Collection, 1907

old enough to have secessions from its ranks," a reference to the 1897 resignation of membership at the Society by a group of Impressionists and the formation of The Ten.[62] Also in 1899, a critic for the *Tribune* proclaimed, "Something direful has happened." This, he explained, was partly due to the absence of the "best men," among them The Ten, "who had held a brilliant exhibition of their own."[63]

Reviewers frequently related the growing similarity of the Academy and Society to an increase in artists showing at both venues. In 1891, the *Art Interchange* offered what sounded like a widely held opinion on how this worked out on a practical level: "The most ambitious or successful canvases are generally reserved for the Society of American Artists by all who think they have sufficient talent or influence to hope for admission to that exclusive and not always impartial convocation."[64] In 1896, W. D. Howells at *Harper's* thought that "the level of the Artists seemed evener if not higher than that of the Academy" but that "certain painters who contributed to the excellent quality of the Artists, as a whole, were better represented at the Academy."[65]

The strengths and weaknesses of the various categories of subject matter and their proportional breakdown also greatly interested reviewers. During a majority of years, many responded positively to the numerous portraits and other figurative works shown by the Society. In 1883, the *Times* wrote that portraits by John Singer Sargent, Wyatt Eaton, and J. Alden Weir were "to the fore" and then proclaimed: " . . . it is certain that American art can show very excellent stuff in the way of portraiture."[66] In 1897, James B. Townsend, writing for the *Times*, believed that there could "hardly be any just comparison drawn between the few figure works at the Academy and the many in the Society's display." Although he maintained that the draftsmanship of "the younger American figure painters" was sometimes careless and that they strove "perhaps too much after "effects and novel poses," he stressed their drawing ability and felt compelled to admit that "many of the older American artists have not improved in drawing the figure in lo! these many years."[67] In reviewing the previous annual for *Harper's* in 1896, Royal Cortissoz had paid considerable attention to Frank Benson's decorative figure—

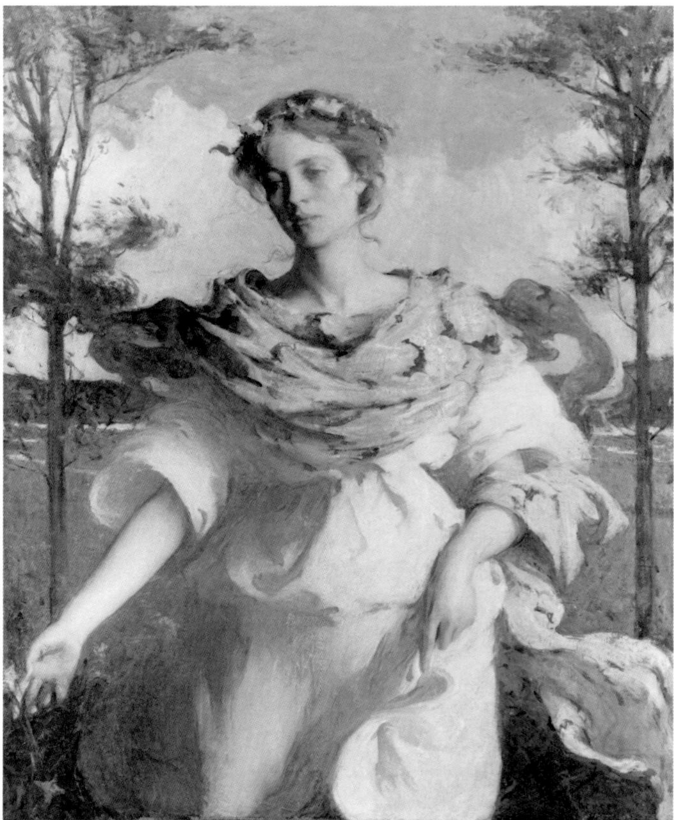

Fig. 70 Frank Benson, *Summer,* 1890, oil on canvas, 50⅛ x 40, National Museum of American Art, Smithsonian Institution, Gift of John Gellatly

Summer (fig. 70), which was hung in a place of honor, by then an aspect of the Society's exhibition policy. The critic felt that this work, like those by almost all of the other artists in the exhibition, was "not necessarily of great spiritual import or dramatic significance" but rather "so sincere, so strong, and so artistic that its importance could hardly be overestimated."[68]

At certain of the Society annuals of the 1880s, and particularly ones of the mid-1890s when Impressionism was a significant factor, reviewers noted an increase in the number of landscapes. In 1897, Townsend wrote, "The contrast between the smoothly painted, carefully detailed, and highly finished landscapes in the Academy and the broadly handled ones of the Society show is indeed a marked one."[69] In 1901, it was the eclectic nature of the Society's subjects that was reported by the *Times*: "Figure pieces, portraits, religious and pagan compositions, and more especially marines, have 'taken the wall' of the landscapes and forced them into a minority." The critic was happy with the change, feeling that it was "as it should be," for there had been "too much of the landscape pure and simple, at least too much of the ordinary landscape."[70] The *Commercial Advertiser* called the exhibition "strong in landscape work" but noted, significantly, that "the impressionistic element" was "almost entirely absent."[71]

Critics also evaluated the subject matter at the Academy, where landscapes did predominate each year, although they were rivaled in number by genre paintings.[72] The *Daily*

Tribune reported that the Academy's 1878 annual was "remarkably poor in portraits," of which only approximately 24 were shown.[73] Two years later, when landscapes numbered 124 and portraits 55, the *Art Interchange* seemed weary of the most prevalent subject matter at the Academy: "There is the usual amount of landscapes which makes us wish that green paint had never been discovered, and the countless repetitions of the same old subjects."[74] The same paper gave this assessment in 1891: "There is a plentiful assortment of all the various lines of painting, excepting the historical—for which the American painter generally feels himself incompetent."[75] (Historical subjects had represented a small percentage at the Academy since its inception.) Also in 1891, the *New York World* noted that it was rather strange for an Academy exhibition to have landscapes in the position of secondary importance, but "portraits and figure compositions were well to the fore" (probably meant in terms of quality considering the numerical breakdown). The writer found this development encouraging and felt that, if "followed up" the next year, there would be "reason to believe that the old reproach that American artists could paint nothing but landscapes, and poor ones at that [would] cease to have any force."[76] Among the notable figurative works presented at the Academy two years later, in 1893, was *The Ameya* (fig. 71) by Robert Blum, who previously showed six times at the Academy and seven times with the Society. Inspired by a trip to Japan, the painting depicts a Japanese candy-blower. Well-received and probably responsible for Blum's election to full membership at the Academy that year, the work was described by the *Times* as "a kaleidoscope of colors, nicely adjusted, and admirably painted, not alone for color, but for composition and variety of characters."[77]

From the late 1890s through 1906, the reviews of the Society annuals were so mixed that the organization's future could not have been safely predicted. It continued to receive the most numerous and most strongly stated positive comments. In 1898, the *Post* wrote that it was maintaining a high standard of excellence as it "always" had.[78] The same year, the *Times* called it the "most talked-of art organization in America," adding that respect was of course "due and awarded to the old Academy" but that the spring exhibition of the "younger rival [had] come to overshadow that of the older institution." Even though it had experienced secessions, it had "grown strong enough with age to maintain its position and to go on serenely from strength to strength."[79] The *Brooklyn Daily Eagle* considered the 1901 offering "fresher and more exhilarating than any previous show in New York" and praised it for what would seem to be contradictory characteristics—the "cleverest use of brush and paint" and its "restoration to respectability of the good old faculty of imagination." The best aspects of it were the pictures that "preach."[80] In 1904, Sargent's *The Misses Hunter* (fig. 72) became one of his best received portraits shown by the Society. The *Post* called it "a great masterpiece," and the *Tribune* considered it "an oasis of brilliance"—but "in a desert of humdrum works."[81] The organizers of the annual

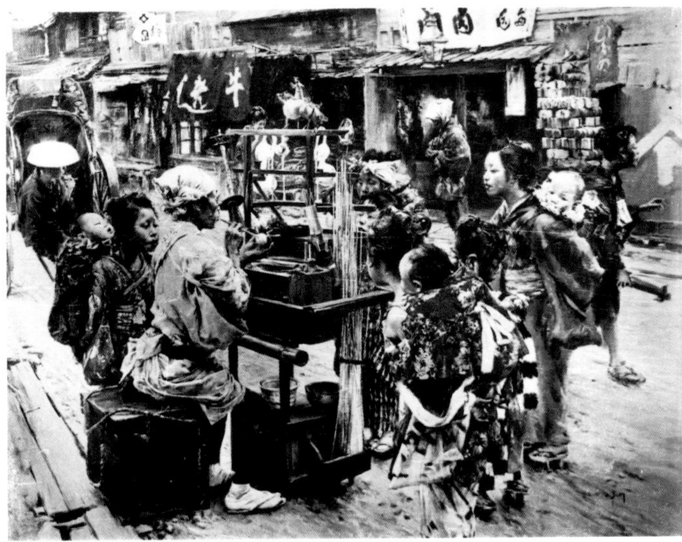

Fig. 71 Robert Blum, *The Ameya,* oil on canvas, 25¹/₁₆ x 31¹/₁₆, The Metropolitan Museum of Art, Gift of the Estate of Alfred Corning Clark, 1904 (National Academy of Design, 68th Annual, 1893, no. 274)

would have known of the work's drawing power because it had attracted considerable attention when shown at the Royal Academy in London in 1902 and at the Pennsylvania Academy of the Fine Arts slightly earlier in 1904.

In 1905, various critics noticed that the Society had an open attitude to certain young, controversial realists, some of whom would rally as The Eight and present a groundbreaking independent exhibition in New York in 1908. The *Sun* wrote that the Society had "come round to Mr. [Robert] Henri" and was "on its way to a reasonable appreciation of Mr. [William] Glackens."[82] John Sloan and George Luks were also represented in the exhibition, the latter with a portrait and *The Spielers* (fig. 73).

Even in the year of the Society's demise, 1906, when it culled 448 works from 1,500 submissions (350 works were shown at the Academy), the press still took the organization seriously, although there was no current of sentiment that it should continue. The commentary ranged from references to "amateurish contributors" to "excellent exhibition . . . with no funeral wreaths or other signs of death."[83] A painting by Childe

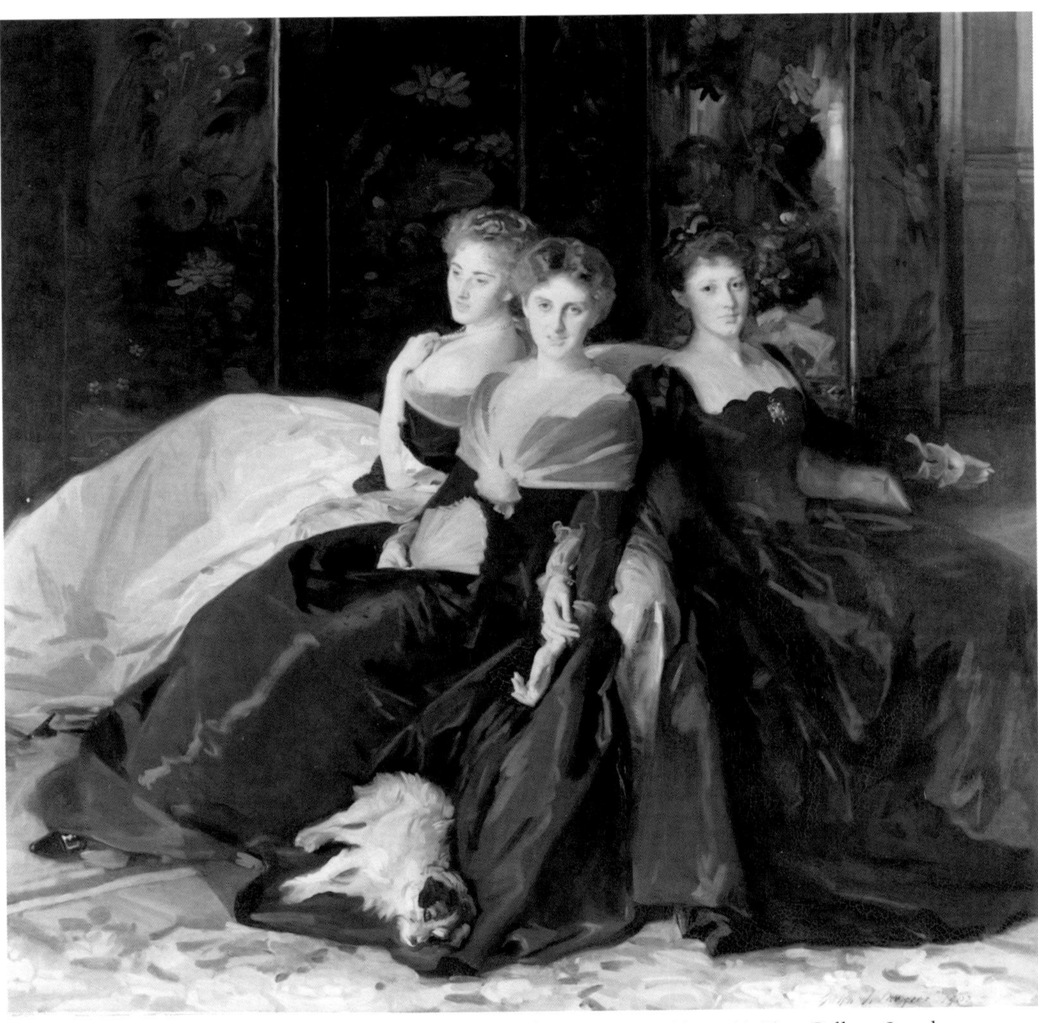

Fig. 72 John Singer Sargent, *The Misses Hunter,* 1902, oil on canvas, 89¼ x 89¼, Tate Gallery, London

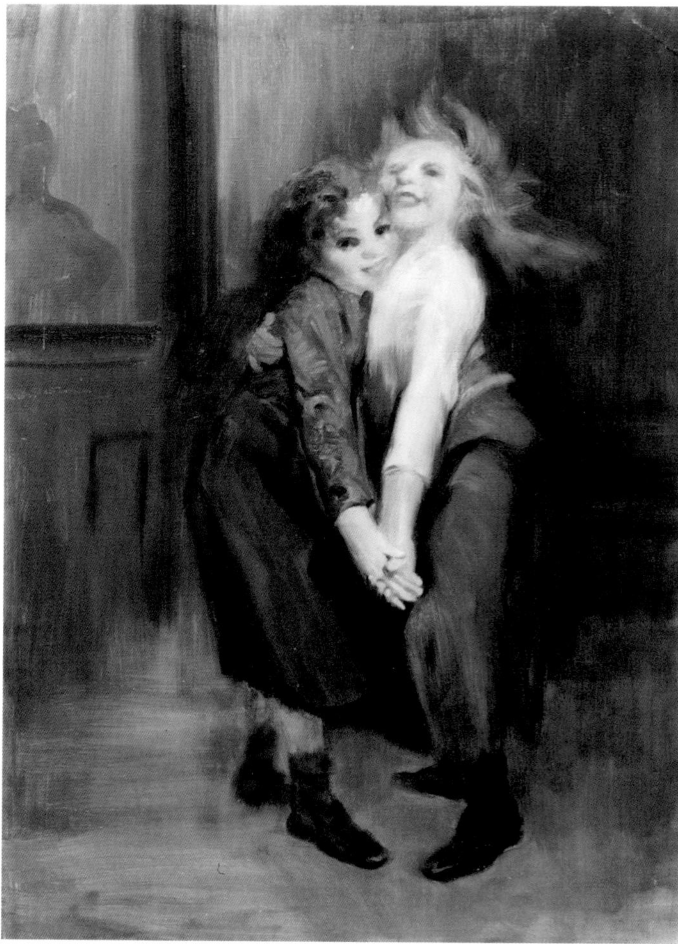

Fig. 73 George B. Luks, *The Spielers*, 1905, oil on canvas, 36 1/16 x 26 1/4, Addison Gallery of American Art, Phillips Academy, Andover, Massachusetts

Hassam was given a place of honor. For *American Art News*, James Townsend wrote that the Society had "brought about what can truly be called a Renaissance of American art."[84]

By at least 1904, critics were reporting other developments, besides issues of quality, that suggested a decline in the Society. In that year, the *Daily Tribune* pointed not only to the defection of members who held shows as The Ten but also to the 1903 deaths of "two of [the Society's] strongest members," Alfred Q. Collin and Robert Blum; it also listed many absentees.[85] At the same time, a critic for the *Sun* took a rather philosophical approach: "To put it briefly, the Society has grown old, as the Academy grew before it; it has lost its youthful enthusiasm and has fallen into lazy habits of self-seeking, or at least self-satisfactions, as the Academy fell in the course of time, as all institutions of the kind have fallen sooner or later." He went on to quote a press agent for the Society about how it never had an endowment and how its members' dues and receipts had "never put a surplus into the treasury."[86] In 1906, the *Tribune* referred to the "excellent services" of the Society but suggested a pragmatic approach to the situation: "Sentiment has its uses, no doubt, but as Whistler used to say, art is art and mathematics is mathematics."[87]

Specific plans for a union of the Academy and Society were worked out in 1905, and, among the critics who reported them, at least a few tried to correct inaccuracies and misconceptions. In the *Burlington Magazine for Connoisseurs,* Charles Fitzgerald wrote of a time of "grandiose ideas and vast plots for the advancement of art in America." The way he saw it, "the contrivers and projectors of schemes" were "accustomed to make light of the rivalry that formerly existed between the two organizations." The truth, in his view, was that "in the course of its vicissitudinous career the Academy never received a severer blow than in the establishment of this rival body." Fitzgerald wanted everyone to know that, "if the Society was not a result of revolt within the Academy, it was nevertheless conceived in a lively apprehension of the Academy's limitations and of the particular dangers of a constitution essentially similar to that of the Royal Academy [the London model for the Academy]." He maintained that, "in its decrepitude" and "no longer sensible of the spirit that gave it meaning," the Society "would be glad enough to forget the past."[88]

In June 1905, the painter/critic Kenyon Cox, a twenty-two time exhibitor at the Society and an eleven-time exhibitor at the Academy, was the first to explain in print the many practical and logical reasons for the merger of the two organizations. He also tried to convey the significance of the Society when he described it as having "had a checkered but, on the whole, an honorable, even a glorious career." And, giving his overall estimation of it, he wrote: "Many of the most notable works of art produced in this country have been first shown to the public in its exhibitions, and some of these exhibitions will forever remain as landmarks in the history of American art." He believed that the Society had "prospered and strengthened itself," beginning in 1892 when it commenced holding exhibitions at the Fine Arts Building on West Fifty-seventh Street, even though, there had been "the regrettable secession of ten of its more vigorous members." Not wanting to deny that "some bitterness of feeling" had existed between the Society and the Academy, Cox described it as having "gone so far, at times, that membership in the one was almost a sufficient reason for non-election to the other." But, "the revolutionaries" of the past were "now among the most respected and authoritative of American artists" and "prominent and influential in both bodies."[89] He also pointed out that the Society's and the Academy's exhibitions were even held in the same building (since 1900).

Cox's discussion, which included issues involving liberalization of rules as well as compromises, was reprinted, almost verbatim, as the report of a committee of artists from both the Academy and the Society. In January 1906, it was presented to members of each to review prior to a vote for or against union. The *Tribune* ran large portions of the report, which indicated that 95 of the 193 members of the Academy, Academicians and Associates, were members of the Society and that 95 of the 134 members of the Society were in some way connected with the Academy. Four members of the Academy's leading body, its

Council, also served on the Board of Control or the Advisory Board of the Society. The report admitted that the two exhibitions were "so nearly alike that it would sometimes be difficult to know, if one were set down suddenly in one of them without a catalogue, which of the two it was."[90]

Various New York critics attacked parts of the report, but a particularly interesting response came from a writer for the *Boston Daily Evening Transcript*. He joked about the "curious features" in the terms of consolidation—how the Society would be absorbed and yet would somehow live on by having its name preserved and inaccessible to "the hands of strangers or unscrupulous people." He saw "this perpetuation of the society" as a "a sop to the members of the society, who might otherwise feel that being absorbed at all is an unpleasant experience." Preserving the Society's name was "a hollow concession," considering that the absorption remained a fact and that the Academy was described in the document as "the surviving organization." The critic flippantly added: "The lion has been known before now to lie down with the lamb, but everybody knows where the lamb goes. . . ."[91]

The day after the nearly seventy-one year old John La Farge, the president of the Society and a founding member, gave the valedictory for the organization in March 1906, the *Sun* quoted him extensively, including his opinion that the last annual was "the best the Society had ever had." The artist appreciated the fact that "more methods" were represented than in the past and cited "the direct influence of the old Italian masters" on "the last group of young men" who had been studying abroad. This influence, he maintained, was "plain and noticeable," whereas two years previously "the influence was all modern." He seemed particularly interested, though, in the possibility of protest against conservatism and saw "a grand chance for the young and original men," those who were struggling for recognition, to do just that. According to him, there was "room for a new group of painters to start the work all over again." Then, almost as if offering a rallying cry, he said: "I am telling that to young painters now."[92]

The day after La Farge's statements appeared in the *Evening Sun*, a critic for the same paper seems to have ignored his stance that the last exhibition was the Society's best. Instead, he detected a "conscious ambiguity" in a remark La Farge had made about the 1906 exhibition being "a good one to go out with." The critic also expressed appreciation of La Farge's "relatively cool forecast" for the future of the organization and contrasted it with "the enormous quantity of nonsense" that he had heard hitherto trickling from the lips of those who currently were and had been "the spokesmen of a new Academy." He liked the fact that La Farge had "no insane illusions"—did "not pretend to think that an Academy twice as big as the old one means a renaissance in art," or to maintain that "its progress had been glorious." La Farge had "indulged in none of the silly talk about a growth of tolerance in the old institution and a saner sobriety in the new." His "temerity" in

suggesting that a new group of painters might start the work over again was also applauded by the critic. In general, he contrasted La Farge's discourse with the "enthusiastic rubbish" that the public had been accustomed to. He himself did "not see the need of a big Academy" and thought that it could not be of the "slightest importance except in a mischievous way like the Royal Academy of London." His hope had been that "there would be some opposition to the obsolete and utterly vulgar idea of a big annual artistic debauch, an idea loathsome to every one of a tolerably discriminating taste." He added that several artists who disliked "such orgies" had put up "the most whimsical argument in the world" when pretending "that a great institution of artists with the inevitable abuses and prejudices that it creates, is bound to result in a wholesome disgust and bring about a reasonable and satisfactory opposition." "And that," he wrote, "is the best excuse they have to give for the existence of the new Academy of Design."[93]

Once the union was completed in 1906, critics were of course interested in analyzing the new situation. The *Boston Daily Evening Transcript* writer previously quoted claimed that, "With 125 painters entitled to all the privileges and emoluments of academicians, not to speak of an unlimited number of associates, the outsiders will [be] more hopelessly outside than ever; and any future secession will have a hard row to hoe."[94] In 1907, at the time of the first post-union annual, critics indicated the anticipatory excitement over it and evaluated the overall effect of the merger.[95] In *American Art News*, Charles H. Dorr wrote that "the combined strength of the two organizations" was "well manifested."[96] The *Herald* noted a "generous recognition of new men," including the landscapist Ernest Lawson.[97] The *Tribune* indicated that "the teapot tempest brewed by the action of one of the younger exhibitors [Robert Henri]," who withdrew certain paintings in protest against the exclusion of certain other artists, did not signify "anything in the least alarming in the character of the show." According to him, "no heroic efforts" on the part of members of the Academy and the Society had been necessary by way of adjustment to "the new regime." The Impressionists and the Academicians were "evidently at ease," while "the representatives of other 'movements'" were "sufficiently in evidence to reassure those observers who may have fancied, from the recent airing of grievances, that the world of art in this city was coming to an end."[98]

And so, the Academy, with a still large number of conservative members, survived the formation of the Society. Undoubtedly the voices of the press, whether praising or bluntly, even at times startlingly, critical, influenced the course of events to a substantial extent. In a multitude of reviews and articles, critics had evaluated the two most important venues for American art during a period when the forces of liberalism and conservatism were in a complicated state of flux. Although they came to no agreement on artistic persuasions or policy matters, they did often strongly express or imply hope for greatness on the part of American artists.

Soon after the union of the Academy and the Society, many critics took the opportunity to cheer new developments—first the independent exhibition of The Eight, held in New York in 1908, and then the nearly full, and in some cases unprecedented, representation of those artists at the Academy within a month.[99]

NOTES

1. For a study of the Society of American Artists during its early years, see Jennifer A. Martin Bienenstock, "The Formation and Early Years of The Society of American Artists: 1877–1884," (Ph.D. diss., City University of New York, 1983; facsimile, Ann Arbor, Michigan: University Microfilms International, 1983).

2. The Academy's annuals included around 500 to 800 works from 1878 through 1891, and around 300 to 500 from 1891 through 1906. At both venues, artists could submit and have accepted more than one work.

3. "NAD," *New York Daily Mail*, April 9, 1878.

4. S. N. [Susan Nichols] Carter, "The Academy Exhibition," *Art Journal* 4 (May 1878): 158.

5. William A. Coffin, "The Academy Exhibition," *Harper's Weekly* 35 (April 18, 1891): 287.

6. Delta, "The Academy Exhibition," *Boston Daily Evening Transcript*, May 6, 1878.

7. M. G. v. R. [Mariana Griswold Van Rensselaer], "NAD, New York. Fifty-Third Annual Exhibition," *American Architect and Building News* 3 (April 27, 1878): 149.

8. The Society's annuals started out at 124 works in 1878 and then stayed under 200 through the 1880s (expect for 1884 when 88 works were shown). From 1890 through 1897, two shows topped 300, whereas the others remained below that figure. The count was then below 400 through 1904; it reached 479 and 448 during the last two years of the organization's existence.

9. Among the locations where the Society presented its exhibitions prior to 1892 were the Kurtz Gallery (1878–79), the American Art Gallery (1882–83), Yandell Gallery (1887–88), and Fifth Avenue Galleries (1889–91). From 1892 on, the Society showed at the galleries of the American Fine Arts Society in the Fine Arts Building on West Fifty-seventh Street.

10. Between 1878 and 1882, the Society did not list the selection committee names in its exhibition catalogues. In 1883 and 1884, the number of participants was nine; in 1886, it was twenty-five.

11. From 1887 through 1891 and in 1896, the Academy's jurors numbered either twelve or thirteen. From 1892 through 1895, the figure was at twenty.

12. This work was painted after Chase returned from a trip to Europe in the summer of 1883. He had been president of the Society in 1880 and later served in that position from 1887 through 1895.

13. "Seventh Exhibition of the Society of American Artists," *Art Interchange* 12 (June 5, 1884): 136.

14. J. M. T., "The American Artists' Exhibition," *Art Amateur* 11 (July 1884): 30.

15. "The Society of American Artists," *New York Sun*, June 1, 1884.

16. Charles H. Caffin, "Exhibition of the Society of American Artists," *Harper's Weekly* 43 (April 1, 1899): 320.

17. "The Society of American Artists," *Art Collector* 9 (April 1, 1899): 166.

18. "The Art World," *New York Ccommercial Advertiser*, March 25, 1899.

19. The Gilder, "Palette and Brush: The Society of American Artists," *Town Topics* 41 (April 13, 1899): 17. The Carnegie Art Galleries is listed as the lender in the exhibition catalogue.

20. "Fine Arts. The National Academy Exhibition. Final Notice," *Nation* 26 (May 30, 1878): 363.

21. "Fine Arts. Fifty-Fifth Annual Exhibition of the NAD—Sixth Notice," *New York Herald*, April 26, 1880.

22. "In the World of Art: Exhibitions Past, Present, and Future, with General News," *New-York Times*, March 29, 1896.

23. "Art Gossip," *Art Interchange* 26 (April 25, 1891): 129.

24. F. G. I., "Fine Arts. NAD," *New York Mail*, April 1, 1878.

25. "The Academy of Design. Figures at the Sixty-eighth Exhibition," *New York Sun*, March 27, 1893. This review also gave the number of submitted versus accepted works.

26. "Fifty-Sixth Academy. First Notice. *Art Interchange* 6 (March 31, 1881): 74.

27. William A. Coffin, "The Academy Exhibition," *Harper's Weekly* 35 (April 18,

1891): 287. He continued with, "It has always been so, and it will no doubt continue to be so, and we can only be thankful when the result of placing pictures under such conditions is not altogether tawdry and unsatisfying."

28. "Society of American Artists," *New York Daily Tribune*, March 16, 1880.

29. "The Society of American Artists. Sixth Annual Exhibition," *New York Daily Tribune*, March 25, 1883.

30. The Fine Arts. The Society of American Artists," *Critic* 8 (May 8, 1886): 232. In "Fine Arts. The Society of American Artists. I," *Independent* 38 (July 22, 1886): 913, Mrs. Schuyler [Mariana Griswold] Van Rensselaer indicated the positive effect of the exhibition space itself: " . . . the room was the best and the best-lighted in the city."

31. Early on, critics sometimes mentioned artists' interests in old master paintings. And in "The Society Exhibition," *Harper's Weekly* 27 (April, 14, 1883): 231, G. W. Sheldon complained that, "There was so much in previous Society exhibitions that smacked of the nomadic shepherd." He went on, though, to praise the Society for succeeding "more nearly than ever before in presenting Nature, not as the nomadic shepherd sees her, but as the artist feels her."

32. "By the Younger Artists," *New York World*, April 23, 1887.

33. Whistler was also represented in the Society exhibitions of 1878, 1882, 1886, 1897, 1899, and 1902. In most cases, the works were borrowed from their owners.

34. "Art Exhibitions. The Society of American Artists," *New York Daily Tribune*, March 29, 1902.

35. "The American Artists," *New-York Times*, April 16, 1880.

36. S. N. [Susan Nichols] Carter, ""The New York Spring Exhibitions. II. The Society of American Artists," *Art Journal* 6 (May 1880): 155.

37. G. W. Sheldon, "The Society Exhibition," *Harper's Weekly* 27 (April 14, 1883): 231.

38. "Art Exhibitions. The Society of American Artists," *New York Sun*, March 25, 1883.

39. Strix, "Our Feuilleton. The Academy Exhibition," *New York Evening Express*, April 3, 1880.

40. G. W. H., "Fine Arts. The Academy Exhibition. Third Article.," *New York Evening Express*, April 2, 1881.

41. "Pictures at the Academy," *Harper's Weekly* 25 (April 9, 1881): 235.

42. "Fine Arts: Fifty-sixth Annual Exhibition of the NAD—Second Notice—A View by Daylight," *New York Herald*, March 21, 1881.

43. "Art Notes," *New York Commercial Advertiser*, April 4, 1881.

44. "Pictures at the Academy," *Harper's Weekly* 25 (April 9, 1881): 235.

45. "Exhibition of the Academy of Design," *Art Amateur* 4 (May 1881): 116.

46. "Fine Arts: Fifty-sixth Annual Exhibition of the NAD," *Nation* 32 (March 31, 1881): 229. The writer also called the work a masterpiece.

47. S. G. W. Benjamin, "A Representative American," *Magazine of Art* 5 (1882): 490.

48. Charles de Kay, "Ninth Exhibition, Society of American Artists," *Art Review* 1 (April 1, 1887): 9.

One of the most consistent exhibitors at both venues was William Merritt Chase, who showed at twenty-five Society annuals from 1898 through 1906 and at eighteen Academy annuals in 1878 and 1879, 1888 through 1895, 1897 through 1899, and 1902 through 1906.

49. "The Society of American Artists," *New-York Times*, April 9, 1888.

50. "The Fine Arts. The Society of American Artists' Exhibition," *Critic* 17 (May 7, 1892): 270.

51. The Gilder, "Palette and Brush: Some Effects of a Color Blindness—and a Highly-Colored Nymph," *Town Topics* 31 (March 29, 1894): 18.

52. "The Society of American Artists," *New-York Times*, March 23, 1895.

53. "Society of American Artists," *New York Sun*, March 24, 1895.

54. "All for Art's Sake," *New York Herald*, March 30, 1889.

55. There was also considerable attention paid to the influx of Impressionism at the Academy's autumn exhibitions, particularly in 1891. These exhibitions, which during the period under study ran from 1882 through 1898, were less prestigious than the ones in the spring; however, many members of the Academy and the Society, as well as other artists, showed in both. Critical responses to the autumn exhibitions were sometimes poles apart, but many revealed the willingness of the Academy to show young artists. In "Monthly Record of American Art: The NAD," *Magazine of Art* 15 (January 1892): v, a critic reported that one reason for the "onslaught" of works at the autumn show of 1891 was "the presence of many, many artists more or less affected by the latest school of Impressionists, or of Affectationists," as Charles H. Miller, a landscape painter, was "said to have dubbed them."

56. "The Academy Exhibition," *New York Evening Post*, April 6, 1892.

57. Cropsey, then sixty-eight, had shown yearly at the Academy since 1863,

with only one exception; Twachtman, then thirty-eight, had shown at the Society from 1878 through 1883 and 1887 through 1890, and at the Academy in 1879 and 1880, 1882 and 1883, and 1888. Figure 69 fits well aspects of the descriptions of Twachtman's work in various reviews, a few of which were very positive. Figure 69 was definitely shown at the exhibitions of The Ten in 1900 and in 1903, under the title *February*.

58. Augustus van Cleef, "At the American Artists Show," *Illustrated American* 19 (April 18, 1896): 531. In "Society of American Artists," *New York Evening Post*, March 24, 1898, J. C. V. D. [John C. Van Dyke] put forth a related general view of American art: "There is a lull just at present in art novelties, and everywhere there is a tendency toward conservatism."

59. Royal Cortissoz, "The Society Exhibition. A Conservative Collection with Portraiture in the Van," *New York Daily Tribune*, March 28, 1897.

60. "Clever Pictures," *New York Herald*, March 28, 1897.

61. "Annual Society of American Artists' Display," *New-York Times*, March 25, 1899.

62. Ibid.

63. "The Society of American Artists," *New York Daily Tribune*, March 25, 1899.

64. "Art Gossip," *Art Interchange* 26 (April 25, 1891): 129.

65. W. D. Howells, "Life and Letters," *Harper's Weekly* 40 (April 18, 1896): 390.

66. "The Society of Artists," *New-York Times*, March 25, 1883.

67. James B. Townsend, "National Academy and American Artists' Spring Exhibitions Described," *New York Times*, April 4, 1897.

68. Royal Cortissoz, "Spring Pictures. Exhibition of the Society of American Artists," *Harper's Weekly* 40 (April 18, 1896): 392.

69. Townsend, *New York Times Sunday Supplement*, April 4, 1897.

70. "Society of Artists," *New-York Times*, April 25, 1901.

71. "The Art World," *New York Commercial Advertiser*, March 30, 1901.

72. For information on subject matter at the Academy's annuals, see Paul Douglas Schweizer, "The Genteel Manner: A Study of the Major Styles and Classes of American Painting Exhibited at the National Academy of Design's Annual Exhibitions, between 1891 and 1910" (Master's thesis, University of Delaware, 1974).

73. C. C. [Clarence Cook], "Fine Arts. NAD. Fifty-Third Annual Exhibition," *New York Daily Tribune*, May 8, 1878.

74. "NAD Exhibition, First Notice," *Art Interchange* 4 (March 31, 1880): 54.

75. "Art Gossip," *Art Interchange* 26 (April 25, 1891): 129.

76. "Many Strong Portraits," *New York World*, April 6, 1891.

77. "The National Academy: Noteworthy Paintings at the Spring Annual," *New-York Times*, March 24, 1893. Blum's work was lent by its owner. The artist never showed again at the Academy.

78. "Society of American Artists," *New York Evening Post*, March 24, 1898.

79. "Annual Society of American Artists' Display," *New-York Times*, March 25, 1899.

80. "Society of American Artists," *Brooklyn Daily Eagle*, March 31, 1901.

81. WAC, "The American Artists," *New York Evening Post*, March 30, 1904. "Art Exhibitions. Annual Show of the Society of American Artists," *New York Daily Tribune*, March 26, 1904. Sargent's work was borrowed from its owners in England, Mr. and Mrs. Charles Hunter.

82. "Certain Painters at the Society," *Evening Sun*, April 1, 1905.

83. "Art Exhibitions. The Last Appearance of the Society of American Artists," *New York Daily Tribune*, March 20, 1906. "The Society of Artists. The Twenty-eighth and Last Exhibition Is Worthy of Its Traditions," *New-York Times*, March 16, 1906. The writer of the latter review did humorously suggest that the only exception concerning signs of death might be Abbott H. Thayer's painting *A Winged Figure*, which was a full-length allegorical figure of an angel.

84. James Townsend, "Society Exhibition," *American Art News* 4 (March 17, 1906): 4.

85. "Art Exhibitions. Annual Show of the Society of American Artists," *New York Daily Tribune*, March 26, 1904. The absentees included John White Alexander, Otto H. Bacher, Cecilia Beaux, John La Farge, Daniel French, Will Hicok Low, and Abbott Thayer, among others. Of those named, only Alexander showed at the Academy that spring.

86. As quoted in "The Society of American Artists," *Evening Sun*, March 26, 1904.

87. "Art Exhibitions. The Last Appearance of the Society of American Artists," *New York Daily Tribune*, March 20, 1906.

88. Ch.[Charles] Fitzgerald, "Plans for a Union of Artists in New York," *The Burlington Magazine for Connoisseurs* 8 (December 1905): 219. This article appeared in the "Art in America" section of the magazine, which was edited by Frank J. Mather, Jr.

89. Kenyon Cox, "The New York Union of Artists," *Harper's Weekly* 49 (June 10, 1905): 833.

90. As quoted in "Urge Art Union," *New York Daily Tribune*, February 11, 1906.

91. "Fine Arts. The Academy—Society Marriage of Convenience," *Boston Daily Evening Transcript*, Feb. 23, 1906. From 1907 through 1944, deceased members of the Society who died before 1906 and had not been members of the Academy were listed separately in the Academy's annual catalogues. From 1918 through 1977, an asterisk was placed next to the names of former Society members in the list of deceased Academy members to indicate their previous membership. This list was discontinued as of 1978.

92. As quoted in "Back to the Academy Now: John La Farge Recalls the Revolt of the Youngsters," *New York Sun*, March 23, 1906.

93. "The Extinct Society of American Artists," *Evening Sun*, March 24, 1906.

94. "Fine Arts. The Academy—Society Marriage of Convenience," *Boston Daily Evening Transcript*, Feb. 23, 1906.

95. At the time of the Academy's winter exhibition of 1906, a *Tribune* critic wrote of the expectation that there would be a sign of change at this, the first, exhibition of the "new regime." His report was: "Nothing has happened." In fact, he saw greater weakness: "This is no occasion for talking about the lion and the lamb lying down together. The tone of the 355 pictures is altogether lamblike." He felt that the exhibition was not more broadly representative of American art and that the "prevailing note" was one of "comfortable mediocrity." He also noted that "some significant pictures" were dated earlier, including Winslow Homer's *The Gulf Stream* (1899), and that they suggested the committee was anxious to bring in "at the last moment, a few striking things with which to enliven a commonplace exhibition." "Art Exhibitions. The Academy and the Society Since Their Fusion," *New York Daily Tribune*, December 29, 1906.

96. Charles H. Dorr, "Annual Academy Exhibition.," *American Art News* 5 (March 16, 1907): 1.

97. "National Academy Exhibition: Varnishing Day in Academy of Design" *New York Herald*, March 16, 1907.

98. "The Academy of Design," *New York Daily Tribune*, March 16, 1907.

99. In "Academy of Design Opens Its Eighty-Third Exhibit," *New York American*, March 14, 1908, "'The Eight' Win Art Victory" was in bold italics above the main title of the review. The painter/critic Guy Pène du Bois indicated that, "Artists and critics who crowded the galleries on varnishing day . . . were astounded." The reason was that the exhibition was "one of the most representative" at the Academy in many years, a point strongly made by other critics as well. There were on hand "many new pictures and innumerable new names." Du Bois went on to note that works by many of the "old Academicians" were present but not "starred" and that paintings representing different schools were "wisely" hung together. A part of one wall was "devoted to the usually slighted realists," and he saw this presentation as "a great victory for the new movement in the art of painting." The "element of modernity" in the exhibition would, he felt, surely make the National Academy "a really national institution." In conclusion, he wrote that, with the 1908 exhibition, "the official salon," New York had "risen far above a great many of the foreign exhibitions."

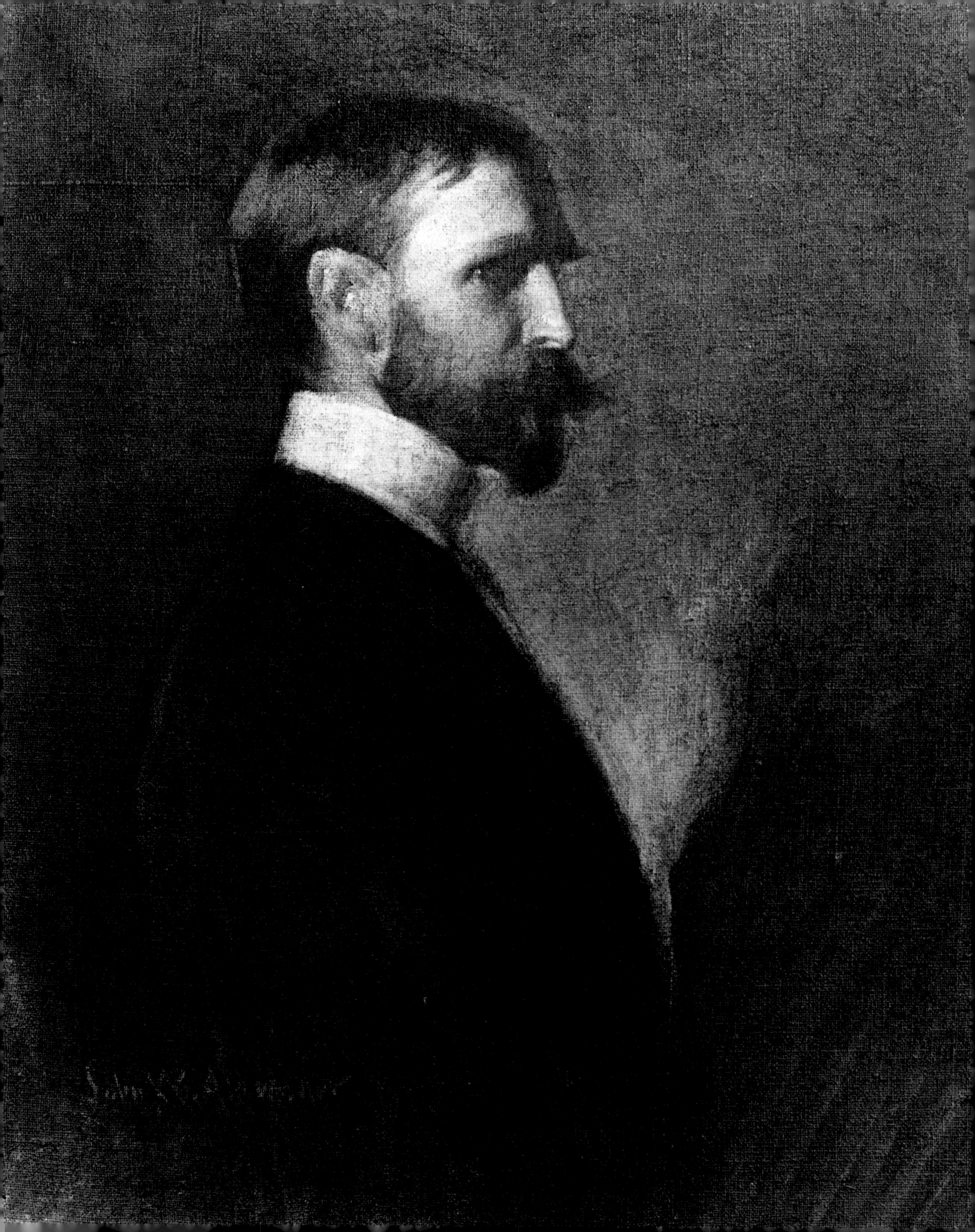

A "Salon of America"? Defining Nationalism at the National Academy of Design, 1909–1915

SARAH J. MOORE

In the spring of 1909, John White Alexander was unanimously elected president of the National Academy of Design, succeeding Frederick Dielman, who had been the president of the Academy from 1900 to 1909.[1] Alexander's election was widely applauded in art circles in the United States as a ray of hope for the revitalization of the flagging institution and for its transformation into a genuinely national center for American art. For example, fellow artist Leon Dabo wrote:

> *You have it in your power to make the National Academy of Design really national, to remove the stigma that rightly or wrongly attached itself to Art societies—and most important of all you, your personality—your great talent should impress the art world of our country that there is no need for a "Secession"—for a rival institution in our midst but that the Academy will admit that there are many expressions of beauty—that "art" is not in the keeping of a few men, no matter how refined their tastes, nor how profound their learning. . . . A new era should begin for this historic society, and under your guidance, I am sure a new era will begin for American art.*[2]

Alexander's commitment to constructing a clear national identity in American art paralleled broader artistic trends and critical concerns in the first decade and a half of the twentieth century. These included the gradual erosion of the internationalism of American art and the radical decline of the expatriate movement. Moreover, Alexander's relationship to and expression of this fundamental shift in American art from internationalism to nationalism is paradigmatic of the complicated movement as a whole.

During the last quarter of the nineteenth century, internationalism and cosmopolitanism were American art's most defining features. Informed by a generation of artists who sought foreign training and who self-consciously aligned themselves with international art ideals and practices, American art redefined itself and in fact reveled in its very lack of "Americanness." As Henry James wrote in 1887: "It sounds like a paradox, but it is a very simple truth, that when today we look for 'American art' we find it mainly in Paris. When we find it out of Paris, we at least find a great deal of Paris in it."[3] Conversely, cultural nationalism re-emerged during the first years of the twentieth century and informed a generation of artists who rejected the internationalism and cosmopolitanism of the previous generation's art and looked not to Europe but rather to their own cities and landscapes for aesthetic sustenance and a national identity.

With the resurgence of nationalism in the early twentieth century, the international spirit of American art in the last decades of the nineteenth century—the context in which Alexander's career and those of his colleagues flourished—was redefined as the backdrop on which to cast new light on national traits and distinctions between American art and that of other nations. Foreign training had been *de rigueur* for American artists in the 1870s and 1880s. They went abroad to learn academic techniques, to find exotic and artistic subject matter, and, generally, to learn what they needed to know to become competitive with European artists. By the turn of the twentieth century, however, vastly improved art conditions in the United States diminished the urgency for extended European study and travel. Moreover, the desire to imprint a distinctly national voice, however difficult that was to define, inspired American expatriates to return home. After more than a decade in Paris, that is exactly what John White Alexander (1856–1915) did in 1901 (fig. 74).

After nearly a quarter of a century of engagement with and emulation of international art trends and practices, art in the United States had come of age and was, many argued, prepared to generate an artistic dialogue that was both vital and self-referential. Such optimism was shared by many, including art critic Mary Fanton Roberts, writing under the pseudonym Giles Edgerton, who in 1908 declared the dissolution of American art's internationalism. This, she believed, was irrefutable testimony of its coming of age. She wrote:

> *We dare to proclaim a man an artist even if he has never crossed the Atlantic or studied at [the Academie] Julien [sic] nor starved in the Latin Quarter. Our artists have come to study* American *conditions and scenery and have recklessly proclaimed them picturesque . . . It is not unnatural that Europe should resent a little the fact that America has ceased, or is beginning to cease, her ardent occupation of copying the works of their great men.*[4]

Alexander assumed his role as president of the National Academy of Design in 1909 with a clear and motivating

OPPOSITE: Fig. 74 John White Alexander, *Self-Portrait* [1901–02], oil on canvas, 30¼ x 25, National Academy of Design

nationalist agenda. His prime objective became the search for a site for a new and adequate building for the Academy and its exhibitions. This project became Alexander's rallying call, and he used it to articulate his understanding of nationalism in American art and the role the Academy was to play in its promotion.[5] In 1910, for example, he wrote "The Need of a National Academy and Its Value to the Growth of Art in America," (fig. 75) an article in which he argued that a national academy should provide an institutional structure and legitimate forum for the development of American art. "All great movements progress through civilization through the aid of an institution," he wrote,

> *It is the means by which ideas are held back from the disintegrating forces of change. . . . The effort of the intelligent to conserve a progressive idea results in the upbuilding of the institution, which for the time being becomes the needed nursery of the idea. . . . It is from the wider point of view that we should regard the existence of the National Academy, and its value to the art of America.[6]*

In the same article, Alexander acknowledged that compared with the negligible conditions of art in America two decades earlier, when artists were driven abroad for artistic sustenance and training, "the great awakening wave of interest now sweeping over the United States in regard to art matters seems little short of miraculous."[7] However, he bitterly regretted the lack of proper accommodations for the exhibition of contemporary American art in New York in comparison with cities such as Philadelphia, Buffalo, and Pittsburgh. He asked, "What is the use of all this preparation if its outcome cannot be made public? About 3,500 pictures are annually submitted to the Academy jury, a very small portion of which can be hung."[8] Alexander concluded that as a truly national organization, the Academy had the obligation to erect a building that could properly house what he called the "Salon of America." Several shorter articles appeared contemporaneously that carried Alexander's urgent appeal for a new home for the Academy and chronicled his frustration in fulfilling his objective. His dismay was palpable in the article entitled, "Even Richmond, Ind., Has a Better Exhibition Than New York" (fig. 76). [9]

Alexander's use of the term "Salon of America" was suggestive of the degree to which he was engaged in current debates about the role of institutions in the formulation and promotion of American art while alluding to the international context within which his own artistic career flourished. Indeed, the term resonated with the complex shifts in American art priorities during the first years of the twentieth century and the construction of a distinctly national profile, in contrast to the previous generation's internationalism and cosmopolitanism. It is perhaps not surprising that the term "Salon of America" was first used widely in critical discussions of and comparisons between the American art displays at the 1900 Paris Universal Exposition and the 1901 Pan-American Exposition in Buffalo.

In striking contrast to the American display at the 1889 Paris Universal Exposition, which defined American art's triumph in international terms, the demonstration of nationalism within an international context was the agenda of the American art display at the 1900 Exposition. Although the paintings themselves were not fundamentally different from those displayed in 1889—decorative and/or academic figure painting dominated as they had in the previous Exposition— the organizers of the 1900 American art section sought to present American works as representative of a distinct national expression, and they imposed the assumption of nationalism as a unifying principle on the official discourse. In his prefatory statement to the catalogue of the American fine arts exhibit, H. Hobart Nichols, a member of the United States Commission of Fine Arts of the Exposition of 1900, stated: "In forming the present exhibition, the object . . . has been to place before this conclave of nations a truly representative American exhibition."

In order to distinguish the present exhibition from its predecessor and to redefine the international context of the Exposition as the backdrop on which to cast light on national distinctions between American art and that of other nations, Nichols detailed the rapid progress of American art in the past decade, in particular the growth of educational institutions that were now fully capable of training American artists at home. He stated confidently:

> *Since the Exposition of 1889 American art has to a great degree emancipated itself from foreign trammels, and entered upon a career of its own—expressing American thought and reflecting American nature. Today we have many well-equipped institutions in which the student can develop an artistic temperament on his native soil, in which individuality is recognized and encouraged, while the necessary methods of expression are being learned.[10]*

The preoccupation with the expression of nationalism in the American art displayed at the 1900 Exposition was shared by French commentators as well, who acknowledged both American art's considerable debt to the French and its nascent liberation from previous dependence.[11] For example, critic and aesthetician Louis de Fourcaud, who had often deprecated *l'école américaine* in Salon reviews, found the American display at the 1900 Exposition worthy of considerable praise, in particular its artists whose works were painted in "*la terre natale.*" He discussed American art's growing independence from foreign influence and quoted an often-repeated criticism of American art—"that America could have artists but it could never have an art"—in order to disclaim its accuracy. He concluded: "The American school of art will probably play one day—and maybe sooner than one imagines—an important role."[12]

In contrast to the French commentators who had a vested interest in asserting the vital role that French art played in the development of American art, American critic Ellis Clarke broadly condemned the American display at the 1900

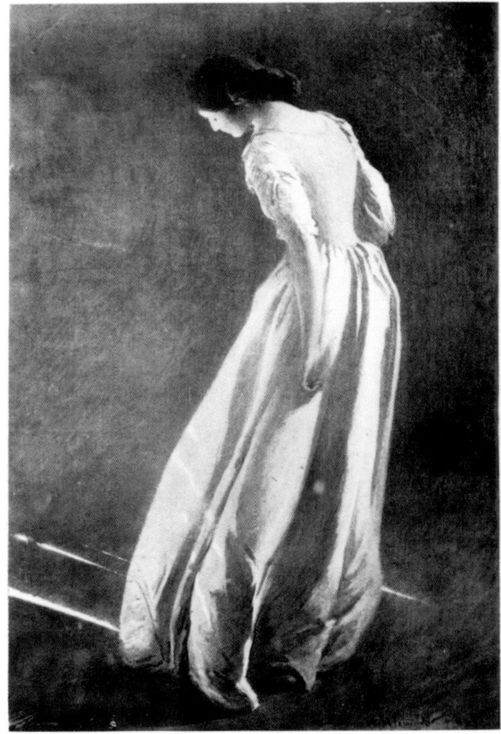
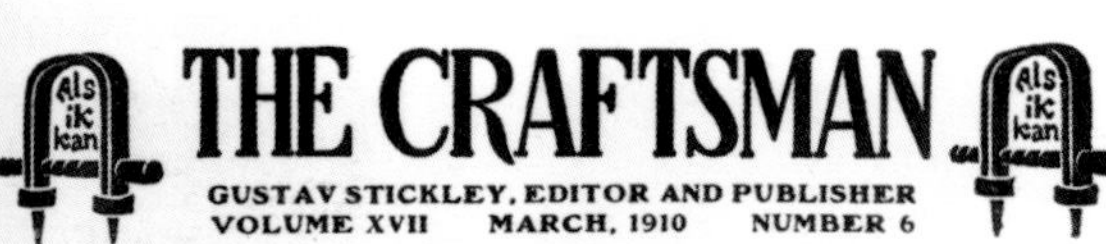
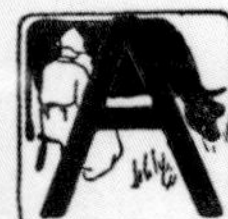

Fig. 75 John W. Alexander, "The Need of a National Academy, and Its Value to the Growth of Art in America," *Craftsman*, March 1910, The New York Public Library, Astor, Lenox and Tilden Foundations

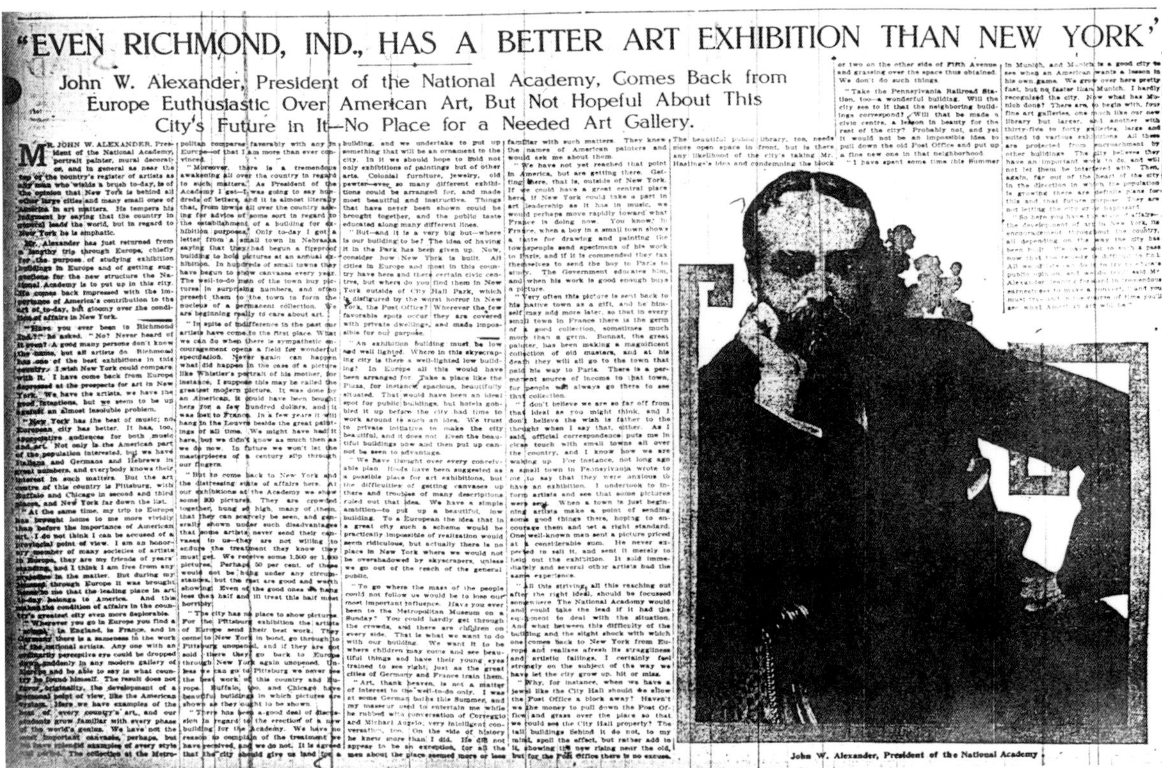

Fig. 76 "Even Richmond Has a Better Art Exhibition Than New York," *New York Times Sunday Magazine*, September 25, 1910, The New York Public Library, Astor, Lenox and Tilden Foundations

Exposition as distinctly "un-national and un-American." Clarke identified expatriatism as the main cause of the protracted "alien element" in American art and strongly advised a commitment to American scenes painted in the United States. He warned: "Extensive, varied, magnificent as is the American art exhibit at Paris, rich as it is in evidence of personal ability, this, therefore, is its lesson: Expatriation is a mistake, both as regards the future of the individual artist and as regards the future of American art."[13]

Appearing in the same issue of *Brush and Pencil* as Ellis Clarke's article was a brief essay, "Strays of Opinion," that addressed the need for an American Salon in order to provide artists in the United States with a venue for exhibition of their work that was as dignified and honorable as those in Europe. The author argued:

> *The project of establishing an American Salon, comparable with the great exhibitions of Europe, is one that should meet the approval and command the support of all who take pride in American work. A national art presupposes a national art center. England has its Royal Academy and France its Paris Salon, and the art of both countries is distinctively and laudably national. America has no such institution, and its art, while robust and progressive, is more the exponent of foreign influences and ideals than the embodiment of national aspiration.*[14]

Arguing that conditions were never more favorable or popular interest more pitched than at the present time for the establishment of such a Salon, the author concluded: "The essential thing is to inaugurate a movement that will give to America a national art center and a great representative salon."[15]

Nowhere was the growing concern with nationalism and the articulation of a distinctly American language of art made clearer than at the Pan-American Exposition held in Buffalo in 1901. Carefully crafted as an elaborate allegory of the New World's coming of age, the Pan-American Exposition revealed the heady confidence of the United States at the beginning of the new century with respect to advances in technology, industry, and science and in light of its position as a new imperial world power and a culture in the full flush of civilization. Unlike earlier expositions that were international in scope, the Pan-American was limited to participation by Americans—North and South. Paralleling the tone of national chauvinism and American cultural imperialism that informed the Exposition as a whole, and designed to confirm the unquestionable merit of American art, the fine arts display did not include any works by European artists. Following the trajectory of nationalism that had informed the American art display at the 1900 Universal Exposition in Paris, William A. Coffin, director of the Division of Fine Arts, sought to establish a model for art exhibitions in the United States that would parallel the prestige of the Parisian Salons while providing the setting within which to articulate a national profile in American art. Coffin, who had served on the Fine Arts Committee for American Art at the 1900 Exposition in Paris, was current with critical discussions about the creation of an American Salon and recognized the potential of the Buffalo Exposition to provide the prototype. He noted: "After 1901 people must look to Buffalo as the standard."[16]

Indeed, references to and questions about American art's national profile characterized many discussions of the American art display at the exposition in Buffalo; the term American Salon seemed to pop up everywhere. In her review of the fine arts display at the exposition, for example, critic Katherine V. McHenry noted: "For the first time in the history of the United States, the artists of Pan-America will be given an opportunity at Buffalo to exhibit their best works and demonstrate that it is not necessary to ransack the galleries and ateliers of Europe to make a creditable display." She continued: "In view of the unquestionable merit of much of the art work done by Americans of the present day, and of the fine outlook for the growth of artistic culture and for a greater degree of patronage of native artists, if the Pan-American Exposition should lead to the establishment of such an institution as an American Salon it will have done an incalculable service to American art."[17] Another contemporary observer referred to the fine arts display as "the first American Salon," adding: " . . .[it] should do honor to the increasing artistic sense of nation."[18] In addition to creating a model for a so-called American Salon, economic imperatives informed the fine arts display in Buffalo, as well. As art historian Joann Marie Thompson observed, "The Pan-American promoters recognized the need for a type of American salon which would encourage patronage from American collectors for hitherto slighted American artists."[19]

Despite the rhetoric of nationalism that informed the agenda of the 1901 Pan-American Exposition, a clear definition of what made American art American, outside of the overly simplistic notion of residency, remained surprisingly vague. Although it was true that many American expatriate artists had returned home by the turn of the century and that the number of American artists traveling to Europe for extended periods of training was dramatically lower than a decade earlier, all of the gold medalists, with the exception of Winslow Homer, had significant tenures in Europe, particularly in Paris. And while more and more artists were painting so-called American subjects on American soil, decorative and/or academic figure painting dominated the Exposition, and especially those works that were awarded medals, much as it had in the American displays at the Paris Salons throughout the 1890s.

With the resurgence of nationalism in the early twentieth century, the international spirit of American art at the end of the nineteenth century was redefined as the foil against which national traits and distinctions between American art and that of other nations would become evident. Indeed, the accomplishments of the cosmopolitan artists of the 1880s and 1890s were recontextualized to highlight not their international status but their prominent position on a trajectory of nationalism in American art.[20] Moreover, the newly-won sense of freedom from foreign influences was credited to the accomplishments of the artists of the post–Civil War generation who, in their desire to participate in the international art arena, significantly raised the level of American art, to the point where it could identify a national tradition and thus declare "independence." As critic Christian Brinton noted in 1908:

> To any sensitive and observant student of American conditions it must have been for some time apparent that radical changes were taking place regarding the status of native painting, sculpture, and architecture. The triumphs achieved by our men in Paris in 1900 have been supplemented by renewed activity at home and by splendid showings at the Buffalo and St. Louis expositions. Interest in art and in matters artistic have been rapidly spreading, rich endowments have poured in upon our museums and schools, and the standard of merit in various yearly displays has risen. Art in America, which was once practically non-existent . . . is to-day the proud possession of the many and throughout all of its manifestations, there can be felt the throb of a new spirit.[21]

Alexander was not alone in his desire for the creation of an American Salon or his concern with issues of nationalism and the role the National Academy of Design played in its articulation and promotion. In fact, several critics addressed these issues; exhibition reviews often gave way to inquiries into the Academy's function in the development of a distinctly American expression in art. In reviewing the Academy's annual exhibition in the winter of 1908–09, for example, critic Mary Fanton Roberts questioned what the National Academy of Design stood for and what its value was to the American public. She asked:

> Should it be an opportunity for our nation to inform itself as to its real progress in art, its development in the past, its hope for the future? Should it thus from year to year stand as a record of the best we can achieve? Should we look to it for an opportunity to understand accomplishment and find inspiration? Should our mature men go to it to watch the progress of our national art, and our students to realize the high standards demanded of them? . . . Or must we accept this famous institution merely as the art opinion of the academic few who invariably see originality coupled with anarchy, and who reticently offer the public year after year a program of cold-served repetition?[22]

Recognizing the vast potential of the Academy to encourage and express the vitality of American art, she criticized its present policies of entropy, insularity, and mediocrity and said one must look to the one-person or small group exhibitions for evidence of the vigor and individuality of artists working in the United States. She concluded, "The Academy should be the final tribunal of justice for growing American art—an art which is even now throbbing with the most vital, most extraordinary civilization the world has ever seen, and the Academy should be seeking out those men, urging them to newer and stronger efforts."[23]

Although harsher in her criticism of the Academy than was Alexander, Roberts shared with the institution's president a desire for the Academy to act as a center for American art activities, hospitable to individual expression and, thus, genuinely representative of the broad range of contemporary art in the United States. At the same time, their writing as well as that of several others, responded to the increasingly varied and ever mounting number of exhibitions—the exhibition of "The Eight" at the Macbeth Gallery in 1908 being the most noteworthy—which signaled the dwindling hegemony of the National Academy of Design as the arbiter of contemporary art in New York only two years after its reunification with the formerly dissident Society of American Artists. In fact, Roberts's article was, in part, a response to one by Robert Henri, written after the Macbeth Gallery exhibition. On those pages, Henri called for the development of national art outside of the confines of the Academy, an institution, he argued, that stifled individuality of ideas and freedom of artistic expression.[24] The dispersion of artistic activity and increasing critical attention to exhibitions other than those at the National Academy continued to erode the institution's prestige and dominance throughout the period, even with exhibitions and organizations not overtly hostile to the Academy, such as The Ten, organized in 1898, and the National Association of Portrait Painters, organized in 1912.

In 1912, critic and author James Gibbons Huneker (1860–1921) asked, "What is the matter with our National Academy?" (fig. 77) and, in comparing its annual exhibitions with those of the Pennsylvania Academy of the Fine Arts, the Corcoran Gallery of Art, and the Carnegie Institute, came to the following conclusion: "You can't see the Academy because of the Academicians."[25] Huneker was not arguing for the Academy's unquestioned hospitality to all new eccentricities but denounced its perpetuation of the academic privilege of exhibiting *hors concours*, a policy that transcended and thus invalidated the will of even the fairest jury of selection. Granting Alexander's admirable and genuine intentions for the progress of art in the United States under the auspices of the National Academy of Design, Huneker disagreed with Alexander's claim that it was only a lack of adequate space that prohibited the Academy from playing a vital role in contemporary American art. He said:

> As spokesman President Alexander has asserted, and not without reason, the exhibiting space is the principal evil to be overcome. He points to the Pittsburgh (Carnegie Institute), Washington (Corcoran Gallery), and Philadelphia (Pennsylvania Academy) exhibitions as confirming his argument. We need a building adequate in size for the Academy, he says, and there is no disputing the fact. But give the Academy its building, give it 2,000

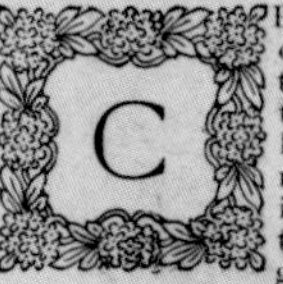

Fig. 77 James Huneker, "What is the Matter with our National Academy," *Harper's Weekly,* April 6, 1912, The New York Public Library, Astor, Lenox and Tilden Foundations

pictures to hang instead of 300, and will the result be different than what it is now—dispiriting mediocrity? Mr. Alexander believes it will be; many people believe the opposite.[26]

The on-going debate about nationalism in American art and the creation of an American Salon continued outside the context of the National Academy of Design as well. For example, the term American Salon was often used in critical discussions of the annual exhibitions held at the Carnegie Institute, Pittsburgh. The history of the Carnegie Institute's international exhibitions, which began in 1896, forms a vital chapter in the discussion of American art's articulation of a national profile within an international context at the turn of the twentieth century. Although internationalism was fundamental to the exhibitions from their inception—the eighth annual exhibition held in the winter of 1903–1904 was the only one in which American art was shown exclusively—the Carnegie Institute "Internationals" were designed to offer a comprehensive view of the varied and complex topography of contemporary American work while providing a distinguished forum within which to present American art alongside of, and more important, equal to that created by contemporary European artists. Noting the parallels between the Parisian Salons and their embrace of nationalism within an international context and the Carnegie Institute annual exhibitions, one critic referred to the latter as "the American Salon," and praised the efforts of John Beatty, Director of Fine Arts, Carnegie Institute, in demonstrating the vitality of Pittsburgh as a center for American art.[27] In a review of the fifth annual exhibition at the Carnegie Institute, another critic observed: "In a sense, the exhibition at the Carnegie Art Galleries is the American Salon. Being international in character, it commands more attention than any other American exhibition, and foreign artists are beginning to feel it a privilege to send their choicest work to it."[28] Alexander must surely have had the Carnegie Institute Internationals in mind in his call for the formation of an American Salon in New York under the auspices of the Academy. Alexander was a frequent exhibitor and prize winner at the Pittsburgh Internationals, a member of the Parisian and later American jury of awards, and he acted as foreign advisor to John Beatty for the inaugural exhibition in 1896.

Disappointment at the failure of the Academy to secure a site for a new building to house exhibition galleries ultimately led Alexander to resign his position as president on March 20, 1915, less than two weeks before his sudden and untimely death. A letter from fellow Academician Henry B. Snell, who had been a close associate of Alexander's since 1900 when he served as assistant director of the United States Commission of Fine Arts of the 1900 Paris Universal Exposition, expressed regret shared by many:

> *Perhaps no one at the Academy knows more than myself how much we owe for your untiring energy and efforts in the interest of the organization. I know you have lifted the Institution from a dead level to a real live one and the Academy is at this moment more in the public mind and in better standing than ever before. . . . It will always be my regret if you leave the chair before the consummation of our hopes, for the ball which you have set rolling is surely on the run, and sooner or later will bear fruit. You will, however, step down with a jolly good clear conscience and I know I voice the opinion of most of the Academicians that you are about the best ever.*[29]

With the outbreak of World War I and the entrance of the United States into the European conflict, all efforts for the acquisition of a new building for the National Academy of Design were halted. Addressing the national effects of the war on art in 1918, then-president J. Alden Weir noted: "It was felt that any attempt at this time to push the project of a new building would not only be futile but unwise, and no effort has been put forth in this direction."[30] Indeed, it would be another twenty-five years before the National Academy of Design would find a permanent home.[31] Given the changing political and cultural climate, and the shifting priorities in American art in the post–World-War-I period, the creation of an American Salon remained an even more elusive goal.

NOTES

1. For a history of the National Academy of Design, see Eliot Clark, *History of the National Academy of Design, 1825–1953* (New York: Columbia University Press, 1954). In 1975, two catalogues were published celebrating the 150th anniversary of the founding of the Academy: Lois Marie Fink and Joshua Taylor, *Academy: The Academic Tradition in American Art* (Washington, D.C.: National Collection of Fine Arts, Smithsonian Institution Press, 1975); and National Academy of Design, *A Century and a Half of American Art* (New York: National Academy of Design, 1975).

2. Letter, Leon Dabo to John White Alexander, May 15, 1909, John White Alexander Papers, Archives of American Art, reel 1728, frames 727–38.

3. Henry James, "John Singer Sargent," *Harper's New Monthly Magazine* 75 (October 1887): 683.

4. Giles Edgerton [Mary Fanton Roberts], "American Art Scores a Triumph at International Exhibition of Painting in Pittsburgh," *Craftsman* 14 (August 1908): 463.

5. As a founding member of the Fine Arts Federation of New York in 1897, whose mission was to unify the art societies in the city and to promote civic interest, the National Academy of Design spearheaded the effort to obtain a new building that would house exhibitions of the members of the Federation (the name was later changed to National Academy Association). See Clark, *National Academy of Design*, 164–67.

6. John W. Alexander, "The Need of a National Academy and Its Value to the Growth of Art in America," *Craftsman* 17 (March 1910): 607.

7. Ibid., 607.

8. Ibid., 608.

9. See, for example, "There is No Art Center, J. W. Alexander Says," *New York Times*, February 3, 1910; "Suggests New Site for Art Home Here," *New York Times*, February 26, 1910; "National Academy Seeks a New Site," *New York Times*, July 7, 1910; "Says We Need Art Galleries," *New York Times*, September 19, 1910; and "Even Richmond Has a Better Art Exhibition Than New York," *New York Times Sunday Magazine*, September 25, 1910.

10. Quoted in H. Hobart Nichols, "Prefatory," in *Fine Arts Exhibit, United States of America, Paris Exposition of 1900. Official Illustrated Catalogue* (Boston: Noyes, Platt, and Company, 1900) xv–xvi. See also Diane Fischer, "The American School in Paris: The Repatriation of American Art at the Universal Exposition of 1900" (Ph.D. diss., Graduate Center, City University of New York, 1993).

11. See, for example, Léonce Bénédict, "*Les Arts à l'Exposition Universelle de 1900: L'Exposition Décennale. La Peinture Étrangère, III,*" *Gazette des Beaux-Arts* 24 (December 1900): 581–82; and Georges Lafenestre, "*L'Exposition Universelle. La Peinture I, Les Écoles Étrangères,*" *La Revue de l'Art Ancien et Moderne* 8 (October 1900): 218.

12. L. de Fourcaud, "*Les Peintres Américaines à l'Exposition,*" *Le Gaulois du Dimanche*, September 15–16, 1900.

13. Ellis T. Clarke, "Alien Element in American Art," *Brush and Pencil* 7 (October 1900): 36, 47. See also N. N. [Elizabeth Robins Pennell], "The Paris Exposition—V. The American Section," *Nation* 71 (August 2, 1900): 88–90.

14. "Strays of Opinion," *Brush and Pencil* 7 (October 1900): 64.

15. Ibid., 64.

16. Quoted in Joann M. Thompson, "The Art and Architecture of the Pan-American Exposition, Buffalo, New York, 1901" (Ph.D diss., Rutgers, The State University of New Jersey, 1980), 169. See also Sarah J. Moore, "Mapping Empire in Omaha and Buffalo: World's Fairs and the Spanish-American War," in *The Legacy of the Mexican and Spanish-American Wars: Legal, Literary, and Historical Perspectives* (Bilingual Press: Arizona State University, forthcoming).

17. Katherine V. McHenry, "Fine Arts at the Pan-American Exposition," *Brush and Pencil* 7 (January 1901): 217, 219.

18. William H. Hotchkiss, "The Pan-American on Dedication Day," *Review of Reviews* 23 (June 1901): 683.

19. Thompson, "Pan-American Exposition," 169. See also Buffalo, Pan-American Exposition, *Catalogue of the Fine Arts* (Buffalo: David Gray, 1901).

20. See for example, Charles H. Caffin, "The Picture Exhibition at the Pan-American Exposition," *International Studio* 14 (August 1901): xiii; and Charles De Kay, "Paintings at the Pan-American," *New York Times Sunday Magazine*, July 7, 1901. See also Kenyon Cox, "Some American Figure Painters," *Cosmopolitan* 32 (April 1902): 585–600, and idem., "American Art at Buffalo," *Nation* 73 (August 15, 1901): 127–28.

21. Christian Brinton, "The New Spirit in American Painting," *Bookman* 27 (June 1908): 351. See also John C. Van Dyke, "Preface," in *American Painting and Its Tradition* (New York: Charles Scribner's Sons, 1919), vi.

22. Giles Edgerton [Mary Fanton Roberts], "What Does the National Academy of Design Stand For, Has it at Present a Value to the American Art Public?" *Craftsman* 15 (February 1909): 520.

23. Ibid., 530.

24. See Robert Henri, "Progress in Our National Art Must Spring From the Development of Individuality of Ideas and Freedom of Expression: A Suggestion for a New Art School," *Craftsman* 15 (January 1909): 386–401. For a discussion of "The Eight" and its role in the nationalist debate in American art, see Elizabeth Milroy, *Painters of the New Century: The Eight and American Art* (Milwaukee: Milwaukee Art Museum, 1991).

25. James Gibbons Huneker, "What is the Matter with our National Academy? Two Spring Picture Shows Compared," *Harper's Weekly* 56 (April 6, 1912): 8.

26. Ibid., 8.

27. James B. Townsend, "Carnegie Institute at Pittsburgh Presented as the American Salon," *Craftsman* 16, no. 4 (July 1909): 383–90. For general information on the Carnegie Institute annual exhibitions, see Kenneth Neal, *A Wise Extravagance: The Founding of the Carnegie International Exhibitions, 1895–1901* (Pittsburgh: University of Pittsburgh Press, 1996); Department of Fine Arts, Carnegie Institute, *1896–1955. Retrospective Exhibition of Paintings From Previous Internationals* (Pittsburgh: Department of Fine Arts, Carnegie Institute, 1958); Henry Adams, "Introduction," in Carnegie Institute, *American Drawings and Watercolors in the Museum of Art, Carnegie Institute* (Pittsburgh: Museum of Art, Carnegie Institute, 1985), 6–10; and Gabriel Weisberg, "Tastemaking in Pittsburgh: The Carnegie Internationals in Perspective, 1896–1905," *Carnegie Magazine* 56 (July/August 1983): 20–26, 40–41.

28. Austin E. Howland, "The Pittsburgh Art Exhibition," *Craftsman* 7 (December 1900): 129.

29. Letter, Henry B. Snell to John White Alexander, April 13, 1915, Alexander Papers, reel 1728, frames [735–850].

30. Clark, *National Academy of Design*, 167.

31. The National Academy's permanent home was given to the institution in 1939 by Archer Milton and Anna Hyatt Huntington. See *A Century and a Half of American Art*, 15.

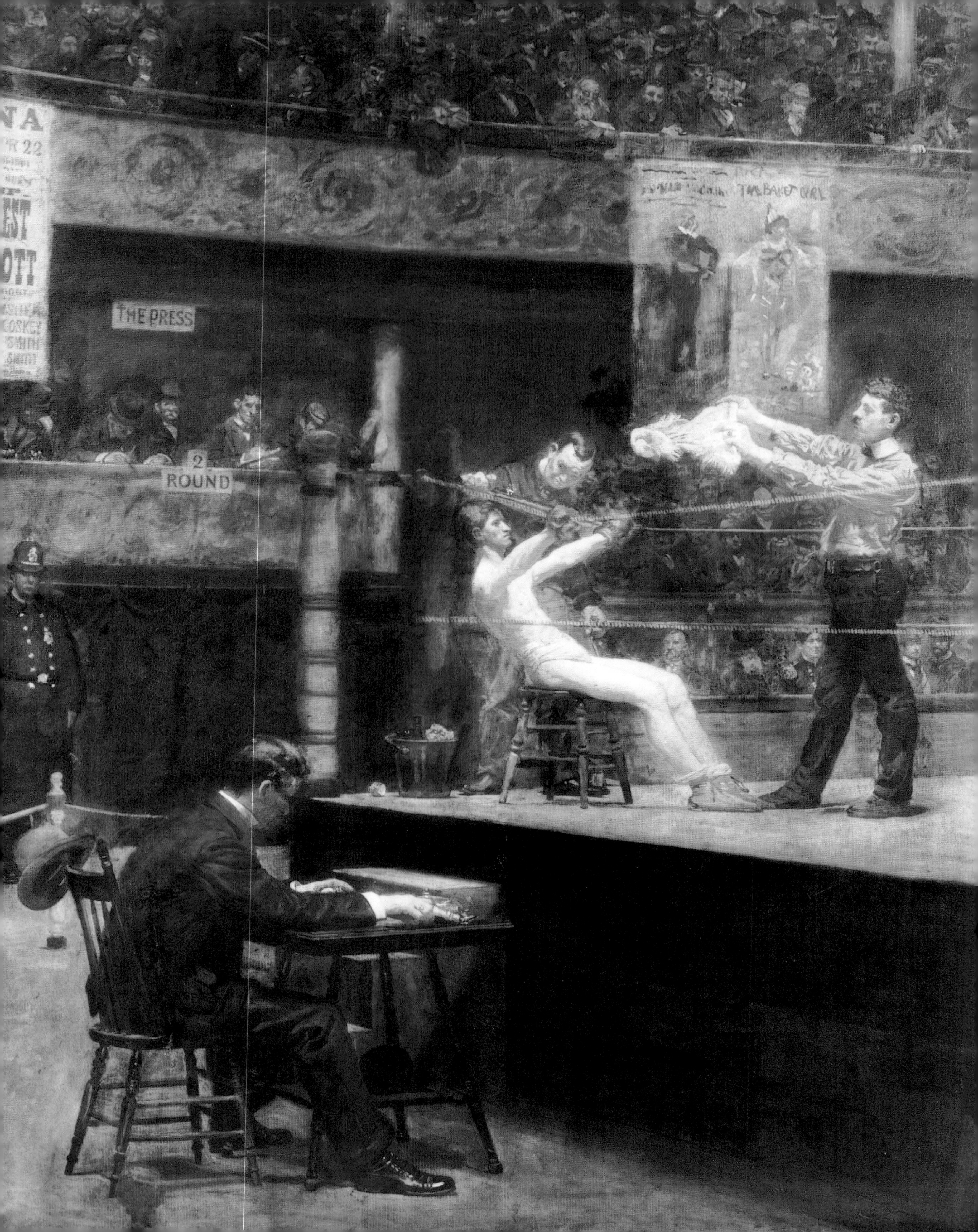
THE PRESS
2 ROUND
THE BAKET GIRL

"As National as the National Biscuit Company": The Academy, the Critics, and the Armory Show[1]

AVIS BERMAN

After the Armory Show, the American art world was irrevocably transformed. The exhibition, which contained nearly thirteen hundred works of art, with every progressive tendency in Europe and America on view, was declared "the most stimulating episode in this city's art history up to the present time" within weeks of its opening on February 17, 1913.[2] It continued to be recognized as a landmark occasion that would resonate long into the future.[3] Just as American artists had to confront the impact and implications of what they had just seen, so too did the critics who covered the event. The reviewers, like the painters and sculptors, had to consider the conflict between modern and traditional styles and ponder if contemporary art could set aside the mimetic representation of nature as an ultimate ideal. They had to absorb the vocabulary and syntax of modern art as practiced by the European avant-garde and consider the obligations of American artists and art institutions to probe or ignore it. As they wrestled with the ramifications of the Armory Show, working critics in New York could not fail to use it as a measure of other major art events. Well before 1913, the National Academy of Design's annual spring and fall exhibitions had become an important staple of the exhibition calendar, and during and after that year comparisons with what had transpired within the 69th Regiment Armory were inevitable. Was the Academy adjusting to Cubism, Fauvism, and Expressionism, or even to Post-Impressionism? Was it taking note of the new in its admission and exhibition policies? By definition, did it even have to? Or, as it had in the past, would the Academy recover from attacks by co-opting the rebels banging on its gate? Such questions lingered on in the New York art columns for a year or two after the big show. After that, these issues were an implicit part of all journalistic art discussion, and, as will be seen by a survey of a half-dozen critics who shaped opinions in the opening years of the twentieth century, the degree to which these writers accepted modernism directly influenced their attitudes toward the Academy.

The Armory-Academy linkage was made explicit by critics for several reasons. First, the ground swell of artist-organized independent exhibitions in New York that distinguished the first decade of the twentieth century was staged in reaction to the Academy's exclusionary membership and exhibition policies, and one of the primary purposes of the Armory Show was to destroy the Academy's hegemony over sales and commissions. During the course of these rebellious efforts, the activists announced that the Academy was their target, and the critics listened.

The second reason rested on a happenstance of timing. The International Exhibition of Modern Art, as the Armory Show was formally known, closed in New York on March 15, 1913, by which time seventy thousand people had seen it. Hundreds of artists and a number of open-minded critics had not so much visited it as lived in it. The Academy's spring annual opened on that same March 15, and the adventure of the Armory Show, which one reporter said "has made men stop and think . . . [and] set New York and its artists by their ears,"[4] shimmered in radiant contrast to the Academy's offerings. The spring exhibition, another paper lamented, did not "present either ideas or emotions that stir[red] the spectator."[5] It did not help the Academy that some prominent members, including its president, John White Alexander, and the venerable Edwin Blashfield and Kenyon Cox, endorsed a parody exhibition that debuted on March 22, 1913. Billed as the work of the "Academy of Misapplied Arts," the show featured examples of the "Cubistic, Post-impressionist, Futuristic, Neurotic, Psychotic, and Paretic" schools, and the proceeds were earmarked for the local association for the blind.[6]

The third reason to posit an Academy–Armory Show nexus is that several of the writers who were to emerge as leading art critics—and, as it happened, champions of the American and European avant-garde—got their most important newspaper jobs in or just before 1913. Thus they were confronted with the leviathan of art experiences at the dawn of their journalistic careers and spheres of influence, and the big show colored their points of view for years to come. Over the ensuing months and years, as the Armory Show grew in importance as a critical birthing ground, any art institution that did not sufficiently take its message into account was bound to suffer from the salvos of outraged pens. As a stronghold of conservative and reactionary elements, and standing, as it often did, as a stuffy rebuke to the Armory Show, the Academy lent itself to journalistic caricaturing, destined to become the object of ridicule or condemnation. "Academic," as the critics customarily defined it, noted the *New-York Times* in reviewing the 1916 winter exhibition, meant that a work of art "follows a well-known formula and brings to mind many paintings that have preceded it."[7] Points could be scored by picturing the institution as full of dangerously narrow and power-hungry art politicians, and in the hands of a good writer, the Academy was a whetstone on which to sharpen one's rhetorical skills; a critical position taken against it, if argued boldly and cleverly enough, could burnish a career.

The Academy's motives and authority had been a focus of artistic and critical discontent since the waning years of the nineteenth century. The organization was well aware of the ire it could arouse, and it had already survived a vigorous challenge to its prestige from the Society of American Artists, which had been founded as a protest against it in 1877, by amalgamating with the group twenty-nine years later.

But even after the merger, complaints persisted outside the Academy from the next generation of artists. They charged that the institution effectively censored opposition through the selection process for exhibitions. The spring and fall annuals were nominally open to all comers, but nonmembers had to undergo a trial by a jury of academicians; if their work appeared to be outside certain formulas and traditions, they were likely to be rejected, whereas members' submissions, no matter how feeble, were *hors concours*. Moreover, one could not be elected an academician or an associate academician unless he or she had been approved for the spring or fall exhibitions of that year.[8] Therefore the Academy's domination ensured the virtual disenfranchisement of the more innovative or independent artists.

Why this mattered so much to the outsiders is that New York, although the art capital of the country, offered extremely limited possibilities for painters and sculptors who had not yet established a reputation. Fewer than six commercial galleries showed or sold the work of living American artists, and only three of them were willing to represent anyone besides salable names. The sole remedy for this stifling state of affairs was the occasional show initiated and paid for by the excluded artists themselves.[9] However, lack of funding or a permanent exhibition space kept these independent salons sporadic occurrences, and artists were at the mercy of the various exhibiting societies that held shows throughout the year. The Academy, the most illustrious and powerful of these bodies, was the one organization that could be counted on to provide regular and well-attended exhibitions, and acceptance or rejection from them could mean the difference between survival and failure. So when the Academy exempted members' contributions from the scrutiny of a jury and rejected or "skied" everyone else's work above eye level, its actions rallied the dissidents. The Academy's claims that it spoke for the breadth of the community of artists in establishing standards also angered its adversaries because, in reality, it was a private institution. As John Sloan once put it, the Academy was "no more a National agency than the National Biscuit Company."[10]

By 1906, the year that the Academy thought it was safe from trouble because it had absorbed the Society of American Artists, two breakaway groups emerged as threats to it, organizationally and aesthetically. One circle was constituted of the painters and photographers clustering around Alfred Stieglitz, who showed painting, sculpture, photography, and graphic art of the most advanced nature at "291," his gallery on Fifth Avenue. He introduced Cézanne, Matisse, and Picasso to America, as well as such pioneering American modernists as Marsden Hartley, Arthur Dove, John Marin, Max Weber, and Abraham Walkowitz. Stieglitz simply discounted the Academy as irrelevant, and gambled that in the future the world would come round to him.

The other group, the band of artists marshaled by the firebrand painter and teacher Robert Henri, preferred to battle the Academy head-on. The nucleus of his coterie consisted of his old friends Sloan, William Glackens, George Luks, and Everett Shinn; they later were joined by Henri's prize students—George Bellows, Rockwell Kent, Edward Hopper, and Guy Pène du Bois. Most of them were bracketed as New York realists, known for their firsthand observation of the hard facts of urban existence. Considered in relation to what was happening in Europe in 1906—the Fauves and Expressionists had already made their debuts, and Picasso was moving toward Cubism—the American Realists were provincial, and their rebellion moderate. But given the somnolence of the great majority of American artists, including the leaders of the Academy, the Henri group provided a bracing alternative to the *status quo*.

Henri, who was elected to the Academy in 1906, began lobbying for his followers to be included in its shows. But when some of his friends' work was rejected, he, as well as Glackens, Luks, Sloan, Shinn, Arthur B. Davies, Ernest Lawson, and Maurice Prendergast, planned, in response to the Academy's slights, to show together in February 1908 as "The Eight." This historic exhibition was the opening wedge in the struggle to democratize the process by which American artists could put their work before the public. Henri, Sloan, Luks, and Shinn had many friends in the press, and Charles Fitzgerald, then a critic for the *New York Sun*, was Glackens's brother-in-law. The artists tutored the newspapermen as to their intentions, and in articles discussing The Eight's insurrection, which began in 1907, many brickbats were flung at the Academy. President Frederick Dielman complained about the "ignorant abuse and willful misrepresentation" by the press, characterizing it as

irresponsible and unjust. . . . Is it anything less than unblushing impudence that emboldens any newspaper writer on art . . . to set his individual judgment against that of thirty professional painters and sculptors and to represent that body as incompetent, ignorant, or jealous and afraid to encourage new genius?[11]

Henri successfully enlisted the writer, critic, and editor Mary Fanton Roberts (1864–1956) (fig. 78) to his cause.

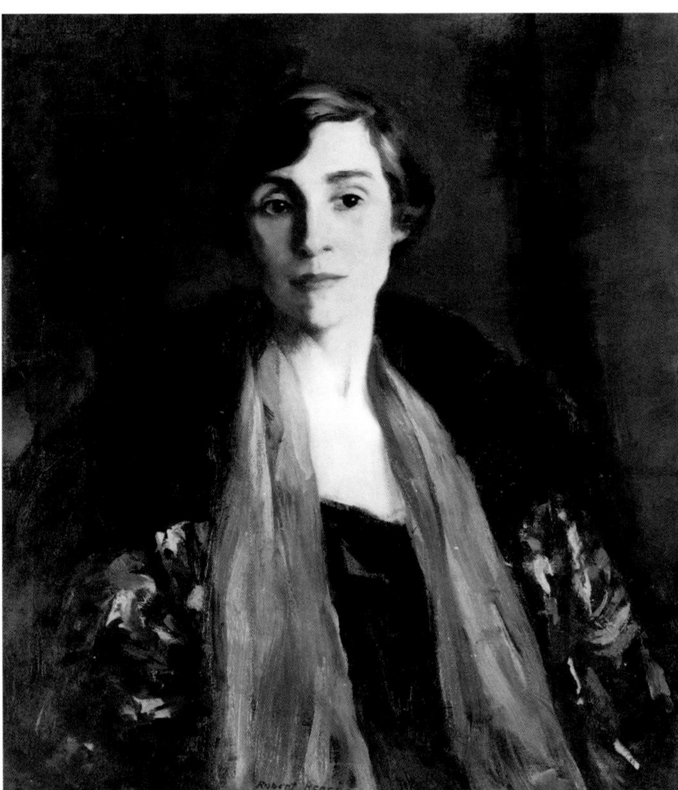

Fig. 78 Robert Henri, *Portrait of Mary Fanton Roberts*, 1917, oil on canvas, 32 x 26, The Metropolitan Museum of Art, Bequest of Mary Fanton Roberts, 1957

Roberts, unlike some of the men in the dailies, did not end her fight against the Academy or her advocacy of the New York Realists in 1908. Nor did she have to wait for an exhibition to express her views. As editor of the *Craftsman* from 1905 to 1916, Roberts moved the journal, which was published by the Arts-and-Crafts furniture manufacturer Gustav Stickley, from its emphasis on gracious living and social reform toward more extensive coverage of progressive tendencies in literature, drama, dance, photography, and art. A friend and partisan of Sloan, Henri, and Glackens, she was decidedly not an impartial journalist. She essentially turned the magazine over to the Henri circle, whom she viewed as the art-world trustbusters of the Roosevelt era, whenever she could. In February of 1908, using the pseudonym "Giles Edgerton," Roberts wrote an important article on The Eight, which was illustrated by the now famous portrait photographs commissioned from Gertrude Käsebier. Headlining them as the creators of "a national art,"[12] Roberts praised their strength and fearlessness, and tartly noted that these artists were "occasionally seen at the Academy—not often."[13] Similarly, when reviewing the spring 1908 exhibition at the Academy, she awarded the show a pat on the back because the jury had been liberal "in the hanging of so many paintings of the younger and more virile men. The Eight, for instance, were treated exceptionally well. . . . Surely such an exhibition as this should open the eyes of the Academy to the value and significance of the younger school of American painters."[14] Roberts hammered away at

the same point throughout 1909, even though Glackens had become an associate member of the Academy in 1906, Lawson in 1908, and Bellows in 1909. From then on, she used the occasion of each Academy exhibition to press for ever greater representation of the artists close to her.

In March 1910, Roberts ran an article by John White Alexander, the Academy's new president. In "The Need of a National Academy and Its Value to the Growth of Art in America," Alexander intimated that if the institution got the bigger building it deserved, the jury could accept more pictures. Yet Roberts chose to illustrate Alexander's text with paintings by artists who had been adversarial to the system—namely, Henri, Glackens, Sloan, and Lawson. She further undercut Alexander's message by proclaiming that she had elected to reproduce paintings "of the pioneer spirit, possibly witnesses to revolutionary ideas which in the end may breed a new and interesting institution for its own preservation."[15] Sloan was represented by *Chinese Restaurant* (fig. 79), and after Roberts used it in the *Craftsman*, the artist marveled that he had been able to spot the painting in the exhibition because it was hung above the line[16]; the year before his *Haymarket, Sixth Avenue* (see no. 61) had been "skied."[17] *Chinese Restaurant* represented Sloan's last successful submission to the Academy; he had only begun to show there in 1906 as a result of Henri's activism.

Two months later, in May 1910, Roberts printed an article by Henri on the Independents Exhibition, the ultimate precursor to the Armory Show, and organized by his former student, Rockwell Kent. The first paragraph proclaimed that the show was not "an exhibition of people who have had their pictures accepted or refused by the Academy." Rather, it was "an opportunity for individuality, an opportunity for experimenters."[18] The rest of the essay continued to harp on the theme of the Academy as an art dictatorship.

For Roberts, the Academy was deficient as long as it did not do well enough by the Henri school, which she continued to discuss in 1912, even though she was pleased that works by Glackens, Shinn, and Jerome Myers were no longer skied. Nevertheless she pinpointed the basic problem of the Academy as being a prisoner of outworn precedents—original high purposes had ossified into rigidity.

If Roberts was in Henri's pocket, the English-born Charles Henry Caffin (1854–1918) was unequivocally aligned with Stieglitz and the "291" set. Caffin was a proponent of modernism who began his journalistic career in America working for the *Evening Post*. He was also an art editor for *Harper's Weekly* (1897–1901), *International Studio* (1901–1905), and after he left the *Post,* he worked for the *New York Sun* until 1904. During this hiatus from the newspapers, he wrote several books on art history, criticism, and appreciation, including *Masters of American Painting* and *Masters of American Sculpture*, as well as a daring book for its time (1901), *Photography as a Fine Art*. From 1913 until his death in 1918, he was art critic for the *New York American*.[19]

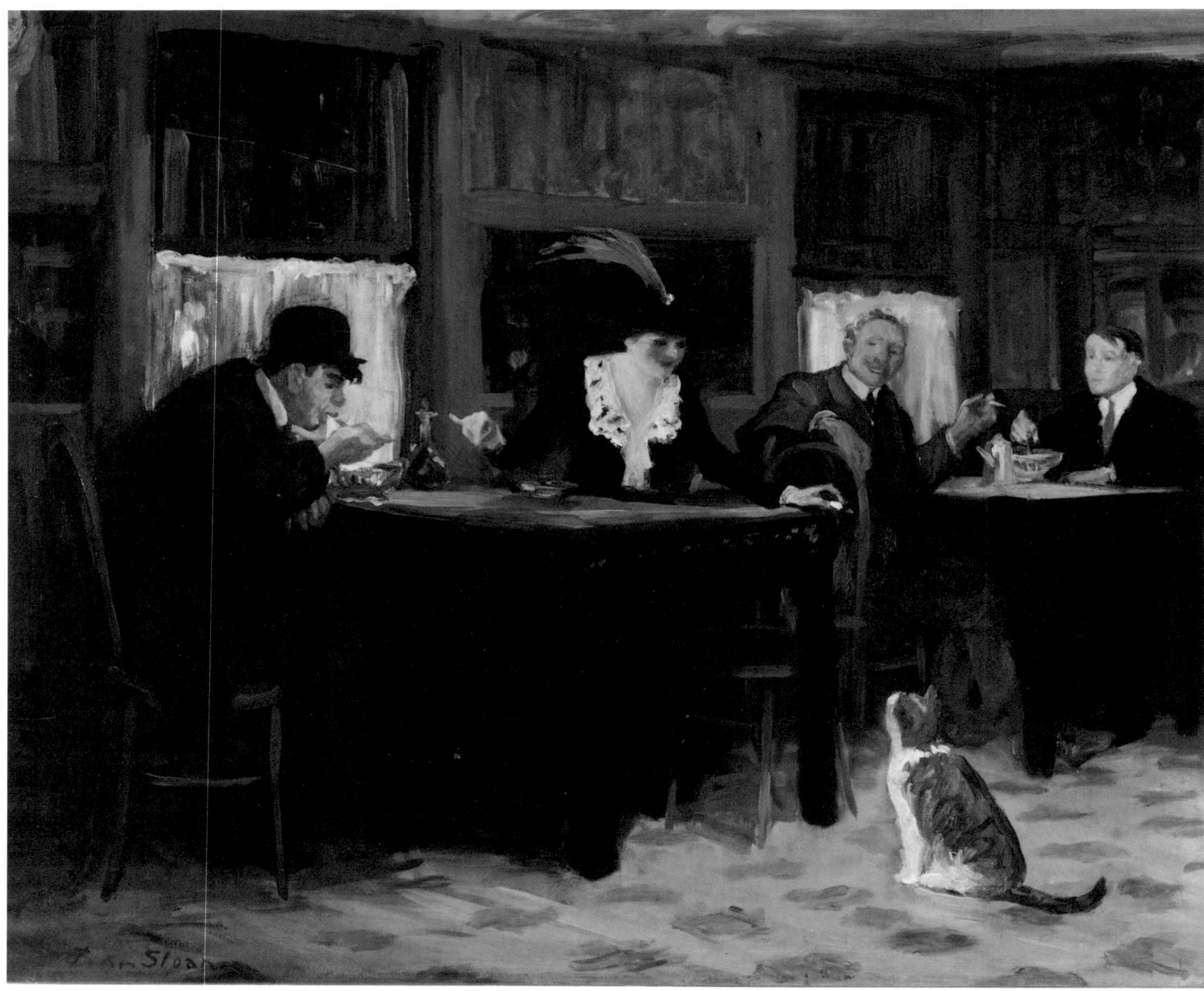

Fig. 79 John Sloan, *Chinese Restaurant*, oil on canvas, 26 x 32¼, Memorial Art Gallery of the University of Rochester, Marion Stratton Gould Fund (National Academy of Design, Winter Exhibition, 1909, no. 248)

Throughout these years Caffin contributed to the two journals associated with Stieglitz, *Camera Notes* and *Camera Work*, and he was a fixture in his gallery. He was aware of—and endorsed—the European avant-garde early; he deeply admired Cézanne, and in 1909 he visited Matisse's studio in Paris, which he wrote about for *Camera Work*. He also published early articles admiring of the Stieglitz stable. And, like Roberts, he was a seasoned campaigner against the Academy. Writes his biographer, "From the beginning of his work as an art critic . . . [h]e found the showing at the National Academy of Design less progressive than the several other exhibitions which he reviewed, and he judged that the academic hold was weak and failing."[20] Besides being on record as early as 1898 for his distrust of the Academy's dogmatism, he also castigated the institution for its mediocrity in 1899 and 1901 and had not grown any fonder of it as the years passed. Thus when

Caffin, who had embraced abstraction to a far greater degree than Roberts, took over the art page of the *New York American* in January of 1913, it would have been thought that he would have been even more radical than she was in his excoriation of the Academy's product when compared with the Armory Show and related events on the contemporary art scene. But both had fairly similar responses.

In fact, Caffin's manner was extremely relaxed. He refused to be impressed by the Armory Show, and in a review appearing on March 17, 1913, called "The National Academy Opens; Exit the International Show," he reported that the academicians

generally agreed that after the fitful fever of the past . . .
we were settling down again to sanity; that the delirium
of modernity had abated and the sober common sense of

Caffin had written off the Academy, and accepted it for
what it was. He had little wish to try to rehabilitate it,
acknowledging that such labors would be a waste of energy.
Indeed, in that same notice, he lavished his scorn on The
Eight, whom he derided as arrogant and too literary. Roberts
was far more enthusiastic about the Armory Show, calling it
"fearless" and "inspired," a display of "the most revolutionary
art work the art world has ever seen,"[22] and she prophesied
that the event would bring a much wider liberation in all art
matters. Granting that the Academy committee had made its
choices before the Armory Show exploded on the world, she
nonetheless remarked on the dull palette of the average
Academy fare in comparison to the colors employed by the
Post-Impressionists and Fauves that New Yorkers had just
seen. Roberts tactfully described the 1913 spring annual as
"pleasant and peaceful" as well as "a curious contrast to the
Armory Show, and possibly the last so simple and gentle
in color."[23]

Roberts, Caffin, and their younger and more forward-
looking peers proved to be the critics whose voices would be
vindicated, but the traditionalists were the ones faithfully
heeded by the public at large because its tastes changed more
slowly.[24] Although the conservative wing of the art-critics'
fraternity also included the academician Kenyon Cox (1856–
1919) (fig. 80) and the *New York Times* reviewer Elizabeth
Luther Cary (1867–1936), the most influential to hold the anti-
modernist line was Royal Cortissoz (1869–1948), the art critic
of the *New York Tribune*. He began writing in 1891, and his
vision was not only formed then, but "never . . . wavered from
his youthful commitment,"[25] even though he remained on the
paper until World War II. Thus Cortissoz was predictable—he
consistently did not like art to "depart from a recognizable
reality or create an antagonistic response from the viewer."[26]
Reluctant to abandon the familiar, he represented "common
sense" attitudes to middle-class readers and commanded a
mass audience. As long as no drastic breaks were made with
tradition, Cortissoz could tolerate change, but he was much
happier with the well known and the reassuring; the last
major movements he unequivocally accepted were Impressionism and Tonalism, and he became the primary protector
of the Academy's prestige and spokesman for its case.[27]

Accordingly, Cortissoz was appalled by the Armory Show,
which disturbed rather than soothed, and scourged its participants for their "egotism," "freakishness," and "eccentricity."

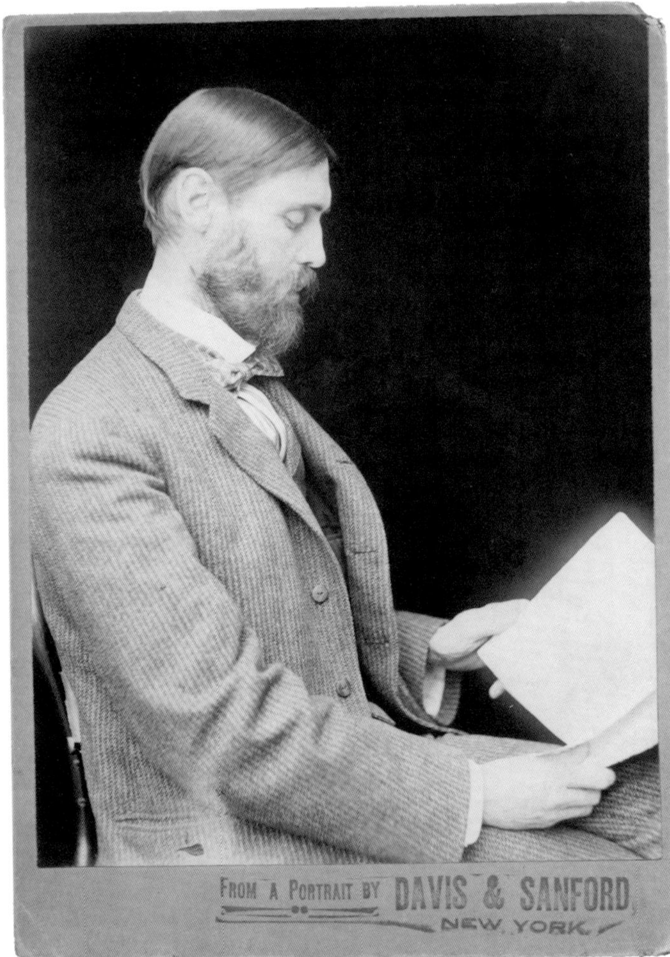

Fig. 80 Davis & Sanford, *Kenyon Cox,* photograph, Archives, National
Academy of Design

His fiercest wrath was reserved for Cézanne, van Gogh, and
Matisse. Indeed, his denunciations of the Armory Show now
live in infamy in the publications of art historians who have
written about the event. As the relentless defender of the
Academy, he emphasized to his readers that it had adjusted
just beautifully to the commotion on Lexington Avenue, and
he was full of praise for what was on the walls.

Two other respected critics, both of them younger than
Caffin, also received important berths in or around 1913, and
they would become the two leading advocates for modern
European and American art. After a career as a painter, illustrator, and art teacher, Henry McBride (1867–1959) joined the
New York Sun as an art critic in 1913 and remained so until
1950. From the first he stood out as the most prescient—and
effective—proponent of modern art in New York. Keenly
interested in avant-garde experimentation, McBride started
as he meant to go on, especially in regard to the Academy.
Eyeing the institution "as though it were the skeleton of some
prehistoric monster,"[28] he gently poked fun at it, talked in
generalities, and never mentioned a specific work of art if he
could avoid doing so. His attitude was made apparent in one
of his first articles, which was on the Academy. It was titled

"Spring Academy Show Comes: International Exhibition Just Ended; Remembered as Most Stimulating Episode in City's Art Life." After noting that it had been roundly proved that the public would flock to a first-rate exhibition of modern art, he hoped the Academy would learn a lesson about how to attract an audience. "Without reference to this new exhibition more than to past ones," he concluded, "it may be said that when the Academy shows more pictures that people wish to look at its attendance will increase."[29]

Whereas McBride's critical disposition tended toward the genial, that of Forbes Watson (1880–1960), another provocative presence on the American art scene in the teens and 1920s, was acerbic. From the first, Watson, who distrusted authority in all forms, was a born fighter; he was like Henri in that respect, and he admired what Henri, Sloan, Glackens, and Davies stood for in art politics as well as in art. He threw thunderbolts of scathing sarcasm at the exclusionary policies of the Academy, whose power, though vitiated by the Armory Show, had by no means crumbled. He was a partisan of the School of Paris, but he saw American art as his real cause, and the Academy in all its phases, not merely its twice-yearly exhibitions, earned his antipathy. In late 1912, Watson became an art critic for the *New York Post* and chief art critic for the paper a few years later; in one of his first pieces he took the Academy's measure. He commended two portraits by Bellows, though he thought the more important one was unfairly skied. He then suggested how interesting it would be to have, in conjunction with the institution's annual, the opportunity to hold a "Salon des Refusés," because he imagined that pictures that did not pass muster might be more stimulating than those that did. Yet Watson was wise enough to allow, in contemplating the winter 1912 annual, which "maintain[ed] the average standard," that the Academy could not hold a radical exhibition because genuinely radical or original pictures were unlikely to be submitted to it.[30]

When the Armory Show opened, Watson was shaken by it. He later wrote, "My first visit to the Armory Show made it clear that the conventional world of art was living in a false and unprotected security."[31] Instead of lashing out at the unfamiliar things before him, as Cortissoz did, he realized that he could not base his judgments on previous standards. He revisited the Armory numerous times until he had mastered the epic exhibition and absorbed Picasso, Matisse, Brancusi, and their peers. In his first notice, Watson immediately sized up the undertaking as one of unparalleled significance, and made a key point on which critical arguments would hinge for years: "The most important achievement of the exhibition is that it brings forward to the attention of the visitor the . . . fact that the artist is not a rival of the camera, that his chief function is not to represent, but to express a point of view."[32] Watson was one of the few writers not to mention the Armory Show in his review of the Academy's spring 1913 exhibition, but his first paragraph was not promising. "Important pictures are no more prevalent than usual," he wrote,

but the dead picture, manufactured without impulse, has been a little more rigorously excluded. Among the works which remain to be mentioned few new-comers of vigor and promise appear, but many of the regular contributors send just the sort of work that is expected of them.[33]

When the Academy's next exhibition opened in December 1913, the critics continued to use it as a vehicle for their own agendas. Roberts gauged it by its devotion to the Henri group, Caffin conceded that the Academy was always going to be the Academy and judged it on those terms, Cortissoz went on with his cheerleading, and Watson and McBride shook their heads in despair. Caffin, for example, allowed that the show was "carefully conservative," and had "many pictures and sculptures of conspicuous merit." Among the works he found worthy were *Centaur and Dryad* by Paul Manship (fig. 81), and *The Path of Gold* by Jonas Lie (location unknown).[34]

Cortissoz reminded readers that the question of the Armory Show's impact on "American art in general and upon the Academy exhibitions in particular" still remained to be answered. He reported that the organization "recognized the fact . . . that something had to be done." Citing *The Widow* by Charles Hawthorne (1914; Huntington Museum of Art, Huntington, West Virginia) and Lawson's *Hudson River, Palisades*—a favorite among most of the reviewers that season—as examples of the Academy's having seen the light while still not giving into "the freakishness which had its chance at the Armory" and which "has properly failed to make any impression." Cortissoz argued that "fairness dictates that

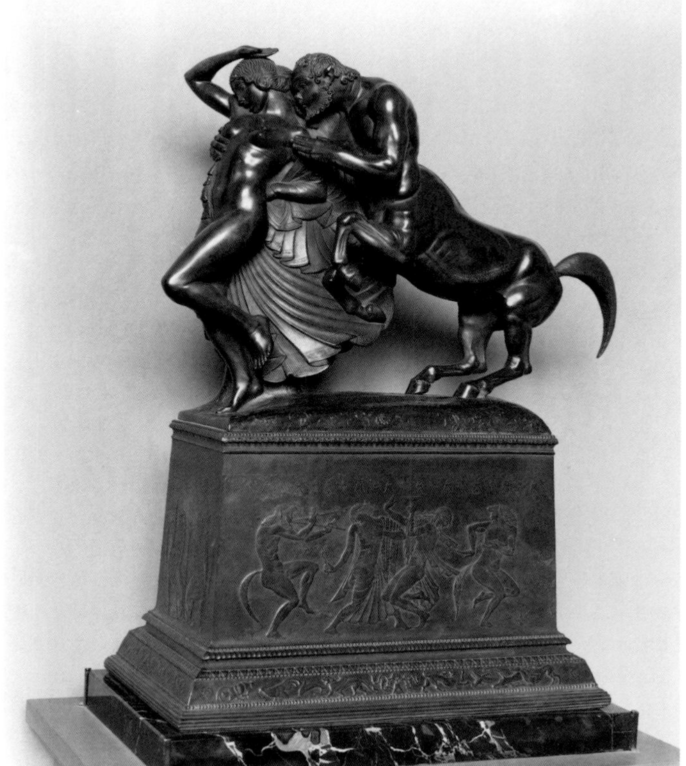

Fig. 81 Paul Manship, *Centaur and Dryad,* 1913, bronze, 28 (height), The Metropolitan Museum of Art, Amelia B. Lazarus Fund, 1914 (National Academy of Design, Winter Exhibition, 1913, no. 72)

some recognition should be made of the smallest step in the right direction."[35]

Watson also singled out Manship's prize-winning *Centaur and Dryad*, but he expressed an opinion opposite of Cortissoz's through almost the same words. The exhibition, he said, "will make more than one heart glad. Fears have been whispered . . . that the purity of the National Academy was to be defiled" by the "horrid influences" of the winter before. "To be able to allay such fears," Watson continued, "is a gratifying task. All is well at the Fine Arts building. A definite stand has been taken. The Academy will have none of it. . . . [I]t is not making the slightest pretence at having any of it."[36]

In the *Sun*, McBride did not have the stomach to mention anything on the walls except a landscape by John Singer Sargent, nor did he wish to fire an arsenal of eloquence against a lumbering old dinosaur. Instead, he was content to sigh,

The general level: Academies have to do with the general level. It is at once their function and their weakness.

The general level is very safe but not particularly interesting. . . . there isn't a bad picture there, nor a great one. Not a single one that will make history nor even a sign of a newcomer with something enthusiastically discovered.[37]

The critics had not moderated their stances for the spring 1914 exhibition. Roberts was happy because the Academy's doors seemed to be ajar—"so many of the younger men," she proclaimed, "were given an opportunity to express their own joy and enthusiasm in life."[38] Cortissoz could be counted on to like the exhibition, no matter what its contents—the subtitle of his review read, "American Pictures of Interest for Clever and Conservative Workmanship," hardly a compliment to a twentieth-century consciousness—and he went on to twist himself into more knots to pump it up. "The average is good, no doubt, but not poignantly interesting. . . . Yes, this is decidedly a good academy, if the only test is that which can be met by good taste and an adroit brush."[39] It is interesting to notice that none of the critics spotted what today would be considered to be the most substantial painting in the show—*Between Rounds*, by Thomas Eakins (fig. 82)—but in fairness, the canvas was painted in 1899, and did not qualify as a contemporary expression.

The reviews of the winter 1914 exhibition revealed that the specter of the Armory Show had not yet been laid to rest. Cortissoz again had kind words for the incremental quality of the Academy's efforts in making its display "a little more interesting, a little more suggestive."[40] Caffin jumped on the same issue, but made his point more bluntly. The Academy had taken note that a new style of painting had come into the world, although "a few years after the world at large begins to appreciate them." He was pleased that a prize had been awarded to Hayley Lever for *St. Ives Bay* (c. 1905; Yale University Art Gallery) because the picture was distinctly Post-Impressionist in inspiration. "On the whole," Caffin explained,

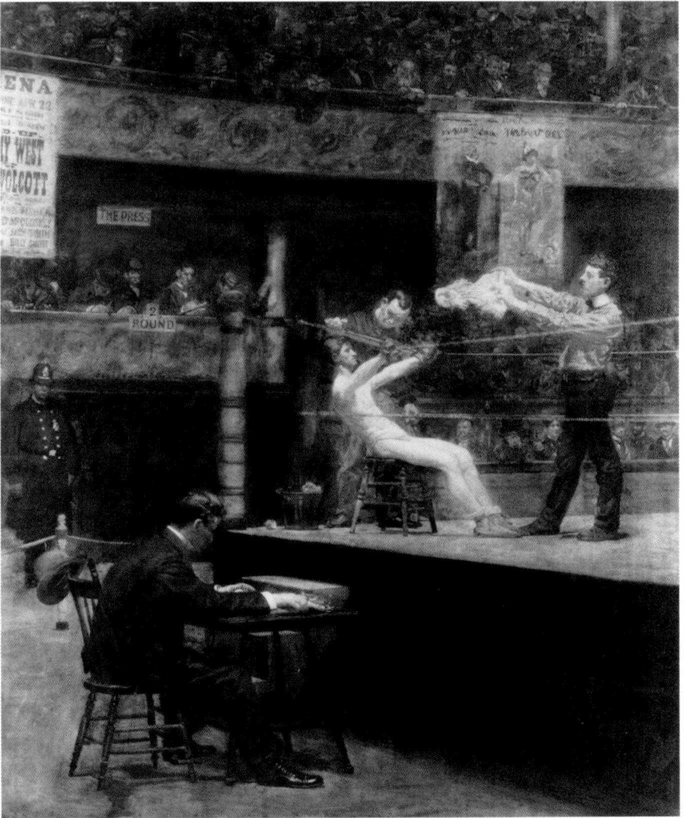

Fig. 82 Thomas Eakins, *Between Rounds*, 1899, oil on canvas, 50⅛ x 39⅞, Philadelphia Museum of Art, Gift of Mrs. Thomas Eakins and Miss Mary Adeline Williams (National Academy of Design, 89th Annual Exhibition, 1914, no. 90)

it cannot be said that the exhibition is higher in merit than in previous years. It is merely different. There is no endless succession of fresh, sweet spring landscapes, golden autumnal commonplaces and pink lights and blue shadows on snow. There are very few such pictures, but to take their places are many commonplace pictures painted in the broader, looser style [derived from modernism], without any inspiration.[41]

By late 1915 Lawson was the lone member of The Eight who regularly made an appearance at the Academy, and Bellows was the only gifted painter of the next generation who remained an exhibition mainstay. (Two years earlier, his *Little Girl In White* [fig. 83] had won the Hallgarten Prize at the Academy.) Provocative artists had gone elsewhere, notwithstanding the Academy's futile hope that in electing as its president Julian Alden Weir, who had also been president of the artists' association behind the Armory Show, it would attract innovative painters and sculptors. Even the critics who were more likely to be kindly disposed toward the Academy were losing patience, as the issues of disenfranchisement and exclusion were still very evident. Only Cortissoz rallied to the Academy's side, contending that the "test of an academy does not lie in what is not there."[42] The normally equable Caffin reported that several academicians had implored him to write about the need to expand their premises: they alleged that

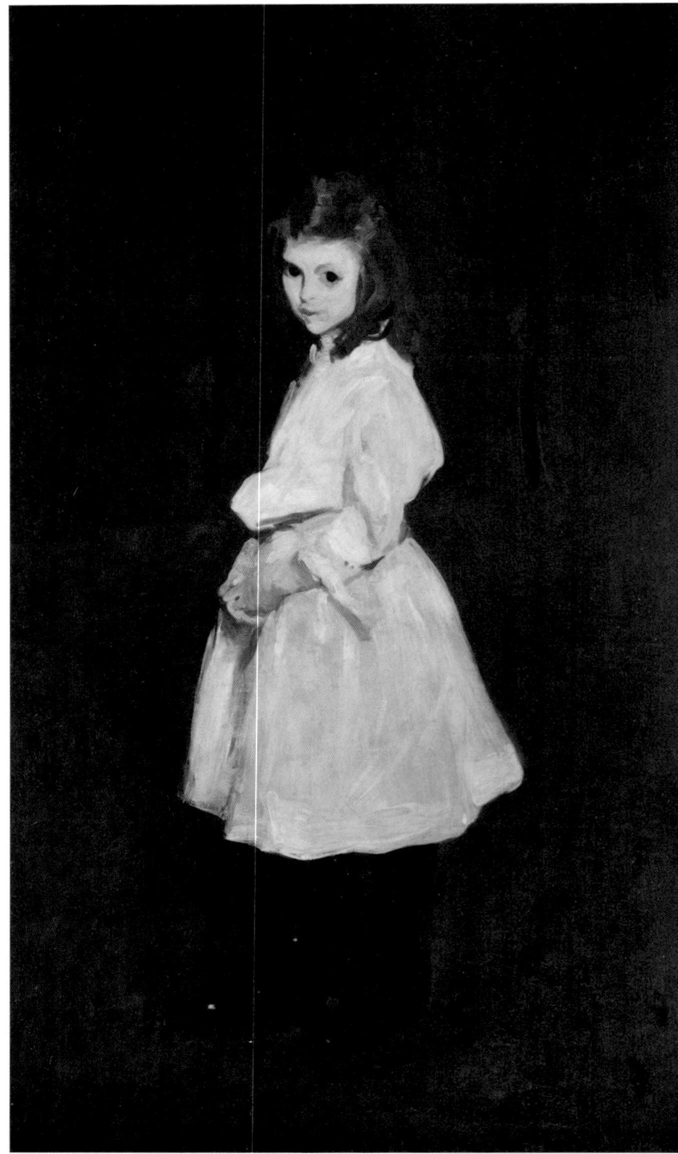

Fig. 83 George Bellows, *Little Girl in White (Queenie Burnet)*, 1907, oil on canvas, 62¼ x 34¼, National Gallery of Art, Washington, D.C., Collection of Mr. and Mrs. Paul Mellon (National Academy of Design, 88th Annual Exhibition, 1913, no. 216)

their shows were unsatisfactory because they did not have enough room to hang nonmembers' submissions. But Caffin felt that Academy members should admit that the representation of artists in the modernist camp was insufficient for reasons other than a paucity of wall space, declaring,

> *If they would frankly admit they are a close* [sic] *corporation, existing for the maintenance of certain artistic convictions and for the financial benefits that are to be received from solidarity of prestige, we could understand their position. . . . On the other hand, if they desire to be actually representative and to extend opportunity to artists whose ideals and methods vary from their own, why do they permit privilege or preference to block the way?*[43]

McBride, displaying a little more asperity than usual, followed up on his dismal headline, "Winter Exhibition Lacking in Spirit," by saying, "There are no pictures or sculptures that make the pretence of greatness, and there are none seen that will be talked about. No single artist who exhibits exceeds his past performance and no new artist makes a 'first appearance' with sufficient eclat to suggest that he will have a future."[44] He then described the show's prize winners with a distinct lack of brio. A second notice was even more scathing and rather than running a picture of a work from the Academy's show, McBride illustrated the article with reproductions of a sculpture by Brancusi and a canvas by Max Weber, both on view in commercial galleries.

Nor was Watson, who had become an eager surveyor of newer artistic terrains, to be contained. "Were it not for a corps of energetic dealers a whole realm of artistic endeavor . . . vital . . . to the creative spirit of to-day, would remain practically unseen," he began. "For, outside of the studios and the dealers' galleries, only one or two examples crop up in the large general exhibitions throughout the country, which, for the most part, take their cue from the National Academy of Design."[45] Warming to his subject, which would be the focus of his critical objections for years to come, Watson once more connected the Academy to the Armory Show, saying that now that its organizers "have dropped by the wayside," artists who would not knuckle under to official standards could only show at small, informal exhibitions. "And," he continued, "while their works individually are better seen in such places than they could be in the big heterogeneous affair, they can only win a comparatively restricted public. Meanwhile, the great general public remains ignorant of much of the real development of to-day."[46]

Watson complained that those who flocked to the Academy and beheld canvases by artists "Daniel Garber, Cecilia Beaux, Paul Doherty, Charles Hawthorne—have these paintings not won large sums of money?—will go away feeling that they know what's what in American art. . . . and they will know nothing of the great forces tormenting and uplifting the men of the future. . . ."[47] Watson was glad to see *Bathers at Blue Point* by Glackens, along with canvases by Prendergast, Lawson, and Childe Hassam, but he took care to say that such artists, whose pictures departed from formula, were "accidents" of the Academy "rather than a spiritual part of it." He characterized them as academicians "merely by title."[48] In the teens, Hassam and Lawson consistently earned good notices. Even when the reviews of the spring and winter shows were universally bleak, which occurred during 1918, a painting like Hassam's *Allies Day, May 1917* (see no. 67) was heralded as a dynamic exception to its drab companions.

By the spring 1916 show, McBride was no longer tiptoeing around the Academy in his reviews; the pose of mock seriousness could not be sustained. His patience had vanished, because the institution had failed to respond to the times. The infinitesimal steps that contented Cortissoz bored and annoyed him. A "low level . . . has been characteristic of the official institution since the outbreak of the war," he wrote. "There are no new names in the exhibition and certainly no new subjects. . . . So featureless a show has seldom been seen." Lawson deserved a prize for *Chicken Coop* (location unknown) and McBride also enjoyed *The Spinner* by Eakins ("a slight work by a thoughtful painter")[49] and Bellows's *The Sawdust Trail* (see no. 66). *Truth*, a nude sitting on a well by Kenyon Cox (fig. 84), he dismissed as unfortunate and foolish. The sooner that the painting "gets back where she belongs, i.e., at the bottom of a well," he wrote, "the better it will be for all concerned."[50] Perhaps because McBride denounced Cox as well as the Academy in general, in his most sardonic words to date, the conservative *American Art News* reprinted his essay with implied disapproval.[51] Yet by the end of the year, even that journal, which had been almost as dependable as Cortissoz in extolling the Academy, had grown disenchanted. One of the reviewers summed up the winter show as an "acreage of mediocrity."[52]

This already lamentable situation deteriorated noticeably in 1917. No one shaping the development of American painting and sculpture—for example, Dove, Hartley, Charles

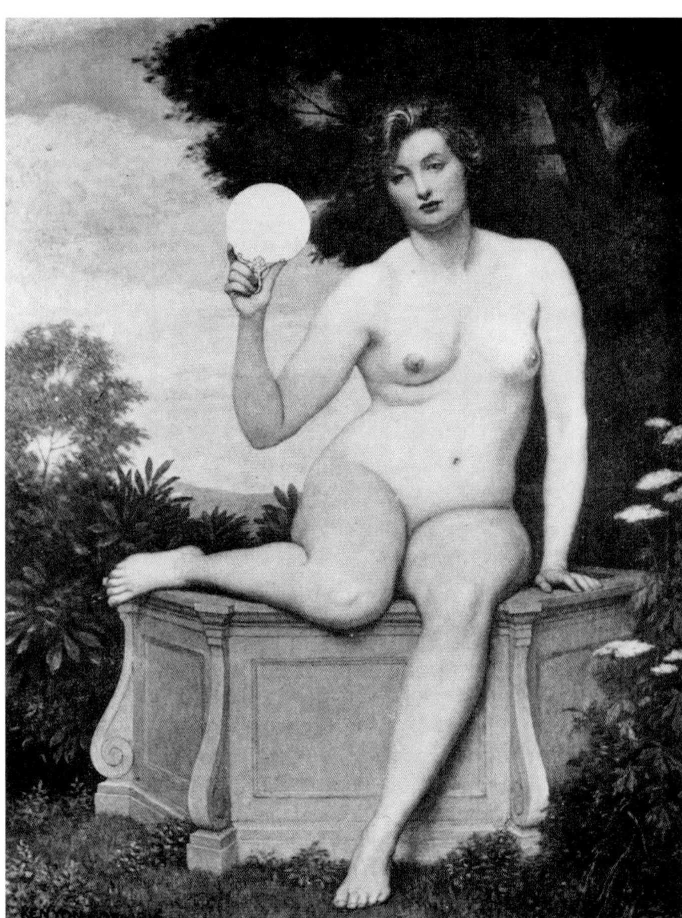

Fig. 84 Kenyon Cox, *Truth*, frontispiece from National Academy of Design, *Illustrated Catalogue, Ninety-First Annual Exhibition*, 1916, Archives, National Academy of Design (The painting was no. 123 in the exhibition.)

Sheeler, Charles Demuth, Elie Nadelman, or Gaston Lachaise—was seen at the Academy, and the possibility of their appearing there diminished even more sharply with the advent of two salons conceived as antidotes to the Academy's monopoly on large exhibitions. The Society of Independent Artists, an artist-run exhibition cooperative devised as a haven for anyone outside the Academy, came into being in 1916. Its first show, which opened on April 10, 1917, with 2,125 entries, instantly leapt into art and social history when Marcel Duchamp tested the much-vaunted guarantee that any object submitted would automatically be accepted for public display by anonymously entering the now-notorious porcelain urinal as a work of art under the name of R. Mutt. The Independents survived this controversy and became a thriving competitor on the spring exhibition calendar; after 1917, critics often contrasted the fresh and frequently eccentric talents they had seen there with the smoothly executed but unmemorable paintings on view at the Academy. Also flourishing in response to the Academy's stagnation were the Whitney Studio and the Whitney Studio Club, two galleries established in Greenwich Village by the sculptor and art patron Gertrude Vanderbilt Whitney to give young and unknown artists without dealers a chance to show their work. The Studio was inaugurated in December 1914, but it did not become expansive or sufficiently professional until 1917; the Club was founded in early 1918.[53] Whitney's enterprises were soundly backed in print by Roberts, Watson, and McBride, increasing their standing exponentially.

The Independents and the Whitney Studio and Club offered the first lasting routes to success around the Academy since the Armory Show. It was Cortissoz, of all people, who put the dilemma most succinctly, though he could not refrain from softening his dire conclusions with a questionable rationale.

> There was a time when this [the spring 1917 exhibition] was the salient event of the season—one went to the Academy to see how American art was getting on. Now its status is of almost any miscellaneous collection of pictures, for works that might revive its old prestige are displayed elsewhere. . . . [But] in these days of innumerable exhibitions there are not enough good paintings to go round, and the Academy suffers first. Perhaps, therefore, it is not, as an institution altogether to blame. . . . [54]

In his caustic review of the spring 1916 annual, McBride referred to the outbreak of World War I in Europe in dating the Academy's decline and, during the last two years of the war, changes bearing on the Academy were wrought among the critics as well. The *Craftsman* folded in 1916, and Roberts founded a new magazine, the *Touchstone*, which she began publishing in May 1917. Later that year Watson volunteered to drive an ambulance at the French front; he did not return to New York until 1919, and when he did it was as critic of the *New York World*, a livelier paper that gave him jurisdiction over an entire page. Caffin died in January of 1918. McBride and Cortissoz, however, continued on their courses: McBride danced around the Academy's dullness and Cortissoz confected reasons to excuse it.

In 1919 the Academy's authority was so devalued that a contingent of members, led by Bellows and Hassam, vainly attempted to reform the institution's exhibition and admission practices. Bellows was frustrated enough to turn critic, and he published a devastatingly candid letter in the *American Art News*. It was nothing less than an indictment:

> *Now, it is my decided opinion that at least 50%, yes 75%, of the finest artists in America are not only not members of the academy but are not even welcomed on its walls. Add this to the fact that some of the best artists who are members think the exhibitions so bad they are not willing to display works therein, and we find some reason for . . . the small allotment of interest and life which characterize year in and out the exhibitions of the National Academy of Design.*[55]

The Bellows-Hassam faction was defeated, and shortly afterwards Bellows, who had brought the weight of his reputation to the quarrel, defected from Academy shows. He did not resign his membership, but the organization effectively lost one of its most brilliant exhibitors.

While the Academy was losing ground from within, Watson added to his might on the art scene. He became the chief art advisor to Gertrude Vanderbilt Whitney and Juliana Force, the director of the Whitney Studio and Whitney Studio Club, and through this connection he too gained control of a magazine. With Whitney's financial backing, Watson was appointed editor of the *Arts*, a monthly magazine of art news and criticism, in 1923. He was a dynamic and enterprising editor, and he molded the magazine into one of the best art journals of the day. Its coverage of art ranged from Lascaux and Altamira to Max Beckmann and John Marin. McBride did not come into a magazine of his own, but in 1920 he was appointed art critic for the *Dial*, an outstanding cultural periodical dedicated to the avant-garde.

The critics were obliged in the dailies to include Academy exhibitions, but their editors recognized the institution's fading imprint on the city's intellectual life, and the notices devoted to it were cut from two to one. And in their own publications, the critics elected not to provide steady coverage at all; they assumed that the Academy was not germane to their special readers, the art-conscious public. Condemning provincialism, Roberts announced that the *Touchstone* would be "particularly interested in modern art, in the youth of all art," and it would be watching "for every expressionism of freshness and originality in the art of America." She would "care above all about the men who have made the world know that America has her own art—men like Henri and Glackens and Sloan, Borglum, Bellows and a host of others whose opinion and accomplishments will be the backbone of this maga-

zine."[56] Roberts made good on her words. Articles and reviews profiled Henri, Sloan, Glackens, the Society of Independent Artists, the Daniel, Macbeth and Montross galleries, Bellows, George Grey Barnard, Mahonri Young, Hunt Diederich, and Max Weber, as well as Steinlen, Cézanne, Rodin, Degas, Gauguin, and Boris Anisfeld, but neither the activities nor the exhibitions of the Academy were ever chronicled during the lifetime of the magazine, which lasted until June 1921, when it was taken over by the *Arts*.

McBride's column in the *Dial* was called "Modern Art," and he wrote about the Society of Independent Artists, Matisse, Lachaise, the Arensberg collection, Dada, Jules Pascin, Joseph Stella, Nadelman, Yasuo Kuniyoshi, and Jacques Villon, among others. With his mandate to talk about the new and innovative, his allegiance to reviewing the Academy was nil. In the January 1923 issue he briefly alluded to "a more than usual negligible Winter Academy,"[57] and, in a monthly column over three years, he only mentioned it again twice. As he would humorously explain in the June 1925 issue,

> *There has been very little comment in THE DIAL upon the activities of the National Academy of Design and no evidence upon the part of the readers of THE DIAL that this sin of omission has been greatly deplored. In fact the interest in the Academy is not intense. There has been a tendency to regard the aged officers of the aged institution as harmless, and they have been permitted to amuse themselves after their fashion without interference.*[58]

Watson had no interest in omissions or gentle mockery when it came to an avowed foe. The Academy, he believed, was the principal antagonist of modern art in America, and his duty was to thwart its influence. The *Arts* was an unrestricted forum for the editor's views and, given Whitney's and Force's encouragement of artists who eschewed the Academy, he was prepared to be pugnacious. In his first editorial, Watson declared that he intended "to stand with the American artist against timidity and snobbery."[59] A month later, he pledged his support of modern art. Even articles on other topics were occasions for throwing punches against the Academy. In writing about Glackens, an artist he deeply admired, Watson scored points by contrasting his hero to "[m]ediocrities" who tended to "organize, play politics . . . secure official plums and direct the policies of public artistic undertakings."[60] In expounding on the Armory Show, he noted that "the academies that trembled momentarily to their foundations have settled back into something like their old positions."[61]

Mercifully, Watson overlooked the spring Academy, letting the event pass with a cursory squib by the artist Alexander Brook. But he had one of his young and feisty associate editors, Virgil Barker, take on the winter exhibition. Barker reported,

> *Many members whose work could have been counted upon to raise the present level sent nothing; many of*

those who did send are responsible for some of the worst pictures shown. From the burden of this double handicap there could be no relief through the work by non-members which was sufficiently commonplace to meet the requirements of the jury of selection.[62]

However, Barker did draw a trenchant distinction in his notice, saying, " . . . it is the mediocrity of this Academy exhibition which is to be deplored, not its conservatism; for conservatism can be positive and distinguished when it is forceful and intelligent."[63]

The *Arts* pretty much ignored the 1924 exhibitions. This decision was not unique to Watson, as that year the Academy was considered at rest while it readied itself for its hundredth anniversary in 1925. Even the normally reliable *American Art News* didn't bother with its own review; instead it printed a negative one by McBride. Though Watson may have made effective copy by sniping at the Academy as a fortress, it was one whose walls were tumbling down. The newer members of the art press registered a sense that the organization was beleaguered. Its only dependable advocates besides Cortissoz, whose own standing was waning, were the less impressive Peyton Boswell, who had taken over at the *American*, and occasionally James B. Townsend, the antediluvian senior reviewer at the *American Art News*. Helen Appleton Read, who became art critic of the *Brooklyn Eagle* in 1922, took a middle to liberal position. She had studied with Henri and had imbibed his principles, but she was a great friend of Eugene Speicher, an academician of the Bellows generation, and her reviews reflected both influences. Her early assessments did not castigate, but they were not apt to inspire readers to visit the Academy galleries. Margaret Breuning, the new critic of the *Post* who would go on to fill the position honorably for many years, felt sorry for an institution she saw as unduly pilloried. Even McBride, in a state of mock alarm, reported that none of the people he had talked to during the opening of the winter 1923 Academy had attended the show but commiserated with him for being obliged to visit it. "This indifference alarms me," he wrote. "I am not exactly noted as a champion of the Academy, but I assure you I have no desire to see it dwindle utterly."[64] He then proceeded to suggest a list of improvements and changes.

Watson, however, was raring to deliver a neat uppercut to the collective academic jaw. The time for a knockout was handed to him in 1925, on the occasion of the Academy's centennial. Its council decided to use the anniversary to secure an endowment that would enable the organization to present exhibitions throughout the nation and obtain a bigger building in New York; the goal was $6 million. Watson vehemently protested the proposed campaign in his March 15, 1925, column in the *World* and in the April 1925 issue of the *Arts*. None of his rhetorical firepower was spared, for he saw a sinister side to these schemes, coming as they did from a body of artists who applied censorship in the form of a jury system. In

the longest editorial he had ever written for the *Arts*, Watson pounced on the Academy for claiming to be "significantly official." On the contrary, he argued, the Academy was never responsible to the public because works of art by members, no matter how inferior in quality, were invariably admitted to its exhibitions. It was not speaking nationally as it pretended; rather, it was "a private institution upholding one particular phase of art." But its unforgivable transgression was the power the organization had appropriated in making such a claim:

> *Only when the Academy branches out and takes unto itself the position of the leading national institution of art, only when it carefully evolves a scheme whereby it can control the principal exhibitions throughout the country and secure, for its own members exclusively, the commercial advantages belonging to such control, only when it asks the public to give it $6,000,000 in order that it can obtain a power and influence that would be dangerous for any art organization of this type to have, does it become necessary for every artist in this country, who believes in freedom of expression to put his back into a fight against the dangerous presumptions of the National Academy.*
>
> *The National Academy of Design is an exceedingly well organized private institution whose fundamental object is to sell the works of art of its members. The more important the institution can make itself, the better will the works of its members sell. Always awake to the opportunity to secure greater privileges, on the basis that it is not a private but a national institution, it now emerges once more with the cleverest scheme that it has ever propounded.*[65]

Watson added that the Academy's galleries were, in reality, too big as they were. To fill them the jury had to accept second-rate submissions as no one with true standing among artists was a member.

Several of the more liberal critics in New York allied themselves with Watson. McBride supported him in the *Sun* as well as in the *Dial*, lauding Watson's frankness and noting that while it took no special courage to oppose the Academy anymore, mettle was required to counter a noble-sounding subscription fund. He was concerned enough to drop his customary, disarming style:

> *When one thinks for a minute of the immense impetus that could be given American life by merely spending the income of $6,000,000 in the purchase of contemporary American art, the absurdity becomes apparent of handing such a sum of money over to a set of fossils who cannot recognize art when they see it; and would probably blow most of it on needless buildings and paraphernalia.*[66]

Read also addressed the Academy's drive in the *Brooklyn Eagle*, and she seconded Watson. Yet the accolade that pleased him most was a letter, which he published in the June 1925 issue of the *Arts*, from the Washington collector and patron Duncan Phillips, the one force for contemporary art in the nation's capital. After congratulating Watson on his "splendidly courageous editorial," which he perceptively recalled as being foreshadowed in the article on Glackens two years before,[67] Phillips exclaimed, "More power to you in fighting this desperate move of politicians who dishonor the painters' profession! . . . Please let me enlist for such a fight."[68]

On October 17, 1925, the Academy's centennial opened at the Corcoran Gallery of Art in Washington, D.C., under the patronage of President and Mrs. Calvin Coolidge, and in New York it was staged at the Grand Central Galleries. Because of the historic nature of its contents, the exhibition transcended the conventional spring and fall affairs. Distinguished paintings, sculptures, drawings, and prints by artists of the past, from Gilbert Stuart to the recently deceased Bellows, were borrowed for the occasion, including Winslow Homer's *Eight Bells* (fig. 85), *Frosty Morning, Montclair* by George Inness (1892; private collection), and *Caritas* by Abbott Thayer (1893; Museum of Fine Arts, Boston). Aside from the *Arts*, the critics were united in their appreciation of the show.

Yet the fund-raising drive failed, on account of the adverse publicity that had been created and because the Art Students League fought against the strengthening of the Academy's art school at the expense of its own. Watson had won, and the future was on his side. In the January 1926 *Arts*, he wrote about the dispersal of the great modern art collection of John Quinn, who had died in 1924. Watson wished that someone had purchased everything and used it as the nucleus of a museum of modern art. One reader of this editorial was the painter and connoisseur Alfred Gallatin, and Watson's plea led him to establish the Gallery of Living Art a year later. In 1929, the Museum of Modern Art was founded, and in 1930 Gertrude Whitney consolidated her galleries into the Whitney Museum of American Art. These institutions were created in the Academy's despite. Its exhibitions were supplanted, and the right to place "N.A." after one's name no longer meant a mark of superior attainment, let alone a professional advantage. Indeed, as early as 1927, the Academy, tired of watching artists who had ignored them develop into painters of stature, invited, "as a concession to modernism," younger and more progressive artists to the spring annual without subjecting them to the jury. But it was too late—many rebuffed the gesture.[69]

These new museums of contemporary and modern art were the fruits of the Armory Show and the controversial epoch it engendered. In particular, in the Museum of Modern Art, the critics were given a new focus for their energies.[70] It would dominate the New York art scene, just as the Academy had twenty-five years before. Indeed, between the opening of the Armory Show and the establishment of the Museum of Modern Art, the positions of the Academy and its adversaries were entirely reversed. No longer was the avant-garde the province of a handful of cognoscenti and the Academy and its activities comfortably familiar to the general public. Vanguard art increasingly became the creed of the majority, and the Academy's sphere of influence dissolved. Neither its exhibitions nor history would be paid sustained critical attention again for another half century.

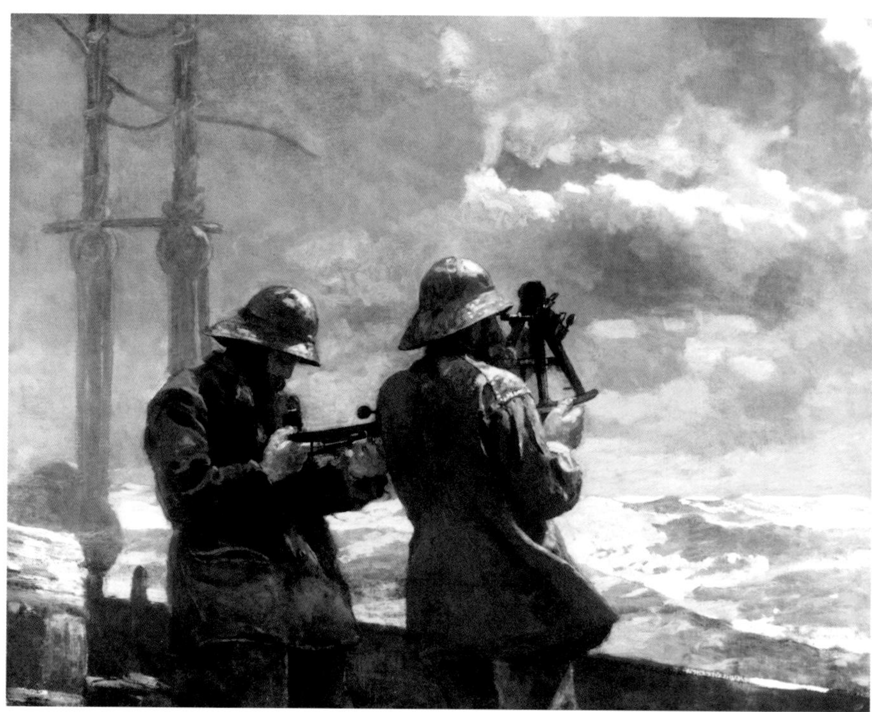

Fig. 85 Winslow Homer, *Eight Bells*, 1886, oil on canvas, 25³/₁₆ x 30³/₁₆, Addison Gallery of American Art, Phillips Academy, Andover, Massachusetts, gift of an anonymous donor (National Academy of Design, 63rd Annual Exhibition, 1888, no. 370)

NOTES

1. It is a pleasure to thank David Dearinger and Trudie Grace of the National Academy of Design for their unstinting help in procuring primary research materials that otherwise would have been difficult to locate. I am likewise grateful to the staffs of the Whitney Museum of American Art and Cooper-Hewitt Museum libraries, who also went out of their way to provide assistance.

2. Unsigned [Henry McBride], "Spring Academy Show Comes: International Exhibition Just Ended," *New York Sun*, March 16, 1913.

3. For example, see Forbes Watson, "Painting and Sculpture," *The Year 1913—New International Yearbook*, clipping in Forbes Watson Papers, Archives of American Art (AAA), and an unsigned notice by Mary Fanton Roberts, "Als Ik Kan; Book Reviews; Notes," *Craftsman* 23(March 1913): 726.

4. Quoted in Milton W. Brown, *The Story of the Armory Show* (New York: Abbeville Press, and The Joseph H. Hirshhorn Foundation, 1988), 182.

5. Ibid.

6. Ibid., 141–42.

7. "Some of the National Academy Pictures," *New York Times Magazine*, December 17, 1916.

8. Eliot Clark, *History of the National Academy of Design, 1825–1953* (New York: Columbia University Press, 1954), 161.

9. See Avis Berman, *Rebels on Eighth Street: Juliana Force and American Art* (New York: Atheneum Publishers, 1990), 4–5, 68.

10. John Sloan, *Gist of Art: Principles and Practise Expounded in the Classroom and Studio* (New York: Dover Publications, 1977), 28.

11. Quoted in Clark, 163.

12. Giles Edgerton [Mary Fanton Roberts], "The Younger American Painters: Are They Creating a National Art?," *Craftsman* 13 (February 1908): 512.

13. Ibid., 522.

14. The Editor [Mary Fanton Roberts], "Als Ik Kan; Notes; Book Reviews," *Craftsman* 14 (June 1908): 340-41.

15. Editor's note to John W. Alexander's article, "The Need of a National Academy, and Its Value to the Growth of Art in America," *Craftsman*, 17 (March 1910): 618.

16. John Sloan, letter to Mary Fanton Roberts, December 16, 1909, Mary Fanton Roberts Papers, AAA.

17. Bruce St. John, ed., *John Sloan's New York Scene, 1906–1913* (New York: Harper & Row, 1965), 205. In his diary entry for December 10, 1909 (p. 359), Sloan recorded that *Chinese Restaurant* was "in the artificially lighted Society room with the 'overflow' pictures."

18. Robert Henri, "The New York Exhibition of Independent Artists," *Craftsman* 18 (May 1910): 160.

19. Sandra Lee Underwood, *Charles H. Caffin: A Voice for Modernism, 1897–1918* (Ann Arbor, Mich.: UMI Research Press, 1983), 3. Unless otherwise stated, details of Caffin's life and career are drawn from this volume.

20. Ibid., 2.

21. Charles H. Caffin, "The National Academy Opens; Exit the International Show," *New York American*, March 17, 1913.

22. Mary Fanton Roberts, "Science in Art, as Shown in the International Exhibition of Painting and Sculpture," *Craftsman* 24 (May 1913): 216.

23. [Mary Fanton Roberts], "The Quality of the Spring Academy," *Craftsman* 24 (June 1913): 315.

24. H.Wayne Morgan, *Keepers of Culture: The Art-Thought of Kenyon Cox, Royal Cortissoz, and Frank Jewett Mather, Jr.* (Kent, Ohio: Kent State University Press, 1989), ix. Unless otherwise stated, information about Cortissoz's life and career is taken from this volume.

25. Arlene R. Olson, *Art Critics and the Avant-Garde: New York, 1900-1913* (Ann Arbor, Michigan: UMI Research Press, 1980), 19.

26. Ibid., x.

27. Morgan, 69-72.

28. Daniel Catton Rich, "Introduction," in *The Flow of Art: Essays and Criticisms of Henry McBride* (New York: Atheneum Publishers, 1975), 26.

29. [Henry McBride], "Spring Academy Show Comes: International Exhibition Just Ended," *New York Sun*, March 16, 1913.

30. [Forbes Watson], "Academy Exhibition," *New York Evening Post*, December 18, 1912.

31. Forbes Watson, unpublished manuscript, 1946, Forbes Watson Papers, AAA. For more information about Watson, see Berman, 164-67, 185-88.

32. [Forbes Watson], "International Art," *New York Evening Post*, February 20, 1913.

33. [Forbes Watson], "National Academy," *New York Evening Post*, March 18, 1913.

34. Charles Caffin, "Winter Exhibition of the National Academy," *New York American*, December 22, 1913.

35. Royal Cortissoz, "Matters of Art," *New York Tribune*, December 28, 1913.

36. [Forbes Watson], "The National Academy," *New York Evening Post*, December 20, 1913.

37. [Henry McBride], "Gems from the National Academy of Design," *New York Sun*, December 21, 1913.

38. [Mary Fanton Roberts], "At the Spring Academy," *Craftsman* 26 (May 1914): 148.

39. Royal Cortissoz, "The Academy in Fair Form," *New York Tribune*, March 21, 1914.

40. Royal Cortissoz, "The Winter Show at the Academy," *New York Tribune*, December 20, 1914.

41. Charles Caffin, "National Academy Influenced by New Art; Pictures Once Extreme Now Commonplace," *New York American*, December 19, 1914.

42. Royal Cortissoz, "The Winter Exhibition of the Academy of Design," *New York Tribune*, December 19, 1915.

43. Charles Caffin, "National Academy Winter Exhibition; First Review," *New York American*, December 20, 1915.

44. Henry McBride, "Winter Exhibition Lacking in Spirit," *New York Sun*, December 18, 1915.

45. Forbes Watson, "The National Academy," *New York Evening Post*, December 18, 1915.

46. Ibid.

47. Ibid.

48. Ibid.

49. Eakins was a member of the Academy, but it was a source of outrage to the Henri group that he had not been elected to the rank of associate academician until the age of 58. (See Bennard Perlman, *Painters of the Ashcan School: The Immortal Eight* [New York: Dover Publications, 1988], 183.)

50. McBride, "National Academy Lacking in Thrills," *New York Sun*, March 19, 1916.

51. "Critic Bombards Academy," *American Art News*, April 15, 1916.

52. James Britton, "The Winter Academy," *American Art News*, December 30, 1916.

53. See Berman, 142-44, 155-58.

54. Royal Cortissoz, "The Spring Exhibition of The Academy of Design," *New York Tribune*, March 18, 1917.

55. George Bellows, "Bellows Answers Butler," *American Art News* 17 (May 3, 1919): 4.

56. Mary Fanton Roberts, "Art Notes," *Touchstone* 1 (May 1917): 114.

57. Henry McBride, "Modern Art," *Dial* 74 (January 1923): 115.

58. Henry McBride, "Modern Art," *Dial* 78 (June 1925): 527.

59. Forbes Watson, "Editorial," *Arts* 3 (January 1923): 1.

60. Forbes Watson, "William Glackens," *Arts* 3 (April 1923): 246.

61. Ibid.

62. Virgil Barker, "Notes on the Exhibitions," *Arts* 4 (December 1923): 341.

63. Ibid., 342.

64. Henry McBride, "Art News and Reviews," *New York Sun*, November 25, 1923.

65. Forbes Watson, "Editorial," *Arts* 7 (April 1925): 183.

66. Henry McBride, "Modern Art," *Dial* 78 (June 1925): 528.

67. Duncan Phillips, "A Letter from Duncan Phillips," *Arts* 7 (June 1925): 299.

68. Ibid., 300.

69. Henry McBride, "National Academy of Design's Concession to Modernism," *New York Sun*, March 26, 1927; Berman, 239.

70. Susan Noyes Platt, *Modernism in the 1920s: Interpretations of Modern Art in New York from Expressionism to Constructivism* (Ann Arbor, Michigan: UMI Research Press, 1985), 142.

THE
POETS AND POETRY
OF
AMERICA

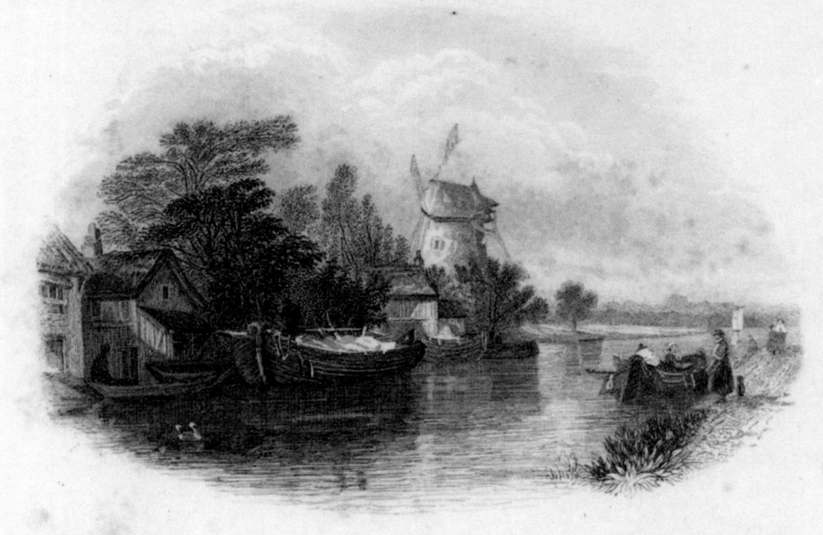

BY RUFUS WILLMOT GRISWOLD.

PHILADELPHIA

PARRY AND McMILLAN.

(SUCCESSORS TO A HART.)

Ekphrasis: A Non-critical Look at Early Nineteenth-century Portraiture through Poetry[1]

W I L L I A M   H .   G E R D T S

Ekphrasis: the literary representation of the visual arts.[2] More narrowly, the term has often been used, and its ramifications explored by writers such as John Hollander, to relate specifically to *poetic* representations of works of art.[3] Ekphrasis, if not as old as the hills, is at least as old as the Greeks, for it would seem, according to its theorists, to start with the description of the shield of Achilles by Homer (and not *Winslow* Homer!). But American poets, well known and anonymous, did acknowledge the achievements of our painters and sculptors from far back in Colonial times, and aspects of this phenomenon, too, have been studied and "catalogued" by recent scholars.[4]

The association of painting specifically with poetry, and the identification of what has come to be known as "The Sister Arts," has its own historical construction also, most celebrated probably in Rensselaer Lee's renowned article of 1940, "Ut Pictura Poesis."[5] Lee's concern was with Renaissance art, but later scholars such as Roy Park have carried this discussion into more recent times,[6] while the interplay between the two is the subject of Jean Hagstrum's brilliant volume, *The Sister Arts,* though this concern is with the interplay of poetry and painting only in England.[7] Twentieth-century scholarly treatment of American reflections on this subject has centered especially, and logically, on the work of Thomas Cole and the Hudson River School landscape painters, vis-à-vis the nature poets of the second quarter of the nineteenth century, especially William Cullen Bryant—the poetic painter and the painterly-poet.[8]

There are many approaches to the interaction between the sister arts that could be explored here. A good many of our artists, including those active in the first half of the nineteenth century, the subject of this essay, were poets themselves, sufficiently celebrated that whole volumes of their poetry appeared in print, as with Allston's *The Sylphs of the Seasons, with Other Poems,* published in 1813.[9] Allston's own poetry was also included in catalogues of exhibitions in which their pictorial counterparts were shown, such as his *Tuscan Girl* (1831; private collection), lent by David Sears to the Sixth Annual Exhibition held at the Boston Athenaeum in 1832, *The Young Troubadour* (1832; location unknown) lent by John Bryant, Jr., to the Ninth Annual Exhibition held there in 1835,

and *Rosalie* (1835; Society for the Preservation of New England Antiquities, Boston), lent by Nathan Appleton to the Twenty-third Annual in 1850. The Athenaeum's first annual exhibition even brought forth a separate publication by William George Crosby of *Poetical illustrations of the Athenaeum gallery of paintings,* twenty poems inspired by American and European biblical subjects, genre scenes, and especially landscapes.[10] Allston, again, was the most prominent painter, with poems dedicated to his *Saul and the Witch of Endor* (c. 1820; Mead Art Museum, Amherst College, Amherst, Massachusetts), *Rising of a Storm at Sea* (fig. 87) (1804; Museum of Fine Arts, Boston), *Landscape [Time] after Sunset* (c. 1891; Corcoran Gallery of Art, Washington, D.C.), and *[Miriam] the Prophetess* (1821; William A. Farnsworth Library and Art Museum, Rockland, Maine). Portraiture made only a meager appearance in this compilation, one poem devoted to Rembrandt Peale's *Portrait of George Washington* (1824; United States Senate Collection, Washington, D.C.),[11] and another to *A Lady* by Francis Alexander.[12]

Verses by other artists, such as Cole, were published in magazines and journals. One of the loveliest of these, this time by a portrait specialist, Henry Inman, appeared in *The Gift* for 1844, though it is a landscape image reflecting the artist's current state of mind, and actually inspired by his colleague Cole's famous pictorial series on *The Voyage of Life* (fig. 88) (1840; Munson-Williams-Proctor Institute, Utica, New York):

> Now listless o'er time's sullen tide
> > My bark of life floats idly on;
> Youth's incense-laden breeze has died,
> > And passion's fitful gusts are flown.
>
> While sadly round her aimless course
> > Now lowering brood the mental skies,
> The Past but murmurs of remorse,
> > And dim the ocean-future lies.
>
> And must this be? My soul, arouse!
> > See through the passing clouds of ill
> How Fame's proud pharos brightly glows,
> > And gilds thy drooping pennant still!

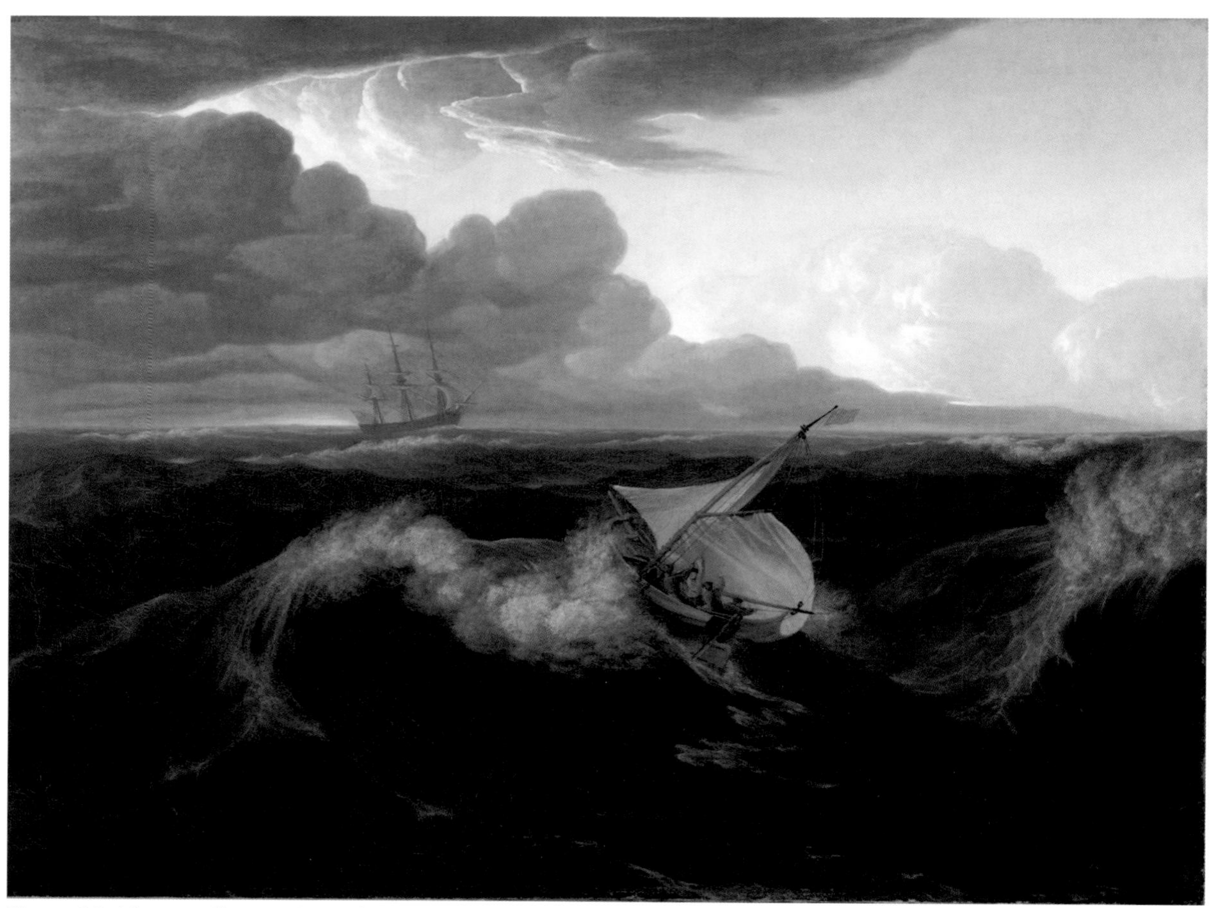

Fig. 87 Washington Allston, *Rising of a Thunderstorm at Sea*, 1804, oil on canvas, 38¼ x 51, Museum of Fine Arts, Boston, Everett Fund

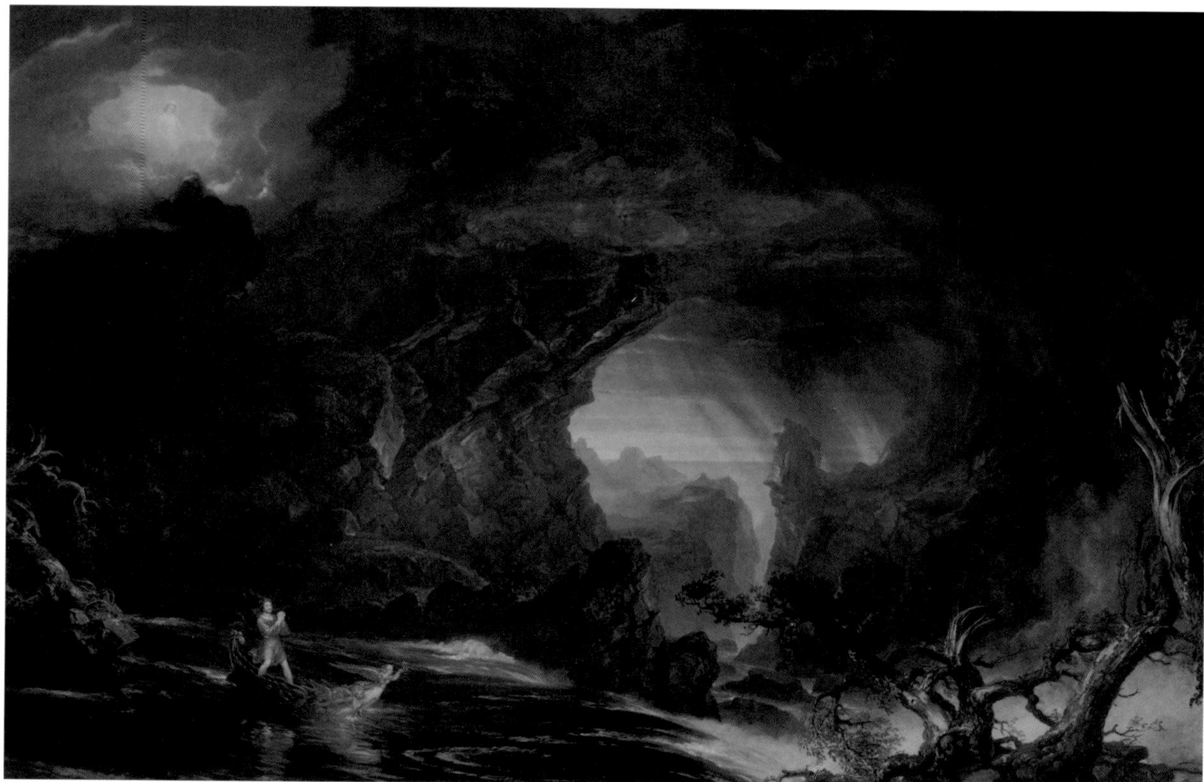

Fig. 88 Thomas Cole, *The Voyage of Life: Manhood*, c. 1840, oil on canvas, 52 x 78¼, Munson-Williams-Proctor Institute, Utica, New York, Museum Purchase

> Stretch to thine oar yon beam thy guide,
>   Spread to Ambition's freshening gale;
> Friendship and love are at thy side,
>   While glory's breathings swell thy sail.[13]

Another body of art-related verse concerns the poetic memorials bestowed upon recently deceased artists. Inman is again a case in point, for the catalogue of his memorial show, held at the rooms of the American Art-Union in New York in February 1846, included poetic tributes from the Albany *Argus* and the *New-York Evening Mirror*.[14] While American fiction, both novels and short stories concerning artists, abounded, there were also poems written and published about artists and the artistic life, such as "The Astonished Painter" of 1839, Mary Arthur's poem, "The Young Artist," published in 1850, and "The Painter's Travel Song," which appeared in 1867.[15]

And there were occasional compilations pairing paintings and poetry, as in *The American Gallery of Art,* published in Philadelphia in 1848 by John Sartain, which featured his engravings after the work of Philadelphia painters (including Sartain's own design of *The Artist's Dream.)*[16] The text was composed of both poetry and prose. In some cases, such as with Samuel Osgood's 1847 painting *The Maid of Frascati* (then owned by J. Francis Fisher, an important Philadelphia collector) and the poem, "The Peasant Girl of Frascati," by the artist's wife, Frances [Locke], a noted poet, the two were completely aligned, as were the painting by William Winner, owned by Sartain himself, and the poem by Sarah Josepha Hale, both entitled "Taking Sanctuary," and Joshua Shaw's picture (owned by G. W. Plantou) and Alice G. Lee's poem "The First Ship." On the other hand, a poem in the volume was inspired by Benjamin West's *Picture of "Death on the Pale Horse,"* but the painting itself was not reproduced.

There were articles that appeared in the American periodical press during the eighteenth century, both before and after the American Revolution that, at least by inference, referenced the concept of the Sister Arts.[17] Reviews of Allston's 1813 *The Sylphs of the Seasons, with other Poems* generated discussions of the connection of the two.[18] Reciprocity and/or contrast between the two artistic forms were the subject of numerous articles, lectures, and discourses, sometimes, as in the case of Samuel F. B. Morse's "Lectures on the Affinity of Paintings with the Other Fine Arts," presented in March and April of 1826, considered in a broader context.[19] But the analogy of the two arts of painting and poetry had been discussed several decades earlier, with most writers favoring one or the other. In 1809, a writer claimed the superiority of the painter, who united the talents of both poet and actor, concluding that: "His are the superiorities of Imitation over Description, of Sensation over Reflection…[one who] approaches nearest to the powers of the Creator in the noblest imitation of his works."[20] In turn, it is not unlikely that Morse's lectures may have inspired the article "Poetry and Painting" that appeared in the *New-York American,* where the anonymous writer

divided the palm of superiority. He noted that "In the sublimest regions of imagination poetry reigns triumphant," but that "Painting takes precedency of poetry in grouping the most attractive and imposing objects of nature's varied scenes . . . not simply by fascinating the organs of sense, & thereby more strongly impressing the mind, but by presenting at once a whole; whereas, in poetical description, object succeeds object."[21] A decade later, another writer grouped Sculpture along with Poetry and Painting among the Sister Arts, allowing each to record their histories and their spiritual potency.[22]

Several discussions concerning the Sister Arts appeared in 1856 in the *Crayon,* the country's first sustained specialized art publication. The first, published in October, emphasized their interrelationship, including music and architecture, as well as poetry, painting, and sculpture.[23] Two months later, a writer investigated "the old question, never likely to be settled—which is the worthier Art . . . Painting or Poetry?" He contrasted the different spheres of the two arts, invoking a host of authorities from the Greek poet Simonides to the seventeenth-century English clergyman Thomas Fuller and the German eighteenth-century critic, aesthetician, and dramatist Gotthold Lessing to the more recent writers Coleridge, Goethe, and Ruskin.[24]

If Morse integrated painting among the other fine arts, his colleague and fellow specialist in historical painting (at least in ambition), the South Carolinian John Blake White, presented his lecture on "the Moral Excellence of Painting and showing the superiority of its powers over those of Poetry," before the Philosophical Society of Charleston in March of 1832. White's essay was provoked by the numerous champions of poetry who had exalted its charms at the expense of painting, but he maintained the primacy of painting, which "enlarges the mind, purifies the heart, chastens the manners, polishes the tastes, corrects & improves the understanding"—in short, painting's moral superiority. And while he invoked such historical examples as those biblical epics by his fellow–South Carolinian Washington Allston, *The Dead Man Revived by Touching the Bones of the Prophet Elisha* (1811–14; Pennsylvania Academy of the Fine Arts, Philadelphia) and *Saul and the Witch of Endor,* White also dealt with landscape painting and portraiture. In regard to the latter, White determined that "No description, surely, can reach the various lineaments, and the *infinitely delicate shades and expressions* of the human countenance; while Painting is able to delineate them with surprising, nay, even with *miraculous truth.*" Compared to poetry, portrait painting could perpetuate "the tenderest sympathies of Love and Friendship" as well as "the freshness of youth, the *vigor* of manhood, [and] the *sanctity* of age. . . ." White found "the high-wrought efforts of Poetry . . . spiritless and unprofitable" compared with the portrait which "transports us into the very Elysian Groves, where, in all the glow and freshness of life, and health, and grace, and beauty, our departed Friends are exhibited to our enraptured eyes."[25]

Portraits and portraitists, in fact, inspired poetical rapture

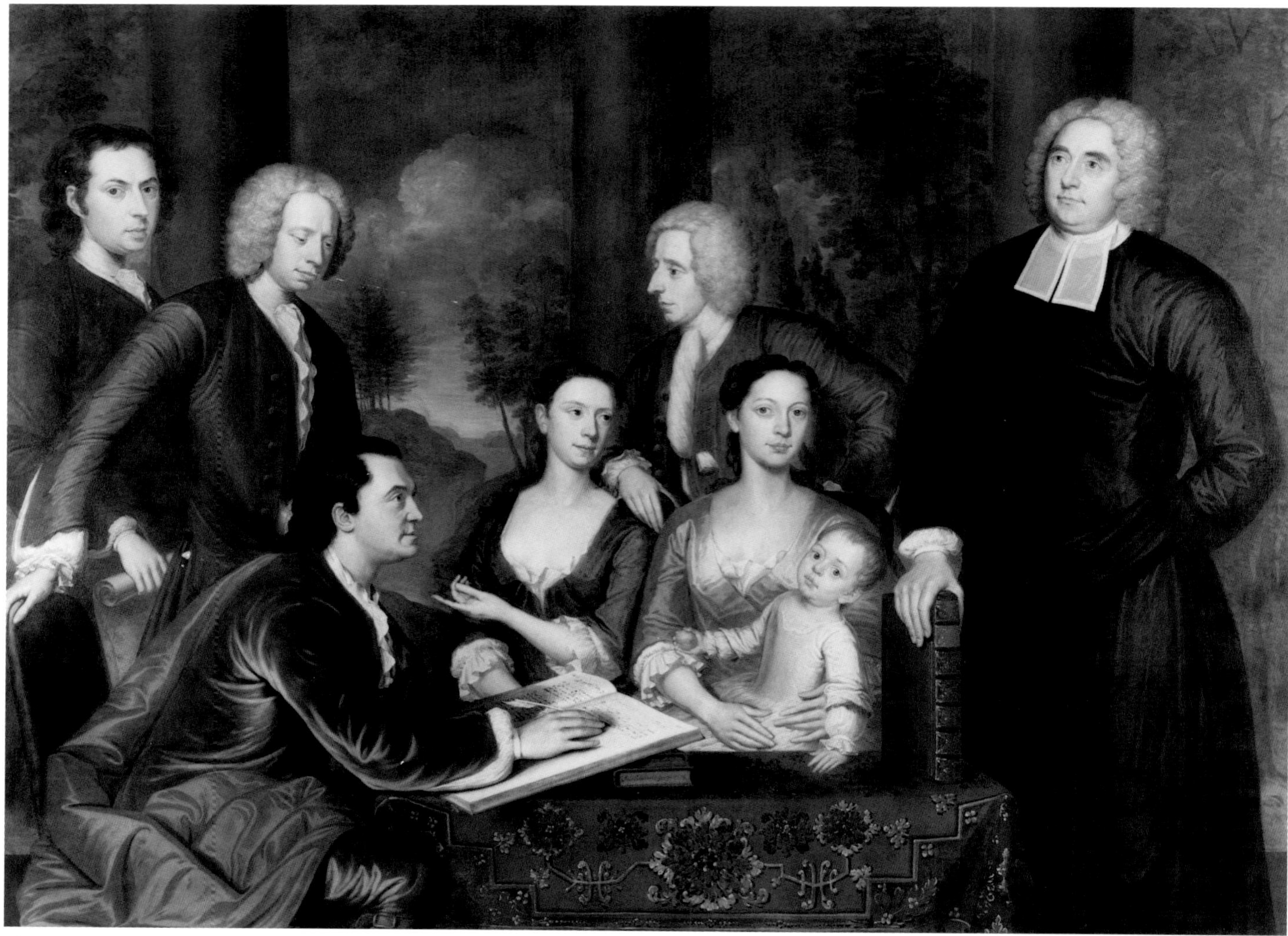

Fig. 89 John Smibert, *Dean Berkeley and His Entourage (The Bermuda Group)*, 1729–31, oil on canvas, Yale University Art Gallery, Gift of Issac Lothrop

that appeared in the American press from early in the eighteenth century—logical enough, since the great majority of pictorial achievement in Colonial times was grounded in portraiture.[26] Several of these poems stand out both for their historical significance in identifying the work and range of the artists, and for their hyperbole, beginning with Mather Byles's eighty-line poem written probably early in 1730, "To Mr. Smibert on the sight of his Pictures" (fig. 89).[27] As Jessie Poesch has pointed out, Byles, in his poem, alluded to the concept of the Sister Arts when he wrote:

> Alike our Labour, and alike our Flame,
> 'Tis thine to raise the Shape;
> 'Tis mine to fix the name.[28]

Among the next generation of painters to emigrate from Great Britain to the American colonies, John Wollaston, who was one of our more peripatetic portraitists, appears to have received the greatest number of panegyrics. In March of 1753, a "Dr. T. T." published "Extempore: On seeing Mr. Wollaston's Pictures in Annapolis," and five and one-half years later,

Francis Hopkinson published in Philadelphia "Verses inscribed to Mr. Wollaston."[29] Hopkinson's poem actually concluded with a paean to the young Benjamin West, logical enough since West had just then begun to adopt Wollaston's high-style British rococo manner of portraiture. Hopkinson enjoined West:

> May'st thou ever tread
> The pleasing paths thy Wollaston has lead,
> Let his just precepts all your work refine,
> Copy each grace, and learn like him to shine.

West had actually been the subject of an earlier eulogy in the same magazine, a poem inspired by one of his female portraits: "Upon seeing the portrait of Miss **—** by Mr. West."[30] The identity of the subject here is not known, but West's *Portrait of Jane Galloway* inspired the poem by John Thomas, "To a Lady of Maryland," and Hopkinson later honored West in a long poem entitled "Genius."[31] West was not the earliest native-born American to be eulogized in poetry; Robert Feke's portrait of *Mrs. James Bowdoin II* inspired a

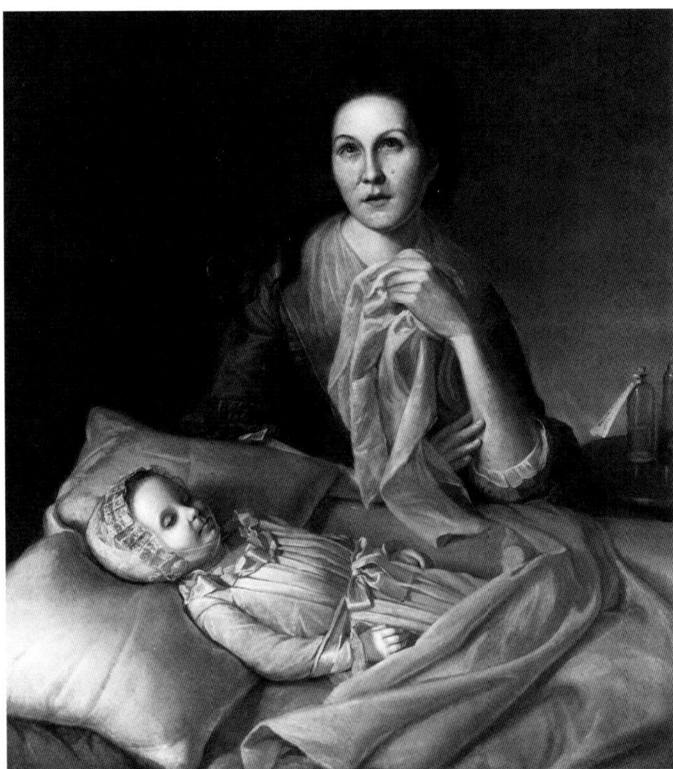

Fig. 90 Charles Willson Peale, *Rachel Weeping Over Her Deceased Child,* 1772/76, oil on canvas, 37⅛ x 32¼, Philadelphia Museum of Art, Given by the Barra Foundation, Inc.

poem written by her husband, probably around 1748, when they married, though it was not published until 1759.[32] And an elegy in Latin to Smibert's short-lived artist-son, Nathaniel Smibert, written by John Beveridge, appeared in the *Boston Gazette* on May 2, 1757.[33]

Charles Willson Peale may have been the Colonial artist to receive the greatest number of poetical tributes, beginning with that published in the *Maryland Gazette* in September 1770, praising his likeness of the actress Nancy Hallam, depicted in the role of Imogen in Shakespeare's *Cymbeline* (1771; Colonial Williamsburg Foundation), a painting that was celebrated again in verse the following year.[34] Peale himself may have written the poem published in the same journal in April 1771, inspired by his painting of his wife and child.[35] And just before the Revolution, still another tribute to Peale appeared in the Maryland Gazette, this time devoted to his portrait of his wife, Rachel, lifting her naked, sleeping child from its bath.[36] The most spectacular, if lugubrious poem regarding Peale's work is a later, shorter one, relating to Peale's portrait of Rachel weeping over her deceased child (fig. 90), which appeared in 1782:

Draw not the curtain, if a Tear,
Just trembling in a Parent's eye,
Can fill your awful soul with fear,
Or cause your tender Breast to sigh.

A Child lies dead before your eyes
and seems no more than moulded clay,
while the affected mother cries
and constant mourns from day to day.[37]

The majority of eighteenth-century American poetry devoted to art referenced specific artists and/or specific paintings. And this continued into the early years of the nineteenth century as well; one of several such effusions was penned by Mrs. Perez Morton in regard to one of the several likenesses of her by Gilbert Stuart[38] (fig. 91):

STEWART, thy portrait speaks! With skill divine
Round the light graces flow the *warming line;*
Expression in its finest utterance lives,
And a new language to creation gives.
Each varying trait the gifted artist shows—
Wisdom majestic in his bending brows;
The Warrior's open throat, his eyes of fire—
As where the charms of bashful youth retire:
Or patient, plodding, and with wealth content,
The man of commerce counts his cent per cent;
'Tis *character* that breathes, 'tis soul that twines
Round the rich canvass, traced in living lines,
Speaks in the face, or in the form displayed,
Warms in the tint and mellows in the shade.

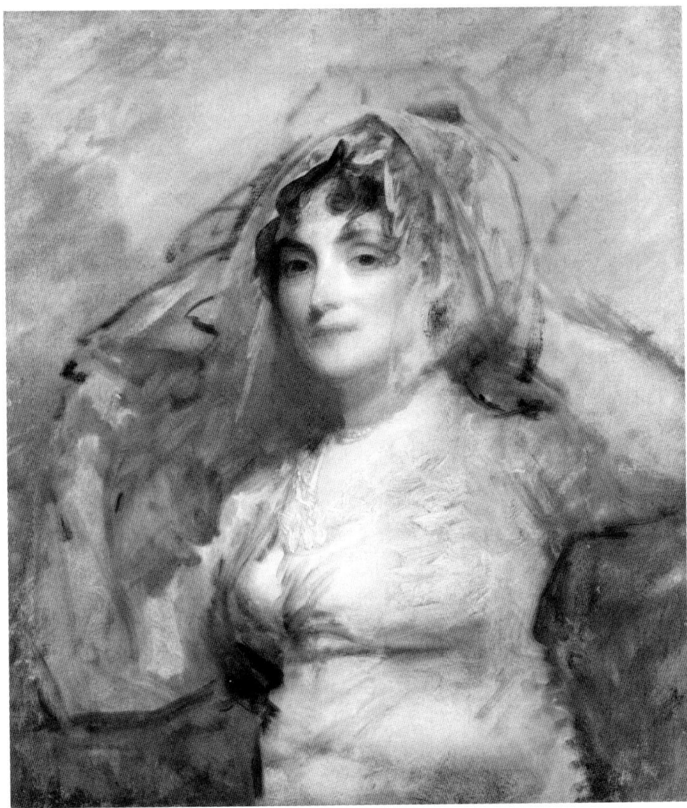

Fig. 91 Gilbert Stuart, *Mrs. Perez Morton,* c. 1802, oil on canvas, 29⅛ x 24¼, Worcester Art Museum, Worcester, Massachusetts, Gift of the grandchildren of Joseph Tuckerman

These touching graces, and that front sublimes,
Thy art shall rescue from the spoil of time
Thence the fair victim scorns the threatening rage
And trembling step of slow advancing age,
Still on her cheek the rose of beauty blows,
Her lips deep tint its breathing crimson shows;
Like the magicians wand, thy pencil gives
Its potent touch, and every feature lives.[39]

Such poems were produced in ever-increasing numbers, of course, throughout the nineteenth century and into our own times,[40] and, as we have seen, sculptors such as Hiram Powers also attracted lyrical effusions, once Americans became professionally identified with this medium, beginning in the second quarter of the century. But what may possibly be identified with the appearance of regular public exhibitions such as those instituted by the National Academy of Design is a body of poetry reflecting more general increased public awareness of art. And since these exhibitions were dominated by portraiture in the early years of the Academy, there is correspondingly a significant body of poetry concerning the portrait, both the life-size oil likenesses and the more intimate miniature watercolors on ivory (figs. 92 and 93). See, for instance, a poem that appeared in a New York newspaper in 1826, the year of the National Academy's first show:

THE PORTRAIT:
Oh yes! These lips are very fair,
   Half lifted to the sky,
As if they breathed an Angel's prayer,
   Mix'd with mortal's sigh;
But theirs is not the song that flings
O'er evening's still imaginings
   Its cherish'd witchery;
No these are not the lips whose tone
Sad memory has made her own!

And these long curls of dazzling brown
   In many a fairy wreath,
Float brightly, beautifully down
   Upon the brow beneath;
But these are not the locks of jet,
For which I sought the violet,
   On that remembered heath;
No, these are not the locks that gleam
Around me in my twilight dream!

And these blue eyes—a very saint
   Might envy their pure rays—
Are such as limners learn to paint,
   And poets long to praise;

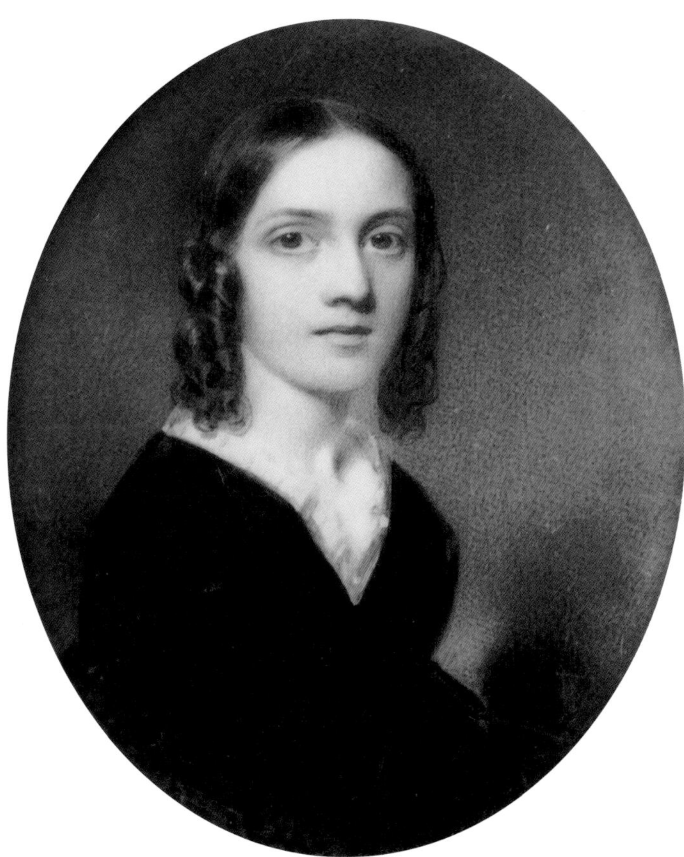

Fig. 92 Samuel Fanshaw, *Mrs. Cornelius Ver Bryck*, watercolor on ivory, 3⅛ x 2¾ (oval), Private collection, New York

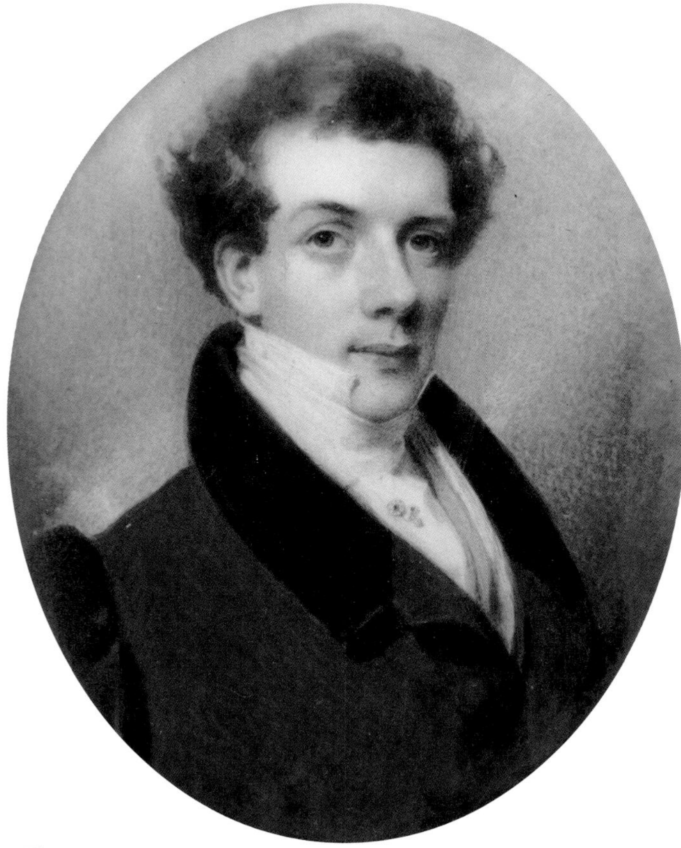

Fig. 93 Henry Inman, *Portrait of a Gentleman*, watercolor on ivory, 3⅛ x 2¾ (oval), Private collection, New York

But theirs is not the speaking glance,
On which, in all its young romance,
    My spirit loves to gaze;
No, these are not the eyes that shine,
Like never setting stars on mine!

By those sweet songs I hear at night,
    Those black locks on the brow,
And those dark eyes, whose living light
    Is beaming o'er me now.
I worship nought but what thou art!—
Let all that was decay—depart,—
    I care not when, or how;
And fairer far these hues may be—
They seem not half so fair to me![41]

Such poetry not infrequently compared, as here, the painted to the living likeness, and we notice that the anonymous author did not neglect to reference the Sister Arts, allying the limner and the poet. Even more touching was the following, written by the noted American scholar and poet James Gates Percival,[42] and published in the *Knickerbocker* in 1836:

As those blue eyes upon the canvass throw
Their watery glances to me, where thy tear
Seems gathering to a starry drip, to flow
Down the soft damask of her cheek, I hear
From her moved lips, a voice salute my ear,
That was so kind so confiding; pain
Which once did throb within me, now doth veer
To a clam stillness; the delirious brain
Seems by cool drops renewed to life's young bliss again.

Ah! I would then that pictured form could talk
Of hours, that once were happy in the round
Of thought still growing, as at each new walk,
With deeper hue the early bud is found,
Till it unfolds its leaves, and scatter round
Its purest incense; so our lives steal by,
Catching new loves and hopes, which closely wound
With every blended thought and wish, will try
The heart to its last throb, when loved ones leave or die.[43]

Some poems referencing portraits continued to be written to specific works of art, tributes to particular American masters, as in this example by one "G. L."[44]:

Lines To a Portrait of a Roman Girl: by F. Alexander

Those deep, deep, fervent eyes, whose gaze intense
    Is fixed on vacancy—that youthful brow,
    Where thoughts of pain are gathering even now,
And long have gather'd, 'till the very sense

Of thought is agony—that ripe full mouth,
    Scarce open, and the lone distracted air
    On thy sweet face all tell how sullen care
Hath marr'd thee, daughter of the sunny South!
Say, doth thou miss thy lover's hand among
    Those rich brown tresses, that the winds of Heaven
    Play with so rudely? Hath the false one given
His cold heart to another? Hath he flung
Away that fiery heart of thine, that swells
    And burns within that full and glowing breast,
    Where never more sweet peace, nor tranquil rest
Shall cleanse the fount of its embittered wells!

No legend speaks the story of thy days;
    Yet there is that inwrought upon thy brow,
    Which far more eloquent than words avow,
All the long anguish of thy soul betrays.
Alas, the tale it tells! For blighted youth—
    Heart crush'd—hope lost—life wasted—all things
      gone,
    But the deep sense of wretchedness alone,
Impictured here to tell the living truth—
Say the hard world has been too hard with thee,
    Oh, fitting emblem of Rome's crumbled wall,
    In ruins still most beautiful! And all
Look sadly on thee, and sigh, 'Misery!'[45]

Of course, the painting that inspired this poem, though designated a portrait, was not a formal commission and was surely based on a model hired by Francis Alexander during his long Italian residence. Thus, it could embody more narrative and even allegorical significance than could a formal commission. Still, even poetry derived from more traditional portraits sometimes shared with such verse as the above a surprising degree of sensuosity and passion, qualities to which most viewers today are blind, but which contemporaries identified in all artistic manifestations.[46] Such poetry might not be of the highest artistic quality, but it often embodied great ardor: the following excerpt, by "Thekla," written specifically for the *New Mirror,* is a case in point:

"A Portrait"

Her brow had the transparent hue
    Of marble 'neath the moonbeam's glow,
And the blue veins peep'd softly through,
    Like violets from the snow.
Now o'er that brow a beam would stray,
    And now a cloud arise,
As light and shade alternate play
O'er changeful April skies.

Her eyes were dreamlike, soft and bright;
    Their colour none might tell,

For now they danced in rapture's light,
    And now 'neath sorrow's spell
They droop'd; but whether mirth
    Or sadness slumbered there
No other eyes in the wide earth
    Could boast of charms so rare.

Her voice, like a melodious lute,
    Echoed in music 'round,
And tuned to measure grave or glad,
    Still woke harmonious sound;
We thought while rose its song of glee
    We could not love it more,
Yet when it thrilled to sorrow's key
    'Twas dearer than before.

Her smile! How shall I seek to paint
    A thing so wondrous bright?
As well might painter's hand attempt
    To sketch the rainbow's light.
A sudden splendour, like the rays
    From morning's rising sun;
A beam that deck'd in dazzling hues
    The face o'er which it shone.[47]

While "Thekla" may remain anonymous, such poetic effusions to portraiture were sometimes penned by authors such as James Gates Percival, who were highly regarded in their own day. Another was Emma Embury, whose poem, "A Portrait," was published in the *Literary World* in July of 1847.[48] Here the moral virtue of the subject was paramount, as the last of Embury's five verses avows:

There dwelleth in the sinlessnesses of youth
    A sweet rebuke that vice may not endure.
And thus he makes an atmosphere of truth,
    For all things in her presence grow more pure;
She walks in light,—her guardian angel flings
A halo round her from his radiant wings.

What all of these, and other poems to portraits have in common is the feminine gender of their subject; men were seldom so singled out, even if, as in the case of Embury, the author was female.[49] This is true, again, for instance, in George H. Clark's "The Portrait," a poem published in the *Knickerbocker* in July of 1858. There is a surprisingly rakish spirit to this poem, the author contrasting the appearance of a mother holding a sleeping child with her younger portrait likeness, noting:

The maid has such a conscious look
    Of bashfulness and fun,
That one would guess her half-coquette
    And half demurest nun;

Or deem some merry devil lurked
    Within those angel eyes,
To tempt deluded man astray
    With hopes of Paradise.
And did you really, truly wear
    That charming bodice-waist,
With its provoking open front,
    So exquisitely laced?
If low-necked dresses then were cut
    So wonderfully low,
Pray tell me why it is that now
    You never wear them so?[50]

Of course, portraiture inspired prose fiction as well as poetry during these same years, and again such writing can be traced to the predominance of portraits in contemporary exhibitions. In "The Portrait: A Sketch," which appeared in *Godey's Lady's Book* in June of 1832, the narrator announces immediately that he has fallen in love with a portrait when "The exhibition had only opened; I had gone to see it on the third day. . . ." And later: "Not a day did I miss the Exhibition."[51] And again, in a short story, "The Portrait," that was published in the *Knickerbocker* two years later, it was Fletcher, the narrator's friend, who fell in love with Miss Ellen Vincent, no. 73 in the catalogue of the exhibition where the two viewed this "most beautiful painting,—a female head,— perfectly Grecian. She might have been the Sybil, when Apollo first beheld her. . . ."[52]

The poetry and prose discussed so far have been directed toward traditional oil portraits "in large"—usually life-size paintings that both commanded the professional efforts of the majority of our artists during the eighteenth and early nineteenth centuries, and correspondingly dominated the early exhibitions of the National Academy of Design. But also prominent in those shows, and in some ways, of equal or even greater appeal and of more intimate significance, were the small portrait miniatures—usually, though not always, water-colors on ivory. This art form had its own specialists, though of course some oil portraitists also painted miniatures or had specialized in painting them in some phase of their careers. Inman, for instance, had done both in the early 1820s, and then took on his pupil, Thomas Seir Cummings, as a partner in 1824, Inman painting the large oils and Cummings the miniatures. After several years, Inman pretty much relinquished miniature painting, and Cummings became New York's leading specialist for many decades. And this was significant for the National Academy, since Inman was the organization's first vice-president, and Cummings its treas-urer for many decades.

Miniatures began to be painted in the American Colonies at least in the 1740s, but the art reached its apogee at the end of that century and into the 1840s. The exhibition records of the National Academy testify to this. The first annual show, held in 1826, offered miniatures by Cummings, Anson Dickinson, and

Charleston's most renowned artist, Charles Fraser. The number of miniature painters gradually increased in each successive exhibit, and by 1829 there were a dozen painters showing miniatures, reaching to almost twenty in the late 1830s. Then the numbers show a gradual decline in the mid-1840s, and by 1850 there were few, if any, miniatures exhibited. During the following decade there were never more than four miniature painters represented and usually only two; for the record, Henry Colton Shumway was the most consistent exhibitor, first displaying miniatures in 1829, and continuing through 1861. One interesting facet among these statistics is the large number of women artists, both married and unmarried, who showed from the earliest years through the mid-1840s, this, in addition to Anne Hall, the first professional female Academician and the New York area's most renowned female miniature specialist.

The decline of miniature painting can be attributed to a number of factors. First, there was the general criticism of the dominance of portraiture in the early annual exhibitions, writers expressing their dismay both at the repetitiousness of the imagery and the projected vainglory implicit therein. There was also the rise of other genres, particularly landscape, with its implicit celebration and even glorification of the distinctive characteristics of the nation. But most of all, in regard to miniatures, was the rivalry of photography beginning in the 1840s, a form of likeness-taking that was quicker, cheaper, and could embody the exactitude that increasingly was demanded for the more clinical aesthetics of the mid-century, akin to the pictorial changes in landscape painting—from the romantic sensibilities of Thomas Cole to the scientific specificity of Frederic Church.

While both the large oil portrait and the small miniature shared the stylistic characteristics and temporal changes that occurred over the approximately sixty-year period of the popularity of the small portrait images, the miniature evoked more emotional, personal, even intimate resonances among viewers. As Robin Bolton-Smith, one of our leading contemporary specialists in this art form has noted: "The miniature as a vessel for the exchange of sentiments was an exclusive and highly personal mode of portraiture. . . ."[53] While the miniature did, indeed, inspire prose effusions—see, for instance, "The Miniature," which appeared in *Atkinson's Casket* in April of 1831[54]—Romantic poetry became the ideal form of literary equation for the subjective and intimate sentiments projected by the miniature. And a rich trove of such poetry appeared in American literature at exactly the time of the greatest display of miniatures in public exhibitions. "Lines Suggested by a Miniature," which was published in the *New-York Mirror* in October of 1833, serves as an example:

> Soul of my soul! though seas dispart
> Our bosom's mutual sigh;
> Thanks to the painter's magic art,
> I see—I feel thee nigh!

Thanks to that skill whose godlike power
    Transcends the tyrant Fate's,
Fills the cold void that absence leaves,
    And space annihilates.

How sweet in that ideal type
    Each cherished look to trace;
O with what fond idolatry
    I gaze upon that face!
Whose blended charms of shape and hue,
    In radiant beauty glow,
As meet the sister beams of light,
    In summer's graceful bow.

Hers is that dark and glossy tress,
    That soft cheek's vermeil dye,
That ruby lip's voluptuousness,
    And that star-molten eye;
Hers, too, that sweet angelic mien,
    Vainly by words defined—
The witchery of beauty's queen,
    The halo of the mind.

'Tis but a breathless shape of art,
    A pictured dream I own;
But then how oft does rapture spring
    From semblances alone!
Which seen by fancy's weirdly eye,
    Whate'er their varied form,
Seem beings of reality
    With life and passion warm.

Image of her in whose pure heart
    Imparadised I reign!
Though, weighed in avarice' gilded scales,
    Thou'rt valueless and vain;
I would not that these charmed eyes
    Should gaze no more on thee,
For all the glittering argosies
    That sweep the sail-white sea:

For though relentless fate has seen
    Thee from my side removed,
And stretched a passless bourne between
    The loving and beloved;
With thy mute portraiture to bless,
    Where'er by fortune thrown,
In earth's most desert loneliness,
    I shall not be alone![55]

The miniature painter might well have felt honored and even inspired by the reference here to his/her "magic art" and "godlike power." And incorporated here are the invariable themes of the temporality of beauty and even life vis-à-vis the

endurance of the painted likeness. On the other hand, miniatures were, themselves, delicate—such likenesses in watercolor were all too easily damaged, often by water, or their
ivory support cracked and broken. And this fragility, along
with the sentimental worth of the miniature, was acknowledged by the well-regarded poet Caroline Gilman in her
poem, "The Disfigured Miniature."

> Alas! I cannot trace the beams
>   That sparkle in thy soft, dark eye,
> Like summer's lightning's chasten'd gleams,
>   That linger on an evening sky.
>
> And lost, too, is the gentle smile,
>   That, like a sunbeam over flowers,
> Has danced upon thy lips the while
>   And charm'd my gay or anxious hours.
>
> The quick idea genius gave,
>   The cold reflection reason wove,
> Study's deep thought, abstruse and grave,
>   And gentler looks that told of love;
>
> The glance benevolent and kind,
>   That banish'd pain, distrust and fear,
> All these in vain I seek to find,
>   And sigh to think they are not here.
>
> And yet I cast thee not away—
>   Poor image of a face divine!
> But clasp thee to my heart, and say,
>   'Deform'd, yet precious, thou art mine!'
>
> Oh! when the hand of withering care,
>   Shall bid, like this, thy beauty fade,
> Or sickness plant her furrows where
>   The bloom of youth has brightly stray'd,
>
> Then may'st thou prize the faithful heart,
>   That like the flower of night—perfume,
> Asks no parterre where sunbeams dart,
>   But blossoms gladly 'mid the gloom.[56]

Only occasionally was the sorrowful, admittedly sometimes maudlin tone of ekphrastic poetry transcended by a
touch of humor and even cynicism, as in George Pope
Morris's "The Miniature," published in 1831:

> William was holding in his hand
>   The likeness of his wife—
> Fresh, as if touched by fairy wand,
>   With beauty, grace, and life.
> He almost thought it spoke—he gazed
>   Upon the treasure still—
> Absorbed, delighted, and amazed
>   To view the artist's skill.
>
> "This picture is thyself, dear Jane!
>   'Tis drawn to nature true—
> I've kissed it o'er and o'er again,
>   It is so much like you."
> "And did it kiss you back, my dear?"
>   "Why—no—my love," smiled he.
> "Then, William, it is very clear,
>   'Tis not at all like me!"[57]

But Morris's poem is the exception to the standard sentiments of ekphrastic poetry devoted to miniature painting. A
short archetypal example, published in 1833 in Morris's
weekly newspaper, the *New-York Mirror,* at the height of the
vogue for the painting and exhibition of miniatures, may conclude our consideration of such literature.

> When far away, though deep impressed,
>   Thy form lies imaged on my mind;
> This dear memento on my breast
>   A place shall find.
>
> When worn by age, or cold decay,
>   For such, alas, is beauty's doom;
> This oft shall wake, in bright array,
>   Thy beauty's bloom.
>
> When death—oh, can it ever be!—
>   That fair original shall blight,
> These speaking eyes shall shed o'er me
>   Their living light.[58]

Such poetic effusions in regard to miniature painting
understandably disappeared as this form of artistry itself fell
into disfavor with the rise of photography. Likewise, the
romantic celebration of portraiture in large gradually diminished as a wholly different sensibility, at once far less sentimental, replaced the romanticism of the pre–Civil War years.
It is far beyond the scope of this essay to investigate this
change of aesthetics and cultural values. American paintings
and poetry continued to be paired in the latter half of the century, as in the 1886 publication *Poetic Thoughts, with Pictures,*
celebrating works by members of the Artists' Fund Society of
Philadelphia.[59] And, of course, poetry continued to be
devoted to specific works of art, if not nearly so often to gen-
eralized art forms, and less often also to works of portraiture.
Let me conclude with one final poem, this of the post–Civil
War era, commemorating a relatively unlikely celebrant of the
portrait form. This is "Love Grown Bold," by Richard Watson
Gilder, the poet and editor of *Scribner's Monthly* and then
Century Magazine, a poem inspired by Winslow Homer's por-
trait of Helena de Kay (c. 1872; Thyssen Collection, Madrid),

who was later to become Gilder's wife.[60] The painting was exhibited at the National Academy of Design, not at one of the annual exhibitions, but in 1894 at the show of *Portraits of Women: Loan Exhibition for the Benefit of St. John's Guild and the Orthopaedic Hospital:*

> This is her picture painted ere mine eyes
> > Her ever holy face had looked upon.
> > She sitteth in a silence of her own;
> > Behind her, on the ground, a red rose lies;
> Her thinking brow is bent, nor doth arise
> > Her gaze from that shut book whose word unknown
> > Her firm hands hide from her;—there all alone
> > She sitteth in thought-trouble, maidenwise,
> And now her lover waiting wondereth
> > Whether the joy of joys is drawing near;
> > Shall his brave fingers like a tender breath
> That shut book open for her, wide and clear?
> > From him who her sweet shadow worshippeth
> > Now will she take the rose, and hold it dear?[61]

Despite the archaisms of language ("ere"; "sitteth"; "doth"; "wondereth"; "worshippeth"), the poem differs from its predecessors quoted here, not only because of the specificity of imagery, but also because of the implicit incertitude both of imagery and response that the author projects. The serenity of the earlier poetry is replaced here by hesitancy and doubt, a fitting distinction for this now more restive era.

NOTES

1. I would like to thank Dr. Carrie Rebora Barrett for sharing with me her ekphrastic file, and Zachary Ross for locating some of the poems and many of the literary references discussed in the present essay.

2. See David Rosand, "Ekphrasis and the Generation of Images," *Arion,* 1, no. 1, 1990, p. 61.

3. John Hollander, "The Poetics of *Ekphrasis, Word and Image* 4 (1988): 209–19.

4. Again by Hollander, see his *The Gazer's Spirit: Poems Speaking to Silent Works of Art* (Chicago: University of Chicago Press, 1995). Among the American artists whose works are celebrated in the poetry quoted here are the painters John Trumbull (poem by Joseph Rodman Drake), Elihu Vedder (by Herman Melville), George Inness (by Walt Whitman), and James A. M. Whistler (by Algernon Swinburne), and the sculptors Thomas Crawford (by John James Piatt) and Hiram Powers (by Elizabeth Barrett Browning). Other pre-twentieth-century American artists whose works are referenced but not elaborated by Hollander include Horatio Greenough (poem by Richard Henry Dana), Robert Weir (by Fitz-Greene Halleck), Thomas Eakins (by Thomas Bolt), and Augustus Saint-Gaudens (by Richard Watson Gilder). In one case, that of Washington Allston, Hollander includes a poem *by* that American poet-painter about a work by Raphael. He also includes Emma Lazarus's famous poem about Auguste Bartholdi's *Statue of Liberty.* I want to thank Deborah Frizzell for first bringing this study to my attention. Hollander himself wrote and published a poem, "A Statue of Something," inspired by Thomas Eakins's *William Rush and His Model* (1908; Honolulu Academy of the Fine Arts). See John Hollander, "Ekphrasis: Words on Pictures," *Art & Antiques* 1 (March 1984): 88–89.

5. Rensselaer W. Lee, "Ut Pictura Poesis: The Humanistic Theory of Painting," *Art Bulletin* 22 (December 1940): 197–269.

6. Roy Park, "*Ut Pictura Poesis:* The Nineteenth-Century Aftermath," *Journal of Aesthetics and Art Criticism* 28 (Winter 1969): 155–64. The literature on the interplay between painting and poetry in America in the twentieth century is enormous. To suggest a typical example, see James E. Breslin, "William Carlos Williams and Charles Demuth: Cross-Fertilization in the Arts," *Journal of Modern Literature* 6 (April 1977): 248–63.

7. Jean M. Hagstrum, *The Sister Arts: The Tradition of Literary Pictorialism and English Poetry from Dryden to Gray* (Chicago: University of Chicago Press, 1958).

8. Here the writings of Donald A. Ringe are especially pertinent. See his articles "Kindred Spirits: Bryant and Cole," *American Quarterly* 6 (Fall 1954): 233-44; "Bryant's Criticism of the Fine Arts," *College Art Journal* 17 (Fall 1957): 43–54; and "Paintings as Poems in the Hudson River Aesthetics," *American Quarterly* 12 (Spring 1960): 71–93. See also William Cullen Bryant, II, "Poetry and Painting: A Love Affair of Long Ago," *American Quarterly* 22 (Winter 1970): 859–82; Donald B. Kuspit, "19th Century Landscape: Poetry and Property," *Art in America* 64 (January–February 1976): 64–71. John C. Riordan's 1970 dissertation for Syracuse University is entitled: "Thomas Cole: A Case Study of the Painter-Poet Theory of Art in American Painting from 1825–1850."

9. Washington Allston, *The Sylphs of the Seasons, with Other Poems* (Boston: Cummings and Hilliard; Cambridge, Massachusetts: Hilliard & Metcalf, 1813). Allston's *Lectures on Art, and Poems,* edited by Richard Henry Dana, Jr. (New York: Baker and Scribner, 1850) was published posthumously. In this case, the writer was a painter whose poetry included a good many poems about art. Poems devoted to Michelangelo, Raphael, Pellegrino Tibaldi, and Rembrandt were contained in both volumes; the later publication also included poems relating to his own paintings, *The Spanish Girl [in Reverie]* (1831; Metropolitan Museum of Art, New York); *A Tuscan Girl* (1831; private collection); and *Young Troubadour* (1832; location unknown); poems about the artists Michelangelo and Rubens; and two on works of sculpture: an *Angel* by the Italian Luigi Bienaimé, and *The Angel and Child* (1833; Museum of Fine Arts, Boston), by Allston's Boston colleague Horatio Greenough.

10. [William George Crosby], *Poetical illustrations of the Athenaeum gallery of paintings* (Boston: True and Greene, 1827).

11. This was Peale's famous *Patriae Pater* portrait of Washington, exhibited at the Athenaeum in 1827 in pointed contrast there to *Washington at Dorchester Heights* (1806; Museum of Fine Arts, Boston, deposited by the City of Boston) by Boston's resident master, Gilbert Stuart. Critics of the show frequently compared the two; Crosby's choice to include a poem to Peale's painting and not to Stuart's may well indicate his personal favoritism.

12. Alexander exhibited six portraits in the Athenaeum's First Annual Exhibition, but only one represented a woman, *Miss Cecilia Eustaphieve* (1827; Colonel Cecil Stewart), presumably the subject of this poem.

13. H[enry] I[nman], "Lines," *The Gift: A Christmas and New Year's Present* (Philadelphia: Carey and Hart, 1844), 148. Engravings after Inman's paintings, *Mumble-the-Peg* (1842; Pennsylvania Academy of the Fine Arts, Philadelphia) and *Early Days of Washington* (location unknown) were reproduced in this gift book, but neither these nor any other illustrations related to the poem.

14. *Catalogue of the Works by the Late Henry Inman; with a Biographical Sketch* (New York: Van Norden & King, 1846), 11–12.

15. "The Astonished Painter," *The Lady's Book* 19 (November 1839): 193-94; Mrs. Mary Arthur, "The Young Artist," *Godey's Lady's Book* 41 (November 1850): 281; "The Painter's Travel Song," *New York Leader,* February 2, 1867. Prose fiction, rather than poetry, is brilliantly discussed in Stephanie Wasielewski Fay, "American Pictorial Rhetoric: Describing Works of Art in Fiction and Art Criticism, 1820–1875" (Ph.D. diss., University of California, Berkeley, 1982).

16. J[ohn] Sartain, ed., *The American Gallery of Art* (Philadelphia: Lindsay and Blakiston, 1848). This publication is briefly discussed in Ann Katharine Martinez, "The Life and Career of John Sartain (1808–1897): A Nineteenth-Century Philadelphia Printmaker" (Ph.D. diss. George Washington University, 1986), 44–45.

17. An important, unpublished study here is Marek Bartelik, "Art Criticism in America. The Doctrine *Ut Pictora Poesis* in Early 19th Century America," Graduate School of the City University of New York, 1993. Bartelik cites "On the Knowledge of Painting," *American Magazine & Historical Chronicle* 2 (March 1745): 114-17; "Painting," *Christian's, Scribner's and Farmer's Magazine* 1 (December–January, 1789–1790): 595; and "On the Superiority of Painting to Poetry," *New York Magazine* 6 (October 1795): 601–2. The first and last of these were not original discussions; rather they were derived from English texts.

18. See, for instance, the review in *American Monthly Magazine and Critical Review* 4 (August 1817): 245, which begins, "Poetry and painting are kindred arts," and goes on to discuss their mutual need for a refined sensibility to beauty, a relish for the luxury of nature, exquisite perception of character, and sentiment, noting also that the "same fervour of fancy is requisite to both."

19. Nicolai Cikovsky, Jr., ed., *Lectures on the Affinity of Painting with the Other Fine Arts* (Columbia, Missouri: University of Missouri Press, 1983). Morse delivered these four lectures at the New York Athenaeum soon after he became the first president of the newly formed National Academy of Design, with which organization the original manuscripts reside. Morse categorized poetry and painting (along with sculpture) among the "fine" as opposed to the "useful" arts; the other "fine arts" were music, landscape gardening, architecture, oratory, and theater, but only poetry, music, and landscape gardening were "perfect arts." Most of the third lecture was devoted to poetry, and lecture four integrated painting with the other "perfect arts."

20. "The Poet and Painter Compared," *Port Folio* 2, no. 4, 1809, p. 367.

21. "B," "Poetry and Painting," *New-York American*, July 5, 1826.

22. "F," "The Sister Arts; or, Poetry, Painting, and Sculpture," *American Monthly Magazine* 7 (October 1856): 297–98.

23. "Sister Arts," *Crayon* 3 (October 1856): 297–98.

24. "Painting and Poetry," *Crayon* 3 (December 1856): 361–63.

25. John Blake White, "An Essay on the Moral Excellence of Painting and showing The superiority of its powers over those of Poetry," manuscript, Charleston, South Carolina Historical Society, March 9, 1832.

26. See J. A. Leo LeMay, *A Calendar of American Poetry in the Colonial Newspapers and Magazines and in the Major English Magazines Through 1765* (Worcester, Massachusetts: American Antiquarian Society, 1972). LeMay first published Part One of this study in the Society's *Bulletin* in 1970, 291–392.

27. [Mather Byles], "To Mr. Smibert on the sight of his Pictures," *American Weekly Mercury* (Philadelphia), February 10–19, 1730. The poem was reprinted in London in the *Daily Courant*, April 14, 1730. Byles's poem, in turn, provoked a satirical response by Byles's contemporary, Joseph Green, "To Mr. B—, occasioned by his verses to Mr. Smibert on seeing his Pictures," *Boston Gazette,* April 13, 1730. Byles's authorship and the response are discussed in Henry Wilder Foote, *John Smibert Painter* (Cambridge, Massachusetts, Harvard University Press, 1950), 56–57; also see LeMay (1970), 335 and 337, and LeMay, op. cit., 1972, p. 24. Green, in fact, in another poem, referenced one of Smibert's portraits, that of John Checkley (last recorded owner, Mrs. Edmund Gosling, Paget, Bermuda), whose likeness was "now redeemed, by Smibert's skilful hand. . . ." See Samuel L. Knapp, *Biographical Sketches of Eminent Lawyers, Statesmen, etc.* (Boston: Richardson and Lord, 1821), 135.

28. Jessie Poesch, "'In just Lines to trace'—The Colonial Artist, 1700–1776," in Ellen G. Miles, ed., *The Portrait in Eighteenth-Century America* (Newark: University of Delaware Press), 72. Poesch's essay, pp. 61–83, is the definitive study of the poetic encomiums devoted to American Colonial artists.

29. Dr. T. T., "Extempore: On Seeing Mr. Wollaston's Pictures in Annapolis," *Maryland Gazette,* March 15, 1753; Francis Hopkinson, "Verses inscribed to Mr. Wollaston," *American Magazine and Monthly Chronicle of the British Colonies* 1 (October 1758): 607–8. "Dr. T. T." may be Dr. Thomas Thorton, see LeMay, *A Calendar of American Poetry* (1972), 158–59.

30. The poem has been variously ascribed to Hopkinson, a Mr. [William?] Hicks, and to Joseph Shippen, and the subject identified as either Jane Galloway (c. 1757; Historical Society of Pennsylvania, Philadelphia) or, more likely, Rebecca Moore (later, Mrs. William Smith) (c. 1758; Mrs. Meyer De Schaunsee). If the latter, the work may relate to the subject's forthcoming marriage, which took place on June 3, 1758, to William Smith, the editor of the *American Magazine.* See Helmut von Erffa and Allen Staley, *The Paintings of Benjamin West* (New Haven: Yale University Press, 1986), 508, 556.

31. Poesch, "'In Just Lines to Trace,'" p. 73, citing George E. Hastings, *The Life and Works of Francis Hopkinson* (Chicago: University of Chicago Press, 1926), 150–51.

32. Marvin S. Sadik, *Colonial and Federal Portraits at Bowdoin College* (Brunswick, Maine: Bowdoin College Museum of Art, 1966), 49–51. The poem does not appear to be referenced in LeMay (1972).

33. John Beveridge, "Nathaniel Smibert…," *Boston Gazette,* May 2, 1757, quoted in Foote, 258–60. See also LeMay (1972) p. 189.

34. [Probably William Eddis], "To Miss Hallam," *Maryland Gazette,* September 6, 1770; "To Mr. Peale, on his Painting Miss Hallam in the Character of Fidele [Imogen's boyish disguise] in Cymbeline," *Maryland Gazette,* November 7, 1771.

35. [Charles Willson Peale?], "On a Picture of Mrs. P—e," *Maryland Gazette,* April 18, 1771.

36. Crito, "Poet's Corner. To Mr. Charles Peale, on his exquisite and celebrated picture of beauty, addressing itself to insensibility," *Maryland Gazette,* July 8, 1773.

37. Printed in the *Freeman's Journal,* December 4, 1782, quoted in Charles Coleman Sellers, *Charles Willson Peale* (New York: Charles Scribner's Sons, 1969), 107. Sellers quotes all the Peale poems here referenced.

38. Sarah Wentworth Apthorp Morton, the most renowned woman poet of the period, known as the "American Sappho," was painted by Stuart in Philadelphia a number of times in c. 1802-03. The best known and most reproduced likeness is that in the collection of the Worcester Art Museum, Massachusetts. It is more likely, however, that Mrs. Morton was commenting not upon this unfinished work but on one of the two more complete and formal representations in the collections of the Henry Francis Dupont Winterthur Museum, Winterthur, Delaware, or on that in the Museum of Fine Arts, Boston.

39. *New-York American,* March 22, 1821. Morton's better-known poem to her likeness by Stuart, "To Mr. Stuart on his portrait of Mrs. M," was published in Philadelphia in the *Port Folio* in June 1803, part of which reads:

> E'en me, by the enlivening grace arrayed,
> Me, born to linger in affection's shade,
> Hast thou, kind artist, with attraction drest,
> With all that nature in my soul expressed.
> Go on, and may reward thy cares attend,
> The friend of Genius must remain thy friend….

Port Folio 3 (June 1803): 193. See Paul S. Harris, "Gilbert Stuart and a Portrait of Mrs. Sarah Apthorp Morton," *Winterthur Portfolio* 1 (1968): 198–220.

40. See, for example, L. H., "The Speaking Picture, Suggested by Vanderlyn's Portrait of Mrs. Allston, Daughter of Aaron Burr," *Knickerbocker* 13 (May 1839): 417. The best-known poet of the period with those initials was Lucy Hooper. Louisa J. Hall was also well regarded, but I do not know if either was living in Brooklyn in 1839, where the author indicated the poem had been written. Three paintings of Theodosia Burr Alston by Vanderlyn are known (c. 1800, New-York Historical Society; 1802, Yale University Art Gallery; c. 1815, location unknown). She married Joseph Alston and died at sea in 1813; she was never the wife of Vanderlyn's friend and colleague Washington Allston.

41. "The Portrait," *New-York American,* June 6, 1826.

42. Percival (1795–1856) was the state geologist for Connecticut and Wisconsin, and assisted Noah Webster in the production of his dictionary.

43. "The Portrait: an Extract," *Knickerbocker* 7 (April 1831): 384.

44. The best-known American poet of the time with those initials was George Lunt (1803–1885).

45. "G. L.," "Lines to a Portrait of a Roman Girl: by F. Alexander," *Knickerbocker* 8 (July 1836): 29. This painting was not exhibited at the National Academy; the poem may have been inspired by *A Roman Lady—From Life,* exhibited at Harding's Gallery in Boston in May of 1834.

46. For a brilliant exposition of similar contemporary implications of emotion and sensibility in a very different medium, that of marble sculpture, see J. Carson Webster, "Erastus D. Palmer: Problems and Possibilities," *American Art Journal* 4 (November 1972): 34–43.

47. Thekla, "A Portrait," *New Mirror* 1 (April 8, 1843): 7.

48. Emma C. Embury, "A Portrait," *Literary World* 24 (July 1847): 588. Embury was a well-known poet and prose writer whose work figures significantly in the classic anthology by Rufus Wilmot Griswold, *Poets and Poetry of America* (Philadelphia: Carey and Hart, 1842) (see fig. 86). Percival and Lunt are also included in this compilation. In the history of American art, Embury is best known as the author of *American wild flowers in their native haunts* (New York: D. Appleton & Company, 1845; Philadelphia: G. S. Appleton, 1845), with superb chromolithographs by Edwin Whitfield, one of the classics of early American still-life printmaking.

49. The gender of the subject of the poem by "G. G.," "Lines On Seeing the Portrait of a Lost Friend," *Knickerbocker* 13 (April 1839): 308, is unclear. The reference to the "round lips beloved" and "the tranquil breast" suggest that the subject is rather a woman than a man. The reference to a "Lost Friend" might denote a woman author, and if that is the case, then the subject might possibly be male.

50. [George H. Clark], "The Portrait," *Knickerbocker* 52 (July 1858): 70. This may be George Henry Clark (1819–1906), the author of a celebrated biography of Oliver Cromwell (1895).

51. "The Portrait: A Sketch," *Godey's Lady's Book* 4 (June 1832): 276–79. The narrator placed himself in an exhibition in Dublin, not New York

52. "The Portrait," *Knickerbocker* 2 (August 1834): 127–29.

53. Robin-Bolton Smith, *Portrait Miniatures in the National Museum of American Art* (Chicago: University of Chicago Press, 1984), 2. Modern-day studies of American miniatures have generally been limited to collection catalogues. See also Martha R. Severens, *The Miniature Portrait Collection of the Carolina Art*

Association (Charleston: Gibbes Art Gallery, 1984); Susan E. Strickler, *American Portrait Miniatures: The Worcester Art Museum Collection* (Worcester, Massachusetts: Worcester Art Museum, 1989); Dale T. Johnson, *American Portrait Miniatures in the Manney Collection* (New York: Metropolitan Museum of Art, 1990). The fullest bibliography on American miniature painting can be found in Johnson, pp. 249–57.

54. "The Miniature," *Atkinson's Casket* 6 (April 1831): 153–56.

55. "Lines Suggested by a Miniature," *New-York Mirror* 11 (October 12, 1833): 116.

56. "The Disfigured Miniature," in Caroline Gilman, *Tales and Ballads* (Boston: William Crosby & Company, 1839), 150. Gilman may have been especially drawn to a consideration of miniatures because, though Boston-born, she had settled in Charleston, South Carolina, where the city's most eminent artist was the miniature specialist Charles Fraser. During the 1830s, Gilman edited the *Southern Rosebud,* one of the first children's papers in the United States.

57. George P. Morris, "The Miniature," *Atkinson's Casket* 6 (August 1831): 360; reprinted in George P. Morris, *The Deserted Bride; and Other Poems* (New York: Adlard & Saunders, 1838), 48. A well-known poet, Morris was even more celebrated as the founder and editor of the weekly newspapers the *New-York Mirror* and later the *Home Journal.*

58. "The Miniature," *Knickerbocker* 5 (May 1833): 284.

59. *Poetic Thoughts, with Pictures* (Philadelphia: J. B. Lippincott Company, 1886). The poems introduced here were not inspired by the paintings by artists such as George Lambdin and William Trost Richards, but were pertinently, if rather randomly, chosen from literature by American and English poets such as Bryant, Longfellow, and Wordsworth. In the single case of Russell Smith's Welsh landscape, *Fernrock,* the artist also provided the two-stanza verse.

60. Gilder met de Kay in May of 1872; since he states in the poem that the picture was painted prior to his acquaintance with the subject, the painting must date from before then. De Kay and Gilder became engaged in November of 1873 and married on June 4, 1874. See Thayer C. Tolles, "Helena de Kay Gilder: Her Role in the New Movement," (M. A. thesis, Newark, University of Delaware, 1990) 8–12.

61. Richard Watson Gilder, *The New Day* (New York: Century Company, 1875), 19. This poem figures in the discussion by Joseph Stanton, "Winslow Homer, Helena de Kay, and Richard Watson Gilder: Posing a Rivalry of Forms," *Harvard Library Bulletin* 5 (Summer 1994): 51–72. The author here conjectures the exceedingly unlikely scenario of Homer's romantic interest in de Kay and rivalry with Gilder, even projecting the possibility of Homer adopting portraiture as a professional pursuit in order to support a family with de Kay! My thanks to Abigail Booth Gerdts, director of the Winslow Homer Catalogue Raisonné, for sharing her material and thoughts on this picture.

CATALOGUE

OF THE

EXHIBITION

NOTES TO THE READER

Works of art in this catalogue and the exhibition that it accompanies were selected based on the critical response that they received at the time of their first public exhibition, which, for many, occurred in the annual exhibitions of the National Academy of Design. As the title of this book implies, most of these works received positive criticism; but some that received primarily negative reviews have also been included. Availability for loan to the current exhibition also influenced selection.

Each entry begins with the artist's name, dates, and places of birth and death, followed by information taken verbatim from the catalogue for the National Academy of Design's annual exhibition in which the work first appeared, including:

- title of the work of art, if it differs from the title in current usage
- number and dates of the exhibition
- object entry number
- owner's name, if indicated

When the object illustrated is not the actual one that debuted at the Academy between 1826 and 1925, but a reasonable substitute for it (a preparatory study, a replica, another version of the same subject by the same artist or, in the case of sculpture, another cast of the same conception), the title of the work is marked with the symbol §.

Measurements are cited in inches, height preceding width.

Abbreviations used in the catalogue footnotes and appendix:

AAA	Archives of American Art, Smithsonian Institution, Washington, D.C.
AAm	Art Amateur
HW	Harper's Weekly
IS	International Studio
LW	Literary World
NAD	National Academy of Design
NYCA	New York Commercial Advertiser
NYDG	New York Daily Graphic
NYDT	New York Daily Tribune
NYEM	New York Evening Mail
NYEP	New York Evening Post
NYET	New York Evening Telegram
NYH	New York Herald
NYL	New York Leader
NYM	New-York Mirror
NYS	New York Sun
NYT	New-York Times

Catalogue entry authors are identified as follows:

DBD	David B. Dearinger
TAG	Trudie A. Grace
AH	Andrea Husby
SK	Sarah Kelly
MM	Mark Mitchell
ZR	Zachary Ross

1

William Dunlap, NA

Perth Amboy, New Jersey 1766–1839 New York, New York

Scene from the Novel of the "Spy," 1st Annual Exhibition,
May 14–July 16, 1826, no. 99

The Detection of Harry Wharton in Disguise, by Jack Lawton.
From James Fennimore Cooper's "Spy," 6th Annual
Exhibition, April 28–July 9, 1831, no. 24, for sale

Scene from Cooper's "The Spy," 1823–24

Oil on canvas, 22 × 27

New York State Historical Association, Cooperstown, New York

William Dunlap was best known as a history painter and portraitist. The thirteen works he sent to the National Academy of Design's first annual exhibition in 1826 included five portraits, a sketch of a biblical painting by Benjamin West, and four studies for an original, monumental exhibition piece called *Christ on Mount Calvary*.[1] Of these, the religious paintings received the most critical attention. This is not surprising, given the taste at the time for didactic images with clear, familiar moralizing lessons. Another work Dunlap showed that year, however, also received some attention. This was his *Scene from Cooper's "The Spy,"* which, as a literary-genre image, was a rare excursion for Dunlap.[2]

Dunlap's choice of subject here is easily explained: besides being a painter, he was also a playwright and theatrical historian. As such, he was part of the New York-based Knickerbocker circle of literary figures that included William Cullen Bryant, Washington Irving, and James Fenimore Cooper. The writings of all of these men served as major sources of inspiration for American artists during the first half of the nineteenth century. Cooper's second novel, *The Spy*, which was published in 1821, is a historical romance written in the style of Sir Walter Scott and set during the American Revolution. As the catalogues for the National Academy's 1826 and 1831 exhibitions clarify, Dunlap chose to illustrate the moment when the disguised Harry Wharton is detected by Jack Lawton, who says to him, "Now, Sir, my principal business being done, may I beg to examine the quality of that wig." Dunlap later remembered the circumstances of his creation of this image. On December 1, 1823, he rented a room at the corner of Nassau and Pine streets in New York and there, during the subsequent winter, painted his scene from *The Spy*. "I had recently become acquainted with [Cooper]," he

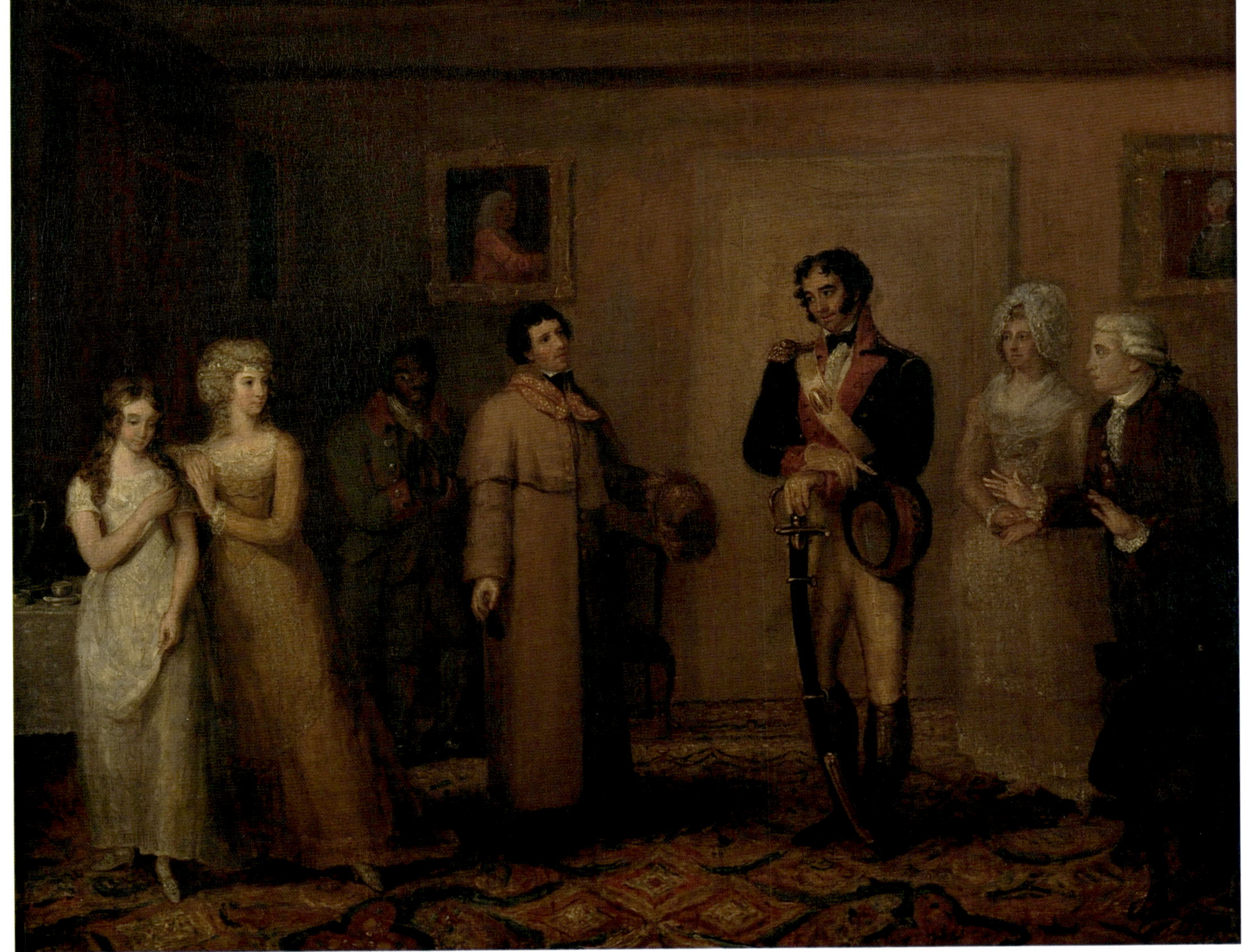

wrote, "and acquaintance has ripened into friendship."[3] He may also have seen the play by Charles P. Clinch based on the novel, which opened in New York to some success in March 1822 and was revived occasionally thereafter, at least into the 1860s.[4]

There was little published criticism of the Academy's first annual exhibition, but one periodical noticed and appreciated Dunlap's efforts with *The Spy*. This was the *New-York Mirror*, which found the painting "very pleasing" and saw it as evidence that Dunlap's "industry appears to be equal to his talents."[5] Evidently, the painting made enough of an impression on the Academicians that it was shown again at the Academy in 1831, on the occasion of the organization's one and only retrospective exhibition.   DBD

1. For at least one journalist, the group of paintings proved Dunlap's versatility, industry, and "variety of invention" (*NYEP*, April 28, 1831).

2. The painting, or perhaps another version of it, actually debuted at the American Academy of Fine Arts in 1824 under the title *A scene from the celebrated novel of the Spy. Jack Lawton detecting Harry Wharton in disguise* (Cowdrey, *American Academy of Fine Arts and American Art-Union Exhibition Record*, 119).

3. William Dunlap, *History of the Rise and Progress of the Arts of Design* (New York: George P. Scott & Co., 1834), 1:293.

4. Joseph N. Ireland, *Records of the New York Stage from 1750 to 1860*, 2 vols. (New York, 1866–1867), 1: 399; and Richard Moody, *America Takes the Stage* (Bloomington: Indiana University Press, 1955), 144. I wish to thank Kevin Lane Dearinger for these citations.

5. "The NAD," *NYM* 3 (June 10, 1826): 366–67.

2

Henry Inman, NA
Utica, New York 1801–1846 New York, New York

Full Length Portrait of Mr. Macready in the Character of Wm. Tell, 2nd Annual Exhibition, May 6–July 16, 1827, no. 4, for sale

Portrait of Macready, 3rd Annual Exhibition, May 6–July 10, 1828, no. 80

Full Length of Mr. M'Cready, in the character of Wm. Tell, 6th Annual Exhibition, April 28–July 9, 1831, no. 32, owner C. Edwards

William Charles Macready as William Tell, 1826–27 §
Oil on canvas, 30 × 25

The Metropolitan Museum of Art, New York, Rogers Fund, 1906

Henry Inman's full-length portrait of the English actor William Charles Macready (1793–1873), painted around 1827 and now lost but known from an engraving by Asher B. Durand, was his earliest life-size, full-length portrait. It was also the first major work Inman exhibited at the National Academy of Design and, as such, established his reputation as one of this country's leading artists.[1]

In the Academy's first annual, of 1826, Inman was represented by eleven portraits of unidentified ladies and gentlemen, probably all of which were bust-length images; a copy of a painting by George Morland; and a historic work called *Death of Mohegan* (location unknown). The following year he showed far fewer works (three), of which the portrait of Macready was certainly the most impressive in both size and subject matter. In 1828, Inman sent another image of Macready to the Academy—the painting now in the collection of the Metropolitan Museum of Art. In 1831, the full-length portrait was shown again in the Academy's retrospective exhibition.

Macready, who was best known for his dramatic portrayals of characters such as Orestes, William Tell, and Macbeth, was on the first of three visits to the United States when Inman painted his portrait.[2] Inman took Macready's likeness from life, producing the painting now at the Metropolitan, which he then expanded into the more imaginative full-length.[3] He chose to show the actor as he appeared in the scene from the play by James Sheridan Knowles during which Tell is arrested and incarcerated in the castle of Küssnacht.[4] Details, such as the shackles and the castle itself, that help to tell the story, are features of Inman's full-length version, but the emotion of the character—his anger and defiance—are apparent in both it and the smaller version.

The fact that Inman's portrait of Macready announced the painter as a major figure in American art was made clear by Samuel F. B. Morse's review of the National Academy's annual exhibition of 1827. The painting, Morse wrote, "would do credit to a more practised artist; there are here to be discovered the elements of a great painter, which persevering industry and study will surely mature." Having said that, Morse then took on the role of mentor by advising the younger Inman to give more attention to detail in his paintings. Morse noted that the upper part of the figure showed energy and expression, but the lower part seemed weak and "too feminine."[5] This was undoubtedly the result of Inman's having painted the bust from life and then having relied on memory or other means to create the rest of the figure. In fact, this was a criticism shared by others. A writer for the *New-York Mirror*, probably its editor George Pope Morris, praised Macready's face, which, he thought, "glows with all the fire and expression of the original." The rest of the body, however, especially the legs, was painted "in an unpardonably careless style."[6]

Inman did what he could to make certain that the favorable press that he had received for his Macready portrait did not evaporate. In 1828, he sent the full-length version of the painting to the annual exhibition of the Boston Athenaeum;[7] and to make sure New Yorkers did not forget him, he sent the life study he had made for the painting to the Academy's annual. Excitement over it—and over Inman as a rising star—was thus maintained. Favorable notice continued in journals such as the *New-York Mirror*, which reported that the smaller Macready portrait "possesses the same traits of faithful and spirited resemblance of the [full-length]; but has evidently been finished with a bolder and more rapid pencil."[8]

When Inman's full-length of Macready returned to the Academy in 1831, it joined a small but impressive group of life-size historical portraits shown that year. These included Samuel Morse's portrait of Lafayette (no. 3) and Inman's own of Martin Van Buren (1830; City of New York, City Hall Portrait Collection). The Academy's hanging committee placed Inman's *Macready* next to Charles Cromwell Ingham's portrait of an elegant young woman (no. 6). The contrast of the two images was not lost on the critics. The *New-York Mirror*, for example, compared the "fierce and lofty" attitude of Macready with the "seducing vision of female loveliness" of *The White Plume*, which the writer felt, was "as soft and soothing as the other is vehement and ferocious."[9]

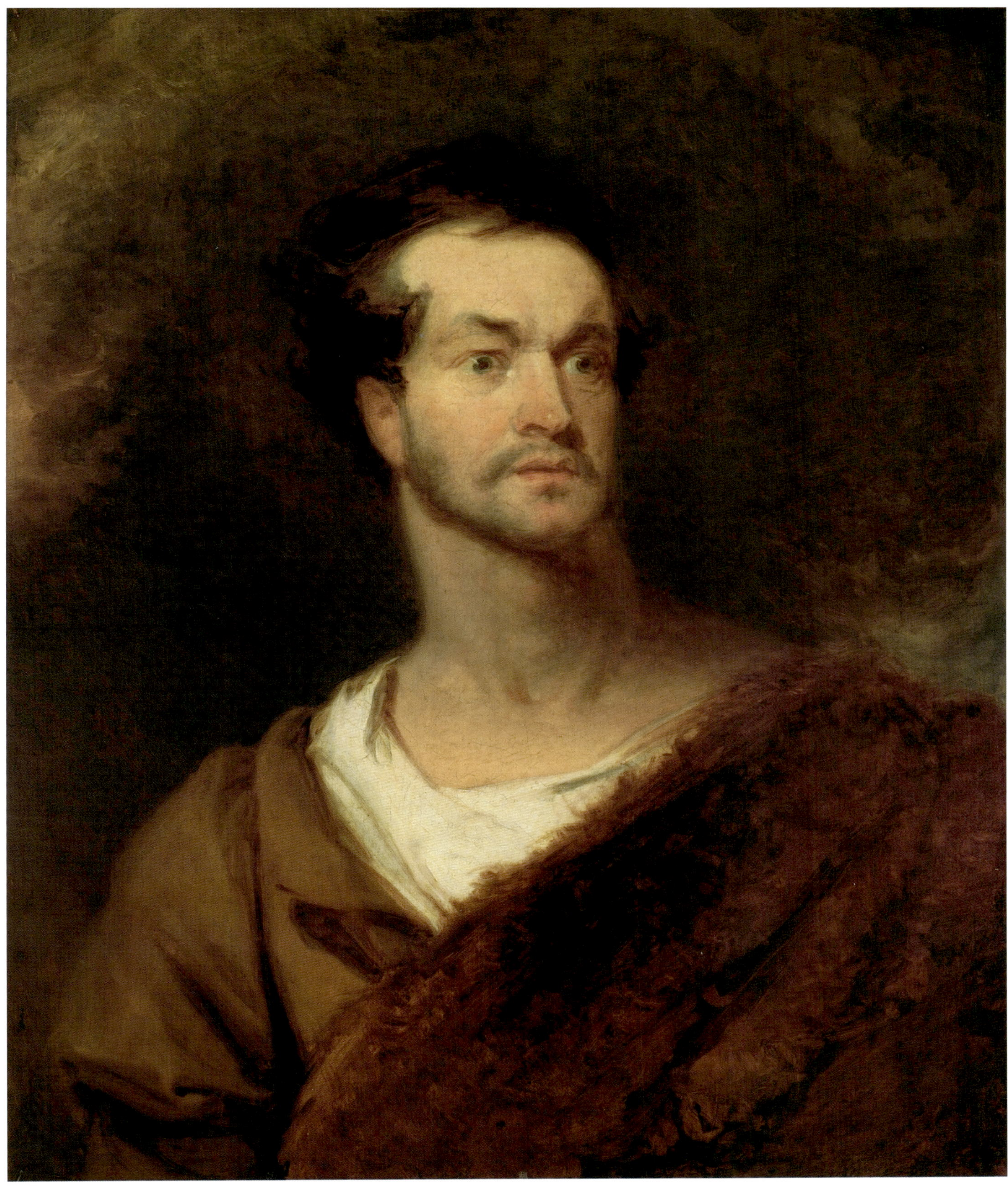

2

For his part, Inman was credited with adding "greatly to the splendour of the exhibition."[10] His *Macready* was said to be "full of fire," and he was praised for capturing the actor's "haughty grandeur of attitude, and the fierce and lofty hate glaring from his features."[11] The awkwardness of the figure that was so apparent to the critics of 1827 seems to have gone unnoticed in 1831; but by that time, Inman had firmly established himself as New York's most innovative and accomplished portraitist.[12]   DBD

1. William H. Gerdts, *The Art of Henry Inman* (Washington, D.C.: The National Portrait Gallery, 1987): 34.

2. Carrie Rebora, catalogue entry in Gerdts, *Art of Henry Inman*, 64.

3. One of these was the sculptor John I. H. Bowere, who printed a handbill excoriating the painting. Writing under the name of Middle-Tint, he told his readers that, while the head in Inman's portrait resembled Macready, the neck, trunk, and legs were not his. Thomas Cummings, who reprinted this handbill in his *Historic Annals of the National Academy of Design* (Philadelphia: George W. Childs, Publishers, 1865), rejoined that the "future reputation of Inman showed how false the critic's conclusions, or how greatly mistaken public opinion" (78).

4. Oswaldo Rodriguez Roque, "Henry Inman," in John Caldwell and Oswaldo Rodriguez Roque, *American Paintings in the Metropolitan Museum of Art* 1 (New York: Metropolitan Museum of Art, 1994): 451.

5. [Samuel F. B. Morse], "Review. *The Exhibition of the NAD*," *United States Review and Literary Gazette* 2 (July 1827): 248.

6. [George Pope Morris?], "The Fine Arts. NAD," *NYM* 4 (June 2, 1827): 354.

7. Robert F. Perkins, Jr., and William J. Gavin III, *The Boston Athenaeum Art Exhibition Index 1827–1874* (Boston: The Library of the Boston Athenaeum, 1980), 84.

8. *NYM* 5 (May 24, 1828): 367.

9. "The Fine Arts. NAD," *NYM* 8 (May 7, 1831): 350.

10. Apollo, "The NAD," *NYEP*, May 7, 1831.

11. "NAD," *NYM* 8 (May 7, 1831): 350.

12. Gerdts, 37.

3

Samuel F. B. Morse, NA

Charlestown, Massachusetts 1791–1872 New York, New York

Full Length Portrait of Gen. Lafayette, the Property of the Corporation of the City of New-York, 2nd Annual Exhibition, May 14–July 16, 1827, no. 2

General la Fayette, Full Length, 6th Annual Exhibition, April 28–July 9, 1831, no. 8, owner Common Council

Marquis de Lafayette, 1825 §

Oil on canvas, 30 × 25
Collection of The New York Public Library, Astor, Lenox, and Tilden Foundations

As the founder and first president of the National Academy of Design, Samuel F. B. Morse was active in all of the organization's affairs during the first several decades of its existence. This included sending an average of four or five works per year to each of its annual exhibitions from 1826 through 1837. While the majority of these works were portraits, he also exhibited genre and literary scenes, landscapes, and large historical paintings. In the last category was his *House of Representatives* (see fig. 30), which was in the Academy's annual of 1827. Also in that exhibition was Morse's life-size, full-length portrait of the Marquis de Lafayette (City Hall, New York), and the pair undoubtedly made it clear that Morse, the president of the nascent National Academy of Design, was the right man for the job.

The circumstances surrounding the commissioning of Morse's life-size image of Lafayette have been detailed elsewhere.[1] Briefly stated, the project was initiated by the Common Council of New York City in 1825 to honor General Lafayette, who, at the time, was on his famous final American tour. The commission was the most coveted one of its kind, and Morse's victory established him as a leader among American artists. In February 1825, he departed for Washington, D.C., where, over the next several weeks, Lafayette sat for the oil study that is now in the collection of the New York Public Library. Morse eventually took the study back to New York, where he used it to develop the full-length portrait, the work unveiled to the public at the National Academy of Design's 1827 exhibition.

That year Morse himself wrote a lengthy review of the National Academy's exhibition. It was published, anonymously, by his friend William Cullen Bryant, who was then editor of the *United States Review and Literary Gazette* (see the essay "Annual Exhibitions and the Birth of American Art Criticism to 1865" in this book). This bit of historical conflict-of-interest provides an opportunity to read Morse's assessment of his own painting, one that, ultimately, is fair, if somewhat defensive. Morse began the discussion of his *Lafayette* by stating that he was pleased with its "conception." After describing the work, he admitted that the execution of the painting was "not so highly finished as it might be." He explained this by recounting that the artist (he was speaking of himself, of course) "had only three sittings of the General . . . the completion being prevented by a most sudden domestic calamity to the artist, which called him immediately home. . . ." The reference is to the sudden death of Morse's wife. Overcoming that tragedy, he succeeded in completing the oil study. Back in New York, however, he found it difficult to catch more than a glimpse of the busy Lafayette, who, Morse remembered, "was almost *fêté* to death." The artist *qua* critic summed up the rest of the story:

> *The execution of the picture was thus necessarily delayed, the time passed, a succession of domestic losses [the deaths of his parents] repeatedly interrupted the artist, the hour at which it was engaged to be finished arrived, the corporation pressed him, and he found himself obliged to finish it with a haste unworthy of his talents. It is only to be wondered at that, under such circumstances, and with so limited opportunity, he was able to do so much.*[2]

Whatever Morse may have thought of his painting, it was a success, at least if we measure it in its effect on potential patrons: it led to several other important portrait commissions.[3] Not everyone was pleased with it, however, even after it became part of New York's visual fabric. In 1831, when it was sent back to the Academy for the institution's one and only retrospective exhibition, a writer for the *New-York Mirror,* possibly its editor George Pope Morris, praised the subject, but damned the painting. "It is to be regretted . . . ," he stated without apology, "that the painting is not worthy the reputation of the president of the academy."[4]

DBD

1. See Edward Lind Morse, ed., *Samuel F. B. Morse, His Letters and Journals,* 2 vols. (Boston and New York: Houghton Mifflin Company, 1914), 1: 259–74; Paul J. Staiti, "Samuel F. B. Morse and the Search for the Grand Style," in Grey Art Gallery and Study Center, New York University, *Samuel F. B. Morse* (New York, 1982), 50–54; William Kloss, *Samuel F. B. Morse* (New York: Harry N. Abrams, Inc., 1988), 94–96.

2. [Samuel F. B. Morse], "Review," *United States Review and Literary Gazette* 2 (July 1827): 247–48.

3. Staiti, 54.

4. "The Fine Arts. NAD. Second Notice," *NYM* 8 (May 14, 1831): 358.

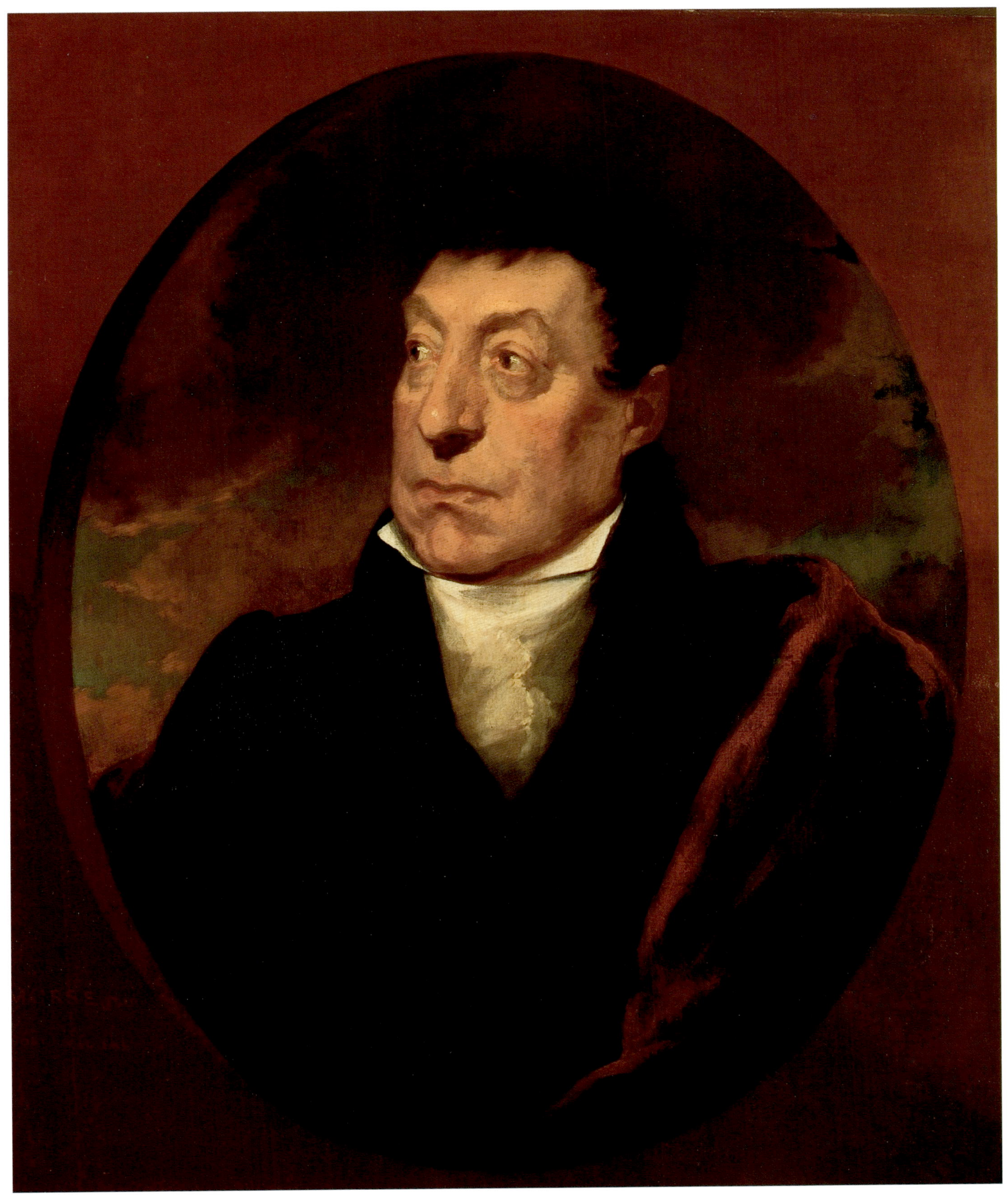

3

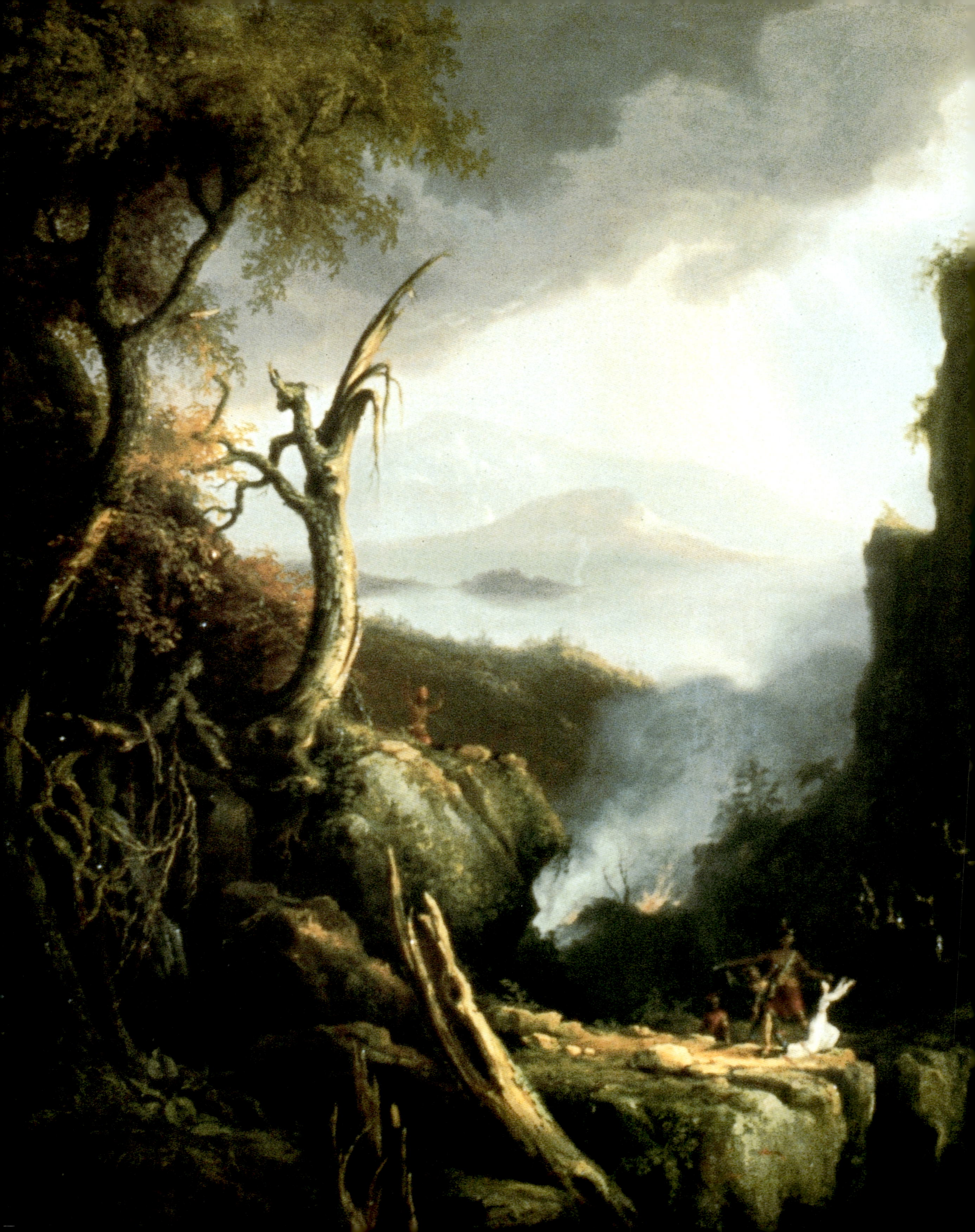

4

Thomas Cole, NA

Lancashire, England 1801–Catskill, New York 1848

Landscape, scene from "The Last of the Mohicans", 2nd Annual Exhibition, May 6–July 16, 1827, no. 11

The Last of the Mohicans, 6th Annual Exhibition, April 28–July 9, 1831, no. 10, owner Doctor Hosack

Last of the Mohicans, 1827

Oil on canvas, 36 × 48

Annenberg Rare Book and Manuscript Library, University of Pennsylvania, Philadelphia

As a founding member of the National Academy, Thomas Cole was an active participant in its early exhibitions. Between 1826 and the year of his death, he sent works to all but one (1839) of the Academy's annuals. For the first, in 1826, he sent three landscapes; but the following year he sent a larger and slightly more varied selection consisting of four pure landscapes and two historical ones. The latter were *St. John in the Wilderness* (1827; Wadsworth Atheneum) and *The Last of the Mohicans.* Of these six paintings, *St. John* received the most critical attention and together with *The Last of the Mohicans* made a pair of paintings—one with a theme from religious history, the other from American history—that impressed contemporaries as being clear evidence of Cole's genius.

Typically, the reviews of Cole's *Mohicans* were positive but cautious. For example, Samuel Morse, although he was not willing to deify Cole quite yet, noted, in the *United States Review and Literary Gazette,* Cole's "fine feeling for the picturesque, and good management of *chiaro oscuro.*"[1] It was generally agreed that Cole's talents were best used when he stayed close to nature; adding tiny figures to paintings, as he did in *The Last of the Mohicans,* only "deformed the noble landscape," according to a writer for the *New-York Mirror.*[2] Morse thought that, although the figures were nicely subordinated to their surroundings, they were badly drawn.[3]

Despite these opinions, Cole, like many of his contemporaries, felt that, when possible, a painting should be more than a picturesque view of familiar terrain. Art could fulfill its traditional purpose to teach and inspire by having a historical or literary source that would furnish the requisite moralizing lesson. To further this agenda, Cole saw to it that the catalogue for the Academy's 1827 exhibition included a rather lengthy quotation from James Fenimore Cooper's novel *The Last of the Mohicans.* The passage helps clarify the particular moment from the story that is being depicted: the attack on Cora Munro that eventually leads to her death and the deaths of several native Americans. The public responded favorably to the painting, and by July it had been bought by Dr. David Hosack.[4] The Academicians, too,

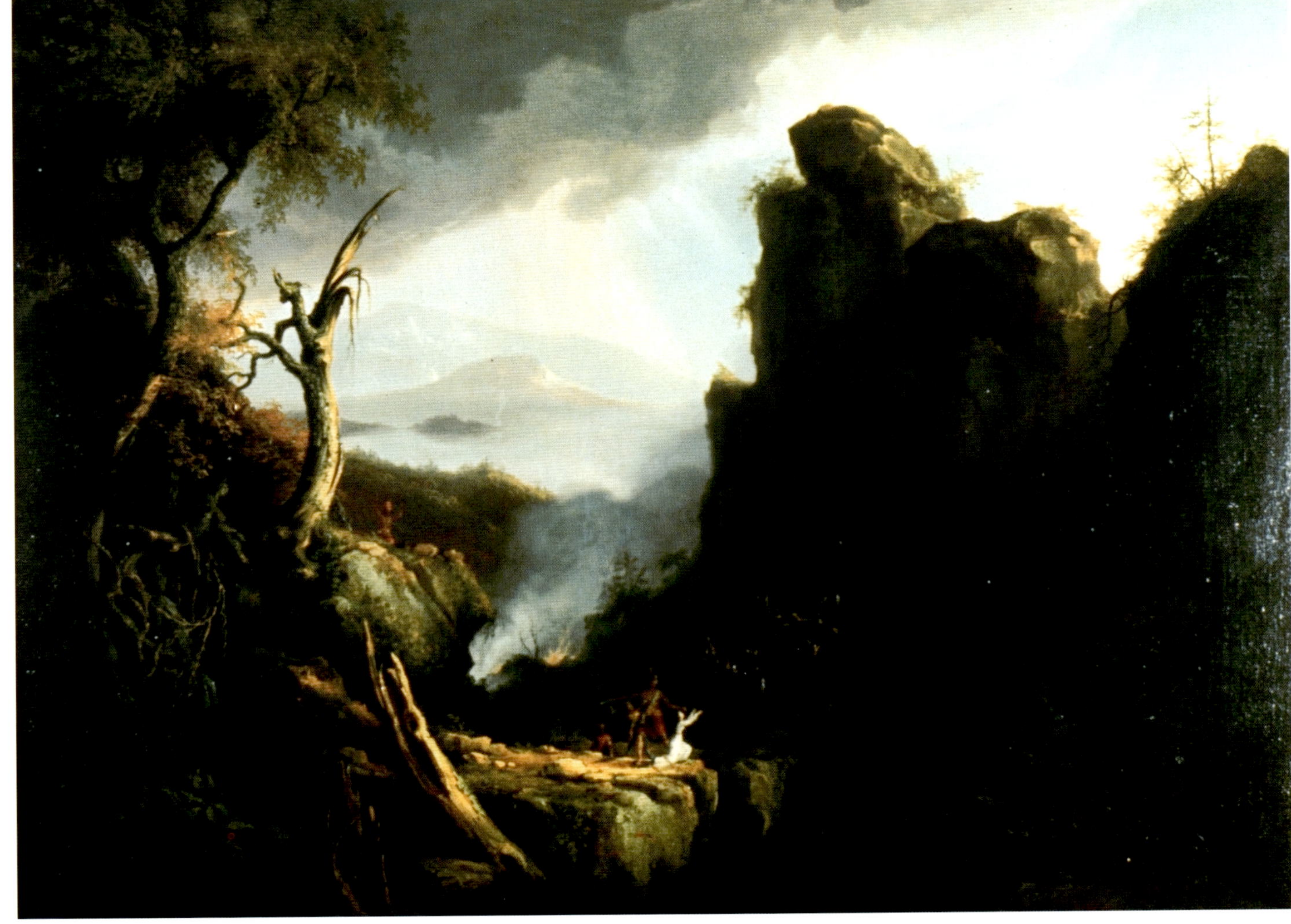

seem to have thought well of it for they included it in the annual of 1831, a retrospective exhibition of works from the five previous annuals.   DBD

1. [Samuel F. B. Morse], "Review. *The Exhibition of the NAD, 1827,*" *United States Review and Literary Gazette* 2 (July 1827): 250.
2. "The Fine Arts. NAD," *NYM* 4 (June 2, 1827): 354.
3. [Samuel F. B. Morse], "Review," *United States Review and Literary Gazette* 2 (July 1827): 232–33.
4. *United States Review and Literary Gazette* (July 1827) reported that the painting was "now in the possession of one, who has not only the means, but, we believe, the disposition, to encourage native talent."

5

Samuel F. B. Morse, NA

Charlestown, Massachusetts 1791–1872 New York, New York

Una and the Dwarf Relating the capture of the Redcross Knight to Prince Arthur and His Squire. (Illustration of Spencer's Fairy Queen, *1st Bk., 7th Canto.),* 3rd Annual Exhibition, May 6–July 10, 1828, no. 10

Scene from Spencer's 'Fairie Queene':
Una and the Dwarf, 1826–27

Oil on wood, 26⁵⁄₁₆ × 42⁷⁄₈

The Toledo Museum of Art, Toledo, Ohio; Purchased with funds from the Florence Scott Libbey Bequest in Memory of her Father, Maurice A. Scott

In 1828, the year after the debut of his *Lafayette,* Samuel F. B. Morse sent *Una and the Dwarf,* one of his rare genre-literary images, to the National Academy's annual exhibition. The artist took his subject from Book I of Edmund Spenser's epic poem *The Faerie Queene* (1590). Here, Prince Arthur consults with Una, whose lover, the Red Cross Knight, is being held prisoner by a giant. The Knight's servant—the dwarf of the title—points toward the castle in which his master is incarcerated. The theme is one of loyalty and undying devotion (Una's and the dwarf's) and heroism (the Prince's). Morse's interpretation was one of thirteen landscapes and historical subjects commissioned from seven artists, including Asher B. Durand and Thomas Cole, by members of the Stevens family of Hoboken, New Jersey. The father, John Stevens (d. 1838), and his two sons, Robert Livingston Stevens (1787–1856) and James Alexander Stevens (1790–1873), operated steamboat lines that ran vessels between New York and Philadelphia and up the Hudson. The paintings were commissioned to decorate the *Albany,* which was soon to be the latest addition to the fleet.[1] To Morse and his contemporaries, the use of thematically advanced paintings to decorate a steamboat must have seemed a very modern, and even a very American, thing to do. Morse indicated as much in a letter to his mother, written in May 1826, in which he called the project "a new and noble channel for the encouragement of painting."[2] In early March of the following year, the *New York Evening Post* announced the completion of Morse's contribution to the project.[3]

Shortly after it was finished, and presumably as he waited for the *Albany* to be completed, Morse sent *Una and the Dwarf* to the National Academy's annual exhibition. It received a comparatively lengthy and mostly positive critique in the *New York*

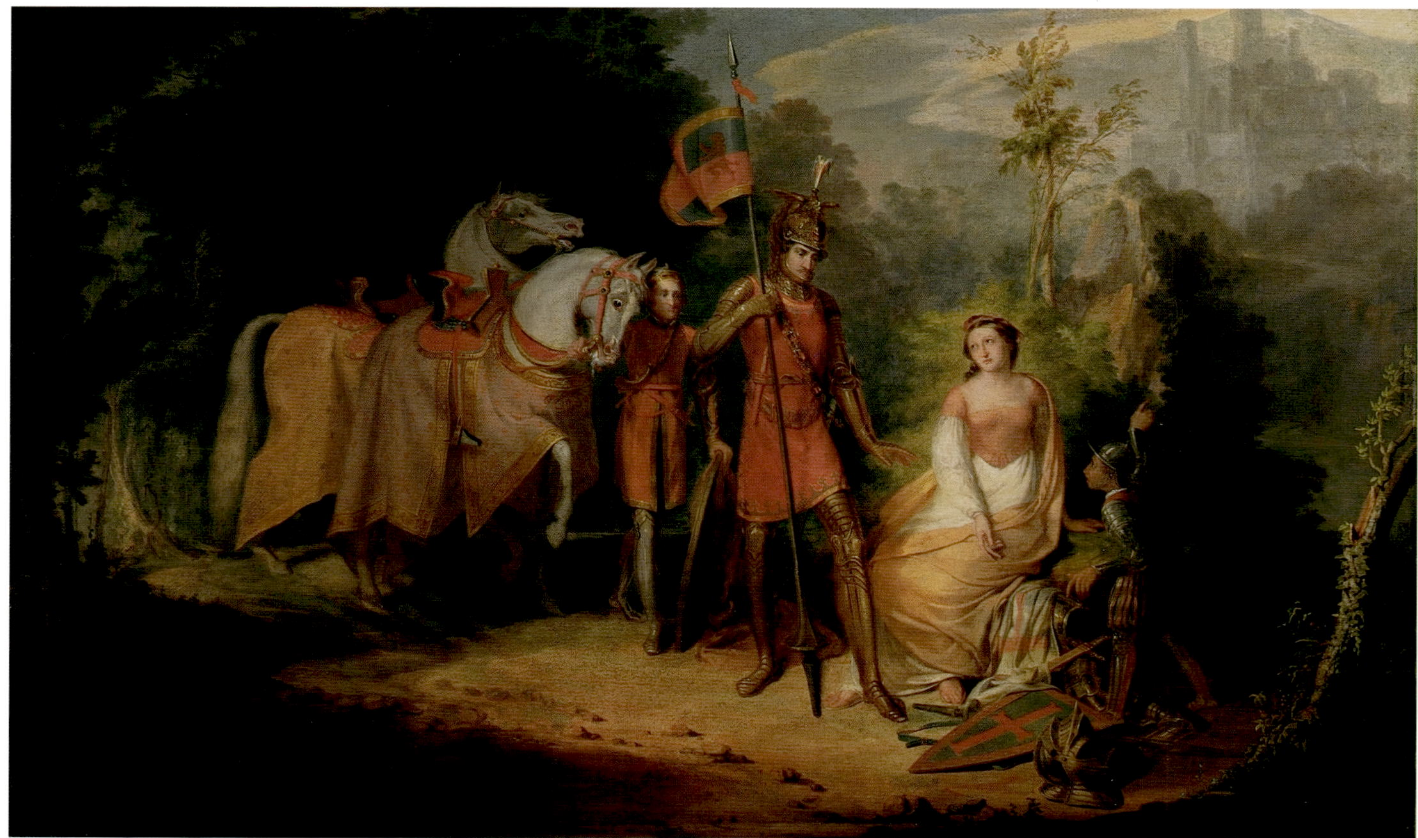

5

Morning Courier. The author of that review was sculptor John I. H. Bowere, writing under the name of Middle-Tint. In that guise, Bowere could be among the most caustic of critics. Nevertheless, he thought Morse's painting was the "best poetic delineation ever made" by the artist and called it "well drawn, spiritedly handled, and beautifully colored." While he found the legs of the Prince to be too long, he admired the effective juxtaposition of the dwarf and the "mild, unassuming" Una. In closing, he advised Morse to seek inspiration from the old masters; in that way, he could raise his already admirable art to the level of the American masters Gilbert Stuart, Washington Allston, Charles Robert Leslie, and Thomas Sully.[4]   DBD

1. *Appleton's Cyclopedia of American Biography,* 5: 673–75. The Stevenses made significant contributions to the scientific advance of shipping technology. They were also active in the railroad business.
2. Samuel F. B. Morse to Elizabeth A. Morse, May 10, 1826, quoted in Edward Lind Morse, ed., *Samuel F. B. Morse: His Letters and Journals* (Boston: Houghton Mifflin Company, 1914), 1:289.
3. "Morse's New Picture," *NYEP,* March 2, 1827.
4. [John I. H. Bowere], "Middle-Tint on the Works of Living Artists, at the NAD. No. 4," *New York Morning Courier,* June 18, 1828.

6

Charles Cromwell Ingham, NA

Dublin, Ireland 1796–1863 New York, New York

The White Plume, 3rd Annual Exhibition, May 6–July 10, 1828, no. 40

The White Plume, 6th Annual Exhibition, April 28–July 9, 1831, no. 31[1]

Asher Brown Durand (1796–1886)

after Charles Cromwell Ingham

The White Plume, c. 1830 §

Engraving, 4½ × 3⅜
Print Collection, Miriam and Ira D. Wallach Division of Art, Prints and Photographs, The New York Public Library, Astor, Lenox and Tilden Foundations

Of all the works portraitist Charles Cromwell Ingham sent to the National Academy of Design's annual exhibitions between its inception in 1826 and his death in 1863, *The White Plume* was probably the best known and the most highly regarded. Although the painting is now unlocated, it is known from an engraving, shown here, made by Asher Brown Durand, the leading engraver of the day and Ingham's friend and fellow founder of the Academy.

The White Plume is undoubtedly a portrait—as opposed to an ideal work, as its rather evocative title might suggest—and it was referred to by contemporary writers as such. One source identified the sitter as a Jane Ricker Lawrence, later Mrs. Benjamin F. Lee.[2] Whoever Ingham's sitter was, it is likely that he idealized her to some degree. By giving her a romantic costume and setting, and by giving the painting its fanciful title, Ingham implies a possible literary source. In fact, at least one contemporary source thought that *The White Plume* had been inspired by Lord Byron's poem *Don Juan.*[3]

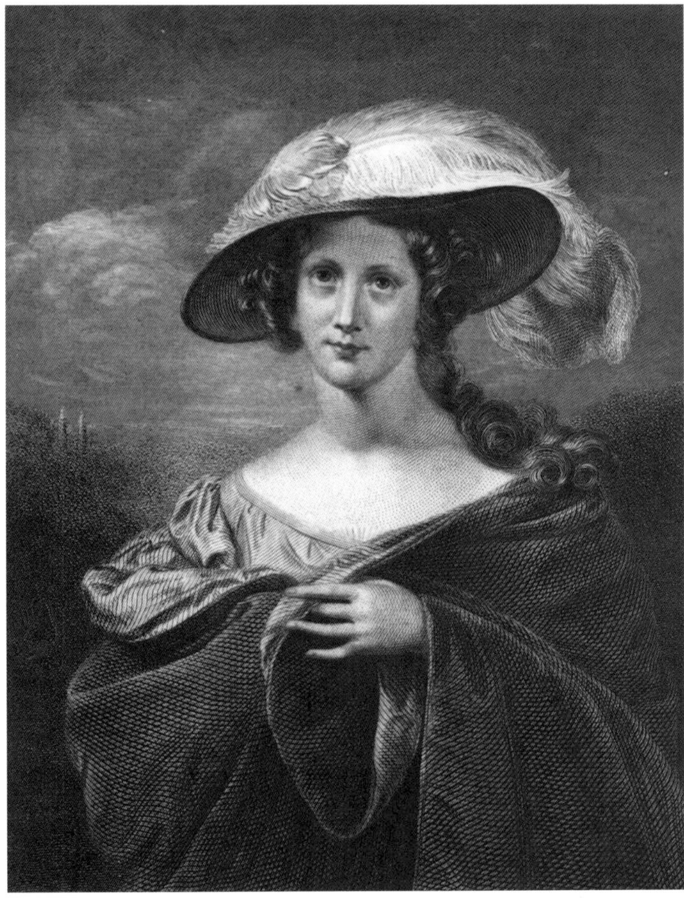

6

From the time of its debut at the National Academy in 1828, *The White Plume* gained Ingham "great applause," as William Dunlap put it.[4] A critic for the *New-York Mirror* called it "most attractive" and was particularly struck by the figure's eyes. These, he observed, have "a glassy brightness and rotundity, that makes it difficult to believe them mere painted counterfeits; the spectator can almost see them move, and reads in them an expression of thought, a light of soul, that the pencil has seldom succeeded in mimicking so closely."[5]

More praise came in 1831 when the painting was again shown at the Academy. *The New York Evening Post* reported that *The White Plume* was among a handful of paintings that drew "the admiration of all" that year,[6] while the *New-York Mirror* continued its earlier praise of the work. Although that journal's critic thought there were too many portraits in the show, he encouraged portrait painters to follow the examples of Ingham and Henry Inman in painting "public men or beautiful women." He was especially impressed with Inman's portraits of William Charles Macready (no. 2) and Martin Van Buren and Ingham's *The White Plume,* all of which were in the 1831 show. He envied Van Buren, whose portrait hung opposite *The White Plume,* because the politician "from one week's end to another, does nothing but look" at her "dangerous" eyes. "It is a seducing vision of female loveliness," he continued,

as soft and soothing as the other is vehement and ferocious. The shadow of a graceful bonnet never fell on a countenance more radiant and beautiful. How perfectly unclouded the features; how lightly the tresses repose on the soft shoulder; what a brilliancy of complexion; a mouth which you wish to fold your arms and gaze on forever, instead of going back to bargaining and business; and the eyes blue and beaming....[7]

After the Academy's exhibition closed, Ingham sent *The White Plume* to exhibitions in Boston and Philadelphia.[8] At the latter venue, the painting encountered a rare dissenter, the entrepreneur and writer Frances Trollope. When Mrs. Trollope wrote her infamous *Domestic Manners of the Americans* (1832), she remembered the painting. Although she recalled that it had been a highly admired work, Mrs. Trollope complained that "the drawing is very defective, and the contour, though the face is a lovely one, hard and unfleshy." She then used the portrait to criticize generally Americans' lack of artistic taste and knowledge. "From all the conversations on painting, which I listened to in America," she wrote, "I found, that the finish of drapery was considered of the highest excellence, and next to this, the resemblance in a portrait; I do not remember ever to have heard the words *drawing* or *composition* used in any conversation on the subject."[9]

None of the catalogues of the various exhibitions in which the painting of the *White Plume* appeared lists an owner, implying that the painting remained with the artist himself. While one might reasonably assume that it eventually was in the possession of the family of the sitter, no evidence for that exists and the provenance of the painting after 1831 is not known.   DBD

1. The reference here is not to Durand's engraving but to Ingham's original painting, which was the object exhibited at the Academy in 1828 and 1831.

2. Grolier Club, *Catalogue of the Engraved Work of Asher B. Durand* (New York, 1895), no. 225.

3. Thomas S. Cummings, *Historic Annals of the National Academy of Design* (Philadelphia: George W. Childs, 1865), 353.

4. William Dunlap, *History of the Rise and Progress of the Arts of Design in the United States* (New York: George P. Scott and Co., Printers, 1834), 2: 273.

5. "The Fine Arts. NAD," *NYM* 5 (May 24, 1828): 366

6. Apollo, "The NAD," *NYEP*, May 7, 1831.

7. "The Fine Arts. NAD," *NYM* 8 (May 7, 1831): 350.

8. *The White Plume* was shown at the Boston Athenaeum in 1829 and at the Pennsylvania Academy of the Fine Arts the following year. See Robert F. Perkins, Jr., and William J. Gavin III, *The Boston Athenaeum Art Exhibition Index 1827–1874* (Boston: The Library of the Boston Athenaeum, 1980); and Anna Wells Rutledge, *Cumulative Record of Exhibition Catalogues. The Pennsylvania Academy of the Fine Arts 1807–1870* (Philadelphia: The American Philosophical Society, 1955).

9. Frances Trollope, *Domestic Manners of the Americans* (London, 1832), 267–68.

7

Charles Robert Leslie, HM
London, England 1794–1859 London, England

Londoners Gypsying, 4th Annual Exhibition, May 11–July 13, 1829, no. 29, owner R. Donaldson

Asher Brown Durand (1796–1886)
after Charles Robert Leslie

Gipseying Party, n.d. §
Engraving, 6 × 8
National Academy of Design, New York

The painting on which this engraving is based, *Londoners Gypsying* (location unknown), was one of the most popular works in the National Academy of Design's annual exhibition of 1829. Charles Robert Leslie began the painting in London in 1819 and had finished it by April of the following year, when he sent it to the annual exhibition of the Royal Academy of Arts.[1] Although the critical success of the painting was a factor in Leslie's election to the Royal Academy in 1821, he despaired at finding a buyer for the work.[2] His fears were soon alleviated, however, when the painting was purchased by American art collector Robert Donaldson, who was visiting London at the time.

By the time *Londoners Gypsying* was shown at the National Academy of Design in 1829, Leslie was considered by most educated Americans to be, with Washington Allston, Gilbert Stuart, and a few others, among the modern masters of painting. Given Leslie's reputation, then, and the fact that *Londoners Gypsying* had already been successfully shown in London, it is not surprising that critics noticed and praised it when it debuted in this country.[3] The subject matter—common folk out in the countryside having fun—was a rare one in art at the time. William Dunlap, this country's first chronicler of artists' lives, wrote in his biographical sketch of Leslie's life, "While my mind is occupied by the pictures of Leslie brought to New-York, I will mention one which has always given me great delight—it is a citizen's family enjoying the delights of the country, and is in the possession of Mr. Donaldson."[4]

Almost every critic who wrote about the National Academy's 1829 annual exhibition raved about Leslie's *Londoners Gypsying*. A correspondent for the *New-York American,* identified only as "C," was typical. Believing that Leslie's work in general would "produce a salutary influence both on the taste of the public and on the study of the artist," he praised *Londoners Gypsying* for its lack of artifice. He wrote, "the soul of the painter appears to have breathed upon the canvas. The moment of conception must have been one of a peculiarly happy nature, as every touch of the pencil shows a brilliant and humorous imagination." The painting succeeded, he concluded, because it was the perfect embodiment of man's relationship with nature. Its achievement was to blend "human character in its happiest moments" with "nature in her usual beauty and loveliness."[5]

Similarly, a writer for the *Critic* devoted an unusual amount of space to Leslie's painting. Like the writer for the *New-York American,* this author was impressed with Leslie's ability to conjoin nature and man. "No painter of the present day," he stated, "shows in his work more careful observation of nature, in her frolic moods . . . than Leslie." The critic described the scene at length and, in doing so, expressed his admiration for Leslie's choice of objects and attention to minute detail, from the flower in the man's buttonhole to the fold of his trousers. These, the critic explained, "are little congruous incidents which beautifully illustrate character."[6]

Leslie's painting was also among those that were highly praised by the critic for the *New-York Mirror,* presumably its editor George Pope Morris. Morris said that he "could devote a page of our journal, did time and dire necessity permit" to Leslie's work. "We stood and pored upon this exquisite composition for a good half-hour," he reported, "and thought that, were our artists paid at home as they are paid in England, such pictures might be produced and purchased here as well as there. . . ." Turning to look at another painting—John Quidor's unsold *Rip Van Winkle*—he concluded that in Europe Quidor's painting,

7

like Leslie's, "would be bought at a handsome price, and the painter be thus encouraged and enabled to produce one still better." The history of these two paintings, hung in the same room at the Academy's exhibition, caused Morris to despair for the future of American art. "How it will be in America," he concluded, "we cannot say."7   DBD

1. Charles Robert Leslie to Miss Leslie, April 9, 1820, in Tom Taylor, ed., *Autobiographical Recollections by the Late Charles Robert Leslie, R. A.* (Boston: Ticknor and Fields, 1860), 216.

2. Charles Robert Leslie to Miss Leslie, June 28, 1820, in Taylor, ed., 219. Also see William Nathaniel Banks, "Edgewater on the Hudson River," *The Magazine Antiques* 121 (June 1982): 1400–10.

3. In fact, Donaldson had already lent the painting to the 1828 exhibition of the American Academy of the Fine Arts in New York. Its popularity was enhanced when, in 1830, it was engraved by Asher Durand for publication in the *Atlantic Souvenir,* and in the following year when it was engraved again, probably by John Sartain, for *Godey's Lady's Book* (Eleanor Broome Green, "Charles Robert Leslie" [Ph.D. diss., The George Washington University, 1973], 253). For many years, the painting hung in Donaldson's house in New York City and then in his home, Edgewater, in Barrytown, Dutchess County, New York. It last appears in the records as part of the Donaldson estate inventory taken in 1872, when it was appraised at $5,000, by far the most highly valued work in Donaldson's collection (Banks, 1402). Leslie also painted a portrait of Donaldson (1821; Edgewater), which was almost certainly the portrait shown at the Academy the same year as *Londoners Gypsying.*

4. William Dunlap, *History of the Rise and Progress of the Arts of Design in the United States* (New York: George P Scott and Co. Printers, 1834), 2: 242.

5. C., "NAD," *New-York American,* June 11, 1829.

6. "Fine Arts. NAD. Fourth Annual Exhibition." *Critic* 2 (May 23, 1829): 47.

7. [George Pope Morris?], "Fine Arts. The Fourth Annual Exhibition of the National Academy," *NYM* 6 (May 16, 1829): 354.

8

William Sidney Mount, NA

Setauket, New York 1807–1868 Setauket, New York

Full Length Portrait of Right Rev. Benjamin T. Onderdonk, Bishop of the Protestant Epis Church, 8th Annual Exhibition, May 8-July 6, 1833, no. 75

Bishop Benjamin T. Onderdonk, 1830 §

Oil on canvas, 34 × 27

Collection of The New-York Historical Society

William Sidney Mount's record as a participant in the annual exhibitions of the National Academy of Design is impressive. He began exhibiting paintings there in 1828, when he was still a student at the Academy's school, and he was represented in every subsequent exhibition until the year after his death. Through 1833, he showed mostly portraits. Exceptions came in 1828 and 1829 respectively, when he sent two paintings with literary sources—*Christ Raising the Daughter of Jairus* (1828; The Museums at Stony Brook, New York) and *Saul and the Witch of Endor* (1828; National Museum of American Art, Washington, D.C.)—and in 1831, when he showed *Boys Quarreling after School* (1830; The Museums at Stony Brook, New York). Although the last brought Mount some prophetic praise as a genre painter, he was best known as an accomplished portraitist through at least the first half of the 1830s. In fact, it was his expertise in this field

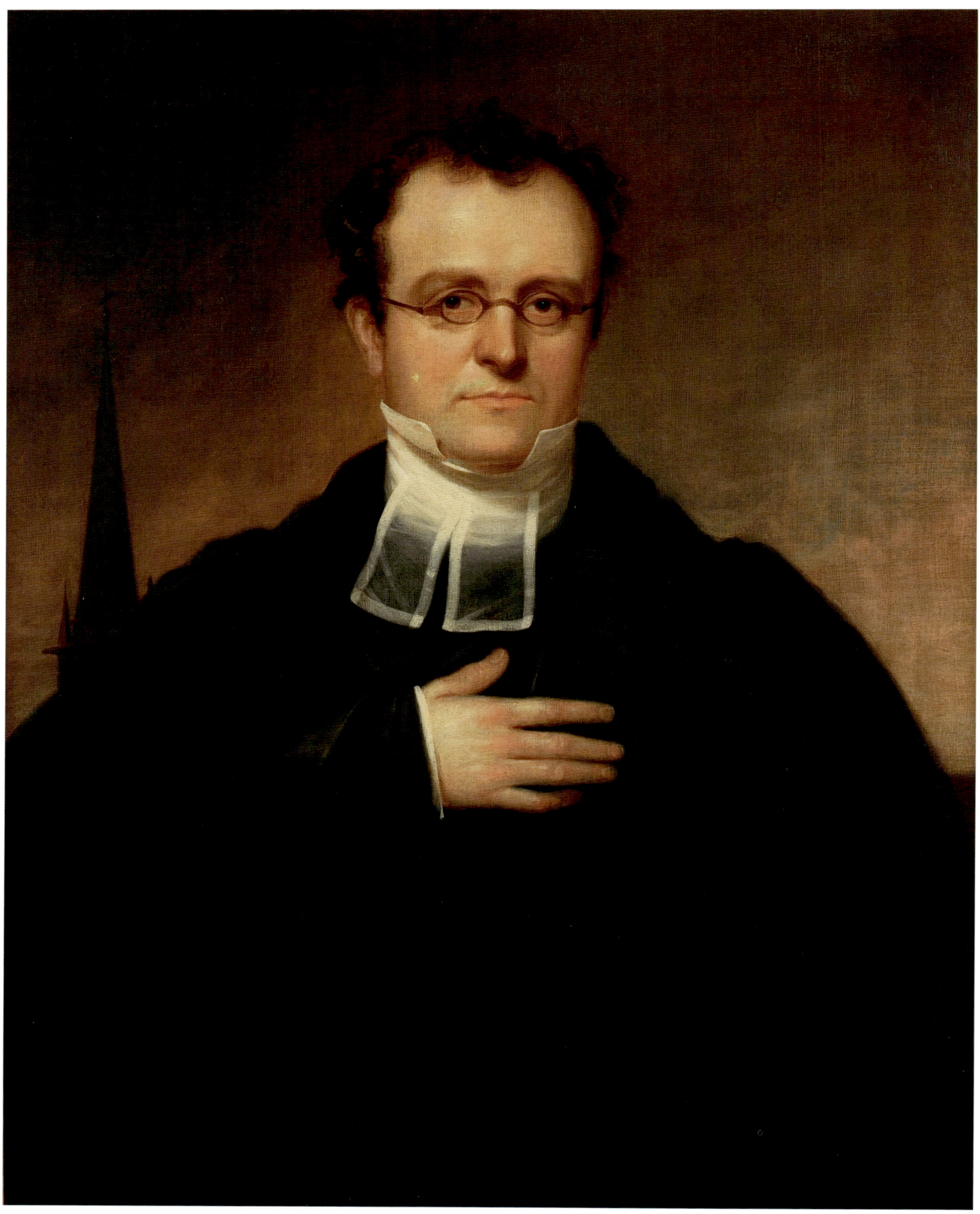

that led to his election as an associate member of the National Academy in 1831 and to full Academician in 1832.

Among Mount's portraits that received notable critical attention during this period was his full-length image of Benjamin Tredwell Onderdonk (1791–1861), bishop of the Protestant Episcopal Church of New York, which was exhibited at the Academy in 1833. As artist and historian William Dunlap reported a few years later, the exhibition of the portrait "elicited a universal burst of applause, and a just tribute of admiration from connoisseurs and artists."[1] Onderdonk was a native of New York City and a graduate of Columbia College, where he studied theology. He was ordained a priest in 1815 and served as such at Trinity Church in New York until he was promoted to the rank of bishop in 1830. That same year, Mount began painting a full-length portrait of him for the bishop's alma mater, Columbia College. Around the same time, he painted the half-length image, shown here, evidently on order from or as a gift for the subject's family.[2]

Almost every critic who covered the National Academy's 1833 exhibition noted and praised Mount's *Onderdonk*. The *New York Evening Post* called it "noble" and stated that the painting "would do credit to any artist."[3] The *Morning Courier and New-York Enquirer* stated that it is "a fine picture" that "tells the decided improvement of the young artist."[4] Likewise, the *New-York Mirror* noted that it had been following the rise of "this pupil and student of the National Academy of Design" and was "happy to see so prominent a work of art in so prominent a situation in the gallery of Clinton-hall." After praising the Academicians for supporting young, talented artists such as Mount, the *Mirror's* writer—probably its editor, George Pope Morris—went on to describe the painting more fully:

The general simplicity of this composition comports happily with the function of the person represented. The likeness is strong. The figure stands well, and arrangement of the hands and book is admirable. The accessories are well chosen, and the silver chalice painted as well as we should think possible, and is kept at the same time in perfect subordination; the precious metal does not attract attention from the bishop or the book.[5]

The only dissenter from these decidedly positive opinions was the *American Monthly Magazine,* which thought that the painting was "good" but objected to the likeness, mostly in terms of Onderdonk's age. "If taken recently," the magazine wrote, "it is too young, and not sufficiently 'filled up' for the bishop. We accord as to its general features, and admire the dignified position and appropriate finish of the drapery, but certainly the artist has done for him, what all who know him will be glad of,— restored him two or three by-gone years."[6]   DBD

1. William Dunlap, *History of the Rise and Progress of the Arts of Design* (New York: George P. Scott & Co., 1834), 2:452.

2. The half-length descended in Onderdonk's family until 1953 when it was given to the New-York Historical Society. See *Catalogue of American Portraits in the New-York Historical Society* (New Haven: Yale University Press, 1974), 2: 587–88. Mount's full-length portrait of Onderdonk is in the collection of Columbia University, New York.

3. "Academy of Design," *NYEP*, May 8, 1833.

4. "NAD," *Morning Courier and New-York Enquirer,* May 10, 1833.

5. "NAD. Fourth Notice," *NYM* 10 (June 8, 1833): 387.

6. "Miscellaneous Notices of Literature, Fine Arts, the Sciences, Drama, &c.," *American Monthly Magazine* 1 (July 1833): 332.

9, 10

John Gadsby Chapman, NA
Alexandria, Virginia 1808–1889 Tottenville, New York

The Bedchamber of Washington, in Which he Died, with the Furniture, as it Was at the Time, Drawn on the Spot by Permission of Mrs. John Washington; View of Yorktown, Virginia; Tomb of Washington; View from the Site of the Old Mansion of the Washington Family; View of the Birth-place of Washington; Residence of Washington's Mother at Fredericksburg, Virginia; Distant View of Mount Vernon, 10th Annual Exhibition, May 5–July 4, 1835, nos. 8, 63, 71, 156, 157, 199, 212

Archibald Dick (c. 1805–1868)
after John Gadsby Chapman (1808–1899)

View of York Town, Virginia, 1835 §

New Tomb of the Washington Family, 1835 §

Engravings, 3 × 4 each

From James Kirke Paulding, *A Life of Washington* 2 (1835)

Private collection, New York City

In 1835, John Gadsby Chapman completed a series of nine paintings of sites associated with George Washington that had been commissioned or at least were quickly purchased from him by poet and author James Kirke Paulding (1778–1860). The paintings, now in a private collection, were based on sketches made in northern Virginia after Chapman's return from Italy in 1831.[1] Seven were exhibited at the National Academy of Design in 1835, and engravings after several of them were used as illustrations for Paulding's *A Life of Washington,* published in two volumes in 1835.[2] The paintings and the engravings, two of which are illustrated here, proved to be tremendously popular and marked Chapman's first success as an artist.

The attention garnered by Chapman's Washington paintings actually began before they debuted at the Academy. A writer for the *New-York Mirror* reported on the completion of the series in March 1835, and briefly described six of the works, which he had seen in Chapman's New York studio.[3] Their subsequent popularity was the result, almost exclusively, of their subject matter. After the group debuted at the National Academy in 1835, they were kept in the public eye when some of the engravings that were made after them appeared in the exhibition of the following year.

When Chapman's paintings were shown at the Academy in 1835, the one that received the most attention was that of Washington's bedroom. What impressed the critics most was that the painting was a success despite—and probably because of—the absence of figures. Like the riderless horse in a funeral procession, the empty room allowed the patriotic viewer to ponder, romanticize, and finally glorify the great man *in absentia.* "To make a picture of a bed-chamber, without one figure to enliven the scene," the *New-York Mirror* reported, "was an arduous task; but Mr. Chapman has successfully achieved it. It is in itself a picture—but the associations connected with it, especially in the bosoms of Americans, render it one of the most precious in the gallery."[4] *The American Monthly Magazine* joined the chorus of praise, calling this "the most remarkable painting in the room." Like the writer for the *Mirror,* this author admired Chapman's ability to make a "most lovely picture" out of "a common bed-

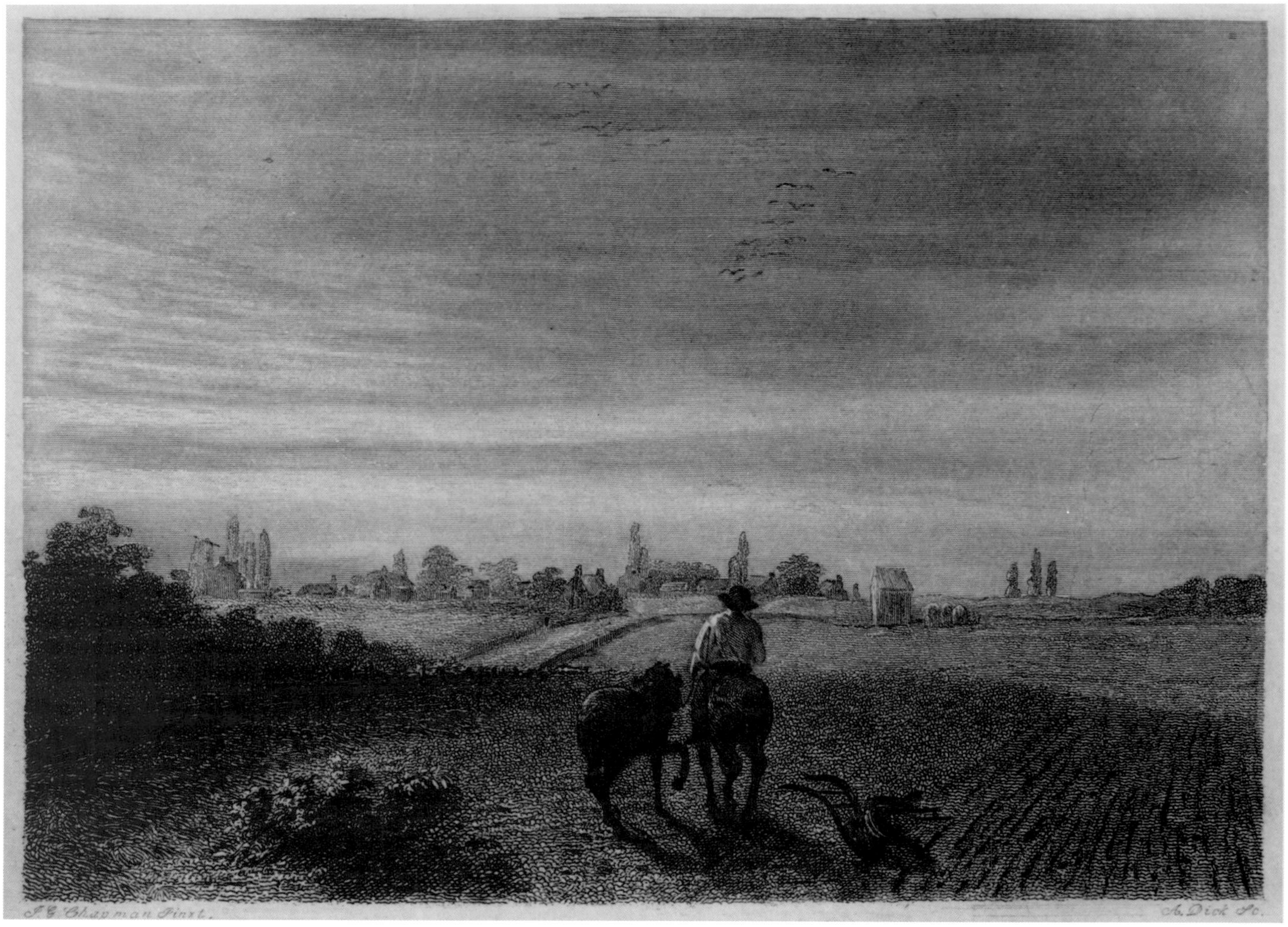

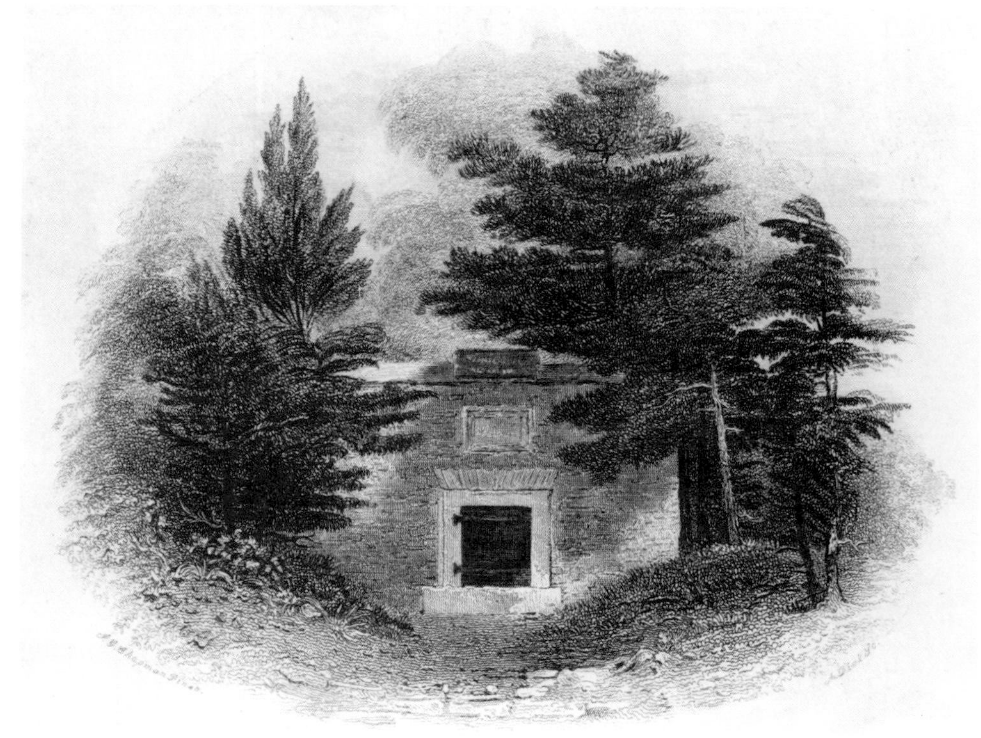

9

10

chamber, with a few articles of furniture, by no means picturesque or striking in themselves"[5] This talent was affirmed in Chapman's image of Washington's mother's home, which offered further proof of "how very little is requisite to make up a lovely picture."[6] In actuality, this was all in keeping with the methodology Chapman used throughout the series. The historic characters are not depicted *in situ*, only the *situ* itself *sans* the former president, his mother, his wife, or his British adversary.

Most critics noted, too, the patriotic didacticism of these paintings. According to the *Morning Courier and New-York Enquirer,* Chapman's works, along with those of John F. Weir and Asher Durand in the same show, "are subjects that not only combine the two highest branches of the art, but address themselves to feelings that find a home in the mind of every American." These paintings placed Chapman "in the first rank of our artists." All of this must have been encouraging to the young Chapman who, most critics admitted, was previously unknown to them. "The publick is indebted to this very excellent artist," the *Mirror* concluded, "for preserving such relicks of the truly great and good as this."[7]   DBD

1. Georgia S. Chamberlain, "John Gadsby Chapman, Painter of Virginia," *Art Quarterly* 24 (Winter, 1961): 379. Chapman befriended members of the Washington family, visited Mount Vernon a number of times, and was permitted to copy paintings in the family's collection. All nine of his original Washington paintings are illustrated in *The Old Print Shop Portfolio* 18 (October 1958): 26–34. They are now in a private collection.

2. Evidently, Paulding was pleased enough with Chapman's Washington series that he was secure in supporting the artist's bid for a commission to paint a historic image for the Rotunda of the U.S. Capitol in 1835. Early that year, he wrote to Richard Henry Wilde about the project: "I *Know* that there are artists in this Country fully competent to the purpose. Among these is my friend Mr. John G. Chapman who has painted several pictures for me & of whose talents I feel so assured, that I would willingly be responsible for his executing a work highly honourable to the Country" (Paulding to Wilde, February 13, 1835, in Ralph M. Aderman, ed., *The Letters of James Kirke Paulding* [Madison: The University of Wisconsin Press, 1962], 164).

3. "Original Notices of the Fine Arts. The Artists' Studio. John G. Chapman," *NYM* 12 (March 21, 1835): 301–02.

4. "The Fine Arts. Exhibition of the NAD," *NYM* 12 (May 16, 1835): 366.

5. "Fine Arts in America. NAD. Tenth Annual Exhibition," *American Monthly Magazine* 5 (June 1835): 316.

6. "Fine Arts in America. NAD. Tenth Annual Exhibition," *American Monthly Magazine* 5 (July 1835): 396.

7. "The Fine Arts. Exhibition of the NAD. Third Notice," *NYM* 12 (May 30, 1835): 379; "The Fine Arts. Exhibition of the NAD. Sixth Notice," *NYM* 12 (June 20, 1835): 406.

11

William Sidney Mount, NA

Setauket, New York 1807–1868 Setauket, New York

> *Farmer's Nooning,* 12th Annual Exhibition, April 21–July 4, 1837, no. 268, owner J. Sturges

Farmers Nooning, 1836

> Oil on canvas, 20¼ × 24¼ in.
>
> The Museums at Stony Brook, New York

Farmers Nooning was painted in 1836 for Jonathan Sturges, a New York grocer and art collector. Sturges was pleased with the painting and, in 1837, wrote to William Sidney Mount of his satisfaction: "I was sitting opposite the 'Farmers Nooning' last evening and enjoyed myself so much I suddenly felt quite anxious to get a peep at some other scene in the same line."[1] Sturges had already expressed his pride in the painting by lending it to the National Academy's annual exhibition earlier that year. There, it received instant acclaim as one of the artist's masterpieces, a "chef-d'œuvre," as the *Knickerbocker* called it, a "gem of the first water."[2]

By 1837, Mount's reputation was shifting from that of a consummate portraitist, as seen in the success of his likeness of Bishop Benjamin T. Onderdonk (no. 8) in 1833, to that of an accomplished genre painter. As judged by the quality of works he was exhibiting at the National Academy of Design each year, Mount's expertise at painting scenes of everyday American life was becoming more and more evident to the public. By 1836, when he showed two paintings in this subject category— *Undutiful Boys* and *Farmer's Bargaining,* both now in the collection of the New-York Historical Society—it was apparent that Mount was on his way to being this country's premier genre painter. Lewis Gaylord Clark, editor of the *Knickerbocker,* for example, was pleased that Mount had not submitted any portraits to the Academy's annual that year and, instead, had sent the two genre scenes. These works, Clark noted, confirmed Mount's talent at painting "domestick scenes, and particularly those of moral life" and his ability to capture truthfulness and humor "both in the faces and the attitudes of his figures."[3]

Mount's success with these two paintings in 1836 was probably surpassed by the exhibition the following year of his *Farmers Nooning.* Just as Clark had praised Mount's earlier paintings, a writer for the *New-Yorker* applauded the "faultless character and truth about this artist's productions which are as attractive as they are excellent." While he wished Mount had handled the light in a more convincing manner, he thought that it was the artist's best work to date. "The expression of the sleeping negro about to be 'tickled with a straw' by the mischievous boy," he wrote, "the looseness of the hay, the satisfied and contented air of the man lying on the ground kicking up his heels, are all excellent."[4]

In fact, it was the African-American man who received the most attention from the critics. After calling Mount "the American Wilkie" and the painting "truly American," the *New-York Mirror* pointed out "the negro who sleeps on a hay-cock in the sun, stretched on his back and raising his arm—which sleeps though in motion—as the arch boy tickles his nose with a straw." "All is nature," the journal concluded, "in the perfection of art."[5] Another writer called the painting "admirable" and declared that "the black fellow is the masterpiece of the composition;—the nettled expression of his countenance as he feels the straw—the foreshortening of his figure—the delighted appearance of the boy— all speak the fact that Mr. Mount is indeed a great painter."[6]

Farmers Nooning quickly became one of Mount's best known canvases. Two engravings of it were made; one appeared in the July 1845 issue of *Godey's Lady's Book,* a popular leisure magazine, and another, tinted, was published for the Apollo Association in New York.[7]   ZR

1. Jonathan Sturges to William Sidney Mount, December 14, 1837, New-York Historical Society, New York, quoted in David Cassedy and Gail Shrott, *William Sidney Mount: Works in the Collection of The Museums at Stony Brook* (Stony Brook, New York: The Museums at Stony Brook, 1983), 53.

2. [Lewis Gaylord Clark?], "Exhibition of the National Academy," *KB* 9 (June 1837): 621.

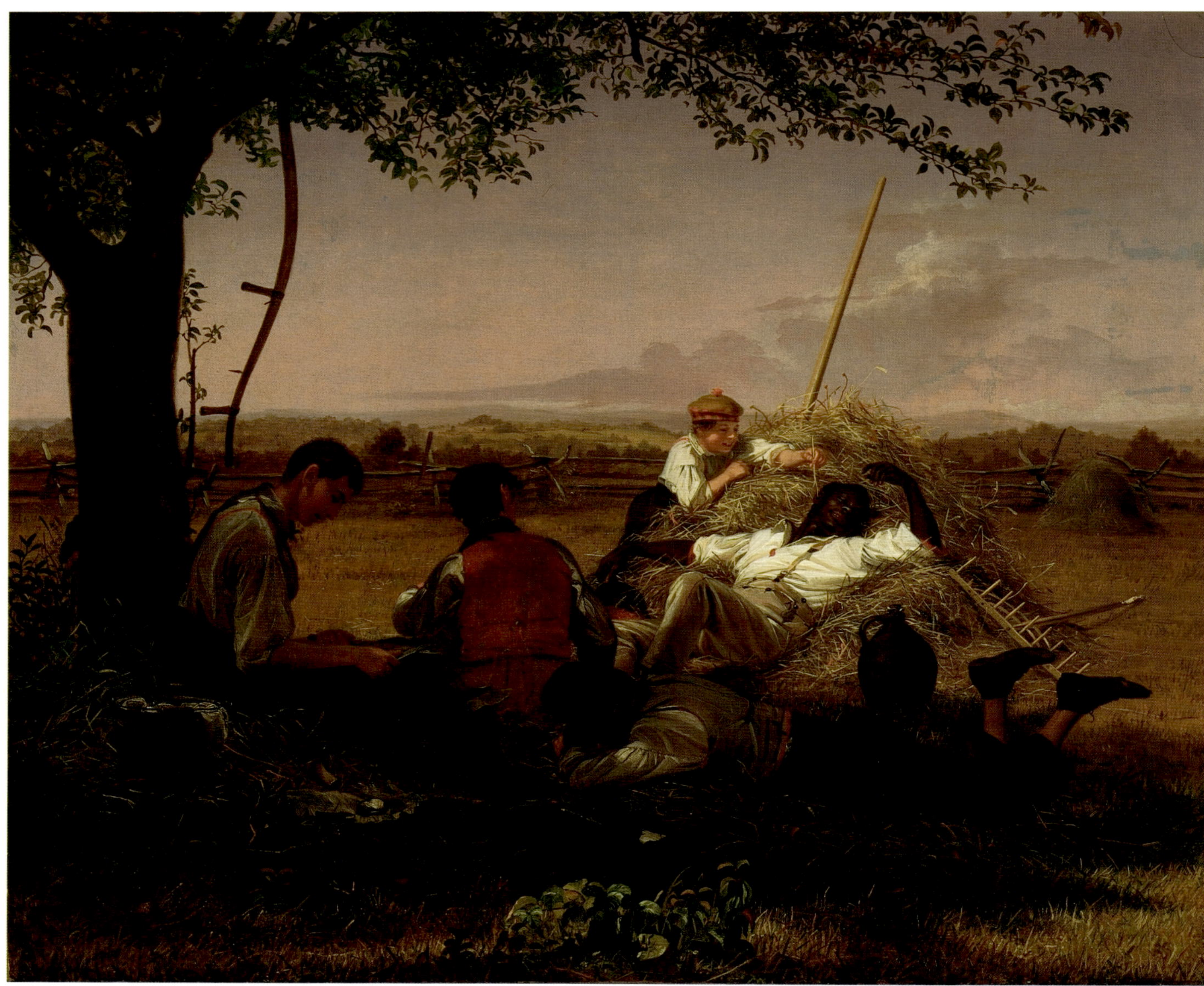

11

3. [Lewis Gaylord Clark?], "Editor's Table. NAD: Eleventh Annual Exhibition," *KB* 8 (July 1836): 115.

4. "The Twelfth Annual Exhibition of the NAD," *New-Yorker* 3 (May 6, 1837): 109.

5. "The NAD," *NYM* 14 (June 17, 1837): 407.

6. Undated clipping, quoted in Cassedy and Shrott, 53.

7. Cassedy and Shrott, 53.

12

Charles Cromwell Ingham, NA

Dublin, Ireland 1796–1863 New York, New York

The Great Adirondack Pass, Painted on the Spot, 14th Annual Exhibition, April 24–July 6, 1839, no. 20

The Great Adirondack Pass, 1838

Oil on canvas, 48 × 40

Adirondack Museum, Blue Mountain Lake, New York

Beginning in the 1810s, when he first showed his paintings in this country at the exhibitions of the American Academy of Fine Arts in New York, Charles Cromwell Ingham made a reputation for himself as a painter of exquisitely detailed, highly linear, and finely polished portraits, especially of women. By the 1830s, he was second only to Henry Inman among the leading portraitists in New York City, a position he held well into the 1850s. Among his greatest critical successes were the portraits he called *The White Plume* (see no. 6) and *Ariel* (location unknown), which were shown at the National Academy of Design's annual exhibitions of 1828 and 1834 respectively. The latter work, a portrait of British actor and singer Mrs. Elizabeth Austin in the guise of her favorite Shakespearean character, was singled out by most critics for praise; an entire article in the *New-York Mirror* was dedicated to it.[1] Ingham was talented in the area of portraiture, and that is the genre in which the public and press expected to see him excel. When he deviated from this path, he was met with silence or, even worse, derision.

As a founding member of the National Academy of Design, Ingham was an unfailing participant in its annual exhibitions, sending as many as eleven paintings per year to the shows, almost

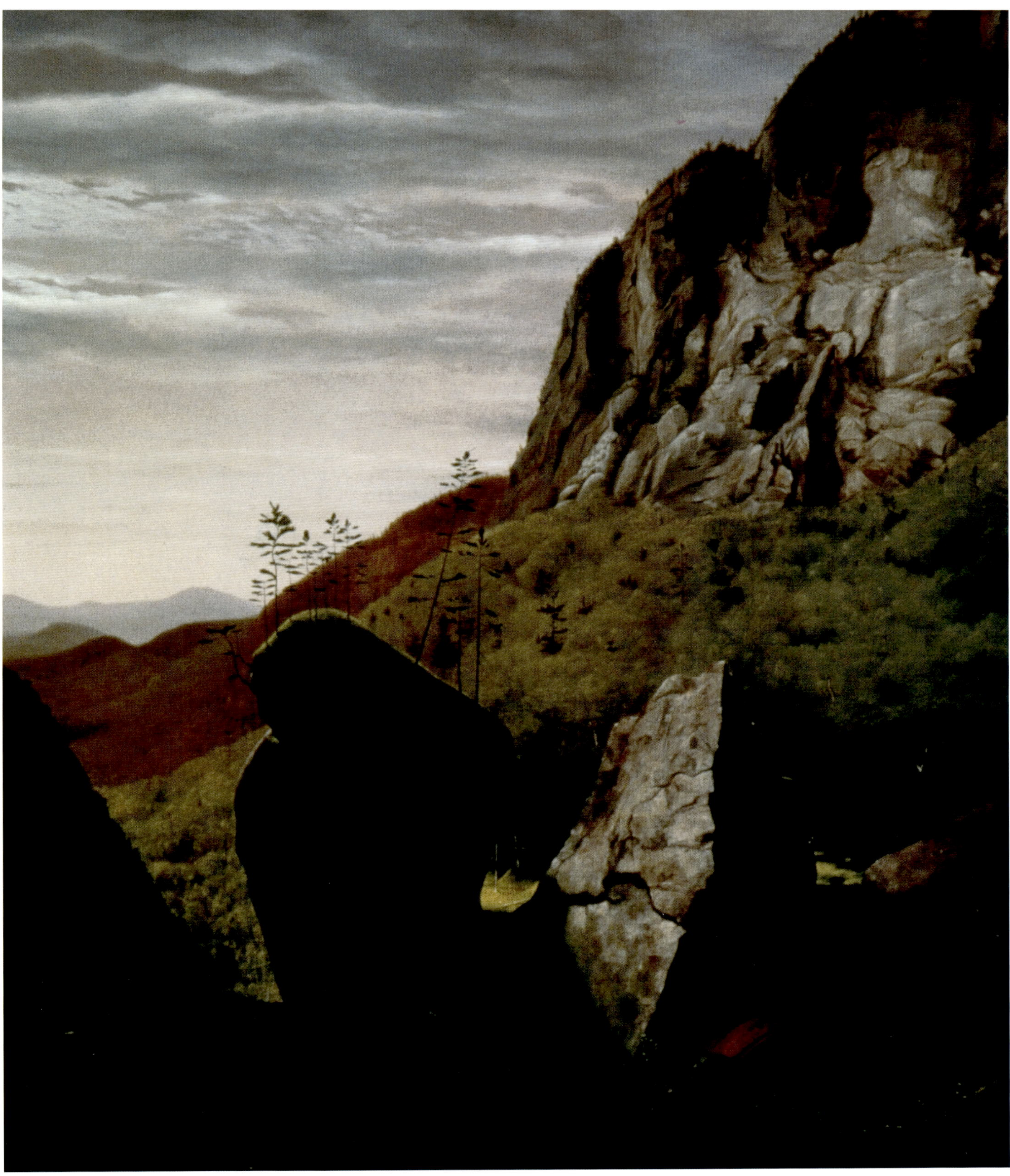

all of which were portraits. In fact, before 1839, he exhibited only three non-portraits at the Academy: in 1832, he sent the literary-genre painting *The Bard Singing "The Isles of Greece," Before Haidee and Juan;* in 1835, he submitted his *Landscape View, Looking Over the Hudson towards Fishkill, from the Seat of J. L. Morton, esq., N.A., at New Windsor;* and in 1837, he included a painting titled simply *Landscape* (locations unknown) among his submissions. None of these received any notable critical attention.

That was not the case with his *Great Adirondack Pass,* which he exhibited at the Academy in 1839. The painting resulted from a trip Ingham made to the mountains of Essex County, New York, in the company of Dr. Ebenezer Emmons and others. Emmons was geologist for the state of New York and was conducting research for what would become his *Report on the Second Geological District,* published by the New York state legislature in 1842. As part of the expedition, Ingham's task was to record accurately the "spot" known as Indian Pass, paying close attention to the rock formations there. His effort seems to have been considered a success from a scientific point of view, since Emmons had the painting engraved as an illustration for his book.[2] Unfortunately, few critics thought the painting was a success from an artistic point of view.

The *New-Yorker* started the tirade against the painting, nastily labeling it "The Great Abominable Pass" and advising Ingham to stick to portraiture.[3] John Fisher, writing for the *Knickerbocker,* called the work "a daub" and stated that it was void of any truth to nature and, instead, was filled with "lilliputian minutiae."[4] Likewise, a writer for the *New York Literary Gazette* punned on the title of the painting by moaning that things had come to "a pretty Pass" when paintings such as this "are allowed to decorate the walls" of the National Academy.[5]

What effect these negative comments had on Ingham is unrecorded. It is known that he had a close association with the leaders of the Hudson River School, such as Thomas Cole and Asher B. Durand, who were also active in the National Academy. A surviving sketchbook used by Ingham in the 1820s and 1830s (National Academy of Design) contains several highly detailed landscape drawings, including a view of Hoboken, "sketched on the spot," another of Kaaterskill Falls, and a third of the Catskill Mountain House. Although these are undeniably accomplished drawings, Ingham was, at the time, aware of his limitations as a landscapist, as he expressed in a letter he wrote to Cole in 1833. There, he almost seems to predict the criticisms that would come six years later when he sent *The Great Adirondack Pass* to the Academy's exhibition. "I think it impossible to look at a landscape and paint it so as to be pleased with the picture . . . ," he wrote.

I sat at a window and painted the view before me, but have failed in giving colour. I find it exceedingly difficult to get the colour of the distance. . . . I have painted it like a miniature, every tree on the horizon, eight miles off, I have painted every house and bush, so that the picture will give pleasure to myself as a memorial or a map, but little pleasure to anybody else.[6]

DBD

1. "Ingham's Ariel," *NYM* 11 (July 13, 1834): 14. Notable reviews of *Ariel* also appeared in "NAD," *NYEP,* June 18, 1834, and "Miscellaneous Notices Of The Fine Arts, Literature, Science, The Drama, &c.," *American Monthly Magazine* 3 (May 1834): 207. I wish to thank Kevin Lane Dearinger for identifying Mrs. Austin for me.

2. Patricia C. F. Mandel, *Fair Wilderness: American Paintings in the Collection of the Adirondack Museum* (Blue Mountain Lake, New York: The Adirondack Museum, 1990), 73.

3. "Exhibition of the NAD. —(Second Notice.)," *New-Yorker* 7 (May 11, 1839): 125.

4. J[ohn] K[enrick] F[isher], "Editor's Table. The Fine Arts," *Knickerbocker* 13 (June 1839): 545.

5. "Exhibition of the National Academy. —No. VI. The Landscapes," *New York Literary Gazette,* no. 21 (June 22, 1839): 165–66.

6. Ingham to Cole, October 24, 1833, Thomas Cole Papers, AAA, reel ACL-1.

13

Francis William Edmonds, NA

Hudson, New York 1806–1863 Bronxville, New York

15th Annual Exhibition, April 27–July 8, 1840, no. 230

The City and the Country Beaux, 1840

Oil on canvas, 20⅛ × 24¼

Sterling and Francine Clark Art Institute, Williamstown, Massachusetts

In 1840, art critics still considered Francis William Edmonds, a banker by profession, to be an amateur artist. The acclaim he received for *The City and the Country Beaux,* however, helped remove any doubts about his talents. Based on the strengths of this painting and *Sparking* (1840; Sterling and Francine Clark Art Institute, Williamstown, Massachusetts), his other entry for 1840, the National Academy of Design rewarded his skill by electing him a full Academician. Although he never painted full-time, Edmonds's yearly contributions to the Academy, and the recognition he received there, helped make him a popular genre painter at mid century.

In *The City and the Country Beaux,* Edmonds depicted a comic exchange between a young lady and her two suitors, who flank her on either side, suggesting the choice she faces. In choosing a courtship scene, Edmonds was reacting to an art market that craved humorous or satirical genre paintings, often with ambiguities that kept audiences guessing at meaning. Inspired by similar scenes by William Sidney Mount and earlier European precedents, Edmonds composed a narrative that relied less on ambiguity than on the obvious contrast of the elegantly dressed, graceful "city beau" and the boorish, comically attired "country beau."[1] Critics, however, commented primarily on the stylistic attributes of the painting, lauding the high degree of finish and Edmonds's impeccable attention to detail. As the critic of the *Knickerbocker* wrote about his two paintings, "They are *finished* pictures; finished in 'the scope and in the detail.' The whole story is told. No part is omitted, or slurred over. And it is here that so many of our artists fail. They become impatient, and spurn those several requirements of detail, and finish, without proper attention to which, no painter can become great." His effusive praise continued with a comparison to David Wilkie (1785–1841) and Dutch masters of genre painting, suggesting that Edmonds drew from them an attention to design, color, and the "correct rules of taste."[2] The association with a European genre painter such as Wilkie, who was popular in America at the time, was high praise for Edmonds.

Although the opinion was by no means universal, many critics were impressed with Edmonds's dual status as a banker and artist. The *New York Herald's* critic called Edmonds's showing at the Academy in 1840 a "capital juncture; and, for an amateur, an astonishing effort." He thought Edmonds's work was "very superior to many by artists who have those cabalistic characters A. and N. A. attached to their names," although he was certainly willing to point out the flaws of Edmonds's painting. He found for example, the woman's face to be "too broad, and too red" and her neck, "none of the cleanest." In the end, however, he conceded, ". . . it is a capital picture, and far better than Inman or Ingham could begin to paint."[3]

SK

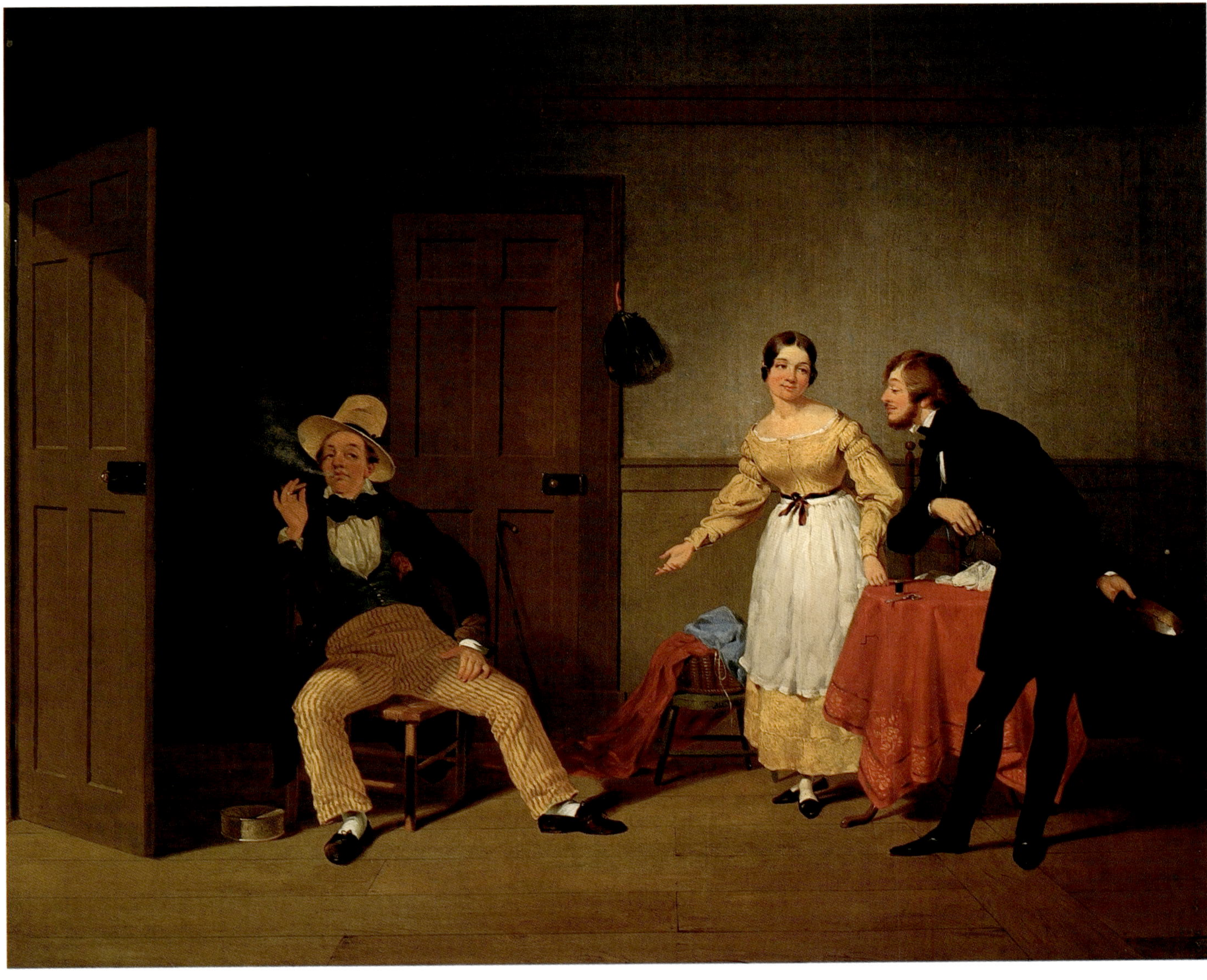

13

1. Sarah Burns, "Yankee Romance: The Comic Courtship Scene in Nineteenth-Century American Art," *American Art Journal* 18 (1986): 64–65.

2. [Lewis Gaylord Clark?], "NAD," *KB* 16 (July 1840): 82–83.

3. "National Academy," *NYH,* July 2, 1840.

14

Daniel Huntington, NA

New York, New York 1816–1906 New York, New York

16th Annual Exhibition, May 3–July 5, 1841, no. 27, owner Edward L. Carey, Esq.

Mercy's Dream, 1841

Oil on canvas, 84⅝ × 66

Pennsylvania Academy of the Fine Arts, Philadelphia, Bequest of Henry C. Carey (The Carey Collection)

Mercy's Dream gave Daniel Huntington an opportunity to combine two of his interests: literary and religious painting. Here, he illustrates a passage from the second part of John Bunyan's *The*

Pilgrim's Progress, a perennially popular book in this country, from its publication in Boston in 1681 until the middle of the nineteenth century.[1] The painting illustrates a dream that Mercy recounts to her friend Christiana wherein an angel, hearing of her troubles and sorrow, brings her peace and leads her to heaven.[2]

The imagery invoked in Bunyan's tale made it possible for Huntington to create a moralizing painting that could take advantage of religious symbolism without retelling a moribund story from the Bible. From its debut at the National Academy of Design in 1841, the painting was a huge popular success and, thanks to engraved reproductions, it rivaled Thomas Cole's series *The Voyage of Life* (1839–40; Munson-Williams-Proctor Institute, Utica, New York) as the best known American image of the 1840s.[3]

Most critics were not impressed with the National Academy's annual exhibition of 1841. The *Knickerbocker,* for example, spoke of "the low character of the exhibition."[4] For almost all who wrote about the show, however, Huntington's *Mercy's Dream* was cited as the most "distinguished," as the *New York Express* put it, work in the exhibition.[5] The *New-York Mirror* called it a "beautiful picture" and noted that it was the favorite of many visitors to

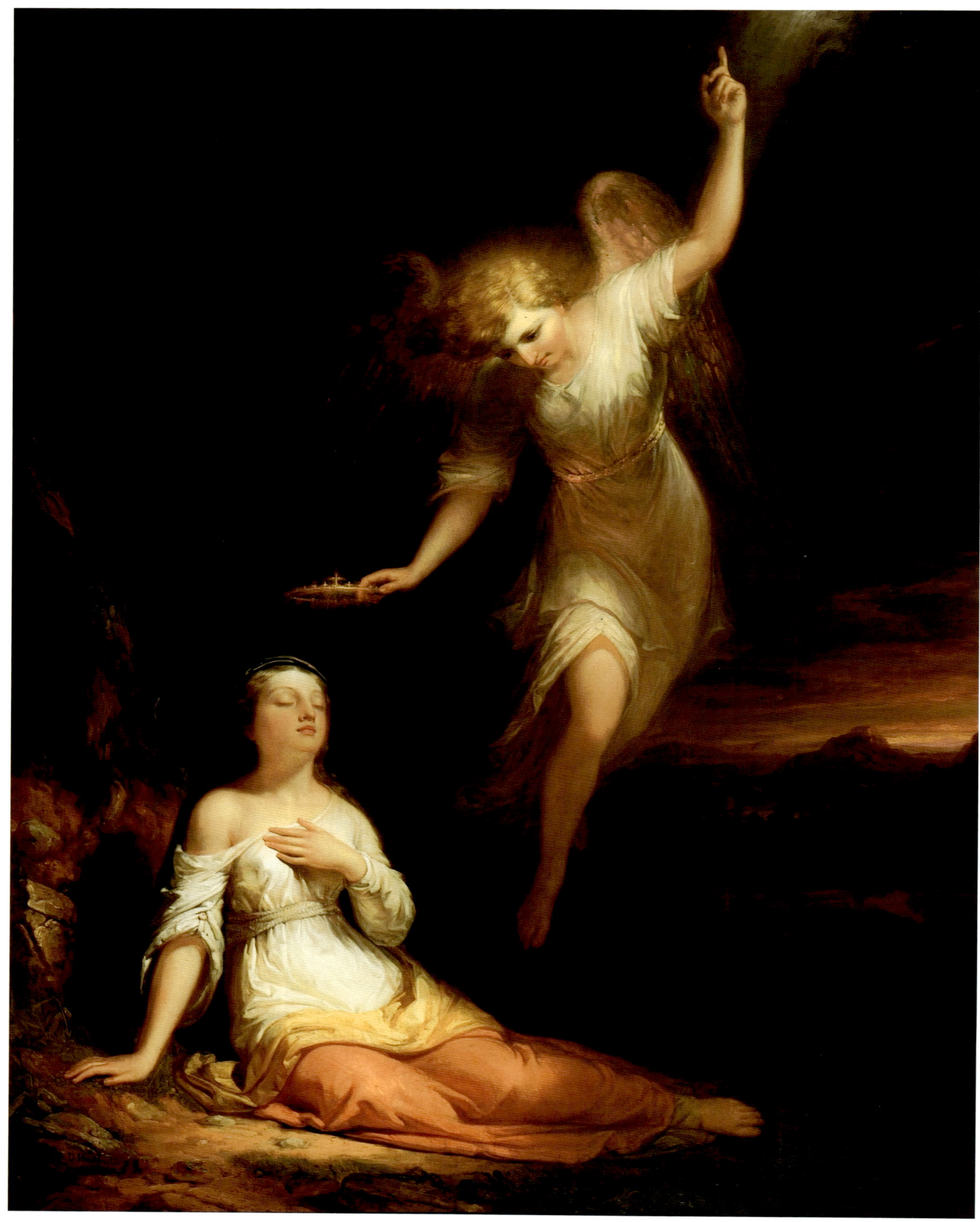

14

the exhibition. "Mercy herself," the journal reported, "is a lovely production of art; graceful, finely coloured and conceived."[6] The only fault the journal found in the work was in the stiffness of the angel's hair. Likewise, the *Knickerbocker* noted that the angel is "felicitously conceived and executed: the head is not beautiful, and the hair is indifferently managed." These were minor problems, however, for the painting's ultimate effect was "very pleasing." "The back-ground is grand," the *Knickerbocker* noted. "The figure of Mercy, too, is exceedingly lovely, and seems as if it were just waking from a sweet sleep." The journal concluded, ". . . this picture reflects great credit upon Mr. Huntington, and we hope it will not be the last subject of the kind which his pencil shall illustrate."[7] Even the *New York Evening Post*, which found only a few works in the exhibition to be worth mentioning, singled out *Mercy's Dream* as a "beautiful" and delightful illustration of Bunyan's "glorious pages."[8]

Perhaps the highest praise came from a writer for the journal *Arcturus*, who called *Mercy's Dream* "the Picture of the Year." "The subject is not one that would have charms for an ordinary Artist, working in the ordinary trading spirit," the writer continued,

> *—it is no well-known scene or story floating on the popular breath, and already embodied in the ideas of beholders. In seeking inspiration at the Dream of our peasant Dante, John Bunyan . . . what the painter will* find, *is determined by the measure of what he* brings. *The pure-hearted simplicity of Stothard, and the stern grandeur of Martin, have found fit employment, in tracing the flowery paths of the Valley of Humiliation, or peopling with strange creation the palpable darkness of the Valley of the Shadow of Death. Remembering these, we rejoice to say that the Artist has not miscalculated his strength. We have rarely seen a picture so full of promise.*[9]

With the close of the National Academy's exhibition, the painting was by no means forgotten, even though it was already part of a private collection. In 1842 and in several subsequent years within that decade, it was shown at the annual exhibition of the Artists' Fund Society at the Pennsylvania Academy of the Fine Arts in Philadelphia;[10] and in 1850, it was one of 130 works by Huntington gathered for a special exhibition organized by the American Art-Union in New York to honor the artist.[11] As a highlight of that presentation, *Mercy's Dream* was again singled out as being of great significance. After warning the reader that Huntington's "*forte* is not historical painting," a critic for the *Literary World* went on to identify *Mercy's Dream* as "a picture which does honor to American art, and the highest credit to the artist." In a long paragraph devoted to the painting, the writer gave it high praise as "a beautiful embodiment of that purity, and innocence, and peace, for which there is an universal recognition and reverence."[12]

DBD

1. Bunyan's book, the full title of which is *The Pilgrim's Progress from This World to That Which Is to Come,* was published in London in two parts, the first in 1678 and the second in 1684. See Frank Luther Mott, *Golden Multitudes: The Story of Best Sellers in the United States* (New York: The Macmillan Company, 1947), 19–20, and David E. Smith, *John Bunyan in America* (Bloomington: Indiana University Press, 1966).

2. A version of this section of Bunyan's tale was quoted in the catalogue of the National Academy of Design's 1841 exhibition in which the painting appeared.

3. The definitive study of *Mercy's Dream* is William H. Gerdts, "Daniel

Huntington's *Mercy's Dream*: A Pilgrimage through Bunyanesque Imagery," *Winterthur Portfolio* 14 (Summer 1979): 172–93. Also see Wendy Greenhouse, "Daniel Huntington and the Ideal of Christian Art," *Winterthur Portfolio* 31 (Summer/Autumn, 1996): 103–40.

4. [Lewis Gaylord Clark?], "The Fine Arts. NAD," *KB* 18 (July 1841): 86–87.

5. "NAD. Sixteenth Annual Exhibition, 1841," *New York Express,* May 18, 1841.

6. "NAD. Second Notice," *NYM* 19 (May 22, 1841): 167.

7. *KB* 18 (July 1841): 86–87.

8. "NAD," *NYEP,* June 12, 1841.

9. "The Fine Arts. Exhibition of the Academy," *Arcturus* (June 1841): 60.

10. Anna Wells Rutledge, *Cumulative Record of Exhibition Catalogues. The Pennsylvania Academy of the Fine Arts 1807–1870* (Philadelphia, 1955), 105.

11. Gerdts, 181.

12. "The Fine Arts. The Huntington Gallery," *LW* 7 (February 16, 1850): 157

15

Robert Walter Weir, NA
New York, New York 1803–1899 New York, New York

16th Annual Exhibition, May 3–July 5, 1841, no. 22, owner Albert Sumner, Esq.

53rd Annual Exhibition, April 2–June 1, 1878, no. 536

Columbus Before the Council at Salamanca, 1884 §

Oil on canvas, 29¼ × 40⅛

West Point Museum Collection, United States Military Academy

The painting that Robert Walter Weir exhibited at the National Academy of Design in 1841 with the title *Columbus Before the Council of Salamanca* is now unlocated, but he made at least two near-replicas of it, both of which are extant and which are dated 1877 and 1884 respectively. A drawing, probably made after one of these paintings and scored with grid lines, also exists and, along with the 1884 painting, is in the collection at West Point. The painting dated 1877 was exhibited at the Academy in 1878 and was engraved for reproduction in George W. Sheldon's *American Painters*, published two years later.[1] Both surviving paintings and the drawing follow the same compositional format, although the types of figures and details of costume, furniture, and background differ considerably from one to the other. Contemporary descriptions of the lost painting, which was shown at the Academy in 1841, make it clear that Weir based the later works on it.[2]

The earlier version of Weir's *Columbus Before the Council of Salamanca*—the one exhibited at the Academy in 1841—was seen in the artist's studio by a writer for the *New-York Mirror* in July 1838. Weir had begun the painting in 1837[3] and, according to the writer for the *Mirror*, had only just completed it when the article was written. At that time, too, it was being prepared for shipment to its owner Hugh Swinton Ball of Charleston, South Carolina, who evidently had commissioned or purchased it from Weir in advance of its completion. Unfortunately, and evidently unknown to the writer for the *Mirror*, Ball had been killed the previous month in the wreck of the steamer *Pulaski*, en route to Baltimore from Savannah,[4] and Weir's painting, instead, entered the collection of Albert Sumner, who lent it to the Academy's exhibition of 1841.

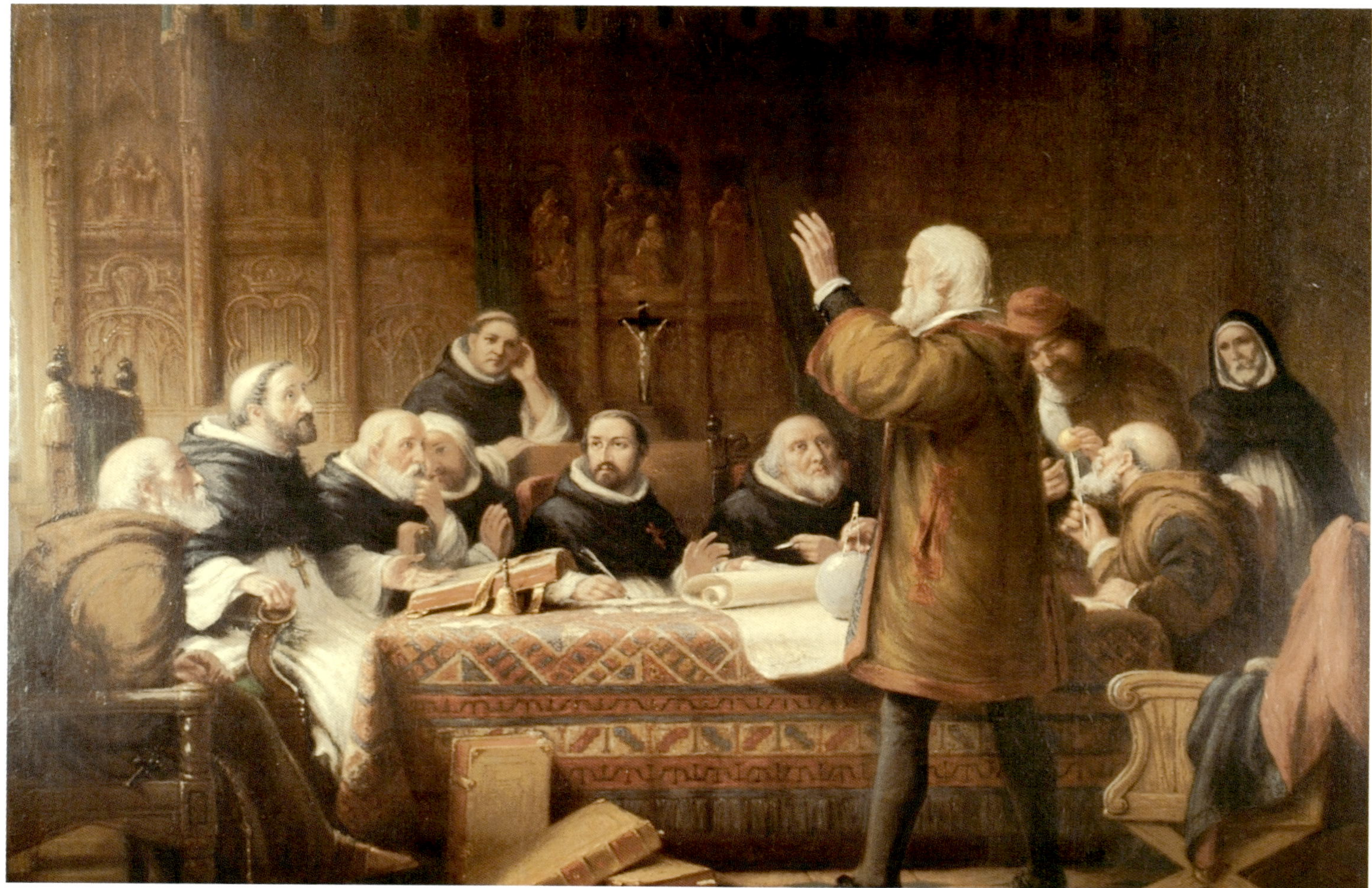

15

The article in the *Mirror* described the painting in detail and highly praised it for its "harmonious" composition and its historical accuracy. The description makes it clear that the extant drawing precisely conforms to the 1837–38 painting.[5] In the background of both, the artist depicted the altar of the Convent of St. Stephen, where Columbus's meeting with the council took place—an image of St. Stephen's martyrdom is clearly visible over the altar.[6] This detail does not appear in the later versions of the painting, which strongly suggests that the drawing is the "tracing" that Weir made of the earlier work in 1859 to send to Montgomery C. Meigs, superintendent of the construction and decoration of the U.S. Capitol. Weir was hoping to get a commission for a second painting for the Rotunda of the Capitol building and thought the Columbus theme would be appropriate.[7]

The writer for the *Mirror,* quoted above, ended his article by expressing regret "that this noble work of art should not be exhibited on the walls of the National Academy." [8] Thanks to the sudden death of Ball, however, the *Mirror* got its wish, and the early praise that the journal gave the painting was verified by almost all the critics who wrote about the Academy's show. In the typical language of the day, and in keeping with its previous assessment of the picture, the *Mirror* called it "the very gem of the exhibition" and again praised the accuracy of the accessories and the thoroughness with which the story is told.[9] The *New York Express* thought it was a fine picture of an honorable subject and particularly praised the expressive quality of the faces. The *Knickerbocker* called it "excellent," "beautiful," and "admirable."[10]

DBD

1. The engraving is by W. H. Morse. For the history of Weir's involvement with the Columbus theme, see Jacob Edward Kent Ahrens, "Robert Walter Weir (1803–1889)" (Ph.D. diss., University of Delaware, Newark 1972), 71–78.

2. Two paintings with the title *Columbus Before the Council at Salamanca* were among those by Weir sold at Orgties & Co., New York, in 1891. The dimensions of these works are given in the catalogue of that sale as 11 × 8½ and 38½ × 28½ respectively. The latter was said to be "an enlarged replica of No. 874 [the smaller work]." Presumably, these are the paintings executed by Weir in 1877 and 1884 (Ortgies & Co., *Catalogue of Oil Paintings and Water Colors by Robert W. Weir, N. A.* [New York, 1891], nos. 874 and 888). The smaller painting was with the Hirschl & Adler Galleries, New York, in 1995, the larger is the one now at West Point.

3. Ahrens, 72.

4. Ball's significance as an art collector was recognized by his being elected as an Honorary Member of the National Academy of Design in 1837. Among the paintings he owned were Washington Allston's *Spalatro's Vision of the Bloody Hand* (1831; location unknown, probably destroyed) and Henry Inman's *The Bride of Lammermoor* (c. 1835; private collection), both of which received significant critical attention when shown at the Academy in 1832 and 1835 respectively.

5. "The Fine Arts. Columbus Before the Council of Salamanca," *NYM* 15 (July 6, 1838): 294.

6. Weir's apparent source for the painting was Washington Irving's *A History of the Life and Voyages of Christopher Columbus,* which had been published in 1828. A quotation from that book was included with the listing for the painting in the catalogue for the National Academy's annual exhibition of 1841.

7. Ahrens, 72–73.

8. "Columbus," *NYM* 15 (July 6, 1838): 294.

9. "NAD. Second Notice," *NYM* 19 (May 22, 1841): 167.

10. "NAD," *New York Express,* May 18, 1841; "The Fine Arts," *KB* 18 (July 1841): 86–89.

Emanuel Gottlieb Leutze, NA

Schwäbisch Gmünd, Baden-Württemberg 1816–1868 Washington, D.C.

The Return of Columbus in Chains to Cadiz, 18th Annual
Exhibition, April 27–July 4, 1843, no. 100

Columbus Before the Queen, 1843 §

Oil on canvas, 38¾ × 51³/₁₆

Brooklyn Museum of Art, Dick S. Ramsay Fund and A.
Augustus Healy Fund

Emanuel Gottlieb Leutze began participating in the annual exhibitions of the National Academy of Design in 1843. He sent two
paintings to the Academy that year—*Sir Walter Raleigh on the
Morning of His Execution* and *The Return of Columbus in Chains
to Cadiz,* both of which are now unlocated. The success of these
paintings, especially the latter, firmly established Leutze's reputation in this country and led to his being designated an honorary
member of the Academy that same year.[1]

The *Return of Columbus in Chains* was the second in a series
of three works illustrating the explorer's wrongful arrest in San
Domingo in 1500 and his subsequent exoneration by Queen
Isabella and King Ferdinand upon his return to Spain. The first

in the series was *Columbus Before the High Council of Salamanca*
(1842; location unknown), and the third, illustrated here, was
Columbus Before the Queen (1843). The most likely source for
these paintings is Washington Irving's best-selling *Life and
Voyages of Columbus,* published in 1828.[2] Irving describes
Columbus's appearance before the king and queen "not as a man
ruined and disgraced, but richly dressed, and with an honorable
retinue." The queen reportedly wept when she saw the explorer,
and Columbus gave "an eloquent and high-minded vindication
of his loyalty, and the zeal he had ever felt for the glory and
advantage of the Spanish crown."[3] The chains depicted in the
foreground of Leutze's painting remind the viewer, however, of
the injustice that Columbus had suffered.

Even before its much-anticipated arrival in New York, *The
Return of Columbus in Chains* was exhibited in Brussels, where it
received a medal *à vermeil* from the king of Belgium.[4] By early
May 1843, the work had been purchased out of the Academy's
exhibition by the Apollo Association for distribution in its annual lottery.[5] It achieved such acclaim that in 1847 Henry Tuckerman
wrote that it was "too well known, and justly appreciated, to
require any description" for his readers to call it to mind.[6]

During the painting's exhibition at the National Academy in
1843, most critics interpreted it in light of its moralizing and
didactic qualities. According to Tuckerman, Leutze believed "that
a thorough poetical treatment of a picture required that the

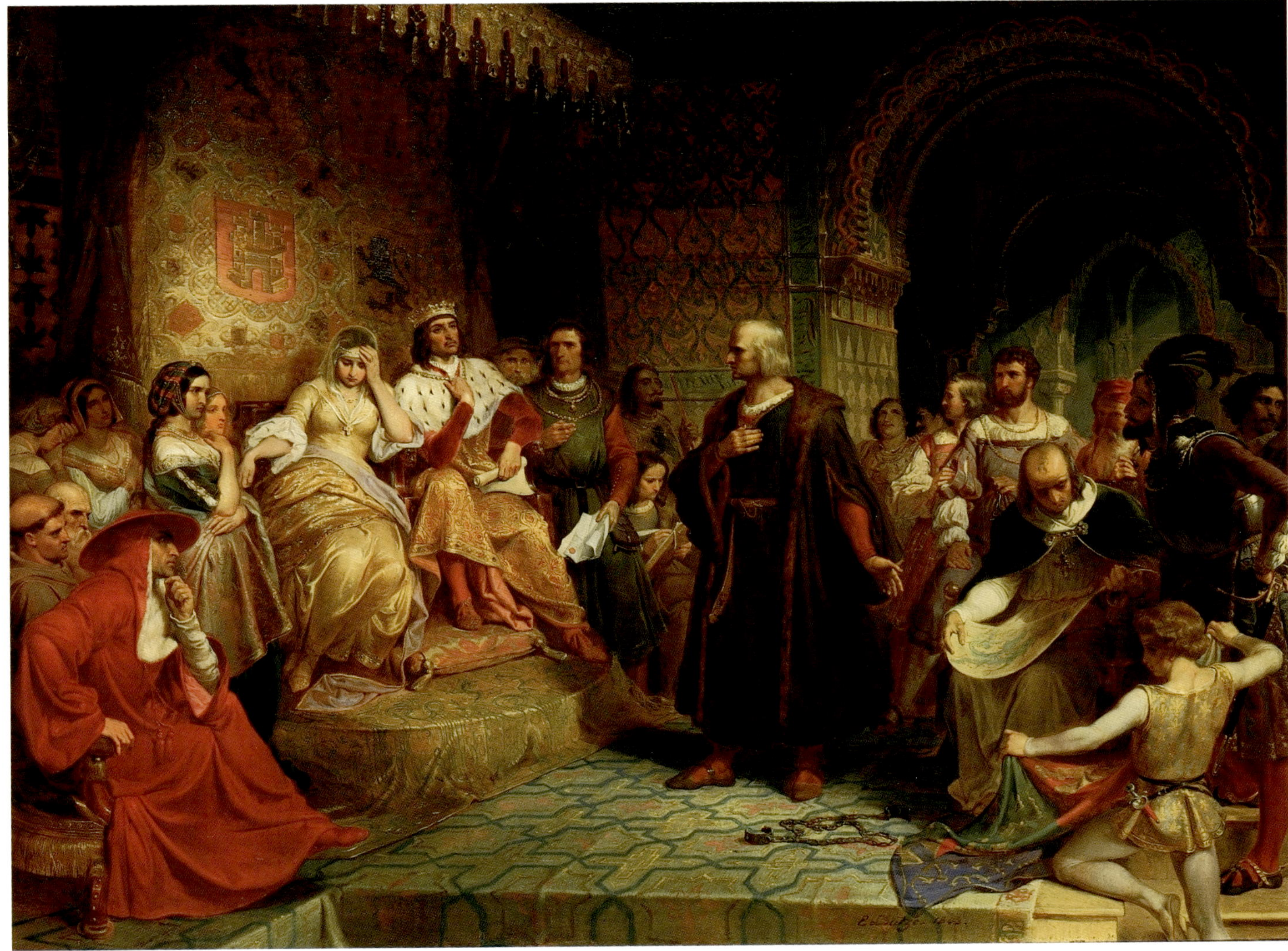

16

anecdote should not be so much the subject, as the means of conveying some one clear idea, which is to be the inspiration of the picture."[7] The critic of the *New York Evening Post* seemed aware of Leutze's intent when he described *The Return of Columbus* as "a painting of great spirit, invention and dignity."[8]

To American eyes, Leutze's painting was a revelation, and most American journalists agreed with the reviewer from the *New Mirror* who described *Columbus in Chains* as "a beautiful production, painted with uncommon care and truth in all its parts." He continued: "The persons of Columbus and his two companions in irons are finely conceived and well executed figures, full of grandeur of expression and appropriate character, and indeed this may be said of every part of the picture."[9] A writer for the *New World* called it a "really fine picture," and a colleague at *Brother Jonathan* praised Leutze by predicting, "From this time forth, every American will be proud of him."[10]

A more balanced review—one that pointed out the faults as well as achievements of the picture—came from the *Anglo-American*. The success of the work was, that journal reported, due mostly to its subject, which is one of "both majesty and firmness." The "dignity and elevation" of character of the three principal figures, as well as the "passions and feelings" of the other figures, allow the work to deliver successfully its requisite moralizing lesson to the viewer. On the other hand, the writer noted, the canvas "is somewhat too crowded, and the figures have not sky enough above them to permit the story to be freely wrought out. In short, it is too much like a picture cut down."[11]

Despite generally glowing reviews from critics, *Columbus in Chains* was drawn into a heated exchange in the pages of the *New World* over the selection committee's exclusion of other works from the exhibition on grounds of "indecency."[12] One critic sarcastically expressed surprise that the committee "did not exclude Leutzer's [*sic*] noble picture of Columbus; it contains a full-length naked figure, exhibiting a much greater surface of flesh" than other works that had been condemned for their impropriety.[13] There is no evidence, however, that Leutze was concerned with the controversy, and it did not deter him from including nudes in later works.[14]

The other work Leutze exhibited at the Academy in 1843, *Sir Walter Raleigh, on the Morning of His Execution*, had been in New York before its appearance at the Academy, and reviews of the work published in the *New World* in February of that year may have whetted the public's appetite for Leutze's art.[15] After praising the painting at length, a critic for the *New World* described Leutze himself in heroic terms, saying, "We are assured that an American public will sympathize with us in the rising fortunes of a young and talented countryman who has struggled manfully against every difficulty, and by the sheer force of *mind*, has raised himself from the humble station of an itnierant [*sic*] portrait painter in Virginia, to the favor of the courts, academies, and the monarchs of Europe."[16] The critic's praise notwithstanding, *Sir Walter Raleigh* was upstaged by *The Return of Columbus* at the Academy's exhibition, and the latter can be credited with vaulting Leutze into the front rank of American artists.   MM

1. "Return of Mr. Leutze," *Bulletin of the American Art-Union* (September 1851): 95; Barbara S. Groseclose, *Emanuel Leutze, 1816–1868: Freedom Is the Only King* (Washington, D.C.: Smithsonian Institution Press, 1975), 74.

2. Friedrich von Boetticher, *Malerwerke des neunzehnten Jahrhunderts* (Leipzig: Pantheon Verlag für Kunstwissenschaft [1891–1901], 1948), 1: 894; Groseclose, 73.

3. Washington Irving, *Columbus, His Life and Voyages* (1828; repr. New York: G. P. Putnam's Sons, 1896), 269–70.

4. "The Young American Artist Leutzi [*sic*]," *New World* 6 (February 25, 1843): 246; Groseclose, 74.

5. "Arts and Artists," *New Mirror* 1 (May 6, 1843): 76. The work remained in the family of the recipient, Richard J. Arnold, until 1978, when it was sold at auction. See C. G. Sloan & Co., Inc., Washington, D.C., Sale Catalogue (September 1978), lot 1628: 133.

6. Henry T. Tuckerman, *Artist-Life: or Sketches of American Painters* (New York: D. Appleton & Co., 1847), 182.

7. Tuckerman, 176.

8. "Exhibition of the Academy of Design," *NYEP*, May 5, 1843.

9. "Arts and Artists," *New Mirror* 1 (May 6, 1843): 76.

10. "National Academy," *Brother Jonathan* 5 (May 20, 1843): 82.

11. "NAD—Annual Exhibition," *Anglo-American* 1 (May 6, 1843): 45.

12. H. F., "The Rejected Picture," *New World* 6 (May 6, 1843): 545–46.

13. H. F., "The National Academy," *New World* 6 (May 20, 1843): 605.

14. For example, see Leutze's *Storming of the Teocalli* (1848, Wadsworth Atheneum, Hartford, Conn.) and *Nude* (1855, private collection, New York; illus. in Groseclose, fig. 73).

15. "The Young American Artist Leutzi," 246; *Sir Walter Raleigh* had already been purchased by A. M. Cozzens and was in his collection when it was reviewed.

16. Ibid.

17

Asher Brown Durand, NA

Jefferson Village [Maplewood], New Jersey 1796–1886 Jefferson Village, New Jersey

25th Annual Exhibition, April 15–July 6, 1850, no. 138

Landscape—Scene from "Thanatopsis," 1850

Oil on canvas, 39½ × 61

The Metropolitan Museum of Art, Gift of J. Pierpont Morgan, 1911

This painting by Asher Brown Durand was one of the main attractions at the Academy's annual of 1850, and almost every critic who visited the show wrote about it, although not always with praise. The *Knickerbocker* thought that the "noble" painting was "itself worth the price of a visit to the Academy."[1] Both the *New York Herald* and the *Morning Express* called it "the gem of the collection," and the former went on to say that the "execution and general finish abundantly testify to the extensive knowledge the artist possesses of nature."[2] The inevitable comparison of Durand to Thomas Cole was made by the *New York Tribune*, with Durand not quite living up to the deceased master's reputation. The *Tribune* conceded, however, that *Thanatopsis* had many pleasing qualities, not the least of which was the sense of quietude with which it was imbued.[3]

The *Albion*, too, praised *Thanatopsis*, but it warned readers that the painting is an allegory, "a class of pictures very objectionable, being rarely able to tell their tales without the aid of textual description." Luckily, the writer continued, Durand incorporated the allegorical elements—"a feudal castle, a gothic church, and the performance of funeral solemnities"—so successfully into the surrounding environment, that the viewer can ignore them and enjoy the painting as a pure landscape.[4] A writer for the *Literary World* agreed about the problems inherent in attempting an allegorical work and, he thought, Durand had failed in that pursuit here. While he considered the theme to be a

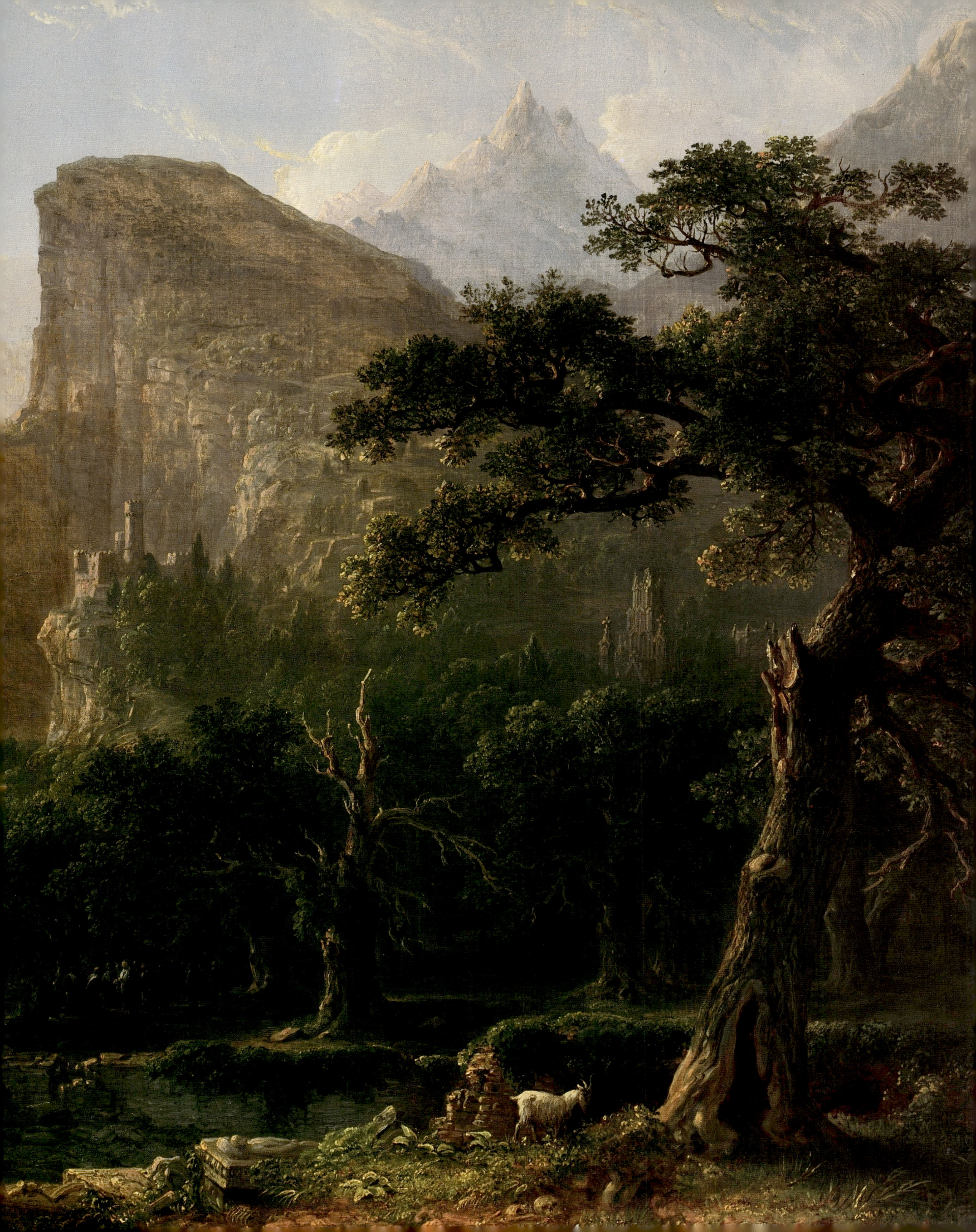

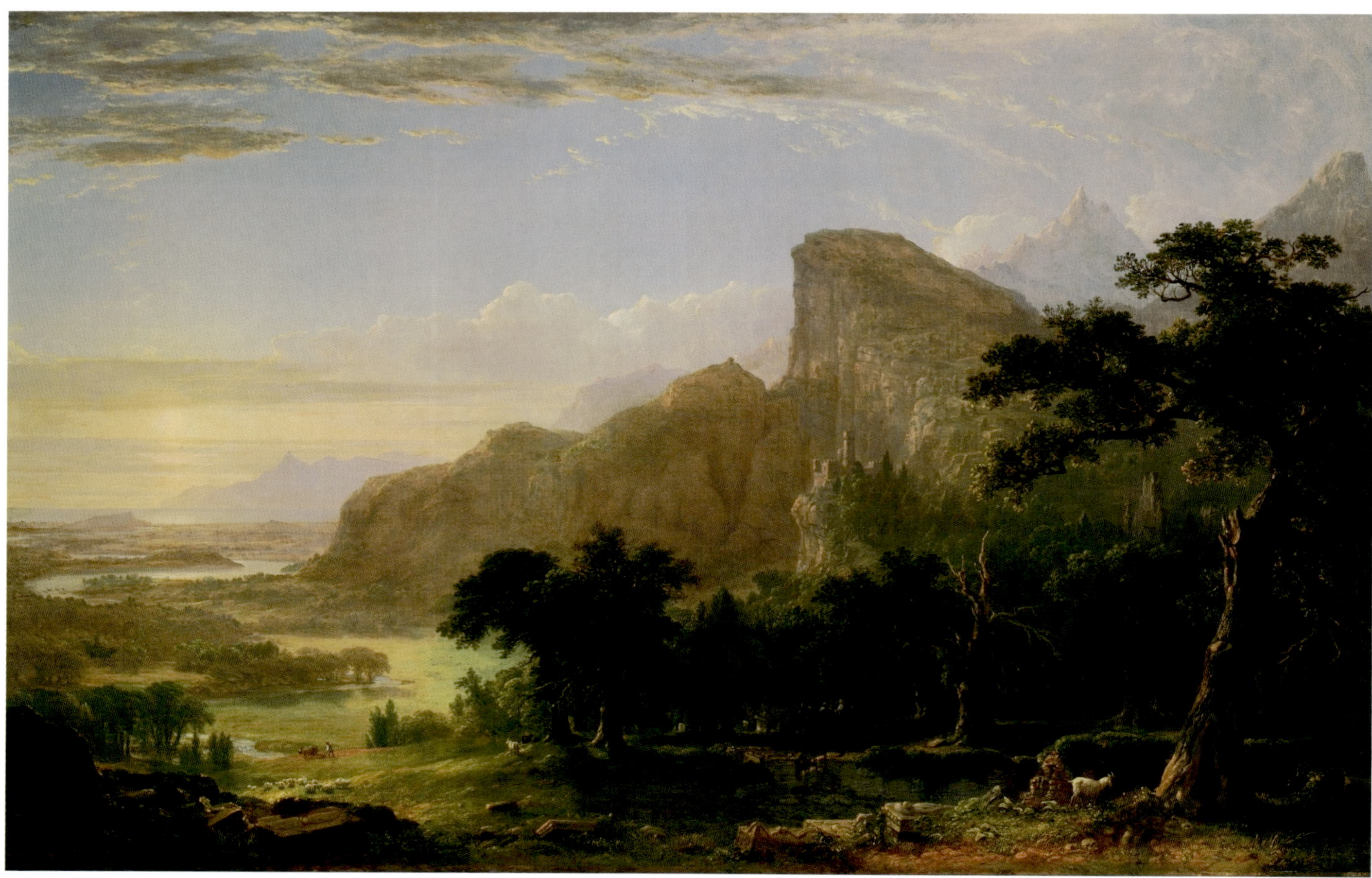

17

worthy one—"the illustration of the finest of American poems, in a kindred Art, by a hand, equally with that of the poet, a master-hand in its sphere of labor"—he felt that the painting "does not explain itself." Without the lines quoted in the catalogue, it "could hardly be understood."[5]

The painting was inspired by one of William Cullen Bryant's best-known poems, *Thanatopsis*, published in 1817. When the painting debuted at the National Academy in 1850, the following lines from that work were printed in the exhibition catalogue:

> *The hills*
> *Rock-ribbed and ancient as the sun,—the vales*
> *Stretching in pensive quietness between;*
> *The venerable woods—rivers that move*
> *In majesty, and the complaining brooks*
> *That make the meadows green; and poured round all,*
> *Old oceans gray and melancholy waste,—*
> *Are but the solemn decorations all*
> *Of the great tomb of man.*

Thanatopsis was purchased from the Academy's 1850 exhibition by the American Art-Union, which distributed it by lottery to one of its members. It was eventually owned by J. Pierpont Morgan, who gave it to the Metropolitan Museum of Art in 1911.[6]

DBD

1. [Lewis Gaylord Clark?], "National Academy Pictures," *KB* 35 (June 1850): 558.
2. "The Fine Arts. NAD," *NYH*, May 12, 1850; "NAD," *New York Morning Express*, April 22, 1850.
3. "NAD. Twenty-Fifth Annual Exhibition," *NYDT*, June 20, 1850.
4. "Fine Arts. NAD," *Albion* 9 (June 27, 1850): 201.
5. "The Fine Arts. The National Academy," *LW* 7 (April 27, 1850): 424.
6. David B. Lawall, *Asher B. Durand: A Documentary Catalogue of the Narrative and Landscape Paintings* (New York: Garland Publishing, Inc., 1978), 82; Oswaldo Rodriquez Roque, in John Caldwell and Oswaldo Rodriquez Roque, *American Paintings in the Metropolitan Museum of Art* (New York: The Metropolitan Museum of Art, 1994), 1:422

18

Junius Brutus Stearns, NA

Arlington, Vermont 1810–1885 Brooklyn, New York

26th Annual Exhibition April 8–July 5, 1851, no. 32, owner N. A. Design

The Millennium, 1849

Oil on canvas, 51 × 68¼

National Academy of Design, New York

Junius Brutus Stearns was an active participant in the National Academy of Design's annual exhibitions from 1838 until his death. Before the Civil War, most of the works he showed there were portraits, although he did send the occasional history painting or genre scene. In the former category, his subjects tended to be either biblical or taken from American history. In 1841, for example, he showed *Cain and Abel* (location unknown) at the

Academy, and in 1848 his *Scene at the Battle of Brandywine* (1848; New York art market, 1979) was exhibited there. After his failure to attract much attention with his large exhibition piece, *The Millennium,* in 1851, however, he abandoned biblical scenes in favor of the more accessible ones from American history.

The subject of Stearns's *The Millennium* is taken directly from the writings of the prophet Isaiah in the Old Testament (11:6):

> *The wolf also shall dwell with the lamb, and the leopard*
> *shall lie down with the kid; and the calf and the young lion*
> *and the fatling together; and a little child shall lead them.*

The Book of Isaiah was a popular source for artists in the late eighteenth and early nineteenth centuries. In America, the best known interpretation of the above passage is Edward Hicks's *Peaceable Kingdom* paintings, of which he did many.

What worked for Hicks, however, does not seem to have worked for Stearns. When *The Millennium* debuted at the National Academy's annual exhibition in 1851, it received little critical attention. Contemporary critics often professed hunger for grand-manner historical and religious works, but, as far as is known, only one, George W. Curtis, writing for the *New York Daily Tribune,* noticed Stearns's painting. However, he praised it not for being an illustration of a well known biblical passage or for any presumed didactic message but for its anatomical and environmental accuracy. "Mr. Stearns's Millennium is admir-

able," Curtis wrote, "for the head of the Lion, which is most faithfully rendered, and has all the leonine regality which belongs to the animal." On the other hand, he thought that Stearns's interpretation of the biblical words was boring. "The treatment of the subject," Curtis continued, "is, however, rather commonplace and apparent."[1]

Unlike Curtis, other writers who reviewed the Academy's exhibition focused their attention on the landscapes and genre paintings in the show. This less than enthusiastic response to *The Millennium* may have influenced Stearns's choice of subject for future works. While he did not forsake the higher category of history painting, he shifted his focus in the following years to scenes from American history. He became especially known for his paintings of the life of Washington, two of which—*Washington, the Farmer* (1851; Virginia Museum of Fine Arts, Richmond) and *Death Bed of Washington* (1851; Dayton Art Institute, Dayton, Ohio)—he showed at the Academy in 1853.[2]   DBD

1. G[eorge] W. C[urtis], "The Fine Arts. The NAD," *NYDT,* June 21, 1851.
2. For Stearns's Washington series, see Mark Thistlethwaite, "Picturing the Past: Junius Brutus Stearns's Paintings of George Washington," *Arts in Virginia* 25 (1985): 12–23.

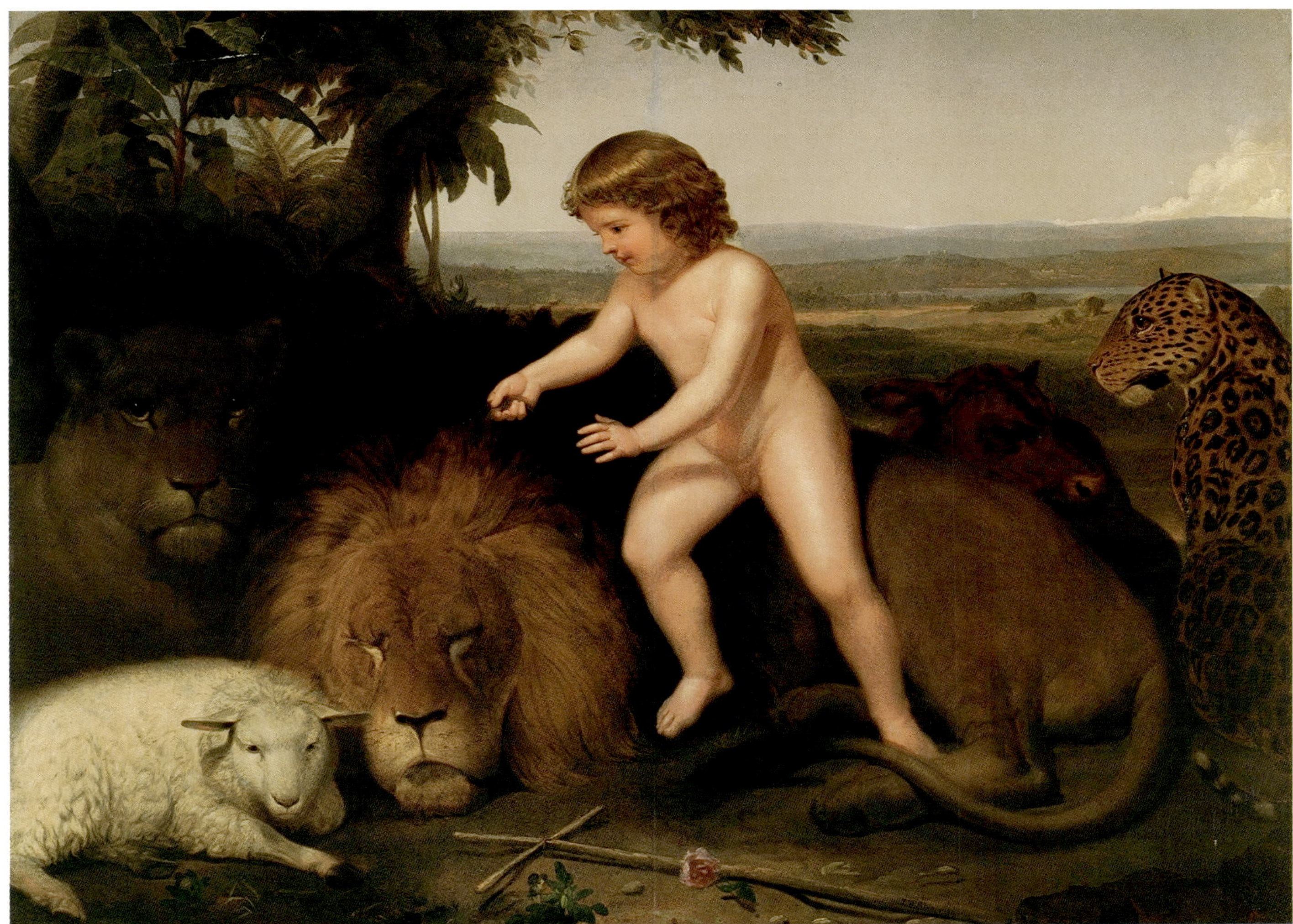

19, 20

Jasper Francis Cropsey, NA

Rossville, New York 1823–1900 Hastings-on-Hudson, New York

27th Annual Exhibition, April 13–July 7, 1852, nos. 48 and 50, for sale

The Spirit of War, 1851

Oil on canvas, 43⅝ × 67⅝

National Gallery of Art, Washington, D.C., Avalon Fund

The Spirit of Peace, 1851

Oil on canvas, 43¾ × 67

The Woodmere Art Museum, Philadelphia, Pennsylvania, Bequest of Charles Knox Smith

In 1855, Jasper Francis Cropsey published an essay, "Up Among the Clouds," in which he exalted the wonders of the sky and stated his belief that, in depicting it, artists "should be led to strive for the noblest truth and beauty."[1] Yet, as Cropsey's *oeuvre* indicates, the faithful study of nature was not his sole concern. As had Cole, Cropsey placed equal emphasis on works with literary or allegorical meaning, and, also like Cole, he was torn between painting faithful depictions of American scenery and proving his ability to create works of an elevated nature, replete with allegorical meaning.

The pendant pair *The Spirit of War* and *The Spirit of Peace* reflects the duality in Cropsey's allegiance. Imaginary landscapes that moralize on the terrors of war and the blessings of peace, the two paintings received enormous critical attention when they were exhibited at the National Academy of Design in 1852. Of *War*, the *New York Herald* noted that the "design and picturesqueness of this painting is good," while the *Albion* thought that the "conception is grand in the extreme, and nothing can exceed the vigour and felicity with which the idea is interpreted and diffused over the larger portions of the canvas."[2] While such comments were common in the critical response to Cropsey's pairs, many critics questioned Cropsey's desire to paint allegorical landscapes. The critic for the *Knickerbocker*, for example, lamented that the paintings "are too large for the amount of thought in them, and have all his faults, with few of his characteristic excellences … there is excellent painting and poetic thought, but they show too ambitious aspirations."[3] Cropsey's aspirations here also engendered unfavorable comparisons with Thomas Cole. The critic for the *Literary World* cautioned, "If we might make a suggestion to him, it would be to avoid with the greatest care whatever subjects Cole has ever treated—he has feeling and power enough to succeed in a way which will provoke no comparisons."[4]

Most critics felt that the pair suffered from an excess of detail, particularly for compositions that attempted to convey allegorical meaning. Obviously impressed with the paintings, a writer for the *New York Tribune* devoted an entire article to them; but he did take exception to certain aspects of the works. "One might say that Cropsey is too conscientious," he noted, "Knowing that the landscape is composed of infinite detail, however grand the general impression, he seems unwilling that every bit of that detail should not have full justice." This critic further felt that the careful delineation of foreground, although appealing, distract-

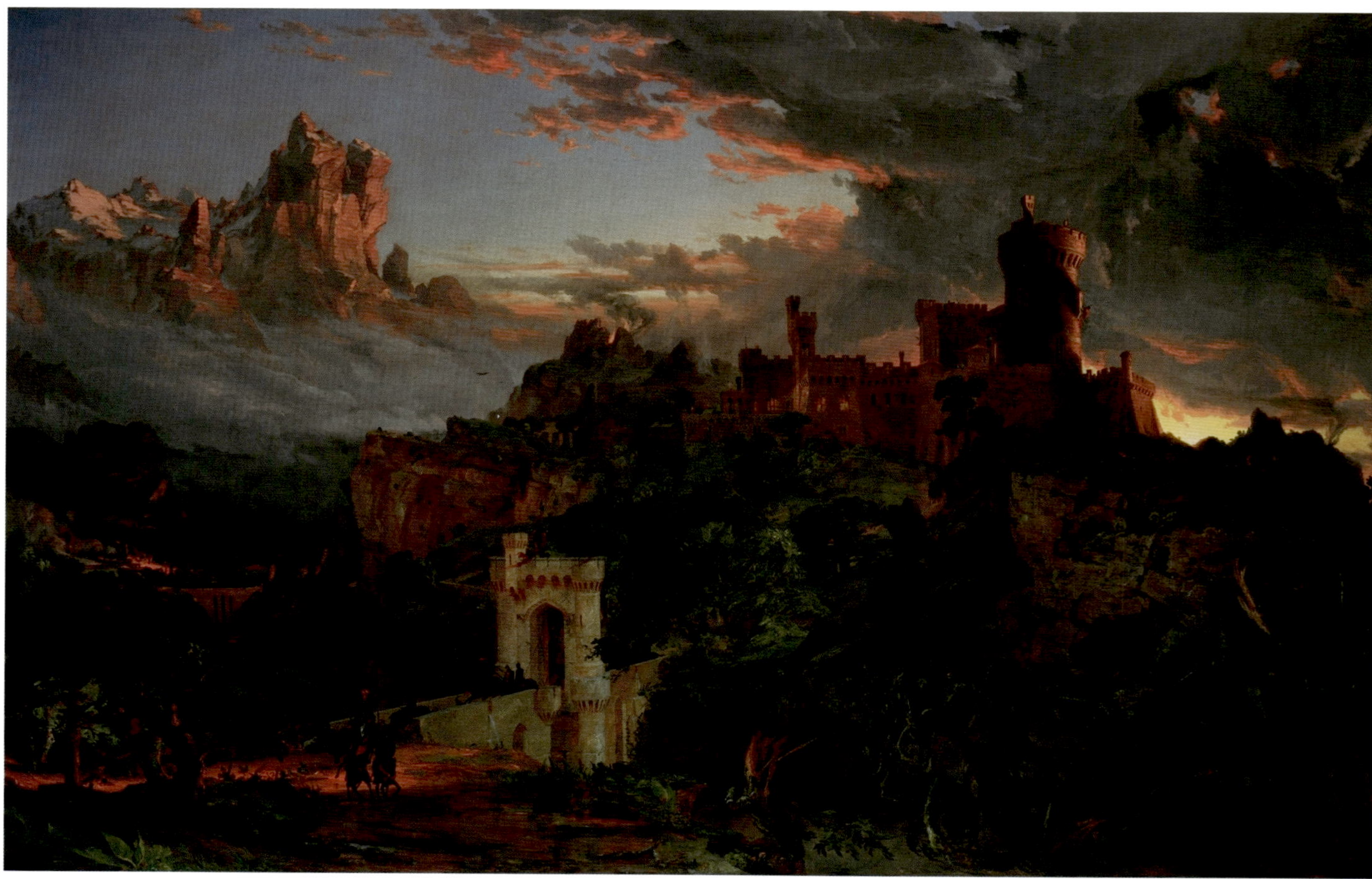

19

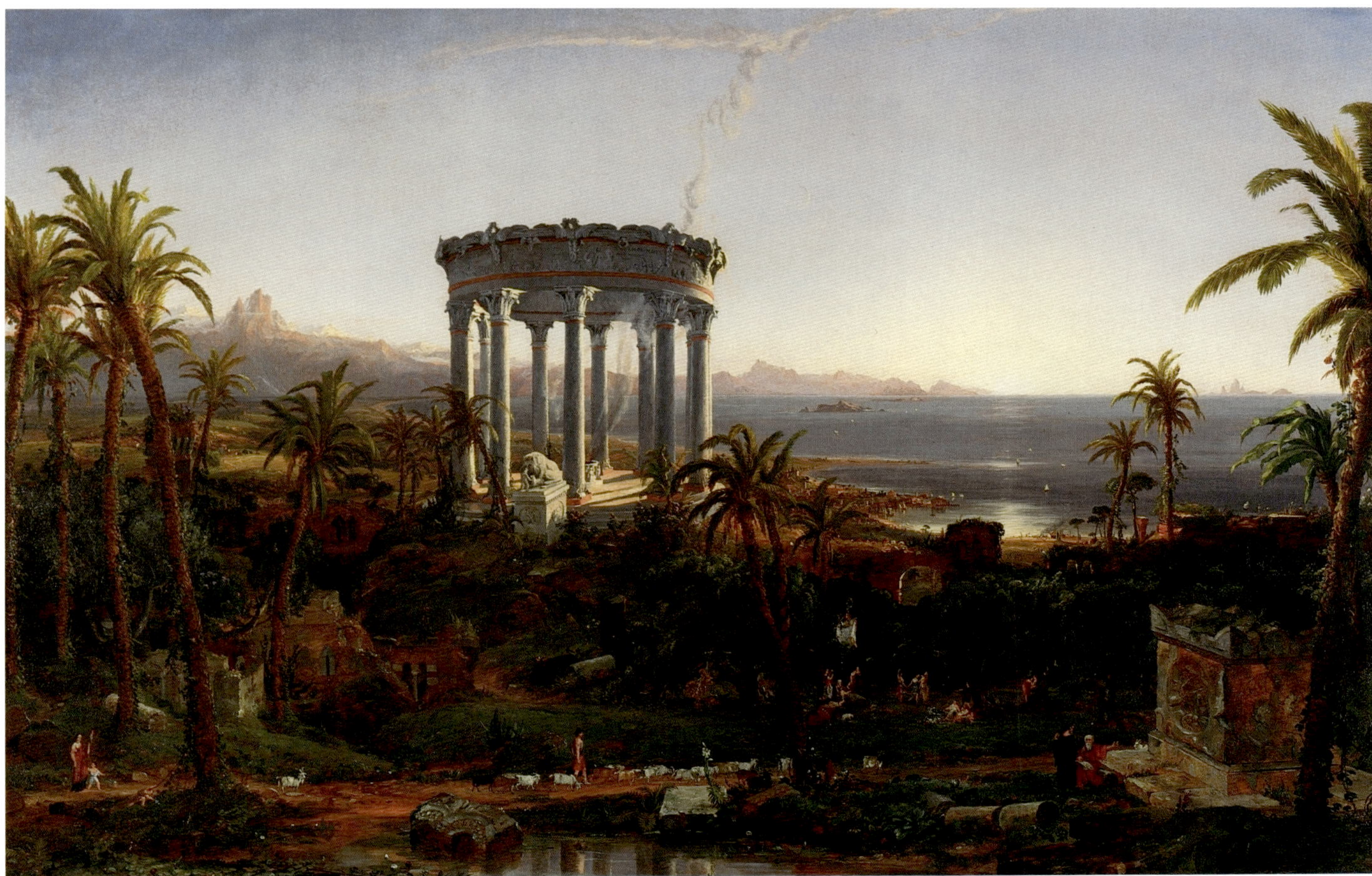

20

ed from the overall message of the painting: "Fine words do not make a poem," he wrote.[5]

Despite some negative reaction, the extensive reviews the paintings inspired indicate that Cropsey succeeded in making them the most important works at the Academy that year. The dramatic subject matter and the large format chosen by Cropsey drew the critics' attention in the midst of the hundreds of other landscapes. The written commentary, both positive and negative, inspired by the paintings, and their later exhibition history and favorable reception by artists, suggests that even in the nineteenth century, publicity of any sort was desirable, and that poor press did not necessarily affect popularity.[6]   S K

1. J. F. Cropsey, "Up Among the Clouds," *Crayon* 2 (August 8, 1855): 80.

2. "The Fine Arts. Exhibition of Paintings by the NAD," *NYH*, April 21, 1852; "Fine Arts. The NAD," *Albion* 11 (April 24, 1852): 201–2.

3. [Lewis Gaylord Clark?], Exhibition of the NAD," *Knickerbocker* 39 (June 1852): 567.

4. "The Fine Arts. Exhibition of the NAD.—No. III," *LW* 10 (May 8, 1852): 332.

5. [George W. Curtis], "The Fine Arts. NAD," *NYDT*, April 24, 1852.

6. The paintings were purchased by the Philadelphia collector Joseph Harrison, in whose collection they remained until 1912 when they were bought by separate parties. They were reunited in a special exhibition at the National Gallery of Art in Washington, D.C., in 1994 (see Franklin Kelly, *Jasper Francis Cropsey: The Spirit of War and The Spirit of Peace* [Washington, D.C.: National Gallery of Art, 1994]).

21

Asher Brown Durand, NA

Jefferson Village [Maplewood], New Jersey 1796–1886 Jefferson Village, New Jersey

> 29th Annual Exhibition, March 22–April 2, 1854, no. 386, owner H. K. Browne [*sic*]

June Shower, 1854

> Oil on canvas, 33⅛ × 48⅛
>
> The Manoogian Collection, Taylor, Michigan

Asher Brown Durand painted *June Shower* for presentation as a gift to his friend and colleague, sculptor Henry Kirke Brown (1814–1886).[1] Ten years after he received the painting, Brown expressed to Durand the regard that he and his family felt for it. "I wish it were in my power," he wrote, "to express to you how much Mrs. Brown and myself prize the landscape. It is the central point of all our possessions . . . . I shall not part with the picture as long as I have a wall to hang it on."[2] Certainly another indication of the sculptor's delight in the painting is that he lent it to the National Academy of Design's annual exhibition in March, 1854, probably within weeks of its having been finished.[3] As soon as the Academy's exhibition closed, Brown sent the work on to the annual exhibition of the Pennsylvania Academy of the Fine Arts in Philadelphia. Later, in 1915, Brown's nephew, the artist Henry K. Bush-Brown, who had inherited it, lent it to the Panama-Pacific International Exposition in San Francisco.

The high opinion that the Brown family had of the work was affirmed by everyone who wrote about it when it debuted at the

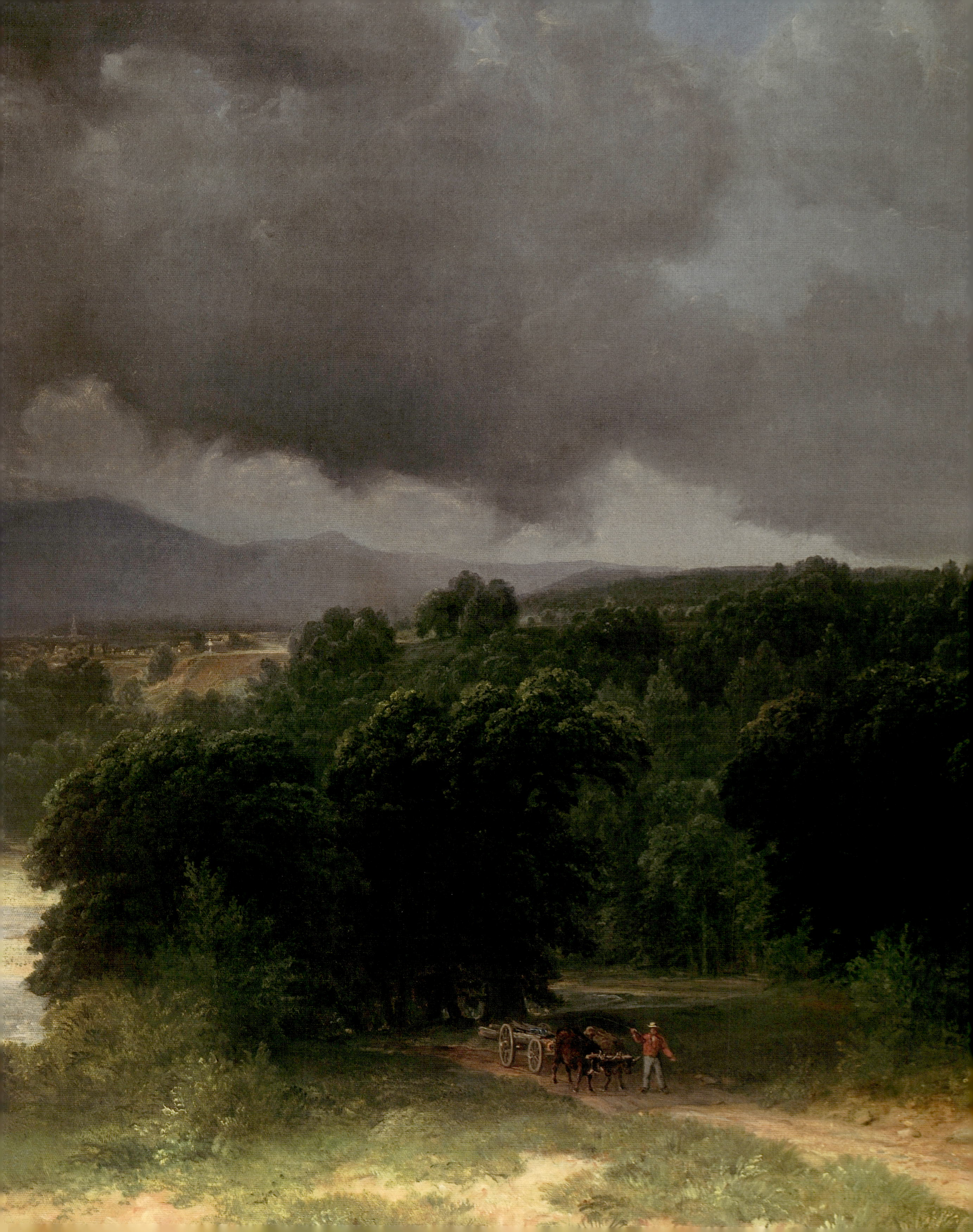

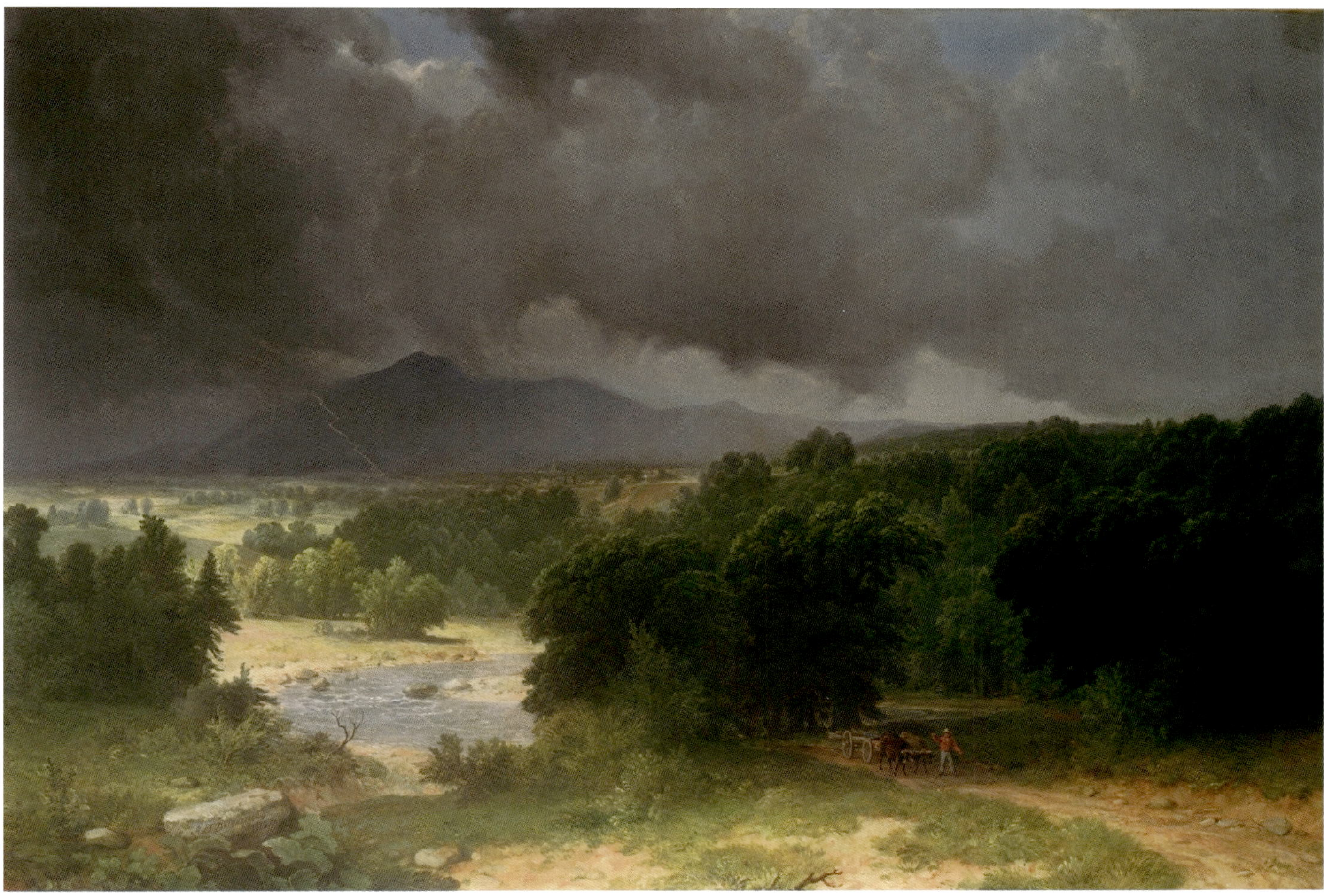

National Academy and for a number of years thereafter. One of the most enthusiastic reviews came from a writer for the *Albion* who was particularly impressed by Durand's ability to depict a storm with such precision that, in looking at the painting, a viewer could have the same experience, physically and emotionally, that he or she would have in the presence of a real storm. "You may almost see and feel and hear the oncoming of the summer thunder-storm," he wrote, "with its floods of rain in the distance, and its premonitory patterings nigh at hand."[4] A critic for the *Photographic and Fine Art Journal* agreed and tried to do in prose what Durand had done in paint. "There is something terrific in that moment," he wrote,

in which brute and human nature sympathizes. The cattle huddled together in the field, the doors and windows are shut, children sit close to their mothers, while the thunder rolls heavily in the distance, the big drops of rain patter among the leaves, the earth grows dark, the furious wind lashes and twists the trees like reeds—there is a lull—and then simultaneous with the white darting fire comes the quick blow of sound as if the very earth had split. Then the clouds break away; the peaceful and clear light falls upon the scene.[5]

Presumably, *June Shower* was returned to the Brown family once the Pennsylvania Academy's annual exhibition of 1854 closed. It did not appear again publicly until Ortgies Gallery staged a memorial exhibition of Durand's work in New York in 1887.[6] In the interim, however, *June Shower* was not forgotten. At the end of 1854, E. Anna Lewis recalled having seen it at the National Academy and reported in *Graham's Magazine* that it "is one of the most perfect and pleasing pictures of its kind ever painted, and the best that Durand has yet produced." Her experience on viewing it was as immediate and emotional as was that of the writer for the *Albion*. "We hear the breeze driving the clouds along the air," she wrote, "and the big drops of rain falling into the lips of the thirsty foliage, and feel the dripping wings of the wind until we imagine ourselves out in a June shower."[7]

In 1871, a writer for *Scribner's Monthly* made a list of those paintings by Durand that had been the most popular in exhibitions and that had brought the painter the most attention, praise, and prizes. Among these was *June Shower*.[8]   DBD

1 Evidence that *June Shower* was painted specifically for Brown is given by John Durand in his biography of his father (John Durand, *The Life and Times of A. B. Durand* [New York, 1894], 175). The role of *June Shower* in the relationship between Durand and Brown and the circumstances of its creation is the focus of David B. Dearinger, "Asher B. Durand and Henry Kirke Brown: An Artistic Friendship," *American Art Journal* 20 (1988): 74–83.

2 Brown to Durand, February 1, 1864. Brown was as good as his word: the painting remained in his family until the 1980s.

3 The catalogue of that show included a brief quotation from a poem with the listing for Durand's painting: "Yon murky cloud is foul with rain, / I see it driving o'er the plain."

4 "Fine Arts. National Academy of Design," *Albion* 13 (April 15, 1854): 177.

5 "The National Academy of Design," *Photographic and Fine Art Journal* 7 (May, 1854): 157.

6 *Studies in Oil By Asher B. Durand, N.A., Deceased* (New York: Ortgies Art Gallery, 1887), no. 380.

7 E. Anna Lewis, "Art and Artists of America. Asher Brown Durand," *Graham's American Monthly Magazine* 45 (October, 1854): 321–22.

8 D. O'C. Townley, "Living American Artists. Asher Brown Durand, Ex-President N. A. D.," *Scribner's Monthly* 2 (May 1871): 43.

22

William Sidney Mount, NA

Setauket, New York 1807–1868 Setauket, New York

Coming to the Point: a Variation of "Bargaining for a Horse," 29th Annual Exhibition, March 22– April 25, 1854, no. 150, owner A. R. Smith

Coming to the Point, 1854

Oil on canvas, 25 × 30
Collection of The New-York Historical Society

Nearly twenty years after the exhibition of his highly acclaimed *Bargaining for a Horse* (1835, New-York Historical Society) at the National Academy of Design, William Sidney Mount showed *Coming to the Point*, a "variation" on the earlier work, at the Academy's exhibition of 1854. As a rule, Mount was averse to such repetition,[1] but the earlier success of the theme prompted him to recycle it. The critics, however, were not impressed with this reincarnation.

The demise of the American Art-Union in 1852 may also have contributed to Mount's decision to revisit *Bargaining for a Horse.* The Art-Union's membership had grown to 13,578 in 1851, the year before the New York Supreme Court ruled that its distribution of art works by lottery was illegal.[2] The managers of the organization believed that the annual distribution of engravings to all subscribers, rather than the lottery for original works, was responsible for this popularity.[3] The success of *Bargaining for a Horse,* in both its original form and in reproduction, gave Mount's publisher and friend William Schaus every reason to believe that another such print, taken from a painting with a similar theme, could be lucrative. Both Schaus and Mount set their sights on *Coming to the Point,* which had been commissioned from Mount by Adam R. Smith, an art collector from Troy, New York.[4]

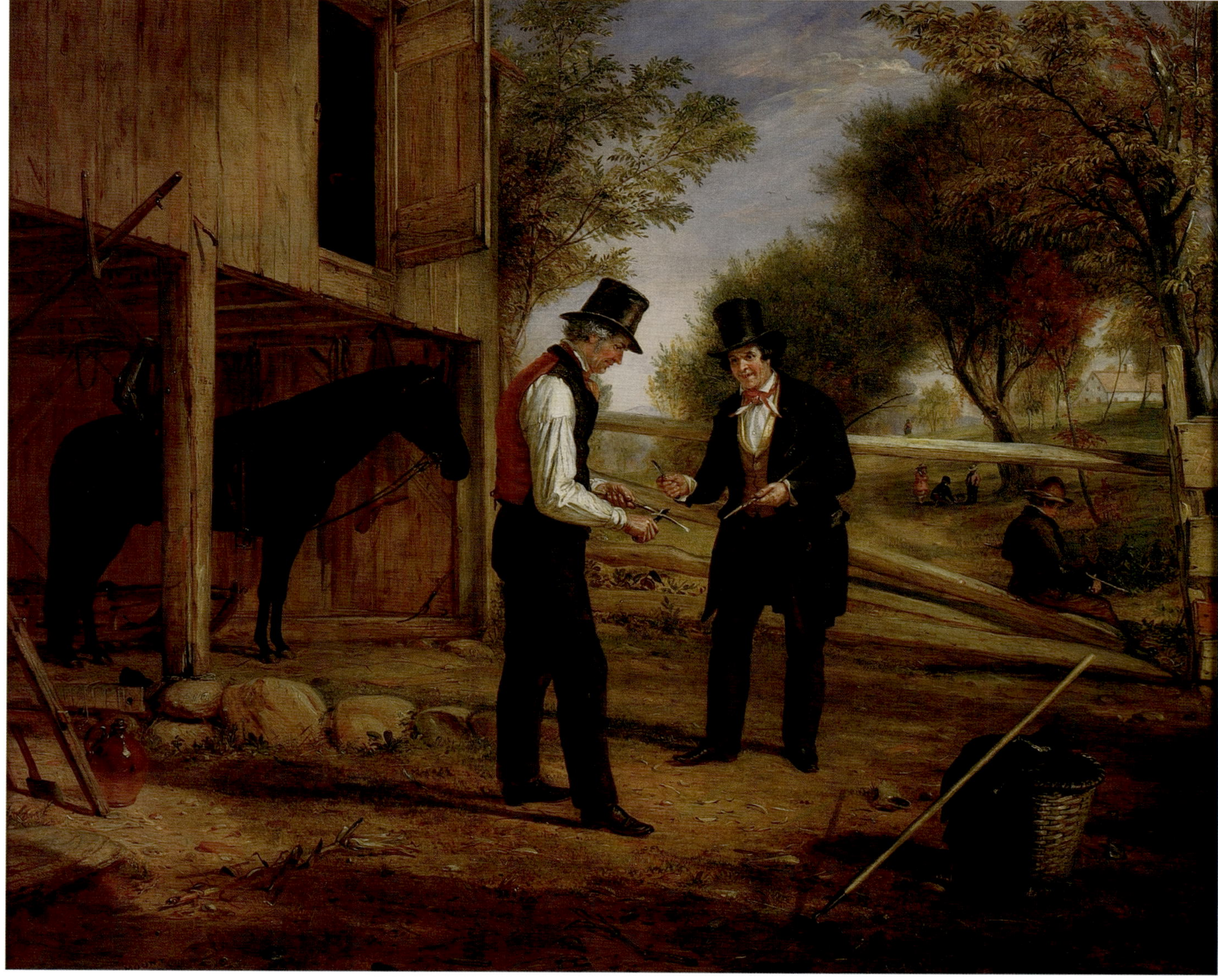

22

Of the few known reviews of *Coming to the Point,* the *New York Tribune*'s assessment was the least charitable. "We are sorry not to compliment Mr. Mount on this production," the paper confessed,

but the truth is, it is a great falling off. The comic humor which illuminated his former works is here very, very feebly reflected, while the landscape of the back ground, the horse under the shed and all the accessories generally are inexpressibly poor. The horse looks like a child's toy, and the wonder is how any body would be so long in settling the price of so worthless an animal.[5]

The critic from the *New-York Times* was not so negative and even thought that a few elements, such as the barn, were "excellently painted." He was not a great enthusiast of Mount's work, though, and went on to say, "The fault which we find with this, as with everything else we have seen by the same artist, is its flatness, and also its peculiar method of treatment."[6] Mount's attempt to recapture the acclaim of his earlier work was, by all accounts, a failure.

Although the painting was assailed by critics when it was first shown at the National Academy's annual exhibition in 1854, Schaus hoped that the relatively limited press coverage of the exhibition would not jeopardize sales of the lithograph.[7] He even published a "press release" in which he boldly—and inaccurately—asserted that the painting "is pronounced by all who have seen it the *chef d'oeuvre* of the artist."[8] The absurdity of his claim is made apparent by one of his own letters to Mount in which he reported "even artists have been unkind to [the] work."[9]

In his correspondence, Mount did not betray much surprise at the bad publicity elicited by *Coming to the Point.* He ascribed the negative reviews to disgust over the amount of money he had received to reproduce the painting. As he wrote to Schaus, "The two hundred dollar copy right, which you gave me, could not be forgiven; that raised the steel pen against me, as you had predicted."[10] Whether or not Schaus had promised to buy the copyright before Mount even took up the commission is unknown. The publisher had, however, paid the artist before the work was exhibited at the Academy, and its inclusion there was clearly understood by the press as a publicity effort for the forthcoming print.[11]

MM

1. Alfred Frankenstein, *William Sidney Mount* (New York: Abrams, 1975), 269.

2. See Maybelle Mann, *The American Art-Union* (Otisville, New York: ALM Associates, 1977), 26, 90.

3. Ibid., 25.

4. Letter from Mount to Schaus, March 15, 1854, New-York Historical Society, repr. in Frankenstein, 167. Although Adam R. Smith, a collector from Troy, New York, commissioned and owned the actual painting, Mount sold the copyright for the work to Schaus without Smith's knowledge (letter from Mount to Smith, March 4, 1854, New-York Historical Society, reprinted in Frankenstein, 165–66).

5. "The Fine Arts. The NAD," *NYDT,* March 30, 1854.

6. "The NAD," *NYT,* April 4, 1854.

7. The exhibition was only open for a month because the Academy had to move out of its building by May 1. Letter from Mount to Schaus dated March 2, 1854, in the collection of the New-York Historical Society, reprinted in Frankenstein, 165; Eliot Clark, *History of the National Academy of Design, 1825–1953* (New York: Columbia University Press, 1954), 70.

8. "Autobiographical Press Release by William Schaus," New-York Historical Society, repr. in Frankenstein, 153.

9. Letter dated April 24, 1854, Museums at Stony Brook, Long Island, repr. in Frankenstein, 167.

10. Letter, April 26, 1854, New-York Historical Society, repr. in Frankenstein, 167.

11. Mount corresponded with Smith and Schaus about the sale of the copyright for the painting in early March, 1854 (see Frankenstein, 165–66)

23

Frederic Edwin Church, NA

Hartford, Connecticut 1826–1900 New York, New York

La Magdalena, 30th Annual Exhibition, March 12–May 10, 1855, no. 131, owner Suydam

Scene on the Magdalena, 1854

Oil on canvas, 28¼ × 42
National Academy of Design, New York

In 1853, Frederic Edwin Church and his friend Cyrus W. Field spent five months touring parts of South America, including what is now Colombia. A major part of the journey was their ascent of the Magdalena River, via canoes and steamers, from its mouth in the Caribbean Sea near Barranquilla, to Honda, the last navigable spot upriver. After returning to the United States, Church spent the following two years working on a number of major paintings based on sketches he had made in South America. He sent four of these—*The Cordileras: Sunrise* (1854; Alexander Gallery, New York); *Tamaca Palms* (1854; Corcoran Gallery of Art, Washington, D.C.); *Tequendama Falls, near Bogota, New Grenada* (1854; Cincinnati Art Museum); and *Scene on the Magdalena*—to the National Academy of Design's annual exhibition of 1855. They introduced the public to an important new phase in Church's career and in the history of American landscape painting. For Church, the venture was a critical and popular success.

By 1855, Church was already familiar to New Yorkers. He had been participating in the National Academy's exhibitions since 1845 and in those of the American Art-Union since 1847, and he had received consistently good notices for the works he showed at these venues. In 1845, the *Broadway Journal* pointed out two small landscapes that Church submitted to the Academy that year as "evidence of genius."[1] Three years later, the artist's *View of Stockbridge* (location unknown) was praised. The *New York Evening Post* called it an "excellent landscape of immense labor" that proved that Church was "very steadily and surely advancing in his profession."[2] This was confirmed in 1849, with his *West Rock, New Haven* (New Britain Museum of Art, New Britain, Connecticut), which received almost universal praise, [3] and in 1851, when his *Beacon Off Mount Desert Island* (1851; private collection) was lauded.[4] In 1852, his *The Wreck* (1852; The Parthenon, Nashville, Tennessee) was singled out from the Academy's exhibition for particularly favorable comment.[5]

With this reassuring record, it is not surprising that Church chose the National Academy as the place to announce his new interest in the landscape of South America. Most critics took the bait. The *Knickerbocker,* for example, observed:

Church shows, this year, that his genius is not confined to painting northern scenes. We have a most brilliant triumph from him. These South-American pictures of his are noble

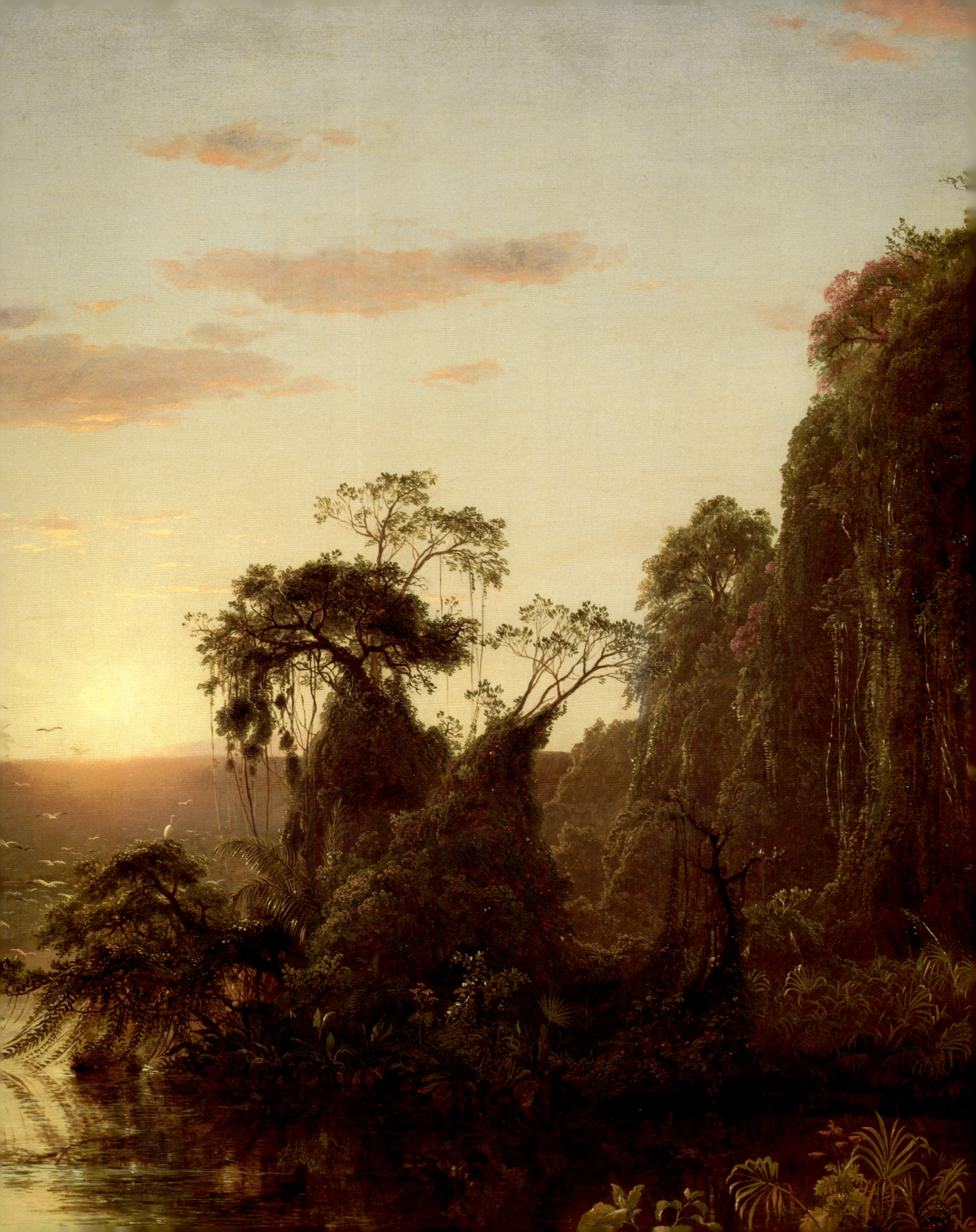

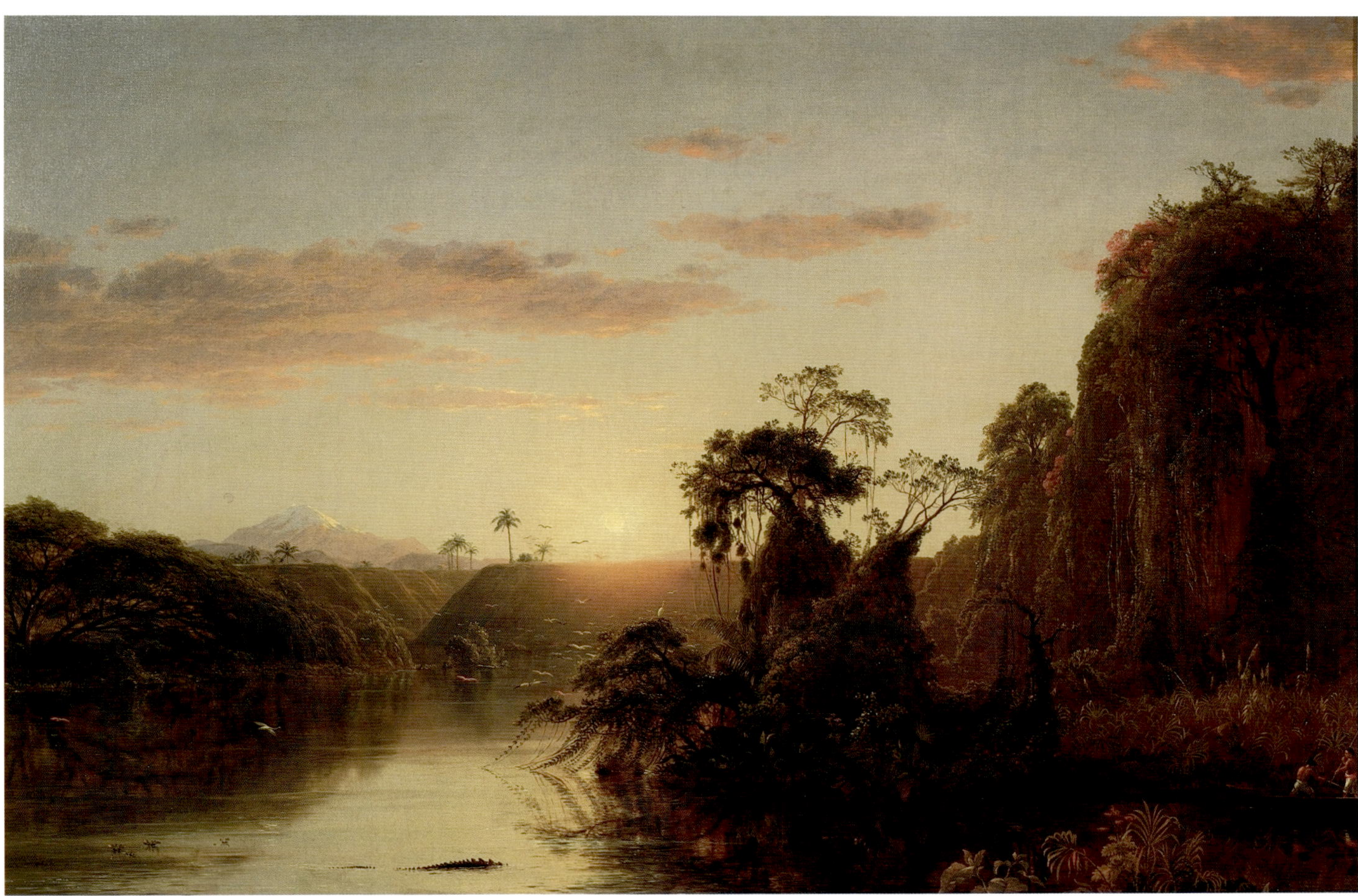

23

*achievements. The golden hues, the painted flowers, the rich
fruit, the luxuriant foliage of the tropics, have been seized by
him and placed lovingly on his canvas.*[6]

The *Crayon* declared that the four paintings made "a great
addition to the attractiveness of the Exhibition, and deserve very
faithful attention."[7] Critic Clarence Cook reported in the
Independent that the paintings "are interesting not only as faithful transcripts of unfamiliar scenery, but as evidences of progress
in the artist. They show careful study and facility of execution."[8]
Most critics praised the works as a group and, while some singled
out *Tequendama Falls*, the largest and most ambitious of the four,
as their favorite,[9] none of the four works went unnoticed. The
Albion told its readers that *Scene on the Magdalena* was a "most
elaborate and apparently most truthful portraiture of that marvelous tropical vegetation, which bedecks the river."[10] The
Knickerbocker challenged critics to "Look at Number 63, 'Tamaca
Palms;' see the clearness, the brilliancy, the depth of atmosphere,
and then say that Church is not a great painter—if you can."[11]
The *New York Daily Tribune* marveled at the manner in which
Church had filled both works with brilliant local color and "animated them with characteristic details, aquatic birds in flocks,
crocodiles on the water, trailing plants entangled in inextricable
knots, and so forth."[12] "What a gush of colors!" the *Knickerbocker*
said of the *Cordilleras*, "How the sun glows in the heavens, and
bathes in the air, like a lover in the lap of beauty!" And of *Tamaca
Palms:* "Aerial distance, and skies, and foreground are Church's
forte, and in this class of subjects he has full opportunity for
displaying it."[13]

Another aspect of his talent that was made apparent by the
South American group was his ability to render exacting, almost
microscopic detail. The *Crayon* expressed its admiration for this.
"We may rely on each plant as a veritable transcript, [and this] is
as it ought to be, for no matter how subtle the treatment of a picture, or how artistic its composition, if it have not this basis of
truth we are only polishing pebbles."[14] *Putnam's Monthly Magazine* was equally impressed with this aspect of Church's talent.
"His perceptions are uncommonly minute," the magazine
observed, "going down into the microscopic range. . . ."[15] The
four South American paintings that Church exhibited in 1855
suggested that he was quickly becoming the acknowledged master of landscape painting in America and the rightful heir of his
teacher, Thomas Cole.   DBD

1. "20th Annual Exhibition of the Academy of National Design: Landscapes,"
Broadway Journal 1 (May 3, 1845): 276. The paintings were *Twilight among the
Mountains* (Olana State Historic Site, Hudson, New York) and *Hudson Scenery*
(location unknown). Church's exhibition history and the present location, when
known, of paintings exhibited during his lifetime are given in Debora Rindge,
"Chronology," in Franklin Kelly, Stephen J. Gould and James Ryan, *Frederic
Edwin Church* (National Gallery of Art, Washington, D.C.: 1989), 158–72.

2. "The Twenty-Third Exhibition of the National Academy," *NYEP*, May 13,
1848; "NAD. Twenty-Third Annual Exhibition," *NYEP*, May 30, 1848. Other positive comments about the painting were made by the *Morning Courier and New
York Enquirer*, May 11, 1848, and *Family Companion* 2 (June 24, 1848): 78–79.

3. See, for example, "The NAD," *Bulletin of the American Art-Union* 2 (May
1849): 13–15; Achille Bonbon, "The Academy Exhibition," *International Art-Union
Journal* 4 (May 1849): 52–59; "Editor's Table. National Academy of Design,"
Knickerbocker 33 (1849): 468–70; "NAD," *Morning Courier and New-York Enquirer*,
May 3, 1849.

4. For example, G[eorge] W. C[urtis], "The Fine Arts. The NAD. III.," *NYDT,* May 10, 1851; and N. N., "The Twenty-Sixth Exhibition of the National Academy of Design," *Bulletin of the American Art-Union* no. 2 (May 1851): 21–24.

5. For example, "Fine Arts. The NAD—No. III," *Albion* 11 (May 8, 1852): 225–26; and "The Fine Arts. NAD. IV," *NYDT,* May 8, 1852.

6. [Lewis Gaylord Clark?], "Editor's Table. Exhibition of the NAD," *Knickerbocker* 45 (May 1855): 532.

7. "Sketchings. The NAD," *Crayon* 1 (March 21, 1855): 186.

8. Clarence Cook, "The Fine Arts. The NAD," *Independent* 7 (April 19, 1855): 121.

9. For example, see "The Fine Arts. The National Academy Exhibition," *NYH,* March 24, 1855; and R. T., "Exhibition of the NAD. [Third Article]," *NYDT,* May 7, 1855. The big painting did not please everyone, however. A writer for the *Knickerbocker,* almost certainly its editor Lewis Gaylord Clark, found it "not quite up to the mark" and even suggested that Church should refrain from painting falling water, "for he cannot" ([Lewis Gaylord Clark?], "Editor's Table. Exhibition of the NAD," *Knickerbocker* 45 [May 1855]: 532). A writer for the *Albion* agreed, stating that Church "has not overcome the difficult tumult of the rushing, bubbling, living, liquid torrent" ("Fine Arts. The NAD," *Albion* 14 [March 24, 1855]): 141). Consciously or not, Church proved these critics wrong when his *Niagara* (Corcoran Gallery of Art, Washington, D.C.), painted in 1857, made him the most famous and successful artist in America at the time.

10. "Fine Arts. The National Academy of Design," *Albion* 14 (March 24, 1855): 141.

11. [Lewis Gaylord Clark?], "Exhibition of the NAD," *Knickerbocker* 45 (May 1855): 532.

12. R. T., "Exhibition of the NAD. [Third Article]," *NYDT,* May 7, 1855.

13. [Lewis Gaylord Clark?], "Exhibition of the NAD," *Knickerbocker* 45 (May 1855): 532.

14. "Sketchings. The Academy Exhibition. —No. I," *Crayon* 1 (March 28, 1855): 202.

15. "The NAD," *Putnam's Monthly Magazine* 5 (May 1855): 507–08.

24

William Morris Hunt

Brattleboro, Vermont 1824–1879 Isles of Shoals, New Hampshire

"*La Marguerite,*" 31st Annual Exhibition, March 14–May 10, 1856, no. 169, owner Martin Brimmer

La Marguerite, 1853[1]

Oil on canvas, 46 × 35½

Museum of Fine Arts, Boston, Bequest of Mrs. Martin Brimmer

William Morris Hunt made his debut at the National Academy of Design in 1856 with three paintings: *The Fortune Teller* (fig. 34), *Girl with Rabbit* (private collection), and *La Marguerite.* The last two were lent by Hunt's patron, the important Boston art collector Martin Brimmer, who had already lent *La Marguerite* to the Boston Athenaeum, where it was first shown publicly two years earlier. The critical reception of Hunt's paintings at the Academy in 1856 was mixed. Most critics weighed in against *The Fortune Teller,* which they found mystifying, at best. A writer for the *New York Evening Post,* for example, thought it was "repulsive and false," caustically adding that it "looks like some aboriginal illumination of a rhinoceros hide."[2] A critic for the *New York Daily Tribune* was not sure what to make of the painting or how to respond to it. "[It] is impossible to discern the meaning of the artist," he explained, "or to divine the reason of his adopting so strange a method of expressing his ideas."[3]

Hunt had only recently returned from studying in France with the progressive teacher Thomas Couture. Couture encouraged his students to paint in a more expressive manner, at least in the planning stages of their work.[4] It was this aspect of Couture's style, as translated by Hunt, that created ambivalence in the reaction of critics to his work. A writer for the *New-York Times,* for example, thought that Hunt's *La Marguerite* was "strange." Nevertheless, he admired the "latent power" that was evident in the painting, even though he was not sure what this "power" might ultimately lead to. "The good that is in these pictures," he concluded, referring to all three paintings Hunt sent to the Academy that year, "is very good and normal, while the bad may be only an accident, or a perverse viciousness. We shall see more of Mr. Hunt by and by, and then we shall know better what he is driving at."[5]

One of the longest analyses of Hunt's submissions to the Academy's 1856 exhibition appeared in the *Albion* under the by-line "Louvre." Whoever the critic was, he or she, noted the "Couturesque" qualities of Hunt's paintings, as did most critics who wrote about them. *La Marguerite,* the critic thought, "is a masterly piece of work," with the best modeling and coloring of any painting in the exhibition. On the other hand, the critic continued, *The Fortune Teller* had been influenced by some of Couture's less admirable qualities, especially in the "morbid flesh tints" that are reminiscent of Couture's best known work, *The Romans of the Decadence* (1847; Musée du Louvre). Despite this, no American painter has a more promising career, the critic concluded, "than Couture's favorite pupil, William Hunt."[6]

The *Albion* critic, it seems, was as concerned about the possible negative impact of Couture on Hunt, as were his colleagues at other journals and newspapers. So, too, was Clarence Cook, the reliably vicious critic who wrote for a number of American newspapers and journals starting in the 1850s. Cook's initial view of Hunt, as seen in his reaction to the works the artist sent to the Academy in 1856, was positive, if cautious. He called *La Marguerite* "very lovely," but, in his more typical way, quickly cautioned his readers that Hunt had just returned from his stint with Couture. "[W]e can only hope," Cook wrote, "that the vicious mannerisms of that great painter have only clung to his pupil's earliest works, and that in the next stride he will shake them off." As far as Cook could see, Hunt's development and assertion of his own style was worth waiting for. "Certainly his pictures are full of hope and promise," Cook continued, "this is the best word we can say for them, but the hope springs alike from the intensity of his conceptions and his power of giving to them form and body. We shall not forget him in the future."[7] Cook was as good as his word, but his future notice of Hunt would never be as positive as it was in 1856. In fact, Cook quickly became one of Hunt's most unrelenting critics, eventually dismissing the artist's oeuvre as "flimsy rubbish."[8]

Clarence Cook notwithstanding, Hunt's *La Marguerite* gained a certain amount of popularity with the public via a lithograph that was made of it in 1863. In his history of American artists, Henry Tuckerman noted the fact and, in passing, explained the title of the painting. It depicts "a beautiful girl," he wrote, "slowly testing her love by nipping leaf after leaf from the flower of that name—simple in action, but so naively true to nature, that it has become a popular lithograph."[9] DBD

1. The painting shown here is the second of three versions of the subject painted by Hunt. He executed the first version in about 1852, when he showed it at the Paris Salon, and the third version around 1872, when he showed it at that

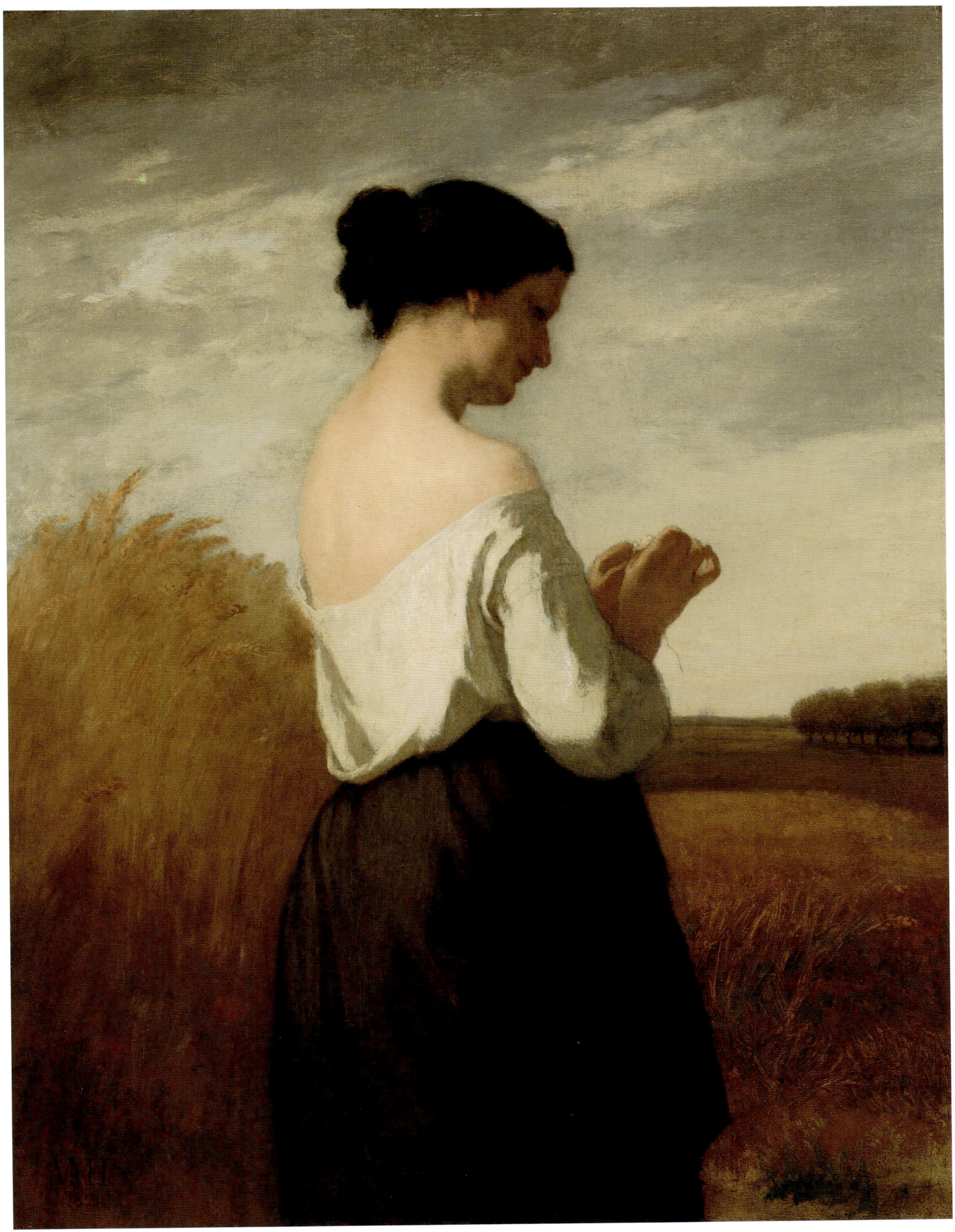

year's exhibition at the National Academy (no. 336). That also happened to be the last Academy exhibition in which he participated.

2 "NAD," *NYEP*, April 7, 1856.

3 "The NAD," *NYDT*, April 12, 1856.

4 Martha J. Hoppin, "The Sources and Development of William Morris Hunt's Painting," in *William Morris Hunt, A Memorial Exhibition* (Boston: Museum of Fine Arts, 1979), 9. As Hoppin notes, "From Couture, Hunt inherited an unusually great stress on technique and on the spontaneity associated with sketches."

5 "NAD," *NYT*, May 10, 1856.

6 Louvre, "Fine Arts," *Albion* 15 (April 5, 1856): 165.

7 Clarence Cook, "NAD. Thirty-First Yearly Exhibition," *Independent*, May 1, 1856.

8 Quoted in Henry Adams, "The Contradictions of William Morris Hunt," *William Morris Hunt, A Memorial Exhibition*, 24.

9 Henry T. Tuckerman, *Artist-Life: or Sketches of American Painters* (New York: D. Appleton & Co., 1847), 449. The lithograph was made by D. C. Fabronius in Boston (*American Paintings in the Museum of Fine Arts, Boston* [Boston: Museum of Fine Arts, 1969], 1:156).

25

George Henry Boughton, NA

Norwich, England 1833–1905 London, England

Winter Twilight, 33rd Annual Exhibition, April 13–June 30, 1858, no. 57, for sale

Winter Scene, 1860 §

Oil on canvas, 15⅛ × 12¼

National Academy of Design, New York

George Henry Boughton received his first notable critical attention when he exhibited a painting called *Winter Twilight* (1858; New-York Historical Society) at the National Academy of Design in 1858. Its success encouraged him to paint a number of similar scenes during the years that followed, one of which, shown here, was bought from the artist by painter and art patron James A. Suydam. The atmosphere, light, and mood of the painting are similar to those in the work that received rave reviews in 1858.

According to the artist, *Winter Twilight* of 1858 was created out-of-doors and depicts an island in or near the Hudson River just south of Albany, New York. Many years after completing the image, the artist recalled its early history:

It was the depth of winter and it struck me that I had never seen a winter landscape painted just as I saw it. I went into a field and worked until I was so cold that I was on the point of giving up. . . . I sent it to the New York National Academy of Design. . . . In a little while I got a letter saying it was accepted and hung. Then I began to think of going to New York to try my luck. . . . As soon as I arrived I met a friend, who said to me, "you're in luck; Your picture has been sold to R. L. Stuart. . . . The picture had been skied, but the president, Mr. Durand, saw it, and said, "That is too good a thing to be put up there. . . . and he said to the hangers, "Suppose you put that down here on the line."[1]

Durand's high opinion of the painting soon found support.

Although Boughton was little known in 1858—a "comparatively fresh hand,"[2] as one writer put it—*Winter Twilight* was noticed and praised by almost every critic who saw it at the Academy that year. The *New-York Times* called it "an exquisite piece of luminous fidelity," while the *Crayon* acclaimed it "one of the best pictures in the collection." It was especially praised for the manner in which it caught "the sentiment" of the time of day and the season.[3] A writer for *Harper's Weekly*, who opened his review of the Academy's exhibition with a discussion of Boughton's painting, described it as a "perfect piece of winter" because it successfully captured "the chill distance, the dark outline of trees against the sky, the house withdrawing as if into itself, the lustre of the ice in the foreground, . . . and the hurry of the woodman homeward."[4]

Likewise, the art journal *Albion* was delighted with the artist's ability to render convincingly the tonalities of winter. "The tint is almost that of blue steel, as reflected from the clouds," the critic wrote, "relieved only by a glimmer of cold yellow light that remains just above the horizon, and is itself caught up by the ice of a frozen stream." Again, however, it was the artist's understanding of the mood of the season that the writer most admired. "The whole is sad and solemn," he went on, "and the dullness of the atmosphere is rather felt than seen." His only worry was that some viewers might find Boughton's impressions of winter too oppressive.[5]

The success of *Winter Twilight* at the Academy in 1858 gave Boughton the self-confidence to move to New York City that same year, taking rooms at the Tenth Street Studio Building. His work caught the attention of some of New York's leading artists and collectors. One of these—either Asher B. Durand or John F. Kensett, depending on which version of the story one reads—recommended *Winter Twilight*, then on view at the Academy, to the important New York art collector Robert L. Stuart. The sale prompted him to be, at least for a time, a specialist in winter landscapes, and many important New York collectors eventually had examples of Boughton's work in their possession. Undoubtedly proud of his acquisition, Stuart sent it to the Paris Exposition in 1867, after which it again appeared at the Academy with fifty-nine other American paintings and sculptures lately returned from that world's fair.[6]   DBD

1. George H. Boughton, quoted in Rudolph de Cordova, "Illustrated Interviews. LXXI—Mr. George Henry Boughton, R. A.," *Strand Magazine* 20 (July 1900): 8. Also see Frederick W. White, "Gallery and Studio. George H. Boughton," *Art Amateur* 7 (March 1883): 48, and James Dafforne, in "The Works of George Henry Boughton," *Art Journal* (London) (1893): 41.

2. [George W. Curtis], "The Lounger. This Year's Pictures," *HW* 2 (May 1, 1858): 275.

3. "The Fine Arts. Exhibition of the NAD" *NYT*, May 8, 1858; [John Durand], "Sketchings. Exhibition of the NAD," *Crayon* (1858): 147.

4. [George W. Curtis], "The Lounger. This Year's Pictures," *HW* 2 (May 1, 1858): 275. Curtis was so moved that he ended his analysis of the painting by quoting a number of lines from Shelley on winter, beginning with "It was a winter such as when birds die . . . ."

5. "Fine Arts. NAD," *Albion* 36 (April 24, 1858): 201.

6. NAD, *Catalogue of First Winter Exhibition, Including the First Annual Collection of the American Society of Painters in Water Colors, and the Works from the American Art Department of the Paris Universal Exposition* (New York, 1867–68), no. 684.

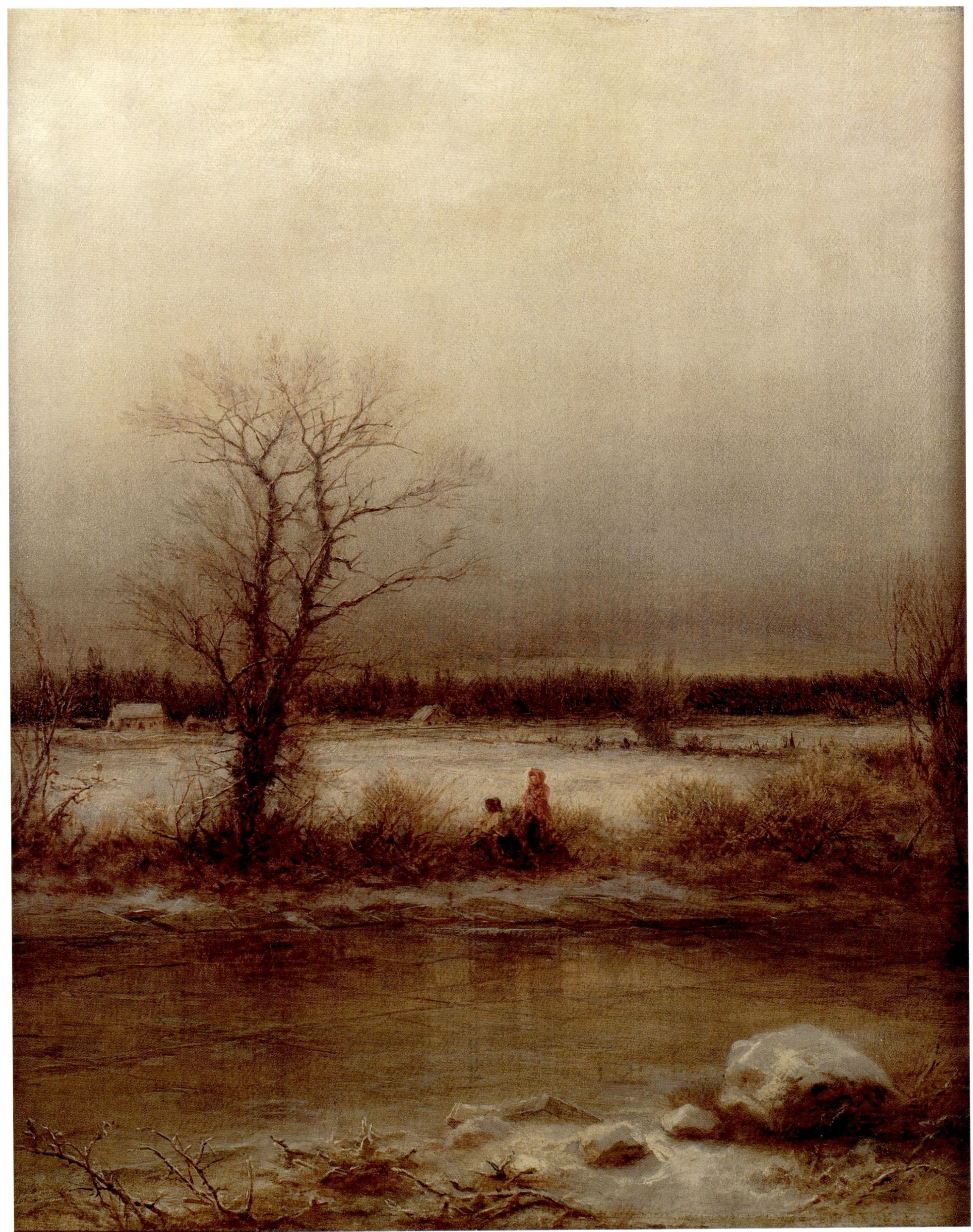

25

26

Eastman Johnson, NA

Lovell, Maine 1824–1906 New York, New York

Negro Life at the South, 34th Annual Exhibition, April
13–June 25, 1859, no. 321

Life in the South, n.d. §

Oil on canvas, 38 × 45
High Museum of Art, Atlanta

In the spring of 1859, with tensions about slavery running high in
the North and the South, and John Brown's raid on Harper's
Ferry to occur that fall, Eastman Johnson's showpiece picture,
Life in the South (1859; New-York Historical Society), created an
enormous sensation at the thirty-fourth annual exhibition of the
National Academy of Design.[1] His timing was impeccable. The
subject of the painting—a family of slaves relaxing behind the
artist's home in Washington, D.C.— was eminently suited to
garner acclaim as one of the foremost pictures of the exhibition.
Regardless of how any particular critic felt about the institution
of slavery, few could ignore Johnson's painting.[2] As one critic
wrote, "… it is a sort of 'Uncle Tom's Cabin' of pictures, and gives
rise, therefore, to quite as many painful as pleasant reflections."[3]
The artist's ability to accurately tap into issues of great relevance

to the nation was to serve him well during the Civil War years and
the next decade, enabling him to become one of the most successful genre painters of the nineteenth century. Between 1859,
with his triumphant exhibition of *Life in the South,* and 1876,
when he exhibited *Husking Bee, Island of Nantucket* (see No. 41)
to equally great acclaim, the artist solidified his reputation by
carefully choosing subjects and turning them out in quick succession so as to keep himself in the public eye.

Johnson's greatest strength was undoubtedly his draftsmanship. His beginnings as a portraitist in crayon, and his European
study, had ensured that he could construct forms naturalistical-
ly. Critics noted Johnson's ability to render details convincingly
and saw this as proof of his "truth" and "sincerity." *Life in the
South* was highly praised for these qualities, especially for capturing truthfully and artistically the institution of slavery. The
New-York Times noted that *Life in the South* "is a composition
essentially naturalistic, studied in all its details with a curious
fidelity worthy of the Pre-Raphaelites."[4] Although Johnson was
not a Pre-Raphaelite, his attention to secondary details heightened the impact of the painting. For critics, and presumably the
public, Johnson's naturalism made his paintings a pleasure to
explore visually, and this was important in establishing the artist
as a preeminent genre painter. As the critic for the *Albion* wrote
of *Life in the South,* "The artist is imbued with his subject. Negro
life is before you."[5]

In keeping with his close attention to details, Johnson's paint-

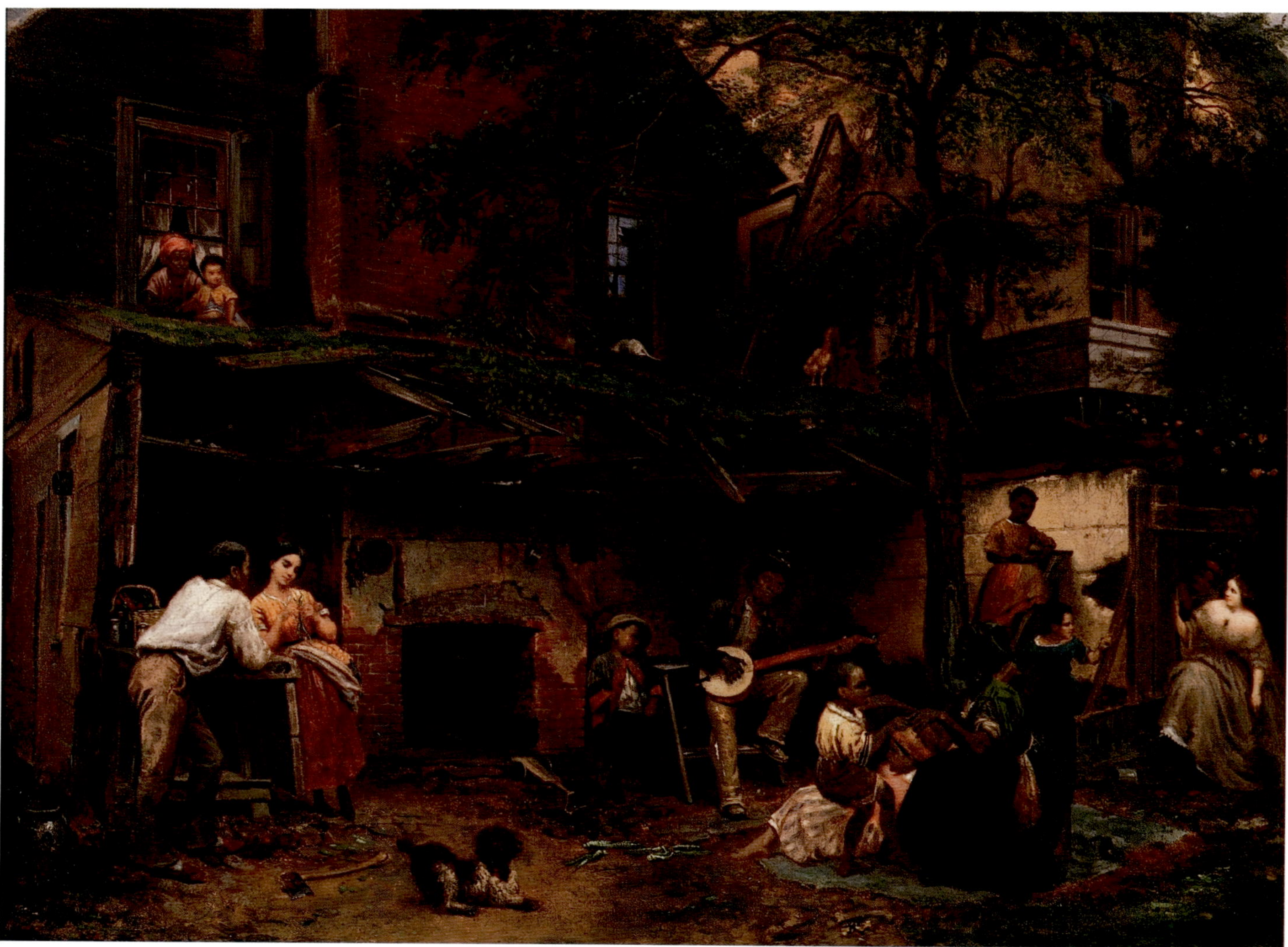

26

27

ings were, until *Husking Bee, Island of Nantucket,* finished to a fairly high degree, with solid definition of forms and inconspicuous brushwork.[6] As comments about Johnson's earlier compositions suggest, critics at the time preferred the tightly constructed, polished appearance of the Düsseldorf school and its American followers. "There is," said the *Albion,* "nothing left to be taken for granted; no dashing-in for the sake of effect; no slurring over of parts."[7] Suspicious of artists who relied upon painterly effects to distract from poor compositions, critics approved of Johnson's "Germanesque elaboration" and "Dutch fidelity" in the finish of *Life in the South.*[8]   SK

1. The painting illustrated here is not the one shown at the National Academy of Design but an undated replica of it. For years, the painting has been popularly referred to as *The Old Kentucky Home.*

2. See John Davis, "Eastman Johnson's Negro Life at the South and Urban Slavery in Washington, D.C." *Art Bulletin* 80 (March 1998): 67–92.

3. "The National Academy Exhibition. Concluding Article," *New York Semi-Weekly Tribune,* May 24, 1859.

4. "The Academy of Design. The Thirty-Fourth Exhibition of the Academy of Design," *NYT,* April 20, 1859.

5. "Fine Arts. NAD. First Notice," *Albion* 37 (May 7, 1859): 225.

6. Although many European artists, notably those of the French Barbizon school, were painting in a looser style by the 1860s, these developments were slow to reach America. Johnson, who had studied with Thomas Couture in Paris and was undoubtedly familiar with contemporary French styles, began moving away from tight handling and local color soon after *Life in the South.* See Sally Mills, "'Right Feeling and Sound Technique': French Art and the Development of Eastman Johnson's Outdoor Genre Paintings," in Marc Simpson, Sally Mills, and Patricia Hills, *Eastman Johnson: The Cranberry Harvest, Island of Nantucket* (San Diego: Timken Art Gallery, 1990), 55.

7. *Albion* 37 (May 7, 1859): 225.

8. "The Academy of Design. The Thirty-fourth Exhibition of the Academy of Design," *NYT,* April 20, 1859; "The Lounger. The Academy Again," *Harper's Weekly* 3 (May 14, 1859): 307.

27

Sanford Robinson Gifford, NA

Greenfield, New York 1823–1880 New York, New York

37th Annual Exhibition, April 14–June 23, 1862, no. 104, owner S. B. Caldwell

Sunday Morning in the Camp of the Seventh Regiment near Washington, D.C., 1862

Oil on canvas, 16 × 30
The Union League Club, New York

As a leader of the second generation of Hudson River School painters, Sanford Robinson Gifford participated in almost every annual exhibition of the National Academy of Design from 1847, when he first showed there, to 1880, the year of his death. Of the works he showed at the Academy during the years before 1862, only one was of a subject other than landscape, and that was a portrait exhibited in 1850. So his introduction of historical elements into the landscapes he exhibited in 1862 was unusual.

The exhibition of 1862 was the first opportunity for artists to submit war-related images to the National Academy's annuals. While works of this kind never dominated the shows, the timeliness of their subject matter almost guaranteed that they would receive attention. Five works of art that can be identified with some assurance as depicting events, real or imagined, of the Civil War were shown at the Academy in 1862. The following year approximately nine war-inspired paintings and sculptures were seen there; a similar number appeared in 1864; and about eleven war images, the largest number of any year, were exhibited in 1865. After that date, with the end of the war, the number quickly dwindled, and within a few years the topic was more or less moribund.

Two of the four paintings Gifford sent to the Academy in 1862—*Bivouac of the Seventh Regiment, Arlington Heights, Va.* (1862; Seventh Regiment, New York) and *Sunday Morning in the Camp of the Seventh Regiment near Washington, D.C*—resulted from direct observations he had made while serving in the Seventh Regiment of the New York State National Guard. Gifford, in fact, was one of only a few artists who actively participated in the Civil War. He was mustered into the Eighth Company of the Seventh Regiment shortly after the war began in April 1861 and subsequently made three tours of duty in defense of the nation's capital.[1] In July 1861, the *Crayon* reported that Gifford had "ready for reproduction, on a large scale, several studies of scenery and picturesque groupings, connected with military events at Washington."[2] The results were the two paintings he sent to the Academy the following year; and his deviation in these works from pure landscape into the realm of historical landscape paid off.

Most critics seemed to admire the manner in which Gifford had combined the general and the specific in these paintings. "The landscape is charming," the *New York Herald* reported, "commencing a long stretch down the Potomac, and the residents of the camp ground are capitally handled."[3] The *Albion* called the painting "one of the few happy fruits of the war" and admired the peacefulness of the landscape and the sense of security implied by the presence of the soldiers guarding the capital, visible in the background. The infusion of religion into the scene, too, only enhanced its value to the critic, who pointed out "the Chaplain officiating as the central figure, and his simply-uniformed audience scattered about at 'magnificent distances,' not so close as fielders at cricket, [says] more for the artist's happy grouping than for the reverend expounder's attractive eloquence."[4]

Harper's Weekly complained that, judging by the contents of the Academy's exhibition, the war had not provided much inspiration for American artists. Gifford's *Sunday Morning* was the exception. It "is remarkable for the fidelity with which the personality of the chaplain, the Rev. Mr. Weston, is rendered," the journal stated, "[T]he individuality of the man is unmistakable." The critic, who was almost certainly editor George W. Curtis, was equally impressed with Gifford himself. He was, Curtis wrote, "one of the artists who, during the year, have preserved the traditions of Michael Angelo, by patriotic service under canvas as well as on it."[5]

DBD

1. Gifford's Civil War paintings are discussed in Ila Weiss, *Poetic Landscape: The Art and Experience of Sanford R. Gifford* (Newark: University of Delaware Press, 1987), 226–29. Also see Ila Weiss, *Sanford Robinson Gifford (1823–1880)* (Ph.D. diss, Columbia University, 1968; New York: Garland Publishing, 1977), 206.

2. *Crayon* 8 (July 1861): 151, quoted in Weiss, 207.

3. "Fine Arts. Thirty-seventh Annual Exhibition of the NAD," *NYH*, April 16, 1862.

4. "Fine Arts. The NAD. Third and Concluding Notice," *Albion* 40 (May 17, 1862): 237.

5. [George W. Curtis], "The Lounger. The National Academy," *HW* 6 (May 3, 1862): 274.

28

Albert Bierstadt, NA

Solingen, Germany 1830–1902 New York

Sunlight and Shadow, 37th Annual Exhibition,
April 14–June 23, 1862, no 34, for sale

Sunlight and Shadow: Study, 1855 §

Oil on canvas, 18½ × 13
Collection of the Newark Museum,
Gift of Dr. J. Ackerman Coles, 1920

Albert Bierstadt first participated in the National Academy's annual exhibitions in 1858. He showed each year thereafter through 1865, and most years during the 1870s. Judging by their titles, all the works Bierstadt exhibited at the Academy were landscapes. Most of these had titles specific to the sites they depicted: *Lake Lucerne* (1858; National Gallery of Art, Washington. D.C.), *View near Newport* (1859; location unknown), *Base of the Rocky Mountains* (1860; location unknown), for example. *Sunlight and Shadow,* exhibited in the Academy's annual exhibition of 1862, and the study for which is shown here, is therefore unusual.[1]

The title *Sunlight and Shadow* (or *Sunshine and Shade* as the painting was sometimes called) focuses on ephemeral—and romantic—aspects of light and shadow. The point of view in the painting further forces the viewer to concentrate on light and the manner in which it passes through and reflects off objects in its path. This distinctive aspect of *Sunlight and Shadow* was noticed and praised by contemporary critics. A writer for the *New-York Times* called it "a wonderful painting" and "one of the finest efforts of the collection," marveling at the way in which the sun "does its work upon an old church and a patriarchal tree in the most satisfactory manner."[2] Most critics understood Bierstadt's intent. The *Brooklyn Daily Eagle* trumpeted it as "a magnificent work, evincing great labor, and a thorough knowledge of the effects of light and shade";[3] and *Harper's Weekly* thought that its solar effects were "more perfectly painted than any sunshine we ever saw."[4]

The *New York Evening Post* agreed, suggesting that *Sunlight and Shadow* is "probably the most perfectly satisfactory painting the artist has ever produced." The newspaper then described the painting:

> And on these old statues, on the church porch, on the
> balustrade and on the tessellated pavement before the porch,
> the sunlight falls, broken in chequered patches by the foliage
> of an old oak tree which is seen at the left of the picture. The
> only figure is that of a woman seated on the step of the
> church, with a sleeping child on her lap, and the whole work
> is one of the happiest delineations of noonday repose which
> we have ever seen. [5]

Both at the time and later, the press acknowledged that *Sunlight and Shadow* was Bierstadt's first artistic success. Henry Tuckerman, for example, noted that the painting had made Bierstadt "generally and favorably known in art" and "added to his popularity, and to the merit of the artist as a fond and faithful student of nature."[6]

The success of *Sunlight and Shadow* did not end with the closing of the National Academy's exhibition. In 1867 it was shown at

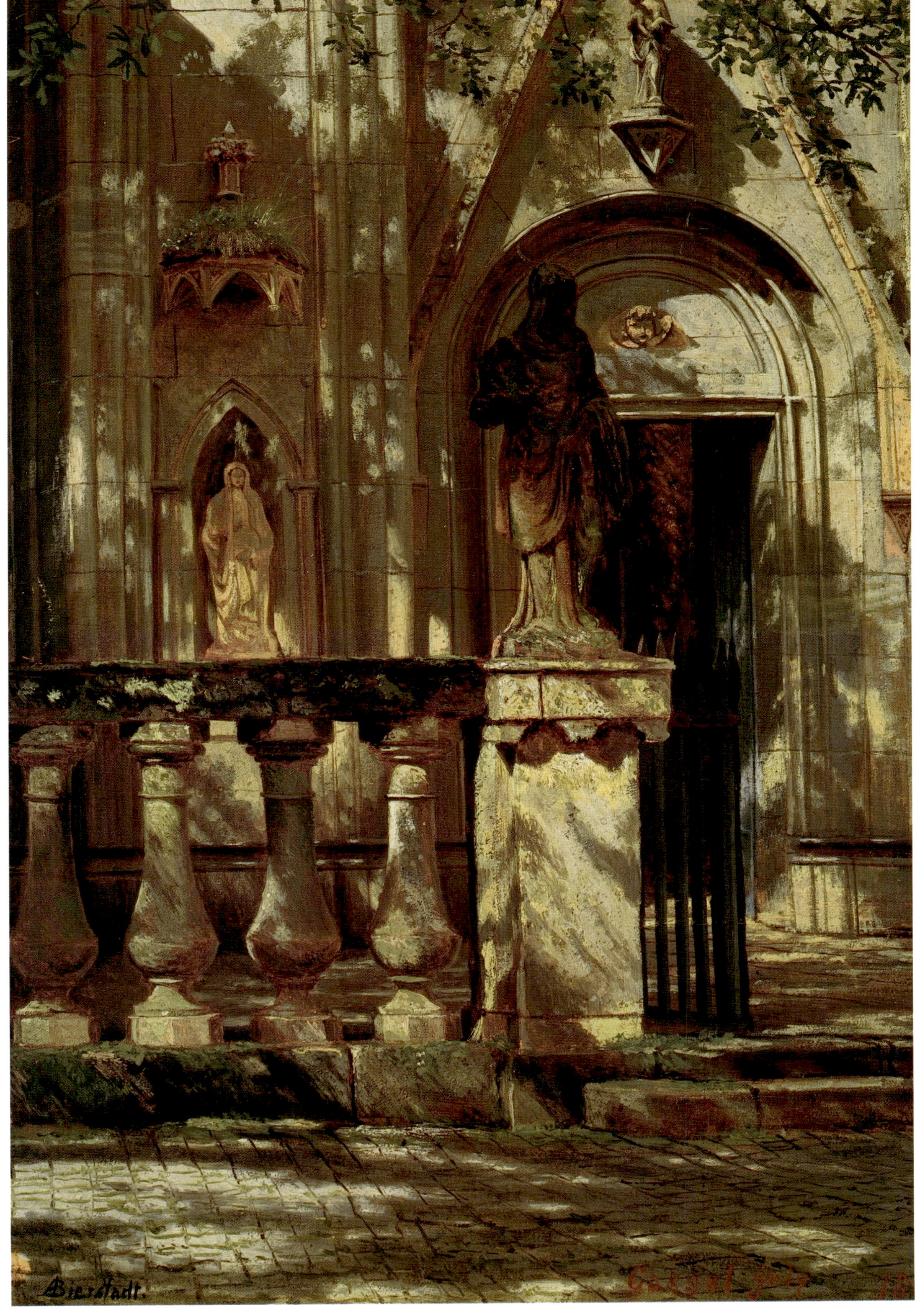

the first exhibition of the Yale School of Fine Arts in New Haven, where the college paper called it "undoubtedly the finest picture in the gallery."[7] Thirteen years later, it was one of two paintings by Bierstadt selected for the exhibition celebrating the opening of the new Metropolitan Museum of Art, and in 1887 it was part of a group of the artist's work shown in the *American Exhibition* in London. The continued popularity of *Sunlight and Shadow* was abetted by the production in Berlin in 1864 of a chromolithograph of it. The chromolithograph, which was the first major reproduction of one of Bierstadt's paintings, was exhibited and offered for sale at Emil Seitz's Broadway gallery in New York later that year.[8]   DBD

1. The painting shown here is the study, made in Germany in 1855, for the larger work that Bierstadt actually showed at the Academy in 1862. That painting (1862; 41½ × 35½) is now in the collection of the Fine Arts Museums of San Francisco. A drawing by Bierstadt, *Sketch after "Sunlight and Shadow* (1862) is in the Whaling Museum, New Bedford, Massachusetts.
2. "The NAD. Paintings in the First Gallery," *NYT*, April 24, 1862.
3. *Brooklyn Daily Eagle*, March 24, 1862, quoted in Nancy K. Anderson and Linda S. Ferber, *Albert Bierstadt: Art & Enterprise* (New York: The Brooklyn Museum, 1991), 166.

4. *HW* 6 (May 10, 1862): 290. Quoted in Anderson and Ferber, 166.
5. "The Academy of Design. Second Notice. The large Room," *NYEP*, April 17, 1862.
6. Henry T. Tuckerman, *Book of the Artists* (New York: G. P. Putnam & Son, 1867), 388.
7. *College Courant* (Yale), September 11, 1867, quoted in Anderson and Ferber, 184.
8. Anderson and Ferber, 180, 249, 252, 271.

29

John Quincy Adams Ward, NA
Urbana, Ohio 1830–1910 New York

Freedman—Model for Bronze Statuette, 38th Annual Exhibition, April 14–June 24, 1863, no. 467

The Freedman, 1862 $

Bronze, 20 × 14¾ × 7
National Academy of Design, New York

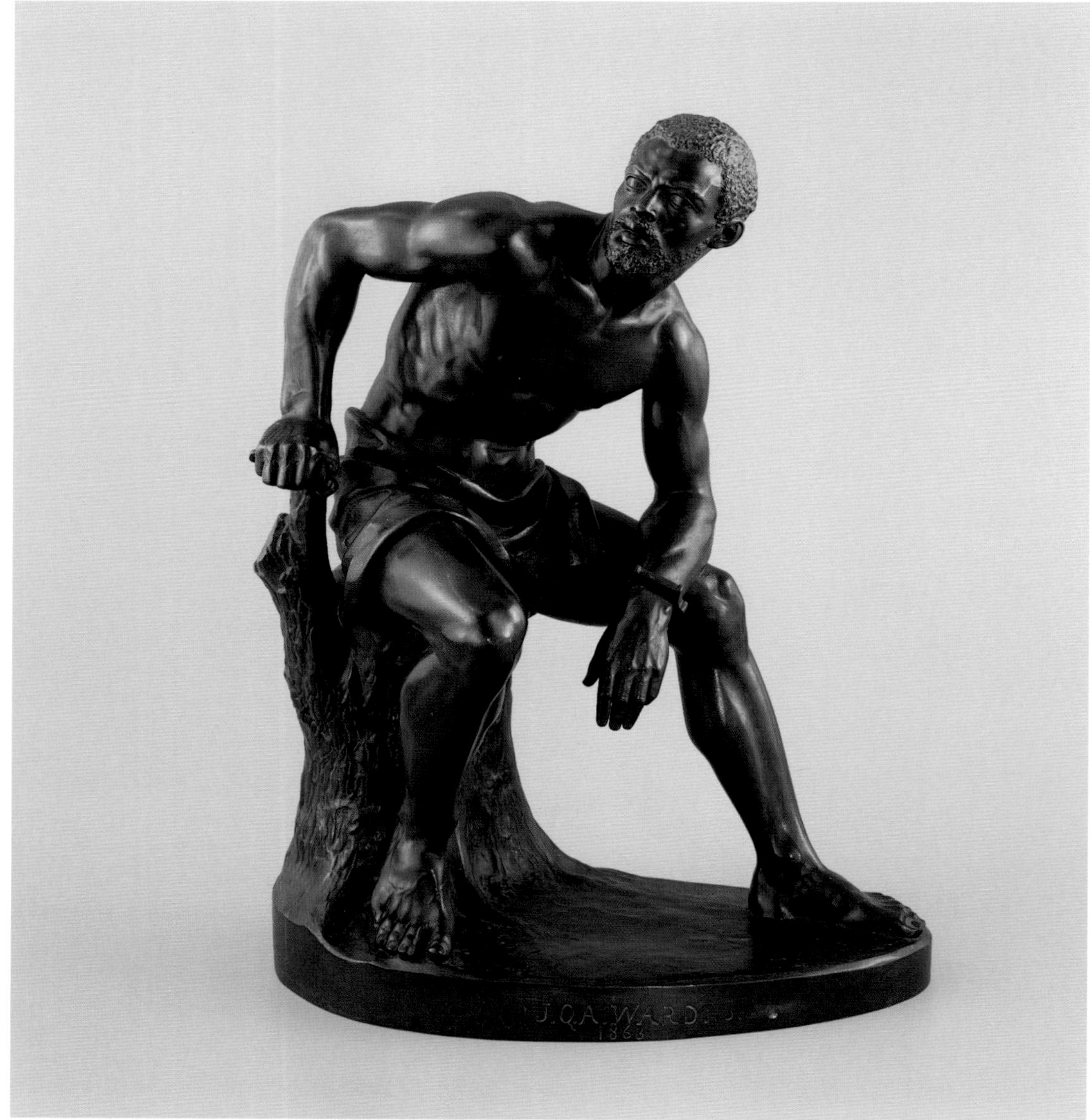

29

J. Q. A. Ward's sculpture *The Freedman* was one of at least ten works of art with themes related to the Civil War that were shown at the National Academy of Design in 1863. Among those that received notable favorable attention was Victor Nehlig's *An Episode of the War: The Cavalry Charge of Lt. Harry B. Hidden* (1862; New-York Historical Society), which depicted a well-known incident of the previous year.[1] The subject was timely, of course, and in fact, was also the focus of another painting in the same exhibition, a collaborative effort by Charles Loring Elliott and Junius Brutus Stearns titled *Lt. Harry B. Hidden, Killed at Sangster's Station, Va., March 9, 1862* (location unknown).

Another popular theme in 1863 was the escaped slave, commonly called contraband. At least three works that addressed this issue were in the Academy's annual that year: a painting— Granville Perkins's *Escape of Contraband* (location unknown)— and two sculptures—John Rogers's *Union Refugees* (1864, Yale University Art Gallery) and Ward's *The Freedman.* The popularity of this theme may have been prompted by Abraham Lincoln's Emancipation Proclamation, issued in September 1862.[2]

Perkins's painting and Rogers's sculpture were highly anecdotal. Ward's sculpture was not, leaving the critics to consider its style, particularly the artist's treatment of anatomy. Predictably, this aspect of the work led to discussions of race. A writer for the *Albion,* for example, called the anatomy "very fine" and marveled at the way in which Ward had somehow made the small figure seem "Titanic."[3] A writer for the *New-York Times* also praised the figure's anatomy. Tired of the "insipid and expressionless" products of neoclassicism, with their "delicate and workmanlike" finish, he found Ward's use of idealism "encouraging." Noting that the sculpture had "elicited very hearty appreciation," he reported that Ward had based it on perfect "specimens of the race" in order to show "that the African shares with the European the exalted proportions of the human figure." "We know of no American statue," he concluded, "which more nearly approaches the classic, either in conception or execution."[4]

On the other hand, some critics found the idealism of the figure disturbing. A writer for *Continental Monthly* took issue with the distortion of reality that he perceived in the piece. While he admitted that it probably had "its fine points," he complained that the sculpture lacked any "allegorical relation to the freedmen of our continent." "If the chains of the negro are being broken," the author explained his opinion, "he does not appear in the character of a Hercules, but rather as a patient and enduring martyr, awaiting the day of deliverance appointed by Heaven."[5]

Whatever the critics said, pro or con, Ward seems to have been proud of his achievement with *The Freedman.* He sent it and his sculpture of *The Indian Hunter* (1866; a version is in the collection of the Metropolitan Museum of Art), with which he had made his debut at the National Academy in 1862, to the Paris Exposition of 1867.[6] With other American paintings and sculptures from that exhibition, *The Freedman* was shown again at the National Academy in 1868. DBD

1. For example, see "The NAD. Its Thirty-Eighth Annual Exhibition," *NYEP,* May 14, 1863.

2. This connection was suggested by Lewis I. Sharp in his *John Quincy Adams Ward, Dean of American Sculpture* (Newark: University of Delaware Press, 1985), 153.

3. "Fine Arts. NAD. Third and Concluding Notice," *Albion* 41 (May 9, 1863): 226.

4. "NAD," *NYT,* June 24, 1863.
5. "Visit to the NAD," *Continental Monthly* 3 (June 1863): 718.
6. Sharp, 154.

30

James Henry Beard, NA

Buffalo, New York 1812–1893 Flushing, New York

40th Annual Exhibition, April 24–July 1, 1865, no. 265

The Night Before the Battle, 1865

Oil on canvas, 30¾ × 44¼

Memorial Art Gallery of the University of Rochester: Gift of Dr. Ronald M. Lawrence

Although James Beard would eventually become best known as the author of humorous and allegorical animal paintings, his early submissions to the annual exhibitions of the National Academy of Design revealed a diversity of interest that went beyond that subject category. This was evident in the three works he sent to the Academy's 1846 exhibition, the first in which he participated. Judging by their titles—*Mill Boy, North Carolina Emigrants,* and *Portrait of a Gentleman*—the works were, respectively, a figure painting, a genre image, and a portrait. Beard continued to exhibit portraits and genre paintings, augmenting them with the occasional animal painting or landscape, into the 1860s. The appearance, therefore, in 1865 of his *The Night Before the Battle,* with its blend of real and surreal allusions to contemporary events, was probably a surprise to most critics and, we might assume, to the public as well. At any rate, they were impressed with the painting.

The Night Before the Battle was the only Civil War scene Beard exhibited at the National Academy. Although the painting referred to a very public conflict, it was also a personal expression based on experience: Beard was serving as a captain on the staff of General Lew Wallace when he conceived of the image. Undoubtedly, this allowed Beard to imbue the painting with both realism and, in its allegorical elements, surrealism. The contrast of these qualities, in fact, is exactly what attracted the attention of the critics. Cara Montane, writing for the *New York Leader,* called the work a "startlingly wild, original painting." She then described it in some detail:

Within a redoubt, on the bare ground, wrapped in their worn and tattered blankets, lie some dozen or more Federal soldiers; a fire smolders on the left, around which the men lie closer than beyond it. One man, whose face shows white and resolute in the moonlight, has fallen while writing home; the letter, inkstand and pen lie on a powder-cask, which he has used in lieu of a desk. Some have been playing cards, and the cards lie scattered on the ground. The dim figure of the sentry can be discerned far off, on the right. To the centre, and beyond the sleeping soldiers, is a cannon, yawning open-mouthed, waiting for the battle in which to do its duty. Close by this cannon a grinning skeleton, wrapped in a long, dark pall, half kneels, sighting the enemy. . . .[1]

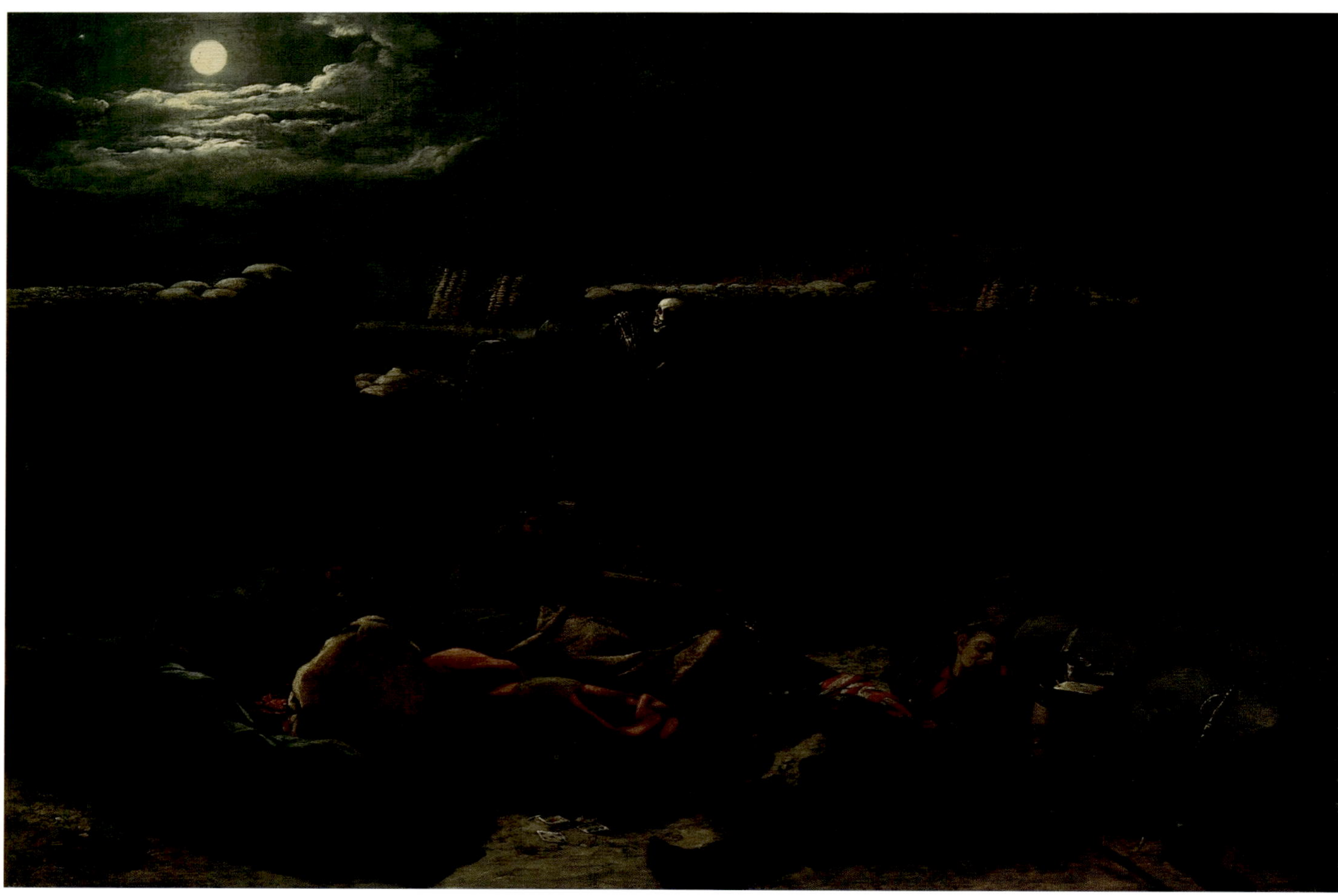

30

In a similar voice, *Harper's Weekly* called the painting a "solemn and striking" one. The writer was impressed with the contrast between the men, at rest or writing a letter, and "the cold moonlight" that "gleams upon a gun which Death, the skeleton, is sighting." This foreboding of death and the overall eeriness of the work prompted the critic to conclude: "It is a picture which makes the spectator glad that peace is come."[2]   DBD

1. Cara Montane, "Another Woman's View of the New Academy of Design," *New York Leader*, June 3, 1865. Montane gave special attention to those works in the show that related to the war. This included Thomas Nast's *General Sherman's March through Georgia* and Constant Mayer's *North and South, an Episode of the War*, both of which she admired.

2. "The Exhibition of the National Academy," *Harper's Weekly* 9 (May 13, 1865): 291.

31

Frederic Edwin Church, NA

Hartford, Connecticut 1826–1900 New York, New York

> *Twilight*, 40th Annual Exhibition, April 24–July 1, 1865, no. 310

Twilight (Mt. Desert Island, Maine), 1865

Oil on canvas, 31¼ × 48½

Washington University Gallery of Art, St. Louis, Bequest of Charles Parsons, 1905

Before the exhibition of his *Twilight (Mount Desert Island)* at the National Academy of Design in 1865, Frederic Edwin Church had shown at least one other painting of Maine's Mount Desert Island there. His *Coast Scene, Mount Desert* (1863; Wadsworth Atheneum) had been at the Academy in 1863 and had been praised for the "pure power" of its crashing waves, among other things. By contrast, two years later, *Twilight*, which is a far more tranquil image, received relatively little attention.[1] The heroic, elemental drama and vibrant palette that had come to typify Church's work seems to have been tamed by the end of the Civil War. *Twilight* reflects this change: as a sort of testament to this newfound peace, a deer emerges from the woods at the lower right of the painting while a potentially dangerous storm passes into the distance.[2]

If many critics felt that Church's painting lacked merit, at least they were consistent, for most of them also felt that the 1865 exhibition, as a whole, was not a success. Their immense enthusiasm for the opening of the new Academy building on Twenty-third Street that year ran headlong into their belief in "the curious infelicity" of works included in the annual.[3] For example, the reviewer from the *Albion* wrote of his hope "that established favourites would surpass themselves in honour of this new temple; that the promising crop of new-comers would at length put out their force; that young men of genius would cease to play at painting, and show that they could execute as well as imagine." He was sadly disappointed, however, when he had to admit that "none of all this has come to pass."[4] The critic for the *New York Evening Post* was the only one to write at any length about *Twilight (Mount Desert Island)*, and even he was ambivalent: "Though this example of Mr. Church's talent is not a masterpiece," he remarked, "at least it is not commonplace or vulgar."[5]

A shift in taste during the early 1860s may have influenced the critical response to Church's work. By 1865, another depiction of Mount Desert, this one by Andrew W. Warren (d. 1873) garnered significantly more coverage in the press than did Church's composition. To the critic from the *New Path*, probably Clarence Cook, Warren's work accurately rendered the subject and even had "a fresh, breezy, out-of-door look about it which is most refreshing."[6] These were precisely the traits that Church was criticized for neglecting.

Unlike Warren's work, Church's 1865 depiction of the island was not based upon any recent trip to the site but, instead, on memory.[7] The *Evening Post* critic ascribed the painting's faults to the fact that it was a studio composition. "The untrue color of the landscape," he wrote, "is the legitimate result of a system of study which scarcely admitted of painting from nature, but which forced the painter to rely upon memory for color and study for outline."[8] While Church's *Twilight (Mount Desert Island)* was clearly not a critical success, its reception is nevertheless telling about what distinguished his own earlier works, as well as those of his followers, in the eyes of his contemporaries.   MM

1. "The NAD. Its Thirty-ninth Annual Exhibition; Third Article," *NYEP*, May 21, 1863. More recent assessments of *Twilight* invariably concur that the work, "despite certain merits, is ultimately an unconvincing recapitulation of a theme that Church had treated so many times before" (Franklin Kelly, *Frederic Edwin Church and the National Landscape* [Washington, D.C.: Smithsonian Institution Press, 1988], 126).

2. John Wilmerding has suggested that the painting may have been mis-titled when it appeared at the Academy. He asserts that the view in the composite landscape may just as easily be interpreted as being to the east. If this is true, the subject of the painting is an optimistic sunrise, rather than a more bleak sunset (Wilmerding, *The Artist's Mount Desert, American Painters on the Maine Coast* [Princeton, New Jersey: Princeton University Press, 1994], 103).

3. "Fine Arts. The New NAD. Second Notice," *Albion* (May 13, 1865): 225.

4. Ibid.

5. Sordello [Eugene Benson], "National Academy of Design, Fortieth Annual Exhibition," *NYEP*, May 3, 1865.

6. "NAD—Fortieth Annual Exhibition," *New Path* 2 (June 1865): 87. There was at least one dissenting voice on this count, however. The *New-York Times* critic wrote briefly of Warren's painting that it was "a painfully distinct production. The rocks look like inlaid work" ("NAD," *NYT*, June 13, 1865).

7. Wilmerding, 103.

8. *NYEP*, May 3, 1865.

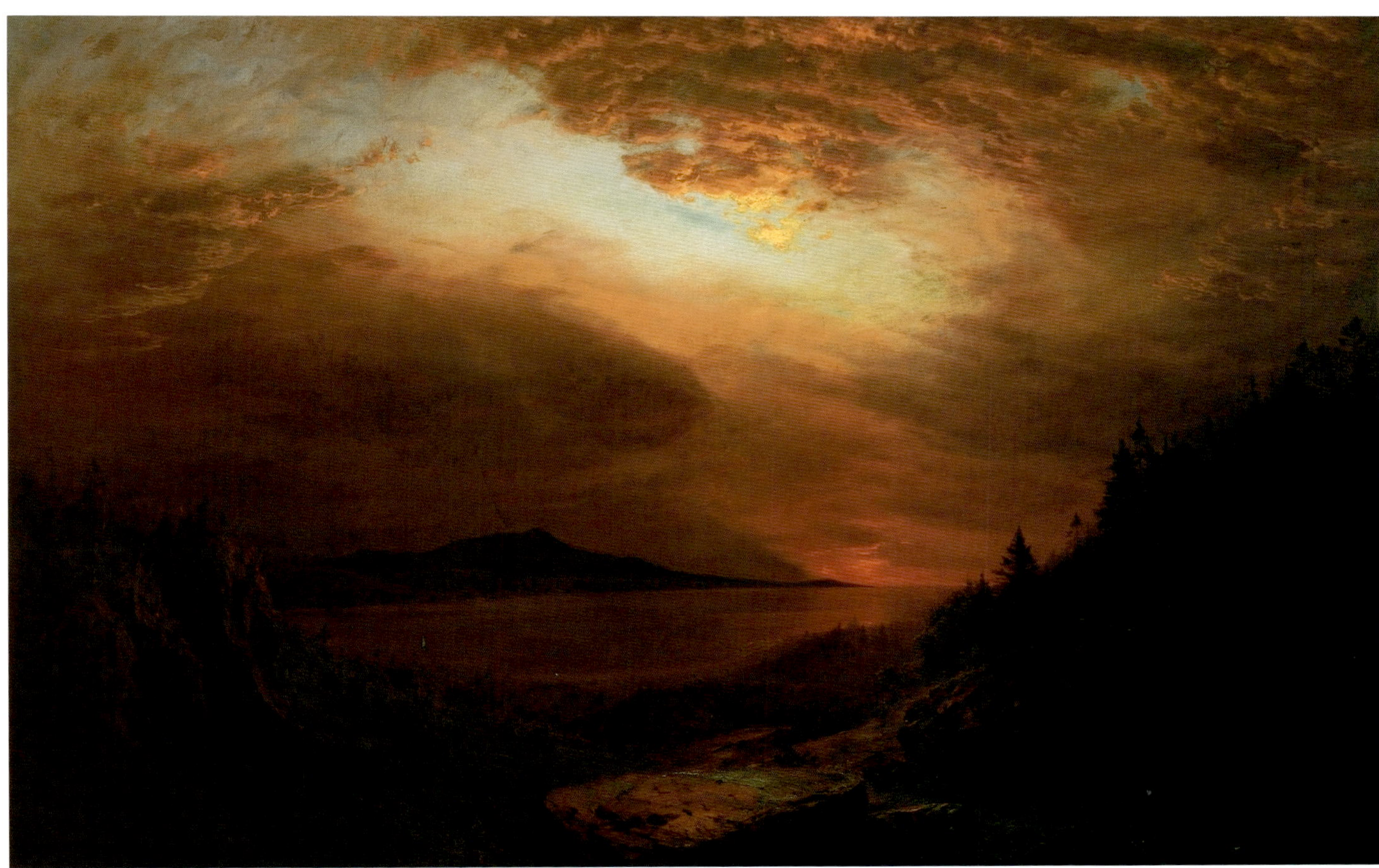

31

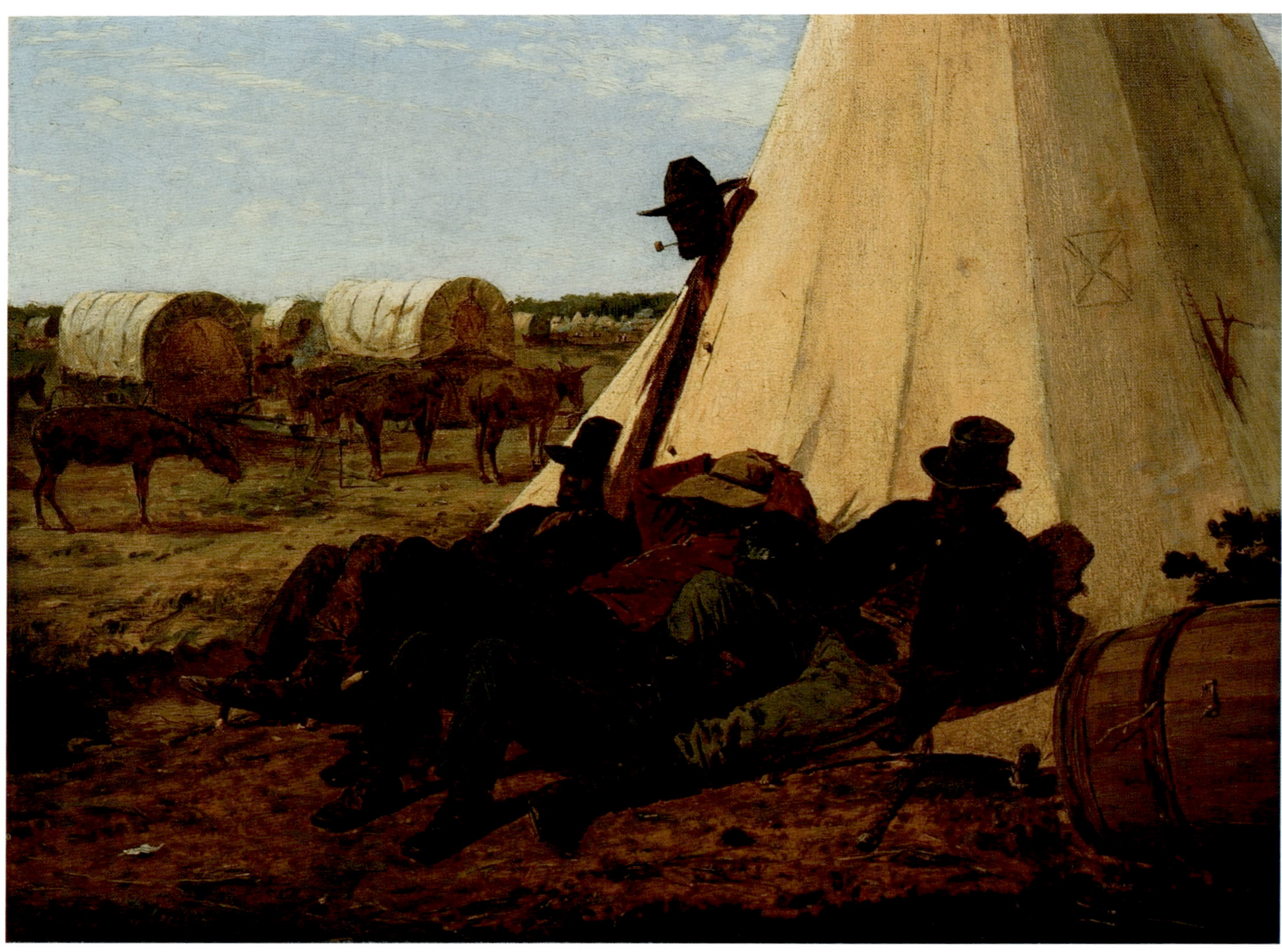

32

Winslow Homer, NA

Boston, Massachusetts 1836–1910 Prout's Neck, Maine

> 40th Annual Exhibition, April 24–July 1, 1865, no. 190, owner William H. Hamilton

The Bright Side, 1865

> Oil on canvas, 12¾ × 17
>
> The Fine Arts Museums of San Francisco, Gift of Mr. and Mrs. John D. Rockefeller III

Winslow Homer first participated in the annual exhibitions of the National Academy of Design in 1860 with a work entitled *Skating on the Central Park,* presumably a work on paper.[1] In 1863, he began submitting paintings to the Academy. The works he sent that year, and again in 1864, 1865, and 1866, were directly or indirectly related to the Civil War.

Of these, the first to receive notable critical and public attention was *The Bright Side,* which was shown at the Academy in 1865.[2] Eugene Benson, the artist and critic, characterized the reaction of most journalists when, in his review of the painting for the *New York Post,* he confessed to having been invigorated "to find boldness and truth amid the trivial and false."[3] In fact, phrases and words such as "truth to nature" and "realism" became standards in most discussions of *The Bright Side.* Clarence Cook, writing for the *New York Daily Tribune,* called the painting a "right sterling piece of work." He thought it was the best thing that Homer had produced so far and hoped the young man would continue to "paint every picture with the loyalty to nature and the faithful study that marks this little square of canvas." These qualities, Cook felt, had made Homer "the best chronicler of the war, so far."[4]

The artist's "faithfulness" to reality impressed a writer for the *New-York Times,* as well. Referring to *The Bright Side's* subject matter, he called the painting "almost grotesque," but praised the realism that came from Homer's "accurate knowledge of African habits and peculiarities."[5] A writer for the *Nation* agreed with these reactions. Homer "paints the scenes and incidents of our great war," he noted, "and paints them well, with a true perception of their character and meaning and with unusual technical skill." He continued, "No improvement could be suggested that would make this picture a more expressive work or more effective as a representation of the scene. The nearest man and the most distant mule are equally good, and both as true and full of expression as if Mr. Homer could paint like Gérôme."[6]

For some critics, Homer's accurate "representation of the scene" gave the painting a humorous bent. This reaction relies upon and reflects contemporary attitudes toward race. George

Arnold, a writer for the *New York Leader,* pointed out, inaccurately, that "nearly all [Homer's] works contain a grotesque element: witness particularly the comic old darkey with the pipe, poking his head through the tent opening."[7] In another article, Arnold, who had seen the painting in Homer's studio several weeks before it was on view at the Academy, stereotyped the figures as revelers in the "warmth" of their "Ethiopean comfort."[8] Other authors referred to the "broad" or "dry" sense of humor evident in the painting.[9] While the subtleties of these effects might be lost to most modern viewers, *Watson's Weekly Art Journal* summed them up in 1865: "The lazy sunlight, the lazy, nodding donkeys, the lazy, lolling negroes, make a humorously conceived and truthfully executed picture."[10] Evidently, the parallel that Homer is credited with having made between men and donkeys in the painting is what, at least for some viewers, made the image funny and, in part, explains its popularity.

DBD

1. This was probably the same image that had been published in Harper's Weekly on January 28, 1860, under the title *Skating on the Ladies' Skating Pond in Central Park, New York.* See William Howe Downes, *The Life and Works of Winslow Homer* (Boston: Houghton Mifflin Company, 1911), 37–38.

2. Marc Simpson, *Winslow Homer: Paintings of the Civil War* (San Francisco: The Fine Arts Museums of San Francisco, 1988), 47. Also see Lucretia Giese, "Winslow Homer: 'Best Chronicler of the War,'" in Nicolai Cikovsky, Jr., ed., *Winslow Homer: A Symposium* (Studies in the History of Art. 26. Center for Advanced Study in the Visual Arts. Symposium Papers XI) (Washington: National Gallery of Art, 1990): 15–31.

3. Sordello [Eugene Benson], "NAD. Fortieth Annual Exhibition," *NYEP*, May 31, 1865.

4. [Clarence Cook], "NAD—Fortieth Annual Exhibition. [Sixth Article]," *NYDT*, July 3, 1865.

5. "NAD. North Room," *NYT*, May 29, 1865.

6. "Fine Arts. The Fortieth Annual Exhibition of the NAD. Second Notice," *Nation* 1 (July 13, 1865): 56–59. Later, Homer's biographer, William Howe Downes, would note that *The Bright Side* was "the first work in color to show any positive promise of what Homer's talent for actuality might become" (Downes, 52).

7. George Arnold, "Art Matters," *NYL*, June 3, 1865.

8. George Arnold, *NYL*, March 11, 1865, quoted in Giese, 17–18. To Arnold's credit, he did suggest that Homer paint a companion piece for *The Bright Side* that would show the plight of black people who come North and "find themselves condemned to saw wood and pile brick in the driving snow, in order to procure a somewhat more miserable subsistence than that of which a mistaken and ferocious philanthropy has deprived them."

9. For example, see "Fine Arts. The NAD. Third Notice," *Albion* 43 (May 27, 1865): 249; and Sordello [Eugene Benson], "NAD. Fortieth Annual Exhibition. Fourth Article," *NYEP*, May 31, 1865.

10. "NAD. Seventh Article," *Watson's Weekly Art Journal* 3 (July 1, 1865): 148–49, quoted in Simpson, 51.

33

Elihu Vedder, NA

New York, New York 1836–1923 Rome, Italy

Jane Jackson, formerly a Slave—Drawing in Oil Color, 40th Annual Exhibition, April 24–July 1, 1865, no. 589

Jane Jackson, Formerly a Slave, 1865

Oil on canvas, 18 × 18

National Academy of Design, New York

Elihu Vedder returned to the United States in 1860 after spending several years studying and working in Europe. He settled in New York, where, in 1862–63, he enrolled in the school of the National

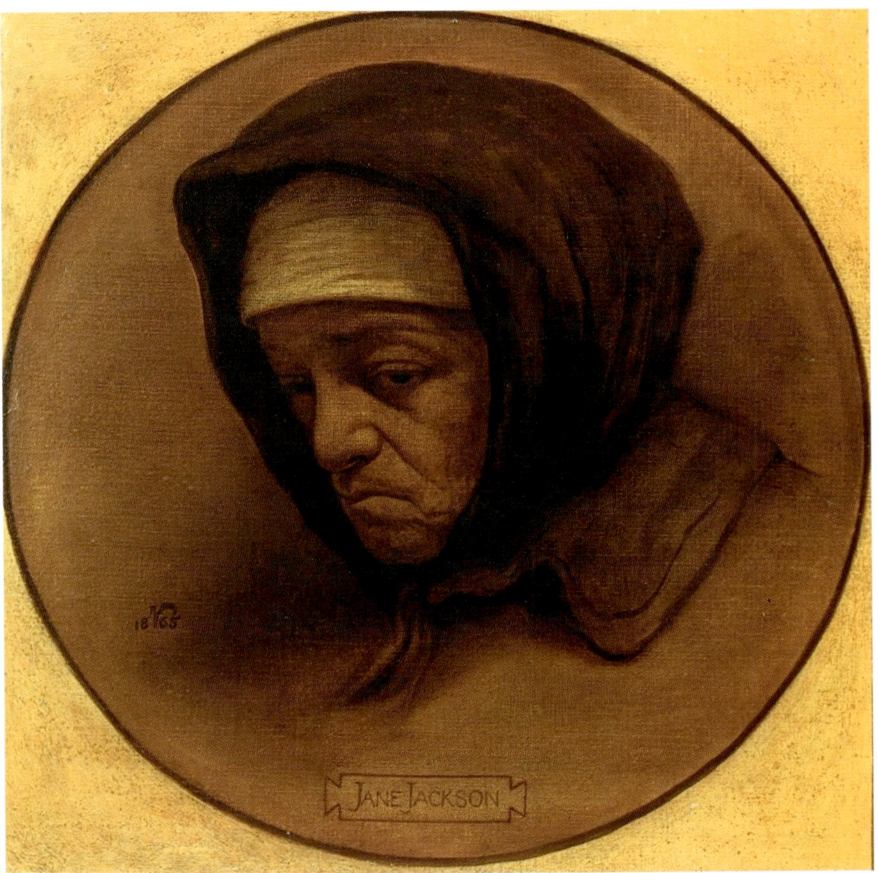

33

Academy of Design. It was at that time, too, that he made his debut at the Academy's annual exhibition of 1862 with six paintings, most of which were based on his Italian sojourns. By the following year, when he showed *The Questioner of the Sphynx* (1863; Museum of Fine Arts, Boston) at the Academy, he had impressed the members of the organization enough that they elected him as an Associate National Academician. Vedder did not disappoint his new colleagues. In 1864, he gained his first public acclaim with *Lair of the Sea Serpent* (1864; Museum of Fine Arts, Boston), which he sent to the Academy's annual that year. The painting's success came from the allegorical and even religious interpretations that it inspired.[1]

The Civil War ended only a few weeks before the opening of the Academy's annual in 1865 and the carnage that had resulted was undoubtedly uppermost in the minds of most Americans, victors or not. Of the eight paintings that Vedder submitted that year, most of which were genre images (although they were not the usual fare in that subject category), three suggest the workings of the subconscious and the presence of a darker side of the human psyche. Their titles—*The Gloomy Path* (location unknown), *The Lonely Spring* (1865, private collection), and *A Lost Mind* (1864–65; Metropolitan Museum of Art, New York)—make this apparent. In fact, of Vedder's eight submissions to the Academy that year, it was these three, especially the last, that garnered the most attention from the press.[2]

The subject matter of another of his works shown at the Academy in 1865 was timely, too. This was his *Jane Jackson, Formerly a Slave,* an unusual rendering, for this period, of an African American. It is devoid of stereotyping and reveals the woman's emotions and the experiences her elderly age implies by focusing on her face instead of showing her in an environment that might suggest her plight. Vedder later recalled the circumstances, circa 1864, that led to the creation of this image:

> At the time I had my studio in the old Gibson Building on Broadway; I used to pass frequently a near corner, where an old negro woman sold peanuts. Her meekly bowed head and a look of patient endurance and resignation touched my heart and we became friends.[3]

The pathos of Jane Jackson caught the attention of some New York critics. Writing for the *New York Leader,* George Arnold called it a "faithfully-studied head of a characteristic old Southern servant" and noted that the "peculiar manner in which it is executed shows the fertility of Mr. Vedder's talent and his power over all the materia [*sic*] of art."[4] In a similar vein, a writer for *Harper's* was impressed with Vedder's ability to capture so much in the face. It is "a head merely," the journal reported, "but there is a quaint vigor in the sketch which well befits the strange, dusky, tragical face. Yet our great romancer, Hawthorne, thought we had no material for romances in this country!"[5]

The literary reference here was not altogether out of place, for another kind of positive reaction to the painting came in the form of a poem, written by Herman Melville. It reads in part:

> *The sufferance of her race is shown,*
> *And retrospect of life,*
> *Which now too late deliverance dawns upon;*
> *Yet is she not at strife.*

> *Her children's children they shall know*
> *The good withheld from her;*
> *And so her reverie takes prophetic cheer—*
> *In spirit she sees the stir.*[6]

Vedder's success with the eight paintings he sent to the National Academy in 1865 coincided with his election to the status of full National Academician that same year. To fulfill the requirements of membership in the Academy, he presented the institution with *Jane Jackson* early in 1866.   DBD

1. For example, see "Art. Exhibition of the NAD," *Round Table* 1 (April 23, 1864): 312, the author of which saw the reptile in the painting as "a symbol of the serene purity of the soul threatened or subjected to a horrible evil."

2. For example, see Sordello, [Eugene Benson] "NAD. Fortieth Annual Exhibition. First Article," *NYEP,* May 3, 1865. Benson noted that, with these paintings, Vedder had "suggested something outside our everyday life, and he has again asserted his peculiar and emphatic genius."

3. Elihu Vedder, *The Digressions of V* (Boston and New York: Houghton Mifflin Company, 1890), 236-240.

4. George Arnold, "Art Matters," *NYL,* June 10, 1865.

5. "The Exhibition of the National Academy," *HW* 9 (May 20, 1865): 307.

6. Herman Melville, *Battle-Pieces, and Aspects of the War* (New York: Harper & Brothers, 1866), 154.

34
Harriet Hosmer
Watertown, Massachusetts 1830–1908 Watertown, Massachusetts

"Puck"—Statue in Marble, 40th Annual Exhibition, April 24–July 1, 1865, no. 635, owner Mrs. Smith Clift

Puck, c. 1855–56 $
Marble, 30⅞ × 15½ × 19¾
The Chrysler Museum, Norfolk, Virginia, Gift of James H. Ricau and Museum Purchase

Until the last quarter of the nineteenth century, sculpture was comparatively rare in the exhibitions of the National Academy of Design, and critical response to what little sculpture was shown there was even rarer. A cursory analysis of these exhibitions prior to the Civil War reveals that an average of four or five sculptures appeared in each exhibition. One of the reasons for this was the fact that most American sculptors at the time worked in the neoclassical style, a preference that practically required them to live and work in Italy for at least part of their careers in order to find the pure white marble they needed for their work and the craftsmen to carve it, and to be able to study the ancient Greek and Roman sculptures that had inspired the neoclassical style. Once ensconced in Italy, they were less likely to send their somewhat cumbersome works back to New York for exhibition. As a result, major sculptors such as Horatio Greenough, Hiram Powers, and Thomas Crawford participated in the Academy's annual exhibitions only sporadically, if at all.[1]

One American critic who signed herself "Esperance" did write about sculpture, in a review of the National Academy's annual exhibition of 1865 for the *New York Leader.* While she mentioned other artists, including sculptors, she was particularly taken with Harriet Hosmer and her marble sculpture of *Puck,* which was

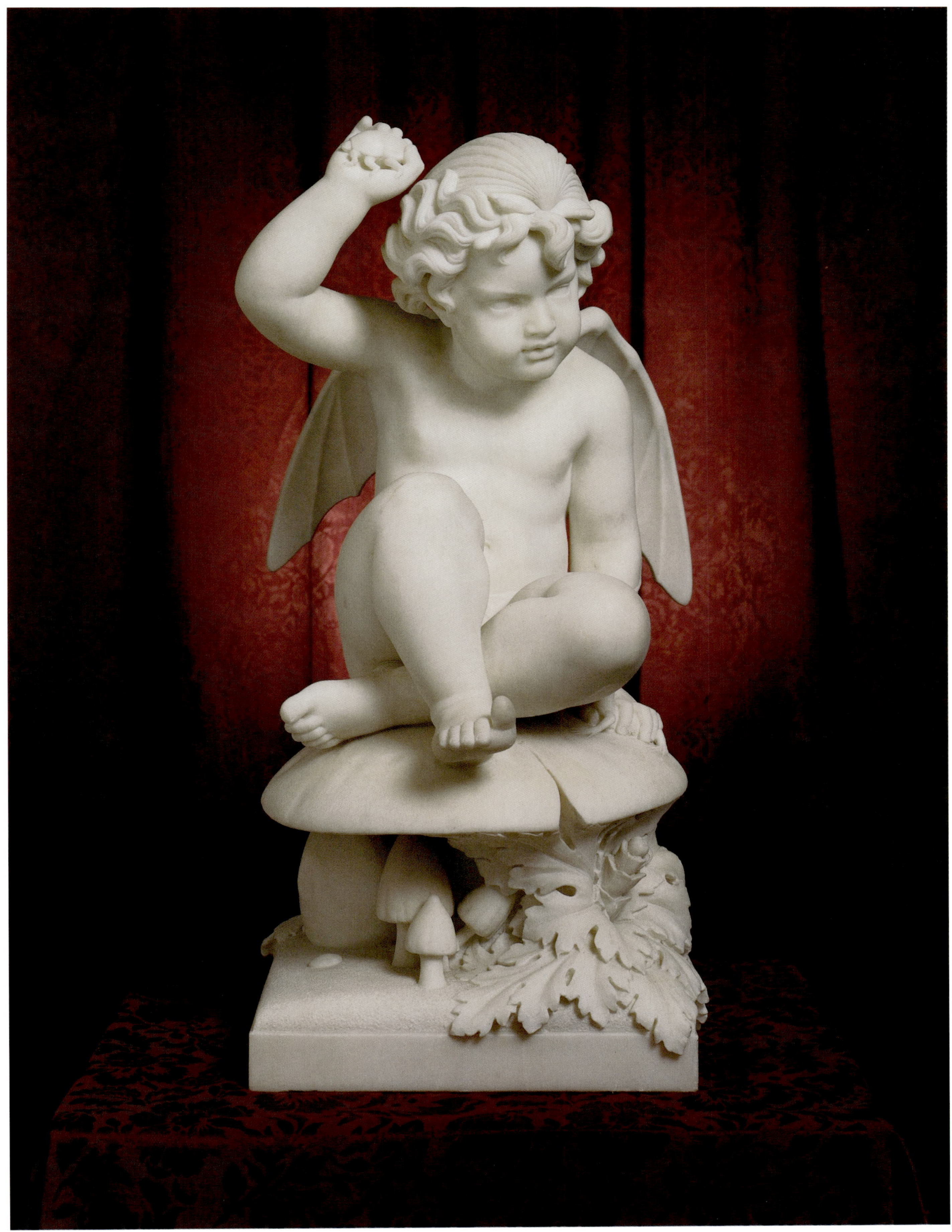

34

shown in the Academy's annual exhibition that year and which had already made the sculptor famous.[2]

Hosmer conceived of *Puck* in 1855.[3] She eventually oversaw the carving of about thirty replicas of it, at least ten of which are extant and one of which is shown here.[4] *Puck's* fame was assured when the Prince of Wales (later Edward VII) visited Hosmer's studio in Rome in 1859 and ordered a replica of the sculpture to display in his rooms at Oxford.[5] Each replica was probably slightly different from the others, mostly in terms of accessories such as the plant and animal forms. The one that Esperance saw at the National Academy in 1865 was lent to the exhibition by Mrs. Smith Clift.[6] The writer thought it was delightful and wrote at length about it. "[W]ho would fail to linger over Miss Hosmer's delicious 'Puck,'" she wrote, "a truly delightful little fairy with which by a sort of miracle, both the admirers and the detractors of this artist contrive to be pleased, those on account of its rare merit, and these because the idea elaborated is said to be borrowed from a painting on a similar subject by Sir Joshua Reynolds."[7]

Esperance was referring here to an accusation, made in the *New Path*, that Hosmer had simply lifted her conception of Puck directly from Reynolds's painting of the same subject.[8] As reported by Esperance, the *New Path* had denied Hosmer "almost all artistic merit, and advised her to become a carver of flowers, etc." On the contrary, the writer for the *New York Leader* believed, Hosmer's name stood "with the few of those who are foremost in her art."[9]

Clarence Cook also noticed Hosmer's *Puck* at the National Academy's exhibition of 1865, but his reaction was positively vicious. While Cook thought the work itself was "a pretty enough bit of fancy," he did not think that Hosmer had represented the character, as drawn by Shakespeare, accurately. The extreme youth of Hosmer's interpretation was the main sticking point for Cook, who felt that Hosmer's Puck "couldn't do the half of what Oberon and Titania set for him." As others had done, Cook linked the sculpture more to Reynolds's version of the sprite than to Shakespeare's. He went so far as to state that Hosmer could easily have conceived of *her* sculpture without having read Shakespeare, but that she could not possibly have made it without looking at Reynolds's painting. Having started on this tack, Cook concluded by dismissing the work as "a pretty toy" and bemoaned the "waste [of] such a beautiful piece of marble" on a toy.[10] In fact, Cook was more a person of his times than was Esperance. By 1865, the neoclassical style had long passed from the European scene; and it was in its very last moments of popularity in this country.   DBD

1. Greenough's work appeared in only six of the Academy's exhibitions, Crawford's in four, and Powers's in three. The most active sculptor at the Academy during this period was Henry Kirke Brown. While he showed in only seven of its exhibitions, one of these (1850) included thirteen of his works. In addition, the Academy was the venue for a special exhibition of fifteen of Brown's sculptures, the first documented solo exhibition of the work of an American sculptor (*Catalogue of Statues, Busts, Bas Reliefs, &c. by H. K. Brown* [New York: Israel Sackett, 1846]).

2. *Puck* made its American debut in Boston, where it was exhibited at Cotton's on Tremont Street in February, 1857. The version shown there was owned by Samuel Hooper, of that city ("Sketchings," *Crayon* 4 (February 1857): 56.

3. H. Nicholas B. Clark, *A Marble Quarry: The James H. Ricau Collection of Sculpture at the Chrysler Museum of Art* (New York: Hudson Hills Press, 1997),

217–20; Dolly Sherwood, *Harriet Hosmer, American Sculptor, 1830–1908* (Columbia, Missouri: University of Missouri Press, 1991), 118–20.

4. Clark, 218.

5. "Miss Hosmer's Studio at Rome," *HW* 3 (May 7, 1859): 293–294; and Sherwood, 119.

6. Evidently, the version of *Puck* shown at the Academy in 1865 had been ordered from Hosmer by Mr. Clift, a resident of New York, in 1857, probably while he was visiting Rome. See Cornelia Crow Carr, ed., *Harriet Hosmer: Letters and Memories* (New York: Moffat, Yard and Co., 1912), 78.

7. Esperance, "A Woman's View of the New Academy of Design," *NYL*, May 27, 1865.

8. The attack had come in "Miss Hosmer's Statue of Zenobia," *New Path* 2 (April 1865): 49-55. Reynolds painted his *Puck* (private collection, England) in 1789. It was well known through an engraving made of it (Clark, 218). The resemblance to Hosmer's sculpture is only general.

9. *NYL*, May 27, 1865.

10. [Clarence Cook], "NAD—Fortieth Annual Exhibition. [Second Article]," *NYDT*, May 20, 1865.

35

Winslow Homer, NA

Boston, Massachusetts 1836–1910 Prout's Neck, Maine

41st Annual Exhibition, April 17–July 4, 1866, no. 490

Prisoners from the Front, 1866

Oil on canvas, 25 × 38

The Metropolitan Museum of Art, Gift of Mrs. Frank B. Porter, 1922

With the successful exhibition of *The Bright Side* in 1865, Winslow Homer, consciously or not, had prepared the way for the even greater success of *Prisoners from the Front* the following year.[1] Although the former certainly received impressive notices in 1865, its small size and supposed humorous subject discouraged viewers from taking it too seriously. No such problems existed for *Prisoners from the Front*. It was large enough to make a memorable impression and, as with all great works of art, its subject invited various interpretations, a characteristic made obvious by the range of critical response that it received when it debuted at the National Academy of Design in 1866. In fact, no other single work of art shown at the Academy's forty previous exhibitions had received the quantity or quality of critical attention that was garnered by *Prisoners from the Front*. It was called "Homer's truly Homeric reminiscence of the war," was said to be a work of genius, and was identified as "the most valuable and comprehensive art work that has been painted to express some of the most vital facts of our war."[2] Critics noted that the painting was "hardly to be bettered" and was "the most thoroughly pleasing picture in the Exhibition."[3]

Predictably, many critics discussed *Prisoners from the Front* in terms of its subject, often by identifying the figures in it by name. Such specificity suggests that some critics interpreted the work as a history painting that recorded a real event, presumably one witnessed by the artist. A writer for the *New York Evening Post* took this approach. "A picture by Homer represents a Union officer—an excellent portrait of General Barlow," he reported, "receiving a group of rebel prisoners who have evidently just been brought in from the front."[4] The *Albion* followed suit:

35

"There is great individuality of character in the group of wild and haggard Confederates, their escort, and the youthful general before whom they are brought. The latter, is we believe, a portrait of General Barlow."[5] George William Curtis, editor of *Harper's,* allowed for a more general interpretation, stating that the men in the painting "may be easily taken as types" but went on to admit that it would "not diminish the interest of the picture if the spectator should see in the young Union officer General Barlow."[6] In another article in the *Post,* the artist/critic Eugene Benson declared the painting to be "a genuine example of true historical art—the only kind of historical art which is trustworthy in its facts, free from flimsy rhetoric and barbaric splendor; sensible, vigorous, honest."[7]

Another interpretation, however, and one adopted by a number of critics, sees the men in the painting as representatives of the region or class from which they came rather than as identifiable individuals. In this light, the painting becomes a summation of the war and an explanation of its outcome. Further comments by Eugene Benson are typical in this regard:

Mr. Homer shows us the North and South confronting each other; and looking at his facts. It is very easy to know why the South gave way. The basis of its resistance was ignorance, typified in the 'poor white;' its front was audacity and bluster, represented by the young Virginian;—two very poor things to confront the quiet, reserved, intelligent, slow, sure North, represented by the prosaic face and firm figure and unmoved look of the Union officer.[8]

A writer for the *New York Leader* also pointed out the "contrast between the various slouching and insolent attitudes of the prisoners and the erect and manly bearing of the Union officer."[9] Likewise, critic Clarence Cook praised the way in which Homer epitomized "the two sides in our late war" and explained how the artist had achieved this:

The leaders are contrasted, not merely without exaggeration, but one may almost say, with judicial impartiality. The two other prisoners, the old man and the boy, are keys to explain the issue of the struggle; they indicate the real weakness of the South, which lay in the character of the people. An ignorant and brutalized society, truly typed by these figures, as all of us who saw Southern prisoners can testify, is no real strength; and accordingly the strength of the South lay, not in her people, but in her officers; while ours lay, not in our officers but in our people.[10]

Cook also expressed the hope that three of the pictures in the exhibition—John F. Weir's *The Gun Foundry* (1864-66, Putnam Country Historical Society, Cold Spring, New York) Eastman Johnson's *Fiddling His Way* (1866, The Chrysler Museum of Art, Norfolk, Virginia), and Homer's *Prisoner's from the Front*—would be among the American paintings sent to the 1867 Paris Exposition.[11] He got his wish: all three paintings went to Paris that year.[12] Appropriately, Homer's was accompanied by *The Bright Side.* Acclaim for both of his entries, but especially for *Prisoners from the Front,* continued abroad.[13] Eugene Benson reported that it "arrested the attention of polished Parisians and fixed itself in the memory of so many of us."[14]

In fact, the popularity of *Prisoners from the Front* has never waned. Art critic Charles Caffin, writing almost one hundred years ago, cogently catalogued the reasons:

DBD

1. Homer's first biographer, William Howe Downes, acknowledged this when he wrote that, with its debut at the National Academy in 1866, *Prisoners from the Front* "served to confirm the favorable impression which had been made by 'The Bright Side' in the Academy's annual exhibition of the previous year (Downes, *The Life and Works of Winslow Homer* [Boston: Houghton Mifflin Company, 1911], 54).

2. *New York Independent*, April 26, 1866, quoted in Natalie Spassky, *American Paintings in the Metropolitan Museum of Art* (New York: The Metropolitan Museum of Art, 1985), 2: 440; Sordello [Eugene Benson], "NAD. Forty-first Annual Exhibition. First Article," *NYEP*, April 28, 1866.

3. "Fine Arts. The Fifty-first Exhibition of the NAD. [First Notice]," *Nation* 2 (May 11, 1866): 603; [George W. Curtis], "Editor's Easy Chair," *Harper's New Monthly Magazine* 33 (June 1866): 117.

4. "Fine Arts. Opening of the NAD," *NYEP*, April 17, 1866. General Francis Channing Barlow was commander of the First Division of the Second Corps of the Army of the Potomac. He was a friend of the Homer family. See Nicolai Cikovsky, Jr., "Winslow Homer's Prisoners from the Front," *Metropolitan Museum Journal* 12 (1977): 155–72; Natalie Spassky's essay on the painting in Spassky, 437–45; Marc Simpson, *Winslow Homer: Paintings of the Civil War* (San Francisco: The Fine Arts Museums of San Francisco, 1988), 247–59; and Lucretia H. Giese, "Prisoners From the Front: An American History Painting?," in Simpson, 65–81.

5. "Fine Arts. NAD. II," *Albion* 44 (May 12, 1866): 225.

6. [George W. Curtis], "Editor's Easy Chair," *Harper's New Monthly Magazine* 33 (June 1866): 117–18.

7. Sordello [Eugene Benson], "NAD. Forty-first Annual Exhibition. First Article," *NYEP*, April 28, 1866.

8. Ibid. A writer identified only by the initials E. B.—almost certainly Benson again—expressed similar thoughts in the *Round Table*, May 12, 1866, 295.

9. "NAD. Forty-First Annual Exhibition," *NYL*, May 12, 1866.

10. [Clarence Cook], "NAD—Forty-First Annual Exhibition," *NYDT*, July 4, 1866.

11. [Clarence Cook], "NAD—Forty-First Annual Exhibition," *NYDT*, June 27, 1866.

12. See Carol Troyen, "Innocents Abroad: American Painters at the 1867 Exposition Universelle, Paris," *American Art Journal* 16 (Autumn 1984): 3–29.

13. See Simpson, 258–259.

14. Eugene Benson, "Historical Art in the United States," *Appleton's Journal* 1 (April 10, 1869): 46, quoted in Spassky, 440.

15. Charles Caffin, *American Masters of Painting* (New York, 1902), 75.

36, 37

Eastman Johnson, NA

Lovell, Maine 1824–1906 New York, New York

The Boy Lincoln, 43rd Annual Exhibition, April 15–June 20, 1868, no. 366.

The Boy Lincoln, 1867 §

Oil on canvas, 26⅞ × 21½

The Manoogian Collection, Taylor, Michigan

The Wounded Drummer Boy, an incident of the late war, 47th Annual Exhibition, April 12–July 4, 1872, no. 205

The Wounded Drummer Boy, 1871 §

Oil on canvas, 47⅞ × 38½

The Collections of the Union League Club, New York City

The Civil War provided Eastman Johnson with some of his most critically acclaimed and popular subjects. He visited the front several times, and events seen there became the subject of some of his paintings. Only one, however, *The Wounded Drummer Boy*, traditionally thought to be an incident of the Battle of Antietam in 1862, clearly depicts a conflict in progress.[1] The painting, which Johnson sent to the Academy's exhibition of 1872, was based on a charcoal and pastel drawing that he had made in 1863 (Century Association, New York).[2] A quotation from an unidentified source was printed in the Academy's 1872 exhibition catalogue beneath the entry for the painting. Since there is no evidence that Johnson was at the Battle of Antietam,[3] the literary source from which the quotation was extracted had probably served as his inspiration:

> In one of the battles of the late war a drummer boy was dis-
> abled by a shot in the leg. As he lay upon the field he called
> to his comrades, "Carry me and I'll drum her through."
> They tied up his wound, a big soldier took him upon his
> shoulders, and he drummed through the fight.

At the Academy, the painting was placed opposite an identical subject, *The Recall* by Julian Scott (location unknown). Johnson's painting received a more effusive notice than the one by the less accomplished Scott. Johnson's figures were "drawn with unerring hand and characterized by a vigilant eye, the group wonderfully alive and moving," while Scott's were executed with "none of that marvelous skill and certainty of light and of drawing which long study and experience have given to Mr. Johnson."[4] In Johnson's painting, the battle is of secondary importance to the portrayal of the inspiring central pair of a soldier and his charge. For one critic, the painting had "the merit and the attraction of a dra-matic incident in which the heroism is itself picturesque."[5] While the subject pleased most critics, the painting received some mixed reviews based on its technical qualities. Another author noted that it was a "spirited group," but he thought "both man and boy have a little air of standing for their pictures."[6]

Many of Johnson's Civil War images related less to battles than to the impact the conflict had on American society or to major players in the political events behind the war. Such was the case with Johnson's many versions of *The Boy Lincoln*. With this sub-ject, Johnson could not fail to reach a sympathetic audience.[7] Not

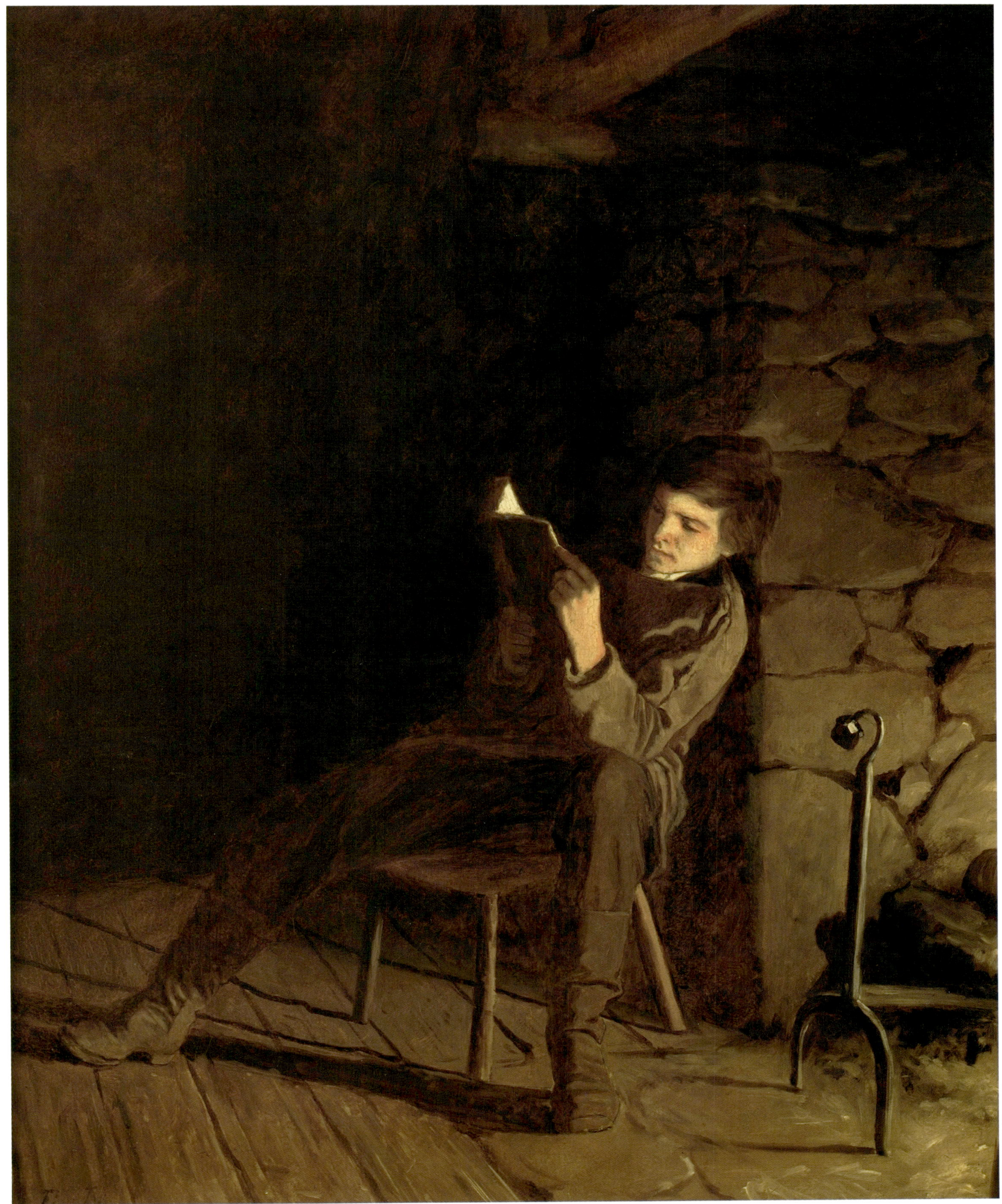

36

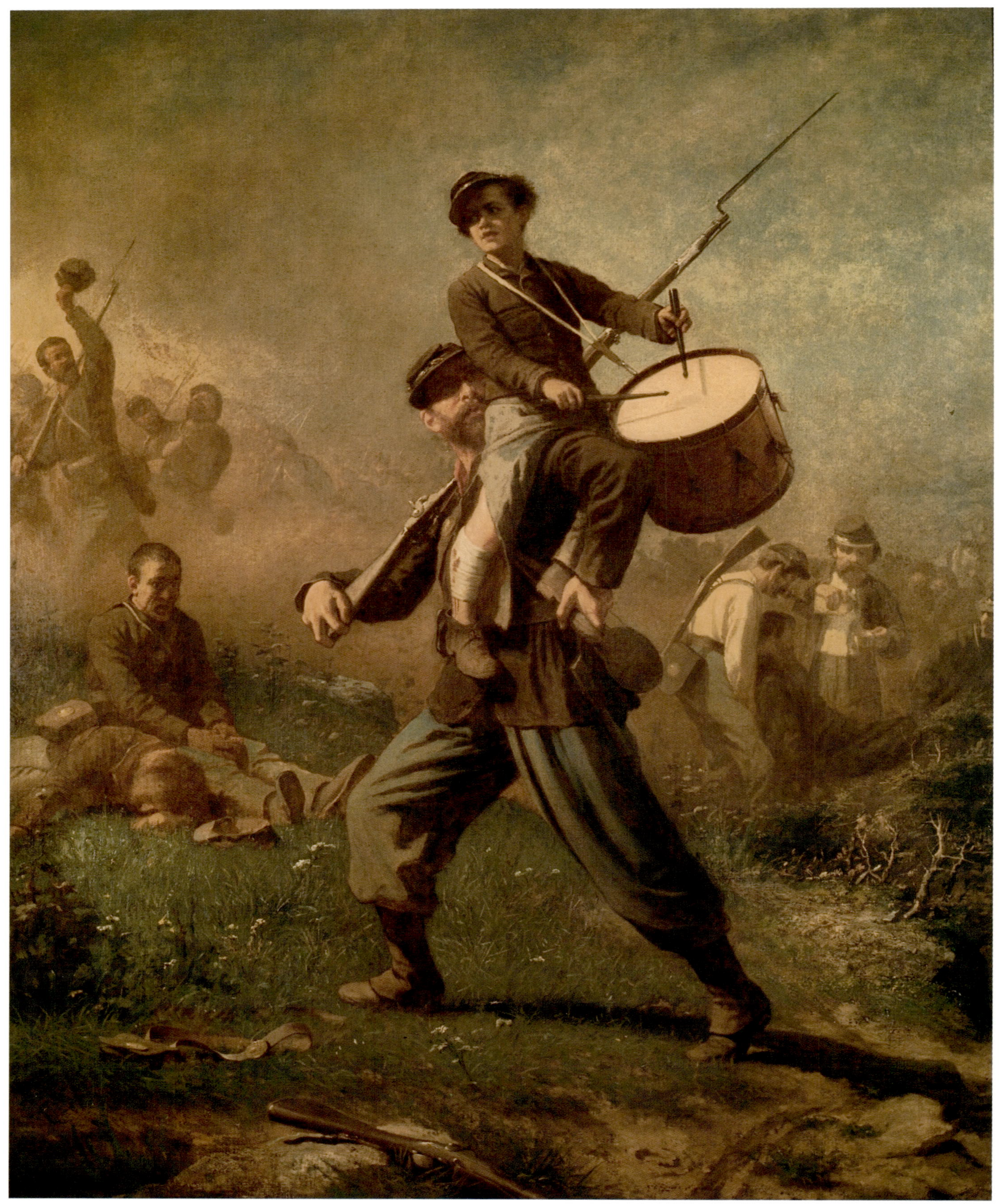

37

only did the painting rely on national veneration for the late president, but by depicting him as a young boy attempting to better himself, Johnson further broadened its appeal.[8] The critic for the *Nation* was aware of this charm when he wrote, "As a delightful and characteristic picture of a typical American youth, reading by the firelight of the farm-house kitchen-fire, it is welcome to all who love pictures with meaning and sincerity behind them."[9]

Apropos to both *The Boy Lincoln* and *The Wounded Drummer Boy,* critics admired Johnson's ability to draw figures, which were frequently noted for being highly expressive, especially in comparison to those of other genre paintings hanging at the exhibitions. Russell Sturgis of the *Galaxy* remarked, "… it is noticeable in Mr. Johnson's pictures that he never avoids the human face, or shuns to give full human expression. Scarcely ever does he evade difficulties of pose and gesture, but will draw an arm abruptly foreshortened rather than disturb his group to get it in profile."[10]

SK

1. John I. H. Baur, *Eastman Johnson, 1824–1906: An American Genre Painter* (Brooklyn: Brooklyn Institute of Arts and Sciences, [1940]), 19.

2. Teresa A. Carbone, "The Genius of the Hour: Eastman Johnson in New York, 1860–1880," in Teresa A. Carbone and Patricia Hills, *Eastman Johnson Painting America* (Brooklyn: Brooklyn Museum of Art, 1999), 59.

3. Carbone, "The Genius of the Hour," in Carbone and Hills, 114, n. 42.

4. "Fine Arts. Exhibition of the Academy of Design. [Third Article.]," *NYDT,* April 22, 1872.

5. A.C.W., "Gossip in a Gallery. A Visit to the Academy of Design," *New York World,* April 21, 1872.

6. "Culture and Progress. Some of the Pictures at the Academy," *Scribner's Monthly* 4 (June 1872): 253.

7. In addition to the one exhibited here, others include the *Boyhood of Lincoln,* the largest and most finished, which is in the University of Michigan Museum of Art (Baur checklist, No. 83), the smaller *Lincoln as a Boy* (Baur, No. 117a; current location unknown), and *The Boy Lincoln Reading,* a charcoal on paper version in the Detroit Institute of Arts (Baur, No. 396).

8. See Patricia Hills, "Genre Painting of Eastman Johnson," in Carbone and Hills, 94–95, on Johnson's successful combination of Lincoln worship and the appeal of children.

9. "Fine Arts. Forty-Third Exhibition of the NAD. Second Notice," *Nation* 6 (May 7, 1868): 377.

10. Russell Sturgis, Jr., "American Painters. The National Academy Exhibition," *Galaxy* 4 (June 1867): 231.

38
Sanford Robinson Gifford, NA

Greenfield, New York 1823–1880 New York, New York

48th Annual Exhibition, April 15–June 7, 1873, no. 236, owner Wm. I. Peake

The Golden Horn, Constantinople, 1880 §

Oil on canvas, 9 × 16

Munson-Williams-Proctor Institute, Utica, New York

In January of 1873, the journal *Arcadian* reported that there "is now on the easel of Sanford R. Gifford, in the Tenth Street Studio building, a fine picture of the 'Golden Horn,' one of the results of Mr. Gifford's travels in the East some time since." The author admired the painting's atmosphere, which he described as a "light, warm haze, through which the mosques and minarets of the city loom up with magic effect," and praised the reflections in "the lightly rippled water in the foreground."[1] The original work is unlocated, but the small painting now in the collection of the Munson-Williams-Proctor Institute and shown here, is probably an accurate, though smaller, replica of it.[2]

The *Arcadian's* reaction to Gifford's painting is typical of that of most critics who wrote about *The Golden Horn* once it appeared in the National Academy of Design's annual exhibition. It is the sort of response that might be expected from viewers accustomed to the works of members of the Hudson River School, such as Gifford. Light and atmosphere were usually the focus in such discussions and, indeed, this is the approach taken by a writer for the *New York Sun* who thought the painting was "one of the finest" in the exhibition. He reported that the "canvas glows with the warm tropical sunshine that transfuses and illuminates the scene."[3] Likewise, the *New York Evening Post* described the painting as "glowing with color and with that tender effect of golden light which radiates over nature just before the close of day." He described the effect of light in impressionist terms: Gifford, he noted, "gives us a succession of waves of light through which the towers and minarets of the great city are indicated, and yet their form is lost in the general glow…."[4]

The *New York Evening Mail* gave the painting its most detailed appraisal, pairing it with John F. Kensett's *Italy,* in the same exhibition. These paintings, the critic wrote, "are both summer pictures in sunny climes. Both are characteristic examples of the artists, and both well deserve the places of honor which have been allotted to them." Gifford's, he went on to report,

is wonderful in its luminous atmosphere. The mists of morning are clearing away before the shafts of the sun god, his rays are bursting forth in triumph over the city of the Sultan and have shed a glorious glamour over the cordage of the vessels, and tuned the waters of the Sea of Marmoa to a rippled expanse of gold. It may be said that the misty treatment which Mr. Gifford has adopted is theatrical and conventional, the monotony of color may be censured, but, for all that we seek in vain for any artist who possesses the same power over aerial sunlight, who is able to perpetuate with equal felicity the fleeting breath of the uprising day king. Other artists arrange their chiaro-oscuro *horizontally, he vertically. The light does not dart out in solid beams, it is diffused from the source whence it emanates, and where it would gleam forth between the interstices of the terraced domes and minarets, there the transparent pencils shoot forth, expanding as they go, until they are lost in the glowing morning air.*[5]

Not all critics were so positive about Gifford's *The Golden Horn* and, in fact, the writer for the *Mail* may have been giving direct response to some of the negative criticism leveled at the painting, rare though it was. The *New-York Times* called the atmosphere in the painting "sickly" and the *New York World* accused Gifford of simply "throwing off" this type of picture "to appease the appetite for color which he has himself created."[6] Surprisingly, given its earlier praise for the work, the *Arcadian,* or at least one of its writers, turned against the painting once it was hanging in the galleries of the Academy. The journal accused

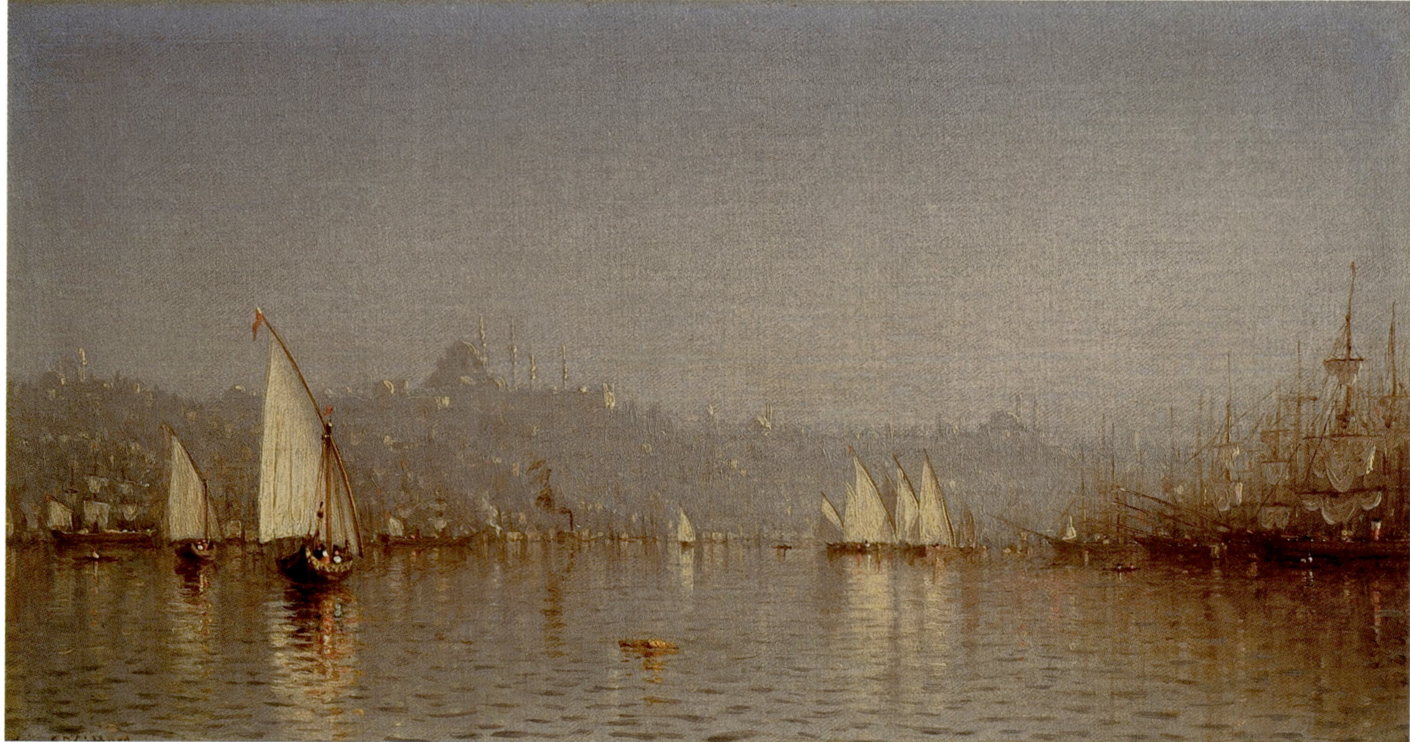

38

both Gifford and Louis Comfort Tiffany, who had also just returned from a trip to the Middle East, of "re-producing Moorish scenes with such assiduity that it is really becoming monotonous." The writer called for "something else besides sunlight effect upon stretches of blank wall and fanciful costumes."[7]

DBD

1. "Fine Arts," *Arcadian* 1 (January 23, 1873): 10.
2. Ila Weiss suggests that the smaller work "may have been an intermediate version, completed later" and possibly "a rethinking of the earlier idea" (Ila Weiss, *Poetic Landscape: The Art and Experience of Sanford R. Gifford* [Newark: University of Delaware Press, 1987], 274). It may have been the work bought from an 1881 sale of Gifford's paintings by a Mr. J. W. Wheeler for $96.00 (Thomas E. Kirby, & Co., *Catalogue of Valuable Oil Paintings, Works of the Famous Artists, Sanford R. Gifford, N.A., Deceased* [New York, 1881], 43; "Fine Arts," *New York Herald*, April 13, 1881).
3. "Fine Arts," *NYS*, April 15, 1873.
4. "NAD," *NYEP*, May 15, 1873.
5. "Fine Arts," *NYEM*, April 29, 1873.
6. "Fine Arts: The Academy of Design," *NYT*, April 20, 1873; "Fine Arts: NAD," *New York World*, April 19, 1873.
7. "Fine Arts: The Academy of Design," *Arcadian* 1 (April 24, 1873): 10. William J. Peake, who lent the original version of *The Golden Horn* to the National Academy's 1871 exhibition, also sent it to the Centennial Exposition in Philadelphia in 1876 (United States Centennial Commission, *International Exhibition. 1876. Official Catalogue. Part II. Art Gallery, Annexes, and Out-Door Works of Art* [Philadelphia: John R. Nagle and Company, 1876], 22).

39
William Page, NA
Albany, New York 1811–1885 Staten Island, New York

49th Annual Exhibition, April 9–June 6, 1874, no. 301, for sale

Shakespeare, 1873 §

Oil on canvas, 27 × 21
Folger Shakespeare Library, Washington, D.C.

In the late 1860s, the painter William Page became interested in creating an accurate likeness of William Shakespeare. It was a pursuit that would occupy the artist for much of the rest of his life, eventually bordering on obsession.

Page began his quest by modeling several busts and even attempting a life-size sculpture of Shakespeare.[1] He then painted a number of bust-size portraits of the man, one of which is shown here, evidently on commission from "four or five New-York gentlemen."[2] These were based on existing images of Shakespeare, especially photographs of a supposed death mask that was then in a private collection in Germany and which Page believed to be authentic.[3] These early efforts led to Page's most ambitious likeness of Shakespeare, a three-quarter-length portrait that he exhibited at the National Academy of Design in 1874 under the title *Shakespeare Reading*.[4] Page had been an active participant in the Academy's annuals since 1827 and had been receiving significant attention from critics and the public since 1835 when his *Portrait of a Lady and Child* (Pennsylvania Academy of the Fine Arts) was one of the successes of that year's exhibition.[5] None of Page's paintings, however, had received as much attention or created as much controversy as did his portrait of Shakespeare in 1874.

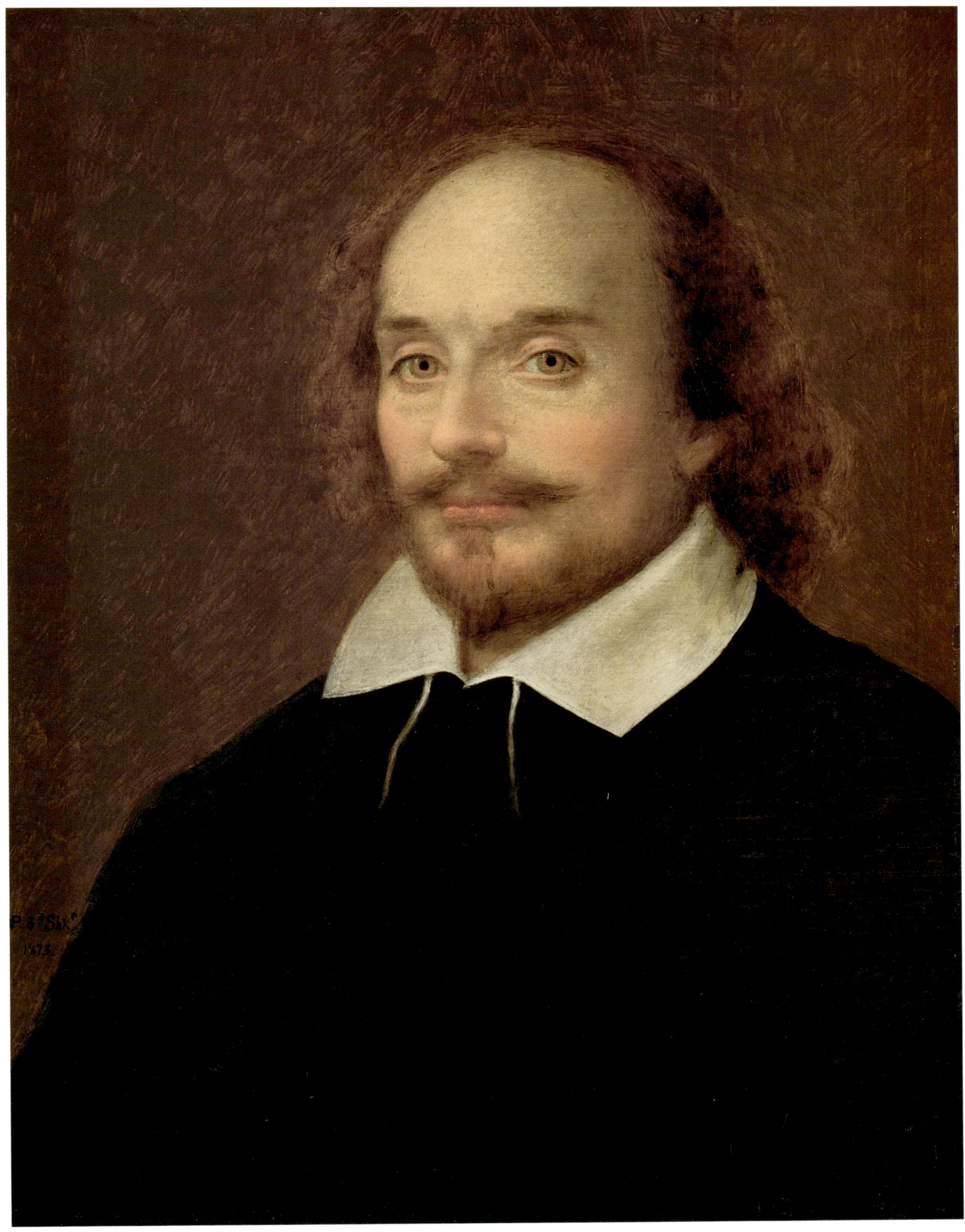

39

Oddly, given what was to follow, the advance word on *Shakespeare Reading* was good. Several critics got a preview of it in Page's studio and declared it a success. The *New-York Times* actually called it "a noble picture" and predicted that it would "create great interest," while *Appleton's Journal* praised Page's interpretation of Shakespeare's "quiet, thoughtful form," the sense of movement that Page gave the figure, especially in the placement of the hands, and the sensitive way in which Shakespeare's eyes were rendered.[6]

Despite these statements, this was the only time the painting would receive unqualified positive responses. Once it was unveiled to the public at the Academy's annual exhibition, few writers were willing to concede that it had any redeeming qualities. The closest thing to praise was the conciliatory but slightly sarcastic comments of the *New York World* which at least gave Page credit for the "erudition and laborious skill" that he had put into the image. If nothing else, the newspaper remarked, the portrait was "an authoritative fabrication, patiently, learnedly, and conscientiously built."[7] A writer for the *Nation* gave Page the benefit of the doubt by assuming that the portrait was meant to be nothing more than a summation of all known images of the playwright—a historical work rather than a true work of art. "Mr. Page has collected the flesh and bones of his subject," the critic wrote, "let him next breathe into it the breath of life."[8]

Far more typical of the critical response to *Shakespeare Reading* was the declaration of *Watson's Art Journal* that the portrait has "as much resemblance to flesh and blood, and looks as much like Shakespeare as a lump of butter does."[9] The *New York Evening Mail* began its assessment of the painting by stating simply that it was "not a success." This, the newspaper reported, was primarily due to Page's attempt to combine the characteristics of all the known portraits of Shakespeare into his version of the man, an effort that resulted in "a combat of intentions and characterizations in the face and consequent weakening of effect."[10] A critic for the *New York Herald* felt that Page had failed to create a truly historical portrait, one that, because of its link to the past, would fulfill the traditional purpose of art to inspire. "Mr. Page presents to us rather a namby pamby personage with a weak rather than poetic expression," the critic wrote. "There is neither in face nor figure that commanding dignity of person which might be put in an ideal creation at the outward symbol of the genius and majestic thought of the man. The position of the figure is awkward and unnatural and unpleasantly suggestive of a lay figure."[11]

As was so often the case during this period, the most caustic writer was Clarence Cook. In his role as art critic for the *New York Daily Tribune,* Cook, "after long and charitable seeking," thoroughly condemned Page's portrait. He called the figure "wooden . . . incapable of motion, vapid and feeble beyond comprehension." The face, which he thought was the worst part of the painting, was lifeless. "The mask has hampered Mr. Page in his conception of Shakespeare, not helped him," Cook explained. "He has anatomised it, with a Boswellian reverence that is a little ludicrous, that luckless scar over the eye, for instance, which those who have studied the mask itself, and not merely the photo-

graphs, declare positively does not exist, being painted with such emphasis that were it really on the living Shakespeare it would create the gravest apprehension. Mr. Page may most powerfully and potently believe in this scar, but we must hold it not honestly to have it thus set down."[12]

Page evidently ignored the bad press created by his *Shakespeare Reading.* In the summer of 1874, he went to Germany to see the death mask for himself.[13] Convinced of its authenticity, he returned to this country and created other images of the man, including another sculpted bust; continued to give public lectures on the history of portraits of Shakespeare; and wrote at least one article on the subject.[14] He even exhibited another portrait of the Bard at the National Academy in 1876 after which he sent it to the Centennial Exposition in Philadelphia.[15]   DBD

1. "A Work of Art. William Page's Bust of Shakespeare," *New York Commercial Advertiser,* July 24, 1871.

2. "Fine Arts," *Appleton's* Journal 12 (November 28, 1874): 701. A letter from Page to Sarah Shaw, dated March 22, 1873, is attached to the stretcher of the version of Page's *Shakespeare* shown here. In the letter, Page tells Mrs. Shaw that the painting is almost finished but that the "gentleman" who commissioned it has not paid for it, despite Page's entreaties. The artist then offered the painting as a gift to Mrs. Shaw (William Pressley, *Catalogue of Paintings in the Folger Shakespeare Library* [Washington, D.C., 1993], 308).

3. Page proselytized about the death-mask by giving public lectures on it. See, for example, "William Page's Lecture," *NYT,* November 14, 1873, and "Shakespeare's Portrait," *NYEM,* November 17, 1873.

4. The details of Page's various Shakespeare portraits are given in Joshua C. Taylor, *William Page, The American Titian* (Chicago: University of Chicago Press, 1957), 196–203, 257–58.

5. Among the favorable reviews of this painting was "Fine Arts in America. NAD," *American Monthly Magazine* 5 (July 1835): 398, which devoted several paragraphs to it. The painting is discussed in Taylor, 14–16.

6. "Fine Arts. The Academy Exhibition. Anticipations of Triumph by the Academicians," *NYT,* April 6, 1874; "Art," *Appleton's Journal* 11 (May 2, 1874): 572; "Art," *Appleton's Journal* 11 (March 21, 1874): 411. *Appleton's* was especially supportive of Page and responded to the negative criticism of his *Shakespeare* by declaring that "it is better to be hated than forgotten."

7. "NAD," *New York World,* April 17, 1874.

8. "Fine Arts. The National Academy Exhibition," *Nation* 18 (May 14, 1874): 320.

9. "Exhibition of the NAD," *Watson's Art Journal* 21 (May 23, 1874): 30.

10. "Fine Arts. The Exhibition at the National Academy. The North Room," *New York Evening Mail,* April 25, 1874.

11. "The Academy of Design," *NYH,* April 20, 1874.

12. [Clarence Cook], "Fine Arts. NAD," *NYDT,* April 25, 1874. In a similar manner, a writer for the *New York Sun* blamed the "unpleasant expression of deadness" that he perceived in the portrait on Page's "too long brooding over the post mortem cast" ("Fine Arts," *NYS,* April 15, 1874). Other reviews that negatively criticized Page's portrait are "Fine Arts," *Daily Graphic,* April 10, 1874, and "Fine Arts," *NYT,* April 13, 1874.

13. "Art Notes," *NYEP,* July 25, 1874.

14. William Page, "A Study of Shakespeare's Portraits, *Scribner's Monthly* 10 (1875): 225.

15. United States Centennial Commission, *International Exhibition. 1876. Official Catalogue. Part II* (Philadelphia, John R. Nagle and Company, 1876), 21. *Shakespeare Reading* returned to the Academy in December 1877 as part of a small exhibition of paintings by Page. One of his busts of Shakespeare was in that exhibition as well and, the press reported, " . . . photographs of the cast and bust are offered for sale for the benefit of Mr. Page, in whose aid this little exhibition is given" ("Mr. Page's Pictures," *NYH,* December 14, 1877).

40

Henry Peters Gray, NA
New York, New York 1819–1877 New York, New York

50th Annual Exhibition, April 8–May 29, 1875, no. 384

The Birth of Our Flag, 1874
Oil on canvas, 72 × 48

National Academy of Design, New York

Henry Peters Gray executed two versions of this painting, each of which contained an allegorical female figure, an eagle, and a flag.[1] Both were inspired by the first stanza of Joseph Rodman Drake's poem, "The American Flag," published in 1843:

When Freedom from her mountain height, unfurled her
    banner to the air,
She tore the azure robe of night, and set the stars of glory
    there.
Then from his mansion in the sun, she called her eagle
    bearer down,
And gave into his mighty hand the chosen emblem
    of our land. [2]

Gray's first painted interpretation of this poem (location unknown), was exhibited in the Academy's annual exhibition of 1863. Probably due to its small size (12 × 8 inches), it did not receive much attention, but what was written about it was positive. *Harper's Weekly* admired the "fine dashing movement in the erect figure;" and the *Albion* admired Gray's "fine female figure."[3]

Given the painting's blatant patriotic allusion to the Union, such praise, however succinct, is certainly not surprising for critics writing in 1863. As the Civil War ended and the centennial of the founding of this country approached, the theme remained timely. In fact, the coming of that anniversary may have been Gray's impetus for recycling the image in 1874. This time, however, he chose a larger format, undoubtedly in hopes of getting attention. He succeeded, but probably not in the way that he had hoped.

At first, the climate looked promising for *The Birth of Our Flag.* A writer for *Appleton's Journal* saw it in Gray's Florence studio shortly after it was finished and predicted a favorable reception for it in the United States. "American history and traditions should have their own symbolical representations in art," he explained, "and in this point of view Mr. Gray's choice of a subject appears perfectly legitimate, even if it be not in perfect accord with the realistic spirit of the age."[4]

Once the painting made its way to the United States and appeared in the National Academy's annual exhibition of 1875, matters turned ugly. The Academy gave *The Birth of Our Flag* a place of honor in its large South Gallery.[5] From the start, it received much attention from the public;[6] but its prominence in the South Gallery also seems to have made it an easy target for the critics. One of these was Clarence Cook, who was especially vitriolic, lambasting the painting not once but twice. His first ranting against it was in a report he filed to the *New York Daily Tribune.* He told his readers that, on entering the South Gallery where the painting hung, he felt like the newly awakened Rip Van Winkle. *The Birth of Our Flag,* he said, has "no more relation to the nineteenth century and to America than a stuffed Dodo

would have."[7] Cook bemoaned lack of growth and development in Gray's talents, concluding that the artist's problems stemmed from his faith "more in Titian than in Nature" and his preference for the "so-called ideal" over the real. Cook failed to see nobility or beauty in the head of the female figure and thought the eagle looked like an "exasperated crow."[8]

Of course, not all critics agreed with Cook and several came to Gray's defense. A writer for the New York edition of the *Art Journal* happily saw *The Birth of Our Flag* as evidence that Gray's visits abroad had not "led him into any of the vagaries of the present fashionable European schools of art."[9] Taking an opposite tack from Cook's, the critic for the *Daily Graphic* felt, rather amazingly, that Gray's allegorical female was not at all idealized but instead was "unmistakably of the earth, earthy."[10] More realistically, the *Nation* admitted that certain aspects of the painting were bound to result in ridicule; but, the writer stated hopefully, " . . . our art will rise above the art of the illustrated-newspaper sort only by the studies, the aspirations, the conflict and the success of which this picture is no mean product."[11]

Despite these comparatively feeble attempts, it was a losing battle and derision of *The Birth of Our Flag* did not end with Clarence Cook. When the painting was shown at the Union League Club in 1877, a writer for the *New-York Times* advised his readers to look at it only on "the Fourth of July, in the morning." To do otherwise, he stated, might cause the viewer to "fall into vain and annoying speculations as to how a handsome girl came to be caught out on a windy slope, a very windy slope, 'mid modings on' but the American flag, and why she smiles and looks so sweet when, beyond all doubt, the large and determined looking eagle over her head is about to bury his hooked beak in her white shoulder."[12]

Fortunately, such vicious criticism did affect the artist, who had died the previous month.   DBD

1. The first, smaller version of the theme, titled *The Origin of Our Flag,* was in the collection of Thomas B. Clarke by 1886. Evidently, it was very close in composition to the later *The Birth of Our Flag.* See Pennsylvania Academy of the Fine Arts, *Catalogue of the Thomas B. Clarke Collection of American Paintings* (Philadelphia, 1891), 52.
2. This is the verse order as quoted in the catalogue of the Academy's 1875 exhibition. The original poem, published in Rufus Willmot Griswold, *The Poets and Poetry of America* (Philadelphia: Carey and Hart, 1843), 147, is slightly different.
3. "The Academy Exhibition," *HW* 7 (May 9, 1863): 290; "Fine Arts. NAD," *Albion* 41 (May 9, 1863): 225.
4. "Notes from American Studios in Italy," *Appleton's Journal* 12 (August 8, 1874): 188-89.
5. "The Fine Arts. Exhibition of the Academy of Design," *NYT,* April 10, 1875.
6. *NYEP* (April 8, 1875), which reported that, at the opening reception of the Academy's exhibition, Gray's painting was one of about seven that attracted the most attention.
7. [Clarence Cook], "Fine Arts. The NAD," *NYDT,* April 9, 1875.
8. [Clarence Cook], "Fine Arts: NAD," *NYDT,* May 1, 1875. Unlike the writer for *Appleton's,* quoted above, Cook railed against the possible purchase of *The Birth of Our Flag* by a public institution. In fact, he confessed that the reason he felt it necessary to express himself so plainly and at such length was that he had heard a rumor that the U.S. government or the Corcoran Gallery of Art might purchase *The Birth of Our Flag.*
9. "The NAD," *Art Journal* (1875): 157.
10. "The Academy Exhibition," *New York Daily Graphic,* April 10, 1875.
11. "Fine Arts. Fiftieth Annual Exhibition of the Academy of Design," *Nation* 20 (April 15, 1875): 264.
12. "The Exhibition of Paintings," *NYT,* December 22, 1877.

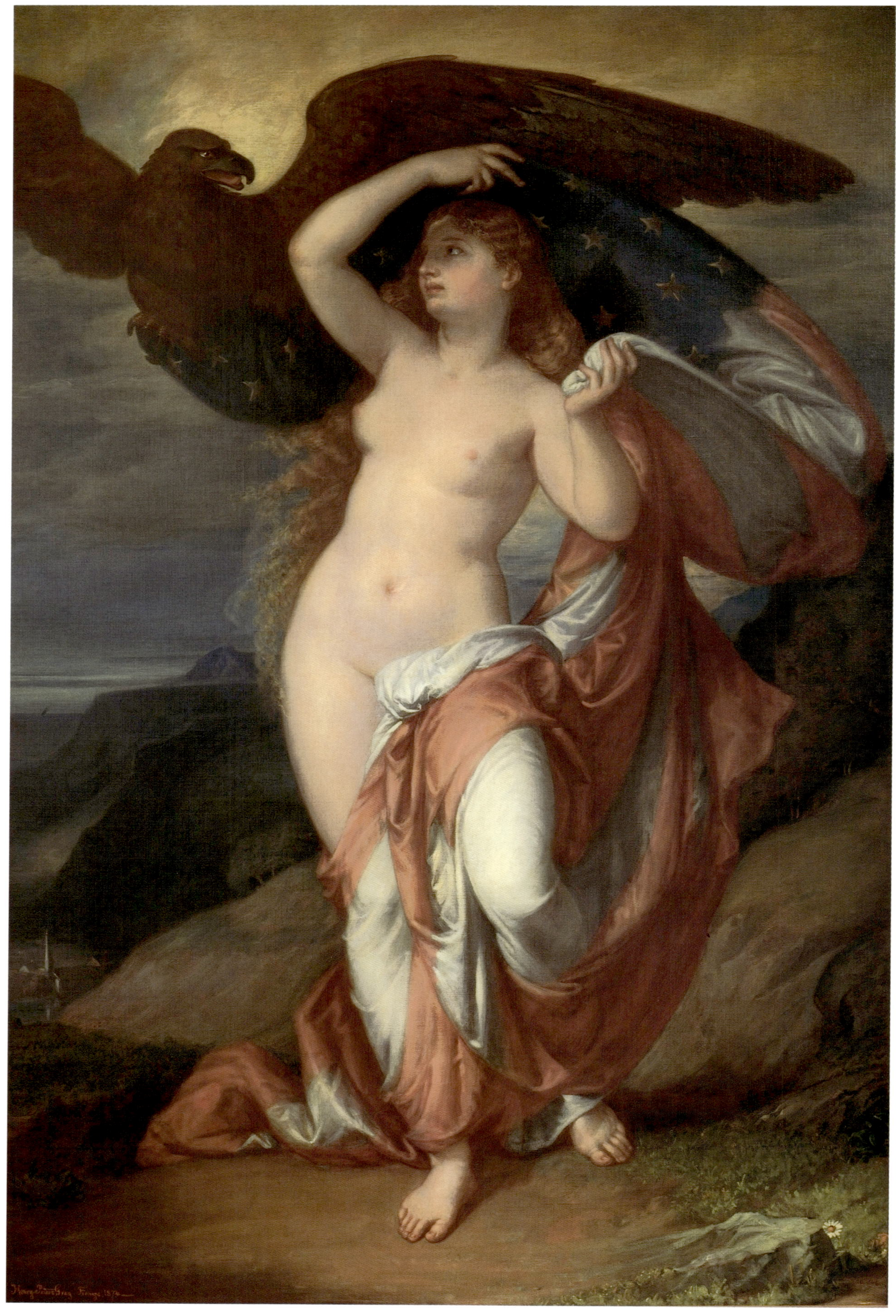

40

41

Eastman Johnson, NA

Lovell, Maine 1824–1906 New York, New York

Husking Bee, Island of Nantucket, 51st Annual Exhibition,
March 28–May 31, 1876, no. 285[1]

Corn Husking at Nantucket, [1875] §

Oil on canvas, 27⅝ × 54½

The Metropolitan Museum of Art, Rogers Fund, 1907

During the 1870s, Eastman Johnson began spending increasing amounts of time on Nantucket, where he found inspiration for his paintings in the island's people and their traditions. By focusing on the regional labors of corn husking, maple-sugaring, and cranberry picking, he was able to explore the social interactions of country people, thereby bringing to his urban viewers scenes of a quaint way of life no longer available to many. This is seen in paintings such as *Husking Bee, Island of Nantucket* (1876; Art Institute of Chicago), which was exhibited at the National Academy of Design in 1876. (An oil study done for the painting the previous year is shown here). On the occasion of that exhibition, a writer for the *New-York Times* called *Husking Bee* "a careful record of a peculiar phase of American country life," while another critic described it as "replete with picturesque life."[2]

By 1876, Johnson's style had shifted from a rather tight linearism to one that involved a looser handling of paint and a more visible brushwork. Much of the critical response to *Husking Bee* focused on these aspects of the painting, with some critics applauding Johnson's effort as progressive while others found it disgraceful. Primarily, the painting was seen as an unusual one for Johnson. One critic noted that it was "painted in a style that reminds one of Dieffenbach, or anybody, rather than Eastman Johnson," and another remarked that it "would hardly be recognized as coming from his hand, even by those who know him best."[3] Most critics pointed out the strong contrast with Johnson's other contribution to the Academy that year, *The New Bonnet* (1876; The Metropolitan Museum of Art), which retained the tight handling and somber tones of his earlier paintings. One comment offers a particular insight into Johnson's awareness of the importance of the annual exhibitions, and the way in which he tried to appeal to different types of viewers: "This 'Husking Bee' seems done to please artists and connoisseurs; the 'New Bonnet' to please the world as it goes."[4]

The reaction to *Husking Bee* is worth exploring, for the critical commentary offers insight into how Johnson fit into what was rapidly becoming a very cosmopolitan art world. One perturbed critic wrote that the "execution is slovenly enough to suggest a sketch, rather than a finished painting," but others were willing to accept it as a completed, if not highly polished, painting.[5] Clarence Cook, writing for the *New York Tribune,* defined "finish" in terms of contemporary developments in French painting, and according to his standards, Johnson's painting was, in a modern interpretation of the word, finished.[6] As such, it fit well with contemporary European painting and, in fact, had a chance to do just that when it was chosen for exhibition at the Paris Exposition in 1878. Certainly, this honor was an indication of Johnson's popularity in general and the cosmopolitan appeal of *Husking Bee.* Furthermore, the Chicago businessman Potter Palmer purchased it for his collection, which also contained works by French artists and younger and more progressive American artists such as William Merritt Chase (1849–1916). As one critic put it, Johnson had taken "no insignificant step in the right direction."[7]

SK

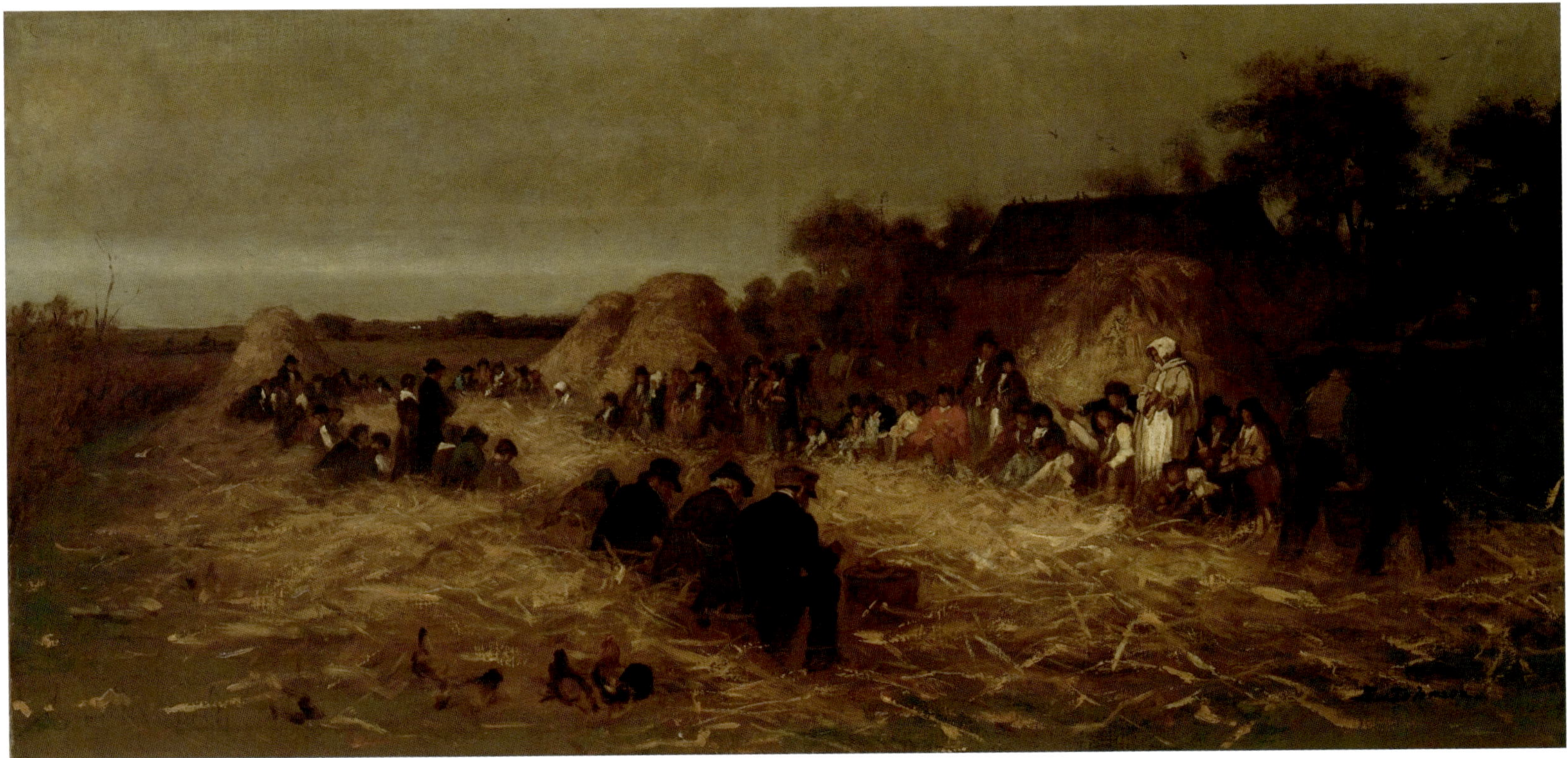

1. The painting in this exhibition is probably the final oil study for the finished version exhibited by Johnson in 1876. That version is *Husking Bee, Island of Nantucket*, now in the Art Institute of Chicago, and is substantially the same, though with tighter brushwork and greater definition of forms. See Natalie Spassky's essay on the painting in Spassky et al., *American Paintings in the Metropolitan Museum of Art* (New York: The Metropolitan Museum of Art, 1985), 2: 227–29.

2. "The Fine Arts. The Academy Exhibition," *NYT*, April 3, 1876; "Art Matters. A Hasty Glance at the Academy Exhibition," *New York Evening Express*, April 20, 1876.

3. "The Fine Arts. The Academy Exhibition," *NYT*, April 8, 1876; [Clarence Cook], "Fine Arts: Fifty-first Annual Exhibition of the NAD," *NYDT*, April 8, 1876.

4. [Clarence Cook], *NYDT*, April 22, 1876.

5. "The NAD," *New York Sun*, April 30, 1876.

6. [Clarence Cook], *NYDT*, April 22, 1876.

7. "Art," *Atlantic Monthly* 37 (June 1876): 760.

42

William Rudolf O'Donovan, ANA

Preston County, Virginia (now West Virginia) 1844–1920 New York, New York

Portrait—Bust of William Page, N.A., 53rd Annual Exhibition, April 2–June 1, 1878, no. 722

William Page, 1877

Bronze, 24¾ × 14 × 10½

National Academy of Design, New York

When the sculptor William O'Donovan came to New York from his native Virginia in 1867, his first impressions of the art establishment—meaning the National Academy of Design and its members—were far from positive. He expressed his frustrations in a letter he wrote to his sister in 1871, when he complained that the Academicians " 'run' the clubs, and have formed themselves into a 'ring' for the purpose of keeping to themselves all the art patronage of the Country."[1] Even after his sculptures began to be accepted into the Academy's exhibitions, his experiences with the organization remained, for the most part, unpleasant. In 1874, he wrote to his sister about his debut there with his bust of Peter Gilsey. The sculpture, he reported, "was not mentioned by a single one of the so-called critics. Nor so far as I could see during repeated visits to the Academy, did it attract the attention of the visitors."[2]

Given this attitude, it is not surprising that O'Donovan joined other artists in forming new, independent organizations such as the Tile Club and the Society of American Artists, both founded in 1877. O'Donovan was an active participant in these somewhat rebellious groups, but he did not discount the importance of affiliation with the Academy. He continued to exhibit works there, albeit sporadically, through 1900. Another connection with the organization was made when, in 1877, he modeled a bust of the Academy's former president William Page.

Page and O'Donovan met in the early 1870s and immediately began a life-long friendship.[3] In 1875, O'Donovan wrote to his mother that Page was of "the very highest rank as an artist" but had an admirable humility; he was one of a group of men "whose works live, for they have been born of love and are part and parcel of their own beings; and of beings made lofty by a clear appre-

hension of spiritual truth."[4] When Daniel Huntington and other Academicians decided to commission a sculpted portrait of their former president, O'Donovan probably seemed like a natural choice. The bust was finished late in 1877 and was sent to the Academy's annual exhibition early the next year. The critical success it had there—not to mention the mere fact that the Academy had commissioned it from him to begin with—probably gave O'Donovan a sense that justice, at least to some degree, had been served.[5]

The bust was first hailed by the *Art Journal* in 1877. A writer for that periodical reported that the work had been completed and cast and would soon be presented to the National Academy. It is, the writer noted, "worthy of the venerable institution that will offer it welcome and shelter." The critic continued in terms that probably pleased O'Donovan since the honesty implied here is in keeping with what the sculptor admired about his sitter:

> It is executed in a truly artistic spirit—the spirit of the healthiest epoch of Greek Art—and is at the same time a thoroughly modern piece of sculpture, without even a hint of the conventionality of the antique. Page's character, the character that those who know him best will the most easily recognize, is depicted with faithfulness and with feeling.[6]

Once the bust was on public view in the Academy's exhibition, the *Nation* used adjectives such as "heroic," "stately," "marvelous," "noble," and "Phidian" to describe it. The portrait's "expression of flesh-texture and that of sparse blowing locks of hair," the journal declared, "are as happy as the facial expression and bearing."[7] Clarence Cook, writing for the *New York Daily Tribune*, was "impressed with the mechanical skill of this performance compared with the crudeness" of the other busts in the exhibition. As he usually did, however, Cook qualified his praise, since, he believed, "mechanical skill" was not enough to make a great work of art. "Mr. O'Donovan's heads will not increase the demand for pedestals," he quipped. "This sculptor is a Pygmalion, whose statue is vexatiously near coming to life. His bust is a watched pot that won't boil."[8] On the other hand, the *New-York Times* felt that O'Donovan's technical abilities were not as high as those of sculptor Olin Levi Warner, whose work was in the same exhibition. Nevertheless, the *Times* concluded, O'Donovan's bust of Page "marks his highest advance so far."[9]

The bust was formally presented to the National Academy in 1879[10] and was unveiled at a ceremony featuring journalist Parke Godwin as the keynote speaker. Godwin congratulated the members of the Academy for commissioning this "image that may remind you that the highest aim of Art is not to do what others have done . . . but to consult your own impressions and sentiments, and to bring out in the best way you can what is deepest and truest in your own souls."[11]

DBD

1. O'Donovan to his sister, April 7, 1871, Historical Society of Pennsylvania, AAA, microfilm roll P23.

2. O'Donovan to his sister, June 8, 1874, Historical Society of Pennsylvania, AAA, microfilm roll P23.

3. Their friendship is evidenced by a group of letters from O'Donovan to Page and Mrs. Page that are among the William Page Papers, AAA, microfilm rolls 22–24. Also see Joshua C. Taylor, *William Page, The American Titian* (Chicago: The University of Chicago Press, 1957), 211–12.

4. O'Donovan to his mother, May 11, 1875, Historical Society of Pennsylvania, AAA, microfilm roll P23.

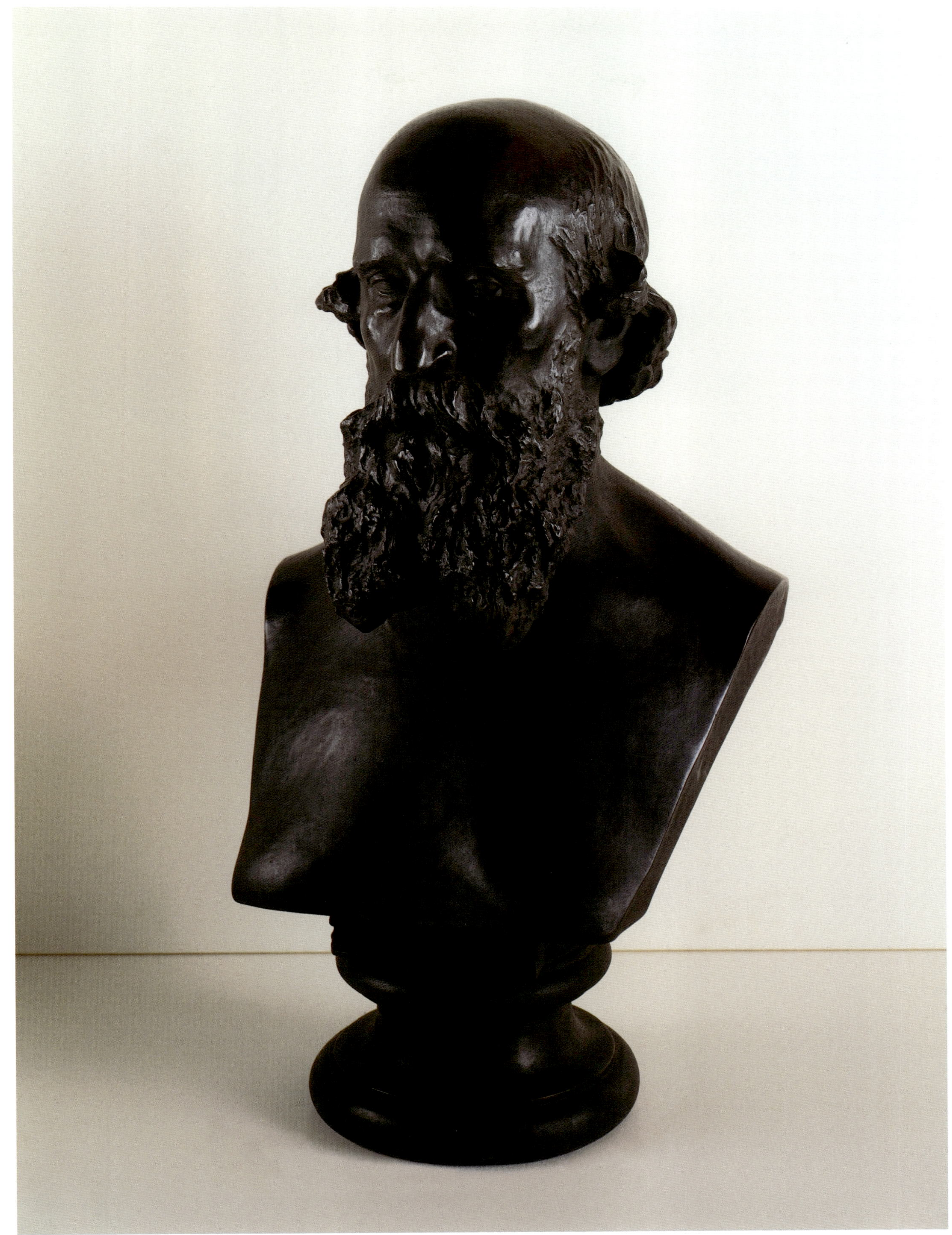

42

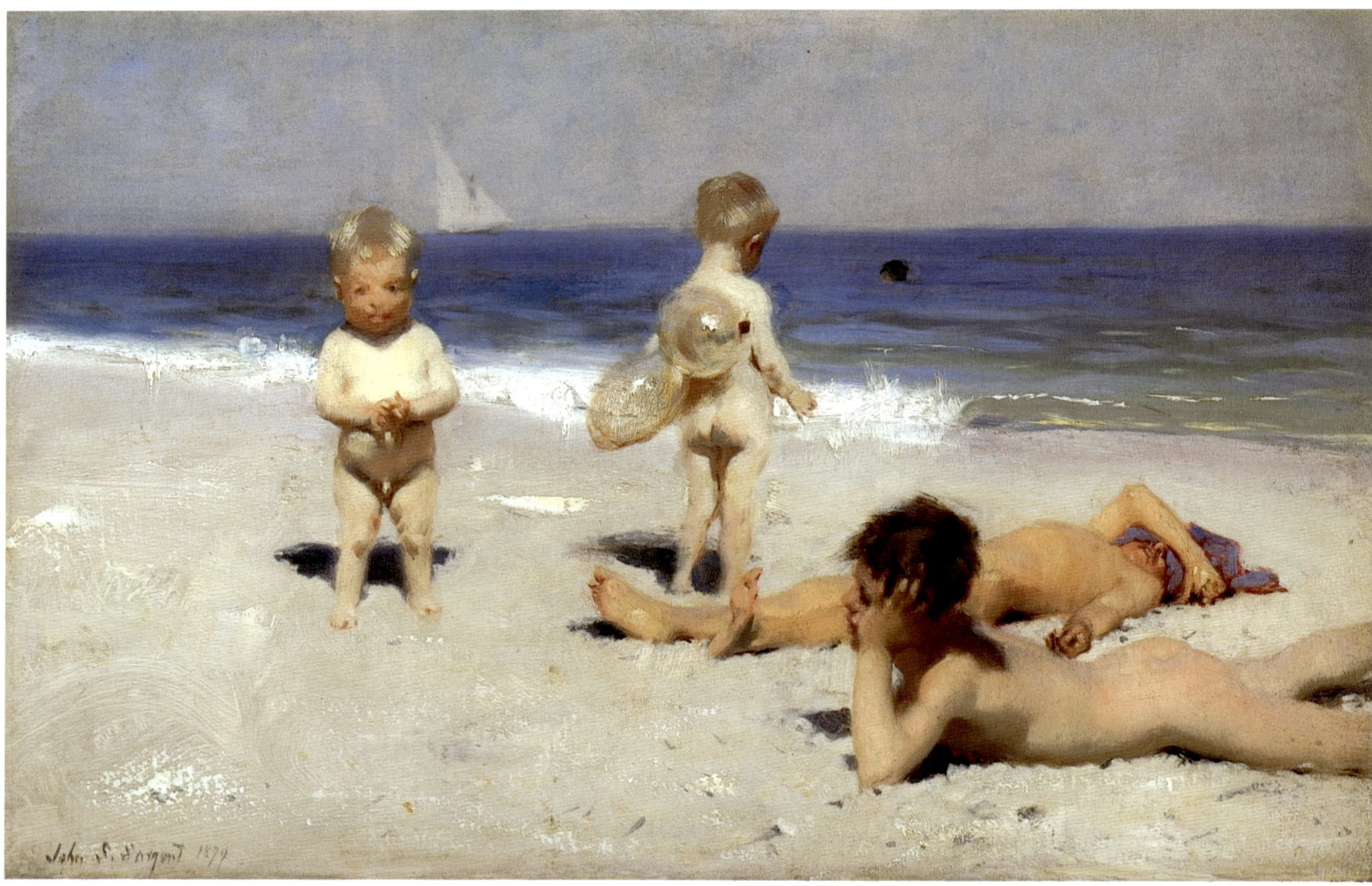

43

5. Besides his bust of Page, O'Donovan also sent portrait busts of his artist friends Winslow Homer and William H. Beard to the Academy's annual that year.

6. "Mr. William R. O'Donovan," *Art Journal* (New York) 3 (1877): 384.

7. "Fine Arts: The National Academy Exhibition. Final Notice," *Nation* 26 (May 30, 1878): 363–64.

8. C[larence] C[ook], "Fine Arts: NAD. Fifty-third Annual Exhibition, II," *NYDT*, April 9, 1878.

9. "The Academy Exhibition. The Sculpture Room," *NYT*, May 20, 1878.

10. Evidently, O'Donovan initially sent a bronze cast of his bust of Page to the Academy annual of 1878 but, being dissatisfied with the casting, he replaced it with a plaster version during the run of the exhibition. (See "Fine Arts: The National Academy Exhibition. Final Notice," *Nation* 26 [May 30, 1878]: 363). He probably then destroyed the first cast and had a new one made for presentation to the Academy. This would explain the delay in the Academy's receiving the bust, which did not come into its possession until 1879.

11. "A Bronze Bust of Mr. William Page," *Art Journal* (New York) 5 (1879): 128.

43

John Singer Sargent, NA

Florence, Italy 1856–1925 London, England

54th Annual Exhibition, April 1–May 31, 1879, no. 431, owner G. M. Williamson

Neapolitan Children Bathing, 1878

Oil on canvas, 10⁹⁄₁₆ × 16³⁄₁₆

Sterling and Francine Clark Art Institute, Williamstown, Massachusetts

Sargent made his American debut with his painting *Oyster Gatherers of Cancale* (1878; Museum of Fine Arts, Boston), which he sent to the Kurtz Gallery for the first exhibition of the Society of American Artists in 1878. The following year he showed *A Capriote* (1878; Museum of Fine Arts, Boston), also at the Society. Neither of these works was ignored by the critics and, in fact, *Oyster Gatherers* received particularly favorable reviews. However, Sargent's next painting, *Neapolitan Children Bathing* was even more of a critical hit when it debuted at the National Academy of Design in 1879.[1]

Not surprisingly, some writers compared *Neapolitan Children* to one or both of the other two paintings mentioned above, usually to its benefit. Edward Strahan, for example, writing for *Art Amateur*, thought it "more felicitous and warm and pleasurable" than *Oyster Gatherers* and "more harmonious in color" than *A Capriote*.[2] Similarly, the *New-York Times* felt that *Neapolitan Children* was "a much better picture than the one shown at the Kurtz Gallery, although not so cautiously painted."[3]

The color and light in the painting were the aspects of the work that captured the most attention, just as they were for the French Impressionists who had been exhibiting as a group in Paris for only a few years. A writer for the *New York Tribune* was one of many to address the method with which Sargent handled the water. For the visitor "who only knows the gray seas that welter round our inhospitable Northern coast," he wrote, Sargent's treatment of the sea might seem "grossly exaggerated, for never, even in the transforming eyes of the most poetical Summer-boarder, do our waters look so beautifully blue as this artist has painted the Mediterranean." He assured his readers, however, that "the blue of this picture is not in the least exaggerated, as everybody knows who has passed even a few weeks of Summer at Naples."[4]

Commenting on the color of the painting, which, the *Art Journal* reported, is "most exquisite as a palette of tints with its azure sea, its white waves . . . combined with the lovely fleshtints of the children." The writer also noticed the "positively purple, dark shadows" in the painting, yet another characteristic that linked it to the contemporary work of the Impressionists. He made another stylistic connection, calling *Neapolitan Children* "an imitation, or, perhaps we should say, an adaptation, from some of the Spanish-Roman work," by which he almost certainly meant paintings by artists such as Mariano Fortuny y Marsal (1838–1874).[5]

With this painting, then, Sargent was able to display a number of qualities of his style and his "growing technical proficiency."[6] In other words, with the exhibition of *Neapolitan Children Bathing* at the National Academy in 1879, the twenty-three-year-old Sargent made it clear that he was an artist of great promise.

DBD

1. Margaret C. Conrads, *American Paintings and Sculpture at the Sterling and Francine Clark Art Institute* (New York: Hudson Hills Press, 1990), 163–64. Also see Marc Simpson, *Uncanny Spectacle: the Public Career of the Young John Singer Sargent* (New Haven: Yale University Press, 1997), 77–78, 89–90.

2. Edward Strahan [Earl Shinn], "The Art Gallery: The NAD. First Notice," *AAm* 1 (June 1879): 4–5.

3. "The Academy Exhibition," *NYT*, May 2, 1879.

4. "Academy of Design: Fifty-fourth Annual Exhibition, Fourth Article," *NYDT*, April 26, 1879.

5. "The Academy Exhibition," *Art Journal* 5 (May 1879): 159.

6. Conrads, 164.

44

Thomas Eakins, NA

Philadelphia, Pennsylvania 1844–1916 Philadelphia, Pennsylvania

A Pair-oared Shell, 54th Annual Exhibition, April 1–May 31, 1879, no. 463, owner Dr. Brinton

The Pair-Oared Shell, 1872

Oil on canvas, 24 × 36

Philadelphia Museum of Art, Gift of Mrs. Thomas Eakins and Miss Mary Adeline Williams

The Pair-Oared Shell was one of the earliest works that Thomas Eakins sent to the National Academy of Design's annual exhibitions and the only one of his paintings depicting rowers on Philadelphia's Schuylkill River ever to be shown there.[1]

The critical notice given *The Pair-Oared Shell* was slight. This may have been due in part to the high position in which it was hung at the Academy, as well as to its unobtrusive character—like some of Eakins's earlier outdoor canvases, it is quite dark. Relative lack of attention was perhaps also attributable to the fact that, at the same time, Eakins's large and far more impressive *The Gross Clinic* (1875; Jefferson Medical College, Philadelphia) was being shown in New York at the second annual exhibition of the Society of American Artists, where it was receiving extensive press coverage. A critic from the *Daily Graphic* maintained that no figure painting in the Academy's annual that year compared "in intellectual power and serious thought" with *The Gross Clinic*.[2]

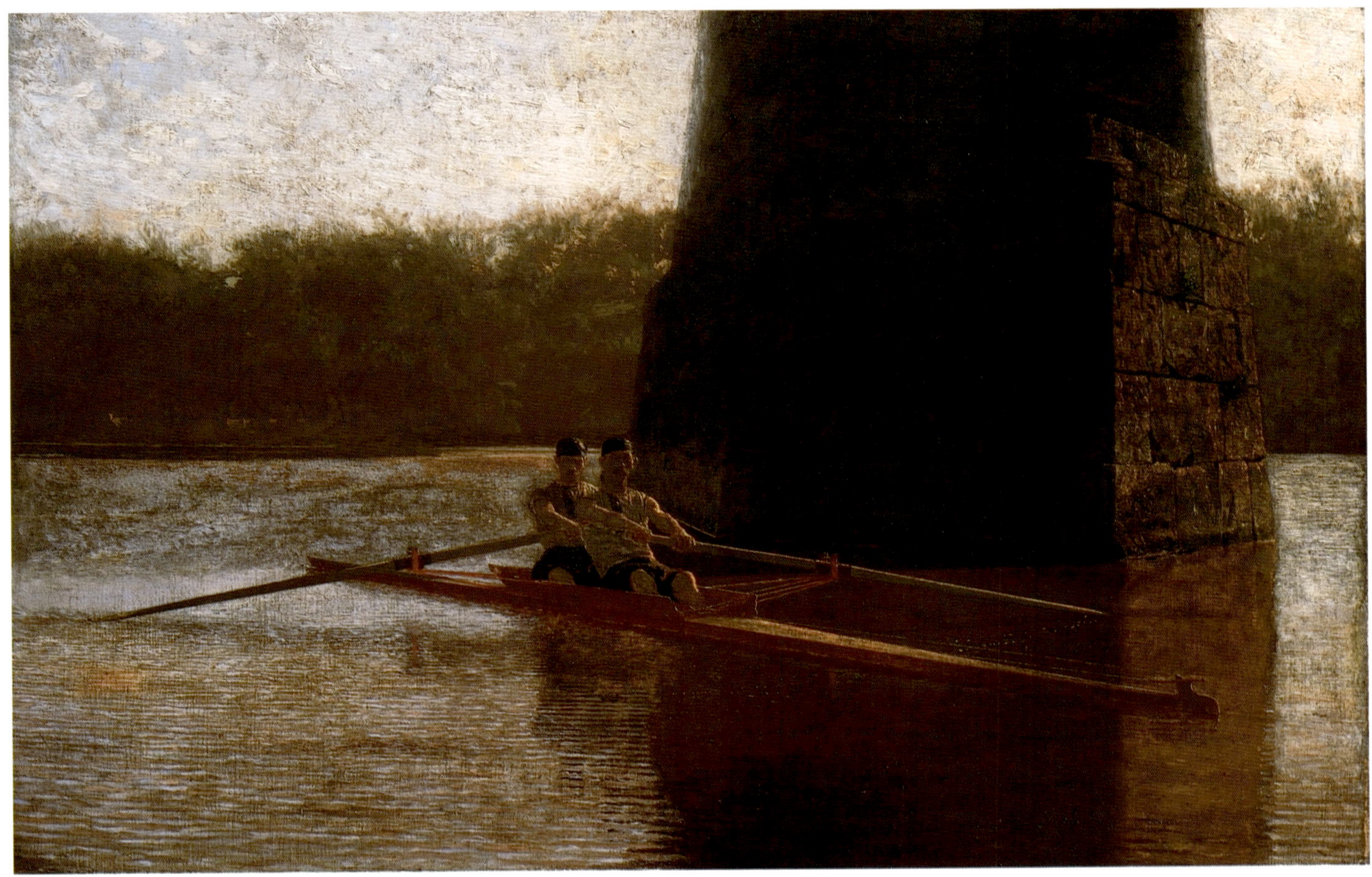

44

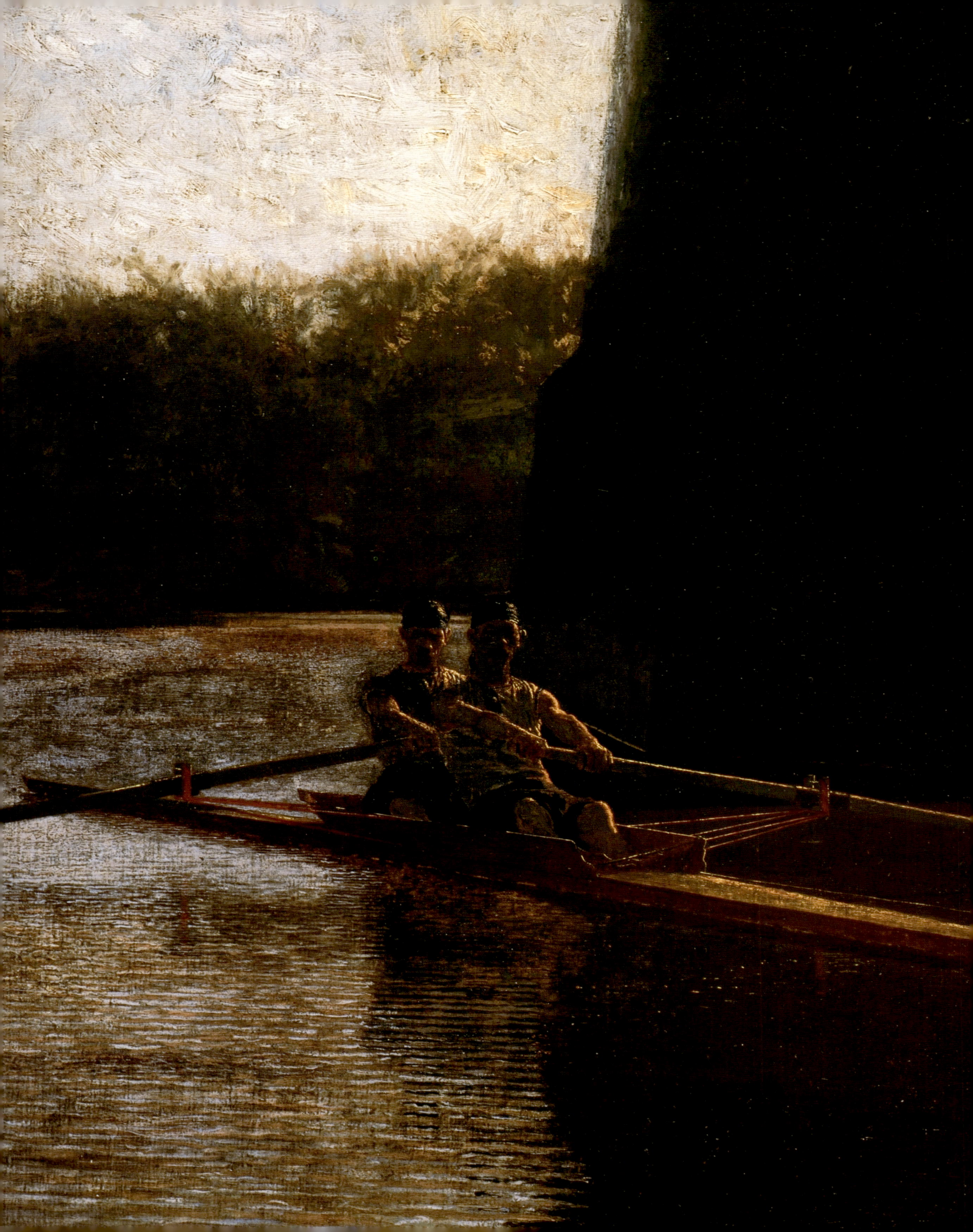

A review of the Academy's exhibition that appeared in the *New-York Times* made up, at least to some degree, for the disinterest and criticism from other quarters. Under the title "Budding Academicians," a critic complained in his first paragraph that Eakins's painting was hung "so far above the line [eye level]" that it could be "scarcely appreciated except on a brilliant day." If a visitor did manage to get a good look at it, he or she would be impressed with its "good drawing, natural and quiet composition, and a pleasant feeling in color." On the issue of originality, he noted that the work depicted a type of activity "where one might have expected that artists would have sought for subject long ago." After describing the work, the critic returned to its style and, with a whiff of criticism, remarked that, as he had found in all of the Eakins's paintings, "there is a slight constraint in the handling, the merest suspicion of conventionality and commonplace." He quickly followed, though, with the observation that these characteristics must be accepted "as part of this strong painter's individuality."[3]

The same critic also contrasted Eakins's painting with a series of six studies by the older and more traditional artist John G. Brown, maintaining that Brown's attempt to capture outdoor effects produced "harsh and painty" results. Pleased that Eakins avoided doing so, the critic cited Eakins's success in handling the shadow of the bridge. Not convinced that Eakins had "poetic expression" in mind, he suggested that the artist may have "tried to express the peculiar charm that every one has experienced when rowing out of the sunlight into a shadow of a great bridge."[4]

The critic for the *New York Herald* mixed positives and negatives: "There is extreme cleverness and knowledge shown in Thomas Eakins' 'Pair-Oared Shell'. . . . It is intensely real and unfortunately decidedly photographic."[5] The last negative struck directly at what would become one of Eakins's major interests. His works of the early 1870s had a stylistic kinship with photography and foreshadowed his active use of the camera in the early 1880s.

Eakins continued to exhibit at the National Academy for many years: seven more times before the turn of the century and then almost annually through 1916, the year of his death. Although he was held in high esteem by Academy members, evidenced in part by his election to both associate and full membership in the same year, 1902, he received only one prize at the Academy annuals. In 1905, he was awarded the Thomas R. Proctor Prize for his portrait of Prof. Leslie Miller (1901; Philadelphia Museum of Art). After 1900, most of the paintings that Eakins submitted to the Academy were portraits, which, in his later years, were his exclusive subject. TG

1. The best known painting from this series is *Max Schmitt in a Single Scull* (1871; The Metropolitan Museum of Art, New York). For a discussion of Eakins's rowing pictures, see Lloyd Goodrich, *Thomas Eakins* (Cambridge, Massachusetts: Harvard University Press for the National Gallery of Art, Washington, D.C., 1982), and Darrel Sewell, *Thomas Eakins: Artist of Philadelphia* (Philadelphia: Philadelphia Museum of Art, 1982).

2. "The Academy Exhibition," *NYDG*, March 29, 1879.

3. "Budding Academicians," *NYT*, April 20, 1879.

4. Ibid.

5. "Fine Arts," *NYH*, April 28, 1879.

45
Thomas Hovenden, NA
Dunmanway, County Cork, Ireland 1840–1895 Plymouth Meeting, Pennsylvania

56th Annual Exhibition, March 22–May 14, 1881, no. 300, for sale for $3,000.00

In Hoc Signo Vinces (La Vendée, 1793), 1880
Oil on canvas, 39 × 54
The Detroit Institute of Art, Gift of Mr. and Mrs. Harold O. Love

Thomas Hovenden began to establish a reputation while studying in France, especially during the late 1870s when he was working at Pont Aven in Brittany. He received his first notable critical attention in 1878 for *The Vendéan Volunteer* (also known as *Breton Interior in 1793*; 1878; private collection), which was shown at the International Exposition in Paris that year.[1] His fame in America, however, began with *In Hoc Signo Vinces*, which took its subject from the Wars of the Vendée, a popular uprising against the French revolutionary forces in the mid-1790s. The political nature of its subject made it unpopular with the French when it debuted at the Salon of 1880.[2]

When the painting was first exhibited in the United States at the National Academy of Design's annual exhibition of 1881, Americans had no such problems with the painting. Obviously impressed with the work, the National Academicians gave it a place of honor on the long wall of the institution's East Gallery, just opposite the main door of the room, and the critics supported this decision.[3] A writer for the *American Art Review* gushed: "Never have we seen a painting by an American artist exhibiting more feeling for suffering and heroic humanity, expressed with greater artistic excellence."[4] The *Evening Post* thought the painting was "a serious and noble performance" and the *Brooklyn Daily Times* called it "superb."[5] For a review of the exhibition in the *New York Evening Express*, the author devoted one of his longer paragraphs to the painting. He noted that, while "Mr. Hovenden has put his foreign study to good advantage," *In Hoc Signo Vinces* showed that he possessed a distinct originality as well. The expressions, firmness of drawing, and appropriately somber coloring in the painting were all admired.[6] Another writer declared, " . . . when the public gaze upon it they will know full well that a star has risen in Israel."[7]

The *Studio and Musical Review* singled out three paintings in the Academy's exhibition for praise that year: Alexander Wyant's *An Old Clearing* (1881; The Metropolitan Museum of Art), Eastman Johnson's *Funding Bill* (1881; The Metropolitan Museum of Art) and Hovenden's *In Hoc Signo Vinces*. In fact, these were the three works that were most consistently identified as the exhibition's best landscape, genre painting, and historical work, respectively. Concerning Hovenden's work, the writer agreed with most of his contemporaries. "As a composition showing fine drawing, a vivid appreciation of dramatic situations, vigorous painting and a splendid rendering of character this picture has never been excelled by an American artist."[8]

A lengthy analysis of the painting was published in the *New York Evening Post*. There, the author identified Hovenden as one of the most promising of the younger artists in the exhibition. *In*

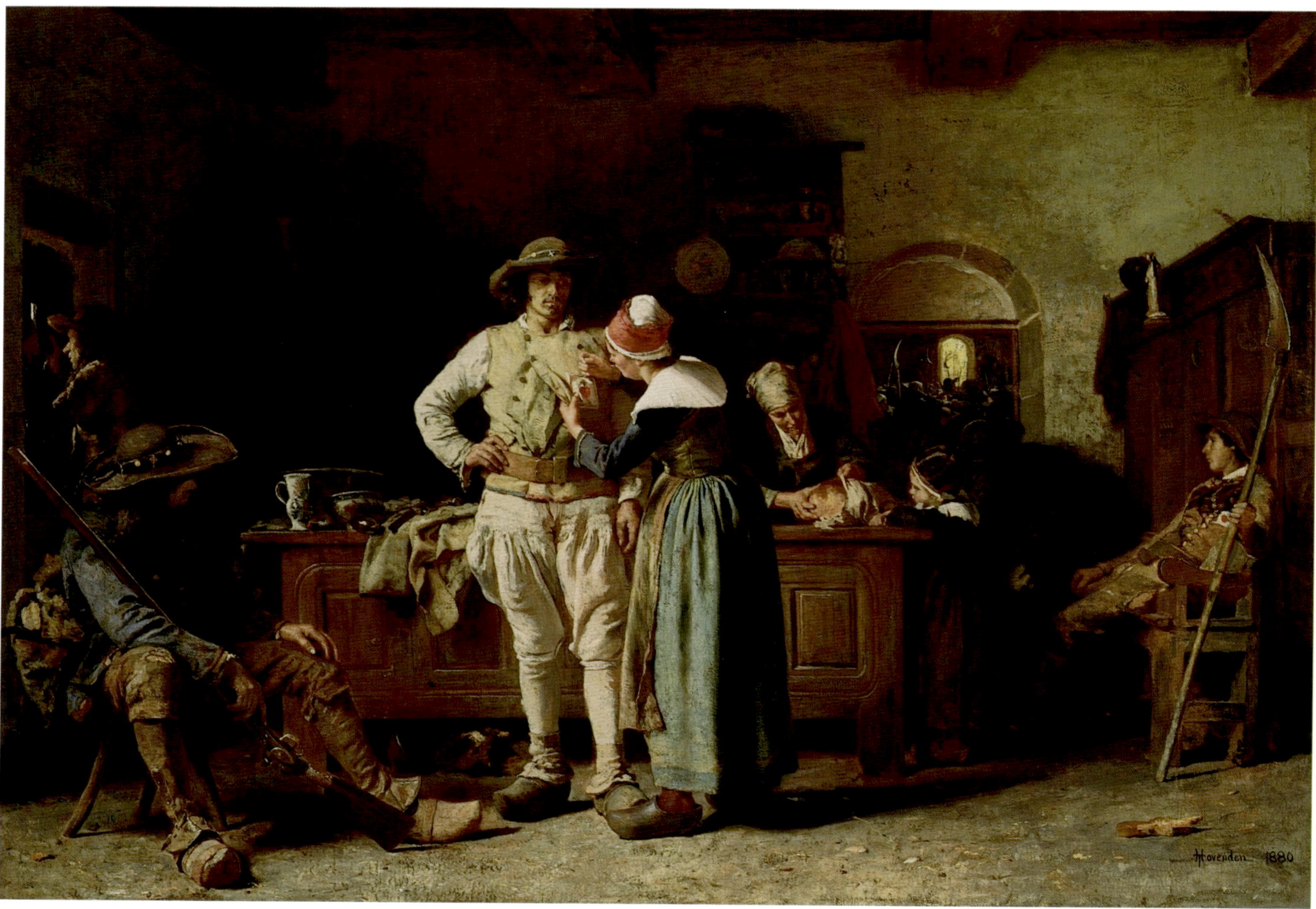

45

Hoc Signo Vinces was praised for its "intelligent and firm" draw-ing, its "wholesome and appealing" subject matter, and its "sense of nature and of life," which, the author found, was extraordinary for a studio picture, "that is to say, for a representation of a scene which the eyes of the artist never saw."[9] The only complaints that were leveled at the painting—and these were few—concerned the less important details of background and shadows.[10]

Perhaps the best tribute to the painting's success, however, was the fact that by the first week of April, about half way through the exhibition's run, the painting had sold for its asking price of $3,000.[11] This event was acknowledged as one of the most impor-tant sales of the exhibition.[12] An immediate result of all of this success was Hovenden's election as an Associate of the Academy. The following year, partially due to the popularity of his *Elaine* (no. 47), which was shown at the Academy in 1882, he was advanced to full National Academician.   DBD

1. Exposition Universelle Internationale, *Catalogue Officiel* (Paris, 1878), 1: 204, no. 62.

2. Anne Gregory Terhune, "Thomas Hovenden, Images of Heritage and Hope," in Woodmere Art Museum, *Thomas Hovenden (1840–1895) American Painter of Hearth and Homeland* (Philadelphia, 1995), 8–34. Also see Lee M. Edwards, "Noble Domesticity: The Paintings of Thomas Hovenden," *American Art Journal* 19 (1987): 5–38; and Tara Tappert's entry on the painting in *American Paintings in the Detroit Institute of Arts* (New York: Hudson Hills Press, 1997), 2: 130.

3. Charles M. Kurtz, *American Academy Notes* (New York, 1881), 28.

4. S. G. W. Benjamin, "The Exhibitions. VII.—National Academy of Design Fifty-sixth Exhibition," *American Art Review* 2 (May 1881): 23.

5. *NYEP*, April 9, 1881; "Fine Arts. The Academy Exhibition," *Brooklyn Daily Times*, April 1, 1881.

6. "Fine Arts. The Academy Exhibition," *New York Evening Express*, April 2, 1881.

7. Unidentified newspaper clipping, AAA, P13, quoted in Edwards, 13.

8. "The Academy of Design. Fifty Sixth Annual Exhibition," *Studio and Musical Review* 1 (March 26, 1881): 130.

9. *NYEP*, April 9, 1881.

10. *New York World* (March 3, 1881), for example, pointed out that the back-ground was too dark.

11. "Art Notes," *Art Journal* 7 (May 1881): 159.

12. 'Work of the Painters. Exhibitions and Sales," *NYDT*, April 17, 1881.

46

Francis Davis Millet, NA

Mattapoisett, Massachusetts 1846–1912 At sea, on board H.M.S. Titanic

Portrait of Miss Kate Field, 56th Annual Exhibition, March 19–?, 1881, no. 413, owner Miss Field

Kate Field, 1887

Oil on canvas

Boston Public Library

Although mostly forgotten today, Mary Katherine Field (1838–1896), was said to have been "continuously in the public

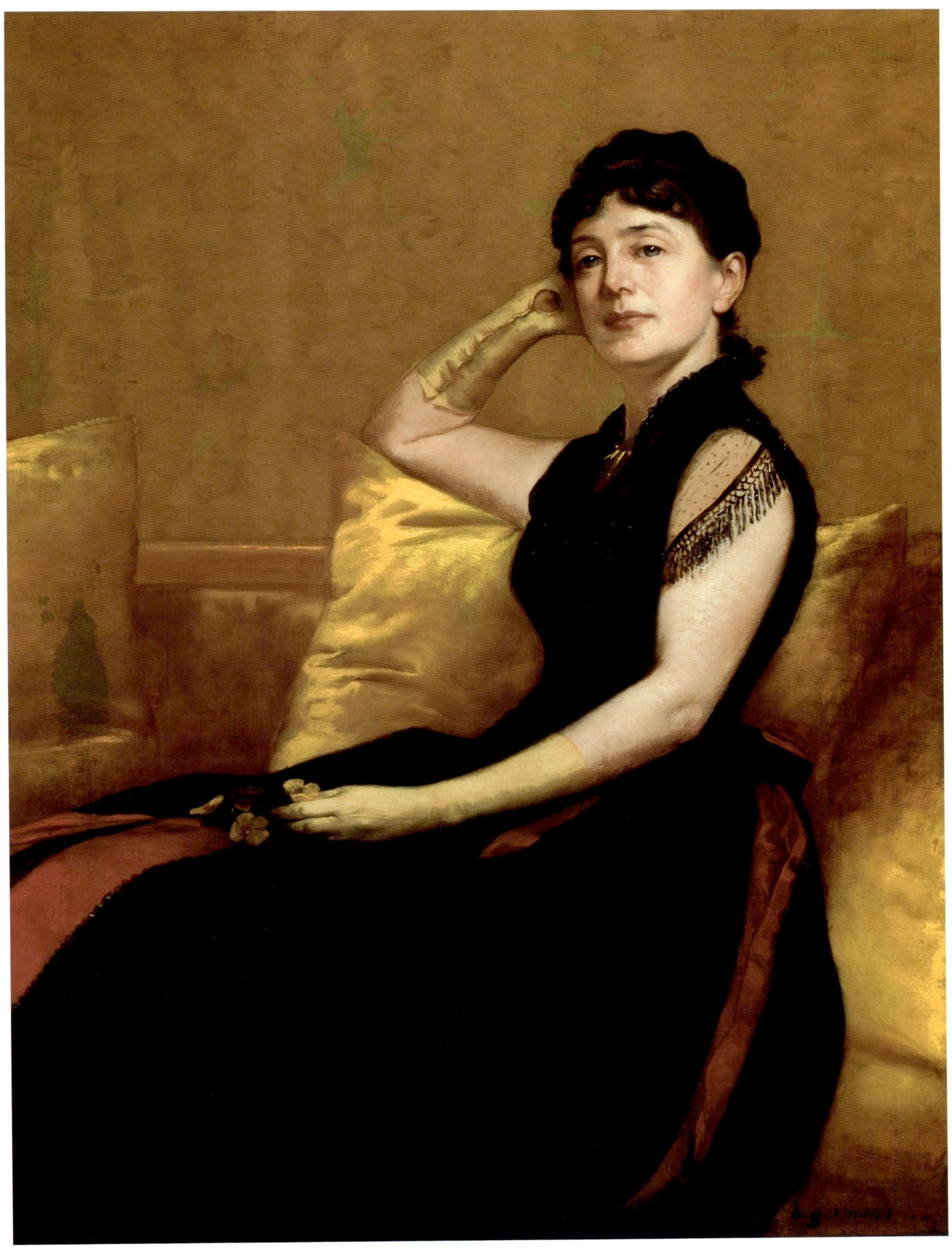

eye and mind" during her lifetime. A daughter of actors, she was schooled in Boston and then moved to London, where she, too, became an actress, as well as a newspaper correspondent, writer, and art critic.[1] Like several of Francis Davis Millet's other portrait subjects—Samuel L. Clemens and Charles Francis Adams, Jr., for example—Kate Field was a life-long friend of the artist. In 1879, Millet and Lily Merrill, whom he had recently married, stayed at Field's London home for several months, and the couple's first child was named Katharine Field Millet, partly in the actress's honor.[2]

Millet's portrait of Kate Field played an important role in his career. It was singled out by some critics as "one of the most prominent works" in the National Academy of Design's exhibition of 1881."[3] In the Academy's gallery, where it was said to arrest "the eye of the viewer with great peremptoriness," the imposing canvas was placed directly opposite an equally large portrait of Millet himself, dressed as a war correspondent.[4] That image, now in the National Portrait Gallery, Smithsonian Institution, Washington, D.C., was painted in 1878 by George Maynard (1843–1923), Millet's friend and former fellow student at the Antwerp Academy. Together, the portraits announced Millet's arrival on the New York art scene, and regardless of whether the critics liked the young artist's portrait of Field, few failed to notice it.

As was usually the case, the reviews of the Academy's 1881 exhibition varied. The *New York Sun,* echoing a chronic complaint about the exhibitions, thought it "the worse hung exhibition that the Academy has seen in years."[5] Except in terms of portraiture, some critics did not find the exhibition to be as strong as that of the Society of American Artists, which was held simultaneously. Others found hope only in the work of the several non-academicians and "new artists" who were making their debut at the Academy that year.[6] On the other hand, the *New York Evening Express* found it to be "one of the best exhibitions that has been held in many years."[7]

Similarly, Millet's portrait of Kate Field, which was extensively reviewed in the press, received uneven responses from the critics. Several, such as a writer for the *New York Evening Mail,* focused on the formal elements of the canvas and praised its draftsmanship. At the same time, however, that writer faulted the painting's bright coloring, which he described as "harsh, hard, and discordant." Nevertheless, he thought the painting was worthy of "careful study for the abrupt transitions that are made from one strong color to another."[8] Similarly, the critic for the *New-York Times* had mixed feelings about the canvas. Ultimately, however, he felt that, "in spite of the stiff pose and theatrical effects," the painting "has force and good technique and human reality."[9]

A H

1. *Dictionary of American Biography* (1959 ed.), 3:368.

2. Joyce A. Sharpley-Schafer, *Soldier of Fortune: F. D. Millet, 1846–1912* (Utica, New York: 1984), 55–57. According to another source, the child was named for both Kate Field and Kate Merrill, Lily Merrill's sister (Hilda Millet Booth and John Parsons Millet, "Frank Millet: A Versatile American," John A. P. Millet Papers, AAA, reel 1100).

3. "Fine Arts: Fifty-sixth Annual Exhibition of the NAD—I," *Nation* 32 (March 31,1881): 229. Millet's portrait of Field does not completely correspond to the contemporary descriptions of the works that appeared in the *Nation* and elsewhere when the painting was shown at the National Academy in 1881. The painting was said to by approximately five by six feet in size, much larger than the current canvas. The painting now in the collection of the Boston Public Library is

either the original work, cut down to its current size, or a partial replica of it. Whatever the case, in terms of color, the current painting corresponds to descriptions of the work shown at the Academy in 1881.

4. *Nation* 32 (March 31,1881): 229; "Fifty-sixth Academy: First Notice," *Art Interchange* 6 (March 31, 1881): 74.

5. *NYS,* March 27,1881.

6. *NYT,* March 28,1881.

7. *New York Evening Express*, March 23, 1881.

8. *NYEM,* April 15,1881.

9. *NYT,* April 3, 1881.

47
Thomas Hovenden, NA
Dunmanway, County Cork, Ireland 1840–1895 Plymouth Meeting, Pennsylvania

Elaine, 57th Annual Exhibition, March 27–May 13, 1882, no. 311, for sale for $10,000.00

The Death of Elaine, 1882
Oil on canvas, 46 × 71
Westmoreland Museum of American Art, Greensburg, Pennsylvania

Thomas Hovenden's *Elaine* was inspired by Alfred Lord Tennyson's Arthurian poem "Lancelot and Elaine," which was published as part of the poet's *Idylls of the King* in 1859. The artist began the painting in Europe in 1879 and brought it back, unfinished, to America the following year.[1] He evidently had hoped to have it ready to send to the National Academy's exhibition in 1881.[2] As the deadline for the exhibition approached, however, *Elaine* remained unfinished and, in March, the *New York World* reported that Hovenden had decided to send *In Hoc Signo Vinces* to the Academy instead.[3] Within the year, Hovenden finished *Elaine* and was able to send it to the Academy's annual in 1882. There it garnered almost as much attention as had *In Hoc Signo Vinces* the year before. The painting was well received by the public and admired by Hovenden's fellow artists, even prompting Hovenden's promotion to full Academician; the press, on the other hand, was less admiring of the work.

Elaine had begun to earn praise from American critics even before it came to the Academy. It was shown to the public at a reception at Hovenden's studio in the Sherwood Building in New York in the winter of 1881 and although it was still not quite finished, it was, according to the *Brooklyn Daily Times,* "greatly admired."[4] A writer for the *Studio and Musical Review* called it "the greatest picture of [Hovenden's] artistic life" and predicted that it would be "one of the art sensations of the last quarter of a century in this country."[5]

At the National Academy, it was given every chance to be just that. It was hung in the "chief place of honor," along the long wall opposite the main entrance to the South Gallery, the Academy's largest and most important exhibition space.[6] Few paintings in the exhibition earned the kind of lengthy analysis—favorable or not—that *Elaine* received. The *New York Mail and Express* devoted an entire article to *Elaine,* which, the critic noted, was successfully "sustaining the burdens" of its having been given the place of honor. "The sincerity of its inception" and "its com-

47

pleteness for an imaginative piece of work," by which he meant the careful delineation of expression and successful choice of figural type, assured this. He concluded that *Elaine* was "one of the greatest pictures of the year" and promised "of far greater things to come" from Hovenden.[7]

Similarly, the *Art Interchange* opened its serial review of the Academy show with a discussion of Hovenden's *Elaine*. This time, however, the attention was not completely favorable. The writer admired the painting's mellow colors, careful draughtsmanship, and excellent composition, although he felt *Elaine* suffered from being over-worked. Hovenden had taken too long in finishing it, the critic reported, and the lengthy delay had damaged the picture.[8]

Another, more serious problem for *Elaine* was that, at the Academy, it hung in the same room as Gilbert Gaul's *Charging the Battery* (1882; New-York Historical Society). Although Gaul's painting was in a less prominent spot than Hovenden's, the critics did not fail to see it and, for the most part, to praise it above all others in the exhibition. After all, Gaul's painting was a seemingly realistic recreation of a Civil War battle—a distinctly timely and *American* subject—and Hovenden's was a stagy, medievalinspired melodrama. Many writers preferred the modern subject to the moribund one. The critic for *Art Amateur* declared Gaul's painting to be the best in the Academy's South Gallery. Meanwhile, he lambasted Hovenden's "large and patient canvas" as being "full of absurdities." The models used for the major figures, he wrote, are vulgar and too "commonplace," the setting is like that of an "old stage-play," and Lancelot's head looks as though it were "on a ball and socket joint that enables it to turn any way its owner wills."[9]

After the close of the Academy's exhibition, Hovenden sent *Elaine* to the Inter-State Industrial Exposition in Chicago in 1882 and to the Society of Artists fourth annual exhibition in Philadelphia in the early months of 1883. In the spring of that year, it was shown at Bendann's art rooms in Baltimore. At all three venues, *Elaine* continued to receive much critical attention and was finally purchased while at the last site by Hovenden's major patron, John W. McCoy of Baltimore.[10]   DBD

1. For the history and a thorough analysis of the painting, see Anne Gregory Terhune, "Thomas Hovenden (1840–1895) and Late-Nineteenth-Century American Genre Painting" (Ph.D. diss., City University of New York, 1983), 219–44.

2. See *NYDT*, February 20, 1881; and "Fine Arts," *Brooklyn Daily Times*, February 28, 1881.

3. *New York World,* March 3, 1881.

4. "Fine Arts," *Brooklyn Daily Times,* February 28, 1881.

5. "Advent of a Great American Painter," *Studio and Musical Review* 1 (February 19, 1881): 52.

6. Charles Kurtz, *Illustrated Art Notes upon the Fifty-Seventh Annual Exhibition of the NAD* (New York, 1882), 44, 52. Kurtz devoted almost two full pages to the painting, including quotations from Tennyson and the *New York Tribune,* and illustrated the entry with a drawing by James D. Smillie of the painting's central figures.

7. "Fine Arts. Notes on the Academy Exhibition," *New York Mail and Express,* April 24, 1882.

8. "Fifty Seventh Academy," *Art Interchange* 8 (March 30, 1882): 74.

9. "The National Academy Exhibition," *AAm* 6 (April 1882): 117.

10. Terhune, (1983), 219, 238. Also see *Baltimore Telegram*, May 19, 1883; "A Superb Picture," *Baltimore Sun,* May 19, 1883; and other clippings in the Thomas Hovenden Scrapbook, Thomas Hovenden Papers, AAA P13.

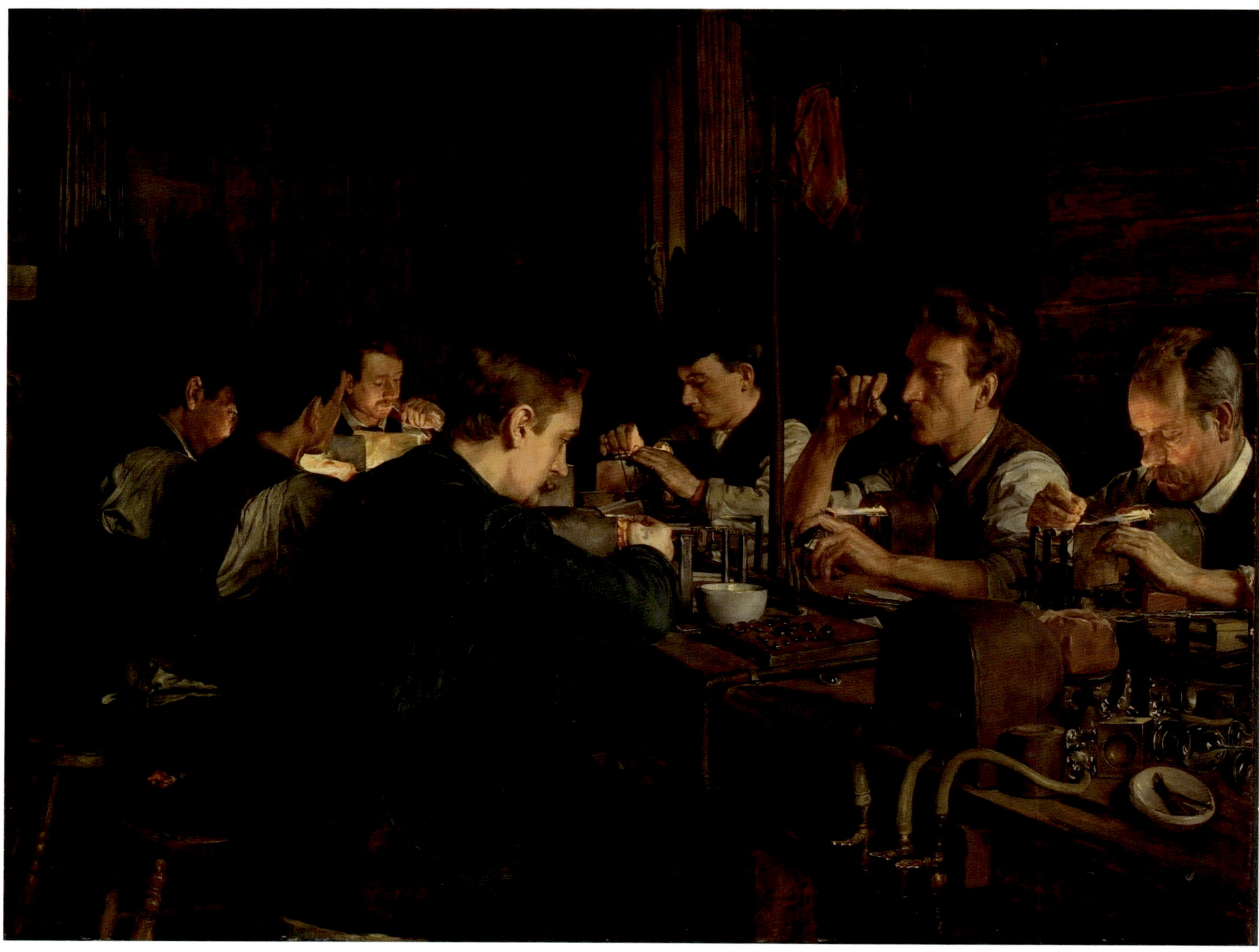

48

Charles Ulrich, ANA

New York, New York 1858–1908 Berlin, Germany

Glass-blowers, 58th Annual Exhibition, April 2–May 12, 1883,
no. 25, owner Thos. B. Clarke

The Glassblowers, 1883

Oil on panel, 18 × 23

Museo de Arte de Ponce, Puerto Rico

While some critics thought that the National Academy of Design's annual exhibition of 1883 was "monotonous" and even "depressing," and others went so far as to declare that the "galleries contain an uncommon amount of rubbish,"[1] none dismissed the event as a total loss. Praise almost always eventually emerged for individual works, and at the top of almost every critic's list was Charles Ulrich's *The Glassblowers*. A writer for *Harper's Weekly*, for example, selected it as "one of the two or three most notable successes of the year," and the writer Charles Kurtz called it "an exceptionally excellent picture."[2]

The reasons for the painting's popularity are easy enough to see and understand. It was respected for its carefully delineated composition, high realism, and working class subject. The *New York Times* thought the faces of the men in the painting were "so typical that they may well have been portraits," and *Art Amateur* found it "remarkable for its extremely careful work."[3] Mariana Van Rensselaer, one the most perceptive and respected critics of her time, wrote:

[W]e should not forget to mark the course of another young American—Mr. Ulrich. He has but lately finished his course at Munich, yet he has already turned to home themes for his inspiration, and shown what thankful pictorial materials they afford. In Mr. Clarke's collection, now on view in New-York, we find several of his works,—among them that which is as yet, perhaps, his best—the Glass-Blowers. . . . His handiwork shows an extremely acute perception of the requirements of the small scale on which he works. It is sufficiently detailed to serve his every purpose, yet never hard, over-elaborate, or wanting in freedom, spirit, or respect for textures. We may indeed look with hopeful pride to the future of an art which can already produce painters of this stamp.[4]

The Glassblowers was lent to the National Academy's exhibition by its owner, Thomas B. Clarke, who, in the second half of the nineteenth century, was one of this country's most important art collectors.[5] After the close of the Academy's exhibition, Clarke generously lent it to other major exhibitions, including the 1883 annual exhibition of the Pennsylvania Academy of the Fine Arts, and the Paris Salon of the following year.[6] In 1888, it was in the first annual exhibition at the Art Institute of Chicago; and in 1893 Clarke sent it to the World's Columbian Exposition in Chicago.[7] Another, more unusual, measure of its success is that it was admired by Vincent Van Gogh, who saw a two-page reproduction of it in the April 21, 1883, issue of *Harper's Weekly*. Van Gogh clipped the reproduction and saved it.[8]   ZR

1. "The Fine Arts: Academy of Design—48th Annual Exhibition," *Critic* 3 (April 7, 1883): 161; "Fifty-eighth Academy," *Art Interchange* 10 (April 10, 1883): 94.

2. "Mr. Ulrich's 'Glass-Blowers,'" *HW* 27 (April, 21, 1883): 251; Charles M. Kurtz, ed., *Illustrated Art Notes upon the 58th annual exhibition of the NAD* (New York, 1883), 19.

3. "Pictures at the Academy: Viewed in the Quiet of Varnishing Day," *NYT*, March 31, 1883; "The Academy Exhibition," *AAm* 8 (May 1883): 126.

4. Mariana Griswold Van Rensselaer, "Henry Mosler and Charles Ulrich," in *A Catalogue of Oil Paintings Exhibited by the Brooklyn Art Association in Aid of the Bartholdi Pedestal Fund, in the Galleries of the Brooklyn Art Association* (New York: Theodore L. DeVinne, 1884), 104.

5. Clarke owned several works by Ulrich (see H. Barbara Weinberg, "Foremost Patron of American Art from 1872 to 1899," *American Art Journal* 8 [May 1976]: 81) and, in 1884, the year that *The Glassblowers* appeared at the Academy, Ulrich painted a portrait of his patron (National Portrait Gallery, Smithsonian Institution, Washington, D.C.). In a sense, Clarke supported Ulrich in another way, too. In 1884, Clarke established the Thomas B. Clarke Prize for figure painting at the Academy. Somewhat appropriately, Ulrich's *Castle Garden* (1884; Corcoran Gallery of Art) was the first recipient of that prize.

6. Lois Marie Fink, *American Art at Nineteenth Century Paris Salons* (1990), 222–23. Fink notes that Ulrich's painting was one of "relatively few urban subjects" in the exhibition, "which depict modern industry or occupations, themes more common to French artists."

7. National Museum of American Art and National Portrait Gallery, *Revisiting the White City: American Art at the 1893 World's Fair* (Washington, D.C., 1993), 334.

8. Brooklyn Museum, *Van Gogh's Sources of Inspiration: 100 Prints from His Personal Collection* (1971), n. p.

49

Francis Davis Millet, NA

Mattapoisett, Massachusetts 1846–1912 At sea, on board H.M.S. Titanic

The Story of Oenone, 58th Annual Exhibition, April 2–May 12, 1883, no. 462, for sale for $2,500.00

Reading the Story of Oenone, c. 1883

Oil on canvas, 30 × 57⅞

Detroit Institute of Arts, Purchase, Art Loan Fund and Popular Subscription Fund

By the time Frank Millet sent *Reading the Story of Oenone* to the National Academy's 1883 annual exhibition, his name was familiar to the public. Besides being known as a consummate portraitist and painter of the human figure, he was acknowledged as an expert on classical costume. During the 1880s and 1890s, he displayed this latter talent in several ways, including delivering a series of lectures on the subject at the Museum of Fine Arts in Boston, the National Academy of Design in New York, and elsewhere; designing classical costumes for the great dramatic actress Mary Anderson; and painting his interpretation of the Greek myth of Oenone. The last illustrated a tale that would have been familiar to educated Americans, based as it was on the writings of Ovid as filtered through the poetry of Alfred Lord Tennyson.[1] Although Millet was to paint a number of images of classically-garbed figures during the 1880s and 1890s, *Reading the Story of Oenone* was his first and most ambitious treatment of the theme.[2]

The beautiful nymph Oenone, so the story goes, fell in love with and married Paris; but the unfaithful shepherd soon deserted her for Helen, whose abduction started the Trojan War. During that conflict, Paris was wounded and, in his distress, called out for Oenone to heal his wounds. Stung by his infidelity, the nymph refused, only to repent too late. Paris died and his

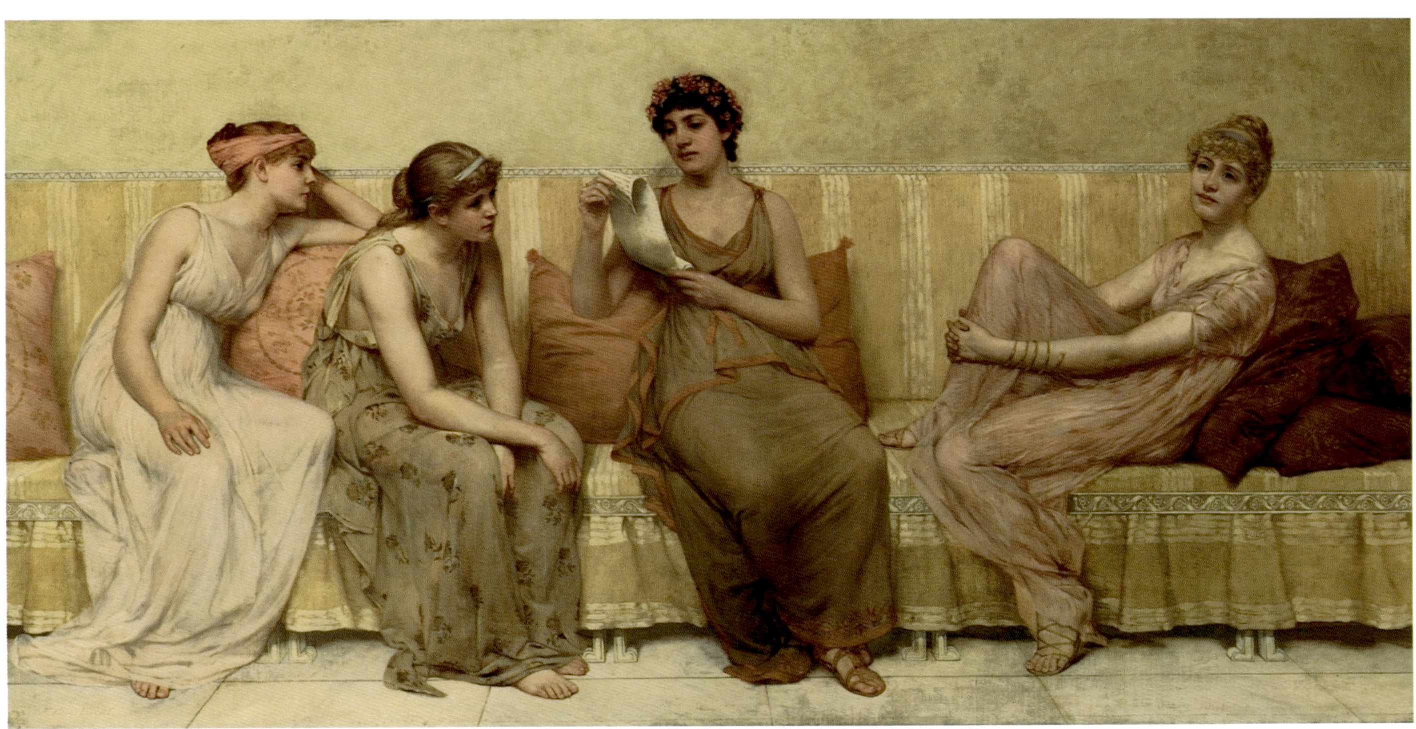

49

inconsolable widow killed herself. Interestingly, instead of illustrating the story itself, Millet focused on the reactions of the young women who listen to the reader and react to the myth's pathos.

Millet had been participating in the National Academy's annual exhibitions since 1876, showing mostly portraits. *Reading the Story of Oenone* was the largest and most impressive work he showed to date, and the positive reviews it received helped to establish the artist in the New York art world. Certainly, the National Academicians themselves thought well of the painting: they hung it on the line (at eye level) in the middle of one of the short walls in the Academy's North-West Gallery, which it dominated.[3] *Art Interchange* noted that "while it is strictly true that the galleries [at the Academy] contain an uncommon amount of rubbish, it is also true that many good pictures are displayed." This included, the journal reported, Millet's *Story of Oenone*, which, "as a study in composition, refined facial expressions and the blending of light tints of draperies, is admirable."[4] Straying from conventional formal analysis and placing Millet in an international context, the writer for the *Critic* noted the influence on him of British artists such as Albert Moore and Lawrence Alma-Tadema, both of whom Millet greatly admired.[5] The critic also favorably compared Millet's treatment of the human figure to that of the tonalist artist Thomas Wilmer Dewing (1851–1938), whose work was concurrently on view in New York at the annual exhibition of the Society of American Artists.[6]

It was, in fact, the cosmopolitan links apparent in Millet's work that prompted the nascent Detroit Museum (now the Detroit Institute of Art) to make *Reading the Story of Oenone* the first purchase for its permanent collection. After leaving the Academy's exhibition in 1883, the painting was shown at the Detroit Art Loan Association's exhibition later that year, and it was out of that show that the Detroit Museum purchased it.[7]

AH & DBD

1. Mary Beth Kriener, "Francis Davis Millet's *Reading of Oenone*," *Bulletin of the Detroit Institute of Arts* 69 (1995): 18; and Tara Tappert, "*Reading the Story of Oenone*," in *American Paintings in the Detroit Institute of Arts* (New York: Hudson Hills Press, 1997), 2: 184. Also see Hilda Millet Booth and John Parsons Millet, "Frank Millet: A Versatile American," John A. P. Millet Papers, AAA, reel 1100.

2. See Deborah Fenton Shepherd's entry on the painting in the Detroit Institute of Arts' *The Quest for Unity: American Art Between World's Fairs 1876–1893* (Detroit: 1983), 122–23.

3. Charles M. Kurtz, *Illustrated Art Notes upon the Fifty-Eighth Annual Exhibition of the NAD* (New York: Cassell, Petter, Galpin & Co., 1883), 69.

4. *Art Interchange* 10 (April 10, 1883): 94.

5. Shepherd (123) has noted the similarity between Millet's painting and Alma-Tadema's *A Reading from Homer* (1885; Philadelphia Museum of Art).

6. "Pictures at the Academy," *NYT*, March 31, 1883. Dewing's *Prelude* (1883), now lost but known through photographs, was his single entry in the Society of American Artists' 1883 exhibition (Society of American Artists, *Sixth Annual Exhibition* [New York, 1883], no. 36). However, his *A Garden* (Museum of Fine Arts, Boston), which was also painted in 1883, is even closer to Millet's painting in composition and content than was *Prelude*.

7. Tappert, 186.

50

Winslow Homer, NA

Boston, Massachusetts 1836–1910 Prout's Neck, Maine

The Life-line, 59th Annual Exhibition, April 7–May 15, 1884, no. 23

The Life Line, 1884

Oil on canvas, 28¾ × 44⅝

Philadelphia Museum of Art, The George W. Elkins Collection

From the time of its debut at the National Academy of Design's annual exhibition of 1866 and for almost twenty years afterward, Winslow Homer's *Prisoners from the Front* (no. 35) remained his greatest critical success. In 1884, however, when *The Life Line* debuted at the Academy, Homer again enjoyed the level of popular acclaim he had reaped with the earlier painting. *The Life Line* also announced to the world that he was moving away from the more predictable genre images that had dominated his work of the 1870s. Critics hailed *The Life Line* as "the most important and the most hopeful picture in the exhibition," "a remarkable success," and "the picture of the year."[1]

Most critics recognized immediately that the true subject of Homer's painting, and the obvious protagonist, is the sea. The "sea fills the greater part of the picture," Robert Jarvis noted in *Art Amateur.* A writer for *Art Interchange* pointed out that the painting was as much a marine as it was a figure study. "Nothing is seen," he wrote, "except obscurely by glimpses through the water."[2]

In fact, the critics' responses, positive or negative, to *The Life Line* were often guided by their opinion of the manner in which Homer handled the water. The *New York World,* for example, called the viewer's aural as well as visual attention to the power of the water in the painting. "One can almost hear the angry roar of the breakers," the paper claimed, "as they dash around the two figures of the rescuer and the girl in his arms, suspended by the line between sky and sea."[3]

On the other hand, the *New York Daily Tribune,* which otherwise praised the painting, thought the water looked "motionless" and the waves "absurd." These deficiencies, the paper reported, were due to Homer's "clumsiness in expression and . . . technical shortcomings."[4] Even more vitriolic in this regard was a writer for the *New York Post* who called Homer's sea a "smooth, slaty mass, heaved into artificial billows."[5]

Such attacks did not go unchallenged. Referring directly to the *Post*'s remarks, the *New York Herald* called the painting "Homer's masterwork" and countered, "It is easy to say that his tremendous surf rolling in huge waves to break on the rocky shore is hard and slaty, but how few that make this criticism have carefully examined water under similar conditions!"[6] The *New-York Times* summed up the issue succinctly: "Dull water or not dull water, Mr. Homer has marked a great triumph with this group."[7]

In fact, almost every critic who wrote about the painting, even those who found it odd, gave, in the end, a positive opinion. "One of the strangest works in the exhibition," a "lady correspondent" from San Francisco wrote, "is Winslow Homer's. . . . It is a powerful work, showing the painter at his best."[8] At least one other woman agreed. Catherine Lorillard Wolfe, one of this country's

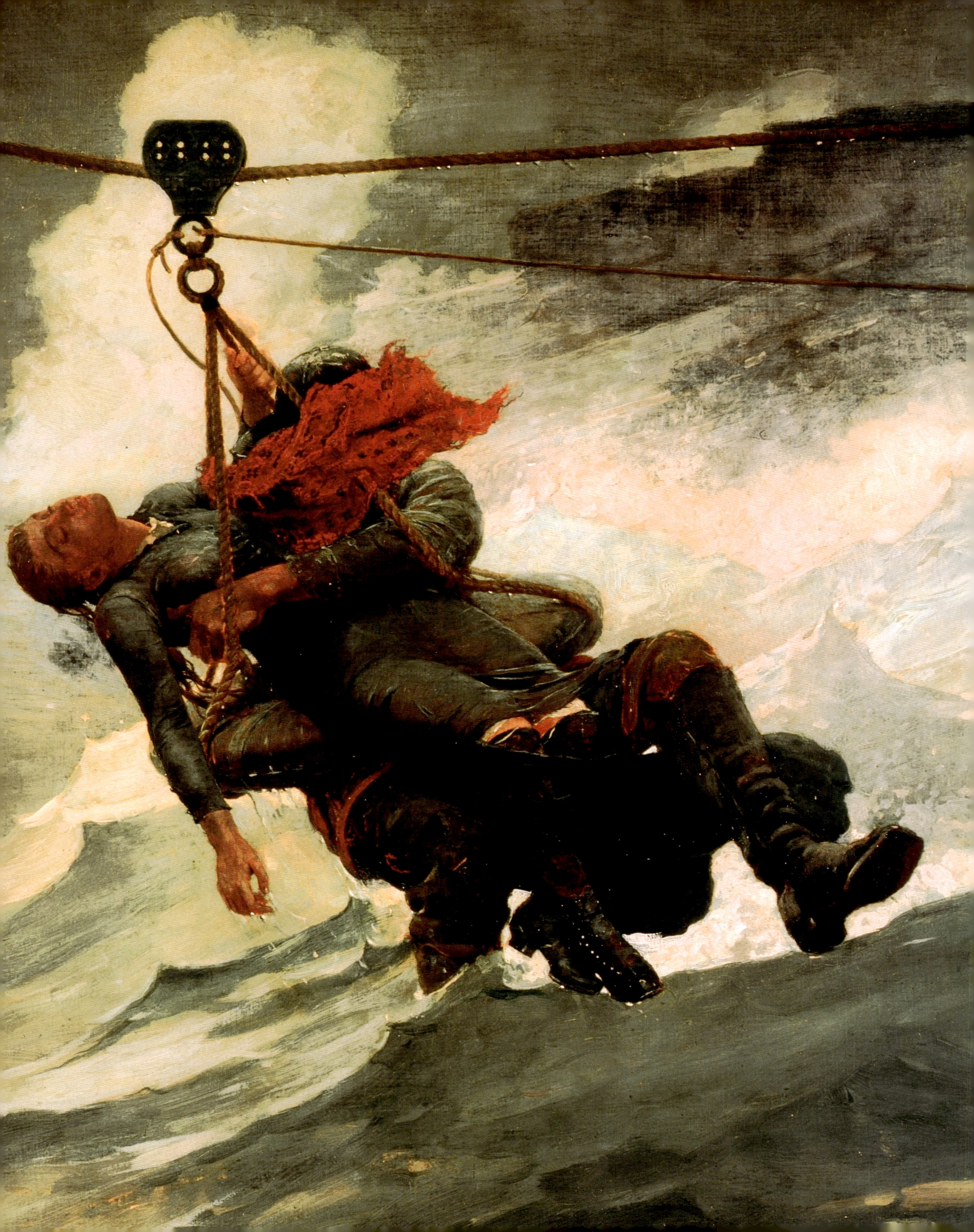

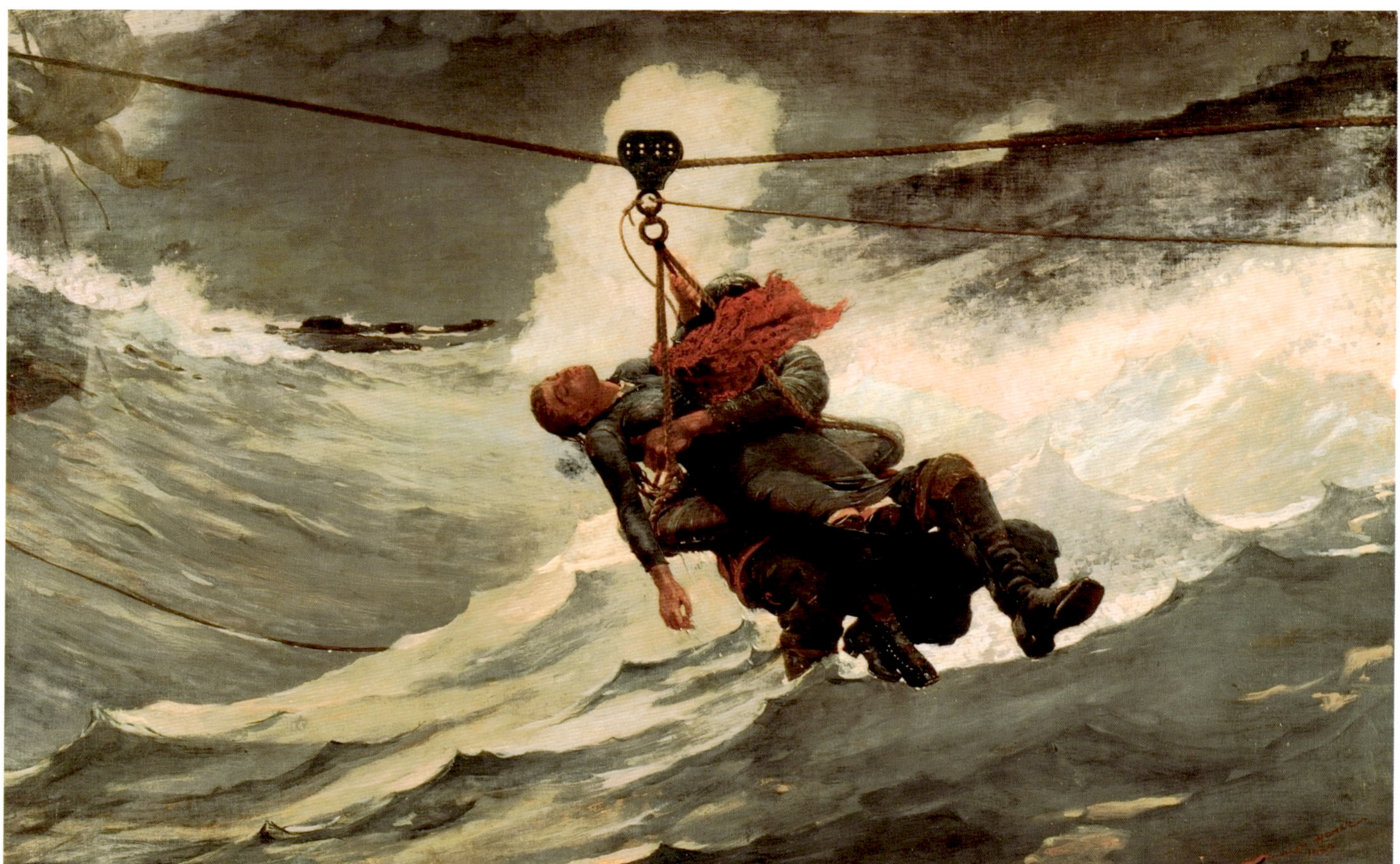

50

most important art collectors of the time, purchased *The Life Line* for $2,500 just as the Academy's exhibition was preparing to open. The press took this as a favorable omen, and not only for the artist. "This purchase," the *New York Herald* reported optimistically, "shows that the tide is turning, and that our richer collectors are beginning to patronize American as well as foreign art."[9]

DBD

1. "The Academy Exhibition," *Critic* 1 (May 3, 1884): 209; Robert Jarvis, "Gallery and Studio: The National Academy Exhibition," *AAm* 10 (May 1884): 125–26; "Fine Arts. Fifty-ninth Annual Exhibition of the NAD. The First View," *NYH*, April 5, 1884. For an account of the circumstances under which the painting was executed and an analysis of its content, see Nicolai Cikovsky, Jr., and Franklin Kelly, *Winslow Homer* (Washington: National Gallery of Art, 1996), 223–25.

2. Robert Jarvis, "Gallery and Studio. The National Academy Exhibition," *AAm* 10 (May 1884): 125–26; "Fifty-ninth Academy. First Notice," *Art Interchange* 12 (April 10, 1884): 89.

3. "The Annual Academy Exhibition," *New York World*, April 7, 1884.

4. "The Academy Exhibition. (Last Notice)," *NYDT*, April 28, 1884.

5. "The Academy Exhibition. Second notice," *NYEP*, April 12, 1884. This review was reprinted in *Nation* 38 (April 24, 1884): 371.

6. "Fine Arts. The Exhibition of the NAD," *NYH*, April 13, 1884.

7. "The Spring Academy," *NYT*, April 5, 1884.

8. C. A., "National Art: Notes in the Exhibition of the National Academy (From a Lady Correspondent)," *San Francisco Evening Bulletin*, April 29, 1884.

9. "Fine Arts. The Exhibition at the National Academy Which Opens To-Day," *NYH*, April 7, 1884

51

John Singer Sargent, NA

Florence, Italy 1856–1925 London, England

Venetian Street, 63rd Annual Exhibition, April 2–May 12, 1888, no. 213, owner Stanford White

Street in Venice, 1882

Oil on wood panel, 17¾ × 21¼

National Gallery of Art, Washington, D. C., Gift of the Avalon Foundation

By 1888, John Singer Sargent had made a name for himself as a painter of elegant portraits. He exhibited one of these, a portrait of Louise (Mrs. Charles) Inches (1887; Museum of Fine Arts, Boston),[1] at the National Academy of Design that year and, as Clarence Cook, the editor and art critic for the *Studio,* noted, the painting was "for some days after the opening of the exhibition the talk of the town."[2] Sargent was also represented at the Academy that year with two other pictures, however, and, of the three, it was these that received the most critical attention. Both are scenes of Venice—*Street in Venice,* shown here, and *Venetian Interior (Venetian Bead Stringers)* (1880 or 1882; Albright-Knox Art Gallery, Buffalo)—where Sargent had spent the summer and early autumn of 1882.[3]

The paintings had made their European debut in 1882 at the first exhibition of the Société Internationale des Peintres et Sculpteurs in Paris. The critical response had not been favorable, with one important journal even dismissing them as "trite and unoriginal."[4] They fared far better in the United States, where almost every critic who wrote about them had nothing but positive remarks to make. In fact, these paintings impressed some Americans simply because they were *not* portraits of elegant women. One of these was Clarence Cook, who wrote, "Mr. Sargent, tiring of over-dressed beauties for the nonce, has picked up a few of the slouchiest specimens of woman-kind that Venice produces, but serves them up with such a skillful turn of the wrist, and such a dexterous toss of the pan, that with our eyes shut we should almost take them for duchesses."[5] Another writer pointed out an aspect that made the two Venetian paintings different from the artist's portraits: they were produced "not by cleverness alone, but must have required a certain amount of what artists call 'feeling.'"[6]

Several critics pointed out the unfinished quality of the two Venetian paintings. A reviewer for the *New York Daily Tribune* called them "studies of an accomplished painter rather than his final results"; but, he noted, " . . . they are thoroughly enjoyable."[7] It was probably this aspect of the pair that prompted the critic for the *Nation* to note how different they looked from anything else in the north gallery of the Academy's exhibition space where they were hung that year. The writer admired the "delicacy of obser-

vation and subtle painting" of *Street in Venice,* and felt that *Venetian Interior* was "essentially a work that appeals to those who are capable of appreciating art purely for its own sake."[8] The *Art Amateur* concurred. "Better painters' sketches than these," that journal declared, "have not yet been seen in the Academy."[9] Sargent's sparse use of color, carefully placed within the overall arrangement of grays and blacks, also caught the eye of some writers. The critic for the *Tribune,* for example, noted the "street vista . . . relieved by touches of color" in *Street in Venice.* The other painting was "a study in grays and blacks pitched in a lower key," where "everything keeps its place."[10]

Despite the positive response Sargent received when these two Venetian paintings appeared at the National Academy, he was not represented there by a similar painting for many years. He showed sporadically at the Academy in the 1890s and then much more consistently from the turn of the century until the year of his death. Almost all of his paintings shown there were portraits, and several of them received notable critical praise. Only in 1910, when his *Venetian Water Carriers* (Worcester Art Museum, Worcester, Massachusetts) appeared at the Academy's annual, and in 1913, when his *A Waterfall* was shown in the institution's winter exhibition, was Sargent represented there by non-

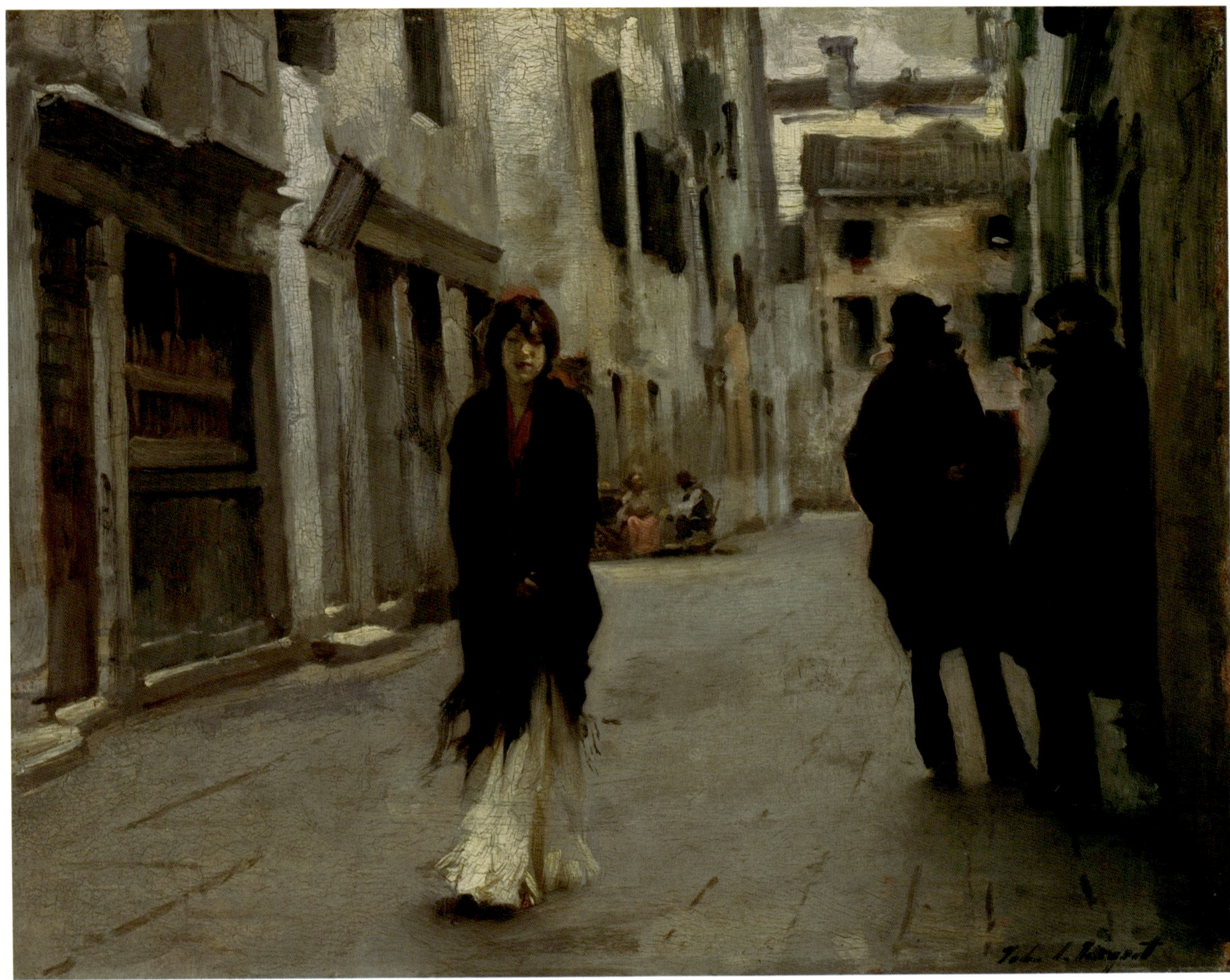

51

portraits. Meanwhile, his *Street in Venice* returned to the Academy in 1892 for the large historic exhibition titled *The New York Columbian Celebration of the Four Hundredth Anniversary of the Discovery of America.* It was shown there again in 1951 for *The American Tradition 1800–1900,* an exhibition commemorating the Academy's 125th anniversary.　　　　　DBD

1. The *Catalogue of the Sixty-Third Annual Exhibition of the National Academy of Design* (New York, 1888) mistakenly lists the painting as *Portrait of Mrs. Charles Vurches* (no. 260). Richard Ormond and Elaine Kilmurry, in *John Singer Sargent: The Early Portraits* (New Haven: Yale University Press, 1998), 1: 260, confirm that the work shown at the Academy that year was Mrs. Inches's portrait.

2. [Clarence Cook], "National Academy of Design: Sixty-third Annual Exhibition. First Notice," *Studio* 3 (May 1888): 88.

3. The paintings were lent to the Academy's exhibition by their owners, painter James Carroll Beckwith, who owned the interior view, and architect Stanford White, who owned the street scene. See Robert Wilson Torchia, *American Paintings of the Nineteenth Century: The Collections of the National Gallery of Art Systematic Catalogue* (Washington: National Gallery of Art), 2: 103–107.

4. Arthur Baignères, "Première exposition de la Société Internationale des Peintres et Sculpteurs," *Gazette des Beaux-Arts* 26 (February 1883): 190, quoted in Linda Ayers, "Sargent in Venice," in Patricia Hills, *John Singer Sargent* (New York: Whitney Museum of American Art, 1986), 68.

5. [Clarence Cook], "NAD: Sixty-third Annual Exhibition, Second Notice," *Studio* 3 (June 1888): 113.

6. "Spring Exhibitions of the `Academy' and the `Society,'" *Arts Review* 3 (July-August 1888): 31.

7. "The Academy of Design: Sixty-third Annual Exhibition," *NYDT*, March 31, 1888.

8. "Fine Arts: The Academy Exhibition," *Nation* 46 (April 19, 1888): 331.

9. "The NAD," *AAm* 18 (May 1888): 132.

10. "The Academy of Design: Sixty-third Annual Exhibition," *NYDT*, March 31, 1888.

52

Robert Frederick Blum, NA
Cincinnati, Ohio 1857–1903 New York, New York

64th Annual Exhibition, April 1–May 11, 1889, no. 132, for sale for $1,200

Two Idlers, 1888–89
Oil on canvas, 29 × 40
National Academy of Design, New York

Robert Frederick Blum was not an active participant in the National Academy of Design's exhibitions, sending only one work to each of eight exhibitions between 1881 and 1897.[1] Nevertheless, he used the exhibitions effectively to promote his career, and several honors and some important patronage resulted from his participation in them. The first of his works to receive notable critical attention at the Academy was *Venetian Bead Stringers* (1887–88), which was shown there in 1888. While reaction to the work was not totally positive, the *Art Amateur* called it "ingenious and dramatic,"[2] and the *Nation* declared it

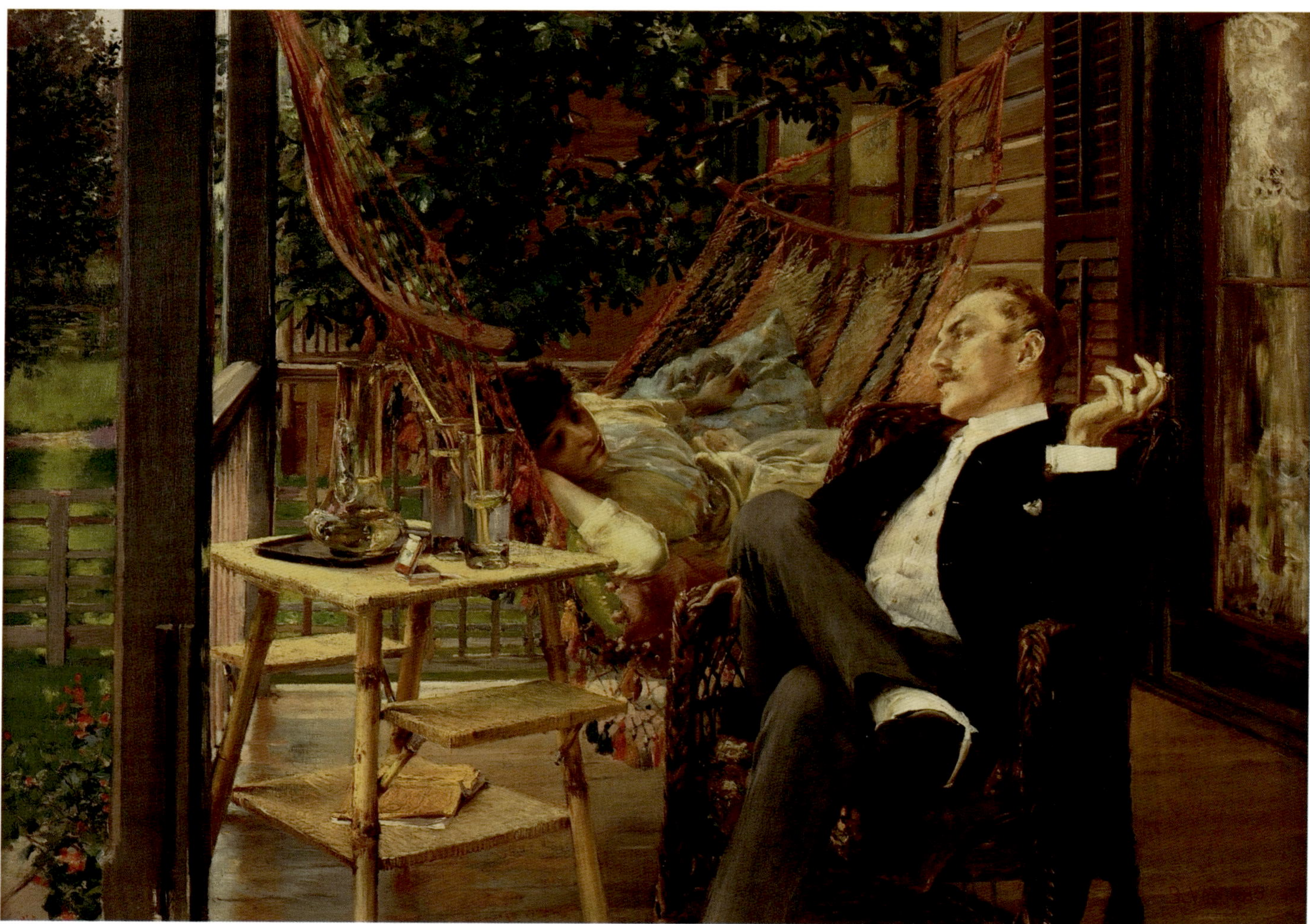

52

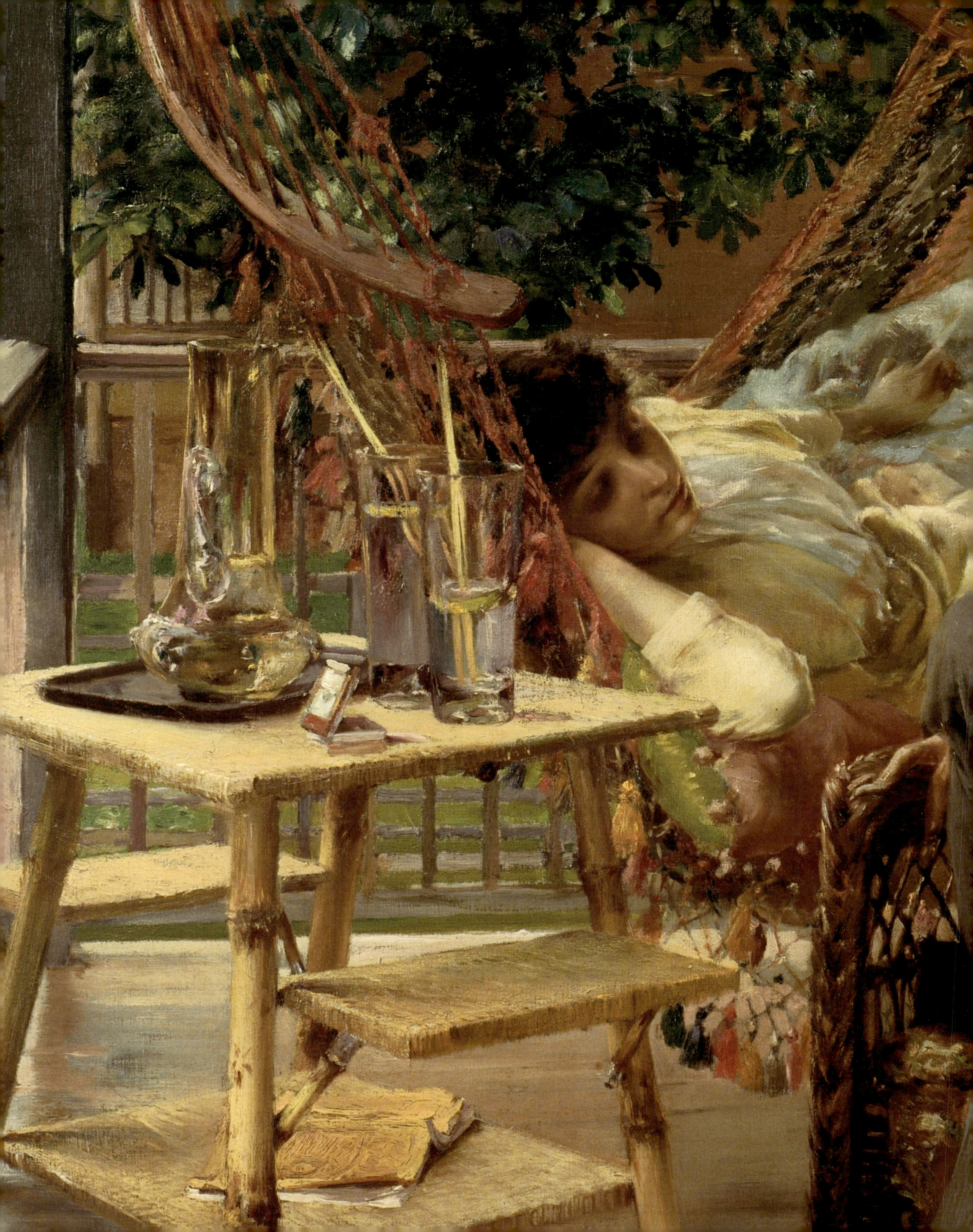

"brilliant and gay in effect without being gaudy."[3] *Harper's Weekly* identified the picture as "a work of unusual importance" and published an engraving of it.[4]

In 1889, Blum was again represented at the Academy by a single canvas, *Two Idlers*. He had begun working on the painting at the home of his friends William and Laura Baer near Brick Church, New Jersey, and finished it in his New York studio.[5]

In terms of critical reaction, Blum was not quite as fortunate with *Two Idlers* as he had been in 1888 with *Venetian Bead Stringers*. Reviews were decidedly mixed—even the most positive of them were not totally so. The columnist for the *Nation* declared that the two best genre paintings in the Academy's exhibition that year were Blum's *Two Idlers* and Irving Wiles's *Sonata* (1889; The Fine Arts Museums of San Francisco) but went on to state that Blum's "is astonishingly clever and able, and contains delightful bits of painting, which for technical quality could not be surpassed by [Giovanni] Boldini himself, but he has either not cared for or not succeeded in preserving the truth of value, and some of the tones in the foreground are much lighter than they should be in relation to the sunlight beyond. . . . Both pictures are so good that the Clarke prize would be well bestowed upon either."[6]

A writer for *Art Interchange* stated that Blum "has painted a large picture empty of air and full of color, which seems to have been designed for tobacconists' purposes."[7] The *New York Herald* thought that it was "capital in all but the face of the man."[8] Despite the predictions of the *Nation's* critic, *Two Idlers* failed to garner any awards at the Academy's exhibition, losing out to several other pictures, including the one by Wiles that was mentioned in the *Nation*. Nevertheless, the high quality of *Two Idlers* encouraged the Academicians to elect Blum to associate membership during the run of the 1889 exhibition.

Similarly, four years later, Blum's election to full membership in the Academy was motivated by the success of his *The Ameya* (Metropolitan Museum of Art), which was in that year's annual. Recently back from his celebrated stay in Japan, Blum may have calculated the display of this work as a public demonstration of his development. If so, the ploy worked. *The Ameya* was Blum's greatest critical success at the Academy since the *Venetian Bead Stringers* and garnered rave reviews.[9] Blum's friend William Baer remembered the connection between the success of *The Ameya* and Blum's election to full membership in the Academy. It "was a well-earned election," Baer wrote, "for it may be said, with due respect for the ability of many others, that the "Ameya" is a performance that is more destined to help mark an era in the success of our art as compared with that of Europe than most anything we have yet seen."[10]

ZR & DBD

1. All of these were annual, spring exhibitions, except the one in 1897, which was the Academy's autumn exhibition.

2. "The NAD," *AAm* 18 (May 1888): 132.

3. "Fine Arts. The Academy Exhibition," *Nation* 46 (April 19, 1888): 331.

4. "The Academy Exhibition," *HW* 32 (April 7, 1888): 250, 252. The etching that was reproduced in *Harper's* had originally appeared in Charles Kurtz's *Academy Notes* (New York: Cassell & Company, 1889), 28. Clarence Cook, bored with having seen too many paintings of this or similar subjects, was among those critics who did not care for the painting (Clarence Cook, "NAD. Sixty-Third Annual Exhibition. Second Notice," *Studio* 3 [June 1888]: 113).

5. William Baer was a miniature painter and had known Blum since their early days in Cincinnati. He traveled and shared a studio with Blum and eventually served as executor of his estate (Bruce Weber, "Robert Frederick Blum,"

[1857–1903] and His Milieu" [Ph.D. diss., City University of New York, 1985], 311–15).

6. "Fine Arts. The Academy Exhibition," *Nation* 48 (April 11, 1889): 312–13.

7. "Art Notes," *Art Interchange* 22 (April 13, 1889): 113.

8. "All for Art's Sake," *NYH*, March 30, 1889.

9. For example, the *Herald* proclaimed *The Ameya* as the "Crack Painting of the Show," gushing that it was the "most brilliant painting in the exhibition . . . remarkable for its reality, its color and its brilliant brush work" ("National Academy Makes a Good Show," *NYH*, March 24, 1893).

10. W. J. Baer, "Robert Frederick Blum," *Book Buyer* 10 (October 1893): 354.

53

Augustus Saint-Gaudens, NA
Dublin, Ireland 1848–1907 Cornish, New Hampshire

Portrait, Medallion of Robert Louis Stevenson, 64th Annual Exhibition, April 1–May 11, 1889, no. 495

Robert Louis Stevenson, 1887–1900 §
Bronze relief, diameter 18 × ½
National Academy of Design, New York

Augustus Saint-Gaudens modeled the features of the famous Scottish novelist and poet Robert Louis Stevenson (1850–1894), in New York in 1887 and 1888.[1] At first, he conceived of the portrait in a large, rectangular format, which he modeled in clay; but he quickly adapted it to a circular, medallion form. Saint-Gaudens chose to debut the portrait in the medallion form and sent a plaster cast of it to the annual exhibition of the National Academy of Design in 1889.[2] A later, bronze cast of this version is shown here.[3]

The first public exhibition of Augustus Saint-Gaudens's sculptures had been at the National Academy of Design's annual exhibition of 1875. As an early member of the Society of American Artists, a rival institution to the Academy, Saint-Gaudens was far more active in that organization's exhibitions, however, than he was in the Academy's. Nevertheless, in 1888, he received excellent critical notices when he sent his bust of General William Tecumsah Sherman to the Academy's exhibition. That success was partially responsible for Saint-Gaudens's election to associate membership in the Academy. Coupled with Robert Louis Stevenson's own fame, it also more or less assured a certain level of critical attention for Saint-Gaudens's portrait of the writer.

The brief comments published in *Harper's Weekly* were fairly typical of the press's response to Saint-Gaudens's *Stevenson* relief. The periodical praised Saint-Gaudens's placement of his subject, "reclining on a couch and puffed up with pillows," a position that was necessitated by Stevenson's affliction with tuberculosis and the discomfort that would have resulted if he had assumed a more traditional pose. This realism, typical of Saint-Gaudens's style, charmed the writer for *Harper's* who called the sculpture "delightful in conception and treatment."[4] Similarly, the *New York Herald* said the portrait was the most important sculpture in the exhibition and called it a "masterly medallion."[5]

A more thorough analysis of the work came from the *New York Sun*, which devoted an unusually lengthy paragraph to it. The newspaper's anonymous critic began by comparing the

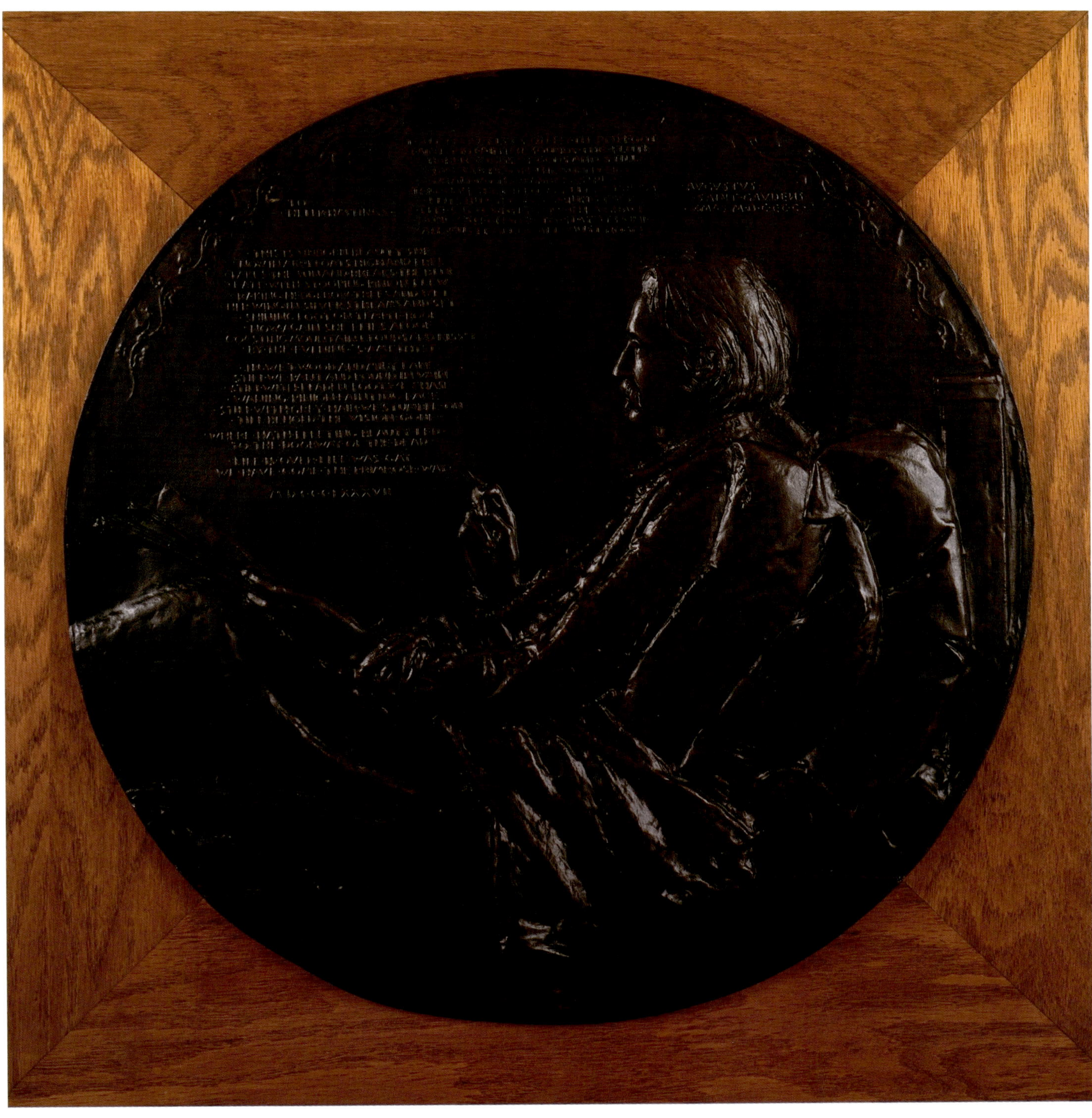

53

sculpture to Saint-Gaudens's bust of Sherman, which had been shown with such success the previous year. While the newer work was not as impressive as the bust of Sherman, the critic believed, it showed the "more graceful, gracious side" of Saint-Gaudens's talent. The writer praised Saint-Gaudens's ability to capture not only Stevenson's "outward aspect," but also his "spirit." This was partially due, the critic continued, to the unusual but thoroughly tasteful and, unfortunately, natural placement of Stevenson in bed. Ultimately, then, it was Saint-Gaudens's ability to combine realism with good taste—even in the details of blankets and pillows—that earned him this praise.

The only regret the *Sun's* critic had was that Saint-Gaudens had not sent the original version of the sculpture—the larger, rectangular one—to the Academy's exhibition. The writer had seen it in clay in the sculptor's studio and had greatly admired it. Compositionally, that format was more conducive to the figure of the reclining Stevenson than the medallion format, which necessitates truncating the figure. Nor was the decorative nature of the round form in keeping with the intent of the sculpture, which, after all, depicted a famous man. Nevertheless, the critic ended by commending the "exquisitely tender if virile handling of this relief, and . . . its character as a patent piece of portraiture."[6]

Saint-Gaudens's portrait of Stevenson was one of his most popular and frequently reproduced sculptures. Following Stevenson's death in 1894, the Church of St. Giles in Edinburgh, Scotland, commissioned Saint-Gaudens to create a memorial to the great literary figure. For that project, Saint-Gaudens remodeled and greatly enlarged his earlier image of Stevenson, and the success of the resulting monument was partially responsible for the sculptor's election to the Royal Academy of Arts in London.[7]

DBD

1. Kathryn Greenthal, *Augustus Saint-Gaudens, Master Sculptor* (New York: Metropolitan Museum of Art, 1985), 119–21.

2. For the various versions and casts of the *Stevenson* relief, see John H. Dryfhout, *The Work of Augustus Saint-Gaudens* (Hanover, New Hampshire: University Press of New England, 1982), 173–76, 261–63.

3. The Academy's cast was a Christmas gift from the sculptor to Helen Hastings, wife of the architect Thomas Hastings. It is inscribed, upper left: *To / Helen Hastings*; upper right: *Augustus Saint-Gaudens / Xmas MDCCCC*; center top and left: *Youth now flees on feathered foot . . . We have come the primrose way.*; center left: *MDCCCLXXXVII*. The poem is from *Underwoods,* a collection of Stevenson's verse, which was dedicated by the author to painter Will Low, who had arranged for Saint-Gaudens to take Stevenson's portrait.

4. "The Academy Exhibition," *HW* 33 (April 6, 1889): 268–69. Stevenson's physical condition is mentioned in Greenthal, 119.

5. "All for Art's Sake: Brilliant Showing at the National Academy Exhibition," *NYH*, March 30, 1889.

6. "The National Academy Exhibition: The Portraits and the Sculpture," *NYS*, March 31, 1889.

7. John H. Dryfhout and Beverly Cox, *Augustus Saint-Gaudens: The Portrait Reliefs* (Washington, D.C.: The National Portrait Gallery, 1969), n.p., nos. 39–41; Greenthal, 119.

54
Kenyon Cox, NA
Warren, Ohio 1856–1919 New York, New York

65th Annual Exhibition, April 7–July 1, 1890, no. 255, for sale for $500

The Approach of Love, 1890–931

Oil on canvas, 18⅛ × 30¼

Cincinnati Art Museum, Gift of Mrs. John DeWitt Peltz and Leonard Updycke in memory of their parents Leonard and Edith Updycke

On his return to the United States from Europe in 1883, Kenyon Cox began painting a series of reclining nudes, of which *The Approach of Love* is an example. As a group, these paintings display the technical skills Cox developed while studying at the Ecole des Beaux-Arts in Paris. Sending *The Approach of Love* to the National Academy of Design's annual exhibition of 1890 allowed him to share his development with the public.

Critics noted that Cox was one of several artists who had sent competent nude studies to the Academy's exhibition that year.[2] One writer noted that Cox was "one of the best draftsmen among American painters,"[3] and most critics agreed that *The Approach of Love* was proof of that.[4]

If his ability to draw the human figure was unquestioned, Cox's handling of color was not. While a writer for the *Critic* called *The Approach of Love* "a brilliant attempt at the splendor of color," a critic for the *New York Sun* noted that, despite Cox's efforts to achieve "a gorgeous scheme of color," the skin of the figures in the work tended to be "disagreeably pink."[5] Other crit-

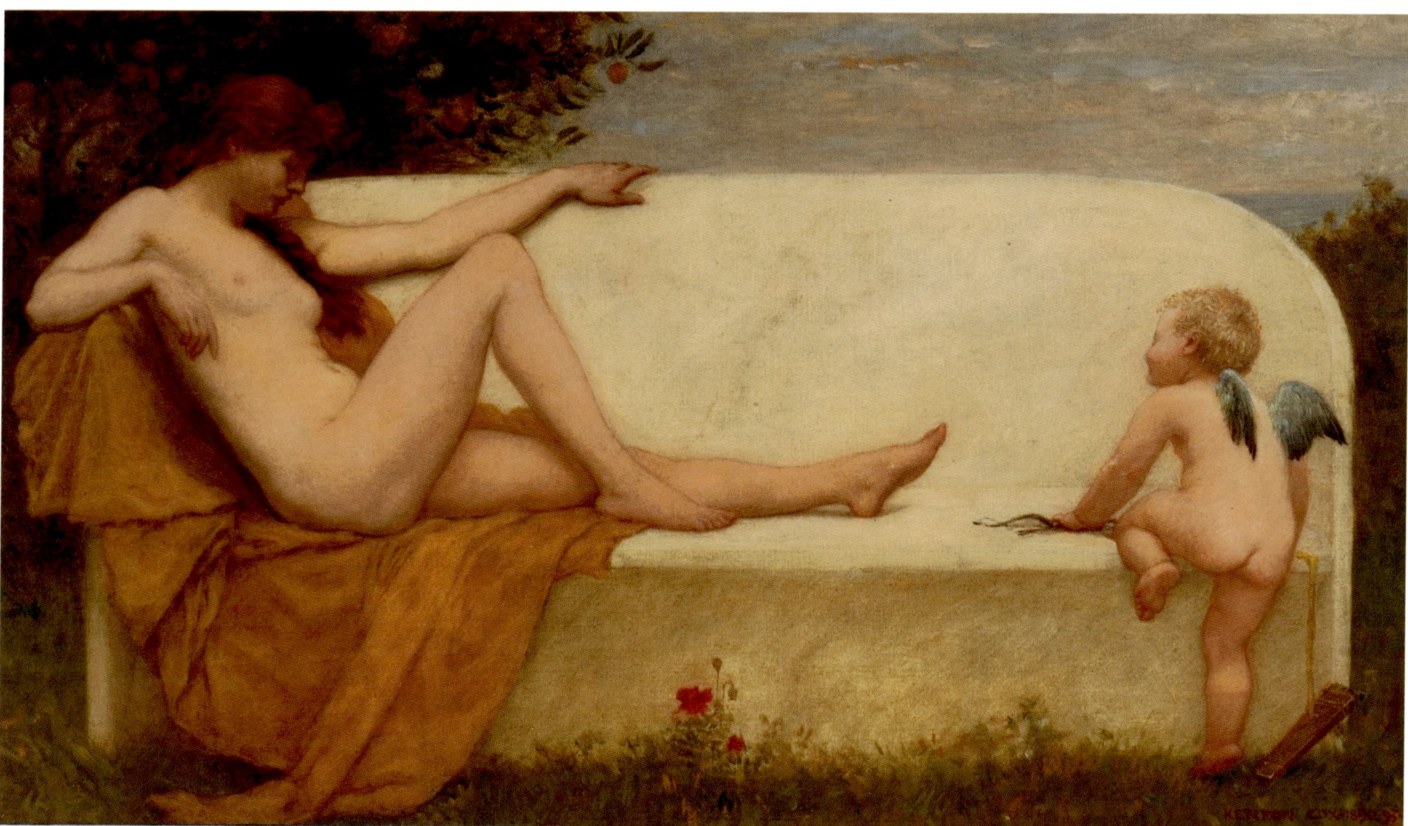

54

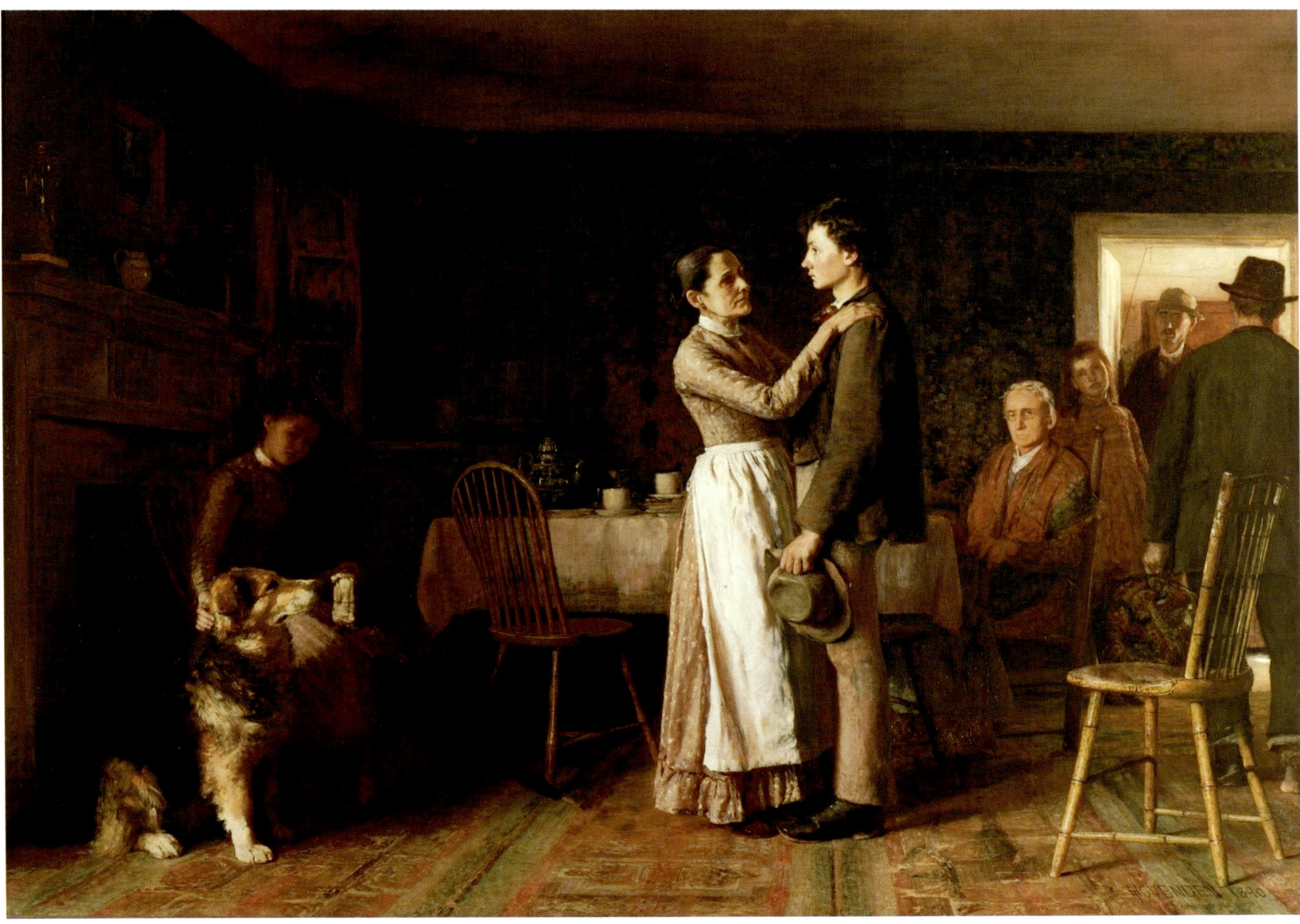

55

ics were less reserved in their displeasure, finding Cox's colors "hot and unpleasant" or "crude and jarring, the oranges warring with reds and blues."[6]

Like many American artists fresh from European academic study, Cox was facing a new, negative attitude toward the nude figure, manifested in such statements as that of the critic for the *New-York Times* who proclaimed *The Approach of Love* to be "brutal." He advised that Cox "stow away such studies as this and keep to portraits until he is able to understand why people find his nude women repulsive."[7] At least partially due to his academic training, Cox's love of the idealized figure, both nude and draped, dominated his art, his teaching methods, and his writings, and classical, idealized figures continued to appear in his murals well into the twentieth century.   AH

1. It is not known why the painting is inscribed, presumably by the artist, with the dates 1890–93. Perhaps Cox made changes or additions to his initial conception after it was exhibited at the National Academy in 1890 and then documented that act by adding the expanded date. Recent examination of the painting by its present owner under ultraviolet light, however, did not reveal evidence of Cox's having done so.

2. "NAD," *Art Amateur* 22 (May 1890): 113.

3. "Kenyon Cox," *Century Magazine* 41 (January 1891): 335.

4. "The Academy Exhibition," *New York Mail and Express*, April 12, 1890.

5. "The Fine Arts: The National Academy's Sixty-fifth Exhibition," *Critic* 13 (April 18, 1890): 186; "Pictures at the NAD: Second Notice," *New York Sun*, April 24,1890.

6. *New York Mail and Express*, April 12, 1890; "The National Academy, New York," *Magazine of Art* 13 (April 1890): xxvi.

7. "The Academy of Design Spring Exhibition," *NYT*, April 4,1890.

55
Thomas Hovenden, NA
Dunmanway, County Cork, Ireland 1840–1895 Plymouth Meeting, Pennsylvania

> "*Breaking the Home Ties,*" 66th Annual Exhibition, April 6– May 16, 1891, no. 321, owner Charles C. Harrison, Esq.

Breaking Home Ties, 1890
> Oil on canvas, 52½ × 72¼
>
> The Philadelphia Museum of Art: Given by Ellen Harrison McMichael in memory of C. Emory McMichael

Whatever ground Thomas Hovenden may have lost among critics with the exhibition of *The Death of Elaine* (no. 47) at the National Academy in 1882, he regained with the appearance of *Breaking Home Ties* in 1891. A critic for the *Art Amateur* summarized the latter painting's composition and theme:

The big, awkward country youth who is about to go out to seek his fortune stands in the centre of the living-room of the farm-house, facing his mother, who lays her hands affectionately on his shoulders and looks up into his face. The bystanders are simply accessories; the pathos of the situation is rendered entirely by these two motionless figures.[1]

The painting's simplicity, sentimentality, familiar subject matter, and nostalgic mood made it an overnight sensation. During Hovenden's lifetime, it brought him national fame.[2]

In fact, thanks to its inclusion in the annual exhibition of the Pennsylvania Academy of the Fine Arts in Philadelphia earlier in 1891, the painting was well on its way to fame by the time it came to the National Academy.[3] In Philadelphia, it was called the "most permanently important work in the exhibition" and was quickly purchased by Charles C. Harrison, Provost of the University of Pennsylvania, for $6,000 in one of the most notable sales of an American painting at the time.[4] Harrison generously allowed his new purchase to go on to New York to the National Academy where, like *Elaine* before it, it was given a place of honor in the center of the east wall in the main, South Gallery.[5] The critics responded accordingly. A writer for the *Art Amateur* admired the painting's composition and the directness and simplicity with which Hovenden dealt with "a difficult theme."[6] The *New York Herald* acclaimed it as the most important figure piece in the exhibition, and the *New-York Times* lauded Hovenden's "power to compose."[7]

Critics for both *Art Interchange* and *Harper's Weekly* agreed, finding *Breaking Home Ties* the best of the artist's work to date. "Mr. Hovenden chooses his subjects with a view of appealing to a sort of cheap popular sentiment," the critic for *Art Interchange* wrote, "but in this instance he has rather risen above his theme."[8] *Harper's* admired the composition and the manner in which Hovenden captured the characters of the two main figures.[9] The subtlety of their expressions, in fact, was something that interested most writers at the time. A typical passage on this topic was written by Charles M. Kurtz for the journal *Truth*:

Rarely does one see in a picture so effective a portrayal as that of this mother and son, each striving to keep back the tears in order to encourage the other to bear the separation more easily. The mother looks as if she were striving to fix in her mind every feature of this boy so dear to her. . . . The boy's attitude suggests eagerness to be off, but his face wears an expression of regret at this last moment. The past comes back to him, simple and peaceful, perhaps now appreciated for the first time.[10]

While a number of writers expressed minor concerns about the sentimentality of the painting, all out negative assaults on it were practically non-existent in 1891.[11] As Anne Terhune has pointed out, however, that situation began to change when the painting, along with Hovenden's *Bringing Home the Bride* (1893; University of St. Thomas, St. Paul, Minnesota), was shown at the World's Columbian Exposition in Chicago in 1893.[12] Partially due to the increasing popularity of Impressionism among the critics, Hovenden's more traditional *Breaking Home Ties* was vulnerable to open attack for its "wooden" figures and "triteness."[13] Nevertheless, the popularity of the painting not only endured but increased with the crowds who attended the fair, bordering at times on the fanatical. A scrapbook kept by the Hovenden family at the time of the Chicago fair contains a seemingly endless number of articles from newspapers and journals, many illustrated with reproductions of the painting or details from it, that chronicle this phenomenal public attention.[14] Poems were written about it and engravings and photogravures of it sold by the thousands.[15] In the gallery at the world's fair, traffic was so great, it was said, that the carpet in front of the painting had to be replaced several times. In fact, for a time, the painting seems to have been a staple at world's fairs, appearing again at both the Louisiana Purchase Exposition in St. Louis in 1904 and the Panama-Pacific International Exposition in San Francisco in 1915.[16]   DBD

1. " 'The Academy' Exhibition," *AAm* 24 (May, 1891): 145.

2. A complete history and analysis of the painting is in Anne Gregory Terhune, "Thomas Hovenden (1840–1895) and Late-Nineteenth-Century American Genre Painting" (Ph.D. diss., City University of New York, 1983), 414–44. Also see Lee M. Edwards, "Noble Domesticity: The Paintings of Thomas Hovenden," *American Art Journal* 19 (1987): 24–29; Sarah Burns, "The Country Boy Goes to the City: Thomas Hovenden's *Breaking Home Ties* in American Popular Culture," *American Art Journal* 20 (1988): 59–73; and Sylvia Yount, "A Pennsylvania Artist: Thomas Hovenden and the Philadelphia Art World," in Woodmere Art Museum, *Hovenden* (1995), 45–47.

3. See, for example, "Hovenden at Home. A Visit to the Artist's Studio at Plymouth Meeting," *Philadelphia Times*, February 23, 1891.

4. "Thomas Hovenden," *Philadelphia Telegraph*, January 31, 1891; and *Philadelphia Sunday Press*, February 22, 1891.

5. "Art Gossip," *Art Interchange* 26 (April 25, 1891): 129.

6. " 'The Academy Exhibition," *AAm* 24 (May 1891): 142.

7. "A Strong Exhibition at the National Academy," *NYH*, April 3, 1891; "The Academy's Exhibition," *NYT*, April 6, 1891.

8. "Art Gossip," *Art Interchange* 26 (April 25, 1891): 129.

9. "The Academy Exhibition," *HW* 35 (April 18, 1891): 287.

10. Charles M. Kurtz, "At the Spring Academy," *Truth* 1 (April 9, 1891), n. p.

11. A rare exception came from a writer for the *New York Evening Post* who thought the painting "not particularly well painted" and, in fact, "almost worthless" ("A Collection of Pictures by American Artists," *NYEP*, March 17, 1891).

12. World's Columbian Exposition, *Official Catalogue. Fine Arts* (Chicago, 1893), 20.

13. Terhune (1983), 428.

14. Thomas Hovenden Papers, AAA, P-13.

15. Frances Forrester, "The Story of a Picture," *Sunday Inter Ocean*, October 29, 1893; *Chicago Post*, November 11, 1893; *Pittsburgh Bulletin*, December 9, 1893, all clippings in Hovenden Scrapbook, AAA, P13.

16. Terhune (1983), 433–35

56

Louis Paul Dessar, NA

Indianapolis, Indiana 1865–1952 Preston, Connecticut

70th Annual Exhibition, April 1–May 11, 1895, no. 134, for sale for $3,000

The Departure of the Fishermen—Early Morning, 1891

Oil on canvas, 63 × 80

The Cooley Gallery, Old Lyme, Connecticut

Writing for the magazine *Brush and Pencil* in 1899, critic Lena M. Cooper stated that *The Departure of the Fisherman—Early Morning* was one of Louis Paul Dessar's more interesting canvases. She was particularly struck by the painting's depiction of the devotion of the men of Brittany as they pause for the ritual bless-

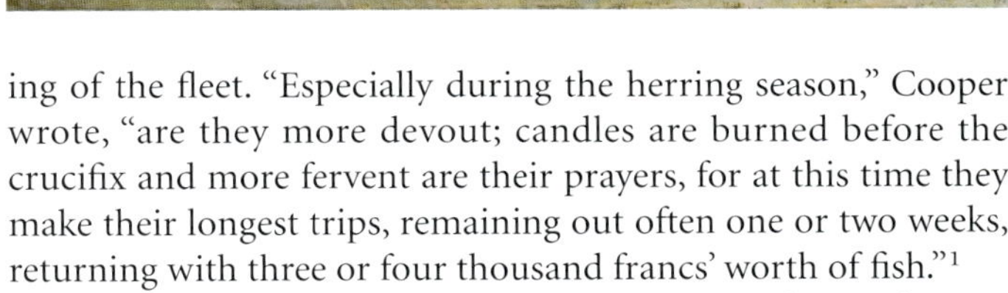

56

ing of the fleet. "Especially during the herring season," Cooper wrote, "are they more devout; candles are burned before the crucifix and more fervent are their prayers, for at this time they make their longest trips, remaining out often one or two weeks, returning with three or four thousand francs' worth of fish."[1]

Dessar's impetus for painting *The Departure of the Fishermen* came from Tony Robert-Fleury, one of his teachers at the Académie Julian, who urged Dessar to paint something specifically for the upcoming 1890 Salon exhibition. Dessar spent the winter and early spring in Etaples, France, where he had already spent several summers painting the fisher folk. He made sketches for his new picture by posing local citizens out-of-doors.[2] With the help of Fleury, the finished painting garnered some positive critical attention at the Salon of 1891 and was awarded a gold medal, third class.[3] It was Dessar's first major success, and two years later, he sent it to the World's Columbian Exposition in Chicago. It won another medal there and, in 1895, it made its New York debut at the National Academy of Design.[4]

Almost all who wrote about the Academy's annual exhibition that year mentioned the works of the American Impressionists, which seem to have dominated the show. One critic referred to "the marked and good influence of the Impressionist movement,"[5] while others were struck by the "general luminosity" of the display. As one writer put it, the exhibition was evidence that "a greater vibration of light and color has been the aim of the painters, and with this, greater truth in rendering the shadows."[6]

Dessar's *The Return of the Fishermen* was not excluded from this discussion. After identifying him as a painter in "the French academical style," *Art Amateur* linked him to the Impressionists and the artists they admired. "Something of the modern preoccupation with states of atmosphere and passing effects of light," the critic wrote, "may be seen in Mr. Louis P. Dessar's 'Departure of Fisherman, Early Morning' . . . in which the effect of mingled twilight and candlelight, so often repeated by Jules Breton and his followers, is very happily introduced."[7]

The *New-York Times* characterized Dessar's painting as showing "cleverness and no little appreciation of good color." While the critic was not fond of its "hackneyed" composition, he admitted that the painting gave Dessar the opportunity to create a tour de force in which he could "exploit his dexterity of brush work." A large painting was not necessary for this display, however; as the critic pointed out, Dessar did the same thing in his much smaller *Almost Home,* his second painting in the exhibition.[8] A writer for *Art Interchange* would probably have agreed; he thought that *Almost Home* was "quite as great" as his *Departure of the Fishermen.*[9]

While these comparisons between Dessar's two paintings—one large, one small—were not meant to denigrate the former, at least one critic was not so generous. Writing for the *New York Evening Post,* this critic compared Dessar's painting to Henry Mosler's *The Last Moments* (location unknown), in the same exhibition. Both paintings, the writer thought, addressed "Salon themes" that were "long since worn threadbare." He admitted that the paintings would receive a lot of attention, due to their size; but, unlike the writer for the *Art Amateur,* quoted above, the critic found Mosler's and Dessar's color schemes somber and "somewhat ancient."[10]

Whatever the case, Dessar's painting was an award winner and a critical success. Nevertheless, Dessar had a difficult time selling it, probably due to its scale. When he sent it to the Chicago world's fair, the asking price was $4,000; but by the time the painting appeared at the National Academy, Dessar had reduced that to $3,000. *The Return of the Fishermen* was eventually bought by the city of Omaha, Nebraska, and hung for a number of years in the city's art gallery and public library.[11]   DBD

1. Lena M. Cooper, "Louis Paul Dessar and His Work," *Brush and Pencil* 5 (December 1899): 101.

2. Interview with Louis Paul Dessar, DeWitt McClellan Lockman Papers, AAA, 502.

3. *Catalogue Illustré de Peinture et Sculpture. Salon de 1891* (Paris, 1891), no. 500. In 1894, Dessar's *The Return of the Fisherman,* probably a companion to his *Departure,* was shown at the Salon. See Lois Marie Fink, *American Art at the Nineteenth-Century Paris Salons* (Washington, D. C.: National Museum of American Art, Smithsonian Institution, 1990), 337.

4. National Museum of American Art and National Portrait Gallery, *Revisiting the White City: American Art at the 1893 World's Fair* (Washington, D.C., 1993), 233.

5. "Ideal in Art at the Academy," *NYH,* March 29, 1895.

6. "The NAD," *Art Interchange* 34 (May 1895): 136.

7. "The NAD," *AAm* 32 (May 1898): 131.

8. "The NAD. Second Notice," *NYT,* April 8, 1895.

9. "The NAD," *Art Interchange* 34 (May 1895): 136.

10. "The Spring Academy," *NYEP,* April 6, 1895.

1.1 The painting was in Omaha by 1924. See William B. McCormick, "Louis Dessar Tonalist," *IS* 99 (July 1924): 295.

57

Daniel Chester French, NA

Exeter, New Hampshire 1850–1931 Stockbridge, Massachusetts

Painting and Sculpture for Hunt Memorial, 76th Annual Exhibition, January 5–February 2, 1901, no. 280

Sculpture and Painting, 1897 §

Bronze, 12½ x 4¼ x 3½

Chesterwood, A National Trust Historic Site, Stockbridge, Massachusetts

At the height of his career, Daniel Chester French was among the most prominent sculptors working in this country. He produced many of America's best known public works, including the colossal statue of Abraham Lincoln for the *Lincoln Memorial* in Washington, D.C., the allegorical figure of *Alma Mater* at Columbia University, and *The Continents* at the Customs House in New York. His first public monument for New York, however, was his *Richard Morris Hunt Memorial.* It was also the first public monument in the United States dedicated to an American artist.[1]

Richard Morris Hunt (1827–1895) was the first American matriculated at the Ecole des Beaux-Arts in Paris, where he studied from 1846 to 1855. After returning to America in 1868, he designed private residences for wealthy East Coast clients and public buildings and monuments, including the Metropolitan Museum of Art and the pedestal for the Statue of Liberty. Hunt was instrumental in establishing professional standards in his field and championing the Beaux-Arts ideal, which called for the integration of the arts into a coherent aesthetic statement. He also served as a mentor to many young architects. As the inscription beneath his bust on French's memorial implies, it is for this, and his "service to the cause of art in America," as much as for the buildings that he designed, that the Municipal Art Society of New York proposed the memorial shortly after his death on July 31, 1895.[2]

By April 1896, French had been appointed the sculptor for the new Hunt memorial; his collaborator was architect Bruce Price (1845–1903). Because the commission came from his peers, French viewed the appointment as one of the highlights of his career. The original site selected for the monument was at Fifth Avenue and Eighty-third Street, close to Hunt's Metropolitan Museum of Art. Another site, Fifth Avenue at Seventieth Street, was soon chosen, however. At the time, this was directly across the avenue from the Lenox Library, another of Hunt's masterpieces. That building was demolished in 1912 to make way for the mansion of Henry Clay Frick, which stands on the site today.

The *Hunt Memorial* epitomizes the Beaux-Arts ideal that both French and Price had learned in Europe. Reflecting the original recommendation of the Memorial Committee, the monument contains a low, semi-elliptical seat, reminiscent of many of Hunt's own memorial designs. In the center stands a bust of Hunt, completed by French in 1898. French was behind schedule on aspects of the project, however, and the memorial was actually dedicated in October, 1898, before he had installed the allegorical figures of *Painting and Sculpture* and *Architecture.* He spent the next several years refining his original conceptions and finalizing the attributes of the allegorical figures.

Although $16,800 had already been raised for the monument by 1900, when the finished figures were cast, the Memorial Committee still owed French $4500, and several pleas were made in the press to raise the needed funds. To assist in this, the statues were sent to the annual exhibition of the National Academy and illustrated in the accompanying catalogue. The figures were praised as being "full of sentiment, showing refined imagination, a scholar's grasp of the requirements and an artist's appreciation of fitness." They clearly demonstrated French's right to "a foremost position for the excellence of his work." The critics advised the public to attend the Academy's exhibition, for, as one wrote, it would "not take long to raise this amount if many who visit the exhibition and admire the statues of Mr. French contribute."[3] By the time the maquettes were exhibited at the 1901 annual exhibition of the Pennsylvania Academy of the Fine Arts, the subscription was successfully raised. The figures were installed on the Hunt monument by June 1901.[4]   AH

1. Lewis I. Sharp, *New York Public Sculpture by Nineteenth-Century American Artists* (Metropolitan Museum of Art: New York, 1974), 49.

2. The standard biography of Hunt is Paul R. Baker, *Richard Morris Hunt*

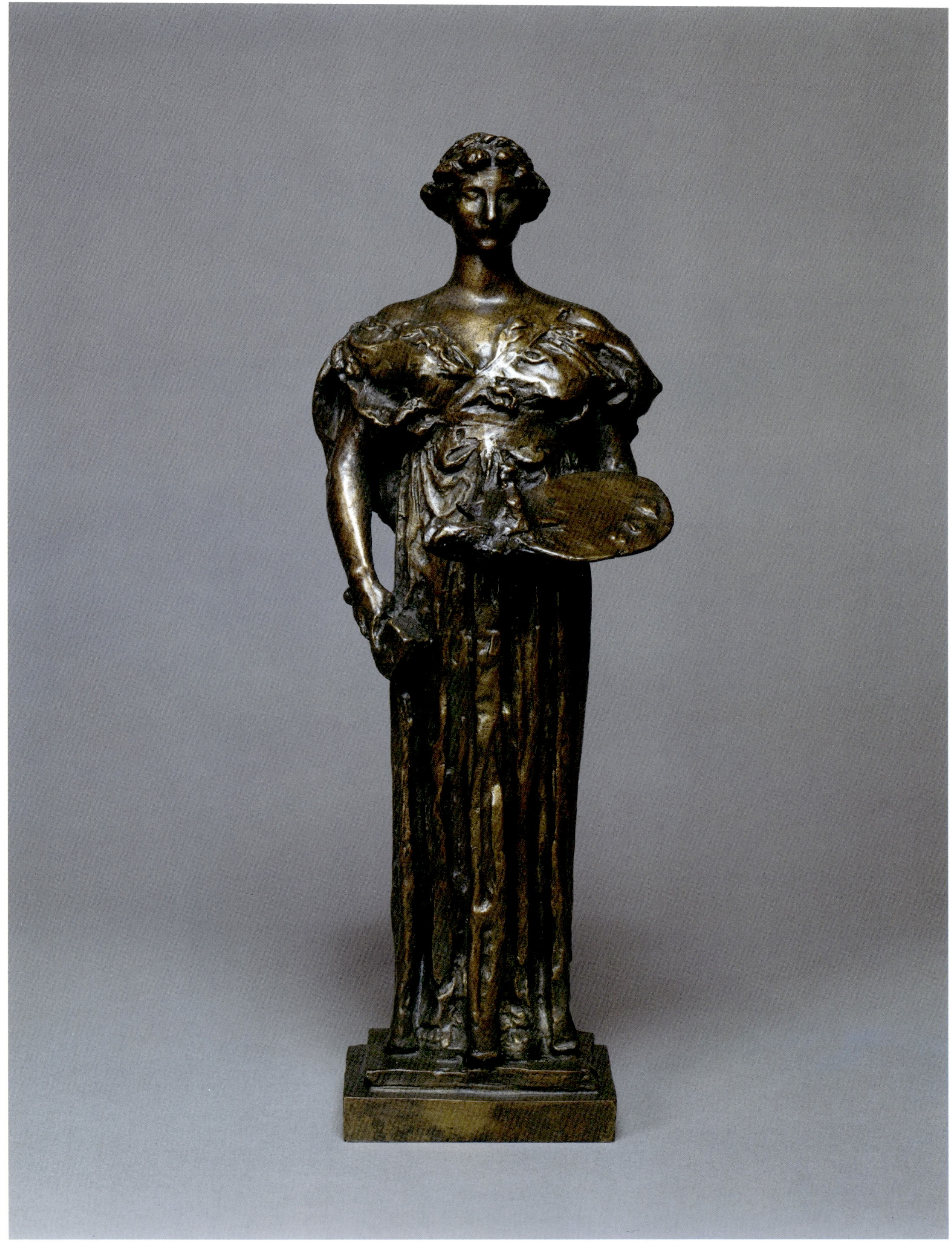

57

(Cambridge, Mass.: Massachusetts Institute of Technology Press, 1980). Also see Susan R. Stein, ed., *The Architecture of Richard Morris Hunt* (Chicago: The University of Chicago Press, 1986).

3. "The Art World, " *NYCA*, January 1, 1901.

4. Michael Richman, *Daniel Chester French: An American Sculptor* (Washington, D.C.: The Preservation Press, 1976), 88.

58

Horatio Walker, NA

Listowel, Ontario 1858–1938 Ile d'Orléans, Québec

Ploughing: The First Gleam, 76th Annual Exhibition, January 5–February 2, 1901, no. 232

Ploughing—The First Gleam at Dawn, 1900

Oil on canvas, 60¼ x 76⅞

Musée du Québec, Canada

Horatio Walker's *Ploughing—The First Gleam at Dawn* received extensive critical acclaim and had an extraordinary exhibition history. Its first exposure occurred at Walker's solo exhibition in 1900 at the Montross Gallery in New York City. In 1901, after its appearance at the National Academy's annual, the painting hung at the Pan-American Exposition in Buffalo. In 1902, it was shown at the annual exhibition at the Pennsylvania Academy of the Fine Arts in Philadelphia. Other venues included major exhibitions in London (1914), Wembly, England (1925), and Paris (1927). The Musée du Québec acquired the work in 1929. Among its many awards were two gold medals, one in Buffalo (1901) and the other at the Universal Exposition in St. Louis (1904).

The praise began at the time of Walker's solo exhibition in 1900. A critic from the *Artist* was entirely positive in his summation of it: "Superb strength is felt throughout; in the firm earth as well as in the broad backs of the laboring beasts, and even in the newly risen light."[1] His last point was reinforced by his appreciative comment about how the light "creeps up the first red glow of morning, scattering its tongues of fire." Also in 1900, a writer for *Brush and Pencil* declared Walker to be "quite the best" of the American "animal painters," and *Ploughing—The First Gleam at Dawn* to be one of his best works. The writer's description of *Ploughing* moved from general observations about the action and light to more evocative lines: "One feels thoroughly the time and the place. Cool mists rise from the earth; there is the chill in the air, and men and beasts are full of the power and dignity of labor."[2]

In reviewing the Academy's 1901 annual, a writer for the *Commercial Advertiser* remembered that at the time of Walker's

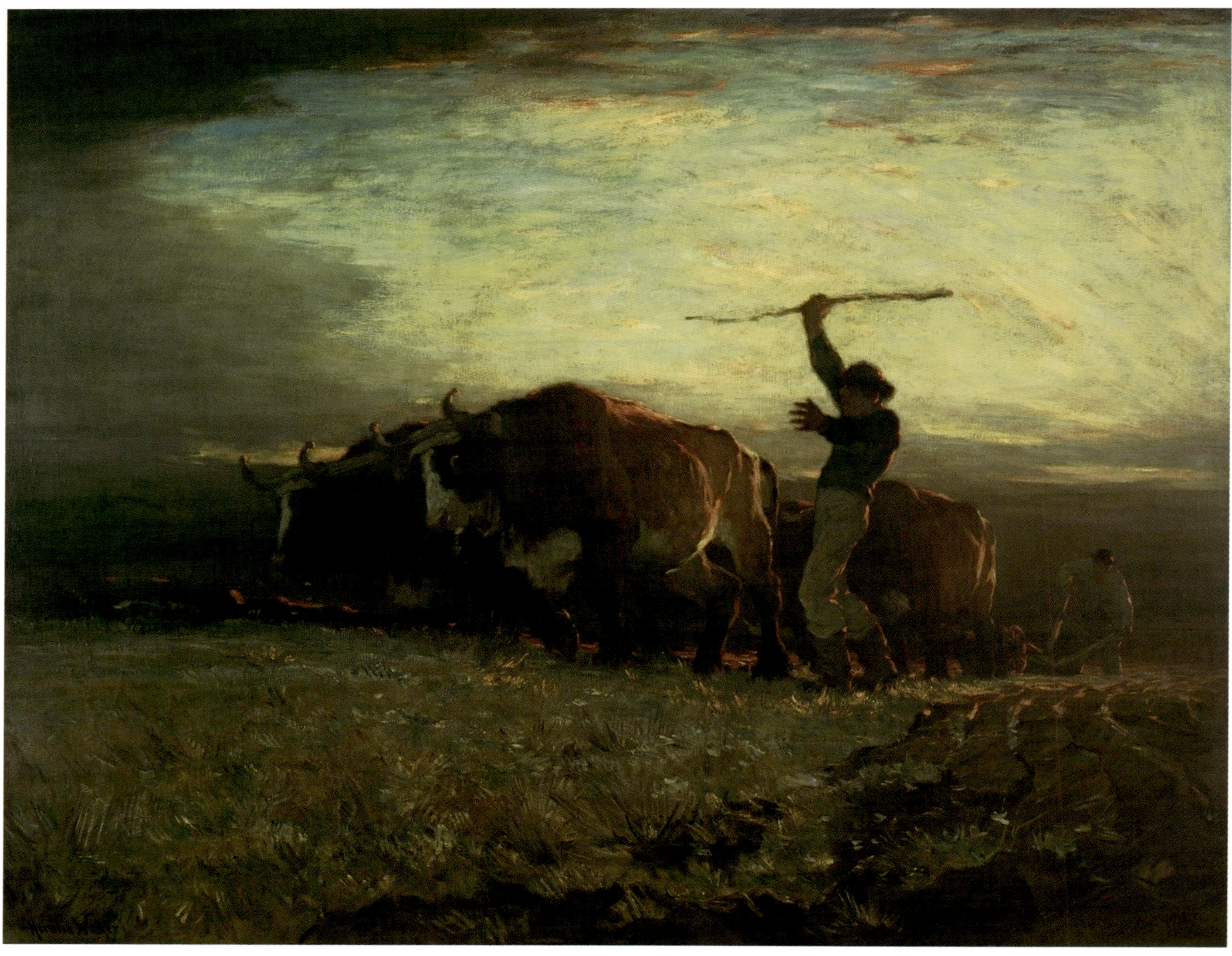

58

solo exhibition the year before, the painting had been praised for its "excellent qualities" and "the almost Homeric rendition of the human and brute element in the composition." He commended the color of the work as "rich, toneful and full of sentiment" and suggested that the picture "ought to be in some museum."[3]

Two years after *Ploughing—The First Gleam at Dawn* received exposure at the annual, Charles H. Caffin published his book *American Masters of Painting,* in which he devoted a chapter to Walker. Caffin paid great heed to *Ploughing.* In this work—as well as in others by Walker—Caffin identified a characteristic he called "heroic suggestion." For Caffin, this gave Walker's work a "universal significance," and he maintained that his paintings "set one's imagination back in the Old World that we call Homeric." Although other critics had mentioned this "Homeric" quality, Caffin lucidly defined it as evocative of "times of spaciousness and simplicity, when we fancy that man's strength was in closest affinity with nature's; times of wholesomeness and poise of mind and body, when man lived by nature's rule and labor was loving."[4]

Although capable of painting works with epic qualities, Walker also depicted peaceful scenes of cheerful looking peasants going about their daily routine with natural ease. In general, his work was most often compared with that of the French Barbizon painter Jean François Millet. Some writers dubbed him the "American Millet," others the "Canadian Millet." In numerous works, as in the example under study, the skies were radiantly luminous, an effect that was inspired by exposure to the work of William Turner, which Walker saw when he spent time in England.[5]   TAG

1. "Exhibition of Works by Horatio Walker," *Artist* (American Supplement) 28 (June 1900): ii.

2. "New York Letter," *Brush and Pencil* 6 (May 1900): 82.

3. "The Art World. Academy of Design Exhibition—Second Notice," *Commercial Advertiser,* January 7, 1901.

4. Charles H. Caffin, *American Master of Painting* (New York: Doubleday, Page & Company, 1903), 180–81.

5. David Karel, *Horatio Walker* (Quebec: Musée du Québec, 1987), 26.

59

Irving Ramsay Wiles, NA

Utica, New York 1861–1948 Peconic, New York

77th Annual Exhibition, January 3–February 1, 1902,
no. 317, owner Julia Marlowe

Miss Julia Marlowe, 1901

Oil on canvas, 74¼ × 55¼

National Gallery of Art, Washington, D.C., Gift of Julia Marlowe Sothern

One would have been in good company if exhibiting a portrait at the Academy's 1902 annual, for there were examples by J. Carroll Beckwith, William Merritt Chase, Thomas Eakins, John F. Weir, and other widely respected artists. A critic for the *Commercial Advertiser* maintained, however, that landscapes not only followed the rule in outnumbering figure paintings in importance but that there were "even fewer figurative works of distinction than usual."[1]

A colleague on the same newspaper noted that Irving Wiles's "attractive canvas" of Julia Marlowe held a position of honor in the Vanderbilt Gallery and was "a most creditable performance, delightful in realizing the personality of the sitter."[2] The word "performance" may have amused some readers, considering that Marlowe was a well-known actress. Born Sarah Frances Frost (1866–1950), she specialized in historical dramas and Shakespeare. Wiles's portrait of her was painted when she was thirty-six and achieving her greatest popular and financial success while starring in a dramatization of Charles Major's novel *When Knighthood Was in Flower* (Indianapolis: Bowen and Merrill, 1898).[3]

A writer for the *New York Herald* could not find any picture of "great note" in the exhibition but conceded that several attracted his attention. He placed Wiles's work first among those and called it the best portrait the painter had done. Wiles had "not alone wielded his brush in a masterful manner" and "been most harmonious in his color scheme" but had also "caught the very expression of Miss Marlowe."[4] The *New York Daily Tribune* critic gushed that Wiles "is gorgeous in his 'Miss Julia Marlowe,'" but complained that, "the color, on close scrutiny, seems cheap and tawdry, and the big canvas is, in respect to style, painfully lacking in distinction."[5]

From the early 1890s on, Wiles was known for his society portraits of women and children and his fashionable genre interior scenes. Although he worked along the same lines as other portraitists of his time such as John Singer Sargent, Cecilia Beaux, and John White Alexander, he generally did not idealize his subjects as much as they did. Nor was dexterous brushwork as important to him as it was to others. A convincing likeness was his aim; and, as the *New York Herald* critic noted, he succeeded brilliantly in his portrait of Marlowe. Of course in this case, there was good reason to stay close to likeness and bring out personality. Not only was Marlowe's appearance familiar to theatergoers, including her large, cleft chin, so clearly seen in Wiles's work, but her charismatic personality was known to them as well. She belonged to the personality school of acting popular at the turn of the century, a method of acting in which the performer put his own personality on display rather than tranforming into another.

Wiles's painting of Marlowe helped significantly to increase his reputation as a portraitist.[6] After the National Academy annual, the portrait received significant exposure at the annual exhibition of the Pennsylvania Academy of the Fine Arts later the same year, the Universal Exposition in St. Louis in 1904, and the Venice Biennale in 1909. Perhaps due to its reception, Wiles portrayed the actress again, in *Julia Marlowe as 'Viola,'* which was shown at the National Academy in 1907.

Wiles's exhibition record at the National Academy was lengthy and remarkably consistent. With the exception of nine years, he showed work, usually at least one portrait, annually from 1879 through 1948, the year of his death. His first of two Academy prizes was awarded for a portrait of his wife, on view in the winter exhibition of 1913. He also exhibited with great frequency at the annual exhibitions of the Pennsylvania Academy of the Fine Arts between 1881 and 1933.   TAG

1. "The Art World," *Commercial Advertiser,* January 8, 1902.

2. "Academy of Design: Opening To-Day of Seventy-seventh Annual Exhibition," *Commercial Advertiser,* January 2, 1902. The painting was also reproduced in the exhibition catalogue, opposite p. 26.

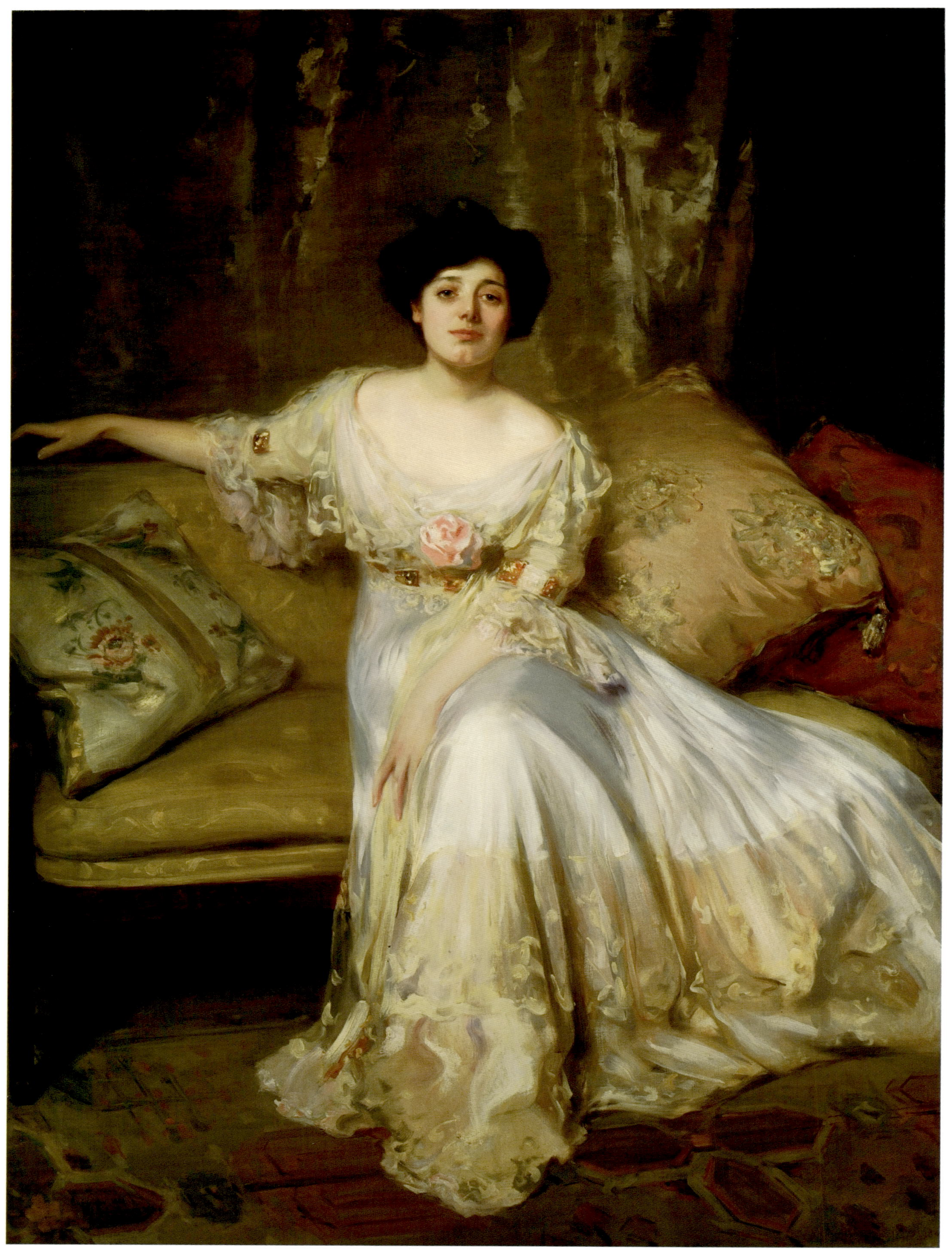

59

3. For a discussion of this work, see Robert Wilson Torchia, *American Paintings of the Nineteenth Century, Part II* (Washington, D.C.: National Gallery of Art, 1998), 264–68. Also see Gary A. Reynolds, *Irving R. Wiles* (New York: National Academy of Design, 1988), 19.

4. "Another Academy Exhibition Opens," *NYH*, January 3, 1902.

5. "Art Exhibitions: The NAD," *NYDT*, January 4, 1902.

6. Reynolds, 19; Torchia, 265.

60

Eanger Irving Couse, NA

Saginaw, Michigan 1866–1936 Albuquerque, New Mexico

77th Annual Exhibition, January 3–February 1, 1902, no. 343

The Peace Pipe, 1901

Oil on canvas, 26 × 31

The Metropolitan Museum of Art, Gift of Mrs. Adolph Obrig in memory of her husband, 1917

Irving Couse was a consistent participant in the National Academy of Design's annual exhibitions from his first showing there in 1891 until his death. In 1902, his submissions were *A Grey Day*, depicting a shepherd minding sheep; a Native American scene entitled *Firelight*; and *The Peace Pipe*, which was awarded the First Julius Hallgarten Prize for "the best oil painted in the United States by an American citizen under thirty-five." The latter work, which undoubtedly contributed to Couse's election to Associate membership at the Academy in 1902, was purchased before the exhibition opened by the New York art collector Adolph Obrig, a friend and patron whom Couse had met in Paris in 1890.

By 1902, Couse was already known as a specialist in Native American themes. He had painted his first such picture in 1891 when he was living on a ranch near the Oregon border in eastern Washington. According to Couse, *The Peace Pipe* represents the chief of the Klikitats sharing a pipe with visiting chiefs of two other tribes.[1]

A critic for the *Commercial Advertiser* considered the theme "well handled" and, more importantly, referred to the "dignity" of the figures.[2] Dignity was exactly what Couse sought in so many of his depictions of Native Americans. Another critic thought the color "excellent" and described the painting as a "serious study of the North American Indian." He noted that its theme was "valuable historically" because few artists had "given the picturesque Indian attention."[3] By "picturesque," he may have been making a

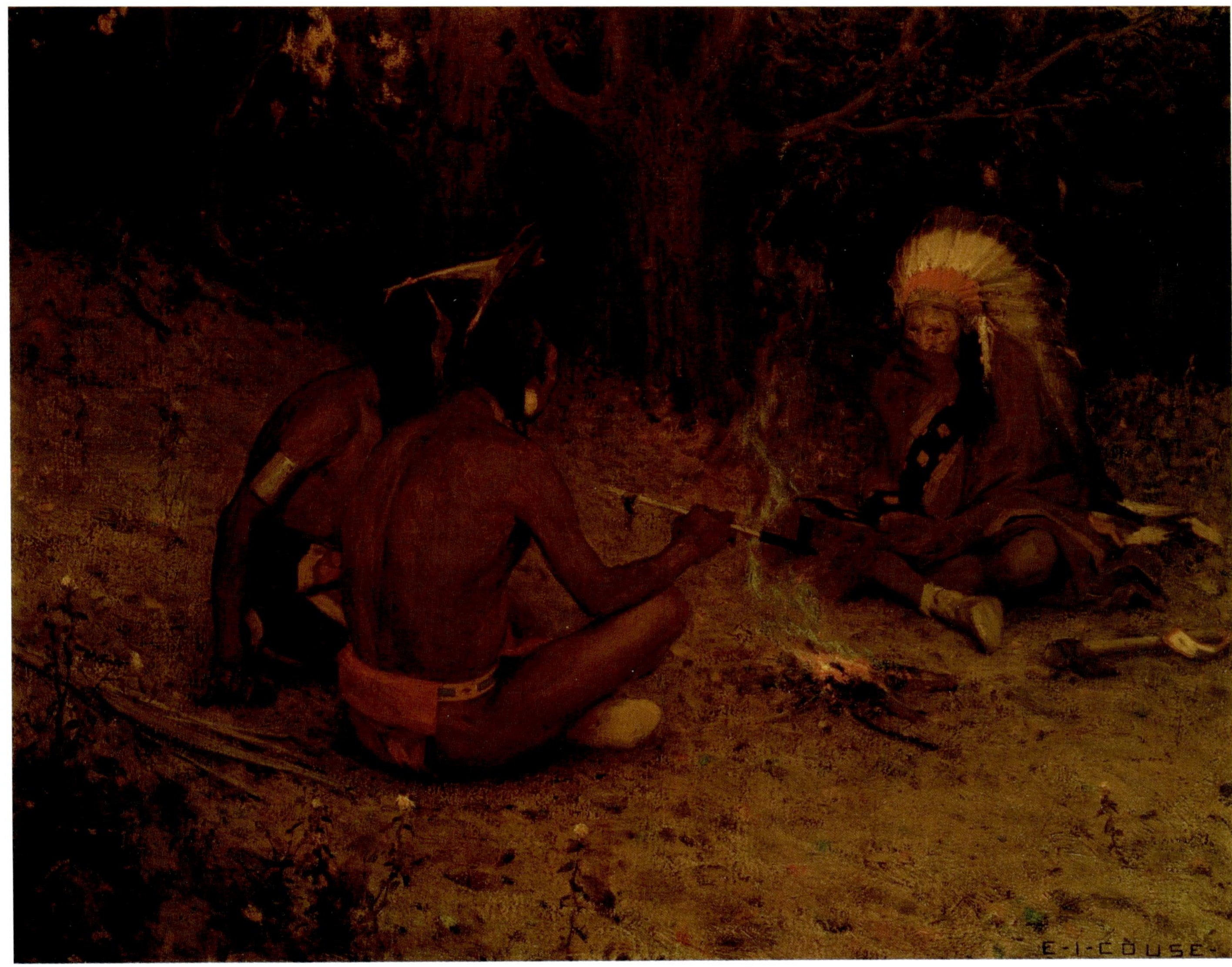

60

distinction between Couse's approach to the Native American versus that of Frederic Remington, who showed several times at the Academy from 1887 to 1899, or Charles Schreyvogel, who exhibited intermittently there from 1892 to 1902.[4]

In 1904, two years after Couse exhibited *The Peace Pipe* at the Academy, a critic for the *American Review* summed up positive opinions of his artistic stature with the observation that he "has earned the high esteem in which his work is regarded by a continuous succession of meritorious pictures making an unusually brilliant record for so young a man."[5] Couse was actually thirty-eight when this was written and had been exhibiting at the Academy since 1891. He eventually had one of the most outstanding exhibition records in the organization's history, and won four prizes at the National Academy for his paintings with Native American themes.   TAG

1. DeWitt McClellan Lockman interview, 12, Couse Family Archives, Tucson, Arizona, quoted in Virginia Couse Leavitt, *Eanger Irving Couse: Image Maker for America* (Albuquerque, New Mexico: The Albuquerque Museum, 1991), 110. For a discussion of *The Peace Pipe*, see Leavitt, 110–11.

2. "Academy of Design: Opening To-Day of Seventy-seventh Annual Exhibition," *Commercial Advertiser*, January 2, 1902. This critic also noted that Edwin Willard Deming had an "excellent Indian picture" on view; it was entitled *Indian Medicine Man.*

3. "The Art World: Academy of Design-First Notice," *Commercial Advertiser*, January 3, 1902.

4. In "A Remote North American Civilization and Its Portrayal in the Art of E. Irving Couse, *Craftsman* 18 (September 1910): 625, Joseph Lewis French observed: "He paints the Indian not primarily as the actor in a wild savage drama as Remington and Schreyvogel have, but as the peaceful dweller in primitive scenes, revealing them often as more poetical and philosophical than the more so-called civilized races."

5. "Eanger Irving Couse," *Art Review* 7 (January 1904): 140.

61

John Sloan

Lock Haven, Pennsylvania 1871–1951 Hanover, New Hampshire

83rd Annual Exhibition, March 14–April 18, 1908, no. 172

The Haymarket, Sixth Avenue, 1907

Oil on canvas, 26¼ × 32 ¹/₁₆

Brooklyn Museum of Art, Gift of Mrs. Harry Payne Whitney

Just one month after the group of mainly realist painters known as The Eight opened their noteworthy independent exhibition at

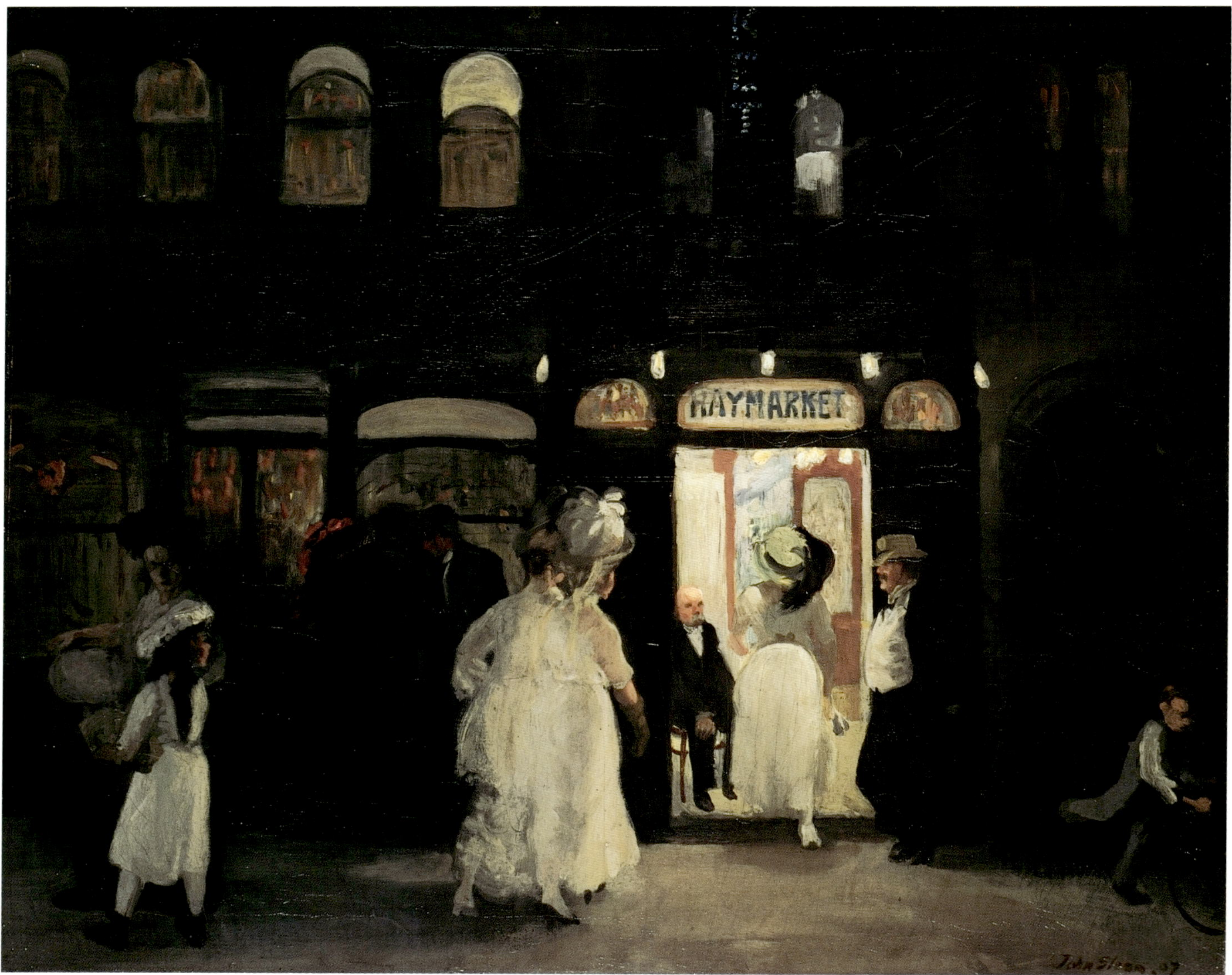

61

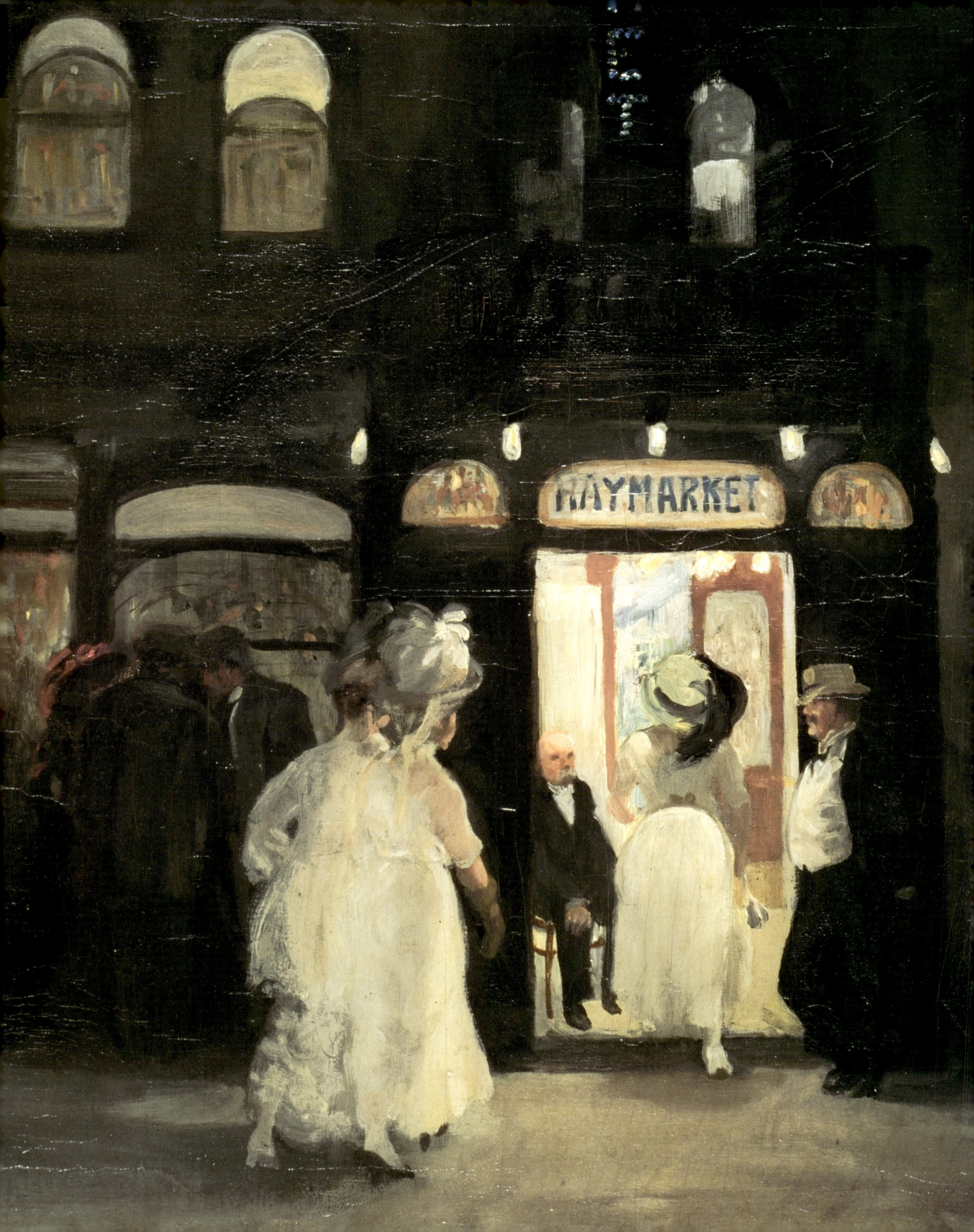

HAYMARKET

the Macbeth Gallery in New York, works by John Sloan and other members of this circle were included in the Academy's 1908 annual exhibition.[1] The *New York American* declared in its headline, "'The Eight' Win Art Victory." In the review that followed, the painter and critic Guy Pène du Bois, who had studied with Robert Henri, the leader of The Eight, noted that the entire section of one of the galleries was devoted to "the usually slighted realists." He considered this "a great victory for the new movement in the art of painting" and felt that the National Academy would surely become "a really national institution" by having this "element of modernity" in its exhibitions.[2] James B. Townsend at *American Art News* wrote that the pictures by The Eight and by those in sympathy with "this intrepid band" constituted a strong group.[3] A critic for the *New York Herald* saw no reason why an artist "disposed to secede" should go any further than the Academy. The proof was the "rebel yell" on one of the walls, which could "be seen far off if not heard." The artists in question had "neglected no picturesquely ugly or disagreeable phase of metropolitan life" but had "contributed wholesome and presentable sides as well."[4]

Sloan was represented at the Academy's 1908 exhibition by two works, a portrait and *The Haymarket, Sixth Avenue*. Charles De Kay, at the *Evening Post*, referred to Sloan and other artists in the exhibition, such as Ernest Lawson and George Bellows, as "the youthful apostles of force." These men, he wrote, "express with by no means equal ability the rush and crush of modern life, the contempt for authority, the disdain of formulas, the endeavor to get there at the quickest and by the shortest road."[5] Indeed, in *Haymarket, Sixth Avenue*, Sloan had freely painted a less than genteel, and hence untraditional, city scene. His subject was a dance hall on Sixth Avenue in Manhattan that he described as "famous through infamy . . . a well known hangout for the underworld." There, he noted, "Ladies whose dress and general deportment were satisfactory to the doorman were admitted free."[6] Du Bois thought that Sloan had captured "the characteristic atmosphere of the place."[7]

Before 1907, Sloan had produced mostly portraits, but in that year he increased his output of paintings of life in New York, executed in his typical painterly manner.[8] Besides *The Haymarket, Sixth Avenue*, this group includes images of working-class people on the city streets, such as *Election Night in Herald Square*, *Hairdresser's Window, Sixth Avenue*, and *Sixth Avenue and Thirtieth Street*. In *The Story of American Painting* (1907), Charles H. Caffin wrote about Sloan's attraction to the "passing show of shops and streets . . . the moving throngs of people, smart and squalid, sad and merry—a phantasmagoria of changing colour, form, and action." He noted, too, that Sloan was able to eliminate some features and emphasize others to produce "a synthesis of effect" that caused confusion to disappear and "the suggestion of vivid actuality" to remain.[9]

Sloan exhibited at the Academy on only five occasions, twice in the winter and three times in the spring, from 1906 through 1909. Some or all of his entries were rejected at various times during this period. After 1909, he never submitted another work to the Academy and later called it "a private institution and no more a National agency than the National Biscuit Company."[10]

TAG

1. Various members of The Eight had shown previously at the Academy, although controversy had occurred in 1907 when Robert Henri protested against the exclusion of certain painters with whom he sympathized. He showed at the Academy in 1898 and then from 1903 through 1908. William Glackens had works included in the annuals of 1905 and 1907; and Ernest Lawson showed there from 1905 through 1908. In the latter year, his painting *Ice on the Hudson* won the First Julius Hallgarten Prize.

2. Guy Pène du Bois, "Academy of Design Opens Its Eighty-Third Exhibit," *New York American*, March 14, 1908.

3. James B. Townsend, "Annual Academy Exhibition," *American Art News* 6 (March 14, 1908): 4.

4. "Academy's Show Wins High Praise," *NYH*, March 14, 1908.

5. Charles De Kay, "The Academy of Design," *NYEP*, March 14, 1908.

6. John Sloan, *Gist of Art* (New York: American Artists Group, 1939), 212.

7. Du Bois, *New York American*, March 14, 1908.

8. Elzea Rowland and Elizabeth Hawkes, *John Sloan, Spectator of Life* (Wilmington: Delaware Art Museum, 1988), 17.

9. Charles H. Caffin, *The Story of American Painting* (New York: Frederick A. Stokes Company, 1907), 373.

10. Sloan, 28.

62

Charles Webster Hawthorne, NA

Lodi, Illinois 1872–1930 Baltimore, Maryland

86th Annual Exhibition, March 11–April 16, 1911, no. 286

The Trousseau, 1910

Oil on canvas, 40 × 40

The Metropolitan Museum of Art, George A. Hearn Fund, 1911

By 1911, Charles Webster Hawthorne had already received two awards at the National Academy of Design's annual exhibitions. With the exhibition of *The Trousseau* at the Academy in that year, he won the coveted Thomas B. Clarke Prize, given for the best figure composition painted in the United States by an American citizen. The painting was further honored when it was purchased by the Metropolitan Museum of Art during the run of the exhibition.

The reviews of the Academy's 1911 annual contain many long comments, mostly positive, about *The Trousseau*. According to a critic for the *New York Daily Tribune*, the Metropolitan Museum had purchased the "the best thing in the spring Academy." The writer felt that *The Trousseau* conferred "distinction upon the exhibition" because it combined "good workmanship" with "thoughtful feeling." The same critic, however, went on to find weakness in the work, specifically in the age of the young woman. For him, the concept of a "school girl" in the role of a bride was "a little disconcerting." Then, in what is virtually a complete contradiction of his earlier point about workmanship united with feeling, he called Hawthorne a "slim artist" who made no more of his subject "than a kind of uninspired exercise in technique."[1]

A *New York Times* critic also delivered a mixed response. Calling Hawthorne's work his best to date, the writer maintained that it was "in many respects a charming piece of very intellectual painting." This was presumably a reference to both its thematic and formal aspects, for he then complained that it comes "perilously near to still life." Explaining the still life quality, he referred to "a kind of stiffness in the drawing, an immobility of contour, a fixity of expression, that interfere with the impression of vital breathing flesh and blood." Then, in a more positive tone, he compared the picture's "psychological suggestion" with that

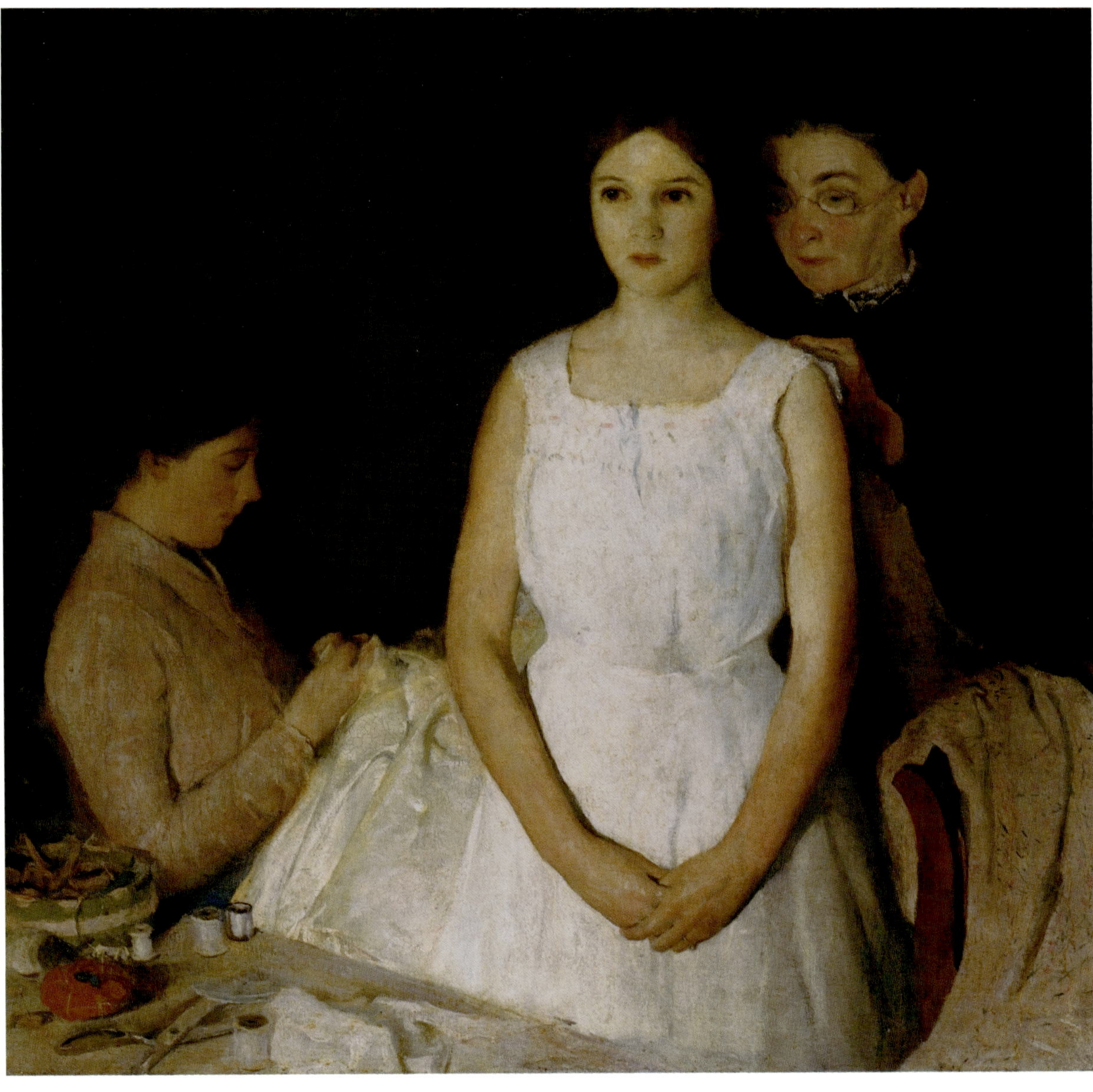

62

found "in the prim little Madonnas of the primitives," adding that Hawthorne "obliterated from the young girl's beautiful little face everything but youth and its mysterious reticence."[2]

A critic for *American Art News*, who thought that the exhibition itself was "not an inspiring one," nonetheless called Hawthorne's painting "almost a masterpiece in composition, feeling, expression and color."[3] For the *New York Sun*, a reviewer revealed the inside information that "some of the painters"—presumably fellow exhibitors at the Academy—"had expressed the opinion" that *The Trousseau* was probably Hawthorne's best work.[4]

Hawthorne so often painted girls or young women in a state of reverie that resultant criticism caused his dealer to ask in 1914 that he reduce his use of this type of figure.[5] He was apparently uninfluenced. In general, his figure compositions included more than one figure and were often inspired by everyday life around Provincetown, Massachusetts, where he summered. One reviewer mistakenly noted that Hawthorne had "found inspiration" for *The Trousseau* among "the simple folk" of this town.[6] Some years later, however, Hawthorne's widow indicated that it was painted in Bermuda.[7] Throughout his career, the beauty of the common-

place interested Hawthorne, who is quoted as saying, "Make a big thing out of a little subject."[8] *The Trousseau* also relates to his fascination with the possibilities of white, expressed in frequent depictions of figures dressed thusly, and by his opinion that there "is nothing in the world so helpful to a young painter as a study of white, if he will but be honest."[9]   TAG

1. "Matters of Art," *NYDT*, March 19, 1911.

2. "This Year's Prize Winners at the Academy," *NYT Magazine*, March 12, 1911: 12.

3. "Annual Academy Display, (First Notice)," *American Art News* 9 (March 11, 1911): 4.

4. "Pictures That Won Prizes," *New York Sun*, March 12, 1911.

5. Marvin S. Sadik, *The Paintings of Charles Hawthorne* (Storrs, Conn.: The University of Connecticut, 1968), n.p.

6. "National Academy Opens," *NYH*, March 11, 1911.

7. Elizabeth McCausland, *Charles W. Hawthorne 1872–1930* (New York: privately printed, 1947), 28.

8. Charles H. Hawthorne, quoted in E. P. Richardson, *Hawthorne Retrospective* (Provincetown, Mass.: The Chrysler Art Museum of Provincetown, 1961), 14.

9. Hawthorne, quoted in Richardson, 15.

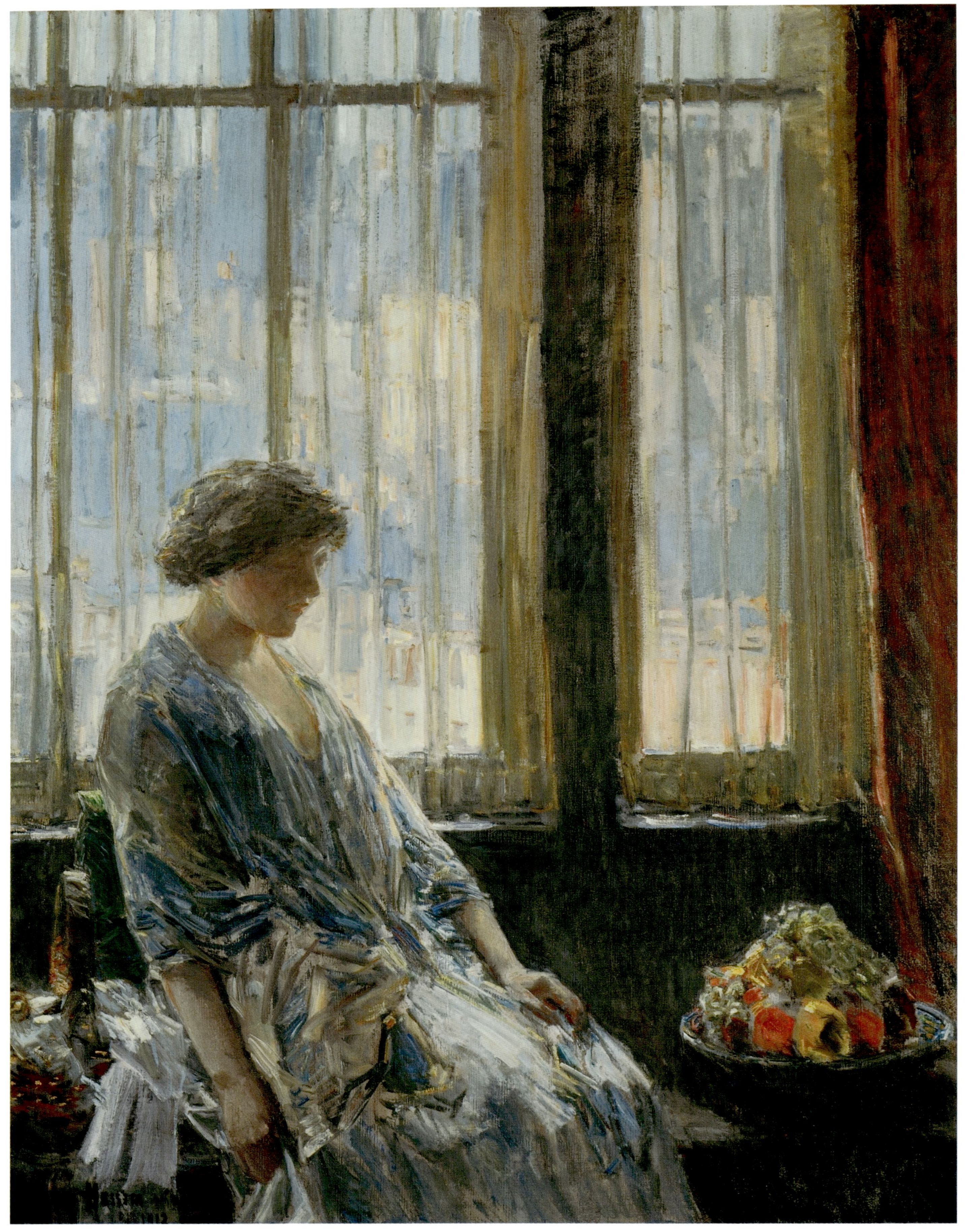

63

63

Frederick Childe Hassam, NA

Dorchester, Massachusetts 1859–1935 East Hampton, New York

87th Annual Exhibition, March 9–April 14, 1912, no. 235

The New York Window, 1912

Oil on canvas, 45⅞ × 35

In the Collection of the Corcoran Gallery of Art,
Washington, D.C., Museum Purchase, Gallery Fund

The New York Window was one of a critically successful series of paintings Frederick Childe Hassam created over a ten-year period beginning in 1909. This series prefigures his better known series of flag paintings, created during and immediately after World War I (see no. 67). Fairly large in scale, the window paintings depict women posed against or near curtained windows through which bright light filters into quiet interiors. They reveal an interest in the seventeenth-century Dutch painter Jan Vermeer, and share their subject and stylistic characteristics with similar images painted at about the same time by American artists such as Robert Reid, Frank Benson, Joseph DeCamp, and Edmund Tarbell. Many of Hassam's examples in this genre are set in the dining or breakfast room of his apartment on West Fifty-seventh Street in New York City. As William H. Gerdts has recently noted, the view from the window is to the south, toward the center of the metropolis.[1]

Hassam had been a consistent participant in the National Academy of Design's annual exhibitions since 1883. His involvement with the Ten American Painters, a somewhat rebellious group of American Impressionists founded in 1898, did not interfere with his association with the Academy. In fact, he sent paintings to the Academy's exhibitions in every year but one from 1895 until the year of his death. He won a number of awards in these exhibitions and was elected an associate member of the Academy in 1902 and a full member in 1906. He was active in Academy affairs, serving on a number of juries of selection for its exhibitions, and by 1912, he was recognized by the press as one of the "leading Academicians."[2]

It was in that year, 1912, that *The New York Window* debuted at the National Academy of Design's annual exhibition to excellent reviews. Writing for the *New York American*, Guy Pène de Bois declared it to be the "masterpiece of the collection." He described it as depicting "a woman whose beauty is doubled by a glorifying sheen of atmosphere. Behind her through faintly indicated curtains may be seen houses of the city that have become similar to the castles of the romanticist's fairyland without the bane of his mysticism and untruth."[3] Likewise, a hurried writer for the *New York Times* noted the painting "with pleasure," and his counterpart at the *New York Herald* thought that Hassam's painting and Robert Reid's *The Goldfish* (private collection; Sonoma, Georgia), "illumine and grace" the gallery.[4] Meanwhile, the critic at the *New York Post* called the work "the most interesting painting on these walls," confiding that it "tempts one to return from time to time" to look at it again.[5] Besides being well received by the critics, the painting was also selected by the Academy for illustration in the catalogue of the 1912 show, only one of a handful of works to be so honored, and for reproduction in *International Studio* that same year.[6]

After its debut at the Academy, Hassam's *The New York Window* went on to win a gold medal at the Corcoran Gallery of Art's biennial exhibition of 1912, after which that museum bought the painting for its permanent collection.[7]   DBD

1. William H. Gerdts, "Three Themes," in Warren Adelson, Jay Cantor, and Gerdts, *Childe Hassam, Impressionist* (New York: Abbeville Press, 1999), 166–68.
2. "National Academy's 87th Display Shows Progress of American Art," *NYH*, March 9, 1912.
3. Guy Pène du Bois, "National Academy Exhibit Decorous. Masterpiece of Show is a Painting by Childe Hassam," *New York American*, March 11, 1912.
4. "Winners of Prizes at Academy Exhibit," *NYT*, March 9, 1912; "National Academy's 87th Display Shows Progress of American Art," *NYH*, March 9, 1912.
5. "Seen at Spring Academy. Fewer Exhibits Than in the December Display," *NYEP*, March 12, 1912.
6. *International Studio* 46 (May 1912): lx.
7. Warren Adelson, "Childe Hassam: Cosmopolitan and Patriot," in Adelson, Cantor, and Gerdts, 60.

64

Jonas Lie, NA

Moss, Norway 1880–1940 New York, New York

89th Annual Exhibition, March 21–April 26, 1914, no. 287

Afterglow, c. 1913

Oil on canvas 50¼ × 60⅜

Art Institute of Chicago, Friends of American Art, 1914

Jonas Lie had been exhibiting at the National Academy almost annually since 1901 when he won the first Julius Hallgarten Prize for *Afterglow* in 1914. Lie was a specialist in marine and landscape painting and was known for his New York City scenes, including views of the Brooklyn Bridge and Manhattan's teeming waterfront. As a critic from the *International Studio* wrote in 1914, "Mr. Lie served his apprenticeship, like many other artists, beneath the Brooklyn Bridge and the city's monster buildings."[1]

Afterglow inspired a number of positive descriptions, which in their length made them unusual for contemporary reviews of the Academy annuals. A *New York Times* critic wrote of the work's "primitive scheme of blue and yellow, its clear-cut patterning, its admirable accenting of windows throwing back the brilliant light, its veil of diffused steam caressing the fronts of the golden buildings and softening their color." He concluded with, "It is a beautiful picture and full of thought and science as well as feeling."[2] A writer for the *New York American* described the painting as "a vision" and the buildings as "golden dreams, rising from gold-laden waters to a blue empyrean, luminous with gold dust." He refused to interpret the work as "an ironical suggestion of Mammon worship" and maintained instead that "it is the glory of aspiration that the picture really symbolizes." His ending made the important point that, "notwithstanding the visionary suggestion, the physical elements in this picture convey a sense of reality."[3]

A critic for the *New York Sun* was also interested in meaning, an issue rarely discussed in reviews of the Academy's exhibitions. The financial district "bathed in golden light," the wharves "indicated in cold blues," and the river "filled with great masses of floating ice" made him suspect "a hint of allegory." Recalling Lie's

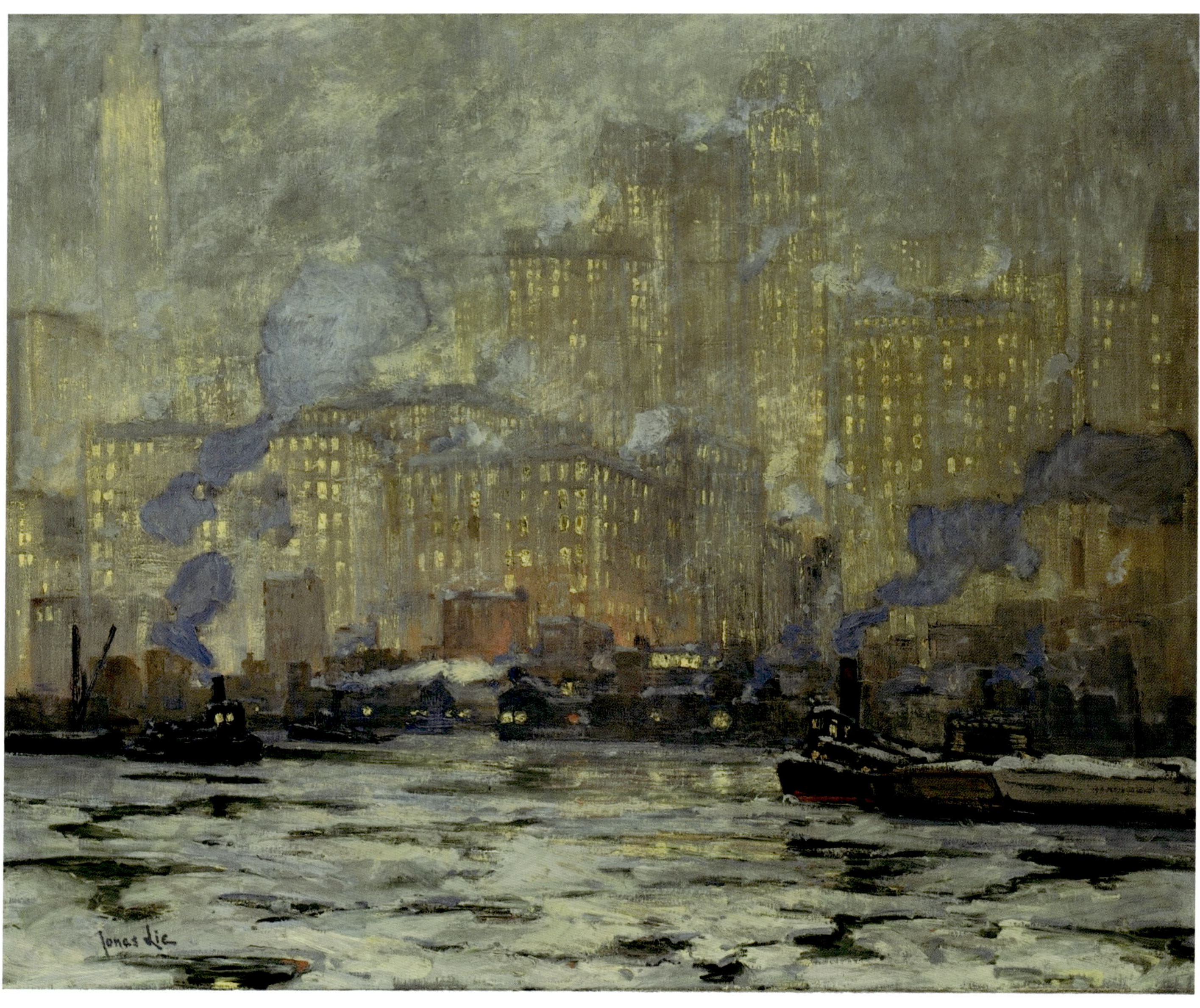

64

A Path of Gold, shown a few months earlier at the Academy's winter exhibition of 1913, he referred to the presence in it of the "same towers" and "same river" but indicated that in *A Path of Gold* "the dying sun had a glittering reflection in the water that pointed to the corner of Broad and Wall streets." In an effort to understand what Lie meant to teach in *Afterglow* ("this second lesson"), he asked: "Does the ice symbolize the hardships we must undergo before we get to the gold? Or does it merely mean that the further one gets from the financial centre the chillier it is?"[4]

Lie showed *Afterglow* during a period when he was also receiving other critical attention. In a review of his solo exhibition at the Folsom Galleries in New York in 1912, a writer for *American Art News* claimed that he had "carried his art to a higher plane than ever before" and then justified the brevity of his remarks with: "This artist's work has now become too well known to the American art public to need comment here."[5] Lie's solo show at Knoedler & Co. in 1914 had drawn considerable notice, in part because his subject in a series of large paintings

was the construction of the Panama Canal. In his review of the Academy's 1914 annual, a critic for the *New York World* referred to that series when writing that Lie had "spared from the wealth of tropical color he found along the Panama Canal to make an 'Afterglow' of New York's castled sky line."[6]   TAG

1. W. H. N. [W. H. de B. Nelson], "A Painter of Panama: Jonas Lie," *IS* 51 (February 1914): cxciv.

2. "Some Old Friends Shown at Vanderbilt Gallery," *NYT Magazine*, March 22, 1914: 11.

3. "Eighty-Ninth Annual Show, National Academy," *New York American*, March 23, 1914.

4. "Many New Artists in Spring Academy," *NYS*, March 21, 1914.

5. J. B. T. [James B. Townsend], "Exhibitions on Now: Works by Jonas Lie," *American Art News* 11 (December 21, 1912): 2.

6. "News of the Art World," *New York World*, March 22, 1914.

Horatio Walker, NA

Listowel, Ontario 1858–1938 Ile d'Orléans, Québec

91st Annual Exhibition, March 18–April 13, 1916, no. 103

De Profundis, 1916

Oil on canvas, 76 × 60

National Gallery of Canada, Ottawa, Ontario

Horatio Walker had been exhibiting with frequency for more than thirty years at the National Academy when he showed *De Profundis* in 1916. The work did not achieve the same level of success as had his *Ploughing—The First Gleam at Dawn* (no. 58) when it appeared in the annual of 1901; however, *De Profundis* was well received by certain critics and was selected for illustration in the exhibition catalogue.

Although the *American Art News* critic James B. Townsend called the painting "another 'poem of toil'" and offered both praise and criticism when describing it as the "best from

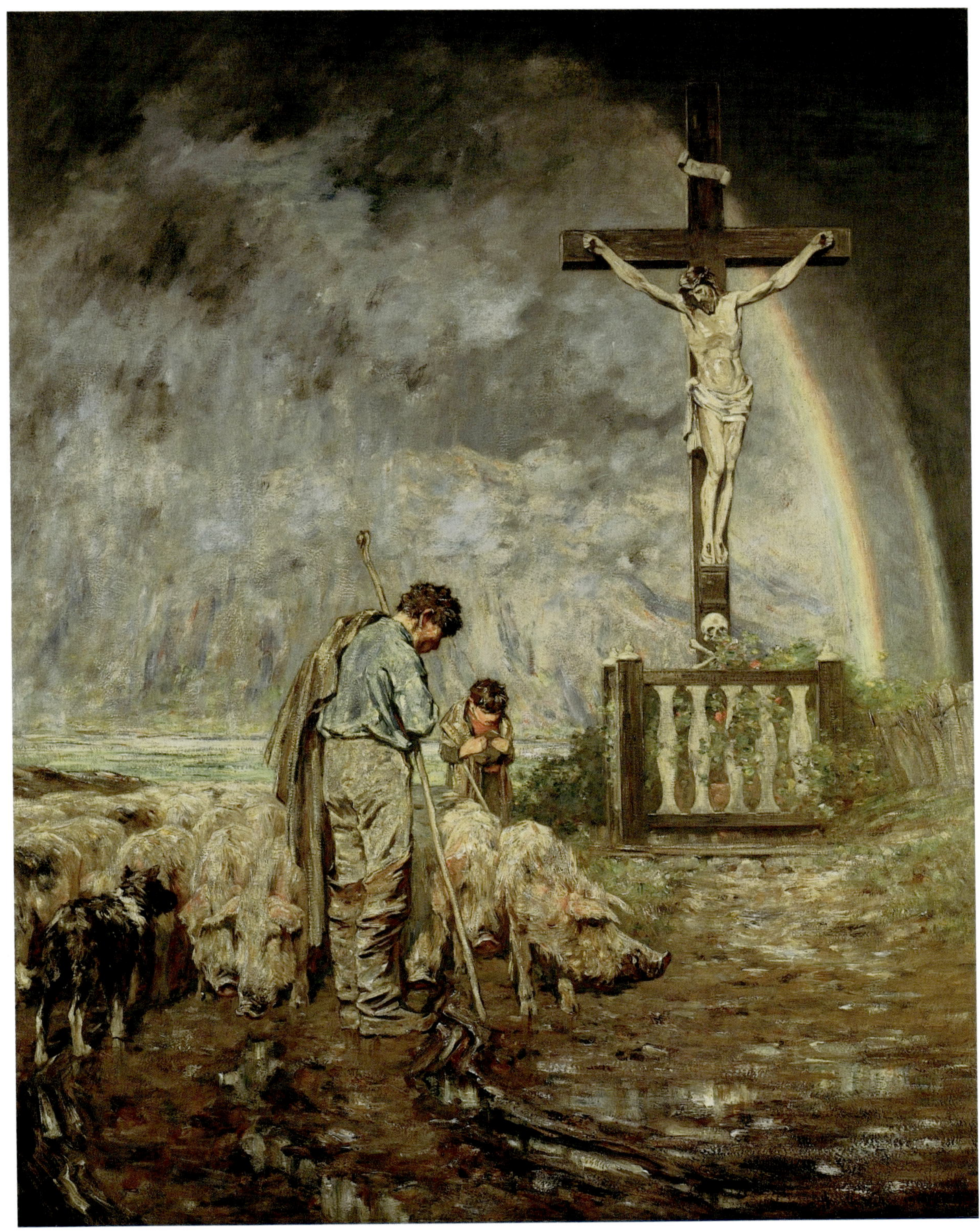

65

[Walker's] able brush in many a day,"[1] a colleague on the same paper, James Britton, was unqualifiedly enthusiastic. Britton began his review by declaring *De Profundis* "the most important picture shown at the Academy in years." The painting was proof for him that Americans had not "entirely forsaken" the "nobly serious field of religious painting." He saw this work as a demonstration that "the mind still exercises dominion over the hand" in painting and expressed his belief that Walker had felt "with genuine profundity the great sentiment of his theme." Not ignoring the artist's technique, he noted that, as usual, it was "masterly." To strengthen his point, he contrasted Walker's handling of paint with the "flaunting skill" of George Bellows. For Britton, Walker's approach was "rather an indigenous, humble capability of rendering dictated by intimate contact with nature." As far as Bellows was concerned, Britton complained that there had been "much blowing" about him. This was undoubtedly a reference to the critical response to the artist's *The Sawdust Trail* (no. 66), a large painting on view in the same annual. Bellows's depiction of gaudily dressed women fainting from excitement while behind them the evangelist Billy Sunday shakes hand with converts at a revival meeting in Philadelphia had its own religious elements but was a sharp contrast to Walker's painting.[2]

While Britton welcomed a work with a serious religious theme, a critic for the *New York Times* was certain that *De Profundis* would attract great attention for other reasons. This would occur in part because of the color, which he described as "striking" and having "the artist's characteristic quality of looking as through [*sic*] the light came from behind it through a translucent medium, such as glass." Attraction to the work would happen primarily, however, because "the man halting in front of the crucifix is a swineherder, and his flock of long-nosed swine are prominent in the foreground of the composition." The critic's point was: "It is the fillip of the unexpected given to a familiar subject which invariably proves arresting." In fact, the swine seem to have been what really interested him, for he went on to call them "really magnificent interpretations of porcine character." Oddly, the critic virtually ignored the religious dimension of the painting except to wonder why the rainbow (actually, two can be seen behind the crucifix) seemed "intrusive." His answer was that this is generally what occurs with "obvious symbolism."[3]

TAG

1. James B. Townsend, "The Spring Academy," *American Art News* 14 (March 18, 1916): 2.

2. James Britton, "Exhibitions Now On: The Spring Academy," *American Art News* 14 (April 1, 1916): 3.

3. "Academy Exhibits Its Prize Paintings," *NYT*, March 18, 1916.

66

George Wesley Bellows
Columbus, Ohio 1882–1925 New York, New York

91st Annual Exhibition, March 18–April 23, 1916, no. 132

The Sawdust Trail, 1916
Oil on canvas, 63 × 45⅛
Milwaukee Art Museum, Layton Art Collection

The *New York Sun's* published review of the National Academy of Design's annual exhibition of 1916 includes a subheading that reads "Bellows Hits the Trail." This was probably intended as a double-entendre, referring to the subject of *The Sawdust Trail* and Bellows's satirical treatment of it. The painting relates to a 1915 series of revival meetings in Philadelphia led by William Ashley ("Billy") Sunday (1862–1935). A former baseball player, Sunday had become a renowned evangelist whose activities were widely covered by the national press. When he called for converts during his revival meetings, hundreds of people would come down the aisles, which were covered with fresh sawdust, to shake hands with him. As seen in Bellows's painting, Sunday often lowered himself into an opening in the platform from which he preached so that he could reach down to his new converts. His wife, "Ma" Sunday, stands nearby, and his choirmaster, known for his flamboyant technique, leads an eighteen-hundred-voice choir in the interior of a huge tabernacle.[1] Swooning and weeping converts occupy much of the foreground.

The *Sun* critic declared *The Sawdust Trail* to be the best work in the exhibition, rating it higher than *The Spinner* by Thomas Eakins (c. 1878; Worcester Art Museum, Worcester, Massachusetts) and the award-winning *Pigeon Coop* by Ernest Lawson (private collection). He thought that the depiction of the events was "as stirring as any" reported by the newspapers and called it "the best thing in the way of satire" that Bellows had done. Appreciative of his ambition in tackling a subject requiring many figures, this critic placed Bellows among a dwindling group of painters who dared "to attack complicated problems." Although he regarded the color as "by no means good as color," its "crudity," he thought, added to "the effect of the burlesque." He also noted that the tall man "being labored with by exhorters" bore a "startling resemblance to Bellows."[2]

Other responses to the painting included a review in the *American Art News* by James Townsend, who dubbed it a "curious canvas," one "full of faults but yet appealing in its remarkable composition, study of character and fine sense of movement."[3] Writing for *International Studio*, W. H. de B. Nelson saw "a very entertaining canvas full of clever painting and observation," in which "lemon-coloured ladies in different stages of religious fervour [are] being propped up or ambulanced out by male enthusiasts."[4] A reviewer for the *New York Herald*, who mistakenly identified the choirmaster as Sunday, called the work "lurid" and noted that the "'trail hitters'" who were in "high emotional excitement" were being "administered to by the exhorter's assistants." He described the women who had fainted as "gaudy in ultra-modern dress, their faces ghastly in the bright light."[5]

The *American Art News* critic James Britton focused praise on another painting in the exhibition, Horatio Walker's *De Profundis* (no. 65), a more traditional representation of religious

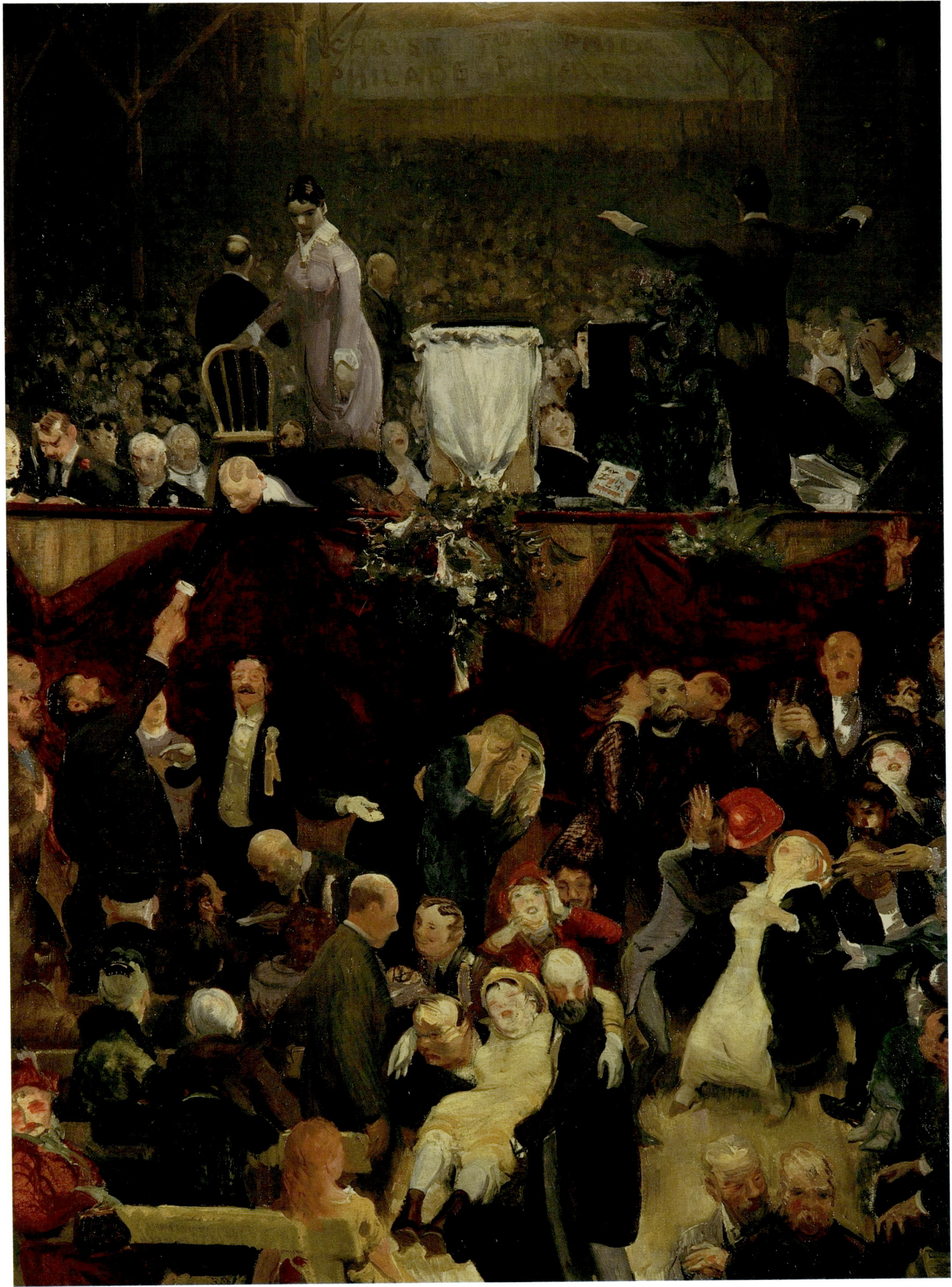

66

sentiment. He found Walker's "skill" different from "the flaunt-ing skill" seen in the painting by Bellows, about whom, Britton wrote, there had been "much blowing."[6]

Writing for the *New York Tribune*, Royal Cortissoz wondered why Bellows had painted a subject for which he had already made a drawing for an illustrated weekly and felt that the work remained "only an illustration."[7] He was referring to a drawing Bellows had made in 1915 on commission from *Metropolitan Magazine*. It and another by him were used as illustrations for an article written by the journalist John Reed on Billy Sunday and his revival meetings.[8] Except for the color, the painting is almost identical to the drawing. In 1917, the year after Bellows showed the painting at the Academy, he produced a lithograph that is likewise different only in some details.[9]

Bellows's satirical approach only hinted at his true feelings about the evangelist. In a 1917 interview for *Touchstone* magazine, he said that Sunday was "the worst thing that ever happened to America," that he was "death to imagination, to spirituality, to art" and "Prussianism personified." He went on: "His whole pur-pose is to force authority against beauty. He is against freedom, he wants a religious autocracy, he is such a reactionary that he makes me an anarchist. You can see why I like to paint him and his devastating 'saw-dust-trail.' I want people to understand him."[10]

TAG

1. For a discussion of this painting and further information about Sunday, see Marianne Doezema, "The 'Real' New York" in Michael Quick et al., *The Paintings of George Bellows* (New York: Harry N. Abrams, Inc., 1992), 121–26.

2. "National Academy Lacking in Thrills," *New York Sun*, March 19, 1916.

3. James B. Townsend, "The Spring Academy," *American Art News* 14 (March 18, 1916): 2.

4. W. H. de B. Nelson, "Springtime at the Academy," *International Studio* 58 (May 1916): xc.

5. "National Academy Opens Exhibition," *New York Herald*, March 18, 1916.

6. James Britton, "Exhibition Now On: The Spring Academy," *American Art News* 14 (April 1, 1916): 3.

7. Royal Cortissoz, "The Spring Show of the Academy of Design," *New York Tribune*, March 19, 1916.

8. John Reed, "Back of Billy Sunday," *Metropolitan Magazine* 42 (May 1915): 9–12, 66–72.

9. For information on the drawings and lithographs related to the painting, see Jane Myers and Linda Ayres, *George Bellows: The Artist and His Lithographs, 1916–1924* (Fort Worth: Amon Carter Museum of Western Art, 1988), 48–51, 53.

10. "The Big Idea: George Bellows Talks About Patriotism for Beauty," *Touchstone* 1 (July 1917): 270.

67

Frederick Childe Hassam, NA

Dorchester, Massachusetts 1859–1935 East Hampton, New York

Allies' Day: May, 1917, 93rd Annual Exhibition, March 13–April 21, 1918, no. 282

Allies Day, May 1917, 1917

Oil on canvas, 36¾ × 30¼
National Gallery of Art, Washington, D.C., Gift of Ethelyn McKinney in memory of her brother, Glenn Ford McKinney

The United States entered World War I in April of 1917. A year later, James B. Townsend, a critic for *American Art News*, noted the seeming haste of artists in making their selections for sub-mission to the National Academy's annual exhibition:

So many artists are in war service of various kinds, here or abroad, or have had their attention and interest diverted from their profession to and by the numerous and various appeals for 'target landscapes,' posters, etc., that there is a seeming sense in the galleries, of hasty preparation, and even of the searching of studio corners for any work that might pass muster and be at all representative to send in.[1]

A writer for the *New York Times* noted that only about half of the number of works usually submitted to the National Academy's annual exhibition were present in 1918 and speculat-ed that the dearth resulted either from war duty or from difficulties the war caused in transporting works.[2] From the *New York Tribune*, a critic commented with annoyance, "The influence of war has crept into art, many of the paintings show-ing khaki-clad figures, battlefields, torpedo boat destroyers and other picturesque sides of warfare."[3] A *New York Herald* reviewer gave a virtually contradictory opinion when he called the annu-al, in general, a "cheerful show" and remarked, "War has not cast its shadow over it, for the very few canvases that relate, directly or indirectly, to the conflict are negligible."[4]

The *Times* critic also gave extended praise to Childe Hassam's *Allies Day, May 1917*, which earned the Second Altman Prize, awarded annually to a landscape painting by an American-born citizen. He began by marveling that "anything so difficult as flags could be manipulated with such skill and produce such a really beautiful picture" and continued with a description of the flags and their colors:

There is the deep red of the large Union Jack directly in the foreground, the Stars and Stripes the flag a little larger, given its proper significance in the etiquette of flags, but with a modified color tone: the deep blue of the French Tricolor striking another deep note, and a wind-crumpled flag breaks the monotony of straight lines.[5]

The scene, he reminded the reader, was historic.

At least a few reviewers responded with little elaboration or faint praise when dealing with Hassam's work. One simply called it "brilliant in color."[6] Another described the color and light: "The gay, crude coloring of the flags is harmonized by a silvery light which quivers over the white façade of the buildings on which they are clustered, distilling a faint echo of their bril-liance."[7] Claiming that none of the best-known painters had "struck any new or resounding note" and that "No 'Modernist'

264 | RAVE REVIEWS

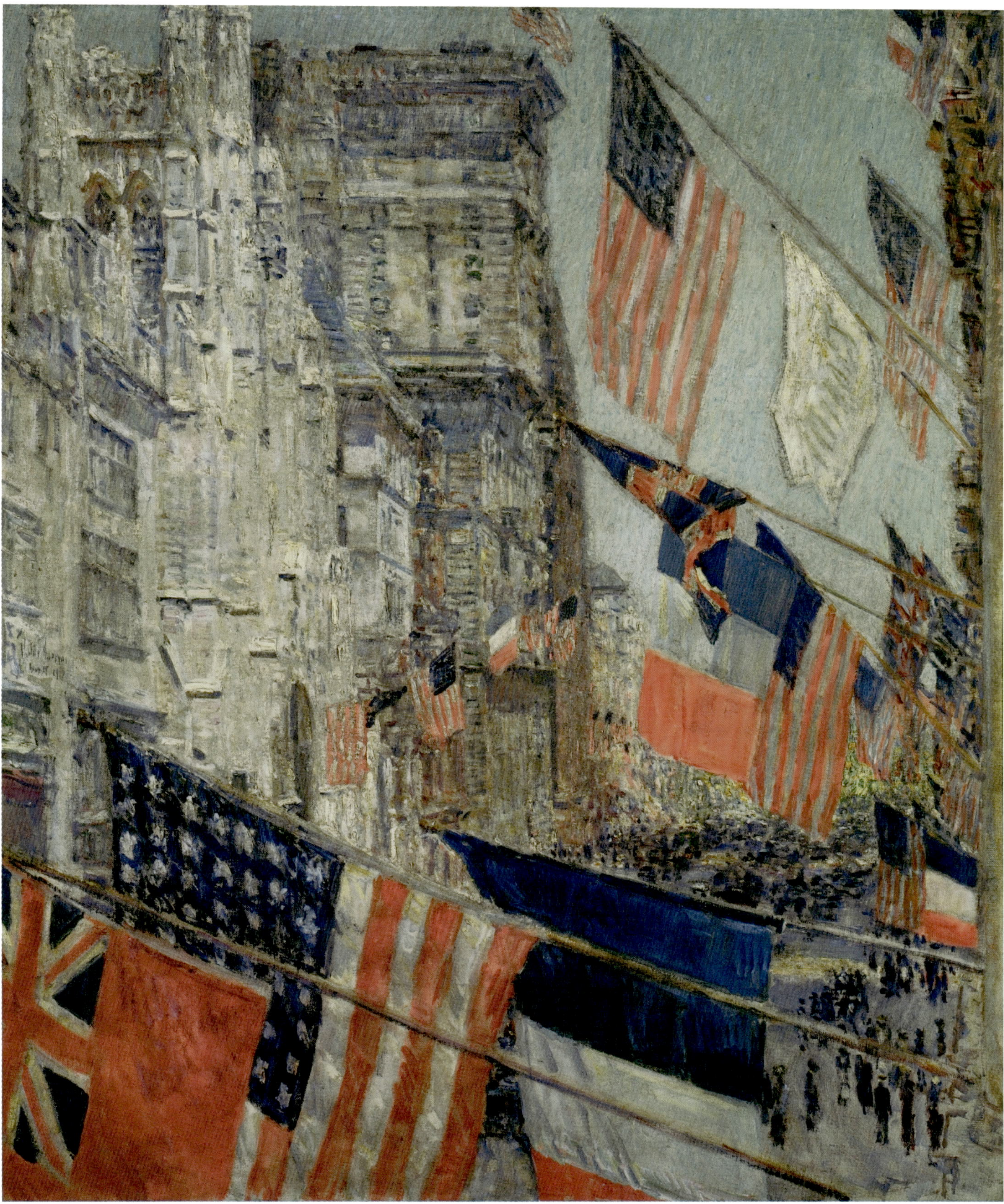

has another year invaded the old Academy," James Townsend referred to Hassam's work as "a clever rendition of strong colors in sunlight."[8] James Britton, his colleague at *American Art News*, restricted his analysis to "clever."[9]

Allies Day, May 1917, showing a view of Fifth Avenue in New York, was one of a group of flag paintings created by Hassam between 1916 and 1919.[10] Eight months after its appearance at the annual of 1918, he exhibited *To the 101st Massachusetts Infantry*

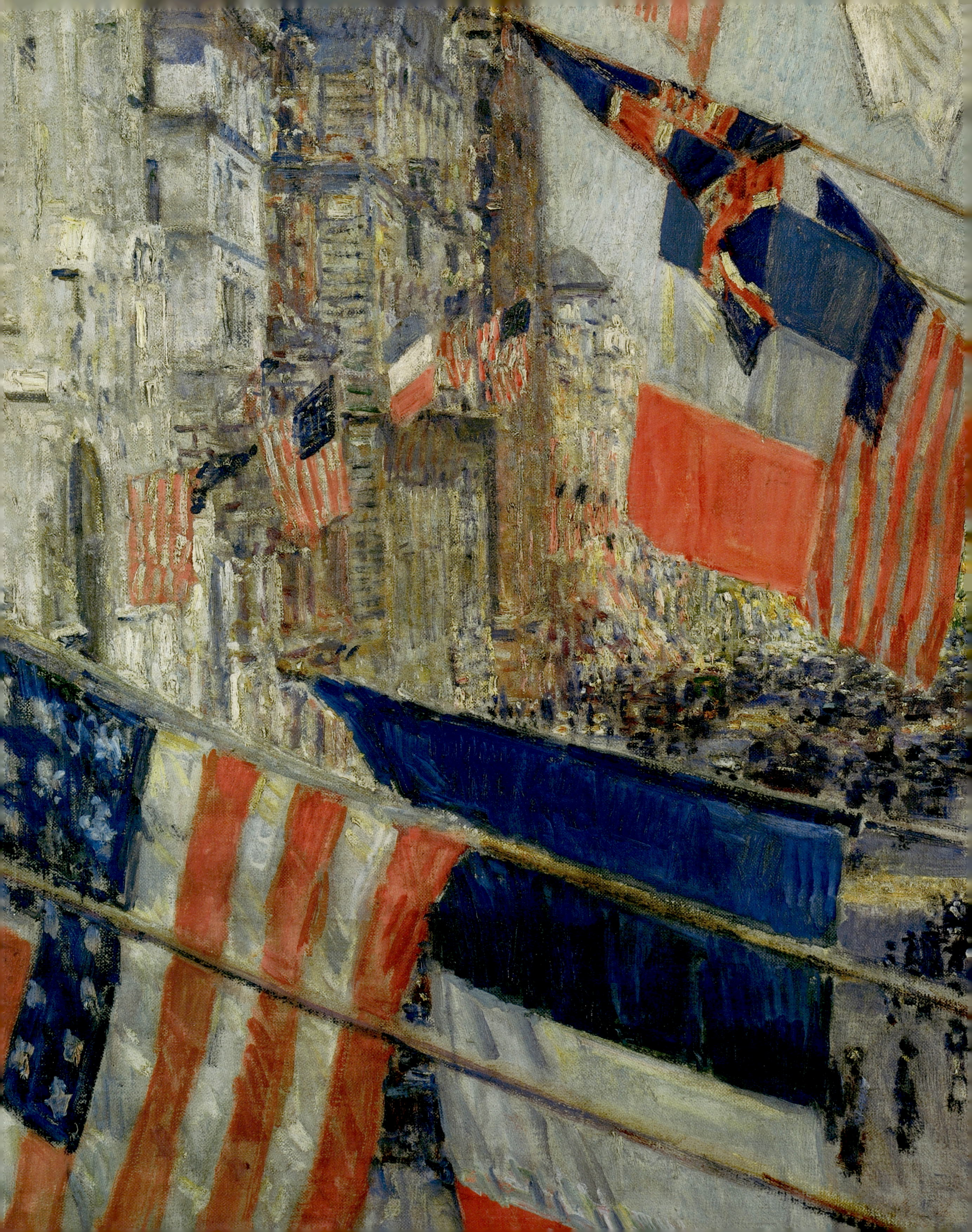

(1918; private collection) at the Academy's winter exhibition. A very different picture, in its depiction of a soldier speaking with a woman before a view of Gloucester, it was ignored by Royal Cortissoz, a writer for the *New York Tribune*, who nonetheless criticized Hassam's flag paintings in general. He pointed out that he had "long been favorably known as a painter of street scenes" but that, although patriotism and the expectation of greater beauty had led him to add a "multitude of flags," no beauty had resulted. With bluntness rarely seen in such reviews, he added: "His flag pictures are on the whole the coldest, least inspired things he ever did in his life."[11] Meanwhile, *Allies Day, May 1917* was becoming Hassam's most famous flag painting. It was the frontispiece for a book of poems by Alfred Noyes entitled *The Avenue of the Allies and Victory* (1918); reproductions of it were sold to help support the Art War Relief fund; and it was reproduced in color in a number of publications about New York or about the war.[12]   TAG

1. James B. Townsend, "A Wartime Academy," *American Art News* 16 (March 16, 1918): 1.

2. "Prize Winners of National Academy," *NYT*, March 13, 1918.

3. "Art," *NYDT*, March 13, 1918. Among the other paintings in the exhibition related to war were *Sacrifice* by Albert Herter, *Out of the West* by Henry Rankin Poore, and *For One of Our Boys* by Helen M. Turner.

4. Gustave Kobbé, "National Academy Opens Its Ninety-Third Annual Exhibition," *NYH*, March 17, 1918.

5. "Prize Winners," *NYT*, March 13, 1918.

6. "Art," *NYDT*, March 13, 1918.

7. "Academy of Design Opens Ninety-third Exhibition, *New York American*, March 13, 1918.

8. Townsend, 1–2.

9. James Britton, "A Wartime Academy," *American Art News* 16 (March 23, 1918): 2.

10. See Ilene Susan Fort, *The Flag Paintings of Childe Hassam* (Los Angeles: Los Angeles County Museum of Art, 1988), 15, 16, 46.

11. Royal Cortissoz, "Winter Exhibition of the Academy," *NYDT*, December 15, 1918. He did praise Hassam's *Tanagra* (1918; National Museum of American Art, Washington, D.C.), which held a place of honor.

12. Fort, 46.

68

Anna Vaughn Hyatt Huntington, NA
Cambridge, Massachusetts 1876–1973 Redding Ridge, Connecticut

Joan d'Arc, 95th Annual Exhibition, April 6–May 9, 1920, no. 890-A

Joan of Arc, 1915 §

Bronze, 49½ × 35 × 13

The National Arts Club, New York

Anna Hyatt became interested in Joan of Arc as the subject for a major sculpture in 1908.[1] In that year, she settled in Paris, where she rented the former studio of French sculptor Jules Dalou. Inspired by French culture and history, she began studying images of Joan of Arc and, from these, produced an equestrian figure of the saint. Heretofore, Hyatt had been an *animalier*—a sculptor of animals. Her *Joan of Arc* was her first major figural work. In 1910, the model for the sculpture was shown at the Paris

Salon, where it received an honorable mention. It was seen by art patron J. Sanford Saltus, an executive of Tiffany and Company, and with his help, Hyatt won the competition for a monument to be erected in New York to honor the 500th anniversary of Joan of Arc's birth. The life-size bronze sculpture was unveiled on Riverside Drive in New York in 1915 to universal acclaim.

In 1920, Hyatt sent a cast of the sculpture to the National Academy of Design's annual exhibition. Again, the conception was well received. James B. Townsend, writing for *American Art News*, for example, called it "striking."[2] At the Academy, it appropriately won the J. Sanford Saltus Gold Medal, an award established by the patron in 1908. This was the first of a number of awards Hyatt won at the Academy; in 1922, she won the Saltus Medal again, this time for her *Diana of the Chase* (1922; National Academy of Design). That recognition led to her election to membership in the Academy. A second full-scale replica of her *Joan of Arc* was installed in Blois, France, in 1921, and Hyatt was made a Chevalier of the Legion of Honor of France.   DBD

1. See Susan Harris Edwards, "Anna Hyatt Huntington: Sculptor and Patron of American Idealism" (M.A. thesis, University of South Carolina, 1979).

2 James B. Townsend, "Spring Academy in Brooklyn (First Notice)," *American Art News* 18 (April 10, 1920): 2.

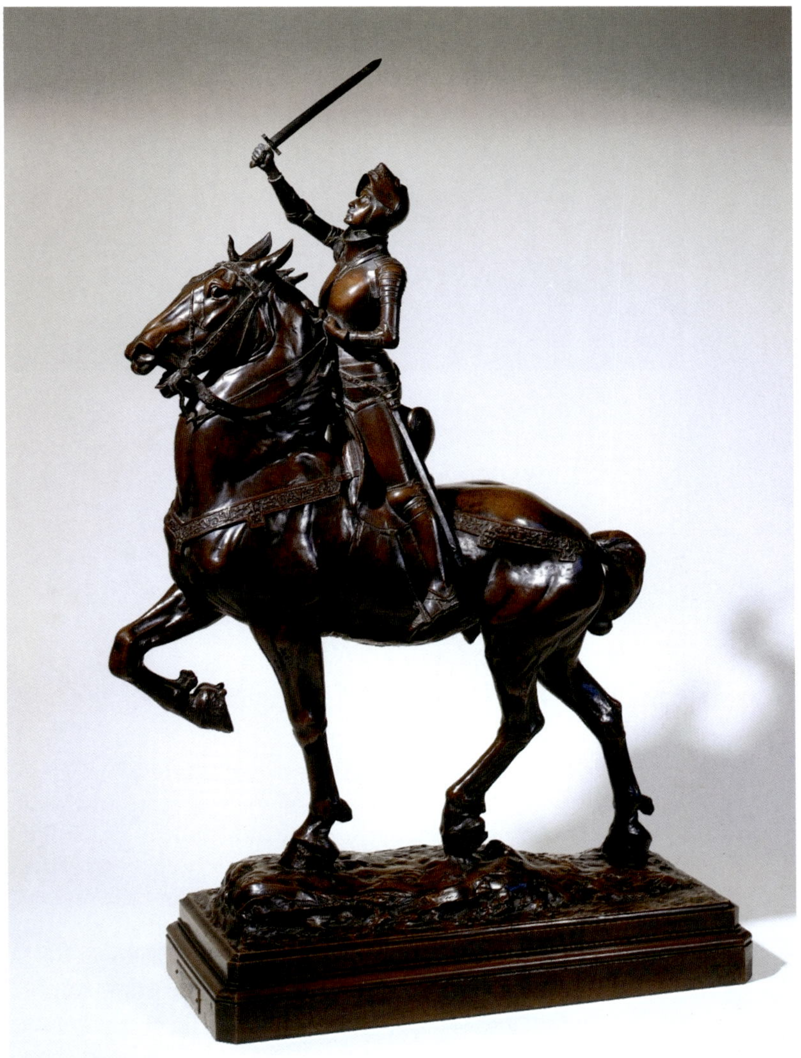

68

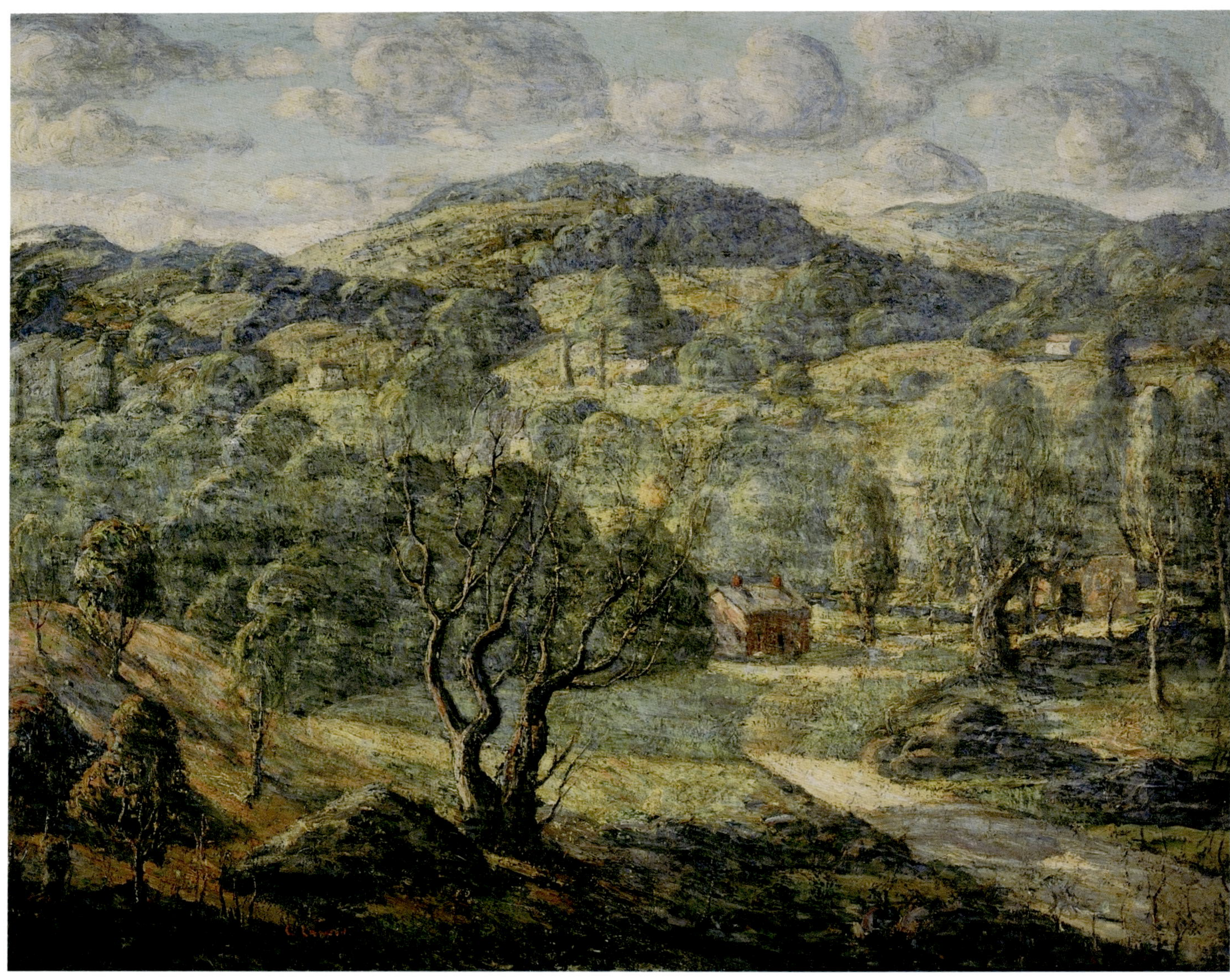

69

Ernest Lawson, NA

Halifax, Nova Scotia 1873–1939 near Miami, Florida

96th Annual Exhibition, March 5–April 3, 1921, no. 201

Vanishing Mist, c. 1916–21

Oil on canvas, 40 × 50

The Carnegie Museum of Art, Carnegie Institute Purchase

Vanishing Mist was one of Ernest Lawson's best-received works. In 1921, it earned the gold medal at the Carnegie Institute's "Twentieth Annual International" exhibition and the First Altman Prize, given for a landscape by an American-born citizen, at the National Academy of Design's annual. Before the year was out, the Carnegie Institute had acquired the painting.[1]

A critic for the *New York Times* gave an extended paragraph to the work, combining praise and lengthy description. With a poetic voice, he began by observing that, "in its pearly floating color," the work was "like a huge opal set in gold"; it illustrated "the power of color to turn artistic prose into artistic poetry." He continued: "His trees and shrubs and boulders climb up the shoulders of his mighty hill, his clouds roll into billows behind its crest, his foreground lies as an obedient hound at his master's word." Indicating one of the ways in which Lawson differed from the Impressionists—his interest in greater solidity of form—he observed that the artist "modeled his hills with a strong and certain touch, boss and hollow rising and sinking up to long hillside in plastic rectitude."[2]

Not so favorably disposed, another *New York Times* critic noted that both Lawson and Robert Spencer, the winner of the Second Altman Prize for landscape that year, had painted better works. Lawson's picture was "less rich than usual in color" and had the appearance of being "niggled with small brushes." What reader would not pause at the latter phrase? The critic did concede that Lawson "can always be relied upon for going after what poetry there is in the 'motif.'"[3] Far more positive was the one sentence given to Lawson's painting by a reviewer for *American Art News*. He described the work as "high-keyed" and "joyous" and added that it was done in his "later and most appealing manner," presumably a reference to Lawson's use of more brilliant color and richer impasto beginning about 1910.[4]

Had the painter/writer Guy Pène du Bois been a reviewer of

the Academy's 1921 annual, Lawson's *Vanishing Mist* would sure-ly have attracted even more attention than it did. In his monograph on the painter published eleven years later, du Bois went so far as to call the work "one of the greatest American landscapes." He also maintained that it "has the lyric peace and quality of a Giorgione."[5]

Lawson exhibited at least once annually at the Academy from 1905 through 1939, and a work was shown posthumously the next year as well. Of the seven awards that he received over the years at the Academy, the first was given to him at the 1908 annual when Lawson and other members of The Eight were invited to submit work after their successful exhibition at the Macbeth Gallery in New York, which had opened a month earlier. Before 1908 had elapsed, Lawson was made an Associate member of the Academy, some vindication since his nomination in 1905 had led to rejection.   TAG

1. For a summary of Lawson's career and a discussion of *Vanishing Mist*, see Diana Strazdes, et al., *American Paintings and Sculpture to 1945 in the Carnegie Museum of Art* (New York: Hudson Hills Press, 1992), 313–14.

2. "Prize Paintings Viewed by Crowd," *NYT*, March 5, 1921.

3. "Academy of Design Exhibition to Open to Public To-day," *NYT*, March 5, 1921.

4. James B. Townsend, "Annual Academy Display," *American Art News* 19 (March 5, 1921): 4.

5. Guy Pène du Bois, *Ernest Lawson* (New York: Whitney Museum of American Art, 1932), 10.

70
Edward Hopper
New York, New York 1882–1967 New York, New York

97th Annual Exhibition, March 25–April 23, 1922, no. 336

American Landscape, 1920
Etching, 7½ × 12½

Whitney Museum of American Art, New York, Bequest of Josephine N. Hopper

In 1920, the National Academy of Design introduced a new feature to its annual exhibitions: a room devoted to works on paper or, as it was commonly referred to at the time, a "black-and-white room."[1] The innovation was immediately recognized as part of a revitalization of the Academy's exhibitions, which, some thought, had been adversely affected by World War I. The *New York Herald,* for example, commented on the "increased liveliness in the atmosphere of the galleries," possibly an indication that "the artists were beginning to shake off the lethargy caused by the war."[2] In the first of these exhibitions in 1920, the inclusion of works on paper prompted critic Peyton Boswell, writing for the *New York American,* to call it "the biggest display of contemporary art that this country has ever seen, and very likely the best...."[3] James B. Townsend at the *American Art News* thought that the inclusion of the 203 "black and whites" that year was "an excellent move" that allowed the exhibition "truly [to] be called a National Salon."[4]

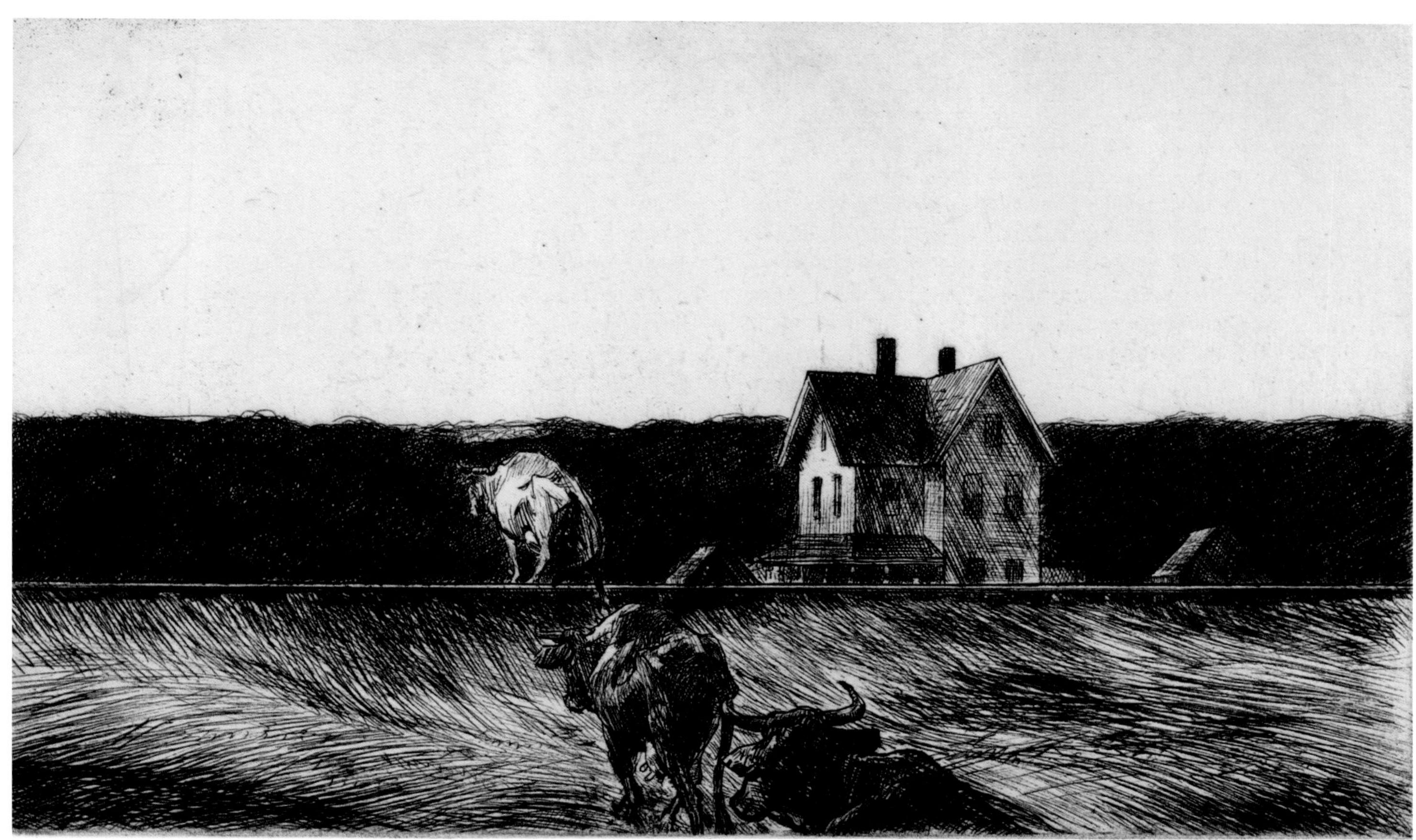

70

The initial success of this innovation evidently encouraged the Academicians to continue it. The next year, 1921, works on paper made up about one-third of the total objects displayed. Especially impressive here were a large lithograph by Joseph Pennell and a group of etchings by Childe Hassam.[5] The grouping pleased some critics, too, because it was relegated to a room that had formerly been used for the display of paintings and sculptures that were the least favorite works of those permitted into the exhibition by the Academy's jurors. That practice had earned the room the title of "the morgue," and the press was generally pleased to see it replaced with the more positive arrangement of works on paper.[6]

The exhibition of 1922 was especially lauded for its inclusion of etchings, engravings, drawings, and prints. A writer for the *New York Tribune* remarked on the difficult but excellent job done by the Academy's jury of selection in choosing the works. Over one thousand had been submitted for consideration, the critic reported, and 422 had been selected. This still considerable number meant that the four galleries in the Fine Arts Building on West 57th Street where the exhibition was held were filled to capacity. Nevertheless, the critic concluded, the arrangement was well "within the limits of good taste."[7]

Among the paintings that received the most attention at the Academy in 1922 were Frank Benson's *Still-Life Decoration* (1922; Art Institute of Chicago) and Daniel Garber's *Tohickon* (1922; National Museum of American Art, Smithsonian Institution, Washington, D.C.) which won the coveted Benjamin Altman Prize in the exhibition. These works were commented on by almost every critic who wrote about the show, but many attended, too, to the installation of works on paper. Critic Peyton Boswell, writing for the *New York American,* believed that the black-and-white group was a "distinguishing mark" of the exhibition and pointed out the work of Helen M. Fanung, Ross Santee, F. Luis Mora, Clifford Adams, and Childe Hassam, among others, in this category.[8]

A writer for the *American Art News* was especially impressed with the inclusion of works on paper in the Academy's annual that year. "After looking at the attractive display of black-and-white pictures in the Academy Room in the Fine Arts Building," he wrote, "no one can say in justice that the National Academy of Design does not respond to new movements and impulses; for this section of the ninety-seventh annual exhibition of our oldest art society is the outstanding feature of the show . . . ." He then reminded his readers that, only a few years before, the Academy would not have considered giving space in its exhibitions to such works. "But now," he marveled, "in response to the arguments of workers in the mediums coming under this general classification, it has arranged the most interesting exhibition of this kind of the current season." He pointed out that among the 130 works on paper in the show were examples by many well-known artists as well as some of newcomers. These included Ross Santee, F. Luis Mora, Clifford Adams, William Auerbach Levy, Childe Hassam, and Edward Hopper.[9] The mention of Hopper in this "exhibition within an exhibition" that the Academy organized in 1922 is interesting. The artist never participated in the Academy's exhibitions as a painter, nor did he have any association with the institution or its school. Nevertheless, once the Academy began including works on paper in its juried annuals, Hopper evidently felt more comfortable submitting works to them, which he did for a number of years during the 1920s. DBD

1. The most recent index of the catalogues of the National Academy's annual exhibition does not include the works on paper that were part of these shows. See Peter Hastings Falk, *The Annual Exhibition Record of the National Academy of Design* (Madison, Connecticut: Sound View Press, 1990).

2. "National Academy Opens Its Spring Exhibition of Art," *NYH*, March 25, 1922.

3. Peyton Boswell, "Arts Academy Has Record Exhibit," *New York American*, April 8, 1920. The exhibition consisted of about 956 objects, making it the largest annual exhibition ever sponsored by the Academy. The main reason that it could be so large was that it was held at the Brooklyn Museum. That institution had offered its galleries for use by the Academy when a fire devastated the rooms at the Fine Arts Building on West 57th Street in Manhattan, where the Academy had been holding its exhibitions since 1900.

4. James B. Townsend, "Spring Academy in Brooklyn," *American Art News* 18 (April 10, 1920): 1.

5. David Lloyd, "Prints on Display at Academy and Library," *NYEP*, March 5, 1921.

6. "Academy of Design Exhibition to Open to Public To-day," *NYH*, March 5, 1921.

7. "422 Pictures Hung in 97th Spring Academy," *NYDT*, March 25, 1922.

8. Peyton Boswell, "Annual Exhibition of Academy of Design Opens," *New York American*, March 25, 1922.

9. "National Academy Opens 97th Annual," *American Art News* 20 (March 25, 1922): 1

71

Guy Rose

San Gabriel, California 1867–1925 Pasadena, California

Rocks and Sea: Point Lobos, 98th Annual Exhibition, March 17–April 1, 1923, no. 26

Point Lobos, c. 1918

Oil on canvas, 24 × 29

Private collection, courtesy of The Irvine Museum, Irvine, California

From its inception, the National Academy of Design attempted to live up to its name. The word *design* would have been understood in the nineteenth century to mean the traditional fine arts—painting, sculpture, and architecture—which are based on the art of drawing. The word *national* was more problematic. The desires of the founders of the Academy in this regard were made clear in the catalogue of the institution's first annual exhibition. There, in 1826, they declared their hopes that the Academy would benefit "all Artists throughout the United States."[1] Whatever they may have proposed in theory, however, was not really carried out in practice, at least at first. This stated geographical inclusiveness was impeded by the Academy's own regulations, spelled out in its early constitutions, which required full members of the Academy to reside in New York City. Non-residents could only attain Honorary Membership, a category that was just that: membership in name only without any benefits, other than the "honor," or responsibilities. This rather strict residency requirement was not remedied until 1870 when, after decades of criticism about the geographic limitations of the Academy, it was removed from the constitution. Although recognizable results from this change were slow in the coming, by around 1900 more and more artists from across the nation were submitting works of art to the Academy's annual exhibitions and, in some cases, being elected to membership in the organization.

A case in point is Californian Guy Rose, who might stand here

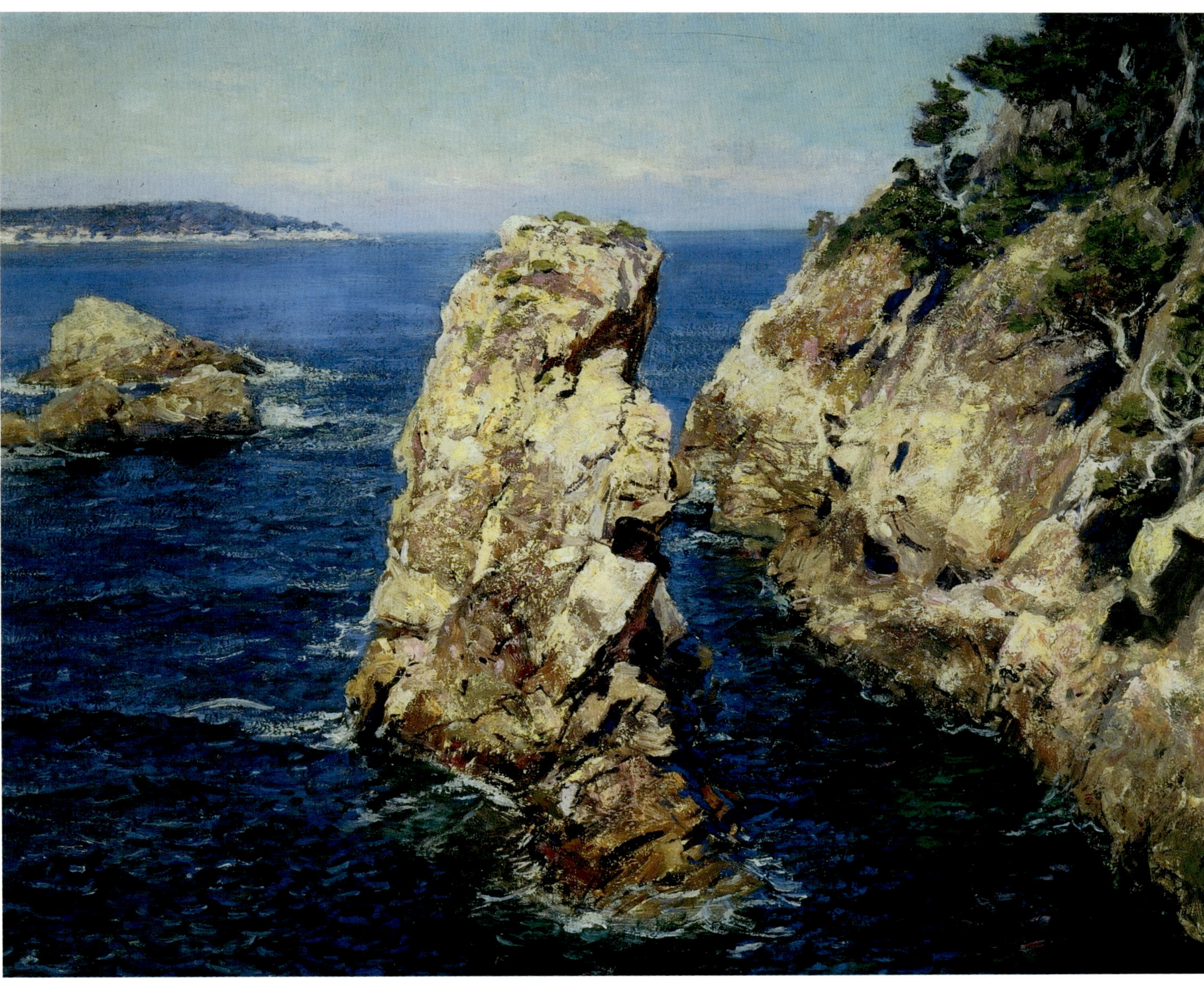

71

as evidence of the Academy's attempts to be more inclusive.[2] Despite his life-long affiliation with his native state, Rose was one of an increasing number of non-New Yorkers who exhibited works at the Academy in the first several decades of the twentieth century. Beginning in 1910, he sent several paintings to the Academy's annuals from Giverny, France, where he was living and working. The first of these was *November Twilight,* which was exhibited at the Academy in 1910. This was followed by a painting entitled simply *November,* which Rose sent to the annual exhibition in 1911, and one called *September Morning,* which was in the Academy's winter exhibition that same year. Rose actually had a brief residency in New York beginning in 1912 and sent works to the Academy's shows in each of the next two years; but he returned to California at the end of 1914 and did not participate in the Academy's annuals again until 1923. In that year, however, he sent a major painting to the Academy, *Rocks and Sea: Point Lobos,* as it was called at the time, which also happened to be the only painting with a California subject that Rose submitted to these exhibitions.[3]

Judging by contemporary reviews of the 1923 exhibition, the organization's goal to make itself truly "national" had been achieved and, finally, was beginning to receive some recognition.

The *New York Tribune,* for example, touted the event as "a national exhibition" and lauded it as "the most venerable and venerated of American art events of the year." The critic was especially impressed with a large group of paintings by "the Taos (New Mexico) group" that included Oscar E. Berninghaus, Walter Ufer, Ernest L. Blumenshein and Julius Rolshaven.[4] The participation of these western artists, along with that of Californians such as Rose and others, would, in the following decades, help to give the Academy the broader geographical scope that it had sought from its inception.   DBD

1. *Catalogue of Pictures, Busts, Architectural Designs & Engravings, in the First Exhibition of the National Academy of the Arts of Design* (New York: D. Fanshaw, 1826), n.p.

2. The definitive study of Rose is Will South, *Guy Rose, American Impressionist* (Oakland and Irvine, California: The Oakland Museum and The Irvine Museum, 1995).

3. See David B. Dearinger, "The National Academy: A California Perspective," in *All Things Bright and Beautiful: California Impressionist Paintings from The Irvine Museum* (Irvine, California: The Irvine Museum, 1998), 141–50.

4. "Annual National Academy Opens Doors To-day," *NYDT,* March 17, 1923. The Taos group was again praised in the *Tribune* by critic Royal Cortissoz (Royal Cortissoz, "Pictures in the Spring Academy," *NYDT,* March 25, 1923).

Appendix A: The Critics

D A V I D   B .   D E A R I N G E R

Deciding who deserves the title "critic" is not always easy, and even the distinction between art historian and critic is often blurred. When does a writer cease to be a historian and become a critic or vice versa? Should the term *critic* be reserved for those writing about the art of their own time, while *historian* be used for those writing about the art of the past? Likewise, at what point does a journalist stop being a reporter and become a critic?

With the intent of leaving these questions for others to answer definitively, brief biographies of selected nineteenth- and early twentieth-century critics are provided here. This group includes major writers who, for part or all of their careers, thought of themselves and were considered by the public to be professional critics. On the whole, their writings were available to a wide audience. This list is not meant to be comprehensive; instead, it focuses on writers who have been mentioned in the essays in this book, but not even all of them are included. Others who could be added are Russell Sturgis, Jr. (1836–1909), Sylvester R. Koehler (1837–1900), Earl Shinn (1838–1886), Eugene Benson (1839–1908), William C. Brownell (1851–1928), William A. Coffin (1855–1925), John C. Van Dyck (1856–1932), Elizabeth Luther Cary (1867–1936), Christian Brinton (1870–1942), Frank Jewett Mather (1868–1953), and Mary Fanton Roberts (1864–1956).

John Neal (1793–1876)

John Neal spent much of his life in his native Portland, Maine, remaining prolific throughout his long career. He was an essayist, novelist, poet, and editor, and is often called America's first art critic. In his witty, often biting style, he strove to do what he believed a critic should do: educate the public. His earliest critical writings appeared in his novel *Randolph* (1823), in which he included commentary on Gilbert Stuart, Rembrandt Peale, and other contemporary American artists. In 1824 he went to London and, pretending to be British, managed to publish a series of literary articles in *Blackwood's Edinburgh Magazine*. After traveling in Europe, he returned to America in 1827. The following year he became editor of the *Yankee*, which soon merged with the *Boston Literary Gazette*. Many of Neal's best essays and exhibition reviews appeared in the publication that resulted—appropriately if unimaginatively titled the *Yankee; and Boston Literary Gazette*. He edited the magazine until 1829. Later, for brief periods in the 1840s, he was editor of the *New England Galaxy* and *Brother Jonathan,* and in the 1860s contributed articles on American artists to *Atlantic Monthly*. Like most early nineteenth-century American writers on art, Neal concentrated more on content than style. Nevertheless, he believed that the freer brushwork of artists such as Gilbert Stuart and Thomas Sully was preferable to the more finished style of Benjamin West or Rembrandt Peale.[1]

George Pope Morris (1802–1864)

A native of Philadelphia, George Pope Morris moved, in his teens, to New York City, where he lived the rest of his life. His earliest employment was in a printing house and, at fifteen, he was contributing poems to the *New York Gazette*. Within a few years, he was also writing novels and lyrics for popular songs. His most successful work in the former category was *Brier Cliff,* which was published in 1826 and made into a popular stage play the following year. His best-known poem remains "Woodman, Spare That Tree," published in 1830. Of the several collections of his poems, the best known is *The Deserted Bride*, first published in 1838 and reissued five years later in an edition with illustrations by Robert W. Weir and John Gadsby Chapman. His collection *Songs and Ballads* was published in 1844 and was an immediate success. In 1823, Morris founded the *New-York Mirror,* one of the most popular literary journals of its day, and he served as its publisher and art critic until 1846. He then served, for a brief time, as editor of the *Home Journal*.[2]

John Durand (1822–1908)

A son of painter Asher Brown Durand, John Durand was born in New York City and died in Paris. With William J. Stillman, he founded the *Crayon*, this country's first true art magazine, in 1855. He wrote a number of books, including a biography of his father (1894), and translated the work of French historian Hippolyte Taine, notably *Ideal in Art* (1868), *Italy, Rome, and Naples* (1869), and *Art of Greece* (1871). He was made an Honorary Member of the National Academy of Design in 1854.

George William Curtis (1824–1892)

George William Curtis was born in Providence, Rhode Island, and moved with his family to New York in 1839. In 1842, he and his brother joined the Utopian community of Brook Farm in West Roxbury, Massachusetts, remaining there for eighteen months. Four years later, Curtis traveled in Italy, Germany, and the Middle East, and then joined the staff of the *New York Daily Tribune* in 1850. He was also one of the founding editors of *Putnam's Monthly* in 1852 and, the next year, began writing a column, "The Editor's Easy Chair," for *Harper's Monthly*. In 1857, he became the leading editorial writer for *Harper's Weekly*. He was a brilliant orator and used his skills to promote various Republican Party candidates, including Abraham Lincoln. He served as a delegate from New York State to a number of national conventions and remained active in politics for the rest of his life. Among his books are *Nile Notes of Howadji* (1851), *Lotus-Eating* (1852), *Potiphar Papers* (1853), and *Trumps* (1862).[3]

James Jackson Jarves (1818–1888)

James Jackson Jarves was a writer, collector, connoisseur, art dealer, diplomat, and critic. As an author, he had no interest in Colonial American art, feeling that American art history really begins with Washington Allston. Although he admired Thomas Cole for introducing historical elements into his landscapes, Jarves generally disliked American landscape painting, especially that of the American Pre-Raphaelites. The future of American art, he thought, lay in the work of artists such as John La Farge and George Inness. Jarves expounded these and other ideas in the five books he wrote, particularly in *Art Hints* (1855), *The Art Idea* (1864), and *Art Thoughts* (1869). He is better known today as one of the earliest collectors of pre-Renaissance Italian paintings; he eventually gave his collection to Yale University.[4]

William James Stillman (1828–1901)

William James Stillman was a painter, journalist, art critic, and photographer. He studied painting with Frederic Edwin Church during the winter of 1848–49, then went to England where he met John Ruskin and Dante Gabriel Rossetti, among others. Two years later, in Paris, he met Eugène Delacroix, Paul Delaroche, Jean-Leon Gérôme, and other leading French artists. At the same time, he became deeply interested in politics and religion, notably transcendentalism. His experiences and wide interests prepared him to write about art, which he began doing for the *New York Evening Post* in 1854 and sporadically over the next few years. He eventually published in the *Nation* and the *Atlantic* in this country and the *Cornhill Magazine* in England. With John Durand, he was a founder and editor in 1855 of the *Crayon*, the first true art journal in the United States. Meanwhile, Stillman continued to paint and to exhibit pictures at the National Academy of Design and elsewhere. Because of his adherence to the teachings of John Ruskin, which were evident in both his paintings and his writings, he was known for a time as *the American Pre-Raphaelite*. He spent his later years in Rome and in England where he died.[5]

Clarence Cook (1828–1900)

Clarence Cook was arguably the most influential American art critic of the nineteenth century; he was certainly one of the most prolific. He studied at Harvard College and, under the influence of Henry Wadsworth Longfellow, began writing and publishing poetry during his college years. After graduation in 1849, he went to New York where he began to write art criticism. In 1854, he was hired as the art critic for the *Independent,* while also writing articles for *Putnam's Monthly*. He left the former periodical in 1856 and, in 1863, became editor of the *New Path*. The following year he became the art critic for the *New-York Daily Tribune,* the most prestigious newspaper in the country. Over the next twenty years, Cook penned hundreds of articles on almost every aspect of the fine arts. After his dismissal from the *Tribune* in 1883, he edited the art journal the *Studio* from 1884 to his retirement in 1893.[6]

Charles De Kay (1848–1935)

Charles De Kay was the principal art critic for the *New-York Times* from 1876 to 1894, and most exhibition reviews published by that newspaper in those years are presumed to be by him. His faith in American art seems to have grown steadily during his years as the *Times* critic, and he was a great promoter of American art organizations, including the National Sculpture Society and the National Arts Club. He was in Germany from 1894 to 1897, but on his return to New York continued to contribute articles to the *Times*, although with less frequency. During those years, he wrote about the sculpture of Paul Bartlett, major private art collections such as those of William T. Evans and Thomas B. Clarke, and French and American Impressionism.[7]

Mariana Griswold Van Rensselaer (1851–1934)

The most influential woman of the American art critics of the last quarter of the nineteenth century, Mariana Griswold was born into a wealthy and socially prominent Connecticut family. Her father took the family to Germany in 1868, and it was in Dresden that she was educated. Her grounding in art was thorough. She was exposed to the writings of German intellectuals such as Johann Winckelmann and Johann Wolfgang von Goethe, and to Europe's great museums. In 1873, she married Schuyler Van Rensselaer, a member of another prominent American family, and they returned to New York. Her earliest writings were poems, published in *Harper's* during the 1870s, but she also began to write art criticism in that decade. With the support of her early mentor, critic Sylvester R. Koehler, her production in this regard increased after the premature death of her husband in 1884. She wrote for *Lippincott's Monthly Magazine, American Architect and Building News,* and *American Art Review,* among other periodicals, and she was a regular contributor to the *Independent* from 1886 to 1889, the *New York World* from 1892 to 1898, and the *Boston Evening Transcript* in 1892. In these and other writings, she often concentrated on themes such as the patronage of art. She wrote a number of exhibition catalogues and books, notably *Book of the American Figure Painters* (1886), in which she concentrated on the development of American art during the previous ten years, and several definitive works on the American architect Henry Hobson Richardson. During her lifetime, she was probably best known for her two-volume *History of the City of New York in the Seventeenth Century* (1909).[8]

Charles Caffin (1854–1918)

Born in England, Charles Caffin matriculated at Oxford University where he studied art and met John Ruskin, who was Slade Professor there at the time. Following a trip to Europe in the early 1880s, Caffin worked in the London theater as an actor and manager. He married in 1888 and four years later took his family to the United States. He was employed as a muralist and decorative artist at the World's Columbian Exposition in Chicago, an experience that brought him into contact with many of the leading American artists of the day. These contacts served him well when, in 1897, he moved to New York, where he became a full-time professional critic. He subsequently served as art critic for the *New York Evening Post* (1897–1900), the *New York Sun* (1901–1904), and the *New York American* (1913–1918). He wrote for

Harper's Weekly (1897–1901) and *International Studio* (1901–1905) and published many books on European and American art, including *American Masters of Painting* (1902), *American Masters of Sculpture* (1903), and *The Story of American Painting* (1907).[9]

Kenyon Cox (1856–1919)

Kenyon Cox was a successful artist, but he also had a career as a writer and respected art critic. He began his art studies at the McMicken School of Design in Cincinnati and the Pennsylvania Academy of the Fine Arts in Philadelphia. In 1877, he went to Paris where he studied with Emile Carolus-Duran and at the Ecole des Beaux-Arts with Alexandre Cabanel and Jean-Leon Gérôme. On his return to the United States, he settled in New York where he illustrated articles for *Century* and *Scribner's* and, beginning in 1884, taught at the Art Students League. He wrote his first art criticism while in Europe and, to supplement his income once he was in New York, he took a job as an art critic with the *Nation*. It was the beginning of a long career as a critic, author, and lecturer. His work appeared in a number of major periodicals and newspapers, including *Harper's, North American Review, Cosmopolitan, Century,* and, notably, the *New York Evening Post.* Many of his essays were eventually anthologized in several books including *Old Masters and New* (1905) and *The Classic Point of View* (1911).[10]

James Huneker (1857–1921)

Huneker has been called the most enlightened American art critic of the early twentieth century. His art education was greatly enhanced when, during an elopement trip he made to Paris in 1878, he met Monet, Degas, and other Impressionists. He joined the staff of the *New York Sun* in 1900 as music and drama critic. In 1906, William Laffan, editor of that newspaper, named him its chief art critic. Huneker promoted the work of the Symbolists and praised Henri Matisse and other avant-garde artists whose works were shown at Alfred Steiglitz's "291" gallery in New York. Huneker was also a supporter of American artists such as Marsden Hartley, John Marin, and Alfred Maurer, and wrote favorable reviews of the exhibitions of The Eight.[11]

Sadakichi Hartmann (1867–1944)

Sadakichi Hartmann was born to a Japanese father and an American mother. He founded two journals in the 1890s, *The Art Critic* and *Art News,* in which he fostered an indigenous American art and promoted artists such as Arthur B. Davies, Arthur Wesley Dow, Robert Henri, and George Luks. He was especially interested in the French Symbolist movement and promoted its American counterpart through his journals. Hartmann also admired American artists of the previous generation—Dwight Tryon, Thomas Dewing, and James Whistler, for example—whom he saw as precursors of modernism. His books include *A History of American Art,* published in Boston in 1901, and *Modern American Sculpture,* published in New York in 1918. Both were largely culled from articles he had published previously. At times, he wrote under the pseudonym of Sidney Allan.

Royal Cortissoz (1869–1948)

Cortissoz evidently educated himself in the arts, but his interest in the field was undoubtedly influenced when he was apprenticed as an office boy in the architectural firm of McKim, Mead and White. In 1889, he was hired as a writer for the *New York Commercial Advertiser* and, two years later, joined the staff of the *New York Tribune* as art editor. He wrote on a wide variety of cultural topics, including reviews of concerts and theatrical events. By the mid 1890s, he was the *Tribune's* main art critic, a role he continued when the paper merged with the *Herald* to become the *Herald Tribune.* Several anthologies of Cortissoz's writings were published during his lifetime, including *Art and Common Sense* (1913) and *American Artists* (1923).[12] The latter included chapters on Abbott Thayer, Thomas Dewing, Thomas Eakins, and Kenyon Cox, along with essays on the histories of American landscape painting and American sculpture. Cortissoz also wrote a monograph on the American painter John La Farge (1911).[13]

NOTES

1. For Neal, see Harold Edward Dickson, ed. *Observations on American Art* (State College: Pennsylvania State College, 1943); Benjamin Lease, *That Wild Fellow John Neal and the American Literary Revolution* (Chicago: University of Chicago Press, 1972); and Neal's autobiography, *Wandering Recollections of a Somewhat Busy Life* (Boston, 1869). Two of Neal's articles from the *Yankee* are reprinted in John W. McCoubrey, *American Art 1700–1960, Sources and Documents* (Englewood Cliffs, New Jersey: Prentice-Hall, Inc., 1965), 125–26, 145–57.

2. A brief biography of Morris precedes eight of his poems, including "Woodman Spare That Tree," in Rufus Wilmot Griswold, *The Poets and Poetry of America* (Philadelphia: Parry and McMillan, 1854), 243.

3. James Grant Wilson and John Fiske, *Appleton's Cyclopaedia of American Biography* (New York: D. Appleton and Company, 1888), 2: 35–36.

4. For Jarves, see Francis Steegmuller, *The Two Lives of James Jackson Jarves* (New Haven: Yale University Press, 1951).

5. For Stillman, see his own *The Autobiography of a Journalist,* 2 vols. (Boston: Houghton, Mifflin & Co., 1901); Simoni, 60–119; and International Center of Photography, *Poetic Localities. Photographs of Adirondacks, Cambridge, Crete, Italy, Athens: William J. Stillman* (New York: 1988), with essays by Anne Ehrenkranz, Colin Eisler, and Linda S. Ferber.

6. For Cook, see Simoni, 123–348; and Jo Ann W. Weiss, "Clarence Cook: His Critical Writings" (Ph.D. diss., The Johns Hopkins University, 1977), which is the most reliable source on Cook to date. Also see Barbara Jean Stephanic, "Clarence Cook's Role as Art Critic, Advocate for Professionalism, Educator, and Arbiter of Taste in America" (Ph.D. diss., University of Maryland, 1997). All three sources include bibliographies of Cook's published writings; Simoni's is annotated, Weiss's is the most extensive.

7. For example, "A Bronze Door by Bartlett," *Times Illustrated Magazine,* November 7, 1897; "The Private Collection of William T. Evans," Ibid., February 19, 1899; and "French and American Impressionism," Ibid., January 31, 1904.

8. For Van Rensselaer, see Cynthia Kinnard, "The Life and Works of Mariana Griswold Van Rensselaer, American Art Critic" (Ph.D. diss., Johns Hopkins University, Baltimore, 1977); and Lois Dinnerstein, "Opulence and Ocular Delight: Splendor and Squalor. Critical Writings in Art and Architecture by Mariana Griswold Van Rensselaer" (Ph.D. diss., City University of New York, 1979).

9. For Caffin, see Sandra Lee Underwood, *Charles H. Caffin: A Voice for Modernism 1897–1918* (Ann Arbor, Michigan: UMI Research Press, 1983).

10 For Cox, see three works by or edited by H. Wayne Morgan and published by Kent State Univeristy Press, Kent, Ohio: *An American Art Student in Paris: The Letters of Kenyon Cox, 1877–1882* (1986); *Keepers of Culture: The Art-Thought of Kenyon Cox, Royal Cortissoz, and Frank Jewett Mather, Jr.* (1989); and *Kenyon Cox 1856–1919: A Life in American Art* (1994).

11. Olson, 37–56.

12. Cortissoz also wrote a history of his long time employer, *The New York Tribune* (New York, 1923)

13. For Cortissoz, see Morgan, *Keepers of Culture,* 63–102; and Olson, 19–36.

Appendix B: National Academy of Design Annual Exhibitions, 1826–1925

SUBJECT CATEGORIES OF WORKS IN THE EXHIBITIONS (all numbers are approximate)

Year	Artists	Total Works	Portraits	History/ Religion	Landscape	Still-life	Genre	Literary/ Figural	Animal	Architecture	Myth	Unknown
1826	32	181	88	10	36	0	2	9	2	28	4	2
1830	51	184	111	2	37	5	4	6	2	14	0	3
1835	79	232	132	5	42	5	15	12	5	13	1	2
1840	123	306	185	4	47	6	26	27	1	6	2	2
1845	145	368	170	12	98	3	37	24	7	14	2	1
1850	144	390	139	15	116	7	47	36	7	14	3	6
1855	140	282	111	5	88	2	21	28	2	15	2	8
1860	265	668	148	26	247	31	94	58	16	32	1	15
1865	289	647	137	13	223	66	96	74	12	22	0	4
1870	244	477	83	10	217	34	50	42	11	17	3	10
1875	272	533	56	12	195	41	116	41	23	32	3	14
1880	406	740	121	16	210	90	155	73	19	30	7	19
1885	429	665	56	6	231	85	180	72	16	17	0	2
1890	445	671	81	6	239	67	179	42	23	4	10	20
1895	322	473	46	5	166	17	147	66	14	4	6	2
1900	203	314	55	1	124	0	79	36	9	7	0	3
1905	276	397	74	3	137	11	107	41	14	8	1	1
1910	309	451	80	5	162	5	110	46	19	7	13	4
1915	347	474	148	4	128	13	74	86	6	7	7	1
1920	417	956	174	13	287	35	181	186	20	39	3	18
1925	331	422	75	4	141	15	82	83	12	3	6	1

Reviews of the Annual Exhibitions of the National Academy of Design, 1826–1925

COMPILED BY DAVID B. DEARINGER AND ELIZABETH BARRY

This compilation contains only those sources that refer to the National Academy's *annual* exhibitions, which were usually held in the spring. It does not contain reviews of the summer, autumn, or winter exhibitions, of which there were a number. Every effort has been made to see that this list is complete. It undoubtedly is not. The compilers would appreciate knowing of additions or corrections to it.

In the following articles, by-lines that are presumed to be pseudonyms, and for which no certain name has been assigned, are left as written in the original publications, without the addition of quotation marks, etc.

It would not have been possible to compile this bibliography without the generosity of William H. and Abigail Booth Gerdts, who allowed us access to their extensive files of NAD reviews. It is with pleasure that we take this opportunity to reiterate our appreciation for the Gerdts American Art Research Library.

Abbreviations

AAm	Art Amateur
HW	Harper's Weekly
IS	International Studio
LW	Literary World
NAD	National Academy of Design
NYCA	New York Commercial Advertiser
NYDG	New York Daily Graphic
NYDT	New York Daily Tribune
NYEM	New York Evening Mail
NYEP	New York Evening Post
NYET	New York Evening Telegram
NYH	New York Herald
NYL	New York Leader
NYM	New-York Mirror
NYS	New York Sun
NYT	New-York Times

1826

"Fine Arts," *NYEP*, May 6, 1826.

"National Academy," *NYEP*, May 15, 1826.

"The National Academy of the Arts of Design," *NYM* 3 (June 10, 1826): 366–67; 3 (June 12, 1826): 375; 3 (July 1, 1826): 391.

1827

"NAD," *NYEP*, June 1, 1827.

"Mr. Morse's Picture of the U. States Representative's Hall," *NYEP*, June 7, 1827.

[George Pope Morris], "The Fine Arts. NAD," *NYM* 4 (June 2, 1827): 354.

[Samuel F. B. Morse], "Review. *The Exhibition of the NAD, 1827. The Second.* New York. D. Fanshaw. 1827," *United States Review and Literary Gazette* 2 (July 1827): 241–63.

1828

"NAD," *NYEP*, May 6, 1828.

"The Fine Arts. NAD," *NYM* 5 (May 24, 1828): 366–67.

Middle-Tint [John I. H. Bowere], "The Works of Living Artists, At the NAD," *New York Morning Courier*, May 17, May 27, June 13, June 18, June 21, June 24, June 26, July 1, July 2, July 8, July 9, July 11, July 12, July 16, 1828.

1829

"Fine Arts. NAD. Fourth Annual Exhibition," *Critic* 2 (May 23, 1829): 46–47.

"Exhibition of the NAD," *NYEP*, May 9, 1829.

"Fine Arts," *NYEP*, June 6, 1829.

C, "NAD," *New-York American,* June 11, 1829.

[George Pope Morris?] "Fine Arts. The Fourth Annual Exhibition of the National Academy," *NYM* 6 (May 16, 1829): 354–55.

1830

"Strictures on the Paintings Exhibited in the NAD—No. 1," *Irish Shield* 2 (June 1830): 235–37.

"Exhibition of the National Academy of the Arts of Design," *NYEP*, May 1, 1830.

"The Fine Arts. NAD," *NYM* 7 (May 15, 1830): 359.

"Living Artists. NAD," *New York Morning Courier,* May 28, June 4, June 12, 1830.

1831

"Exhibition of the NAD," *NYEP*, April 27, 1831.

[No title], *NYEP*, April 28, 1831.

Apollo, "The NAD," *NYEP*, May 7, 1831.

T, "The Progress of the Arts in Our Country," *NYEP*, May 9, 1831.

"The Fine Arts. NAD," *NYM* 8 (May 7, 1831): 350; 8 (May 14, 1831): 358.

"NAD," *New York Morning Courier,* May 6, 1831.

1832

"Communication," *Morning Courier and New-York Enquirer,*
    May 26, 1832.
"Fine Arts," *NYEP,* April 26, 1832.
"Fine Arts. NAD. The Seventh Exhibition," *NYM* 9 (June 2,
    1832): 382–83; 9 (June 9, 1832): 391; 9 (June 16, 1832): 394–95.
*Review of the Seventh Exhibition of the National Academy of
    Design.* New York: Traveller & Times, 1833 (repr. from *New-
    York Traveller*).

1833

"Miscellaneous Notices of Literature, Fine Arts, the Sciences,
    Drama, &c.," *American Monthly Magazine* 1 (July 1833):
    331–34.
"NAD," *Morning Courier and New-York Enquirer,* May 10, 1833.
"NAD," *NYM* 10 (May 18, 1833): 366; 10 (May 25, 1833): 371; 10
    (June 1, 1833): 380; 10 (June 8, 1833): 387; 10 (June 10, 1833):
    398; 10 (June 22, 1833): 406; 10 (June 29, 1833): 410; 11 (July 6,
    1833): 6.
"Critique Upon the Exhibition of the NAD," *Morning Courier
    and New-York Enquirer,* May 18, May 23, 1833.
"Academy of Design," *NYEP,* May 8, 1833.
"NAD," *NYEP,* June 3, 1833.

1834

"Miscellaneous Notices of the Fine Arts, Literature, Science, the
    Drama, &c.," *American Monthly Magazine* 3 (May 1834):
    207–14.
[Lewis Gaylord Clark?], "NAD," *Knickerbocker* 3 (May 1834):
    399–400.
"NAD," *Morning Courier and New-York Enquirer,* May 9, 1834.
"NAD," *NYEP,* May 9, May 18, May 23, June 3, June 5,
    June 18, 1834.
"Original Notices of the Fine Arts," *NYM* 11 (May 10, 1834): 355;
    11 (May 17, 1834): 367.
"Ingham's Ariel," *NYM* 11 (July 13, 1834): 14.

1835

"Fine Arts in America. NAD," *American Monthly Magazine* 5
    (June 1835): 312–18; 5 (July 1835): 391–98.
[Lewis Gaylord Clark?], "The Fine Arts," *Knickerbocker* 5 (June
    1835): 550–56.
"Exhibition of the NAD," *Morning Courier and New-York
    Enquirer,* May 8, 1835.
"NAD," *NYEP,* April 16, 1835.
One of the "Hanging Committee," [Letter to the editor], *NYEP,*
    June 24, 1835.
"Exhibition of the National Academy," *NYM* 12 (May 2, 1835):
    351.
"The Fine Arts. Exhibition of the NAD," *NYM* 12 (May 16, 1835):
    366; 12 (May 23, 1835): 371; 12 (May 30, 1835): 379; 12 (June 6,
    1835): 390; 12 (June 13, 1835): 395; 12 (June 20, 1835): 406; 12
    (June 27, 1835): 413–14; 13 (July 11, 1835): 15.

1836

[Lewis Gaylord Clark?], "Editor's Table. NAD: Eleventh Annual
    Exhibition," *Knickerbocker* 8 (July 1836): 112–15.
[no title], *NYEP,* April 27, 1836.
"NAD," *NYEP,* May 25, 1836.
More Anon, "National Academy," *NYH,* May 9, May 12, May 14,
    May 19, 1836.
"National Academy," *NYH,* May 17, 1836.
"The Fine Arts. NAD," *NYM* 13 (May 7, 1836): 358; 13
    (May 14, 1836): 366; 13 (May 21, 1836): 375; 13 (June 4, 1836):
    390; 13 (June 11, 1836): 398; 13 (June 18, 1836): 406; 13 (June
    25, 1836): 414.
"NAD, Clinton Hall," *New-Yorker* 1 (June 18, 1836): 205.

1837

[Lewis Gaylord Clark?], "Editor's Table. Exhibition of the
    National Academy," *Knickerbocker* 9 (June 1837): 617–23.
[No title], *NYEP,* April 21, 1837.
"NAD," *NYH,* May 8, May 18, May 25, 1837.
"Fine Arts. NAD," *NYM* 14 (April 29, 1837): 351; 14 (May 6, 1837):
    359; 14 (May 13, 1837): 365; 14 (May 20, 1837): 375; 14 (May
    27, 1837): 383; 14 (June 3, 1837): 391; 14 (June 10, 1837): 399; 14
    (June 17, 1837): 407.
"The Twelfth Annual Exhibition of the NAD," *New-Yorker* 3
    (May 6, 1837): 109; 3 (May 13, 1837): 127; 3 (May 20, 1837):
    143; 3 (June 3, 1837): 175; 3 (June 17, 1837): 205.

1838

"Exhibition of the NAD," *American Monthly Magazine* 11 (May
    1838): 469–72.
E. R., "Exhibition of the National Academy," *NYCA,* May 11,
    May 16, 1838.
"The Annual Exhibition of the NAD," *NYEP,* April 25, 1838.
"National Academy," *NYEP,* May 26, 1838.
"NAD," *NYH,* May 5, May 10, May 16, June 1, June 14, 1838.
"The Fine Arts. NAD," *NYM* 15 (May 26, 1838): 382; 15 (June 2,
    1838): 390; 15 (June 9, 1838): 398; 15 (June 16, 1838): 406; 15
    (June 23, 1838): 414; 16 (June 30, 1838): 6; 16 (July 7, 1838): 15.
"Exhibition—NAD," *New-Yorker* 5 (May 12, 1838): 125; 5 (May
    26, 1838): 157–58.

1839

"Pencil Notes on a First Visit to the Gallery," *Corsair* 1 (May 4,
    1839): 121–22.
"The Gallery," *Corsair* 1 (May 18, 1839): 152–53.
"NAD," *Expositor* 1 (May 18, 1839): 261–62.
J[ohn] K[enrick] F[isher], "Editor's Table. The Fine Arts,"
    Knickerbocker 13 (June 1839): 545–49.
"NAD," *NYCA,* April 24, 1839.
E., "NAD," *NYCA,* May 24, May 31, June 11, 1839.
[No title], *NYEP,* May 3, 1839.
"NAD," *NYEP,* May 14, 1839.
"The National Academy," *NYH,* May 4, May 17, 1839.
"Exhibition of the National Academy," *New York Literary
    Gazette,* no. 13 (April 27, 1839): 109–10; no. 15 (May 11, 1839):
    118; no. 16 (May 18, 1839): 125; no. 17 (May 25, 1839): 133-34;
    no. 19 (June 8, 1839): 148; no. 21 (June 22, 1839): 165–66.

"A Glance at the Exhibition of the Academy of Design," *NYM* 16 (May 11, 1839): 367.
"Second Visit to Exhibition at Clinton Hall," *NYM* 16 (May 18, 1839): 375.
"Exhibition of the NAD," *New-Yorker* 7 (May 4, 1839): 109; 7 (May 11, 1839): 125.

1840

[Lewis Gaylord Clark?], "NAD," *Knickerbocker* 16 (July 1840): 81–83.
"National Academy," *NYH*, June 4, June 19, June 25, June 27, July 2, July 4, 1840.
"NAD," *NYM* 18 (July 18, 1840): 30.
"The National Academy," *New-Yorker* 9 (June 20, 1840): 221–22.

1841

"The Fine Arts. Exhibition of the Academy," *Arcturus* 2 (June 1841): 59–62.
[Lewis Gaylord Clark?], "The Fine Arts," *Knickerbocker* 18 (July 1841): 86–89.
"World of Art. NAD," *New World* 2 (May 22, 1841): 365.
"NAD," *NYEP*, June 12, 1841.
"NAD," *New York Express*, May 18, 1841.
"NAD," *NYM* 19 (May 15, 1841): 159; 19 (May 22, 1841): 167.

1842

Sketcher, "The National Academy," *Brother Jonathan* 2 (June 1842): 184–85.
[Lewis Gaylord Clark?], "Editor's Table. NAD," *Knickerbocker* 19 (June 1842): 588–93; 20 (July 1842): 94.
"The Fine Arts. Exhibition of the NAD," *New World* 4 (May 7, 1842): 305; 4 (May 21, 1842): 337.
"The World of Art. NAD," *New World* 4 (May 28, 1842): 352.
"Exhibition of the NAD," *NYEP*, May 3, 1842.
"The Fine Arts," *NYEP*, July 9, 1842.
"The NAD," *NYH*, May 25, 1842.
"NAD—Cutting Criticisms," *NYH*, June 13, June 16, 1842.

1843

"NAD—Annual Exhibition," *Anglo American* 1 (May 6, 1843): 44–45; 1 (May 13, 1843): 70–71; 1 (May 27, 1843): 119.
"National Academy Exhibition," *Brother Jonathan* 5 (May 6, 1843): 8; 5 (May 13, 1843): 49–50; 5 (May 20, 1843): 81–82.
[Lewis Gaylord Clark?], "Editor's Table," *Knickerbocker* 21 (June 1843): 580–83.
"Art and Artists. History of the NAD," *New Mirror* 1 (May 6, 1843): 76–78.
"NAD," *New Mirror* 1 (May 13, 1843): 94; 1 (May 20, 1843): 108–9; 1 (May 27, 1843): 127.
H. F., "The World of Science and Art. The National Academy," *New World* 6 (May 6, 1843): 545–46; 6 (May 20, 1843): 604–5; 6 (June 10, 1843): 693–96; 6 (June 17, 1843): 727–29; 7 (July 15, 1843): 58–60.
"NAD," *NYDT*, May 3, 1843.
"The Exhibition of the NAD," *NYDT*, May 19, 1843.
"Exhibition of the Academy of Design," *NYEP*, May 5, 1843.
"The Paintings in the Atheneum Building," *NYEP*, May 17, 1843.

1844

"Fine Arts. NAD," *Anglo-American* 3 (May 18, 1844): 93; 3 (May 25, 1844): 116–17.
[Lewis Gaylord Clark?], "Editor's Table," *Knickerbocker* 24 (July 1844): 75–77.
"Beautiful Painting by an Untaught Artist," *Morning Courier and New-York Enquirer*, May 1, 1844.
"World of Science and Art. NAD," *New World* 8 (May 4, 1844): 561–62.
"NAD," *NYDT*, April 25, 1844.
"NAD," *NYH*, May 1, May 26, 1844.

1845

"Painting—NAD—Twentieth Annual Exhibition," *Anglo-American* 5 (April 26, 1845): 21; 5 (May 3, 1845): 44; 5 (May 17, 1845): 93.
"20th Annual Exhibition of the Academy of National Design," *Broadway Journal* 1 (April 26, 1845): 257–58; 1 (May 3, 1845): 275–76; 1 (May 10, 1845): 289–91.
"The National Academy," *Broadway Journal* 1 (May 10, 1845), 305–07.
[Lewis Gaylord Clark?], "Editor's Table," *Knickerbocker* 25 (May 1845): 458–59, 468–69; 25 (June 1845): 564; 25 (July 1845): 84.
"NAD," *Morning Courier and New-York Enquirer*, April 21, 1845.
"Our Artists and Their Works," *New World* 9 (April 26, 1845): 269; 9 (May 10, 1845): 297–98.
"City Items," *NYDT*, April 18, 1845.
"NAD," *NYDT*, April 24, April 26, 1845.
"The Fine Arts," *NYEP*, May 10, 1845.
"NAD," *NYH*, April 21, April 22, April 28, April 29, April 30, May 3, 1845.
"National Academy," *NYM* 2 (April 26, 1845), 43.
"Exhibition at the Academy," *NYM* 2 (May 3, 1845): 54, 56.

1846

"Something about Our Painters," *American Review* 4 (August 1846): 180–87.
"NAD—Twenty-first Annual Exhibition," *Anglo American* 7 (April 25, 1846): 22; 7 (May 2, 1846): 45–46; 7 (May 9, 1846): 69–70; 7 (May 16, 1846): 94–95.
[Lewis Gaylord Clark?], "Editor's Table," *Knickerbocker* 27 (May 1846): 463–66; 27 (June 1846): 556–57.
"Academy of Design," *Morning Courier and New York Enquirer*, May 6, 1846.
"The Fine Arts: NAD," *Morris's National Press* 1 (April 25, 1846): 2; 1 (May 2, 1846): 2; 1 (May 9, 1846): 2; 1 (May 16, 1846): 2; 1 (May 23, 1846): 4; 1 (May 30, 1846): 2; 1 (June 6, 1846): 4; 1 (June 13, 1846): 2; 1 (June 20, 1846): 4.
"The National Academy," *NYDT*, April 16, 1846.
"Annual Exhibition of the Academy of Design," *NYEP*, April 15, April 22, 1846.
"The Exhibition at the NAD," *NYH*, April 20, April 21, 1846.
"NAD," *NYM* 4 (April 25, 1846): 46; 4 (May 2, 1846): 58–59; 4 (May 9, 1846): 74–75; 4 (May 16, 1846): 92; 4 (June 6, 1846): 139–40.

1847

"Fine Arts. NAD," *Anglo American* 9 (April 24, 1847): 20–21; 9 (May 1, 1847): 45; 9 (May 8, 1847): 69; 9 (May 15, 1847): 94; 9 (May 29, 1847): 140.

B. C. F., "Fine Arts in America. Twenty-First [sic] Annual Exhibition of the NAD, New York," *Art-Union* (London) (1847): 216.

[Lewis Gaylord Clark?], "Editor's Table," *Knickerbocker* 29 (June 1847): 570–73.

"The Fine Arts," *LW* 1 (April 17, 1847): 256; 1 (April 27, 1847): 279–80; 1 (May 1, 1847): 304; 1 (May 8, 1847): 322–23; 1 (May 15, 1847): 347–48; 1 (May 22, 1847): 370–72; 1 (May 29, 1847): 396–97; 1 (June 5, 1847): 418–20; 1 (June 12, 1847): 447–48; 1 (June 19, 1847): 467–68; 1 (July 3, 1847): 517–18.

"NAD," *NYDT*, April 21, 1847.

"The Exhibition of the National Academy," *New York Evening Mirror*, April 13, 1847.

"The Annual Exhibition of the Academy of Design," *NYEP*, April 2, 1847.

"Exhibition at the National Academy," *NYM* 5 (April 17, 1847): 26; 5 (May 1, 1847): 59; 5 (May 15, 1847): 90.

1848

"NAD," *Family Companion* 1 (April 8, 1848): 127–28; 1 (April 15, 1848): 140; 1 (April 22, 1848): 154; 1 (April 29, 1848): 168–69; 1 (May 6, 1848): 182; 1 (May 13, 1848): 197; 2 (June 10, 1848): 51; 2 (June 24, 1848): 78–79.

"Art-Union vs. The National Academy," *Family Companion* 2 (June 24, 1848): 79.

[Lewis Gaylord Clark?], "Editor's Table," *Knickerbocker* 31 (May 1848): 467–69.

"The Fine Arts," *LW* 3 (March 4, 1848): 106–7; 3 (April 29, 1848): 248–49; 3 (May 6, 1848): 266–67; 3 (May 13, 1848): 287–88; 3 (May 27, 1848): 328–29; 3 (June 3, 1848): 350–51.

"The Twenty-third Exhibition of the National Academy," *Morning Courier and New York Enquirer*, May 11, 1848.

"The Annual Exhibition of the Academy," *NYEP*, April 6, May 13, May 25, May 27, May 30, June 5, June 6, June 17, June 21, 1848.

"The Fine Arts: Exhibition at the NAD," *NYH*, April 15, April 19, 1848.

1849

"NAD," *Albion* 8 (April 14, 1849): 177.

"The NAD," *Bulletin of the American Art-Union* 2 (May 1849): 13–15.

"NAD," *Home Journal* 18 (April 18, 1849): 2.

Achille Bonbon, "The Academy Exhibition," *International Art-Union Journal* 4 (May 1849): 52–59.

"The National Academy," *International Art-Union Journal* 4 (May 1849): 59–61.

[Lewis Gaylord Clark?], "Editor's Table. NAD," *Knickerbocker* 33 (May 1849): 468–70.

"The Colonel's Club," *LW* 6 (April 21, 1849): 358.

"NAD," *Morning Courier and New-York Enquirer*, May 3, 1849.

"The Exhibition at the Academy," *NYEP*, May 2, 1849.

1850

"Fine Arts. NAD," *Albion* 9 (April 27, 1850): 201–2.

N. N., "Exhibition of the National Academy," *Bulletin of the American Art-Union* 3 (May 1, 1850): 18–22.

"NAD," *Graham's Magazine* 36 (May 1850): 344.

[Lewis Gaylord Clark?], "National Academy Pictures," *Knickerbocker* 35 (June 1850): 558–59; 36 (July 1850): 99–100.

"The Fine Arts. The National Academy," *LW* 7 (April 27, 1850): 423–25; 7 (May 4, 1850): 449–50; 7 (May 18, 1850): 497–98.

"NAD. Twenty-fifth Annual Exhibition," *NYDT*, May 1, 1850, May 15, 1850.

H. G., "A Glance at the National Academy," *NYDT*, May 2, June 18, June 20, June 22, July 7, 1850.

"National Academy of the Arts of Design," *NYEP*, April 13, 1850.

"The Fine Arts. NAD," *NYH*, May 12, 1850.

"NAD," *New York Morning Express*, April 22, 1850.

1851

"Fine Arts. The NAD," *Albion* 10 (April 19, 1851): 189.

"Art and Artists in America," *Bulletin of the American Art-Union* 4 (April 1, 1851): 9–16.

N. N., "The Twenty-Sixth Exhibition of the NAD," *Bulletin of the American Art-Union* 4 (May 1, 1851): 21–24; 4 (June 1, 1851): 40–43.

"Figaro's Topic of the Week. The National Academy," *Figaro* 2 (April 12, 1851): 241–42.

"The Fine Arts," *International Monthly Magazine of Literature, Science and Art* 3 (June 1851): 327–29.

[Lewis Gaylord Clark?], "Editor's Table," *Knickerbocker* 37 (May 1851): 469–71.

"Fine Arts. The National Academy," *LW* 8 (April 19, 1851): 320–21.

G[eorge] W. C[urtis], "The Private View of the Academy Exhibition," *NYDT*, April 10, 1851.

G[eorge] W. C[urtis], "The Fine Arts. The NAD," *NYDT*, April 16, April 26, May 10, May 29, June 16, June 21, 1851.

"City Intelligence," *NYEP*, April 7, April 21, 1851.

"Exhibition of the NAD," *Philadelphia Art-Union Reporter* 1 (May 1851): 52.

1852

"Fine Arts. The NAD," *Albion* 11 (April 24, 1852): 201–2; 11 (May 1, 1852): 213–14; 11 (May 8, 1852): 225–26; 11 (May 15, 1852): 237.

[Lewis Gaylord Clark], "Editor's Table," *Knickerbocker* 39 (May 1852): 484–83.

[Lewis Gaylord Clark?], "Exhibition of the NAD," *Knickerbocker* 39 (June 1852): 563–68.

"The Fine Arts. Exhibition at the NAD," *LW* 10 (April 24, 1852): 301–2; 10 (May 1, 1852): 314–16; 10 (May 8, 1852): 331–33.

[George W. Curtis], "The Fine Arts. NAD," *NYDT*, April 17, April 24, May 1, May 8, May 20, May 31, June 7, 1852.

"The Exhibition of the Academy," *NYEP*, April 16, May 28, 1852.

"The Gallery of the Academy of Design," *NYEP*, June 4, 1852.

"The Paintings in the Academy of Design," *NYEP*, June 16, 1852.

"The Fine Arts. Exhibition of Paintings by the NAD," *NYH*, April 21, 1852.

1853

"Fine Arts," *Albion* 12 (April 23, 1853): 201.

[Lewis Gaylord Clark?], "Exhibition of the NAD," *Knickerbocker* 42 (July 1853): 93–96.

"The Fine Arts. The Exhibition of the Academy," *LW* 12 (April 30, 1853): 358–59.

"The Fine Arts. Exhibition of the National Academy," *NYDT*, April 22, 1853.

"City Intelligence. Opening of the Academy of Design," *NYEP*, April 16, 1853.

"Academy of Design. Twenty-Eighth Annual Exhibition," *NYH*, May 8, 1853.

"NAD," *New-York Illustrated News,* May 7, 1853.

"Fine Arts," *Putnam's Monthly* 1 (June 1853): 700–703.

1854

"Fine Arts. The NAD," *Albion* 13 (April 8, 1854): 165; 13 (April 15, 1854): 177.

[George W. Curtis], "Editor's Easy Chair," *Harper's New Monthly Magazine* 8 (May 1854): 846–47.

[Lewis Gaylord Clark?], "The NAD," *Knickerbocker* 43 (May 1854): 539–40.

"The Fine Arts. The NAD," *NYDT*, March 30, April 22, 1854.

"The NAD," *NYT*, March 31, April 4, 1854.

"The Fine Arts. The National Academy," *Putnam's Monthly Magazine* 3 (May 1854): 566–68.

1855

"Fine Arts. The NAD," *Albion* 14 (March 24, 1855): 141; 14 (March 31, 1855): 153.

"Sketchings," *Crayon* 1 (March 21, 1855): 186; 1 (March 28, 1855): 202–3; 1 (April 4, 1855): 218–19; 1 (April 11, 1855): 234–35; 1 (April 18, 1855): 250.

"The Town. Closing Notice of the Academy," *Home Journal* 1 (April 14, 1855): 2.

Clarence Cook, "The Fine Arts. The NAD," *Independent* 7 (April 5, 1855): 105; 7 (April 12, 1855): 113; 7 (April 19, 1855): 121; 7 (April 26, 1855): 129; 7 (May 10, 1855): 145.

[Lewis Gaylord Clark?], "Exhibition of the NAD," *Knickerbocker* 45 (May 1855): 529–33.

R. T., "Exhibition of the NAD," *NYDT*, April 18, April 27, May 7, 1855.

"Fine Arts," *NYEP*, March 7, 1855.

"The Exhibition of the Academy of Design," *NYEP*, March 16, 1855.

"The Fine Arts. The National Academy Exhibition," *NYH*, March 24, 1855.

"NAD," *NYT*, April 12, 1855.

"The NAD," *Putnam's Monthly Magazine* 5 (May 1855): 505–10.

1856

Louvre, "Fine Arts. NAD," *Albion* 15 (March 22, 1856): 141; 15 (March 29, 1856): 153; 15 (April 5, 1856): 165.

"Exhibition of the National Academy," *Crayon* 3 (April 1856): 116–18; 3 (May 1856): 145–50.

"Sketchings. NAD," *Crayon* 3 (May 1856): 157–58.

"Academy of Design," *Frank Leslie's Illustrated Newspaper* 1 (April 12, 1856): 281.

"Topics Astir. National Academy Exhibition," *Home Journal* 1 (April 5, 1856): 2.

Clarence Cook, "NAD," *Independent* 8 (April 24, 1856): 130; 8 (May 1, 1856): 137.

[Lewis Gaylord Clark?], "Editor's Table," *Knickerbocker* 46 (May 1856): 547.

"The NAD," *NYDT*, April 9, April 12, April 19, May 3, May 10, 1856.

"Annual Exhibition of the American Academy of Design," *NYEP*, March 17, 1856.

"NAD," *NYEP*, April 1, April 7, April 12, April 21, 1856.

"The Fine Arts. The Academy of Design," *NYH*, March 18, 1856.

C[larence] C[ook], "NAD. Thirty-first Yearly Exhibition," *NYT*, March 24, April 4, April 21, 1856.

1857

Fidelius, "Art Matters in New York," *Boston Evening Transcript,* May 29, 1857.

[John Durand], "Sketchings. NAD," *Crayon* 4 (July 1857): 220–24.

"Five Minutes in the NAD," *Frank Leslie's Illustrated Newspaper* 3 (June 3, 1857): 424.

"Chat. The National Academy," *HW* 1 (May 30, 1857): 339.

"Topics Astir. NAD," *Home Journal* 1 (June 13, 1857): 2.

"Exhibition of the NAD," *NYEP*, May 30, June 3, June 19, 1857.

"NAD Exhibition," *NYT*, May 27, June 16, June 20, 1857.

1858

"Fine Arts. NAD," *Albion* 36 (April 24, 1858): 201; 36 (May 1, 1858): 213; 36 (May 8, 1858): 225.

[John Durand], "Sketchings. Exhibition of the NAD," *Crayon* 5 (May 1858): 146–48; 5 (June 1858): 175–79.

[George W. Curtis], "The Lounger," *HW* 2 (May 1, 1858): 275; 2 (May 8, 1858): 291; 2 (May 15, 1858): 307; 2 (May 22, 1858): 323.

"Mere Mention. NAD," *Home Journal* 2 (May 8, 1858): 7.

"Editor's Table. Late Words Touching the National Academy Exhibition," *Knickerbocker* 52 (July 1858): 81–84.

"The Exhibition of the American Academy of Design," *NYEP*, April 6, April 29, 1858.

"The Academy of Design," *NYEP*, April 29, 1858.

"The NAD," *NYEP*, April 22, May 1, May 8, 1858.

"The NAD," *NYH*, April 13, April 23, 1858.

"The NAD," *New York Semi-Weekly Tribune*, May 7, 1858.

"The Opening of the Academy of Design. The Fine Arts in the City," *NYT*, April 13, 1858.

"The Fine Arts. Exhibition of the NAD," *NYT*, May 8, 1858.

1859

"Fine Arts. NAD," *Albion* 37 (May 7, 1859): 225; 37 (May 14, 1859): 237; 37 (May 28, 1859): 261.

"National Academy Exhibition," *Cosmopolitan Art Journal* 3 (June 1859): 134.

[John Durand], "Sketchings. NAD," *Crayon* 6 (May 1859):
     152–53; 6 (June 1859): 189–93.
*A Critical Guide to the Exhibition at the National Academy of
     Design, in Tenth Street: For 1859.* New York: Robert M. De
     Witt, Publisher, 1859.
[George W. Curtis], "The Lounger," *HW* 3 (April 30, 1859): 275; 3
     (May 14, 1859): 307.
"Fine Arts. NAD," *Home Journal* 3 (May 14, 1859); 3 (June 4,
     1859).
"The Thirty-Fourth Exhibition of the Academy of Design,"
     NYEP, April 25, 1859.
"NAD," *NYEP,* May 14, 1859.
"NAD," *NYH,* May 8, 1859.
"Exhibition of the Academy of Design," *New York Semi-Weekly
     Tribune,* May 6, May 17, May 24, 1859.
"The Academy of Design," *NYT,* April 20, 1859.

1860

[John Durand], "Sketchings. NAD," *Crayon* 7 (May 1860):
     139–40; 7 (June 1860): 171–73.
"Academy of Design Exhibition," *Cosmopolitan Art Journal* 4
     (June 1860): 81–82.
"NAD: Fourth Gallery," *Home Journal* 4 (May 5, 1860).
"Art Items," *NYDT,* March 10, March 31, May 2, 1860.
"Exhibition of the National Academy," *NYEP,* April 18, 1860.
"City Intelligence. Picture Hanging," *NYEP,* April 19, 1860.
"Fine Arts," *NYEP,* May 3, May 8, 1860.
"Academy of Design. The Cabinet Pictures," *NYEP,* May 15,
     1860.
"The Academy of Design Exhibition," *NYEP,* May 26, 1860.
"The NAD," *NYH,* April 13, April 24, 1860.
"Art and Artists: Thirty-fifth Annual Exhibition of the NAD,"
     NYL, April 21, 1860.
"Art and Artists: Review of the Academy of Design," *NYL,* April
     28, May 26, 1860.
"The Academy of Design of 1860," *NYT,* April 12, 1860.
"NAD," *Sketch Club* (Cincinnati) 1 (May 5, 1860): 5.
Bister, "We Visit the Academy of Design," *Vanity Fair* 1 (April 28,
     1860): 275–76.
Bister, "Our Second Visit to the Academy of Design," *Vanity Fair*
     1 (May 12, 1860): 316.

1861

"Fine Arts. NAD," *Albion* 39 (April 6, 1861): 165; 39 (April 13,
     1861): 177; 39 (April 20, 1861): 189.
"Art Gossip," *Cosmopolitan Art Journal* 5 (March 1861): 35–37.
[John Durand], "Sketchings. NAD," *Crayon* 8 (April 1861):
     94–95.
"Domestic Art Gossip, *Crayon* 8 (May 1861): 151.
[George W. Curtis], "The Lounger. The Academy Exhibition,"
     HW 5 (April 6, 1861): 210–11; 5 (April 13, 1861): 226.
"Academy of Design," *NYDT,* March 20, 1861.
"National Academy Exhibition," *NYDT,* March 27, 1861.
"National Academy Exhibition," *NYDT,* April 5, 1861.
"Fine Arts. The Exhibition of the NAD," *NYEP,* April 9, 1861.
"Fine Arts," *NYH,* March 22, March 31, 1861.
"Art Gossip. NAD," *NYT,* March 22, 1861.

"National Academy Exhibition. The Landscapes of the Present
     Year," *NYT,* April 21, 1861.

1862

"Fine Arts. The NAD," *Albion* 40 (April 26, 1862): 201–2; 40
     (May 10, 1862): 225; 40 (May 17, 1862): 237.
[George W. Curtis], "The Lounger. The National Academy," *HW*
     6 (May 3, 1862): 274; 6 (May 10, 1862): 290.
"The NAD. Thirty-Seventh Annual Exhibition," *NYDT,* April 14,
     1862.
"The Academy of Design. Private View of the Spring
     Exhibition," *NYEP,* April 14, April 17, 1862.
"Fine Arts. Thirty-seventh Annual Exhibition of the NAD,"
     NYH, April 16, 1862.
"NAD," *NYT,* April 15, April 24, April 27, 1862.

1863

"Fine Arts. NAD," *Albion* 41 (April 25, 1863): 201; 41 (May 2,
     1863): 213–14; 41 (May 9, 1863): 225–26.
James Jackson Jarves, "Art and Artist of America. *Catalogue of
     the Thirty-Eighth Exhibition of the NAD,* New York, 1863,"
     Christian Examiner 13 (July 1863): 114–27.
"Visit to the NAD," *Continental Monthly* 3 (June 1863): 715–19.
[George W. Curtis], "Editor's Easy Chair," *Harper's New
     Monthly Magazine* 27 (June 1863): 132–33.
[George W. Curtis], "The Lounger," *HW* 7 (May 2, 1863): 274; 7
     (May 9, 1863): 290.
"Good Work in the Academy Exhibition," *New Path* 1 (June
     1863): 22–24; 1 (July 1863): 22–23.
"Annual Exhibition of the NAD," *NYDT,* April 17, 1863.
"The NAD. Its Thirty-Eighth Annual Exhibition," *NYEP,* May
     14, May 16, May 21, June 3, June 12, 1863.
"Fine Arts. NAD," *NYH,* April 15, 1863.
[Thomas B. Aldrich], "The NAD," *New-York Illustrated News,*
     May 9, May 16, 1867.
Atticus, "Art Feuilleton. Exhibition of the Academy of Design,"
     NYL, April 18, May 2, May 9, May 30, 1863.
"The NAD," *NYT,* June 24, 1863.
"NAD," *New York World,* April 14, April 24, May 2, 1863.

1864

"Fine Arts. The NAD," *Albion* 42 (May 7, 1864): 225.
"An Hour in the Gallery of the NAD," *Continental Monthly* 5
     (June 1864): 684–89.
"The National Academy Exhibition," *HW* 8 (April 30, 1864): 275.
"NAD—Thirty-ninth Annual Exhibition," *New Path* 2 (May
     1864): 9–16.
[Clarence Cook], "NAD—The Thirty-Ninth Exhibition,"
     NYDT, April 23, April 30, May 7, May 14, May 21, June 4,
     June 11, 1864.
William Holbrook Beard, "Art Criticism," *NYDT,* May 21, 1864.
George William Curtis, "Art Criticism," *NYDT,* May 28, 1864.
"The NAD. Thirty-Ninth Annual Exhibition," *NYEP,* May 21,
     May 28, June 3, 1864.
"Literary and Art Gossip. The National Academy Exhibition,"
     New York Illustrated News, May 7, May 28, 1864.

"The Fine Arts," *NYL*, April 16, 1864.

George Arnold, "The Academy Exhibition," *NYL*, April 23, April 30, 1864.

Pictor Ignatus, "Exhibition of the Academy of Design," *NYL*, May 21, 1864.

"NAD. Notices of the Works on Exhibition," *NYT*, May 5, 1864.

"Art. Exhibition of the NAD," *Round Table* 1 (April 23, 1864): 312; 1 (May 7, 1864): 326–27.

"The NAD," *Watson's Weekly Art Journal* 1 (April 30, 1864): 9.

1865

"Fine Arts. The New NAD," *Albion* 43 (May 6, 1865): 213; 43 (May 13, 1865): 225; 43 (May 27, 1865): 249.

"Art Criticism," *HW* 9 (April 15, 1865): 226.

"The Exhibition of the National Academy," *HW* 9 (May 13, 1865): 291; 9 (May 20, 1865): 307.

"The National Academy," *Independent* 17 (June 8, 1865): 4.

"Fine Arts. The Fortieth Annual Exhibition of the NAD," *Nation* 1 (July 6, 1865): 26–28; 1 (July 13, 1865): 56–59.

"NAD—Fortieth Annual Exhibition," *New Path* 2 (June 1865): 81–104.

"Architectural Designs in the Academy," *New Path* 2 (July 1865): 113–16.

[Clarence Cook], "NAD. Fortieth Annual Exhibition," *NYDT*, May 13, May 20, May 31, June 9, June 23, July 3, 1865.

"Forthcoming Exhibition of the NAD," *NYEP*, April 13, 1865.

"NAD. Opening of the New Building," *NYEP*, April 28, 1865.

Sordello [Eugene Benson], "NAD. Fortieth Annual Exhibition," *NYEP*, May 3, May 12, May 22, May 31, 1865.

Esperance, "A Woman's View of the New Academy of Design," *NYL*, May 27, 1865.

George Arnold, "Art Matters," *NYL*, May 6, May 20, June 3, June 10, June 24, 1865.

Esperance, "Academy Gossip," *NYL*, June 10, 1865.

Cara Montane, "Another Woman's View of the New Academy of Design," *NYL*, June 3, 1865.

Esperance, "Academy of Design," *NYL*, June 17, 1865.

"NAD," *NYT*, May 12, May 29, June 7, June 13, June 27, 1865.

"NAD," *Watson's Weekly Art Journal* 3 (July 1, 1865): 148–49.

1866

"Fine Arts. NAD," *Albion* 44 (May 5, 1866): 213; 44 (May 12, 1866): 225.

"Art Criticism," *American Art Journal* 5 (May 2, 1866): 19–20; 5 (May 9, 1866): 35–36; 5 (May 16, 1866): 52–53.

"Exhibition of the National Academy," *American Art Journal* 5 (May 23, 1866): 69.

"NAD," *American Art Journal* 5 (May 31, 1866): 84–85; 5 (June 7, 1866): 100–101; 5 (June 14, 1866): 116.

"The NAD. Forty-first Annual Exhibition," *American Art Journal* 5 (July 5, 1866): 169–70 (reprint from *NYDT*, June 27, 1866).

[George W. Curtis], "Editor's Easy Chair," *Harper's New Monthly Magazine* 33 (June 1866): 117–18.

"NAD. Forty-first Annual Exhibition," *Independent* 18 (April 26, 1866): 4.

"Fine Arts. The Fifty-first Exhibition of the NAD," *Nation* 2 (May 11, 1866): 602–3; 2 (May 13, 1866): 620–21; 2 (May 18, 1866): 635–36; 2 (May 25, 1866): 666–67.

[Clarence Cook], "Soiree at the Academy of Design. Forty-first Annual Exhibition," *NYDT*, April 17, 1866.

[Clarence Cook], "NAD—Forty-first Annual Exhibition," *NYDT*, June 27, July 4, 1866.

"Fine Arts. Opening of the NAD," *NYEP*, April 17, 1866.

Sordello [Eugene Benson], "NAD. Forty-first Annual Exhibition," *NYEP*, April 28, May 11, May 17, 1866.

"Fine Arts. NAD," *NYH*, April 20, 1866.

"NAD. Forty-first Annual Exhibition," *NYL*, April 21, April 28, May 5, May 12, 1866.

"The Academy of Design," *NYL*, May 12, 1866.

"An American Art Feuilleton," *NYT*, May 3, 1866.

"NAD," *NYT*, May 19, 1866.

E. B. [Eugene Benson?], "Art," *Round Table* 4 (May 12, 1866): 295.

1867

"Fine Arts. Exhibition of the NAD," *Albion* 45 (April 20, 1867): 189–90; 45 (April 27, 1867): 201–02; 45 (May 4, 1867): 213–14.

Paletta, "Art Matters. NAD," *American Art Journal* 7 (April 27, 1867): 4–6; 7 (May 4, 1867): 22; 7 (May 11, 1867): 37–38; 7 (May 18, 1867): 53–54; 7 (May 25, 1867): 69–70.

Christopher P. Cranch, "Art Criticism Reviewed," *Galaxy* 4 (May 1, 1867): 77–81.

Russell Sturgis, Jr., "American Painters. The National Academy Exhibition," *Galaxy* 4 (June 1867): 230–31.

Outsider, "The NAD. A Visit to the Exhibition," *Independent* 19 (April 25, 1867): 1.

"Fine Arts. Forty-second Exhibition of the NAD," *Nation* 4 (May 2, 1867): 358–59; 4 (May 9, 1867): 379–80; 4 (May 16, 1867): 398–99.

[Clarence Cook], "The Academy of Design. Private View of the Forty-second Annual Exhibition," *NYDT*, April 16, 1867.

[Clarence Cook], "NAD—Forty-second Annual Exhibition," *NYDT*, May 9, June 14, July 3, 1867.

"NAD. Forty-second Annual Exhibition," *NYEP*, April 26, April 30, May 2, May 22, 1867.

"Fine Art," *NYH*, April 16, April 24, 1867.

"The NAD," *NYH*, April 29, 1867.

"NAD. Forty-Second Annual Exhibition," *NYL*, April 20, April 27, May 4, May 11, May 18, 1867.

"Novel Fine Arts," *NYL*, May 18, 1867.

"The NAD," *NYT*, April 29, May 23, 1867.

"The NAD," *New York World*, April 24, 1867.

"Pictures at the National Academy," *Round Table* 5 (May 11, 1867): 294; 5 (May 18, 1867): 310.

1868

R. M., "Art Matters," *Art Journal* 1 (July 1, 1868): 118–19.

S. S. C., "Art and Artists," *Galaxy* 5 (May 1868): 57–58.

"Art and Artists. The Academy Exhibition—Pictures Elsewhere," *Galaxy* 5 (June 1868): 795–96.

"Opening of the Academy of Design," *HW* 12 (May 2, 1868): 276.

"Fine Arts. Forty-Third Exhibition of the NAD," *Nation* 6 (April 30, 1868): 356; 6 (May 7, 1868): 376–77.

T[heodore] C. G[rannis], *National Academy of Design.
     Exhibition of 1868.* New York: D. Appleton & Company,
     1868 [reprint from *NYCA*].
"Academy of Design. Private View of the Forty-Third Annual
     Exhibition," *NYDT*, April 15, 1868.
[Clarence Cook], "The NAD. Forty-Third Annual Exhibition,"
     NYDT, May 4, May 21, June 13, June 18, 1868.
"The National Academy. The Reception," *NYEM*, April 14, 1868.
"Fine Arts," *NYEP*, April 15, 1868.
"Notes on Art," *NYH*, April 12, April 20, May 3, May 10, May 17,
     June 21, 1868.
"NAD," *NYL*, April 18, April 25, May 2, May 16, May 23,
     May 30, 1868.
"Fine Arts. NAD," *NYT*, May 14, 1868.
"The NAD," *New York World*, April 15, 1868.

1869

"Fine Arts. The NAD," *Albion* 47 (May 1, 1869): 243–44.
"NAD," *Appleton's Journal* 1 (June 5, 1869): 307–9.
"Fine Arts. The NAD," *Galaxy* 8 (June 1869): 910–11.
"Fine Arts. Forty-fifth Exhibition of the NAD," *Nation* 8 (April
     29, 1869): 340.
[Clarence Cook], "Art—Private View of the Spring
     Exhibition—NAD," *NYDT*, April 14, 1869.
[Clarence Cook], "The Fine Arts—The NAD—Forty-fourth
     Annual Exhibition," *NYDT*, May 13, June 5, June 15, 1869.
"Fine Arts. The Forty-fourth Annual Exhibition of the NAD,"
     NYEM, April 14, April 16, May 10, May 12, 1869.
"The Academy of Design. The Forty-fourth Exhibition," *NYEP*,
     April 27, 1869.
"Fine Arts. Forty-fourth Annual Exhibition of the Academy of
     Design," *NYH*, April 26, 1869.
"NAD," *NYH*, April 14, 1869.
R., "NAD. Forty-fourth Annual Exhibition," *NYL*, April 24,
     May 1, May 8, May 22, May 29, 1869.
"Art Items," *New York World*, April 18, 1869.
"Exhibition of the NAD," *Watson's Art Journal* 10 (April 17,
     1869): 299.
"NAD," *Watson's Art Journal* 10 (April 24, 1869): 305–6; 11 (May
     1, 1869): 1–2; 11 (May 8, 1869): 14–15; 11 (May 15, 1869): 32; 11
     (May 22, 1869): 41–42; 11 (May 29, 1869): 57–58; 11 (June 5,
     1869): 73–74; 11 (June 19, 1869): 85–86.

1870

"Topics of the Month: Art," *Aldine* 3 (June 1870): 68; 3 (August
     1870): 92.
John Jones, "The NAD," *HW* 14 (May 14, 1870): 307; 14 (May 28,
     1870): 339; 14 (June 18, 1870): 387.
"The Academy Exhibition," *HW* 14 (May 14, 1870): 316.
"Fine Arts: Forty-fifth Exhibition of the NAD," *Nation* 10 (April
     28, 1870): 278; 10 (June 2, 1870): 357.
[Clarence Cook], "The Academy of Design. The Opening of the
     Season," *NYDT*, April 15, 1870.
[Clarence Cook], "Fine Arts. The Portraits in the Academy,"
     NYDT, April 23, April 30, May 9, 1870.
"Art Matters," *New York Evening Express*, April 15, 1870.

"Fine Arts. The Spring Exhibition of the National Academy of
     Design," *NYEM*, February 4, 1870.
"Art Gossip: The Coming Forty-fifth Annual Exhibition of the
     N. A. D.," *NYEM*, April 12, 1870.
"The NAD: Opening of the Spring Exhibition," *NYEM*, April 15,
     1870.
"The Spring Exhibition: Forty-ninth Annual Exhibition of the
     NAD," *NYEM*, April 18, April 20, May 2, May 4, May 11, May
     24, June 27, July 1, 1870.
"Art Gossip: The True Test of a Good Academy Exhibition,"
     NYEM, April 29, 1870.
"NAD," *NYEP*, April 27, May 9, June 10, 1870.
" 'The Shades of Evening,' " *NYEP*, May 2, 1870.
"Carpenter's Portrait of Alice Cary," *NYEP*, May 20, 1870.
"Annual Exhibition of the NAD," *NYH*, April 18, April 21, May 8,
     May 18, 1870.
"The Butterflies in the Academy," *NYS*, April 15, 1870.
"Fine Arts: Opening of the Forty-fifth Annual Exhibition of the
     Academy of Design," *NYT*, April 17, 1870.
"Fine Arts: Academy of Design," *NYT*, May 1, 1870.
"NAD: Reception and Private View—The Forty-fifth Annual
     Exhibition," *New York World*, April 15, 1870.

1871

"Art," *Aldine* 4 (June 1871): 99–100.
Susan Nichols Carter, "The Spring Exhibition at the Academy of
     Design," *Appleton's Journal* 5 (May 27, 1871): 618–20.
Theodore C. Grannis, "National Academy Exhibition," *Art
     Review* 1 (July 1871): 16.
John Jones, "The Academy Exhibition," *HW* 15 (May 13, 1871):
     427; 15 (May 27, 1871): 476.
"The NAD," *NYCA*, April 14, 1871.
"Art Matters: Annual Exhibition of the National Academy of
     Design," *NYCA*, April 17, 1871.
"Fine Arts. Private View of the Exhibition of the Academy of
     Design," *NYDT*, April 14, April 22, 1871.
"Art Matters: The Academy of Design," *New York Evening
     Express*, April 14, 1871.
"The Spring Exhibition," *NYEM*, April 10, 1871.
"Reception at the NAD: Opening of the Spring Exhibition,"
     NYEM, April 14, 1871.
"Art Gossip: Forty-sixth Annual Exhibition of the National
     Academy," *NYEM*, April 18, April 20, May 8, May 22,
     June 3, 1871.
"Art Notes," *NYEM*, May 5, 1871.
"NAD," *NYEP*, April 13, May 2, May 10, May 26, 1871.
"Fine Arts: The Academy of Design. Opening of the Spring
     Exhibition," *NYET*, April 14, 1871.
"Fine Arts: The Mount Collection," *NYH*, April 10, 1871.
"Fine Arts: Forty-sixth Annual Exhibition of the NAD," *NYH*,
     April 17, 1871.
"The Spring Exhibition at the Academy of Design," *NYH*,
     April 17, 1871.
"NAD," *NYL*, April 15, April 22, April 29, May 6, May 13,
     May 20, 1871.
[No title], *NYS*, April 24, 1871.
"Fine Arts," *NYT*, April 16, April 23, April 30, 1871.

"The Academy of Design: The Forty-sixth Annual Exhibition,"
    New York World, April 23, 1871.
"Culture and Progress at Home: The National Academy
    Exhibition," *Scribner's Monthly* 1 (July 1871): 329–35.
W., "Exhibition of the NAD," *Watson's Art Journal* 14 (April 22,
    1871): 295–96; 14 (April 29, 1871): 307–8; 15 (May 5, 1871):
    6–7; 15 (May 13, 1871): 21; 15 (May 20, 1871): 32–33; 15 (June
    17, 1871): 80–81; 15 (July 15, 1871): 127–28; 15 (August 5, 1871):
    162–63; 15 (August 26, 1871): 199.

1872

"Art: New York," *Atlantic Monthly* 29 (March 1872): 374–77.
"Art in New York," *Boston Daily Advertiser,* April 22, 1872.
"The Spring Exhibition," *Christian Union* 5 (April 17, 1872): 336.
"NAD: Forty-seventh Annual Exhibition," *Fine Arts* 1 (May
    1872): 49–51.
[Clarence Cook?], "Fine Arts," *NYDT,* April 12, April 17,
    April 22, 1872.
"Art Intelligence: The Academy Exhibition," *New York Evening
    Express,* April 12, 1872.
"Art Matters," *New York Evening Express,* April 13, April 18, 1872.
"National Sundays," *New York Evening Express,* April 19, 1872.
"Art Gossip: Spring Exhibition of the National Academy,"
    NYEM, April 18, 1872.
"Art Notes," *NYEM,* April 23, 1872.
"Art Gossip. The Sunday Exhibitions at the Academy," *NYEM,*
    May 6, 1872.
"NAD: Reception Last Evening," *NYEP,* April 12, 1872.
"Fine Arts: Close of the National Academy Exhibition. The Last
    Sunday," *NYEP,* July 6, 1872.
"The Realm of Art," *NYET,* April 13, April 20, April 27,
    May 4, 1872.
"Studio Gossip," *NYH,* March 24, April 7, 1872.
"The Spring Exhibition of the Academy of Design," *NYH,* April
    14, 1872.
"Fine Arts," *NYT,* April 14, April 28, 1872.
"The Academy Exhibition," *New York World,* April 12, 1872.
A. C. W., "Gossip in a Gallery: A Visit to the Academy of
    Design," *New York World,* April 21, April 28, 1872.

1873

"Art: Annual Exhibition of NAD," *Aldine* 6 (June 1873): 127.
"Fine Arts: The Academy of Design," *Arcadian* 1 (April 24, 1873):
    9–10; 1 (May 1, 1873): 9–10; 1 (May 8, 1873): 10.
"Fine Arts: The Academy Exhibition," *Nation* 16 (May 22, 1873):
    358–59.
"NAD," *NYDG,* April 21, 1873.
Orpheus C. Kerr, "Administration Pictures," *NYDG,* May 13,
    1873.
"Female Artists: The Work of Women at the Academy of
    Design," *NYDG,* May 14, 1873.
"Humors of the Academy of Design," *NYDG,* June 6, 1873.
"Art and Its Results: A Lecture by Parke Godwin," *NYDT,*
    February 7, 1873.
[Clarence Cook], "Fine Arts. The NAD," *NYDT,* April 15, April
    25, April 30, 1873.

"Fine Arts," *NYEM,* April 15, April 18, April 22, April 25, April 29,
    May 6, May 16, 1873.
"NAD," *NYEP,* April 14, May 15, 1873.
"Art Matters: Academy of Design—Reception Last Night,"
    NYH, April 15, 1873.
"Fine Arts," *NYS,* April 15, 1873.
"Fine Arts: The Academy of Design," *NYT,* April 20, 1873.
"Hints on Art," *NYT,* April 26, 1873.
"Fine Arts: NAD," *New York World,* April 15, April 18, April 19,
    April 28, 1873.
"Culture and Progress: The NAD," *Scribner's Monthly* 6 (June 18,
    1873): 246–47.
Anglo, "Correspondence: The NAD," *Watson's Art Journal* 18
    (April 26, 1873): 309.

1874

"Art: National Academy Annual Exhibition," *Aldine* 7 (June
    1874): 128.
"Art: The Academy Exhibition," *Appleton's Journal* 11 (April 25,
    1874): 540; 11 (May 2, 1874): 571–73; 11 (May 9, 1874): 603–4;
    11 (May 16, 1874): 636–37; 11 (May 23, 1874): 667–68.
Clarence Cook, "Art. New York National Academy," *Atlantic
    Monthly* 33 (June 1874): 753–57.
"Fine Arts: The National Academy Exhibition," *Nation* 18 (May
    7, 1874): 303–5; 18 (May 14, 1874): 320–21.
"Notes," *Nation* 18 (June 4, 1874): 362–63.
"City Intelligence: The Spring Exhibition, NAD," *NYCA,* April
    20, 1874.
"Fine Arts: Annual Exhibition of the NAD," *NYDG,* April 9,
    April 10, April 14, 1874.
"The New Departure at the National Academy," *NYEM,*
    April 9, 1874.
"The Exhibition: Some of the Notable Pictures," *NYEM,* April
    10, 1874.
"Fine Arts: The Exhibition at the National Academy," *NYEM,*
    April 17, April 25, May 7, 1874.
"NAD," *NYEP,* April 8, April 25, May 4, 1874.
"Art at the Academy," *NYET,* April 11, 1874.
"Second Prep at the Academy," *NYET,* April 23, 1874.
"Studio Notes," *NYH,* April 1, 1874.
"The Spring Exhibition of the Academy of Design," *NYH,*
    April 7, April 9, 1874.
"The Academy of Design: Some of the Gems of the Present
    Exhibition," *NYH,* April 20, 1874.
"Fine Arts: The Exhibition of the Academy of Design," *NYS,*
    April 15, 1874.
"Fine Arts: The Academy Exhibition," *NYT,* April 6, April 9,
    April 13, April 19, 1874.
"Fine Arts: Mr. Moran's New Picture—Academy of Design—
    Notes," *NYT,* May 18, 1874.
[Clarence Cook], "Fine Arts. NAD," *NYDT,* April 9, April 11,
    April 13, April 18, April 24, April 25, May 2, 1874.
"The Academy of Design," *New York World,* April 3, 1874.
"The Academy Exhibition: Private Reception Last Evening,"
    New York World, April 9, 1874.
"NAD: Forty-ninth Annual Exhibition," *New York World,* April
    19, April 27, 1874.

Perdu, "The Fine Arts: The Cloning of the National Academy's
     Exhibition in New York," *Philadelphia Evening Bulletin*,
     June 23, 1874.
"Culture and Progress: The Academy Exhibition," *Scribner's
     Monthly* 8 (June 1874): 245.
"Exhibition of the NAD," *Watson's Art Journal* 21 (May 23, 1874):
     29–30; 21 (May 30, 1874): 42; 21 (June 13, 1874): 5–6.

1875

"Art," *Aldine* 4 (June 1875): 99.
"The Arts," *Appleton's Journal* 13 (April 24, 1875): 534–35; 13 (May
     1, 1875): 567–69; 13 (May 8, 1875): 599–600.
"New-York Studio Notes," *Art Journal* 1 (April 1875): 124–25.
"American Art Notes. NAD," *Art Journal* 1 (April 1875): 126.
"The NAD," *Art Journal* 1 (May 1875): 155–58.
"Art and Artists," *Boston Daily Evening Transcript*, April 9, 1875.
Henry James, "On Some Pictures Lately Exhibited," *Galaxy* 20
     (July 1875): 89–97.
"Fine Arts: Fiftieth Annual Exhibition of the Academy of
     Design," *Nation* 20 (April 15, 1875): 264–65; 20 (April 22,
     1875): 281–82; 20 (April 29, 1875): 301–2; 20 (May 20,
     1875): 352.
"NAD," *NYCA*, April 8, April 9, 1875.
"A Successful Exhibition," *NYCA*, June 2, 1875.
"Fine Arts. The Academy Exhibition," *NYDG*, April 10, April 16,
     1875.
[Clarence Cook], "Fine Arts: The NAD," *NYDT*, April 9, April
     26, April 29, May 1, 1875.
"Art Prizes Awarded: Annual Distribution at the Academy of
     Design," *NYDT*, May 20, 1875.
"NAD," *NYEM*, April 9, 1875.
"NAD: Opening of the Fiftieth Annual Exhibition," *NYEP*,
     April 7, 1875.
"NAD: Reception Last Evening," *NYEP*, April 8, 1875.
"The Academy Exhibition," *NYEP*, April 17, April 24, May 1,
     May 8, May 20, 1875.
"Academy of Design: Opening of the Fiftieth Annual
     Exhibition," *NYH*, April 8, 1875.
"The Fine Arts: The NAD" *NYT*, March 15, April 10, April 17,
     April 25, 1875.
"The Academy of Design," *New York World*, March 22, 1875.
"The Spring Exhibition: Varnishing Day at the Academy of
     Design," *New York World*, April 7, 1875.
H., "Art in New York: Annual Exhibition of the Academy of
     Design," *Philadelphia Evening Bulletin*, April 16, 1875.
H., "The Fine Arts: New York Academy of Design Exhibition,"
     Philadelphia Evening Bulletin, April 28, 1875.
"Culture and Progress: The Academy of Design," *Scribner's
     Monthly* 10 (June 1875): 251–54.

1876

"Notes," *Art Journal* 2 (March 1876): 95–96.
"The NAD," *Art Journal* 2 (May 1876): 157–59; 2 (June 1876):
     189–91.
"Art Matters: Academy of Design," *American Art Journal* 1 (May
     13, 1876): 198.

"The Arts: Representative Pictures at the Academy," *Appleton's
     Journal* 15 (April 15, 1876): 508–10.
"The Arts: The Academy Exhibition," *Appleton's Journal* 15
     (April 22, 1876): 539–50.
"Art," *Atlantic Monthly* 37 (June 1876): 758–62.
"Fine Arts," *Nation* 22 (April 6, 1876): 234–35; 22 (April 20, 1876):
     268.
"NAD. Views of a Visitor," *NYCA*, April 13, 1876.
"The Art Exhibition: The Annual Display of the National
     Academy," *NYDG*, March 29, 1876.
"National Academy Exhibition: Some Landscapes and
     Marines," *NYDG*, April 10, 1876.
"Close of the Academy: Effect of the Admission of Mediocre
     Pictures," *NYDG*, June 2, 1876.
[Clarence Cook], "Fine Arts: Fifty-first Annual Exhibition of
     the NAD," *NYDT*, March 28, April 1, April 8, April 22, April
     29, May 6, 1876.
"Art Notes. The Reception at the Academy of Design," *New York
     Evening Express*, March 29, 1876.
"Art Matters: A Hasty Glance at the Academy Exhibition," *New
     York Evening Express*, April 20, 1876.
"Studio and Academy," *NYEM*, March 10, 1876.
"Fine Arts," *NYEM*, March 30, April 18, 1876.
"NAD: The Fifty-first Annual Exhibition," *NYEP*, March 28, 1876.
"Art Matters: A Glance at Pictures and Remarks about the
     Painters," *NYET*, May 13, 1876.
"The Academy of Design: Another Ramble through the North
     and East Rooms," *NYET*, May 19, 1876.
"Fine Arts. Pictures Exhibited at the Academy of Design," *NYH*,
     April 3, May 26, 1876.
"Fifty-first Exhibition of the National Academy," *NYS*, March
     28, 1876.
"The NAD," *NYS*, April 30, 1876.
"Academy of Design: The Fifty-first Annual Exhibition," *NYT*,
     March 28, 1876.
"The Fine Arts: The Academy Exhibition," *NYT*, April 3,
     April 8, 1876.
"Books, Pictures, Etc: The NAD," *Rod and Gun Late American
     Sportsman* (April 8, 1876): 23–24.

1877

*Academy Sketches: Comprising Reproductions in Fac-Simile from
     Drawings by the Artists, of 110 of the Pictures in the Annual
     Exhibition of 1877 of the National Academy of Design with
     Descriptive Notes by "Nemo."* New York: G. P. Putnam's
     Sons, 1877.
"Art Matters," *American Art Journal* 27 (April 21, 1877): 25; 27
     (April 28, 1877): 42; 27 (May 5, 1877): 57; 27 (May 12, 1877):
     72–73.
"The Academy Exhibition," *Art Journal* 3 (May 1877): 157–60.
"The Academy of Design," *HW* 21 (April 14, 1877): 289–90.
"Notes," *Nation* 24 (April 5, 1877): 207–08; 24 (June 14, 1877):
     352.
"Paintings: The Exhibition of the NAD," *NYCA*, April 2, 1877.
"NAD," *NYCA*, April 3, April 19, April 21, May 10, May 23, 1877.
"The Academy Pictures," *NYDG*, April 3, 1877.
M., "Pictures in the Spring Exhibition," *NYDG*, April 6, 1877.
"Academy of Design," *NYDG*, April 11, 1877.

"At the Academy of Design," *NYDT*, March 24, 1877.

[Clarence Cook], "NAD," *NYDT*, April 3, April 7, April 16, April 21, April 28, May 5, May 19, May 21, May 26, 1877.

William R. O'Donovan, "National Academy Criticism," *NYDT*, June 2, 1877.

C[larence] C[ook], "American Art: Why There Should Be a New Academy," *NYDT*, June 5, 1877.

Clarence Cook, "Academy Criticism," *NYDT*, June 9, 1877.

Clarence Cook, "The Academy and Art," *NYDT*, June 27, 1877.

"Fine Arts: The Academy Exhibition," *NYEM*, March 30, April 16, April 23, May 1, May 7, 1877.

"The Academy Exhibition: The Fifty-second Annual Exhibition," *NYEP*, April 2, 1877.

"The Academy of Design," *NYEP*, April 10, April 21, April 28, May 5, May 12, May 19, 1877.

"Art Matters: The Fifty-second Annual Exhibition of the Academy of Design," *NYH*, April 2, 1877.

"Academy of Design: Private View and Reception Last Night," *NYH*, April 3, 1877.

"Close of the Exhibition," *NYH*, June 3, 1877.

"NAD: The Fifty-second Exhibition," *NYS*, April 15, 1877.

"The Academy of Design: Fifty-second Annual Exhibition," *NYT*, April 3, April 8, April 13, April 15, 1877.

"Imitators in Art," *NYT*, April 22, 1877.

"Academy Exhibition Portraits," *NYT*, April 23, 1877.

"The Private View at the Academy of Design," *New York World*, April 3, 1877.

"The Academy Exhibition," *New York World*, April 10, April 14, April 16, April 23, April 30, May 7, 1877.

"The Academy of Design: Close of the Most Successful Exhibition Since 1866," *New York World*, June 2, 1877.

"Picture-Buyers at the Academy," *New York World*, June 3, 1877.

"Culture and Progress: The National Academy Exhibition, 1877," *Scribner's Monthly* 14 (June 1877): 263–68.

1878

Mariana Griswold Van Rensselaer, "NAD, New York: Fifty-third Annual Exhibition," *American Architect and Building News* 3 (April 27, 1878): 149–50.

"Art Matters: NAD," *American Art Journal* 28 (April 13, 1878): 326–27.

"Notes," *Art Journal* 4 (March 1878): 94–96.

S[usan] N[ichols] Carter, "The Academy Exhibition," *Art Journal* 4 (May 1878): 157–59.

"Fine Arts. The National Academy Exhibition," *Brooklyn Daily Eagle*, April 7, 1878.

Delta, "The Academy Exhibition," *Boston Daily Evening Transcript*, May 6, 1878.

"Fine Arts. The Academy Exhibition. The Portraits," *Independent* 30 (April 11, 1878): 7.

"Fine Arts: In the Academy Exhibit–II," *Independent* 30 (April 18, 1878): 9.

"Notes: The Fifty-third exhibition of the Academy of Design was opened on Tuesday," *Nation* 26 (April 4, 1878): 229.

"Fine Arts: The Fifty-third Exhibition of the Academy of Design," *Nation* 26 (April 18, 1878): 265–66; 26 (May 30, 1878): 363–64.

"Art Notes," *NYCA*, January 9, 1878.

"Art Notes: The NAD Reception Last Evening," *NYCA*, April 2, April 5, April 20, 1878.

"NAD," *NYDG*, April 3, April 11, 1878.

C[larence] C[ook], "Art at the Academy. The Fifty-third Annual Exhibition," *NYDT*, April 2, 1878.

"The Opening Reception," *NYDT*, April 2, 1878.

C[larence] C[ook], "Fine Arts: NAD; Fifty-third Annual Exhibition," *NYDT*, April 2, April 9, April 19, May 8, May 11, May 27, 1878.

"The Academy of Design: Opening of the Fifty-third Annual Exhibition," *NYEP*, March 30, 1878.

"American Art: The Fifty-third Annual Exhibition in the NAD," *NYEP*, April 6, April 20, May 4, 1878.

"Academy of Design: The 53rd 'Private View' and Reception Last Evening," *NYET*, April 2, 1878.

"Art Matters: The NAD," *NYET*, April 9, 1878.

"Pictures and Critics," *NYET*, April 9, 1878.

"Art and Literature: Studio Notes," *NYET*, May 25, 1878.

"Art Matters: Academy of Design—The Close of the Season," *NYET*, June 1, 1878.

"Academy of Design and Its Man," *NYET*, June 7, 1878.

"Fine Arts," *NYH*, March 31, April 2, April 8, April 15, April 22, April 29, May 6, 1878.

"NAD," *New York Mail*, April 4, 1878.

"Social Life: The Academy Opening," *New York Mail*, April 6, 1878.

"Art and Artists," *New York Mail*, May 15, 1878.

"The NAD," *NYS*, April 7, April 14, 1878.

"Varnishing Day," *NYT*, March 4, 1878.

"The Coming Exhibition: Academy of Design Paintings," *NYT*, April 1, 1878.

"The Academy Exhibition," *NYT*, April 7, April 10, April 14, April 21, May 20, 1878.

"The National Academy Exhibition," *New York World*, April 2, 1878.

"The Academy Exhibition," *New York World*, April 14, May 7, May 9, May 19, 1878.

"American Art: The Sale of Pictures Exhibited at the National Academy," *New York World*, June 2, 1878.

1879

M[ariana] G[riswold] Van Rensselaer, "The Spring Exhibitions in New York," *American Architect and Building News* 5 (May 10, 1879): 148–49.

"Editor's Table. The Academy Exhibition," *Appleton's Journal* 6 (May 1879): 469–71.

Montezuma, "My Note Book," *AAm* 1 (July 1879): 25.

Edward Strahan [Earl Shinn], "The NAD. First Notice," *AAm* 1 (June 1879): 4–5; 1 (July 1879): 27–29.

H. H, "The 54th Annual Reception of the Academy of Design," *Art Critic* 1 (April 1879): 2–3; 1 (May 1879): 2; 1 (June 1879): 27; 1 (July 1879): 33–34.

"The Studio: The Spring Exhibition NAD," *Art Interchange* 2 (April 2, 1879): 50; 2 (April 16, 1879): 58.

"Notes," *Art Journal* 5 (March 1879): 95–96.

"The Academy Exhibition," *Art Journal* 5 (May 1879): 158–60.

"The Two New York Exhibitions," *Atlantic Monthly* 43 (June 1879): 781–83.

"Culture and Progress: The Art Season of 1878–9," *Century Magazine* 18 (June 1879): 310–13.

"Fine Arts. The Fifty-fourth Exhibition of the Academy of Design," *Nation* 28 (May 15, 1879): 341–42; 28 (May 22, 1879): 359.

"Art Notes: The Exhibition of Paintings at the National Academy Last Night—A Noteworthy Display," *NYCA*, April 1, 1879.

"The Academy Exhibition," *NYDG*, March 29, 1879.

"An Amateur in the Academy," *NYDG*, May 3, 1879.

"Selections from the Collection of Paintings Now on Exhibition at the Academy of Design," *NYDG*, December 10, 1879.

"NAD: Fifty-fourth Annual Exhibition," *NYDT*, April 1, April 5, April 12, April 26, 1879.

"Art Matters: The Academy Exhibition, First Article," *New York Evening Express,* April 9, 1879.

Strix, "Our Feuilleton. An Old Academician [Letter to the Editor by an Old Academician and Comments]," *New York Evening Express,* April 12, 1879.

"Academy Tactics," *New York Evening Express,* May 15, 1879.

"Artists at Loggerheads," *New York Evening Express,* May 27, 1879.

"The Academy Exhibition: First Impressions and a Hasty Tour of the Galleries," *NYEP*, March 29, 1879.

"The Academy Sculptors: Plastic Art in an Ante-Chamber—Latest Works of O'Donovan, Kemeys, Hartley, and Warner," *NYEP*, April 26, 1879.

"The Academy Painters: Features of the Annual Exhibition at Fourth Avenue and Twenty-third Street," *NYEP*, May 24, 1879.

"Artistic Effervescence: The Cause a Resignation from the National Academy," *NYEP*, May 27, 1879.

"The Academy Paintings: A Better Display Than Has Been Seen for Years," *NYET*, March 31, 1879.

"Academy of Fine Arts: Characteristics Which Make the Present Exhibition a Good One," *NYET*, April 14, 1879.

"The Academy Pictures: Further View of More Prominent Works," *NYET*, April 22, 1879.

"Fine Arts," *NYH*, March 17, March 29, March 30, March 31, April 1, April 7, April 14, April 22, April 28, May 5, June 1, 1879.

"The Academy Exhibition," *New York Mail*, April 1, 1879.

"The National Academy," *NYS*, April 6, April 13, April 20, April 27, May 4, 1879.

"Preparing the Pictures: The Artists' Varnishing Day," *NYT*, March 30, 1879.

"Artists and Their Works: The Academy of Design," *NYT*, April 1, 1879.

Clarence Cook, "Our National Academy," *NYT*, April 4, 1879.

"Artists and Their Works: Around the Galleries," *NYT*, April 7, 1879.

"The Academy of Design: A Little Band of Sculptors," *NYT*, April 12, 1879.

"Budding Academicians: American Genre Pictures," *NYT*, April 20, 1879.

"The Academy Paintings: Flowers and Portraits," *NYT*, April 26, 1879.

"The Academy Exhibition: Sales of Paintings," *NYT*, May 2, 1879.

"The Academy of Design: Last Week of the Exhibition," *NYT*, May 24, 1879.

"Antagonism of Artists: Academy and American Society Painters," *NYT*, May 28, 1879.

"NAD: Close of the Annual Exhibition—The Paintings Sold," *NYT*, June 1, 1879.

"The Academy Exhibition," *New York World*, March 30, April 9, April 27, May 5, 1879.

"The Academy of Design: It Celebrates Its Fifty-fourth Year with a Wreck of Toilets and a Crush of Crowds," *New York World*, April 1, 1879.

"Culture and Progress. The Academy of Design," *Scribner's Monthly* 18 (June 1879): 312–13.

1880

M[ariana] G[riswold] Van Rensselaer, "Spring Exhibitions and Picture-Sales in New York ," *American Architect and Building News* 7 (May 1, 1880): 190–91; 7 (May 8, 1880): 201–2.

S. G. W. Benjamin, "Exhibitions," *American Art Review* 1 (May 1880): 306–13; 1 (June 1880): 348–53.

Montezuma, "My Note Book," *AAm* 2 (May 1880): 113.

"Exhibition of the Academy of Design," *AAm* 2 (May 1880): 112.

"The National Academy Exhibition, Second Notice," *AAm* 3 (June 1880): 2–3.

"NAD Exhibition," *Art Interchange* 4 (March 31, 1880): 54–55; 4 (April 14, 1880): 63.

S. N. Carter, "The New York Spring Exhibitions," *Art Journal* 6 (May 1880): 153–56.

Sidney Hyde, "The Fine Arts: The Academy Exhibition in New York," *Boston Daily Advertiser*, April 9, 1880.

Delta, "The Academy Exhibition," *Boston Daily Evening Transcript*, March 27, May 5, 1880.

"Fine Arts. NAD," *Independent* 32 (April 8, 1880): 6.

William C. Brownell, "Fine Arts: NAD—Fifty-fifth Annual Exhibition—II," *Nation* 30 (April 29, 1880): 334–35.

[Clarence Cook], "NAD. Fifty-fifth Annual Exhibition," *NYDT*, March 27, March 31, April 4, April 18, 1880.

"Pictures Sold at the Academy," *NYDT*, April 15, 1880.

Strix, "Our Feuilleton," *New York Evening Express,* March 27, April 3, April 14, April 24, May 8, May 15, 1880.

"The Academy Exhibition," *NYEP*, March 26, April 17, 1880.

"Art at the Academy," *NYET*, March 27, 1880.

"Academy of Design," *NYET*, April 10, 1880.

"A New Academy of Design," *NYET*, May 18, 1880.

"Fine Arts: Exhibition of the Academy of Design," *NYEM*, March 27, 1880.

"Fine Arts: Fifty-fifth Annual Exhibition of the NAD," *NYH*, March 27, March 30, April 5, April 12, April 19, April 26, May 3, May 10, 1880.

"The National Academy," *NYS*, March 28, 1880.

"NAD," *NYT*, January 28, 1880.

"The Academy Exhibition: The Press View of the Spring Collection," *NYT*, March 27, 1880.

"Artists and Their Work: Pictures in the Academy," *NYT*, April 9, 1880.

"The Academy Exhibition," *New York World*, March 27, 1880.

"Culture and Progress. The Art Season," *Scribner's Monthly* 20 (July 1880): 314–15.

1881

[Clarence Cook], "My Note Book—The Academy 'Private Views,'" *AAm* 4 (April 1881): 91.

"Exhibition of the Academy of Design," *AAm* 4 (May 1881): 115–17.

"The 'Academy' Hanging," *AAm* 4 (May 1881): 112.

S. G. W. Benjamin, "The Exhibitions: VII—NAD. Fifty-sixth Exhibition," *American Art Review* 2 (May 1881): 21–29.

"Fifty-sixth Academy: First Notice," *Art Interchange* 6 (March 31, 1881): 74.

"Art Notes." *Art Journal* 7 (April 1881) 125–28; 7 (May 1881): 157–60; 7 (June 1881): 189–92.

G. P. L., "The Fine Arts: The National Academy Exhibition in New York," *Boston Daily Advertiser*, April 11, 1881.

M. P. N., "Our New York Letter," *Cleveland Plain Dealer*, April 15, 1881.

"The Academy Exhibition," *HW* 25 (April 2, 1881): 219–20.

"Pictures at the Academy," *HW* 25 (April 9, 1881): 235, 237, 239.

"Fine Arts: The NAD: Fifty-sixth Annual Exhibition," *Independent* 33 (March 31, 1881): 8.

"Fine Arts: Fifty-sixth Annual Exhibition of the NAD," *Nation* 32 (March 31, 1881): 229–30; 32 (April 21, 1881): 285–86.

"Art Notes. Poor Pictures by the American Society of Artists— The Great Success of the National Academy Exhibition," *NYCA*, April 4, 1881.

"In Studio and Gallery: What the Painters Are Doing: Another Artists' Reception—Sales of Water-colors—Getting Ready for the Academy," *NYDT*, February 20, 1881.

"NAD: Fifty-sixth Annual Exhibition," *NYDT*, March 20, 1881.

"The Academy Exhibition: Last Night's Private View of the Pictures," *NYDT*, March 22, 1881.

"NAD: Fifty-sixth Annual Exhibition," *NYDT*, March 29, 1881.

"Sales at the Exhibitions: Unusually Large Purchases at the Academy," *NYDT*, April 3, 1881.

"In Studio and Gallery: Notes Among the Painters," *NYDT*, April 10, 1881.

"NAD: Fifty-sixth Annual Exhibition," *NYDT*, April 11, 1881.

"Work of the Painters: Exhibitions and Sales: Paintings Sold at the Academy," *NYDT*, April 17, 1881.

"Notes of Art Work: Close of the Academy Exhibition," *NYDT*, May 15, 1881.

G. W. H., "Fine Arts: The Academy Exhibition," *New York Evening Express*, March 23, March 28, April 2, April 12, April 20, May 13, 1881.

"The Academy Exhibition," *NYEM*, April 5, May 11, 1881.

"The Academy Exhibition," *NYEP*, March 18, 1881.

"Art As Sentiment: Pictures in the Fifty-sixth Annual Exhibition of the NAD," *NYEP*, April 9, 1881.

"Art As Sentimentalism: Pictures in the Fifty-sixth Annual Exhibition of the NAD," *NYEP*, April 16, 1881.

"Fine Arts: The National Academy Exhibition," *NYH*, March 19, 1881.

"Fine Arts," *NYH*, March 20, March 21, March 22, March 28, April 18, May 9, 1881.

W. M. L. [William Mackay Laffan?], "The National Academy Exhibition," *NYS*, March 27, 1881.

[Clarence Cook], "The Academy Exhibition," *NYT*, March 20, 1881.

[Clarence Cook], "The Academy Paintings: Good and Bad Work by New Aspirants to Fame," *NYT*, March 28, 1881.

[Clarence Cook], "The Academy Paintings: More Notable Features of the Exhibition," *NYT*, April 3, 1881.

[Clarence Cook], "Some American Artists: Various Notable Pictures in the Exhibition," *NYT*, April 15, 1881.

[Clarence Cook], "The National Academy: Relations of the Critic and the Artist," *NYT*, April 24, 1881.

"The Academy Exhibition," *New York World*, March 20, 1881.

"The Academy Portraits," *New York World*, April 2, 1881.

"The Figure-paintings at the Academy," *New York World*, April 8, 1881.

"The Academy of Design," *Studio and Musical Review*, March 26, April 9, April 16, 1881.

1882

"Mariana Griswold Van Rensselaer, "Fifty-seventh Annual Exhibition of the NAD, New York," *American Architect and Building News* 11 (April 15, 1882): 174–76.

"Academy Notes," *American Art Journal* 36 (April 15, 1882): 485–86.

Clarence Cook, "Gallery and Studio: The National Academy Exhibition," *AAm* 6 (May 1882): 116–18.

"Drawing Room: Fifty Seventh Academy, First Notice," *Art Interchange* 8 (March 30, 1882): 74.

"The Studio: Fifty-sixth Academy," *Art Interchange* 8 (July 27, 1882): 103.

"Art Notes: New York—NAD," *Art Journal* (May 1882): 157–60; (June 1882): 189–90.

Delta, "New York Topics: The Academy Exhibition," *Boston Evening Transcript*, October 27, 1882.

"The Fine Arts: Fifty-seventh Exhibition," *Critic* 2 (April 8, 1882): 104–5.

"The NAD," *HW* 26 (March 25, 1882): 187, 189.

"Fine Arts: The Two Oil-color Exhibitions," *Nation* 34 (April 20, 1882): 344–46; 34 (April 27, 1882): 366–67.

"800 Pictures Displayed: Complaints Against the Hanging Committee: The Fifty-seventh Annual Exhibition of Paintings," *New York Commercial Advertiser*, March 27, 1882.

"NAD. Fifty-seventh Annual Exhibition—Varnishing Day," *NYDT*, March 25, 1882.

"The Work of the Artists. Sales at the Academy," *NYDT*, March 26, 1882.

"A Private View of the Pictures," *NYDT*, March 26, 1882.

"NAD: Fifty-seventh Annual Exhibition," *NYDT*, April 2, 1882.

"Notes Among the Artists," *NYDT*, April 3, 1882.

"Art Matters of Interest," *NYDT*, April 9, 1882.

"Among the Artists," *NYDT*, April 16, 1882.

"The Work of the Artists," *NYDT*, April 23, 1882.

"Among the Artists," *NYDT*, May 8, 1882.

"The Academy Exhibition," *NYEP*, March 25, 1882.

"Fine Arts: The Fifty-seventh Annual Exhibition of the NAD— and the Fifth Annual Exhibition of the Society of American Art," *NYEP*, April 17, 1882.

"The Two Oil-color Exhibitions—II," *NYEP*, April 27, 1882.

"Fine Arts: Fifty-seventh Annual Exhibition of the NAD," *NYH*, March 25, March 27, April 4, April 10, April 27, 1882.

"Sales at the Academy and the Society of American Artists,"
    NYH, April 9, 1882.
"A Want of Art," *NYH*, April 20, 1882.
"Fine Arts: Notes on the Academy Exhibition," *New York Mail
    and Express*, March 31, April 3, April 24, 1882.
"The National Academy Exhibition," *NYS*, March 26, 1882.
"The NAD," *NYS*, April 2, 1882.
"The Academy of Design," *NYS*, October 24, 1882.
"The Academy Exhibition," *NYT*, March 2, March 30, April 16,
    April 30, 1882.
"Painting As a Profession: Rise of Painters Socially and
    Economically," *NYT*, May 14, 1882.
"NAD, I," *New York World*, March 26, 1882.
"Some Notable Pictures," *New York World*, March 29, 1882.
"NAD, III," *New York World*, April 8, 1882.
"NAD, IV," *New York World*, April 10, 1882.

1883

"The Academy Exhibition," *AAm* 8 (May 1883): 126–28.
"Fifty-eighth Academy," *Art Interchange* 10 (April 10, 1883): 94;
    10 (April 26, 1883): 106.
The National Academy: A Display of Respectable Monotony,"
    Boston Daily Transcript, April 14, 1883.
"The Exhibition of the NAD," *Boston Evening Transcript*, April
    11, 1883.
"Art," *Churchman*, April 14, May 12, 1883.
"The Fine Arts: Academy of Design—48th Annual Exhibition,"
    Critic 3 (April 7, 1883): 161.
G. W. Sheldon, "The Academy Exhibition," *HW* 27 (April 7,
    1883): 214, 220.
"Sketches from the New York NAD," *HW* 27 (April 14, 1883): 229.
"Monthly Record of American Art," *Magazine of Art* 6 (1883):
    xxv–xxx.
"Fine Arts: Fifty-eighth Annual Exhibition of the NAD," *Nation*
    36 (April 18, 1883): 848.
"The NAD: Fifty-eighth Annual Exhibition," *NYDT*, March 31,
    1883.
"Art News and Comments," *NYDT*, April 1, April 8, April 15,
    April 22, 1883.
"The Academy Exhibition," *NYDT*, May 4, May 9, May 12, 1883.
"Fine Arts: Fifty-eighth Annual Exhibition of the NAD," *NYEP*,
    April 19, 1883.
"Fine Arts," *NYH*, April 2, April 8, May 6, 1883.
"NAD: The Fifty-eighth Annual Exhibition," *New York Mail and
    Express*, April 2, 1883.
"Fine Arts: Fifty-eighth Annual Exhibition of the NAD," *New
    York Mail and Express*, April 11, April 17, April 23, 1883.
"Pictures: The NAD," *NYS*, April 2, 1883.
"Pictures at the Academy: Viewed in the Quiet of Varnishing
    Day," *NYT*, March 31, 1883.
"Sales of Pictures at the NAD," *NYT*, April 15, 1883.
"The Academy of Design: Features of the Fifty-eighth Annual
    Exhibition," *NYT*, April 15, 1883.
"The Academy Exhibition," *New York World*, March 31, 1883.
"The Academy," *Studio* 1 (April 7, 1883): 120–23.
"Sales at the Academy," *Studio* 1 (April 15, 1883): 137.
"Exhibition Sales," *Studio* 1 (May 5, 1883): 178; 1 (May 12, 1883):
    192.
"Sales at Exhibitions," *Studio* 1 (May 19, 1883): 204, 206–7.

1884

Robert Jarvis, "The National Academy Exhibition," *AAm* 10
    (May 1884); 125–31; 11 (June 1884): 8–10.
"Fifty-ninth Academy," *Art Interchange* 12 (April 10, 1884):
    88–89; 12 (April 24, 1884): 100–101.
"The Coming Academy Exhibition," *Art Union* 1 (March 1884):
    51–52.
"The National Academy Exhibition," *Art Union* 1 (April 1884):
    75–84.
"The National Academy Exhibition," *Art Union* 1 (May 1884):
    100.
"The National Academy Exhibition: Genre Subjects," *Baltimore
    Sun*, March 1, 1884.
M. H., "The NAD," *Boston Daily Evening Transcript*, April 22,
    1884.
E. W. M., "National Academy Exhibition: Varnishing Day with
    the Academicians," *Boston Evening Transcript*, April 5, 1884.
Art," *Churchman*, May 10, May 17, 1884.
"The Academy Exhibition," *Critic and Good Literature* 1 (May 3,
    1884): 209–10.
The Academy Exhibition," *HW* 28 (April 26, 1884): 271–72.
"The National Academy Exhibition," *Independent* 36 (April 17,
    1884): 488–89; 36 (May 1, 1884): 551–52.
"The Exhibition of the National Academy," *Magazine of Art* 7
    (1884): xxv–xxviii.
"Fine Arts: The Academy Exhibition," *Nation* 38 (April 17, 1884):
    351–52; 38 (April 24, 1884): 370–72; 38 (May 1, 1884): 394
    (reprinted from *NYEP*).
"The Academy Exhibition. First Notice," *NYCA*, April 5, April 8,
    April 12, 1884.
An Artist Who Voted, "The Academy Awards [Letter to the
    Editor]," *NYCA*, May 3, 1884.
"The Academy of Design: Fifty-ninth Annual Exhibition,"
    NYDT, March 5, April 5, 1884.
"The Academy Exhibition," *NYDT*, April 14, April 21, April 28,
    1884.
"The NAD," *NYEP*, April 9, April 12, April 16, April 21, April 22,
    April 29, 1884.
"The Academy Prizes," *NYEP*, April 24, 1884.
Fine Art Notes," *NYET*, April 11, April 21, May 7, 1884.
"Pictures for the Academy," *NYH*, March 16, 1884.
"Fine Arts," *NYH*, April 5, April 7, April 8, April 13, April 20, May
    4, May 18, 1884.
"Fine Arts: Exhibition of the National Academy," *New York Mail
    and Express*, April 5, April 11, April 23, April 29, May 7, 1884.
"The NAD," *NYS*, April 8, 1884.
"The Spring Academy," *NYT*, April 5, 1884.
"More Pictures at the Academy," *NYT*, April 20, 1884.
"Academy of Design," *NYT*, May 18, 1884.
"The Annual Academy Exhibition: To Be Opened to the Public
    To-morrow—The Paintings Hung," *New York World*, April
    7, 1884.
"Pictures over the Doors: A Novel Supplementary Exhibition at
    the National Academy," *New York World*, April 13, 1884.
C. A., "National Art: Notes in the Exhibition of the National
    Academy: Notable Landscapes, Marine Views and Figure
    Painting [From a Lady Correspondent]," *San Francisco
    Evening Bulletin*, April 29, 1884.
"The Reporter. Among the Studios," *Studio* 3 (March 1, 1884):
    101–2.

"Academy Whispers," *Studio* 3 (March 22, 1884): 141.
"[Editorial notes,] *Studio* 3 (April 5, 1884): 157–58; 3 (April 12, 1884): 169–70.
"The National Academy Exhibition," *Studio* 3 (April 12, 1884): 170–73.

1885

"The National Academy Exhibition," *AAm* 12 (May 1885): 128–29.
"The Spring Academy Exhibition," *Art Interchange* 14 (April 9, 1885): 88–89.
M. B. W., "Woman's Work at the Academy," *Art Interchange* 14 (April 23, 1885): 110–12.
"The Spring Exhibition," *Art Union* 2 (January–March 1885): 13.
"Art in Hard Times," *Art Union* 2 (April–June 1885): 36.
E. W. M., "Paintings at the Academy: A Glance at the Fall Exhibitions," *Boston Daily Evening Transcript,* November 21, 1885.
"The Sixtieth Academy," *Critic* 6 (April 11, 1885): 174–75.
"Exhibition of the NAD," *Decorator and Furnisher* 6 (May 1885): 47.
"Fine Arts: The National Academy Exhibition," *Nation* 40 (April 16, 1885): 828–29.
"The Academy of Design: Sixtieth Annual Exhibition," *NYDT,* April 4, April 13, April 20, 1885.
"The National Academy Exhibition," *NYEP,* April 8, April 13, 1885.
"Fine Arts," *NYH,* April 5, April 7, April 13, April 26, 1885.
"Fine Arts," *New York Mail and Express,* April 4, April 15, April 18, 1885.
"The NAD," *NYS,* April 12, 1885.
"The Spring Academy," *NYT,* April 4, 1885.
"The Reception at the Academy," *NYT,* April 6, 1885.
"Sales at the Academy," *NYT,* May 10, 1885.
"The NAD: The Sixtieth Annual Exhibition," *Studio* n.s. 1 (April 11, 1885): 205–11.
"The Clarke and Hallgarten Prizes," *Studio* n.s. 1 (April 25, 1885): 231–32.
"More Scared than Hurt," *Studio* n.s. 1 (May 9, 1885): 237–40.

1886

"The Academy Exhibition," *AAm* 14 (May 1886): 119–20.
"The Spring Exhibition at the Academy," *Art Interchange* 16 (April 10, 1886): 116.
"New York Academy Exhibition: The Annual Spring Show of Paintings," *Boston Daily Evening Transcript,* April 5, 1886.
"Art," *Churchman* 53 (April 24, 1886): 476–77.
"The Fine Arts. Sixty-first Academy Exhibition," *Critic* 8 (April 10, 1886): 182–83.
"The National Academy," *HW* 30 (April 10, 1886): 235–37.
Mrs. Schuyler [Mariana Griswold] Van Rensselaer, "Fine Arts: The NAD," *Independent* 38 (April 15, 1886): 460; 38 (May 6, 1886): 555.
"Fine Arts: The National Academy Exhibition," *Nation* 42 (April 8, 1886): 305.
"The Academy of Design: Sixty-first Annual Exhibition," *NYDT,* April 3, 1886.

"Art News and Comments: The Week in Art Circles," *NYDT,* April 5, May 2, May 3, May 16, 1886.
"The National Academy Exhibition," *NYEP,* April 5, 1886.
"Academy of Design: The Spring Exhibition at the Venetian Art Palace," *NYH,* April 3, 1886.
"At the National Academy: Another Trip around the Galleries of the Sixty-first Annual Display," *NYH,* April 12, 1886.
"Paintings and Sculptures: Autumn Exhibition at the NAD," *NYH,* November 20, 1886.
"The Academy Exhibition," *New York Mail and Express,* April 28, 1886.
"The National Academy," *NYS,* April 3, 1886.
"The Academy of Design: Spring Exhibition of Paintings and Sculptures," *NYT,* April 4, 1886.
"National Academy Notes," *NYT,* April 5, 1886.
"The Spring Academy," *NYT,* April 17, 1886.
"The Academy Exhibition," *New York World,* April 4, April 12, 1886.
"The Clarke and Hallgarten Prizes," *Studio* n.s. 1 (May 1, 1886): 257–58.

1887

"Gallery and Studio: The National Academy Exhibition," *AAm* 16 (May 1887): 125.
Lyman H. Weeks, "Two Academy Exhibitions," *American Art Illustrated* 1 (April 1887): 195–201.
"Art Notes: The Academy Exhibition," *Art Interchange* 18 (April 23, 1887): 129–30.
Ripley Hitchock, "Spring Exhibition, National Academy," *Art Review* 1 (April 1887): 1–6.
"Art Notes," *Art Review* 1 (April 1887): 15–24.
"The Fine Arts: Good Work at the Academy," *Critic* 10 (April 9, 1887): 183; 10 (April 23, 1887): 210–11.
"The Sixty-second Annual Exhibition of the NAD," *Decorator and Furnisher* 10 (May 1887): 41.
"Pictures at the Spring Academy," *HW* 31 (April 9, 1887): 252, 254.
William A. Coffin, "Fine Arts: The Academy Exhibition," *Nation* 44 (April 14, 1887): 327; 44 (April 28, 1887): 373.
"The NAD: Sixty-second Annual Exhibition," *NYDT,* April 2, 1887.
"The Academy Exhibition: Second Notice," *NYDT,* April 14, 1887.
"Art News and Comments: The Week in Art Circles: Notes on the Exhibitions," *NYDT,* April 17, May 15, 1887.
"The Academy of Design: The Pictures in the Spring Exhibition," *NYEP,* April 1, 1887.
"The Academy Exhibition: First Notice," *NYEP,* April 14, 1887.
"The Academy Exhibition, II," *NYEP,* April 26, 1887.
"The NAD: Annual Spring Display of Oil Paintings and Sculptures," *NYH,* April 2, 1887.
"Fine Arts: Various Remarks on the Exhibition Now Open at the National Academy," *NYH,* April 18, 1887.
John R. Tait, "The Academy Exhibition," *New York Mail and Express,* April 11, April 15, 1887.
"The Spring Picture Exhibitions," *NYS,* May 8, 1887.
"The Academy of Design: A Well-Chosen Exhibition," *NYT,* April 2, 1887.

"Pictures at the Academy: Thoughts Suggested by the
     Exhibition," *NYT*, April 10, 1887.
"Close of the Academy Exhibition," *NYT*, May 16, 1887.
"The NAD: The Sixty-second Annual Exhibition," *Studio* 2
     (May 1887): 188–95.

1888

Lyman H. Weeks, "Monthly Record of Art," *American Art
     Illustrated* 2 (March 1888): 26–28.
"The Gallery. The NAD," *AAm* 18 (May 1888): 131–33.
"Recent American Landscape," *AAm* 19 (June 1888): 2–3.
"Art Notes. The Spring Academy Exhibition," *Art Interchange* 20
     (April 21, 1888): 130–31.
"Spring Exhibitions of the 'Academy' and the 'Society,'" *Art
     Review* 3 (July-August 1888): 31–34.
"The Spring Academy," *Catholic World* 47 (June 1888): 424–25.
"The Fine Arts: The National Academy Exhibition," *Critic* 12
     (April 7, 1888): 171–72.
"The Academy Exhibition," *Frank Leslie's Illustrated Newspaper*
     66 (April 14, 1888): 131.
"The Academy Exhibition," *HW* 32 (April 7, 1888): 250, 252.
Mrs. Schuyler [Mariana Griswold] Van Rensselaer, "Fine Arts:
     The Academy Exhibition," *Independent* 40 (April 19, 1888):
     487; 40 (April 26, 1888): 519.
"Fine Arts: The Academy Exhibition," *Nation* 46 (April 19, 1888):
     330–32.
"The Academy of Design: Sixty-third Annual Exhibition,"
     NYDT, March 31, 1888.
"Art News and Comments: The Week in Art Circles: Sales at the
     Academy," *NYDT*, April 1, 1888.
"The Academy of Design: Works in the Sixty-third Annual
     Exhibition," *NYEP*, March 30, 1888.
"The Academy Exhibition," *NYEP*, April 13, 1888.
"Catholicity in Art," *NYH*, March 31, 1888.
"National Academy Exhibition: An Excellent Display by
     American Artists," *New York Mail and Express*,
     March 31, 1888.
"The National Academy Exhibition: First Article," *NYS*,
     April 1, 1888.
"The Academy of Design: Concluding Article," *NYS*, April 8,
     1888.
"The Spring Academy," *NYT*, March 31, 1888.
"Portraits at the Academy," *NYT*, April 8, 1888.
"Winners of Academy Prizes," *NYT*, April 19, 1888.
"The National Academy: Ideal and Genre Pictures," *NYT*, May
     6, 1888.
"The Academy Spring Show: Annual Exhibition of Pictures at
     the Old Institution," *New York World*, March 31, 1888.
Nym Crinkle, "Nym Crinkle's Impressions: His Views about the
     Pictures at the Academy Exhibition," *New York World*, April
     9, 1888.
Gebolt Gibson, "An Artist on American Art: The Academy
     Exhibition As Viewed through Professional Glasses," *New
     York World*, April 22, 1888.
[Clarence Cook], "NAD. Sixty-third Annual Exhibition," *Studio*
     3 (May 1888): 85–89; 3 (June 1888): 109–13.
"Prizes Awarded at the NAD," *Studio* 3 (May 1888): 99–100.

1889

"The Gallery: The Academy Exhibition," *AAm* 20 (May 1889):
     124.
"Art Notes," *Art Interchange* 22 (April 13, 1889): 113–14.
"The Fine Arts: The Spring Exhibition at the Academy," *Critic* 14
     (April 6, 1889): 175.
"The Academy Exhibition," *HW* 33 (April 6, 1889): 268–69.
Mariana Griswold Van Rensselaer, "The Academy Exhibition,"
     Independent 41 (May 16, 1889): 632.
"Fine Arts: The Academy Exhibition," *Nation* 48 (April 11, 1889):
     312–13.
"Art Notes," *New York American*, March 30, 1889.
"The Academy of Design, Sixty-fourth Annual Exhibition,"
     NYDT, March 30, 1889.
"The Academy Exhibition," *NYEP*, April 5, 1889.
"All for Art's Sake: Brilliant Showing at the National Academy
     Exhibition," *NYH*, March 30, 1889.
"The National Academy Exhibition," *NYS*, March 31, April 12,
     1889.
"Spring at the Academy," *NYT*, March 30, 1899.
"The Academy Paintings," *NYT*, April 7, 1889.
"Prizes for Good Pictures," *NYT*, April 18, 1889.

1890

"The 'Academy' Exhibition," *AAm* 22 (May 1890): 113.
"The Fine Arts: The National Academy's Sixty-fifth Exhibition,"
     Critic 16 (April 12, 1890): 186; 16 (April 18, 1890): 186–87; 16
     (May 3, 1890): 224–25.
Susan Hayes Ward, "Fine Arts," *Independent* 42 (April 17, 1890):
     516–17; 42 (May 1, 1890): 583.
"The National Academy, New York," *Magazine of Art* 13 (April
     1890): xxv–xxvi.
"The Academy of Design: Sixty-fifth Annual Exhibition,"
     NYDT, April 4, 1890.
"Sales at the Academy," *NYDT*, April 13, 1890.
"The Academy Exhibition: Paintings Entered for Prizes," *NYDT*,
     April 19, 1890.
"The Academy Exhibition," *NYEP*, April 14, 1890.
"A Remarkably Good Academy Exhibition: Sixty-fifth Display
     of Paintings and Sculptures at the National Institution,"
     NYH, April 4, 1890.
"A Beautiful Art Show: Twelfth and Best Display of the Society
     of American Artists," *NYH*, April 29, 1890.
"The Academy Exhibition," *New York Mail and Express*,
     April 15, 1890.
"Pictures at the NAD: First Notice," *NYS*, April 19,
     April 24, 1890.
"The Academy of Design Spring Exhibition," *NYT*, April 4, 1890.
"The Spring Academy," *NYT*, April 7, 1890.
"The National Academy," *NYT*, April 23, 1890.
"Academy of the Fine Arts," *NYT*, May 17, 1890.
[Clarence Cook], "The Academy of Design Exhibition," *Studio* 5
     (April 5, 1890): 173–74.
[Clarence Cook], "The NAD: Sixty-fifth Annual Exhibition,"
     Studio 5 (May 3, 1890): 214–16.
"American Notes," *Studio* 5 (May 17, 1890): 242–44.

1891

"The Academy Exhibition," *AAm* 24 (May 1891): 142–45.

"Art Gossip," *Art Interchange* 26 (April 25, 1891): 129.

"The National Academy's Sixty-sixth Exhibition," *Critic* 18 (April 11, 1891): 199–200.

William A. Coffin, "The Academy Exhibition," *HW* 35 (April 18, 1891): 287–88.

"NAD," *Magazine of Art* 14 (1891): v–vi.

"The Spring Academy: An Exhibition with Many Good Features (First Notice)," *NYDT*, April 1, 1891.

"The NAD Exhibition," *NYDT*, April 3, 1891.

"Art Notes," *NYDT*, May 17, 1891.

"American Art Exhibited in the NAD," *NYS*, April 12, 1891.

"The Academy's Exhibition," *NYT*, April 6, 1891.

[Clarence Cook], "NAD Sixty-sixth Annual Exhibition," *Studio* 6 (April 11, 1891): 185–86; 6 (April 18, 1891): 193–95; 6 (May 2, 1891): 220.

1892

Royal Cortissoz, "Art in New York," *Arcadia* 1 (April 20, 1892): 12–15.

"The National Academy Exhibition," *AAm* 26 (May 1892): 141; 27 (June 1892): 5.

"Art Gossip," *Art Interchange* 28 (May 1892): 129–30.

"The National Academy," *Critic* 20 (April 9, 1892): 217.

"The Spring Exhibition—The Corridor," *Magazine of Art* 15 (1892): xxii–xxiv.

"Artists and Patrons Meet: Dinner of the Academy of Design," *NYDT*, April 2, 1892.

"The Chronicle of Arts: Exhibitions and Other Topics," *NYDT*, April 10, 1892.

"The Spring Academy: A Strong Impressionist Exhibit (Second Notice)," *NYDT*, April 19, 1892.

"The Chronicle of Arts: Exhibitions and Other Topics," *NYDT*, April 24, 1892.

"The Academy Exhibition: First Notice," *NYEP*, April 6, April 14, 1892.

"Notable Canvases in the Sixty-seventh Exhibition of the National Academy," *NYH*, April 3, 1892.

"World of Art," *New York Mail and Express*, April 4, 1892.

"The Academy of Design," *NYS*, April 9, 1892.

"Varnishing Day at the Academy," *NYT*, April 1, 1892.

"Academy Sculpture and Painting, II," *NYT*, April 5, 1892.

"Academy Prize Pictures," *NYT*, April 18, 1892.

"Two Salons of New-York: Landscapes and Marines at the National Academy," *NYT*, May 1, 1892.

M[ariana] G[riswold] Van Rensselaer, "News of the Week in Art," *New York World*, April 24, 1892.

"The Spring Academy," *New York World*, April 1, 1892.

[Clarence Cook], "The Sixty-seventh Annual Exhibition of the NAD in New York," *Studio* 7 (April 2, 1892): 162–63.

[Clarence Cook], "The NAD: Sixty-seventh Annual Exhibition," *Studio* 7 (April 9, 1892): 173–74.

1893

"The NAD," *AAm* 28 (May 1893): 153–54.

"Art Gossip," *Art Interchange* 30 (May 1893): 129; 30 (June 1893): 154.

"The Fine Arts: The National Academy Exhibition," *Critic* 22 (April 1, 1893): 207.

Charles de Kay, "The National Academy Exhibition," *HW* 37 (April 1, 1893): 299–301.

"Spring Academy at New York," *Magazine of Art* 16 (1893): xxi–xxiv.

"The Chronicle of Arts: Exhibitions and Other Topics," *NYDT*, April 16, 1893.

"The Spring Academy," *NYEP*, March 28, 1893.

"The Hallgarten Prizes," *NYEP*, April 18, 1893.

"The Academy Exhibition: Third Notice," *NYEP*, April 22, 1893.

"The Academy of Design," *NYS*, March 27, April 23, 1893.

"The National Academy: Noteworthy Paintings at the Spring Exhibition," *NYT*, March 24, 1893.

"Shall They Vote Prizes: Exhibitors at the Academy Urged Both Ways," *NYT*, April 19, 1893.

"Art Notes," *NYT*, May 14, 1893.

M[ariana] G[riswold] Van Rensselaer, "Questions of Art," *New York World*, April 9, 1893.

1894

"The National Academy Exhibition," *AAm* 30 (May 1894): 155–56.

"Exhibition of the National Academy," *Art Interchange* 32 (May 1894): 146–47.

Alfred Trumbull, "Springtime Sundries," *Collector* 5 (April 1, 1894): 165.

"Springtime Sundries," *Collector* 5 (April 1, 1894): 165.

"The Fine Arts: The Exhibition of the NAD," *Critic* 24 (April 7, 1894): 244.

"At a Private View," *Harper's New Monthly Magazine* 88 (March 1894): 495.

"The Spring Academy," *Harper's Weekly* 38 (April 7, 1894): 319–20.

"Academy of Design," *NYEP*, April 3, 1894.

"Some of the Principal Pictures at the NAD," *NYH*, April 1, 1894.

"Notable Show of Pictures," *NYT*, March 30, 1894.

"Academy Prices and Prizes," *NYT*, April 9, 1894.

"Last Week of the Academy," *NYT*, May 9, 1894.

"Spring Exhibition at the Academy of Design," *Outlook* 51 (May 4, 1894): 749.

1895

"The NAD," *AAm* 32 (February 18, 1895): 185.

"Recent Prize Awards for Paintings," *AAm* 32 (May 1895): 159.

"The Fine Arts: Exhibition of the NAD," *Critic* 26 (April 6, 1895): 267–68.

Royal Cortissoz, "Spring Art Exhibitions: At the Academy of Design," *HW* 39 (April 6, 1895): 317–19.

W. A. Cooper, "NAD," *Godey's Magazine* 130 (June 1895): 583–89.

"NAD," *NYEP*, March 29, 1895.

"The Spring Academy," *NYEP*, April 6, 1895.

"Ideal in Art at the Academy," *NYH*, March 29, 1895.

"Exhibitions of the Week and General Art Gossip: The Academy Closes Saturday," *NYT*, May 5, 1895.

"The Academy of Design," *NYT*, March 29, April 8, 1895.

"The Academy Exhibition," *New York World*, March 29, 1895.

A. C. W., "At the Spring Art Exhibitions," *New York World*,
April 7, 1895.
"Art Notes and Notices," *New York World*, April 3, 1895.

1896
"National Academy Exhibition," *AAm* 34 (February 1896): 59.
"The NAD," *AAm* 34 (May 1896): 129.
"The Seventy-first Academy Exhibition," *Art Interchange* 36
(May 1896): 114–18.
Lou, "Special New York Letter," *Arts for America* 5 (April 1896):
115.
Van Dyck Brown, "The Spring Exhibition of New York," *Call*,
May 17, 1896.
[Alfred Trumbull], "Small Talk," *Collector* 7 (January 1, 1896): 79.
"The Fine Arts: 71st Exhibition of the NAD," *Critic* 28 (April 4,
1896): 242–43.
Royal Cortissoz, "The Collection at the Academy of Design,"
HW 40 (April 18, 1896): 393–94.
"Art Notes," *Monthly Illustrator & Home and Country* 12 (March
1896): vi, viii, x.
Edward Hildane, "The Academy and Society Exhibitions,"
Monthly Illustrator & Home and Country 12 (May 1896):
351–56.
"A Puzzle for Academicians. Difficulty in Awarding the
Hallgarten Prizes," *NYDT*, March 31, 1896.
"The Spring Academy: Conservative Pictures and Some
Others," *NYDT*, April 1, 1896.
"The Academy of Design (Second Notice)," *NYDT*, April 18,
1896.
"The Spring Academy," *NYEP*, April 1, 1896.
"The Spring Academy," *NYT*, March 27, 1896.
"Exhibitions Past, Present, and Future, with General News,"
NYT, March 29, 1896.
"In the World of Art: The Spring Academy. Second Article,"
NYT, April 3, 1896.
"Art Notes and Notices," *New York World*, March 29,
April 11, 1896.

1897
"The Exhibition of the NAD," *AAm* 36 (May 1897): 107.
"The National Academy Exhibition," *Art Interchange* 38 (May
1897): 118–19.
"Seventy-second Annual Exhibition of the NAD," *Art News* 1
(1897): 4–6.
"The Fine Arts: NAD," *Critic* 30 (April 10, 1897): 259–60.
Royal Cortissoz, "The Academy Exhibition," *HW* 41 (April 17,
1897): 380, 391, 394.
"The Spring Academy," *NYDT*, April 2, April 4, 1897.
"The Spring Academy," *NYEP*, April 7, 1897.
"Pictures Shown in the Exhibition of the NAD," *NYH*, April 11,
1897.
W. A. C., "The Academy Exhibition," *NYS*, April 14, 1897.
"Academy's Spring Exhibition," *NYT*, April 2, 1897.
James B. Townsend, "National Academy and American Artists'
Spring Exhibitions Described," *NYT Sunday Magazine
Supplement*, April 4, 1897.
"The Spring Academy," *NYT Saturday Supplement*, April 3, 1897.

"The Spring Academy," *NYT Saturday Review of Books and Art
Supplement*, April 10, April 17, April 24, May 1, 1897.
"Art Notes and Notices," *New York World*, April 6, 1897.

1898
"The NAD," *AAm* 38 (May 1898): 131.
"National Academy Exhibition," *Art Interchange* 40 (May 1898):
114–16.
"Exhibitions," *Arts for America* 7 (April 1898): 494–95.
Orson Lowell, "Three Important New York Exhibitions," *Brush
& Pencil* 2 (May 1898): 80–92.
"The Fine Arts: The NAD," *Critic* 32 (April 2, 1898): 235.
Charles H. Caffin, "Art: Notes at the Seventy-third Annual
Exhibition of the NAD," *HW* 42 (April 9, 1898): 348–49, 351.
J. C. V. D., "The Spring Academy," *NYEP*, March 30, 1898.
"NAD: Opening of the Spring Exhibition," *NYS*, March 26, 1898.
"Academy of Design: The Spring Exhibition," *NYS*, April 5, 1898.
"The Week in the Art World: The Spring Academy," *NYT
Saturday Review of Books and Art*, March 26, 1898.
"The Week in the Art World," *NYT Saturday Review of Books
and Art*, April 2, 1898.

1899
"The Collector," *AAm* 40 (May 1899): 115.
"The Spring Academy," *Art Collector* 9 (1899): 181.
"Exhibitions," *Art Interchange* 42 (April 1899): 97.
"The Last Exhibition of the Old Academy," *Art Interchange* 42
(May 1899): 114.
"The Observer," *Art Interchange* 42 (June 1899): 138.
"Seventy-fourth Annual Exhibition of the NAD," *Artist* 25
(May–June 1899): ii–vi.
"Exhibitions," *Arts for America* 8 (April 1, 1899): 361–64.
"Art Notes," *Brush and Pencil* 4 (May 1899): 131.
"The Fine Arts. Exhibitions," *Critic* 34 (May 1899): 459–61.
"Art Exhibitions: The Opening of the Academy of Design,"
NYDT, April 1, 1899.
"The Academy's Work," *NYDT Illustrated Supplement*, April 23,
1899.
B. F., "Academy of Design," *NYEP*, April 8, 1899.
"Spring Academy Prize Pictures," *NYH*, April 1, 1899.
"The Last 'Spring Academy' in the Old Home," *NYH*, April 2,
1899.
Henri [*sic*] Pène du Bois, "Last Salon of the Academy of
Design," *New York Journal*, April 5, 1899.
"Art Notes: The Seventy-fourth Exhibition of the Academy of
Design," *NYS*, April 2, 1899.

1900
"Exhibitions: The NAD," *AAm* 42 (February 1900): 58.
"Seventy-fifth Annual Exhibition of the NAD," *Artist* 27
(February 1900): x–xii.
"New York Art News," *Brush and Pencil* 5 (February 1900):
218–22.
Grumbler, "The Grumbler in New York," *Brush and Pencil* 5
(February 1900): 236–39.

"The Art World: Academy of Design Exhibition," *NYCA*,
    January 5, 1900.
"'My Bunkie,' Which Has Made Hoboken Artist Famous," *NYH*,
    January 1, 1900.

1901
"The Collector," *AAm* 44 (February 1901): 62–65.
"The Academy Exhibition," *Art Interchange* 46 (February 1901):
    39.
"Seventy-sixth Exhibition of the National Academy," *Artist* 30
    (February 1901): i–iii.
"Exhibition Notes," *Brush and Pencil* 7 (February 1901): 17.
David C. Preyer, "The New York Art World," *Brush and Pencil* 8
    (April 1901): 26–43.
Charles H. Caffin, "The Seventy-sixth Annual Exhibition of the
    NAD," *HW* 45 (January 19, 1901): 74.
"The Art World," *NYCA*, January 4, January 5, January 7,
    January 12, 1901.
"Art Exhibitions: The NAD," *NYDT*, January 5, 1901.
"Academy's Annual Exhibit Begins," *NYH*, January 5, 1901.
"NAD," *NYT*, January 5, 1901.

1902
John W. Van Oost, "My Note Book," *AAm* 46 (February 1902):
    58.
"The Academy Exhibition," *Art Interchange* 48 (February 1902):
    35.
Harrison N. Howard, "NAD Exhibition," *Brush and Pencil* 9
    (February 1902): 277–89.
A[rthur] H[oeber], "Academy of Design Opening To-day of
    Seventy-seventh Annual Exhibition," *NYCA*, January 2,
    1902.
"The Art World: Academy of Design," *NYCA,* January 3, January
    8, 1902.
"Exhibition of the Academy of Design," *NYCA*, January 11, 1902.
"Art Exhibitions: The NAD," *NYDT*, January 4, 1902.
"Some of the Prize Winners and Other Canvases Now on View
    at the Seventy-seventh Annual Exhibition of the NAD in
    the Fine Arts Building," *NYDT*, January 5, 1902.
"Another Academy Exhibition Opens," *NYH*, January 3, 1902.

1903
John W. Van Oost, "My Note Book," *AAm* 48 (January 1903): 34;
    48 (March 1903): 95.
"Exhibitions," *AAm* 48 (February 1903): 72–73.
"The NAD," *Art Interchange* 50 (February 1903): 37–38.
Harrison N. Howard, "The NAD's Seventy-eighth Exhibition,"
    Brush and Pencil 11 (February 1903): 364–78.
"The Academy Exhibition," *HW* 47 (January 10, 1903): 46.
"NAD," *NYCA*, January 2, January 7, 1903.
"Exhibition of the NAD," *NYCA*, January 10, 1903.
"Art Exhibitions: The NAD," *NYDT*, January 3, 1903.
"Annual Academy Exhibition Opens," *NYH*, January 3, 1903.
"NAD Seventy-eighth Annual at the Fine Arts Building, Fifty-
    seventh Street," *NYT*, January 3, 1903.

1904
"The NAD," *Art Interchange* 52 (February 1904): 34.
Harrison N. Howard, "Exhibition of the NAD," *Brush and Pencil*
    13 (January 1904): 300–13.
Charles H. Caffin, "National Academy Exhibition," *IS* 21
    (February 1904): ccv–ccxx.
Arthur Hoeber, "Academy of Design Seventy-ninth Annual
    Exhibition," *NYCA*, January 2, January 6, 1904.
A[rthur] H[oeber], "Important Paintings at National Academy
    Exhibition," *NYCA*, January 9, 1904.
"Art Exhibitions: The Seventy-ninth Annual Display of the
    Academy," *NYDT*, January 2, 1904.
W. A. C., "NAD Varnishing Day," *NYEP*, January 2, 1904.
"National Academy Opens Exhibition," *NYH*, January 2, 1904.
"National Academy Wakes Up," *NYS*, January 2, 1904.
"The Academy of Design Seventy-ninth Annual Exhibition Is
    Exceptionally Good," *NYT*, January 2, 1904.

1905 [Note: Annual exhibition opened in December 1904]
"The Eightieth Academy," *American Art News* 3 (January 7,
    1905): 2.
W. T. Landers, "The Eightieth Exhibition of the NAD," *Brush
    and Pencil* 15 (February 1905): 73–83.
"Art Exhibitions: The Eightieth Annual Show of the Academy of
    Design," *NYDT*, December 21, December 31, 1904.
"Academy of Design," *NYEP*, December 31, 1904.
M., "The National Academy," *NYEP*, January 7, 1905.
"Annual Academy Exhibition Opens," *NYH*, December 31, 1904.
"Varnishing at the Academy," *NYT*, January 1, 1905.

1906 [Note: Annual exhibition opened in December 1905]
"Annual Academy Exhibit," *American Art News* 4 (December 23,
    1905): 1.
C. E. Townsend, "The NAD's Eighty First Annual Exhibition,"
    Brush and Pencil 17 (February 1906): 75–76.
Arthur Hoeber, "The Exhibition of the NAD," *IS* 27 (February
    1906): lxxxiii–xc.
"American Paintings Exhibited," *NYDT*, December 24, 1905.
M., "The National Academy," *NYEP*, December 23, December 30,
    1905.
"National Academy Exhibition Opens," *NYH*, December 23,
    1905.
"Prize Winner at National Academy Exhibition," *NYH*,
    December 24, 1905.
"Notable Pictures in the NAD Exhibition of 1905," *NYT*,
    December 24, 1905.
"Art and Artists: Talk of the Studios," *NYT*, December 24, 1905.
"Some Reasons Why They Are So Disappointing," *NYT*,
    December 26, 1905.

1907
Charles H. Dorr, "Annual Academy Exhibition," *American Art
    New*s 5 (March 16, 1907): 1, 3, 4.
Charles H. Dorr and W. B. McC., "National Academy Show
    from Opposite Angles," *Brush and Pencil* 19 (April 1907):
    126–36.

Gustav Kobbé, "The Eighty-second Annual Exhibition of the
     NAD," *IS* 31 (April 1907): xli–l.
Frank Fowler, "Impressions of the Spring Academy," *Nation* 84
     (March 28, 1907): 297–98.
"The Academy of Design: Opening of the Eighty-second
     Annual Exhibition," *NYDT*, March 16, 1907.
"Some Paintings in the 82nd Annual Exhibition of the NAD,"
     NYDT, March 24, 1907.
"A Varnishing Day Crush," *NYEP*, March 16, 1907.
"National Academy Exhibition," *NYH*, March 16, 1907.
"Academy's Varnishing Day," *NYT*, March 16, 1907.
"The Spring Exhibition at the National Academy," *NYT*, March
     17, 1907.

1908

James B. Townsend, "Annual Academy Exhibition," *American
     Art News* 6 (March 14, 1908): 1, 4; 6 (March 28, 1908): 3, 4, 6.
"Sculpture at Academy," *American Art News* 6 (March 21, 1908):
     1, 3.
"Low Defends Academy," *American Art News* 6 (March 28,
     1908): 4.
"Notes," *Craftsman* 14 (June 1908): 340–41.
Arthur Hoeber, "Spring Exhibition of the NAD," *IS* 34 (May
     1908): cv–cviii.
Ben Foster, "The Spring Academy," *Nation* 86 (March 19, 1908):
     269–70.
Guy Pène du Bois, " 'The Eight' Win Art Victory: Academy of
     Design Opens Its Eighty-third Exhibit," *New York
     American*, March 14, 1908.
"Some Paintings at the Eighty-third Annual Exhibition of the
     NAD," *NYDT*, March 22, 1908.
C[harles] de K[ay], "The Academy of Design," *NYEP*, March 14,
     1908.
"Art Exhibition Opened: Academy's Show Wins High Praise,"
     NYH, March 14, 1908.
"Art Exhibition Attracts Many: Paintings Shown by NAD
     Marked by Excellence," *NYH*, March 15, 1908.

1909

Henry W. Poore, "The Problem of the Academy," *American Art
     News* 7 (March 13, 1909): 4.
James B. Townsend, "Annual Academy Display," *American Art
     News* 7 (March 13, 1909): 1, 3; 7 (March 20, 1909): 7; 7
     (March 22, 1909): 5–6.
H. W. Watrous, "Academy's Announcement," *American Art News*
     7 (March 22, 1909): 4.
"More of the American Spirit in the Spring Exhibition of the
     NAD," *Craftsman* 16 (May 1909): 176–82.
"The Spring Academy," *Nation* 88 (March 18, 1909): 286–87.
Guy Pène du Bois, "Art Exhibition of Academy of Design
     Lacking in Originality," *New York American*, March 13, 1909.
"Academy Portraits: Painting by Sargent in the Place of Honor,"
     NYEP, March 15, 1909.
"Pictures at the Academy, Genre and Landscape in the
     Exhibition," *NYEP*, March 16, 1909.
"National Academy Ready to Open Annual Exhibition," *NYH*,
     March 13, 1909.
"Pioneer Spirit in Academy Exhibition," *NYT*, March 13, 1909.
"Canvases Shown in Spring Exhibition of the NAD," *NYT*,
     March 14, 1909.

1910

[Leila Mechlin?], "The NAD: Eighty-fifth Annual Exhibition,"
     Art and Progress 1 (May 1910): 196–99.
"Spring Exhibition of the NAD," *IS* 40 (May 1910): lxii–lxv.
Guy Pène du Bois, "NAD Exhibition Has Reached Its Zenith,"
     New York American, March 14, 1910.
R. C., "The Spring Appearance of the National Academy,"
     NYDT, March 12, 1910.
"Academy's Spring Exhibition," *NYEP*, March 12, 1910.
M., "National Academy Pictures: Eighty-fifth Annual
     Exhibition," *NYEP*, March 17, 1910.
"National Academy Opens Crowded Show," *NYH*, March 12,
     1910.
"Art Gossip," *NYS*, March 13, 1910.
"Landscape Portraiture in the Spring Academy," *NYT*, March 27,
     1910.

1911

James B. Townsend, "Annual Academy Display," *American Art
     News* 9 (March 11, 1911): 4; 9 (March 18, 1911): 4; 9 (March
     25, 1911): 4.
"Matters of Art: The Spring Academy," *NYDT*, March 19, 1911.
"Art Notes: Opening of Spring Exhibition of Academy of
     Design," *NYEP*, March 11, 1911.
B. P. S., "The Academy Pictures: Spring Exhibition in the Fine
     Arts Building," *NYEP*, March 15, 1911.
"National Academy Opens Exhibition; Works of Beauty and
     Power Shown," *NYH*, March 11, 1911.
"Pictures That Won Prizes: Leaders in the Spring Show at the
     Academy," *NYS*, March 12, 1911.
"Art Notes," *NYT*, March 11, 1911.
"Art at Home and Abroad: This Year's Prize Winners at the
     Academy," *NYT Magazine Section*, March 12, 1911.

1912

Charles de Kay, "Annual Academy Display," *American Art News*
     10 (March 9, 1912): 7.
L. Merrick, "Annual Academy Display," *American Art News* 10
     (March 16, 1912): 3; 10 (March 23, 1912): 3.
Guy Pène du Bois, "National Academy Exhibit Decorous," *New
     York American*, March 11, 1912.
"Matters of Art: The Academy of Design's Spring Exhibition,"
     NYDT, March 10, 1912.
"Seen at Spring Academy. Fewer Exhibits Than in the December
     Display," *NYEP*, March 12, 1912.
"National Academy's 87th Display Shows Progress of American
     Art," *NYH*, March 9, 1912.
"Notable Pictures at the National Academy's Spring Exhibition
     Just Opened," *NYS*, March 10, 1912.
"Winners of Prizes at Academy Exhibit," *NYT*, March 9, 1912.
"The Prize Winners in the Annual Spring Exhibition of the
     National Academy," *NYT*, March 17, 1912.

"Much Merit in Spring Exhibit of the Academy," *New York World,* March 10, 1912.

1913

"The National Academy Opens. Exit the International Show," *New York American,* March 17, 1913.

"Matters of Art," *NYDT,* March 16, 1913.

"Matters of Art: The Spring Exhibition of the Academy of Design," *NYDT,* March 23, 1913.

"National Academy: The Spring Academy of 1913 Opens to the Public To-day," *NYEP,* March 15, 1913.

"National Academy: The Present Exhibition Indicates an Advance in the Process of Elimination," *NYEP,* March 18, 1913.

"NAD Exhibition Shows Influence of Art Insurgents," *NYH,* March 15, 1913.

"Spring Academy Show Comes," *NYS,* March 16, 1913.

"Prize Paintings in Spring Academy," *NYT,* March 15, 1913.

"A Few of the Paintings at the Spring Academy," *NYT,* March 16, 1913.

Charles Henry Dorr, "This Year's Exhibition of National Academy," *New York World,* March 16, 1913.

1914

A. v. C., "The Spring Academy," *American Art News* 12 (March 21, 1914): 2.

A. v. C., "Exhibitions Now On: The Spring Academy," *American Art News* 12 (March 28, 1914): 3, 6.

"Exhibitions Now on: Sculptures and Miniatures at Academy," *American Art News* 12 (April 4, 1914): 2.

"At the Spring Academy," *Craftsman* 26 (May 1914): 148–55.

"Eighty-ninth Annual Show, National Academy," *New York American,* March 23, 1914.

Royal Cortissoz, "The Academy in Fair Form," *NYDT,* March 21, 1914.

"The National Academy," *NYEP,* March 21, March 23, 1914.

"Many New Artists in Spring Academy," *NYS,* March 21, 1914.

"Gems from the National Academy Exhibition," *NYS,* March 29, 1914.

"Striking Pictures Seen at Academy's Spring Exhibit," *NYT,* March 22, 1914.

"Spring Academy Open," *NYT,* March 21, 1914.

"Art at Home and Abroad. Some Old Friends Shown at Vanderbilt Gallery," *NYT,* March 22, 1914.

"News of the Art World: Spring Exhibition of the National Academy," *New York World,* March 22, 1914.

1915

"New Academy President," *American Art News* 13 (March 20, 1915): 1.

James B. Townsend, "The Spring Academy," *American Art News* 13 (March 20, 1915): 2, 5; 13 (March 27, 1915): 2.

Carroll Beckwith, "Correspondence: Letter to the Council of the Academy of Design from an Academician," *American Art News* 13 (April 3, 1915): 4.

James Britton, "Exhibitions Now On," *American Art News* 13 (April 3, 1915): 2.

"Ninetieth Exhibition of the National Academy," *New York American,* March 22, 1915.

"Landscapes at Academy Exhibit," *New York American,* March 29, 1915.

Royal Cortissoz, "Exhibitions and Other Matters of Fine Art," *NYDT,* March 21, 1915.

"The National Academy," *NYEP,* March 20, March 27, 1915.

"National Academy's Ninetieth Exhibition Opened and Will Be Free to the Public," *NYH,* March 20, 1915.

"Academy Exhibit Now Free to Public," *NYS,* March 20, 1915.

"Annual Spring Exhibition of the NAD," *NYS,* March 28, 1915.

"5,000 at Opening of Design Academy," *NYT,* March 20, 1915.

"Art at Home and Abroad: The Spring Academy Exhibition," *NYT,* March 21, 1915.

1916

James B. Townsend, "The Spring Academy," *American Art News* 14 (March 18, 1916): 1–3.

"Blot on Spring Academy," *American Art News* 14 (March 25, 1916): 3, 4.

James Britton, "Exhibitions Now On: The Spring Academy," *American Art News* 14 (April 1, 1916): 3.

"The Red Ticket," *American Art News* 14 (April 1, 1916): 4.

Henry McBride, "Critic Bombards Academy," *American Art News* 14 (April 15, 1916): 2 [repr. from *New York Sun*].

"Academicians and Modernists," *American Art News* 14 (April 29, 1916): 4.

Member of the National Academy, "Correspondence: Academician Scores *Sun*'s Art Critic," *American Art News* 14 (April 29, 1916): 4.

"Nat'l Academy Sales, \$27,790," *American Art News* 14 (April 29, 1916): 1.

"Hard on the Academy," *American Art News* 14 (April 29, 1916): 1.

Royal Cortissoz, "The Spring Show of the Academy of Design," *NYDT,* March 19, 1916.

"National Academy Opens Exhibition," *NYH,* March 18, 1916.

"National Academy Lacking in Thrills," *NYS,* March 19, 1916.

"Spring Exhibition of the NAD," *NYS,* March 19, 1916.

"Academy Exhibits Its Prize Paintings," *NYT,* March 18, 1916.

"Art at Home and Abroad: Opening of the Spring Academy Exhibition," *NYT Magazine,* March 19, 1916.

1917

James B. Townsend, "The Spring Academy," *American Art News* 15 (March 17, 1917): 1–3; 15 (March 24, 1917): 2.

"Recent Academy Sales," *American Art News* 15 (April 17, 1917): 5; 15 (April 28, 1917): 1.

Charles H. Caffin, "Much of Interest at Academy's Spring Show," *New York American,* March 25, 1917.

Royal Cortissoz, "The Spring Exhibition of the Academy of Design," *NYDT,* March 18, 1917.

"Academy Shows 486 Art Works on Varnishing Day," *NYH,* March 17, 1917.

Gustave Kobbé, "NAD," *NYH,* March 18, 1917.

"Varnish Unused at 92d [*sic*] Academy," *NYS*, March 17, 1917.

Henry McBride, "News and Comments in the World of Art," *NYS*, March 25, 1917.

1918

James B. Townsend, "A Wartime Academy," *American Art News* 16 (March 16, 1918): 1–3.

James Britton, "A Wartime Academy," *American Art News* 16 (March 23, 1918): 1–2.

"Spring Academy Sales," *American Art News* 16 (March 23, 1918): 1.

"Academy of Design Opens Ninety-third Exhibition," *New York American*, March 13, 1918.

"New, Important Things in Art: Second Review of Spring Academy," *New York American*, March 18, 1918.

H.U., "Art," *NYDT*, March 13, 1918.

"Unfinished Chase Group Show on 'Varnishing Day'" *NYH*, March 13, 1918.

Gustave Kobbé, "National Academy Opens Its Ninety-Third Annual Exhibition," *NYH*, March 17, 1918.

"National Academy Opens Exhibition," *NYS*, March 13, 1918.

"Prize Winners of National Academy," *NYT*, March 13, 1918.

Royal Cortissoz, "The Past and Present in American Painting," *NYT*, March 17, 1918.

"Art at Home and Abroad: Exhibitions of Art in Great Variety," *NYT Magazine*, March 17, 1918.

1919

James B. Townsend, "The Spring Academy," *American Art News* 17 (March 22, 1919): 1–2; 17 (March 29, 1919): 2.

"An 'Inside' Academy Row," *American Art News* 17 (March 29, 1919): 1.

Howard Russell Butler, "Proposed Radical Changes in Academy," *American Art News* 17 (April 19, 1919): 4.

"Academy 'Stands Pat'," *American Art News* 17 (April 26, 1919): 1.

"Late Academy Sales," *American Art News* 17 (April 26, 1919): 1.

"The Academy Controversy," *American Art News* 17 (May 3, 1919): 4.

Geo[rge] Bellows, "Correspondence: Bellows Answers Butler," *American Art News* 17 (May 3, 1919): 4, 6.

Royal Cortissoz, "The Opening of the Spring Academy," *NYDT*, March 23, 1919.

Guy Pène du Bois, "Among the Art Galleries," *NYEP Magazine*, March 22, 1919.

G[uy] P[ène du] B[ois], "Academy Exhibition Smaller and Better," *NYEP*, March 22, 1919.

Frederick James Gregg, "Academy Opens Ninety-fourth Show to Crowded Galleries," *NYH*, March 22, 1919.

"Landscape Opening at Spring Academy," *NYS*, March 22, 1919.

"Bolshevism in Our National Academy," *NYS*, March 23, 1919.

1920

Peyton Boswell, "Arts Academy Has Record Exhibit," *New York American*, April 8, 1920.

Royal Cortissoz, "The Spring Academy in Auspicious Form," *NYDT*, April 11, 1920.

"Notes on Current Art," *NYT*, April 11, 1920.

Henry McBride, "News and Reviews of Art," *NYS*, April 11, 1920.

James B. Townsend, "Spring Academy in Brooklyn," *American Art News* 18 (April 10, 1920): 1–2; 18 (April 17, 1920): 1–2; 18 (April 24, 1920): 1–2.

Henry McBride, "*Sun*'s Critic on Academy," *American Art News* 18 (April 17, 1920): 4.

1921

James B. Townsend, "Annual Academy Display," *American Art News* 19 (March 5, 1921): 4; 19 (March 12, 1921): 1–3.

"Notable Exhibit Opened by Academy of Design," *NYDT*, March 5, 1921.

Royal Cortissoz, "Recent Shows of New Pictures and Old Prints," *NYDT*, March 6, 1921.

Royal Cortissoz, "The Contrast Enforced in Two Large Exhibitions," *NYDT*, March 13, 1921.

David Lloyd, "Prints on Display at Academy and Library," *NYEP*, March 5, 1921.

"Academy of Design Exhibition to Open to Public To-day," *NYH*, March 5, 1921.

Henry McBride, "News and Reviews of Art," *NYH*, March 13, 1921.

"Prize Paintings Viewed by Crowd," *NYT*, March 5, 1921.

"From Brush and Chisel," *NYT*, March 6, 1921.

1922

"National Academy Opens 97th Annual," *American Art News* 20 (March 25, 1922): 1–2.

Peyton Boswell, "Annual Exhibition of Academy of Design Opens," *New York American*, March 25, 1922.

"422 Pictures Hung in 97th Spring Academy," *NYDT*, March 25, 1922.

Royal Cortissoz, "The Spring Academy," *NYDT*, April 2, 1922.

David Lloyd, "Portraits of Artists in Spring Academy," *NYEP*, March 25, 1922.

David Lloyd, "'Civic Virtue' a Loss to National Academy," *NYEP*, March 25, 1922.

"National Academy Opens Its Spring Exhibition of Art," *NYH*, March 25, 1922.

"The World of Art: Prize-winning Pictures at the Academy of Design," *NYT*, March 26, 1922.

1923

"National Academy Opens 98th Annual," *Art News* 21 (March 17, 1923): 1–2.

"Annual National Academy Opens Doors To-day," *NYDT*, March 17, 1923.

"Studio and Gallery," *NYDT*, March 24, 1923.

Royal Cortissoz, "Pictures in the Spring Academy," *NYDT*, March 25, 1923.

Margaret Breuning, "Spring Exhibition of Academy on View," *NYEP*, March 24, 1923.

"Academy of Design Has Livelier Air in Annual Exhibit," *NYH*, March 17, 1923.

Henry McBride, "Art News and Reviews," *NYH*, March 25, 1923.

"National Academy Exhibit," *NYT*, March 17, 1923.
"The World of Art: Portraits at the National Academy," *NYT*, March 25, 1923.

1924

"3,000 Attend 99th National Academy Show," *NYH Tribune*, March 22, 1924.
"Academy of Design Exhibition Opens," *NYT*, March 22, 1924.
"The World of Art: The Academy Exhibition and Others," *NYT Magazine*, March 30, 1924.

1925

H. C., "The 100th Annual Brilliant in Color," *Art News* 23 (April 4, 1925).
"Great American Art Exhibition Scheme," *Connoisseur* 72 (May 1925): 52.

William B. McCormick, "100th Show of Academy," *New York American*, April 1, 1925.
[No title], *NYEP*, April 1, 1925.
Margaret Breuning, "Annual Exhibition Marks Centennial of Academy," *NYEP*, April 4, 1925.
"Academy Opens Doors for 100th Annual Show," *New York Herald Tribune*, April 1, 1925.
Royal Cortissoz, "The Spring Academy," *New York Herald Tribune*, April 5, 1925.
Charles Vezin, "The Academy Centennial," *New York Herald Tribune*, April 5, 1925.
Henry McBride, "Academy Has 100th Year Show," *NYS*, April 4, 1925.
"The World of Art: Prize-winning Pictures, Architecture and the Allied Arts," *NYT*, April 5, 1925.
"Art," *New Yorker* 1 (April 18, 1925): 17.

Index to Artists and Works in the Exhibition

Artist	Title	Author	Page(s)
Beard, James H.	*The Night Before the Battle*	DBD	205–06
Bellows, George	*The Sawdust Trail*	TAG	262–64
Bierstadt, Albert	*Sunlight and Shadow: Study*	DBD	202–04
Blum, Robert Frederick	*Two Idlers*	ZR	240–42
Boughton, George Henry	*Winter Scene*	DBD	198–99
Chapman, John Gadsby	*New Tomb of the Washington Family*	DBD	173–75
Chapman, John Gadsby	*View of York Town, Virginia*	DBD	173–75
Church, Frederic Edwin	*Twilight (Mt. Desert Island, Maine)*	MM	206–07
Church, Frederic Edwin	*Scene On the Magdalena*	DBD	193–96
Cole, Thomas Cole	*Last of the Mohicans*	DBD	167–68
Couse, Eanger Irving	*The Peace Pipe*	TAG	253–54
Cox, Kenyon	*The Approach of Love*	AH	244–45
Cropsey, Jasper Francis	*The Spirit of Peace*	SK	188–89
Cropsey, Jasper Francis	*The Spirit of War*	SK	188–89
Dessar, Louis Paul	*The Departure of the Fishermen—Early Morning*	DBD	246–48
Dick, Archibald	*New Tomb of the Washington Family* (after Chapman)	DBD	173–75
Dick, Archibald	*View of York Town, Virginia* (after Chapman)	DBD	173–75
Dunlap, William	*Scene from Cooper's "The Spy"*	DBD	161–62
Durand, Asher Brown	*June Shower*	DBD	189–92
Durand, Asher Brown	*Gipseying Party* (after Leslie)	DBD	170–71
Durand, Asher Brown	*Landscape—Scene from "Thanatopsis"*	DBD	184–86
Durand, Asher Brown	*The White Plume* (after Ingham)	DBD	169–70
Eakins, Thomas	*The Pair–Oared Shell*	TAG	227–29
Edmonds, Francis William	*The City and the Country Beaux*	SK	178–79
French, Daniel Chester	*Sculpture and Painting*	AH	248–50
Gifford, Sanford Robinson	*Sunday Morning in the Camp of the Seventh Regiment*	DBD	201–02
Gifford, Sanford Robinson	*The Golden Horn, Constantinople*	DBD	217–18
Gray, Henry Peters	*The Birth of Our Flag*	DBD	221–22
Hassam, Frederick Childe	*The New York Window*	DBD	258–59
Hassam, Frederick Childe	*Allies Day, May 1917*	TAG	264–67
Hawthorne, Charles Webster	*The Trousseau*	TAG	256–57
Homer, Winslow	*Prisoners From the Front*	DBD	212–14
Homer, Winslow	*The Bright Side*	DBD	208–09
Homer, Winslow	*The Life Line*	DBD	236–38
Hopper, Edward	*American Landscape*	DBD	269–70
Hopper, Edward	*East Side Interior*	DBD	269–70
Hosmer, Harriet	*Puck*	DBD	210–12
Hovenden, Thomas	*Breaking Home Ties*	DBD	245–46
Hovenden, Thomas	*In Hoc Signo Vinces*	DBD	229–30
Hovenden, Thomas	*The Death of Elaine*	DBD	232–33
Hunt, William Morris	*La Marguerite*	DBD	196–98
Huntington, Anna Vaugh Hyatt	*Joan of Arc*	DBD	267
Huntington, Daniel	*Mercy's Dream*	DBD	179–81
Ingham, Charles Cromwell	*The White Plume*	DBD	169–70
Ingham, Charles Cromwell	*The Great Adirondack Pass*	DBD	176–78
Inman, Henry	*William Charles Macready as William Tell*	DBD	162–64
Johnson, Eastman	*Corn Husking at Nantucket*	SK	223–24
Johnson, Eastman	*Life in the South*	SK	200–01
Johnson, Eastman	*The Boy Lincoln*	SK	214–17

Johnson, Eastman	*The Wounded Drummer Boy*	SK	214–17
Lawson, Ernest	*Vanishing Mist*	TAG	268–69
Leslie, Charles	*Gipseying Party*	DBD	170–71
Leutze, Emanuel Gottlieb	*Columbus Before the Queen*	MM	183–84
Lie, Jonas	*Afterglow*	TAG	259–60
Millet, Francis Davis	*Reading the Story of Oenone*	AH	235–36
Millet, Francis Davis	*Kate Field*	AH	230–32
Morse, Samuel F. B.	*Marquis de Lafayette*	DBD	164–65
Morse, Samuel F. B.	*Scene from Spencer's 'Fairie Queene': Una and the Dwarf*	DBD	168–69
Mount, William Sidney	*Coming to the Point*	MM	192–93
Mount, William Sidney	*Bishop Benjamin T. Onderdonk*	DBD	171–73
Mount, William Sidney	*Farmers Nooning*	ZR	175–76
O'Donovan, William Rudolf	*William Page*	DBD	224–26
Page, William	*Shakespeare*	DBD	218–20
Rose, Guy	*Point Lobos*	DBD	270–71
Saint-Gaudens, Augustus	*Robert Louis Stevenson*	DBD	242–44
Sargent, John Singer	*Neapolitan Children Bathing*	DBD	226–27
Sargent, John Singer	*Street in Venice*	DBD	238–40
Sloan, John	*Haymarket, Sixth Avenue*	TAG	254–56
Stearns, Junius Brutus	*The Millennium*	DBD	186–87
Ulrich, Charles	*The Glassblowers*	ZR	234–35
Vedder, Elihu	*Jane Jackson, Formerly a Slave*	DBD	209–10
Walker, Horatio	*Ploughing—The First Gleam at Dawn*	TAG	250–51
Walker, Horatio	*De Profundis*	TAG	261–62
Ward, John Quincy Adams	*The Freedman*	DBD	204–05
Weir, Robert Walter	*Columbus Before the Council at Salamanca*	DBD	181–82
Wiles, Irving	*Miss Julia Marlowe*	TAG	251–53

The full credit line for Eastman Johnson, *Life in the South*, no. 26, is:

High Museum of Art, Georgia; Purchase with funds from the Fine Art Collectors with leadership gifts from Mr. and Mrs. Henry Schwob, Mr. and Mrs. Terry Stent, Mr. and Mrs. Austin P. Kelley, Mr. and Mrs. John L. Huber, Dr. and Mrs. Gerald M. Stapleton, Mr. and Mrs. Noel Wadsworth, and the Collections Council American Art Acquisition Fund, and funds from the Winter Family Foundation, and through prior acquisitions from friends of Belle Newman Howard, Alice M. Rariden in memory of John Russell Bond, Martin Horwitz, William B. and Mary Mobley Fambrough Bequest, Mr. and Mrs. Roy Kaye in memory of Mr. and Mrs. Arnold Kaye, Mr. and Mrs. Harmon L. Barnard, Sr., Mrs. J. K. Ottley in memory of Mr. and Mrs. David Woodward, Friends of Art, Mr. Thomas K. Glenn, Mrs. Armistead Peter III, Mrs. Alfredo Barrili in memory of Mrs. Henry B. Scott, Mrs. William H. Bender, Jr., and Edythe Haskell, Dr. and Mrs. George A. Hyman, Henry Wellington Wack, Hinman Estate, Mr. and Mrs. Walter Beck and Amory Simons, 1997.187